Systems
concepts, languages and architectures

Paolo Atzeni
Stefano Ceri
Stefano Paraboschi
Riccardo Torlone

Database
Systems
concepts, languages &
architectures

The McGraw-Hill Companies

London • Burr Ridge, IL • New York • St Louis • San Francisco • Auckland • Bogotá
Caracas • Lisbon • Madrid • Mexico • Milan • Montreal • New Delhi • Panama • Paris
San Juan • São Paulo • Singapore • Tokyo • Toronto

Published by
McGraw-Hill Publishing Company
SHOPPENHANGERS ROAD, MAIDENHEAD, BERKSHIRE, SL6 2QL, ENGLAND
Telephone: +44(0) 1628 502500
Fax: +44(0) 1628 770224
Web site: http://www.mcgraw-hill.co.uk

British Library Cataloguing in Publication Data
A catalogue record for this book is available from the British Library

ISBN 007 709500 6

Library of Congress cataloguing in publication data
The LOC data for this book has been applied for and may be obtained from the
Library of Congress, Washington, D.C.

Authors' Web site address: http://www.mcgraw-hill.co.uk/atzeni

Publishing Director: Alfred Waller
Publisher: David Hatter
Page design: Mike Cotterell
Typesetting: Mouse Nous
Production: Steven Gardiner Ltd
Cover: Hybert Design

The McGraw·Hill Companies

Printed in Great Britain at the University Press, Cambridge

1   2   3   4   5   CUP   3   2   1   0   9

To our students

Contents

Preface

Databases are essential ingredients of modern computing systems. Although database concepts, technology and architectures have been developed and consolidated in the last decades, many aspects are subject to technological evolution and revolution. Thus, writing a textbook on this classical and yet continuously evolving field is a great challenge.

Key features

This book provides a new and comprehensive treatment of databases, dealing with the complete syllabuses for both an introductory course and an advanced course on databases. It offers a balanced view of concepts, languages and architectures, with concrete reference to current technology and to commercial database management systems (DBMSs). It originates from the authors' long experience in teaching, both in academia and in industrial and application settings.

The book is composed of four main parts and a fifth part containing three appendices and a bibliography. Parts I and II are designed to expose students to the principles of data management and for teaching them how to master two main skills: how to query a database (and write software that involves database access) and how to design its schema structure. These are the fundamental aspects of designing and manipulating a database that are required in order to make effective use of database technology.

Parts III and IV are dedicated to advanced concepts, required for mastering database technology. Part III describes database management system architectures, using a modern approach based upon the identification of the important concepts, algorithms, components and standards. Part IV is devoted to the current trends, focusing on object-oriented databases, active databases, data warehouses and the interaction between databases and the World Wide Web.

Appendices cover three popular database systems: Microsoft Access, IBM DB2 and Oracle.

A number of features make this book unique.

- We make a clear distinction between the basic material (Parts I and II) and the advanced material (Parts III and IV), which often marks the progression from an introductory course to an advanced course. A coherent treatment makes the transition from basic to advanced material quite smooth and progressive and makes this book perfectly suitable to serving the needs of a single, comprehensive course.

- We provide the foundations of the relational model and theory, but we never introduce theory for its own sake. Each concept is immediately applied to SQL, with plenty of examples and exercises.

- The discussion of design techniques starts with the introduction of the elements of the E-R (Entity-Relationship) model and proceeds through a well-defined, staged process through conceptual design to the logical design, which produces a relational schema. Several detailed examples are developed, to help the reader to follow the process.

- We deal with the fundamental issues of database technology (transactions, concurrency control, reliability, recovery) first on a single-server architecture and then on a multi-server architecture with emphasis on distribution, replication and parallelism.

- We emphasize standards (including SQL-2, SQL-3, ODL, OQL, CORBA, ODBC, JDBC, X-OPEN) in order to give to the student an understanding of the way in which the concepts developed in this book are deployed in the commercial world.

- We include appendices on Access, DB2 and Oracle, particularly helpful for hands-on courses. We focus on the ease of use of Access, on the interactive tools of DB2 and the richness of Oracle's PL-SQL as a database programming language.

- We provide a Web site (http://www.mcgraw-hill.co.uk/atzeni/) with slides and exercises with solutions that can be used by lecturers and students.

Detailed Content Overview

Chapter 1 covers the use of database technology in modern information systems. We cover basic aspects, such as the difference between data and information, the concepts of data model, schema and instance, a multi-level organization of the database architecture with the fundamental notion of data independence and the classification of database languages and users.

Part I – Relational Databases

This part introduces the concepts of relational databases and then focuses on SQL programming, one of the main objectives of this textbook.

Chapter 2 describes the relational model, by introducing the basic notions of domain, attribute, relation schema and database schema, with the various integrity constraints: primary key and referential constraints; null values are also briefly discussed.

Chapter 3 illustrates the foundations of the languages for the relational model. First we describe relational algebra, a simple and important procedural language; then we introduce declarative languages like relational calculus (on domains and on tuples with range restrictions) and Datalog.

Chapter 4 provides a thorough description of SQL, by focusing on both the Data Definition Language, used to create the schema of a database and the Data Manipulation Language, which allows for querying and updating the content of the database. The chapter also includes advanced features of SQL, such as programming language interfaces and dynamic SQL.

Part II – Database Design

This part covers the conceptual and logical design of relational databases. The process starts with the analysis of user requirements and ends with the production of a relational database schema that satisfies several correctness criteria. We believe that a student must initially learn about database use before he or she can concentrate on database design with sufficient confidence and therefore we postpone design until after the mastering of a query language.

Chapter 5 introduces the design methodology and describes the E-R conceptual model, with the classical notions of entity, relationship, attribute, identifier and generalization. Business rules are also introduced, as a formalism for the description of additional user requirements.

Chapter 6 illustrates conceptual design, which produces an E-R conceptual description of the database, starting from the representation of user requirements. Simple design principles are illustrated, including methods for the systematic analysis of informal requirements, the identification of the main concepts (entities and relationships), top-down refinement strategies, suggestions for achieving certain qualities of the schemas and schema documentation.

Chapter 7 focuses on logical design, which produces a relational database schema starting from the conceptual schema. We discuss the various design options and provide guidelines that the designer should follow in this phase.

Chapter 8 discusses schema normalization and the correctness criteria that must be satisfied by relational schemas in order to avoid anomalies and redundancies. Normalization is used for verification: although it is an important design technique, we do not believe that a designer can really use normalization as the main method for modelling reality. He or she must, however, be aware of normalization issues. Also, the development is precise but not overly formal: there are no abstract algorithms, but we cover instead specific cases that arise in practice.

Part III – Database Technology

This part describes the modern architectures of database management systems.

Chapter 9   is focused on the technology required for operating a single DBMS server; it discusses transactions, concurrency control, buffer management, reliability, access structures, query optimization and physical database design. This chapter provides a database administrator with the fundamental knowledge required to monitor a DBMS.

Chapter 10   addresses the nature of architectures that use a variable number of database servers dispersed in a distributed or parallel environment. Again, transactions, concurrency control and reliability requirements due to data distribution are discussed; these notions are applied to several architectures for data management, including client-server, distributed, parallel and replicated environments.

Part IV – Database Evolution

This part discusses several important extensions to database technology.

Chapter 11   describes object database systems, which constitute a new generation of database systems. We consider both the 'object-oriented' and the 'object-relational' approaches, which are the two alternative paths towards object orientation in the evolution of database systems. We also consider multimedia databases and geographic information systems. The chapter also describes several standards, such as ODM, OQL and CORBA.

Chapter 12   describes active database systems; it shows active rules as they are supported in representative relational systems (Oracle and DB2) and discusses how active rules can be generated for integrity maintenance and tested for termination.

Chapter 13   focuses on data analysis, an important new dimension in data management. We describe the architecture of the data warehouse, the star and snowflake schemas used for data representation within data warehouses and the new operators for data analysis (including drill-down, roll-up and data cube). We also briefly discuss the most relevant problems of data mining, a novel approach for extracting hidden information from a data warehouse.

Chapter 14 focuses on the relationship between databases and the World Wide Web, which has already had a deep influence on the way information systems and databases are designed and accessed. It discusses the notion of Web information systems, the methods for designing them and the tools and techniques for coupling databases and Web sites.

Appendices

Three appendices conclude the volume, with descriptions of three popular DBMSs:

Appendix A deals with Microsoft Access, which is currently the most widespread database management system on PC-based platforms. Access has a simple yet very powerful interface, not only for programming in SQL and QBE, but also for adding forms, reports and macros in order to develop simple applications.

Appendix B describes the DB2 Universal Database, the latest member of one of the major families of DBMSs produced by IBM. The emphasis of the presentation is on its interactive tools and its advanced functionality.

Appendix C covers Oracle, a major product in the market of DBMSs and specifically focuses on the procedural extension of SQL (called PL/SQL), which is supported by Oracle for writing applications.

Use as a textbook

The book can be covered in a total of approximately 50–70 lecture hours (plus 30–40 hours dedicated to exercises and practical experiences).

Our experience is that Parts I and II can be covered as a complete course in about 30 taught hours. Such a course requires a significant amount of additional practical activity, normally consisting of several exercises from each chapter and a project involving the design, population and use of a small database. The appendixes provide useful support for the practical activities.

Parts III and IV can be covered in a second course, or else they can be integrated in part within an extended first course; in advanced, project-centred courses, the study of current technology can be accompanied by a project dedicated to the development of technological components. Part IV, on current trends, provides material for significant project work, for example, related to object technology, or to data analysis, or to Web technology. The advanced course can be associated with further readings or with a research-oriented seminar series.

An international textbook

Making the book reflect the international nature of the subject has been a challenge and an opportunity. This book has Italian authors, who have also given regular courses in the United States, Canada and Switzerland, was edited in the United Kingdom and is directed to the worldwide market. We have purposely used a neutral version of the English language, thus avoiding country-specific jargon whenever possible. In the examples, our attitude has been to choose attribute names and values that would be immediately understandable to everybody. In a few cases, however, we have purposely followed the rules of different international contexts, without selecting one in particular. The use of car registration numbers from France, or of tax codes from Italy, will make the reader aware of the fact that data can have different syntax and semantics in different contexts and so some comprehension and adaptation effort may be needed when dealing with data in a truly worldwide approach. It should also be noted that when dealing with money values, we have omitted the reference to a specific currency: for example, we say that a salary is '40 thousand', without saying whether it is dollars (and which dollars: US, Canadian, Australian, Hong Kong, …), or Euros, or Pounds Sterling.

Additional support

Supplementary material, including overhead slides, solutions to exercises and additional exercises can be found at the book Web site:

http://www.mcgraw-hill.co.uk/atzeni/

The authors can be contacted through the site.

The Authors

Paolo Atzeni and Riccardo Torlone are professors at Università di Roma Tre. Stefano Ceri and Stefano Paraboschi are professors at Politecnico di Milano. They all teach courses on information systems and database technology and are active members of the research community. Paolo Atzeni and Stefano Ceri have many years of experience in teaching database courses, both in European and in North American universities. They have also presented many courses for professional database programmers and designers. All the authors are active researchers, operating on a wide range of areas, including distributed databases, deductive databases, active databases, databases and the Web, data warehouses, database design and so on. They are actively participating in the organization of the main International Conferences and professional Societies dealing with database technology; in particular, Paolo Atzeni is the chairman of the EDBT Foundation and Stefano Ceri is a member of the EDBT Foundation, VLDB Endowment and ACM Sigmod Advisory Committee. Their appointments include being co-chairs of VLDB 2001 in Rome.

Acknowledgements

The organization and the contents of this book have benefited from our experiences in teaching the subject in various contexts. All the students attending those courses, dispersed over many schools and countries (University of Toronto, Stanford University, Università dell'Aquila, Università di Roma 'La Sapienza', Università di Roma Tre, Politecnico di Milano, Università di Modena, Università della Svizzera Italiana) deserve our deepest thanks. Many of these students have field-tested rough drafts and incomplete notes, and have contributed to their development, improvement and correction. Similarly, we would like to thank people from companies and government agencies who attended our courses for professionals and helped us in learning the practical aspects that we have tried to convey in our textbook.

We would like to thank all the colleagues who have contributed, directly or indirectly, to the development of this book, through discussions on course organization or the actual revision of drafts and notes. They include Carlo Batini, Maristella Agosti, Giorgio Ausiello, Elena Baralis, Giovanni Barone, Giampio Bracchi, Luca Cabibbo, Ed Chan, Giuseppe Di Battista, Angelo Foglietta, Piero Fraternali, Maurizio Lenzerini, Gianni Mecca, Alberto Mendelzon, Paolo Merialdo, Barbara Pernici, Silvio Salza, Fabio Schreiber, Giuseppe Sindoni, Elena Tabet, Letizia Tanca, Ernest Teniente, Carson Woo and probably some others whom we might have omitted. We thank the reviewers of the English edition for a number of very useful suggestions concerning the organization of the book and the specific content of chapters.

We thank the very many people who have contributed to the birth of this book inside McGraw-Hill. We are grateful to Gigi Mariani and Alberto Kratter Thaler who have worked with us to the Italian edition of this work. We are deeply indebted to David Hatter, who endorsed our project enthusiastically and was able to put together an effective team, together with Ellen Johnson and Mike Cotterell. These three people have dedicated an enormous amount of effort to the production process. In particular, we thank Ellen for her support in the translation, David for his careful copy-editing and for the many terminological suggestions and Mike for his professional and patient processing of our manuscript through its numerous revisions.

We would also like to thank our families, for the continuous support they have given to us and for their patience during the evenings, nights and holidays spent on this book. Specifically, Paolo Atzeni would like to thank Gianna, his wife and his children Francesco and Laura; Stefano Ceri wishes to thank Maria Teresa, his wife and his children Paolo and Gabriele; Stefano Paraboschi wishes to thank Paola, his wife; Riccardo Torlone wishes to thank Maria Paola.

1

Introduction

Collection, organization and storage of data are major tasks in many human activities and in every computer-based system. Bank balances, telephone numbers in directories, stock quotations, availability of credit card funds, registers of students enrolled in a university and grades in their exams are all examples of types of data that are fundamental to the activities to which they refer. Computer-based systems ensure that this data is permanently maintained, quickly updated to show changes, and made accessible to the queries of users who can be remote from one another and from the computer where the data is kept. Imagine, for example, queries about the availability of funds on credit cards, asked through simple devices available in millions of businesses (whether hotels, shops or companies), which allow purchases made anywhere in the world to be charged to the credit card owners.

This book is about the management of data through the use of computerized information systems; it describes the concepts necessary to represent information on a computer, the languages for update and retrieval, and the specialized architectures for data management. In this first chapter, the concepts of information systems and databases are introduced, so that we can then deal with the major characteristics of systems for managing databases.

1.1 Information and data

In the pursuit of any activity, whether by an individual or in an organization of any size, the availability of information and the capacity to manage it efficiently are essential; therefore, every organization has an *information system*, which manages the information necessary to perform the functions of the organization. The existence of the information system is partly independent of the extent to which it is automated: note that information systems existed long before the invention and widespread adoption of computers; for example, bank records and electoral rolls have been in place for several centuries. In general, only a subset of the information system of an organization is computerized. The capillary spread of computing technology into almost all human activity, characteristic of the eighties and of the nineties, generates a continuous growth in computerization of information systems.

In the simplest of human activities, information is recorded and exchanged according to the natural techniques typical of the activity itself: written or spoken language, drawings, diagrams, numbers. In some activities, an explicit record might not even exist, the information being − more or less accurately − memorized. In any case, we can say that, as activities have gradually become systematized, appropriate forms of organization and codification have been found.

In computer-based systems the concept of recording and codifying is taken to the limit: the information is recorded by means of *data,* which needs to be interpreted in order to provide information. As with many basic concepts, it is difficult to give a precise definition of the concept of data and of the differences between the concepts of *data* and *information:* roughly we can say that data alone has no significance, but once interpreted and suitably correlated, it provides information that allows us to improve our knowledge of the world.

For example, the string John Smith and the number 25775, written on a sheet of paper, are two pieces of data that are meaningless by themselves. If the sheet is sent in response to the question 'Who is the head of the research department and what is his telephone number?', then it is possible to interpret the data and use it to enrich our knowledge with the information that the person named John Smith is the head of the research department and that his telephone number is 25775.

Having introduced the concept of data in this way, we can move on to that of the database, the main topic of this text. Various definitions are possible; the most general being: a *database* is a collection of data, used to represent information of interest to an information system. In this book, we will mainly consider a far more restricted definition, related to a specific technology, discussed in the next section.

Let us conclude this section with an observation. In many applications, data is intrinsically much more stable than the (manual or automatic) procedures that operate upon it. Returning to an example mentioned earlier, we can observe that the data relating to bank applications has a structure that has remained virtually unchanged for decades, while the procedures that act upon it vary continually, as every customer can readily verify. Furthermore, when one procedure is substituted for another, the new procedure 'inherits' the data of the old one, with appropriate changes. This characteristic of stability leads us to state that data constitutes a 'resource' for the organization that manages it, a significant heritage to exploit and protect.

1.2 Databases and database management systems

Attention to data has characterized computer-based applications since the beginning, but software systems dedicated specifically to the management of data have been in existence only since the end of the sixties, and some applications still do not make use of them. In the absence of specific software, data management is performed by means of traditional programming languages, for example C and FORTRAN, or, more recently, by object-oriented languages, among them C++, Smalltalk and Java. Many applications are written in COBOL, a programming language particularly suitable for 'business applications', that is, applications primarily written for data management.[1]

The conventional approach to data management exploits the presence of *files* to store data permanently. A file allows for the storage and searching of data, but provides only simple mechanisms for access and sharing. With this approach, the procedures written in a programming language are completely autonomous; each one defines and uses one or more 'private' files. Data of possible interest to more than one program is replicated as many times as there are programs that use it, with obvious redundancy and the possibility of inconsistency. Databases were created, for the most part, to overcome this type of inconvenience.

We are now in the position of defining a *database management system* (DBMS) as a software system able to manage collections of data that are *large*, *shared* and *persistent*, and to ensure their *reliability* and *privacy*. Like any software product, a DBMS must be *efficient* and *effective*. A *database* is a collection of data managed by a DBMS.

Let us comment on each of the above listed characteristics of the DBMS and of the databases.

- Databases can be *large,* in the sense that they can contain thousands of billions of bytes and are, in general, certainly larger than the main memory available. As a result, a DBMS must manage data in secondary memory. Obviously 'small' databases can exist, but the systems must be able to manage data without being limited by dimensions, apart from the physical ones of the devices at hand.

- Databases are *shared,* in the sense that various applications and users must be able to gain access to data of common interest. It is important to note that in this way the redundancy of data is reduced, since repetitions are avoided, and, consequently, the possibility of *inconsistencies* is reduced; if more than one copy of the same data exist, it is possible that they are not

---

1. COBOL is a language of the seventies, now largely obsolete; however, many business applications are still written in COBOL. A process of transformation is now in progress that is aimed at rewriting these applications in the more modern languages for database management – the subject of this book.

identical; and vice versa, if every piece of data is stored only once, then the problem of inconsistency is eliminated. In order to guarantee shared access to data by many users operating simultaneously, the DBMS makes use of a special mechanism called *concurrency control*.

- Databases are *persistent;* that is, they have a lifespan that is not limited to single executions of the programs that use them. Conversely, note that the data managed by a program in main memory has a life that begins and ends with the execution of the program; therefore, such data is not persistent.

- DBMSs ensure *reliability;* that is, the capacity of the system to preserve the content of the database (or at least to allow its reconstruction) in case of hardware or software failure. To fulfil this requirement, DBMSs provide specific functions for *backup* and *recovery.*

- DBMSs ensure data *privacy.* Each user, who is recognized by a user name that is specific to that user's access to the DBMS, is qualified to carry out only certain operations on the data, through the mechanisms of *authorization.*

- DBMSs are also concerned with *efficiency,* that is, the capacity to carry out operations using an appropriate amount of resources (time and space) for each user. This characteristic relies on the techniques used in the implementation of the DBMS, and on how well the product has been designed. It should be stressed that DBMSs provide a wide-ranging combination of features that require many resources, and therefore they often put heavy requirements on the resources provided by the operating environment.

- Finally DBMSs increase *effectiveness,* that is, the capacity of the database system to make the activities of its users productive, in every sense. This is clearly a generic definition and does not correspond to a specific function, given that a DBMS provides various services and functions to different users. The task of designing a database and the applications that use it aims essentially to guarantee the good, overall effectiveness of the system.

It is important to stress that the management of large and persistent collections of data is also possible by means of instruments less sophisticated than DBMSs, beginning with the files present in all operating systems. Files were introduced to manage data 'local' to a specific procedure or application. DBMSs were conceived and created to extend the functions of the file system, permitting shared access to the same data by more than one user and application, and also guaranteeing many other services in an integrated manner. Clearly, DBMSs in their turn use files for the storage of data; however, as we shall discuss in Part III of the book, files managed by DBMSs allow the data organization to be of a higher level of complexity.

1.3 Data models

A *data model* is a combination of constructs used to organize data. Each data model provides *structuring mechanisms*, similar to the type constructors of programming languages, which allow the definition of new data types based on constructors applied to predefined, elementary types. For example, Pascal allows the construction of types by means of array, record, set and file constructors.

The *relational data model,* at present the most widespread, provides the *relation* constructor, which makes it possible to organize data in a collection of records with a fixed structure. A relation is often represented by means of a table, whose rows show specific records and whose columns correspond to the fields of the record; the order of rows and columns is irrelevant. For example, data relating to university courses and their tutors and the insertion of the courses into the prospectus of the various degree programmes, can be organized by means of two relations TEACHING and PROSPECTUS, represented by the tables in Figure 1.1. As we can see, a relational database generally involves many relations.

TEACHING

Course	Tutor
Databases	Smith
Networks	Jones
Languages	Robinson

PROSPECTUS

DegreeProgramme	Subject	Year
Information Systems	Databases	4
Information Systems	Networks	4
Information Systems	Languages	3
Electrical Engineering	Databases	4
Electrical Engineering	Networks	4

Figure 1.1   Example of a relational database.

The relational model was proposed in a research setting at the beginning of the seventies, appeared on the market in real systems in the early eighties, and is now, as we have said, the most widespread. Besides the relational model, three other types of model have been defined.

- The *hierarchical data model,* based on the use of tree structures (and hierarchies, hence the name), defined during the first phase of development of DBMSs (in the sixties) but still used in many systems, mainly for continuity reasons.

- The *network data model* (also known as the CODASYL model, after the Conference on Data Systems Languages that gave it a precise definition), based on the use of graphs, developed in the early seventies.

- The *object data model,* developed in the eighties in order to overcome some limitations of the relational model, which extends to databases the paradigm of object-oriented programming; Chapter 11, in Part IV of the book, is dedicated to the object data model.

The data models listed above are all available in commercial DBMSs; they are called *logical*, to underline the fact that the structures used for these models, although abstract, reflect a particular organization (tree, graph, table, or object). Other data models known as *conceptual* models, have been introduced to describe data in a manner independent of the logical model; but these are not available in commercial DBMSs. Their name comes from the fact that they tend to describe *concepts* of the real world, rather than the data needed for their representation. These models are used in the preliminary phase of the database design process, to analyze the application in the best possible way, without implementational 'contaminations'. In Part II of this book, dedicated to the design of databases, we examine in detail a conceptual model, the *Entity-Relationship* model.

1.3.1 Schemas and instances

In a database there is a part that is invariant in time, called the *schema* of the database, made up of the characteristics of the data, and a part that changes with time, called the *instance* or *state* of the database, made up of the actual values. In the example of Figure 1.1, the relations have a fixed structure; the relation TEACHING has two columns (called *attributes*), which refer to courses and tutors respectively. The *schema of a relation* consists of its heading, that is, the name of the relation, followed by the names of its attributes; for example,

TEACHING(Course, Tutor)

The rows of the table vary with time, and correspond to the courses currently offered and their respective tutors. During the life of the database, tutors and courses are added, removed or modified; similarly, the prospectus is modified from one year to the next. The *instance of a relation* is made up of a collection of rows, which vary with time; in the example we have three pairs:

Databases	Smith
Networks	Jones
Languages	Robinson

We could also say that the schema is the *intensional* component of the database and the instance is the *extensional* component. These definitions will be developed and discussed in detail in Chapter 2.

1.3.2 Abstraction levels in DBMSs

The concepts of model and schema described above can be developed further, considering other dimensions in the description of data. In particular, a standardized architecture for DBMSs has been proposed. It is divided into three levels, known respectively as *logical*, *internal*, and *external;* for each level there is a schema.

The *logical*[2] *schema* is a description of the whole database by means of the logical model adopted by the DBMS (that is, one of the models described earlier: relational, hierarchical, network or object).

The *internal schema* describes the implementation of the logical schema by means of physical storage structures. For example, a relation can be physically organized as a sequential file, or a hash file, or a sequential file with indices. We discuss physical structures for the organization of data in Part III of the book, devoted to the technological aspects of DBMSs.

An *external schema* is the description of a portion of the database by means of the logical model. An external schema can offer a different organization of the data in order to reflect the point of view of a particular user or group of users. Thus it is possible to associate various external schemas with a single logical schema: each of the external schemas will provide a specific view of the database (or a subset thereof).

In most of the current systems, the external level is not explicitly present, but it is possible to define derived relations (called *views*). For example, as regards the database in Figure 1.1, a student on the Electrical Engineering degree programme could be interested only in the courses included in the prospectus for that degree programme; this information is present in the relation ELECTRICALENGINEERING, shown in Figure 1.2, which can be derived from the relation PROSPECTUS considering only the rows that refer to the Electrical Engineering degree programme. Mechanisms for *access authorization* can be associated with external schemas, in order to regulate the access of users to the database: a user could be authorized to manipulate only the data described by means of his external schema.

ELECTRICALENGINEERING

DegreeProgramme	Subject	Year
Electrical Engineering	Databases	4
Electrical Engineering	Networks	4

Figure 1.2 A relational view.

1.3.3 Data independence

The multilevel architecture described in the previous section guarantees *data independence*, a major property of DBMSs. In general, this property allows users and applications programs to refer to data at a high level of abstraction, ignoring implementation details. More precisely, data independence presents two aspects, *physical* and *logical* independence.

Physical independence allows interaction with the DBMS independently of the physical aspects of the data. For example, it is possible to modify the

2. This level is called *conceptual* by some authors, following the terminology used originally in the proposal. We prefer the term *logical*, because, as we have seen, we use the term *conceptual* for other purposes.

organization of the files that implement the relations or the physical allocation of files to the storage devices without influencing the high level descriptions of the data and programs that use the data.

Logical independence guarantees that the interaction with the external level of the database is independent of the logical level. For example, it is possible to add a new external schema according to the demands of a new user or to modify an external schema without having to modify the logical schema and therefore the underlying physical organization of the data. At the same time, it is possible to modify the logical level, maintaining unchanged the external schema of interest to a given user (provided that its definition in terms of the logical structures is adjusted).

It is important to underline that access to a database happens only through the external level (which can coincide with the logical level); it is the DBMS that translates the operations in terms of the underlying levels. The multilevel architecture is therefore the fundamental mechanism through which DBMSs achieve data independence.

1.4 Languages and users

DBMSs are complex systems that offer a variety of languages for the management of data and involve, in their life-cycle, a variety of users.

1.4.1 Database languages

Noting the distinction between schemas and instances that we illustrated above, we may distinguish between database languages in a similar way.

- The *data definition language* (DDL) is used to define the logical, external and physical schemas and access authorizations.

- The *data manipulation language* (DML) is used for querying and updating database instances.

It is important to note that some languages, such as, for example, SQL, which we examine in detail in Chapter 4, offer the features of both a DDL and a DML in an integrated form.

Access to data can be specified in various ways.

- Through interactive textual languages, such as SQL.

- Through commands similar to the interactive ones embedded in traditional programming languages, such as C, C++, COBOL, FORTRAN, and so on; these are called *host languages* because they 'host' commands written in the database language.

- Through commands similar to the interactive ones embedded in ad hoc development languages, often with specific features (for example, for the generation of graphs, complex printouts, or forms and menus). These languages vary greatly from one system to another and therefore we can give an idea of only a few of their aspects in the appendices that are devoted to specific systems.

- Through friendly interfaces that allow the formulation of queries without the use of a textual language. These too differ greatly from one system to another and are continually evolving. Again, we touch upon a few simple and important aspects in the appendices.

A large number of programs for data entry, management and printing have a common structure; consequently, the existence of development languages and friendly interfaces considerably simplifies the production of applications, reducing development time and costs.

1.4.2 Users and designers

Various categories of people can interact with a database or with a DBMS. Let us briefly describe the most important.

- The *database administrator* (DBA) is the person responsible for the design, control and administration of the database. The DBA has the task of mediating among the various requirements, often conflicting, expressed by the users, ensuring centralized control over the data. In particular, he or she is responsible for guaranteeing services, ensuring the reliability of the system, and managing the authorizations for access to the data. Part II of the book is about the design of databases, one of the major tasks of the DBA.

- The *application designers* and *programmers* define and create programs that access the database. They use the data manipulation language or various support tools for the generation of interfaces for the database, as described above. Chapter 4 describes SQL as a tool for the design of applications on databases.

- The *users* employ the database for their own activities. They can, in their turn, be divided into two categories.

  o *End users*, who use *transactions*, that is, programs that carry out frequent and predefined activities, with few exceptions known and taken into account in advance.[3]

  o *Casual users*, able to use the interactive languages to gain access to the database, formulating queries (or updates) of various types. They can be specialists in the language they use and interact frequently with the database. Note that the term 'casual' means that the queries are not predefined.

---

3. In database usage, the term *transaction* also has a more specific meaning, which will be discussed in Part III of the book.

1.5 Advantages and disadvantages of DBMSs

We conclude this chapter by summarizing the essential characteristics of databases and DBMSs, and their advantages and disadvantages.

- DBMSs allow data to be considered as a common resource of an organization, available to all its authorized members.

- The database provides a standardized and precise model of that part of the real world of interest to the organization, usable in existing applications and, with the necessary extensions, in future applications.

- With the use of a DBMS, centralized control of the data is possible, which can be improved by forms of standardization and can benefit from an 'economy of scale'.

- Sharing allows the reduction of redundancy and inconsistency.

- Data independence, the fundamental characteristic of DBMSs, favours the development of applications that are more flexible and more easily modifiable.

The use of DBMSs also carries some negative aspects, or at least ones that require careful consideration, including the following.

- DBMSs are expensive products, complex and quite different from many other software tools. Their introduction therefore represents a considerable investment, both direct (the cost of the product) and indirect (the acquisition of the necessary hardware and software resources, application migration, personnel training).

- DBMSs provide, in standardized form, a whole set of services, which necessarily carry a cost. In the cases where some of these services are not needed, it is difficult to extract the services actually required from the others, and this can generate inefficiencies.

In conclusion, we can say that situations can exist in which the adoption of a DBMS can be inconvenient: some applications with one or just a few users without the need for concurrent access can sometimes be achieved more profitably with ordinary files rather than with a DBMS. However, DBMS technology has evolved considerably in recent years, resulting in more and more efficient and reliable systems, on more and more widespread and less expensive architecture, so increasing the convenience of developing applications with a DBMS.

1.6 Bibliography

There are many other books and additional readings on the general aspects of database systems. The more similar in goals to this book, with balanced treatment of methodological and technical aspects, include ElMasri and

Navathe [38], Ramakhrishnan [69], Korth, Silbesrchatz, and Sudarshan [78], and O'Neil [63]. Date's book [33], now in its sixth edition, is very popular in the practitioners' world, since it gives a simple description of many important aspects. Ullman [88] offers an integrated view of existing database technology and possible 'knowledge-based' extensions, a direction that was popular in the eighties. Ullman and Widom [89] focus on a first-level course in databases that includes both a relational and an object-based approach. Additionally, we mention that Stonebraker [80] offers a collection of many influential papers in the field, which can be used to follow the evolution of the technology. For details relating to specific aspects mentioned in this chapter, we refer the reader to the bibliographies of the succeeding chapters, in which they will be explored in more detail.

Part I

Relational databases

2

The relational model

Most current database systems are based on the relational model, which was proposed in a scientific publication by E. F. Codd [26] in 1970, with the intention of providing a basis for data independence. The establishment of the relational model as a *de facto* standard was rather slow, due to its high level of abstraction: efficient solutions were not immediately discovered for relational structures, which were different from those in use at that time. Although the first prototypes of relational systems had already been created in the early seventies, the first relational systems appeared on the market in the early eighties, acquiring a significant share of it only in the mid-eighties.

In this chapter, we illustrate the structural aspects of the model, that is, the way it is used to organize data. After a brief discussion of the various logical models, we show how the concept of a relation can be used to represent the information in a database. Then, we briefly discuss the techniques for the representation of incomplete information and we examine integrity constraints, which allow the specification of additional properties that must be satisfied by the database.

The presentation of the relational model is completed in the next two chapters, the first one dedicated to the principles of query operations on relational databases, and the second one to SQL, the language used in real systems for the definition, updating and querying of relational databases.

2.1 The structure of the relational model

2.1.1 Logical models in database systems

The *relational model* is based on two concepts, *relation* and *table*, which differ in their nature but are highly related. The notion of *relation* is formal, as it comes from mathematics, in particular from set theory, while the concept of *table* is simple and intuitive. Their simultaneous presence is probably the major reason for the great success of the relational model. In fact, tables offer a natural understanding even to end users who come across them in many contexts other than in databases. On the other hand, the availability of a clear and simple formalization has allowed the development of a theory to support the model, with very interesting results.

The relational model satisfies the requirement of data independence, as discussed in Chapter 1: users and programmers make reference only to relations (logical or external level), which are then implemented by means of appropriate physical structures; however, to gain access to the data it is not necessary to know about the physical structures themselves. The relational model was proposed at the end of the sixties in order to provide a higher level of data independence than the network and hierarchical models. These included reference to the underlying structure, by means of the use of pointers and the physical ordering of data.

2.1.2 Relations and tables

Let us recall from basic mathematics courses that, given two sets, D_1 and D_2, the *cartesian product* of D_1 and D_2, in symbols $D_1 \times D_2$, is the set of ordered pairs (v_1, v_2), such that v_1 is an element of D_1 and v_2 is an element of D_2. For example, given the sets $A = \{1,2,4\}$ and $B = \{a,b\}$, the cartesian product $A \times B$ is the set of all the possible pairs in which the first element belongs to A and the second to B. Since A has three elements and B has two, we have six pairs:

$$\{(1,a),(1,b),(2,a),(2,b),(4,a),(4,b)\}$$

In mathematics, a *relation* on the sets D_1 and D_2 (called *domains* of the relation) is a subset of $D_1 \times D_2$. Given the sets A and B above, an example relation on A and B consists of the set of pairs $\{(1,a),(1,b),(4,b)\}$.

The above definition does not indicate whether the sets we are considering may be finite or not, and therefore includes the possibility of infinite sets (and thus of infinite relations). In practice, since our databases must be stored in computer systems of finite size, the relations are necessarily finite. At the same time, it can be useful for the domains to have an infinite size (so that it is always possible to assume the existence of a value not present in the database). Thus, we will assume where necessary that our databases are made up of finite relations on possibly infinite domains.

Relations can be represented graphically in table form. The two tables shown in Figure 2.1 describe the cartesian product $A \times B$ and the mathematical relation on A and B illustrated above.

The definitions of cartesian product and relation refer to two sets, but can be generalized with respect to the number of sets. Given $n > 0$ sets $D_1, D_2 ..., D_n$, not necessarily distinct, the cartesian product of $D_1, D_2 ..., D_n$, represented by $D_1 \times D_2 \times ... \times D_n$, is made up of the set of the n-tuples $v_1, v_2, ..., v_n$, such that v_i belongs to D_i, for $1 \leq i \leq n$. A mathematical relation on the domains $D_1, D_2 ..., D_n$ is a subset of the cartesian product $D_1 \times D_2 \times ... \times D_n$. The number n of the components of

1	a
1	b
2	a
2	b
4	a
4	b

1	a
1	b
4	b

Figure 2.1 Representation in table form of a cartesian product and a relation.

the cartesian product (and therefore of every n-tuple) is called the *degree* of the cartesian product and of the relation. The number of elements (that is, of n-tuples) of the relation is, as usual in set theory, the *cardinality* of the relation. Figure 2.2a shows the tabular representation of a cartesian product on the domains $C = \{x, y\}$, $D = \{a, b, c\}$ and $E = \{3, 5\}$, with degree 3. Figure 2.2b shows a relation on $C \times D \times E$ with degree 3 and cardinality 6.

(a)

x	a	3
x	a	5
x	b	3
x	b	5
x	c	3
x	c	5
y	a	3
y	a	5
y	b	3
y	b	5
y	c	3
y	c	5

(b)

x	a	3
x	a	5
x	c	5
y	a	3
y	c	3
y	c	5

Figure 2.2 A ternary cartesian product and a ternary relation.

Relations (and the corresponding tables) can be used to represent data for any application. For example, the relation in Figure 2.3 contains data relating to the results of a set of soccer matches.

Real Madrid	Liverpool	3	1
Liverpool	Milan	2	0
Real Madrid	Roma	1	2
Roma	Milan	0	1

Figure 2.3 A relation with the results of soccer matches.

It is defined with reference to two domains *integer* and *string,* each of which appears twice. The relation is in fact a subset of the cartesian product:

$$\text{String} \times \text{String} \times \text{Integer} \times \text{Integer}$$

2.1.3 Relations with attributes

We can make various observations about relations and their tabular representations. According to the definition, a mathematical relation is a *set* of ordered n-tuples $(v_1, v_2, \ldots, v_n)$, with $v_1 \in D_1$, $v_2 \in D_2$, $\ldots$, $v_n \in D_n$. With reference to the use that we make of relations for organizing data in our database, we can say that each n-tuple contains various items of data connected to each other, or rather establishes links between them; for example, the first n-tuple of the relation in Figure 2.3 establishes a relationship between the values **Real Madrid, Liverpool, 3, 1**, to indicate that the result of the match between Real Madrid and Liverpool is 3 to 1. We can then remember that a relation is a set and therefore:

- there is no defined order between the n-tuples; in the tables that represent them there is obviously a 'presentation' order, but it is immaterial, since two tables with the same rows, but in different order, represent the same relation;

- the n-tuples of a relation are distinct one from the other, since among the elements of a set there cannot be two identical elements; therefore a table can represent a relation only if its rows are different from one another.

At the same time, each n-tuple has an ordering: the i-th value of each one comes from the i-th domain. This is essential for understanding the meaning of the data in the relation: if we were to swap the third and fourth components around in the relation in Figure 2.3, it would completely change the meaning of our relation, in that the results of the matches would be inverted. This happens because each of the two domains *integer* and *string* appears twice in the relation, and the two occurrences are distinguished on the basis of their positions: the first appearance of the domain *string* refers to the home team, and the second to the visiting team: similarly, the two occurrences of the domain *integer*.

This ordering among the domains of a relation actually corresponds to an unsatisfactory characteristic of the concept of relation as defined in mathematics with regard to the possibility of organizing and using data. Indeed, in computer science there is a tendency to prefer *non-positional* notations to positional ones; the former allows reference to the fields of a record by means of symbolic names, while the latter refers to the same fields through their ordering, and should be used only when the ordering corresponds to an intrinsic feature, as happens, for example, in numerical analysis problems, in which arrays offer an obvious and direct representation of vectors and matrices. The data that we wish to organize in the relations of our databases has a structure that is very similar to that of records: a relation is substantially a set of homogenous records, that is, defined on the same fields. For this reason, we introduce a non-positional notation, by associating names with the domains in a relation, referred to as *attributes*, which describe the 'roles' played by the domains. For example, for the relation concerning the matches, we can use names such as HomeTeam, VisitingTeam, HomeGoals, VisitorGoals; in the tabular representation, we use the attributes as column headings (Figure 2.4). Given the necessity of identifying the components unambiguously, the attributes of a relation (and therefore the column headings) must be different from each other.

HomeTeam	VisitingTeam	HomeGoals	VisitorGoals
Real Madrid	Liverpool	3	1
Liverpool	Milan	2	0
Real Madrid	Roma	1	2
Roma	Milan	0	1

Figure 2.4 A relation with attributes.

By modifying the definition of relation with the introduction of attributes, and still before giving the formal definition, we can see that the ordering of attributes (and of the columns in the tabular representation) is irrelevant: it is no longer necessary to speak of first domain, second domain, and so on; it is sufficient to refer to the attributes. Figure 2.5 shows another tabular representation of the relation in Figure 2.4, with the attributes, and therefore the columns, in a different order (after the American style in which the home team is shown after the visiting team).

VisitingTeam	HomeTeam	VisitorGoals	HomeGoals
Liverpool	Real Madrid	1	3
Milan	Liverpool	0	2
Roma	Real Madrid	2	1
Milan	Roma	1	0

Figure 2.5 Another representation of the relation in Figure 2.4.

To formalize the concepts, let us establish the correspondence between attributes and domains by means of a function $DOM : X \rightarrow \mathcal{D}$, which associates with each attribute $A \in X$ a domain $DOM(A) \in \mathcal{D}$. Then, let us say that a *tuple* on a set of attributes X is a function t, which associates with each attribute $A \in X$ a value of the domain $DOM(A)$. We can therefore give the new definition of relation: a *relation* on X is a set of tuples on X. The difference between this definition and the traditional one of set theory resides only in the definition of tuple: in a mathematical relation we have n-tuples whose elements are distinguished by position, whereas, in the new definition, the elements are distinguished by the attributes, that is, by a non-positional technique. From now on, we will use the term 'relation' to refer to the new non-positional definition.

Let us introduce a useful notation that we will use frequently in the future. If t is a tuple on X and $A \in X$, then $t[A]$ (or $t.A$) indicates the value of t on A. For example, if t is the first tuple of the relation in Figure 2.5, we can say that

$$t[\text{VisitingTeam}] = \text{Liverpool}$$

The same notation is also used for sets of attributes, in which case it denotes a tuple:

$$t[\text{VisitingTeam, VisitorGoals}]$$

is a tuple on two attributes.[1]

2.1.4 Relations and databases

As we have already seen, a relation can be used to organize relevant data for an application. However, a single relation is not usually sufficient for this purpose: a database is generally made up of several relations, whose tuples contain common values where this is necessary in order to establish correspondences. Let us explore this concept more thoroughly by commenting on the database in Figure 2.6:

STUDENTS	RegNum	Surname	FirstName	BirthDate
	276545	Smith	Mary	25/11/1980
	485745	Black	Anna	23/04/1981
	200768	Verdi	Paolo	12/02/1981
	587614	Smith	Lucy	10/10/1980
	937653	Brown	Mavis	01/12/1980

EXAMS	Student	Grade	Course
	276545	C	01
	276545	B	04
	937653	B	01
	200768	B	04

COURSES	Code	Title	Tutor
	01	Physics	Grant
	03	Chemistry	Beale
	04	Chemistry	Clark

Figure 2.6 A relational database.

---

1. There is an overloading in the notation here: if A is an attribute, then $t[A]$ is a value, while if X is a set of attributes, then $t[X]$ is a tuple, that is, a function. Moreover, as we shall see, sets consisting of a single attribute will be denoted by the name of the attribute itself; therefore $t[A]$ denotes both a value and a tuple on an attribute. However, the ambiguity will usually be irrelevant.

- the first relation contains information relating to a set of students, with registration numbers (RegNum), surnames (Surname), first names (FirstName) and dates of birth (BirthDate);

- the third relation contains information on some courses, with code, title and tutor;

- the second relation contains information relating to exams: the student's registration number, the course code and the grade achieved; this relation makes reference to the data contained in the other two: to the students, by means of the registration number, and to the courses, by means of their codes.

The database in Figure 2.6 shows one of the fundamental characteristics of the relational model, which is often expressed by saying that it is 'value-based': the references between data in different relations are represented by means of the values of the domains that appear in the tuples. Instead the network and hierarchical models, which were defined before the relational model, represent references explicitly by means of pointers and for this reason are called 'pointer-based' models. Since in this book we do not have a detailed presentation of these models, we briefly comment here on the fundamental characteristics of a simple model with pointers. Figure 2.7 shows the same database as that in Figure 2.6, where we have used pointers instead of value-based references (the registration numbers of the students and the course codes).

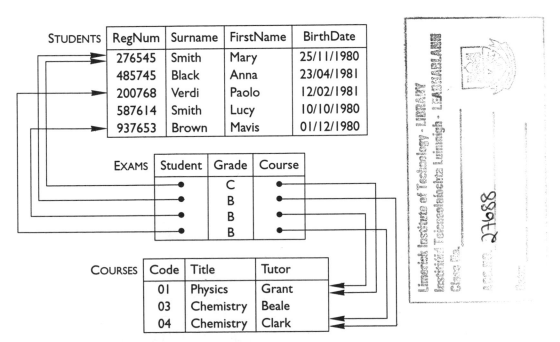

Figure 2.7 A database with pointers.

Compared with a pointer-based model, the relational model has several advantages:

- the logical representation of data (consisting only of values) makes no reference to the physical one, which can also vary with time: the relational model therefore allows physical data independence;

- it represents only what is relevant from the point of view of the application (the user); the pointers are additional, related to implementational aspects; in the models with pointers, the application programmer has to refer to data that is not significant for the application;

- given that all of the information is contained in the values, it is relatively simple to transfer the data from one context to another (for example, if it is necessary to move the database from one system to another); with pointers the operation is more complex, because the pointers have a meaning that is local to each system, and so cannot be just exported directly.

Note that, even in a relational database, on the physical level, the data can be represented by techniques that require the use of pointers. The difference, with regard to pointer-based models, is that the pointers are not visible at the logical level. Furthermore, in the object database systems, which represent one of the evolutionary directions of databases discussed in Chapter 11, object-identifiers show some of the characteristics of pointers, although at a higher level of abstraction.

We can recap at this point the definitions of the relational model, with a few details, distinguishing the levels of the schemas from those of the instances.

- A *relation schema* consists of a symbol, called *name of the relation R* and a set of (names of) *attributes* $X = \{A_1, A_2, \dots, A_n\}$, the whole usually indicated $R(X)$. A domain is associated with each attribute.

- A *database schema* consists of a set of relation schemas with different names:

$$\mathbf{R} = \{R_1(X_1), R_2(X_2), \dots, R_n(X_n)\}$$

- A *relation instance* (or simply *relation*) on a schema $R(X)$ is a set r of tuples on X.

- A *database instance* (or simply *database*) on a schema $\mathbf{R} = \{R_1(X_1), R_2(X_2), \dots, R_n(X_n)\}$ is a set of relations $\mathbf{r} = \{r_1, r_2, \dots, r_n\}$, where every r_i, for $1 \leq i \leq n$, is a relation on the schema $R_i(X_i)$.

To give an example, we can say that the database schema in Figure 2.6 is:

$$\mathbf{R} = \{\text{STUDENTS(RegNum, Surname, FirstName, BirthDate),}$$
$$\text{EXAMS(Student, Grade, Course),}$$
$$\text{COURSES(Code, Title, Tutor)}\}$$

For convenience, we summarize the conventions that we adopt hereafter (and that we have already used in the definitions and in the examples):

- the attributes (when they do not use significant names from the application point of view) will be indicated by letters near the beginning of the alphabet in capitals, possibly with a superscript or a subscript: $A, B, C, A', A_1, \ldots$;

- sets of attributes will be indicated by letters near the end of the alphabet in capitals: $X, Y, Z, X', X_1, \ldots$; a set whose components we wish to highlight will be denoted by the juxtaposition of the names of the attributes themselves: we will write $X = ABC$ rather than $X = \{A,B,C\}$; similarly, the union of sets will be denoted by the juxtaposition of the corresponding names: we will write XY rather than $X \cup Y$; combining the two conventions, we will write XA instead of $X \cup \{A\}$;

- for the relation names we will use the letter(s) R (and S) in capitals: $R_1, S, S', \ldots$; for the relation instances, we will use the same symbols as the corresponding relation names, but in lower case.

In order to illustrate further the fundamental concepts of the relational model, let us discuss two more examples.

First we will note how relations on a single attribute are admissible. This makes particular sense in databases consisting of several relations, in which a relation on a single attribute contains values that appear as values of an attribute of another relation. For example, in a database in which the relation STUDENTS is shown in Figure 2.6, it is possible to use another relation on a single attribute, RegNum, to indicate the students who are also workers (by means of the relevant RegNum, which must appear in the relation STUDENTS) (see Figure 2.8).

STUDENTS

RegNum	Surname	FirstName	BirthDate
276545	Smith	Mary	25/11/1980
485745	Black	Anna	23/04/1981
200768	Verdi	Paolo	12/02/1981
587614	Smith	Lucy	10/10/1980
937653	Brown	Mavis	01/12/1980

WORKERS

RegNum
276545
485745
937653

Figure 2.8 A relation on a single attribute.

Let us now look at a more complex example, which shows how the relational model allows the representation of information with a detailed structure. In Figure 2.9, three receipts from a restaurant are shown. They have a structure that (apart from the preprinted phrases in bold) includes some atomic information (number, date and total) and a variable number of

Da Mario		
Receipt No: 1357		
Date: 5/5/92		
3	covers	3.00
2	hors d'oeuvre	5.00
3	first course	9.00
2	steak	12.00
	Total:	29.00

Da Mario		
Receipt No: 2334		
Date: 4/7/92		
2	covers	2.00
2	hors d'oeuvre	2.50
2	first course	6.00
2	bream	15.00
2	coffee	2.00
	Total:	27.50

Da Mario		
Receipt No: 3007		
Date: 4/8/92		
2	covers	3.00
2	hors d'oeuvre	6.00
3	first course	8.00
1	bream	7.50
1	salad	3.00
2	coffee	2.00
	Total:	29.50

Figure 2.9 Some receipts.

lines, each referring to a homogenous group of dishes (with quantity, description and overall cost). Since our relations have a fixed structure, it is not possible to represent the group of receipts with a single relation: it would not be possible to represent a number of dishes that is not known in advance. We can, however, represent the same information by means of two relations, as shown in Figure 2.10: the relation RECEIPTS contains the data shown only

DETAILS

Number	Quantity	Description	Cost
1357	3	covers	3.00
1357	2	hors d'oeuvre	5.00
1357	3	first course	9.00
1357	2	steak	12.00
2334	2	covers	2.00
2334	2	hors d'oeuvre	2.50
2334	2	first course	6.00
2334	2	bream	15.00
2334	2	coffee	2.00
3007	2	covers	3.00
3007	2	hors d'oeuvre	6.00
3007	3	first course	8.00
3007	1	bream	7.50
3007	1	salad	3.00
3007	2	coffee	2.00

RECEIPTS

Number	Date	Total
1357	5/5/92	29.00
2334	4/7/92	27.50
3007	4/8/92	29.50

Figure 2.10 A database for the receipts in Figure 2.9.

once in each receipt (number, date and total) and the relation DETAILS contains the various lines of each receipt (with quantity, description and overall cost), associated with the same receipt, by means of the appropriate receipt number.

We should point out here that for the database in Figure 2.10 to represent the receipts correctly, two conditions must be satisfied:

- it is not necessary to keep track of the order in which the lines appear on each receipt; in fact, since no order is defined among the tuples of a relation, the tuples in DETAILS are not in any fixed order;

- no duplicate lines appear on any receipt (which could happen in the case of different orders for the same dishes with the same quantity).

Both problems can be resolved by adding an attribute, which indicates the position of the line of the receipt (see Figure 2.11); in this way it is always

DETAILS

Number	Line	Quantity	Description	Cost
1357	1	3	covers	3.00
1357	2	2	hors d'oeuvre	5.00
1357	3	3	first course	9.00
1357	4	2	steak	12.00
2334	1	2	covers	2.00
2334	2	2	hors d'oeuvre	2.50
2334	3	2	first course	6.00
2334	4	2	bream	15.00
2334	5	2	coffee	2.00
3007	1	2	covers	3.00
3007	2	2	hors d'oeuvre	6.00
3007	3	3	first course	8.00
3007	4	1	bream	7.50
3007	5	1	salad	3.00
3007	6	2	coffee	2.00

RECEIPTS

Number	Date	Total
1357	5/5/92	29.00
2334	4/7/92	27.50
3007	4/8/92	29.50

Figure 2.11 Another database for the receipts.

possible to reconstruct perfectly the contents of all the receipts. In general, we can say that the solution to Figure 2.10 is preferable when the information on the receipt is of interest only for its own sake (and in the receipts there are no repeated lines), while that in Figure 2.11 makes it possible to keep track of the actual layout of each receipt. The example demonstrates that in a given situation, the data to be represented in the database can be different according to the specific requirements of the application.

2.1.5 Incomplete information and null values

The structure of the relational model, as discussed in the preceding sections, is very simple and powerful. At the same time, however, it imposes a certain degree of rigidity, in that the information must be represented by means of homogenous tuples of data: in particular, in any relation we can represent only tuples corresponding to the schema of the relation. In fact, in many cases, the available data might not correspond exactly to the chosen format. For example, consider the relation schema:

PERSONS(Surname, FirstName, Address, Telephone)

The value of the attribute Telephone might not be available for all the tuples. It is worth noting that it would not be correct to use a value of the domain to represent an absence of information, as this would generate confusion. In this case, supposing the telephone numbers to be represented by integers, we could, for example, use zero to indicate the absence of the significant value. In general, however, this choice is unsatisfactory, for two reasons.

In the first place, it requires the existence of a value of the domain never used for significant values: in the case of telephone numbers, zero is clearly distinguishable, but in other cases there exists no available value for this purpose; for example, in an attribute that represents the date of birth and that uses as a domain a type Date correctly defined, there are no 'unused' elements that would therefore be usable to denote absence of information.

In the second place, the use of domain values can generate confusion: the distinction between actually significant values and fictitious ones ('place-holders') is hidden, and therefore the programs that have access to the database must take this into account, distinguishing among them (and keeping track of which are the fictitious values in each case).

In order to represent simply, but at the same time conveniently, the non-availability of values, the concept of relation is usually extended to include the possibility that a tuple can assume, on each attribute, either a value of the domain, as seen up to now, or a special value, called a *null value*. The null value denotes an absence of information, and is an additional value, not in the domain. In the tabular representations we will use for the null values the symbol NULL, as in Figure 2.12, which deals with the addresses of

City	GovernmentAddress
Rome	Via Quattro Novembre
Florence	NULL
Tivoli	NULL
Prato	NULL

Figure 2.12 A relation with null values.

government offices in county towns in Italy. Note that all county towns have local government offices, but other towns do not. With reference to the table in the figure, we can note how in effect the three null values that appear in it are assigned for different reasons, as follows.

- Florence is a county town and as such must certainly have a local government office. At the moment we do not know its address. The null value is used because the real value cannot be recorded in the database: for this reason we say that it is an *unknown value*.

- Tivoli is not a county town and therefore has no local government office. Thus the attribute GovernmentAddress can have no value for this tuple. Here the null value denotes the inapplicability of the attribute, or in other words, the non-existence of the value: the value is *non-existent*.

- The county of Prato has been established very recently and we do not know if the local government office has yet been opened, nor do we know its address (whether already operational or planned). In effect, we do not know if the value exists and, if it exists, we do not know what it is. In fact, we find ourselves in a situation that corresponds to the logical disjunction (the 'or') of the two preceding: the value is either non-existent or unknown. This type of null value is usually called *no-information*, because it tells us absolutely nothing: the value might or might not exist, and if it exists we don't know what it is.

In relational database systems no hypothesis is made about the meaning of null values; therefore, in practice, we find ourselves in the third situation, that of the no-information value.

For a further reflection on null values, consider now the database in Figure 2.13, which is defined on the same database schema as Figure 2.6. The null value on the date of birth in the first tuple of the relation STUDENTS is more or less admissible, in that one can accept that the information is not essential in this context. However, a null value for the registration number or the course code creates serious problems, since these values, as we have discussed with reference to Figure 2.6, are used to establish correspondences between tuples of different relations. At this point, the presence of null values in the relation EXAMS actually makes the information unusable: for example, the second tuple, with just the grade and two null values, provides no useful information. Thus, the presence of null values in a relation can in some cases generate doubts as to the actual significance and identity of the tuples: the last two tuples of the relation COURSES can be different or can actually coincide! Hence the necessity for keeping a suitable control over the use of null values in our relations is evident: only certain relation instances should be admitted. In general, when a relation is defined, it is possible to specify that null values are admissible only for some attributes and not for others. At the end of the next section we will present a criterion for the selection of attributes from which null values must be excluded.

STUDENTS

RegNum	Surname	FirstName	BirthDate
276545	Smith	Mary	NULL
NULL	Black	Anna	23/04/1972
NULL	Verdi	Paolo	12/02/1972

EXAMS

Student	Grade	Course
276545	C	01
NULL	B	NULL
200768	A	NULL

COURSES

Code	Title	Tutor
01	Physics	Grant
03	Chemistry	NULL
NULL	Chemistry	Clark

Figure 2.13 A database with many null values.

2.2 Integrity constraints

The structures of the relational model allow us to organize the information of interest to our applications. In many cases, however, it is not true that every set of tuples in the schema represents information that is correct for the application. We have already discussed the problem briefly with regard to the presence of null values. Now, we will look at the problem in greater detail, initially referring to relations without null values. Let us consider, for example, the database in Figure 2.14 and note in it various situations that should not occur.

STUDENTS

RegNum	Surname	FirstName	BirthDate
200768	Verdi	Paolo	12/02/1981
937653	Smith	Lucy	10/10/1980
937653	Brown	Mavis	01/12/1980

EXAMS

Student	Grade	Honours	Course
200768	K		05
937653	B	honours	01
937653	A	honours	04
276545	C		01

COURSES

Code	Title	Tutor
01	Physics	Grant
03	Chemistry	Beale
04	Chemistry	Clark

Figure 2.14 A database with incorrect information.

For the purpose of this exercise, we will assume that the maximum grade is A, for which 'honours' can be awarded, and the minimum is F.

• In the first tuple of the relation EXAMS we have an exam result of K, which is not admissible, as grades must be between A and F.

- In the second tuple again in the relation EXAMS an honours is shown awarded for an exam for which the grade is B. Honours can be awarded only if the grade is A.

- The last two tuples of the relation STUDENTS contain information on two different students with the same registration number: again an impossible situation, given that the registration number exists for the precise purpose of identifying each student unambiguously.

- The fourth tuple of the relation EXAMS shows, for the attribute **Student**, a value that does not appear among the registration numbers of the relation STUDENTS: this is also an unacceptable situation, given that the registration number provides us with information only as a link to the corresponding tuple of the relation STUDENTS. Similarly, the first tuple shows a course code that does not appear in the relation COURSES.

In a database, it is essential to avoid situations such as those just described. For this purpose, the concept of *integrity constraint* was introduced, as a property that must be satisfied by all correct database instances. Each constraint must be seen as a *predicate*, which associates the value *true* or *false* with each instance. In general, we associate a collection of constraints with a database schema and we consider *correct* (or *legal*) the instances that satisfy all the constraints. In each of the four cases discussed above, a constraint would prohibit the undesirable situation.

It is possible to classify the constraints according to the elements of the database that are involved in it. There are two categories, the first of which has some particular subcases.

- A constraint is *intra-relational* if its satisfaction is defined with regard to a single relation of the database; the first three cases above correspond to intra-relational constraints; in some cases, the definition of the constraint considers the tuples (or even the values) separately from each other.

  o A *tuple constraint* is a constraint that can be evaluated on each tuple independently from the others: the constraints relating to the first two cases fall into this category.

  o As a still more specific case, a constraint defined with reference to single values (as in the first example in which, for the attribute **Grade**, only values between A and F are allowed) is called a *value constraint* or *domain constraint*, given that it imposes a restriction on the domain of the attribute.

- A constraint is *inter-relational* if it involves more that one relation; this is seen in the fourth example, in which the unacceptable situation can be prohibited by requesting that a **RegNum** appears in the relation EXAMS only if it appears in the relation STUDENTS.

In the following sections we will examine tuple constraints, key constraints, which are the most important intra-relational constraints, and referential constraints, which are the most important inter-relational constraints.

2.2.1 Tuple constraints

As we have said, tuple constraints express conditions on the values of each tuple, independently of other tuples.

A possible syntax for these constraints permits the definition of boolean expressions (that is, with connectives AND, OR and NOT) with atoms that compare values of attributes (or arithmetical expressions using values of attributes). The violated constraints in the first two examples are described by the following expressions:

$$(\text{Grade} \geq \text{A}) \text{ AND } (\text{Grade} \leq \text{F})$$
$$(\text{NOT } (\text{Honours} = \text{`honours'})) \text{ OR } (\text{Grade} = \text{A})$$

In particular, the second constraint indicates that honours is admissible only if the grade is equal to A (saying that either there is no honours, or the grade is equal to A, or both). The first constraint is in fact a domain constraint, given that it involves a single attribute.

The definition we have given also admits more complex expressions, provided that they are defined on the values of single tuples. For example, on a relation on the schema:

$$\text{PAYMENTS}(\text{Date, Amount, Deductions, Net})$$

it is possible to define the constraint that imposes the condition that the net amount is equal to the difference between the total amount and the deductions, in the following manner:

$$\text{Net } = \text{ Amount} - \text{Deductions}$$

2.2.2 Keys

In this section we will discuss key constraints, which are undoubtedly the most important of the relational model; we could even go so far as to say that without them the model itself would have no sense. Let us begin with an example. In the relation in Figure 2.15, the values of the various tuples on the attribute RegNum are all different from each other: the value of the RegNum *unambiguously identifies* the students; the very idea of the registration number itself was introduced many years ago, well before the introduction of databases, precisely in order to have a simple and effective tool for referring to the students in an unambiguous way. Similarly, in the relation there are no pairs of tuples with the same values on any of the three attributes Surname, FirstName and BirthDate: these pieces of information also identify each person unambiguously.[2] Other sets of attributes also identify unambiguously the tuples of the relation in Figure 2.15: for example, the pair RegNum and DegreeProg, given that RegNum is sufficient on its own.

RegNum	Surname	FirstName	BirthDate	DegreeProg
284328	Smith	Luigi	29/04/59	Computing
296328	Smith	John	29/04/59	Computing
587614	Smith	Lucy	01/05/61	Engineering
934856	Black	Lucy	01/05/61	Fine Art
965536	Black	Lucy	05/03/58	Fine Art

Figure 2.15 A relation to illustrate keys.

Intuitively, a key is a set of attributes used to identify unambiguously the tuples in a relation. More precisely:

- a set of attributes K is a *superkey* for a relation r if r does not contain two distinct tuples t_1 and t_2 with $t_1[K] = t_2[K]$;

- a set of attributes K is a *key* for r if K is a minimal superkey (that is, there exists no other superkey K' of r that is contained in K as proper subset).

In the example, in Figure 2.15:

- the set RegNum is a superkey; it is also a minimal superkey, given that it contains a sole attribute and thus we can conclude that RegNum is a key;

- the set Surname, FirstName, BirthDate is a superkey; furthermore, none of its subsets is a superkey: in fact there are two equal tuples (the first and second) on Surname and BirthDate, two (the last) equal on Surname and FirstName and two (the third and fourth) equal on FirstName and BirthDate; thus Surname, FirstName, BirthDate is another key;

- the set RegNum, DegreeProg is a superkey, as we have seen; however it is not a minimal superkey, because one of its proper subsets, RegNum, is itself a minimal superkey, and thus RegNum, DegreeProg is not a key;

- the set FirstName, DegreeProg is not a superkey, because there are two tuples in the relation, the last two equal, on both FirstName and DegreeProg.

In order to discuss the subject in more depth, let us examine another relation, that shown in Figure 2.16. It contains no pair of tuples that agree on both Surname and DegreeProg. Thus, for this relation, the set Surname, DegreeProg is a superkey. Since there are tuples that agree on Surname (the first two) and on DegreeProg (the second and the fourth), this set is a minimal superkey and therefore a key. Now, in this relation, Surname and DegreeProg identify the tuples unambiguously; but can we say that this is true in

---

2. We assume that first name, surname and date of birth uniquely identify people; this is not true in general, but can be assumed as true within small communities, and it is convenient for the sake of the example.

general? Certainly not, given that there could easily be students with the same surname enrolled on the same degree programme.

RegNum	Surname	FirstName	BirthDate	DegreeProg
296328	Smith	John	29/04/59	Computing
587614	Smith	Lucy	01/05/61	Engineering
934856	Black	Lucy	01/05/61	Fine Art
965536	Black	Lucy	05/03/58	Engineering

Figure 2.16 Another relation to illustrate keys.

Thus we can say that Surname, DegreeProg is 'by chance' a key for the relation in Figure 2.16, while we are interested in the keys corresponding to integrity constraints, satisfied by all the legal relations on a certain schema. When defining a schema, we associate with it constraints that describe properties in the real world, for which information is held in our database. The constraints are defined at the schema level, with reference to all the instances that must satisfy all the constraints. A correct instance can then satisfy other constraints beyond those defined in the schema. For example with a schema:

STUDENTS(RegNum, Surname, FirstName, BirthDate, DegreeProg)

are associated the constraints that impose as keys the two sets of attributes discussed above:

RegNum
Surname, FirstName, BirthDate

Both the relations in Figure 2.15 and Figure 2.16 satisfy both the constraints; the second also satisfies ('by chance', as we said) the constraint that says that Surname, DegreeProg is another key.

We can now make some observations about keys, which justify the importance attributed to them. In the first place, we can note how each relation always has a key. A relation is a set, and thus is made up of elements that are different from each other; as a consequence, for each relation $r(X)$, the set X of all the attributes is a superkey for it. Now there are two cases: either such a set is also a key, so confirming the existence of the key itself, or it is not a key, because there exists another superkey contained within it; then we can proceed by repeating the same argument on this new set and so on; since the set of attributes involved in a relation is finite, the process terminates in a finite number of steps with a minimal superkey. Thus, we can conclude that every relation has a key.

The fact that at least one key can be defined for each relation guarantees access to all the values of a database and their unambiguous identification. Moreover, it allows the effective establishment of the links between data contained in different relations, which characterize the relational model as a 'value-based' model. Let us look again at the example in Figure 2.6. In the relation EXAMS, reference is made to the students by means of RegNum, and to the courses by means of the respective codes: in effect, RegNum is the key of the relation STUDENTS and Code is the key of the relation COURSES. So the values of the key attributes are indeed used to refer to the content of each of the relations from outside (that is, from other relations).

2.2.3 Keys and null values

We can now return to the discussion initiated at the end of Section 2.1.5, regarding the necessity of avoiding the proliferation of null values in our relations. In particular, we will note how, in the presence of null values for key values, it is no longer true that the values of the keys permit the unambiguous identification of the tuples of the relations and to establish connections between tuples of different relations. To this end, consider the relation in Figure 2.17, defined on the same schema as the relation in Figure 2.16. It has two keys, one made up of the sole attribute RegNum and the other of the attributes Surname, FirstName and BirthDate. The first tuple has null values under RegNum and BirthDate and therefore on at least one attribute of each key: this tuple is not identifiable in any possible way; in particular, if we want to insert another tuple into the database relating to a student named John Smith, then we cannot know if we are in fact referring to the same student or to another. Furthermore, it is not possible to refer to this tuple in other relations of the database, since this must be done by means of the value of a key. The last two tuples also present a problem: in spite of the fact that each of them has a key with no nulls (RegNum in the third tuple and Surname, FirstName, BirthDate in the last), the presence of null values makes it impossible to know if the two tuples refer to two different students or the same one.

RegNum	Surname	FirstName	BirthDate	DegreeProg
NULL	Smith	John	NULL	Computing
587614	Smith	Lucy	01/05/61	Engineering
934856	Black	Lucy	NULL	NULL
NULL	Black	Lucy	05/03/58	Engineering

Figure 2.17 A relation with null values on all the keys.

The example clearly suggests the necessity of limiting the presence of null values in the keys of relations. In practice, we adopt a simple solution, which makes it possible to guarantee the unambiguous identification of each tuple and refer to it from within other relations: null values are forbidden on one of the keys (called the *primary key*) and usually (that is, unless specified otherwise) allowed on the others. The attributes that make up the primary key are often underlined, as shown in Figure 2.18. Most of the references between relations are realized through the values of the primary key.

RegNum	Surname	FirstName	BirthDate	DegreeProg
643976	Smith	John	NULL	Computing
587614	Smith	Lucy	01/05/61	Engineering
934856	Black	Lucy	NULL	NULL
735591	Black	Lucy	05/03/58	Engineering

Figure 2.18 A relation with a primary key.

It is worth noting that in most real cases it is possible to find attributes whose values are available for a primary key. However, in some cases this does not happen and it becomes necessary to introduce an additional code attribute that is generated and associated with each tuple at the time of insertion. Note that many identifying codes (including, for example, student registration numbers and social security numbers) were introduced in the past, before the invention or the widespread adoption of databases, precisely to guarantee the unambiguous identification of the subject of a domain (respectively the students and the citizens) and to simplify the reference to them − precisely the goals of keys.

2.2.4 Referential constraints

In order to discuss the most important class of inter-relational constraints, let us consider the database in Figure 2.19. In it, the first relation contains information relating to a set of traffic offences, the second to the police officers who have made the charges and the third to a set of motor vehicles. The information in the relation OFFENCES is given meaning and completeness through reference to the other two relations; to the relation OFFICERS, by means of the attribute Officer, which contains registration numbers (RegNum) of officers corresponding to the primary key of the relation OFFICERS, and to the relation CARS by means of the attributes Registration and Department[3], which contain values that form the primary keys of the relation CARS. The references are significant in that the values in the relation OFFENCES are equal to values actually present in the other two: if a value of Officer in OFFENCES does not appear as a value of the key of OFFICERS, then the reference is not effective (and so useless). In the example, all the references are actually usable.

A *referential constraint* (or *foreign key*) between a set of attributes X of a relation R_1 and another relation R_2 is satisfied if the values in X of each tuple of the instance of R_1 appear as values of the (primary) key of the instance of R_2. The precise definition requires a little care, particularly in the case in

---

3. This is the way registration numbers for cars are organized in France; departments are regions of the country, each with a two-digit code: a registration is made up of the department code and a string (digits and characters) unique within the department. The example illustrates a key composed of two attributes.

OFFENCES	Code	Date	Officer	Department	Registration
	143256	25/10/92	567	75	5694 FR
	987554	26/10/92	456	75	5694 FR
	987557	26/10/92	456	75	6544 XY
	630876	15/10/92	456	47	6544 XY
	539856	12/10/92	567	47	6544 XY

OFFICERS	RegNum	Surname	FirstName
	567	Brun	Jean
	456	Larue	Henri
	638	Larue	Jacques

CARS	Registration	Department	Owner	Address
	6544 XY	75	Cordon Edouard	Rue du Pont
	7122 HT	75	Cordon Edouard	Rue du Pont
	5694 FR	75	Latour Hortense	Avenue Foch
	6544 XY	47	Mimault Bernard	Avenue FDR

Figure 2.19 A database with referential constraints.

which the key of the relation referred to consists of more than one attribute and in the case in which there is more than one key. We will proceed in stages, looking first at the case in which the key of R_2 is unique and consists of a sole attribute B (and therefore the set X is in its turn made up of a sole attribute A): then, the referential constraint between the attribute A of R_1 and the relation R_2 is satisfied if, for every tuple t_1 in R_1 such that $t_1[A]$ is not null, there exists a tuple t_2 in R_2 such that $t_1[A] = t_2[B]$. In the more general case, we must take account of the fact that each of the attributes in X must correspond to a precise attribute of the primary key K of R_2. For this, it is necessary to specify an order both in the set X and in K. Indicating the attributes in order, $X = A_1 A_2 ... A_p$ and $K = B_1 B_2 ... B_p$, the constraint is satisfied if, for every tuple t_1 in R_1 with no nulls in X, there exists a tuple t_2 in R_2 with $t_1[A_i] = t_2[B_i]$, for $1 \leq i \leq p$.

On the schema of the database in Figure 2.19 it makes sense to define the referential integrity constraints:

- between the attribute **Officer** of the relation OFFENCES and the relation OFFICERS;

- between the attributes **Registration** and **Department** of OFFENCES and the relation CARS, in which the order of the attributes in the key sees first **Registration** and then **Department**.

The database in Figure 2.19 satisfies both constraints, whereas the database in Figure 2.20 violates both. The violations are, firstly, that OFFICERS does not contain a tuple with the value on **RegNum** equal to **456** and, secondly, that CARS contains no tuple with the value 75 for Department and 6544 XY for Registration (note that there is a tuple with the value 75 for Department and another with the value 6544 XY for Registration, but this is not sufficient, because there is a need for a tuple with both values: only in this way can the two values make reference to a tuple of the relation CARS).

OFFENCES

Code	Date	Officer	Department	Registration
987554	26/10/92	456	75	6544 XY
630876	15/10/92	456	47	6544 XY

OFFICERS

RegNum	Surname	FirstName
567	Brun	Mavis
638	Larue	Jacques

CARS

Registration	Department	Owner	Address
7122 HT	75	Cordon Edouard	Rue du Pont
5694 FR	93	Latour Hortense	Avenue Foch
6544 XY	47	Mimault Bernard	Avenue FDR

Figure 2.20 A database that violates referential constraints.

With reference to the second constraint, the discussion about the order of the attributes can appear excessive, as the correspondence can be achieved by means of the names of the attributes themselves. In general, however, this need not be possible, and thus the ordering is essential. Let us consider for example, a database containing information on the vehicles involved in road accidents. In particular, let us suppose that we want to include in a relation, together with other information, the Registration and Department of each of the two vehicles involved.[4] In this case, we must have two pairs of attributes and two referential constraints. For example, the schema could be:

ACCIDENTS(Code, Dept1, Registration1, Dept2, Registration2 ...)

In this case, it will obviously not be possible to establish the correspondence in the referential constraint to the relation CARS by means of the names of the attributes, in that they are different from those of the primary key CARS. Only by means of the ordering does it become possible to specify that the reference associates Dept1 (attribute of ACCIDENTS) to Department (attribute of the key of CARS) and Registration1 to Registration and, similarly, Dept2 to Department and Registration2 to Registration. The database in Figure 2.21 satisfies the two constraints, while the one in Figure 2.22 satisfies the one relating to Dept1 and Registration1 and violates the other,

---

4. Let us suppose for simplicity's sake that there are always only two vehicles.

because in the relation CARS there is no vehicle with the registration 9775 GF
and department 93.

ACCIDENTS	Code	Dept1	Registration1	Dept2	Registration2	...
	6207	75	6544 XY	93	9775 GF	...
	6974	93	5694 FR	93	9775 GF	...

CARS	Registration	Department	Owner	Address
	7122 HT	75	Cordon Edouard	Rue du Pont
	5694 FR	93	Latour Hortense	Avenue Foch
	9775 GF	93	LeBlanc Pierre	Rue de la Gare
	6544 XY	75	Mimault Bernard	Avenue FDR

Figure 2.21 A database with two similar referential constraints.

ACCIDENTS	Code	Dept1	Registration1	Dept2	Registration2	...
	6207	75	6544 XY	93	9775 GF	...
	6974	93	5694 FR	93	9775 GF	...

CARS	Registration	Department	Owner	Address
	7122 HT	75	Cordon Edouard	Rue du Pont
	5694 FR	93	Latour Hortense	Avenue Foch
	6544 XY	75	Mimault Bernard	Avenue FDR

Figure 2.22 A database that violates a referential constraint.

A final observation might be useful regarding relations with more than one
key. In this case one of the keys should be indicated as the primary key, and
it is reasonable that the references should be directed towards it: for this
reason, in the specification of the referential constraints, we have been able
to omit the explicit mention of the attributes that make up the primary key.
Moreover, it should be noted that not all DBMSs on the market allow the
explicit indication of the primary key: some allow the specification of more
than one key, but not the highlighting of one as a primary key. In these cases,
the referential constraint must indicate explicitly the attributes that make up
the key to which it refers. For example, let us consider a database on the
schema

EMPLOYEES (EmpNum, Surname, FirstName, Department)
DEPARTMENTS (Code, Name, Location)

in which the relation DEPARTMENTS is identified by the attribute **Code** and,
separately, by the attribute **Name** (no two departments exist with the same
code or with the same name). It is convenient that one of the two keys, for

example **Code**, is indicated as a primary, and used to establish references. If, however, the system does not allow for the concept of a primary key, the constraint must be expressed by the explicit indication of the attributes; we must therefore say that there exists a referential constraint between the attribute **Department** of the relation EMPLOYEES and the key **Code** of the relation DEPARTMENTS.

This is the reason why, as we show in Chapter 4, a more detailed specification is offered for the definition referential constraints in relational systems.

2.3 Conclusions

In this chapter we have defined the structures and constraints of the relational model. First we discussed the concept of relation, with some variations with respect to the concepts of set theory. Then, we showed how relations can be used to organize more complex collections of data using the data itself to create references between different components (without the use of explicit pointers). Then, after introducing the necessity for using null values to denote the absence of information, we discussed the concept of integrity constraints through three fundamental classes: tuple constraints, keys and referential constraints.

In the next two chapters, we complete the presentation of the relational model from two points of view:

- in Chapter 3, we illustrate the foundations of query languages, that is, the languages used to access information in databases;

- in Chapter 4, we show how all the concepts, those relative to the structures and to the constraints, as discussed in this chapter, and those relative to query languages (Chapter 3) are implemented in commercial DBMSs, using SQL.

2.4 Bibliography

It is worth consulting the original article by Codd [26] that contains the original proposal for the relational model: its motivations and the general presentation of the model are still valid. For this work, Codd received the ACM Turing Award, the most important recognition in the computing field; the discussion he developed in such an occasion is also very interesting [30].

Tsichritzis and Lochovsky [87] offer general and comparative discussions on data models.

More formal and detailed treatments on the relational model and its associated theory (which is not developed much in this book) are offered by Maier [58], Ullman [88], Paredaens et al. [67], Atzeni and De Antonellis [3], Abiteboul, Hull and Vianu [1]. Interesting discussions on null values, with the various approaches, were developed by Codd [29] and Zaniolo [93].

2.5 Exercises

Exercise 2.1 Describe in words, the information organized in the database in Figure 2.23.

PATIENT

Code	Surname	FirstName
A102	Harris	Lucy
B372	Rossini	Peter
B543	Johnson	Nadia
B444	Johnson	Luigi
S555	Rose	Jean

ADMISSION

Patient	Admitted	Discharged	Ward
A102	2/05/94	9/05/94	A
A102	2/12/94	2/01/95	A
S555	5/10/94	3/12/94	B
B444	1/12/94	1/01/95	B
S555	5/10/94	1/11/94	A

DOCTOR

Number	Surname	FirstName	Ward
203	Black	Peter	A
574	Bisi	Mavis	B
461	Boyne	Steve	B
530	Clark	Nicola	C
405	Mizzi	Nicola	A
501	Mount	Mavis	A

WARD

Code	Name	Consultant
A	Surgical	203
B	Paediatric	574
C	Medical	530

Figure 2.23 A database for Exercise 2.1 and Exercise 2.2.

Exercise 2.2 Highlight the keys and the referential constraints that exist in the database in Figure 2.23 and that it is reasonable to assume are satisfied by all the databases in the same schema. Highlight also the attributes on which it could be reasonable to admit null values.

Exercise 2.3 Consider the information for the management of loans from a personal library. The owner lends books to his friends, which he records simply by means of the respective names or nicknames (thus avoiding repetition) and refers to the books by title (not having two books of the same title). When he lends a book, he makes a note of the date planned for its return. Define a relational schema to represent this information, highlighting suitable domains for its various attributes and show an instance of it in tabular form. Show the key or keys of the relation.

Exercise 2.4 Represent, by means of one or more relations, the information contained in a timetable of departures from a railway station: show the number, time, final destination, category and stops of every departing train.

Exercise 2.5 Define a database schema to organize the information of a company that has employees (each with Social Security Number, surname, first name and date of birth), and subsidiaries (each with code, branch and director, who is an employee). Each employee works for a subsidiary. Indicate the keys and the referential constraints of the schema. Show an instance of the database and check that it satisfies the constraints.

Exercise 2.6 A family tree represents the structure of a family. Show how the information of a family tree can be represented by means of a relational database, possibly starting with a simplified structure, in which only the male line or only the female line is represented (that is, only the offspring of the male or the female members of the family are represented).

Exercise 2.7 For each of the Exercises 2.3–2.6, evaluate the needs for null values, with the related benefits and difficulties.

Exercise 2.8 Define a database schema that organizes the information necessary to generate the radio programmes page of a daily newspaper, with stations, times and programme titles; besides the name, include the transmission frequency and the location of the radio station.

3

Relational algebra
and calculus

We have seen in the previous chapters that information of interest to data management applications can be represented by means of relations. The languages for specifying operations for querying and updating the data itself constitute, in their turn, an essential component of each data model. An update can be seen as a function that, given a database, produces another database (without changing the schema). A query, on the other hand, can also be considered as a function that, given a database, produces a relation. So, in order either to interrogate or to update the database, we need to develop the ability to express functions on the database. It is important to learn the foundations of query and update languages first, and then apply those foundations when studying the languages that are actually supported by commercial DBMSs.

We will look first at relational algebra. This is a *procedural* language (that is, one in which the data retrieval functions are specified by describing the procedure that must be followed in order to obtain the result). We will illustrate the various operators of the algebra, the way operators can be combined to form expressions, and the means by which expressions can be transformed to improve efficiency. We will also describe the influence that null values have on the relational algebra, and then how a query language can be used to define virtual relations (also known as *views*), which are not stored in the database.

Then, we will give a concise presentation of relational calculus, a *declarative* language, in which the data retrieval functions describe the properties of the result, rather than the procedure used to obtain it. This language is based on first order predicate calculus and we will present two versions, the first directly derived from predicate calculus and the second that attempts to overcome some of the limitations of the first.

We will conclude the chapter with a brief treatment of Datalog, an interesting contribution from recent research, which allows the formulation of queries that could not be expressed in algebra or in calculus.

The sections on calculus and Datalog can be omitted without compromising the understanding of the succeeding chapters.

In the next chapter, dedicated to SQL, we will see how it can be useful, from the practical point of view, to combine declarative and procedural aspects within a single language. We will also see how updates are based on the same principles as queries.

3.1 Relational algebra

As we have mentioned, relational algebra is a procedural language, based on algebraic concepts. It consists of a collection of operators that are defined on relations, and that produce relations as results. In this way, we can construct expressions that involve more than one operator, in order to formulate complex queries. In the following sections, we examine the various operators:

- first, those of traditional set theory, *union, intersection, difference*;

- next, the more specific ones, *renaming, selection, projection*;

- finally, the most important, the *join*, in its various forms, *natural join, cartesian product* and *theta-join*.

3.1.1 Union, intersection, difference

To begin with, note that relations are sets. So it makes sense to define for them the traditional set operators of union, difference and intersection. However we must be aware of the fact that a relation is not generically a set of tuples, but a set of *homogenous* tuples, that is, tuples defined on the same attributes. So, even if it were possible, in principle, to define these operators on any pair of relations, there is no sense, from the point of view of the relational model, in defining them with reference to relations on different attributes. For example, the union of two relations r_1 and r_2 on different schemas would be a set of *heterogeneous* tuples, some defined on the attributes of r_1 and the others on those of r_2. This would be unsatisfactory, because a set of heterogeneous tuples is not a relation and, in order to combine the operators to form complex expressions, we want the results to be relations. Therefore, in relational algebra, we allow applications of operators of union, intersection and difference only to pairs of relations defined on the same attributes. Figure 3.1 shows examples of applications of the three operators, with the usual definitions, adapted to our context:

- the *union* of two relations $r_1(X)$ and $r_2(X)$, defined on the same set of attributes X, is expressed as $r_1 \cup r_2$ and is also a relation on X containing the tuples that belong to r_1 or to r_2, or to both;

- the *difference* of $r_1(X)$ and $r_2(X)$ is expressed as $r_1 - r_2$ and is a relation on X containing the tuples that belong to r_1 and not to r_2;

- the *intersection* of $r_1(X)$ and $r_2(X)$ is expressed as $r_1 \cap r_2$ and is a relation on X containing the tuples that belong to both r_1 and r_2.

GRADUATES

Number	Surname	Age
7274	Robinson	37
7432	O'Malley	39
9824	Darkes	38

MANAGERS

Number	Surname	Age
9297	O'Malley	56
7432	O'Malley	39
9824	Darkes	38

GRADUATES ∪ MANAGERS

Number	Surname	Age
7274	Robinson	37
7432	O'Malley	39
9824	Darkes	38
9297	O'Malley	56

GRADUATES ∩ MANAGERS

Number	Surname	Age
7432	O'Malley	39
9824	Darkes	38

GRADUATES − MANAGERS

Number	Surname	Age
7274	Robinson	37

Figure 3.1 Examples of union, intersection and difference.

3.1.2 Renaming

The limitations we have had to impose on the standard set operators, although justified, seem particularly restrictive. For instance, consider the two relations in Figure 3.2. It would be meaningful to execute a sort of union on them in order to obtain all the 'parent–child' pairs held in the database, but that is not possible, because the attribute that we have instinctively called Parent, is in fact called Father in one relation and Mother in the other.

PATERNITY

Father	Child
Adam	Cain
Adam	Abel
Abraham	Isaac
Abraham	Ishmael

MATERNITY

Mother	Child
Eve	Cain
Eve	Seth
Sarah	Isaac
Hagar	Ishmael

PATERNITY ∪ MATERNITY ??

Figure 3.2 A meaningful but incorrect union.

To resolve the problem, we introduce a specific operator, whose sole purpose is to adapt attribute names, as necessary, to facilitate the application of set operators. The operator is called *renaming*, because it actually changes the names of the attributes, leaving the contents of the relations unchanged. An example of renaming is shown in Figure 3.3; the operator changes the name of the attribute Father to Parent, as indicated by the notation Parent ← Father given in subscript of the symbol ϱ, which denotes the renaming; looking at the table it is easy to see how only the heading changes, leaving the main body unaltered.

PATERNITY

Father	Child
Adam	Cain
Adam	Abel
Abraham	Isaac
Isaac	Jacob

$\varrho_{Parent \leftarrow Father}(\text{PATERNITY})$

Parent	Child
Adam	Cain
Adam	Abel
Abraham	Isaac
Isaac	Jacob

Figure 3.3 A renaming.

Figure 3.4 shows the application of the union to the result of two renamings of the relations in Figure 3.2.

$\varrho_{Parent \leftarrow Father}(\text{PATERNITY}) \cup \varrho_{Parent \leftarrow Mother}(\text{MATERNITY})$

Parent	Child
Adam	Cain
Adam	Abel
Abraham	Isaac
Abraham	Ishmael
Eve	Cain
Eve	Seth
Sarah	Isaac
Hagar	Ishmael

Figure 3.4 A union preceded by two renamings.

Let us define the renaming operator in general terms. Let r be a relation defined on the set of attributes X and let Y be another set of attributes with the same cardinality. Furthermore, let $A_1A_2...A_k$ and $B_1B_2...B_k$ be respectively an ordering of the attributes in X and an ordering of those in Y. Then the renaming

$$\varrho_{B_1B_2...B_k \leftarrow A_1A_2...A_k}(r)$$

contains a tuple t' for each tuple t in r, defined as follows: t' is a tuple on Y and $t'[B_i] = t[A_i]$ for $i = 1, ..., n$. The definition confirms that the changes that occur are changes to the names of the attributes, while the values remain unaltered and are associated with new attributes. In practice, in the two lists $A_1A_2...A_k$ and $B_1B_2...B_k$ we indicate only those attributes that are renamed (that is, those for which $A_i \neq B_i$). This is the reason why in Figure 3.3 we have written

$$\varrho_{Parent \leftarrow Father}(\text{PATERNITY})$$

and not

$$\varrho_{Parent,Child \leftarrow Father,Child}(\text{PATERNITY})$$

Figure 3.5 shows another example of union preceded by renaming. In this case, in each relation there are two attributes that are renamed and therefore the ordering of the pairs (Branch, Salary and so on) is significant.

EMPLOYEES

Surname	Branch	Salary
Patterson	Rome	45
Trumble	London	53

STAFF

Surname	Factory	Wages
Cooke	Chicago	33
Bush	Monza	32

$$\varrho_{Location,\ Pay \leftarrow Branch,Salary}(\text{EMPLOYEES}) \cup \varrho_{Location,Pay \leftarrow Factory,Wages}(\text{STAFF})$$

Surname	Location	Pay
Patterson	Rome	45
Trumble	London	53
Cooke	Chicago	33
Bush	Monza	32

Figure 3.5 Another union preceded by renaming.

3.1.3 Selection

We now turn our attention to the specific operators of relational algebra that allow the manipulation of relations. There are three operators, selection, projection and join (the last having several variants).

Before going into detail, note that selection and projection carry out functions that could be defined as complementary (or orthogonal). They are both unary (that is, they have one relation as argument) and produce as result a portion of that relation. More precisely, a selection produces a subset of tuples on all the attributes, while a projection gives a result to which all the tuples contribute, but on a subset of attributes. As illustrated in Figure 3.6, we can say that selection generates 'horizontal decompositions' and projection generates 'vertical decompositions'.

Figure 3.7 and Figure 3.8 show two examples of selection, which illustrate the fundamental characteristics of the operator, denoted by the symbol σ, with the appropriate 'selection condition' indicated as subscript. The result contains the tuples of the operand that satisfy the condition. As shown in the examples, the selection conditions can allow both for comparisons between

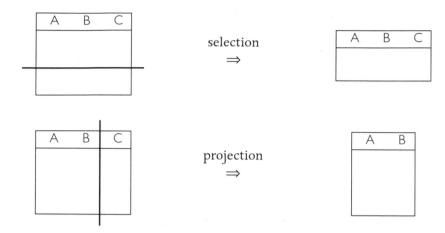

Figure 3.6 Selection and projection are orthogonal operators.

attributes and for comparisons between attributes and constants, and can be complex, being obtained by combining simple conditions with the logical connectives ∨ (*or*), ∧ (*and*) and ¬ (*not*).

EMPLOYEES

Surname	FirstName	Age	Salary
Smith	Mary	25	2000
Black	Lucy	40	3000
Verdi	Nico	36	4500
Smith	Mark	40	3900

$\sigma_{Age<30 \lor Salary>4000}$(EMPLOYEES)

Surname	FirstName	Age	Salary
Smith	Mary	25	2000
Verdi	Nico	36	4500

Figure 3.7 A selection.

More precisely, given a relation $r(X)$, a *propositional formula F* on X is a formula obtained by combining atomic conditions of the type $A\vartheta B$ or $A\vartheta c$ with the connectives ∨, ∧ and ¬, where:

- ϑ is a comparison operator (=, ≠, >, <, ≥, ≤);

- A and B are attributes in X that are *compatible* (that is, the comparison ϑ is meaningful on the values of their domains);

- c is a constant compatible with the domain of A.

Given a formula F and a tuple t, a truth value is defined for F on t:

CITIZENS

Surname	FirstName	PlaceOfBirth	Residence
Smith	Mary	Rome	Milan
Black	Lucy	Rome	Rome
Verdi	Nico	Florence	Florence
Smith	Mark	Naples	Florence

$\sigma_{\text{PlaceOfBirth}=\text{Residence}}(\text{CITIZENS})$

Surname	FirstName	PlaceOfBirth	Residence
Black	Lucy	Rome	Rome
Verdi	Nico	Florence	Florence

Figure 3.8 Another selection.

- $A\vartheta B$ is true on t if and only if $t[A]$ is in relation ϑ with $t[B]$ (for example, $A = B$ is true on t if and only if $t[A] = t[B]$);

- $A\vartheta c$ is true on t if and only if $t[A]$ is in relation ϑ with c;

- $F_1 \vee F_2$, $F_1 \wedge F_2$ and $\neg F_1$ have the usual meaning.

  At this point we can complete the definition:

- the selection $\sigma_F(r)$ produces a relation on the same attributes as r that contains the tuples of r for which F is true.

3.1.4 Projection

The definition of the projection operator is also simple: given a relation $r(X)$ and a subset Y of X, the *projection* of r on Y (indicated by $\pi_Y(r)$) is the set of tuples on Y obtained from the tuples of r considering only the values on Y:

$$\pi_Y(r) = \{t[Y] | t \in r\}$$

Figure 3.9 shows a first example of projection, which clearly illustrates the concept mentioned above. The projection allows the vertical decomposition of relations: the result of the projection contains in this case as many tuples as its operand, defined however only on some of the attributes.

EMPLOYEES

Surname	FirstName	Department	Head
Smith	Mary	Sales	De Rossi
Black	Lucy	Sales	De Rossi
Verdi	Mary	Personnel	Fox
Smith	Mark	Personnel	Fox

$\pi_{\text{Surname,FirstName}}(\text{EMPLOYEES})$

Surname	FirstName
Smith	Mary
Black	Lucy
Verdi	Mary
Smith	Mark

Figure 3.9 A projection.

Figure 3.10 shows another projection, in which we note a different situation. The result contains fewer tuples than the operand, because all the tuples in the operand that have equal values on all the attributes of the projection give the same contribution to the projection itself. As relations are defined as sets, they are not allowed to have tuples with the same values: equal contributions 'collapse' into a single tuple.

EMPLOYEES

Surname	FirstName	Department	Head
Smith	Mary	Sales	De Rossi
Black	Lucy	Sales	De Rossi
Verdi	Mary	Personnel	Fox
Smith	Mark	Personnel	Fox

$\pi_{Department,Head}(EMPLOYEES)$

Department	Head
Sales	De Rossi
Personnel	Fox

Figure 3.10 A projection with fewer tuples than operands.

In general, we can say that the result of a projection contains at most as many tuples as the operand, but can contain fewer, as shown in Figure 3.10. Note also that there exists a link between the key constraints and the projections: $\pi_Y(r)$ contains the same number of tuples as r if and only if Y is a superkey for r. In fact:

- if Y is a superkey, then r does not contain pairs of tuples that are equal on Y, and thus each tuple makes a different contribution to the projection;

- if the projection has as many tuples as the operand, then each tuple of r contributes to the projection with different values, and thus r does not contain pairs of tuples equal on Y: but this is exactly the definition of a superkey.

For the relation EMPLOYEES in Figure 3.9 and Figure 3.10, the attributes **Surname** and **FirstName** form a key (and thus a superkey), while **Department** and **Head** do not form a superkey. Incidentally, note that a projection can produce a number of tuples equal to those of the operand even if the attributes involved are not defined as superkeys (of the schema) but happen to be a superkey for the specific relation. For example, if we reconsider the relations discussed in Chapter 2 on the schema

STUDENTS(RegNum, Surname, FirstName, BirthDate, DegreeProg)

we can say that for all the relations, the projection on **RegNum** and that on **Surname**, **FirstName** and **BirthDate** have the same number of tuples as the operand. Conversely, a projection on **Surname** and **DegreeProg** can have fewer tuples; however in the particular case (as in the example in Figure 2.16) in which there are no students with the same surname enrolled on the same degree programme, then the projection on **Surname** and **DegreeProg** also has the same number of tuples as the operand.

3.1.5 Join

Let us now examine the join operator, which is the most important one in relational algebra. The join allows us to establish connections among data contained in different relations, comparing the values contained in them and thus using the fundamental characteristics of the model, that of being value-based. There are two main versions of the operator, which are, however, obtainable one from the other. The first is useful for an introduction and the second is perhaps more relevant from a practical point of view.

Natural join   The *natural join*, denoted by the symbol ⋈, is an operator that correlates data in different relations, on the basis of equal values of attributes with the same name. (The join is defined here with two operands, but can be generalized.) Figure 3.11 shows an example. The result of the join is a relation on the union of the sets of attributes of the operands: in the figure, the result is defined on Employee, Department, Head, that is, on the union of Employee, Department and Department, Head. The tuples in the join are obtained by combining the tuples of the operands with equal values on the common attributes, in the example the attribute Department: for instance, the first tuple of the join is derived from the combination of the first tuple of the relation r_1 and the second tuple of r_2: in fact they both have sales as the value for Department.

r_1

Employee	Department
Smith	sales
Black	production
Bianchi	production

r_2

Department	Head
production	Mori
sales	Brown

$r_1 ⋈ r_2$

Employee	Department	Head
Smith	sales	Brown
Black	production	Mori
Bianchi	production	Mori

Figure 3.11 A natural join.

In general, we say that the *natural join* $r_1 ⋈ r_2$ of $r_1(X_1)$ and $r_2(X_2)$ is a relation defined on $X_1 X_2$ (that is, on the union of the sets X_1 and X_2), as follows:

$$r_1 ⋈ r_2 = \{t \text{ on } X_1 X_2 \mid \text{exist } t_1 \in r_1 \text{ and } t_2 \in r_2 \text{ with } t[X_1] = t_1 \text{ and } t[X_2] = t_2\}$$

More concisely, we could have written:

$$r_1 ⋈ r_2 = \{t \text{ on } X_1 X_2 \mid t[X_1] \in r_1 \text{ and } t[X_2] \in r_2\}$$

The definition confirms that the tuples of the result are obtained by combining tuples of the operands with equal values on the common attributes. If we indicate the common attributes as $X_{1,2}$ (that is, $X_{1,2} = X_1 \cap X_2$), then the two conditions $t[X_1] = t_1$ and $t[X_2] = t_2$ imply (since $X_{1,2} \subseteq X_1$ and $X_{1,2} \subseteq X_2$) that $t[X_{1,2}] = t_1[X_{1,2}]$ and $t[X_{1,2}] = t_2[X_{1,2}]$ and thus $t_1[X_{1,2}] = t_2[X_{1,2}]$. The degree of the result of a join is less than or equal to the sum of the degrees of the two operands, because the common attributes of the operands appear only once in the result.

Note that often the common attributes in a join form the key of one of the relations. In many of these cases, there is also a referential constraint between the common attributes. We illustrate this point by taking another look at the relations OFFENCES and CARS in the database in Figure 2.19, repeated for the sake of convenience in Figure 3.12, together with their join. Note that each of the tuples in OFFENCES has been combined with exactly one of the tuples of CARS: (i) at most one because Department and Registration form a key for CARS; (ii) at least one because of the referential constraint between Department and Registration in OFFENCES and the (primary) key of CARS. The join, therefore, has exactly as many tuples as the relation OFFENCES.

OFFENCES

Code	Date	Officer	Department	Registration
143256	25/10/92	567	75	5694 FR
987554	26/10/92	456	75	5694 FR
987557	26/10/92	456	75	6544 XY
630876	15/10/92	456	47	6544 XY
539856	12/10/92	567	47	6544 XY

CARS

Registration	Department	Owner	Address
6544 XY	75	Cordon Edouard	Rue du Pont
7122 HT	75	Cordon Edouard	Rue du Pont
5694 FR	75	Latour Hortense	Avenue Foch
6544 XY	47	Mimault Bernard	Avenue FDR

OFFENCES ⋈ CARS

Code	Date	Officer	Department	Registration	Owner	Address
143256	25/10/92	567	75	5694 FR	Latour Hortense	Avenue Foch
987554	26/10/92	456	75	5694 FR	Latour Hortense	Avenue Foch
987557	26/10/92	456	75	6544 XY	Cordon Edouard	Rue du Pont
630876	15/10/92	456	47	6544 XY	Mimault Bernard	Avenue FDR
539856	12/10/92	567	47	6544 XY	Mimault Bernard	Avenue FDR

Figure 3.12 The relations OFFENCES and CARS (from Figure 2.19) and their join.

Figure 3.13 shows another example of join, using the same relations as we have already used (Figure 3.4) to demonstrate a union preceded by renamings. Here, the data of the two relations is combined according to the value of the child, returning the parents for each person for whom both are indicated in the database.

PATERNITY

Father	Child
Adam	Cain
Adam	Abel
Abraham	Isaac
Abraham	Ishmael

MATERNITY

Mother	Child
Eve	Cain
Eve	Seth
Sarah	Isaac
Hagar	Ishmael

PATERNITY ⋈ MATERNITY

Father	Child	Mother
Adam	Cain	Eve
Abraham	Isaac	Sarah
Abraham	Ishmael	Hagar

Figure 3.13 Offspring with both parents.

The two examples taken together show how the various relational algebra operators allow different ways of combining and correlating the data contained in a database, according to the various requirements.

Complete and incomplete joins   Let us look at some different examples of join, in order to highlight some important points. In the example in Figure 3.11, we can say that each tuple of each of the operands contributes to at least one tuple of the result. In this case, the join is said to be *complete*. For each tuple t_1 of r_1, there is a tuple t in $r_1 \bowtie r_2$ such that $t[X_1] = t_1$ (and similarly for r_2). This property does not hold in general, because it requires a correspondence between the tuples of the two relations. Figure 3.14 shows a join in which some tuples in the operands (in particular, the first of r_1 and the second of r_2) do not contribute to the result. This is because these tuples have no counterpart (that is, a tuple with the same value on the common attribute Department) in the other relation. These tuples are referred to as *dangling* tuples.

r_1

Employee	Department
Smith	sales
Black	production
White	production

r_2

Department	Head
production	Mori
purchasing	Brown

$r_1 \bowtie r_2$

Employee	Department	Head
Black	production	Mori
White	production	Mori

Figure 3.14 A join with 'dangling' tuples.

There is even the possibility, as an extreme case, that none of the tuples of the operands can be combined, and this gives rise to an empty result (see the example in Figure 3.15).

r_1	Employee	Department
	Smith	sales
	Black	production
	White	production

r_2	Department	Head
	marketing	Mori
	purchasing	Brown

$r_1 \bowtie r_2$	Employee	Department	Head

Figure 3.15 An empty join.

In the extreme opposite situation, each tuple of each operand can be combined with all the tuples of the other, as shown in Figure 3.16. In this case, the result contains a number of tuples equal to the product of the cardinalities of the operands and thus, $|r_1| \times |r_2|$ tuples (where $|r|$ indicates the cardinality of the relation r).

r_1	Employee	Project
	Smith	A
	Black	A
	White	A

r_2	Project	Head
	A	Mori
	A	Brown

$r_1 \bowtie r_2$	Employee	Project	Head
	Smith	A	Mori
	Black	A	Mori
	White	A	Mori
	Smith	A	Brown
	Black	A	Brown
	White	A	Brown

Figure 3.16 A join with $|r_1| \times |r_2|$ tuples.

To summarize, we can say that the join of r_1 and r_2 contains a number of tuples between zero and $|r_1| \times |r_2|$. Furthermore:

- if the join of r_1 and r_2 is complete, then it contains a number of tuples at least equal to the maximum of $|r_1|$ and $|r_2|$;

- if $X_1 \cap X_2$ contains a key for r_2, then the join of $r_1(X_1)$ and $r_2(X_2)$ contains at most $|r_1|$ tuples;

- if $X_1 \cap X_2$ is the primary key for r_2 and there is a referential constraint between $X_1 \cap X_2$ in r_1 and such a key of r_2, then the join of $r_1(X_1)$ and $r_2(X_2)$ contains exactly $|r_1|$ tuples.

Outer joins   The fact that the join operator 'leaves out' the tuples of a relation that have no counterpart in the other operand is useful in some cases but inconvenient in others, given the possibility of omitting important information. Take, for example, the join in Figure 3.14. Suppose we are interested in all the employees, along with their respective heads, if known. The natural join would not help in producing this result. For this purpose, a variant of the operator called *outer join* was proposed (and adopted in the last version of SQL, as discussed in Chapter 4). This allows for the possibility that all the tuples contribute to the result, extended with null values where there is no counterpart. There are three variants of this operator: the *left* outer join, which extends only the tuples of the first operand, the *right* outer join, which extends those of the second operand and the *full* outer join, which extends all tuples. In Figure 3.17 we demonstrate examples of outer joins on the relations already seen in Figure 3.14. The syntax is self-explanatory.

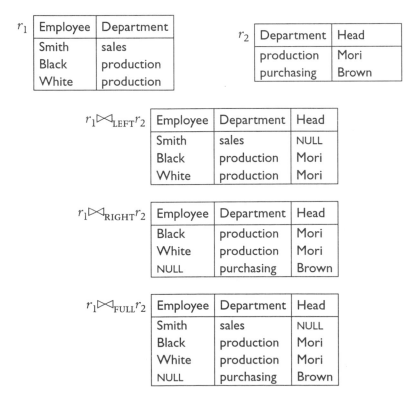

Figure 3.17 Some outer joins.

N-ary join, intersection and cartesian product   Let us look at some of the properties of the natural join. (We refer here to natural join rather than to outer join, for which some of the properties discussed here do not hold.) First let us observe that it is commutative, that is, $r_1 \bowtie r_2$ is always equal to $r_2 \bowtie r_1$, and associative, $r_1 \bowtie (r_2 \bowtie r_3)$ is equal to $(r_1 \bowtie r_2) \bowtie r_3$. Thus, we can write, where necessary, join sequences without brackets:

$$r_1 \bowtie r_2 \bowtie \ldots \bowtie r_n \quad \text{or} \quad \bowtie_{i=1}^{n} r_i$$

Note also that we have stated no specific hypothesis about the sets of attributes X_1 and X_2 on which the operands are defined. Therefore, the two sets could even be equal or be disjoint. Let us examine these extreme cases; the general definition given above is still meaningful, but certain points should be noted. If $X_1 = X_2$, then the join coincides with the intersection

$$r_1(X_1) \bowtie r_2(X_1) = r_1(X_1) \cap r_2(X_1)$$

since, by definition, the result is a relation on the union of the two sets of attributes, and must contain the tuples t such that $t[X_1] \in r_1$ and $t[X_2] \in r_2$. If $X_1 = X_2$, the union of X_1 and X_2 is also equal to X_1, and thus t is defined on X_1: the definition thus requires that $t \in r_1$ and $t \in r_2$, and therefore coincides with the definition of intersection.

The case where the two sets of attributes are disjoint requires even more attention. The result is always defined on the union $X_1 X_2$, and each tuple is always derived from two tuples, one for each of the operands. However, since such tuples have no attributes in common, there is no requirement to be satisfied in order for them to participate in the join. The condition that the tuples must have the same values on the common attributes is always verified. So the result of this join contains the tuples obtained by combining the tuples of the operands in all possible ways. In this case, we often say that the join becomes a *cartesian product*. This could be described as an operator defined (using the same definition given above for natural join) on relations that have no attributes in common. The use of the term is slightly misleading, as it is not really the same as a cartesian product between sets. The cartesian product of two sets is a set of pairs (with the first element from the first set and the second from the second). In the case here we have tuples, each obtained by juxtaposing a tuple of the first relation and a tuple of the second. Figure 3.18 shows an example of the cartesian product, demonstrating how the result contains a number of tuples equal to the product of the cardinalities of the operands.

Theta-join and equi-join   If we examine Figure 3.18, it is obvious that a cartesian product is, in general, of very little use, because it combines tuples in a way that is not necessarily significant. In fact, however, the cartesian product is often followed by a selection, which preserves only the combined tuples that satisfy the given requirements. For example, it makes sense to define a cartesian product on the relations EMPLOYEES and PROJECTS, if it is followed by the selection that retains only the tuples with equal values on the attributes Project and Code (see Figure 3.19).

EMPLOYEES

Employee	Project
Smith	A
Black	A
Black	B

PROJECTS

Code	Name
A	Venus
B	Mars

EMPLOYEES ⋈ PROJECTS

Employee	Project	Code	Name
Smith	A	A	Venus
Black	A	A	Venus
Black	B	A	Venus
Smith	A	B	Mars
Black	A	B	Mars
Black	B	B	Mars

Figure 3.18 A cartesian product.

EMPLOYEES

Employee	Project
Smith	A
Black	A
Black	B

PROJECTS

Code	Name
A	Venus
B	Mars

$\sigma_{\text{Project=Code}}$(EMPLOYEES ⋈ PROJECTS)

Employee	Project	Code	Name
Smith	A	A	Venus
Black	A	A	Venus
Black	B	B	Mars

Figure 3.19 A cartesian product followed by a selection.

For this reason, another operator is often introduced, the *theta-join*. It is a *derived* operator, in the sense that it is defined by means of other operators. Indeed, it is a cartesian product followed by a selection, as follows:

$$r_1 \bowtie_F r_2 = \sigma_F(r_1 \bowtie r_2)$$

The relation in Figure 3.19 can thus be obtained using the theta-join:

$$\text{EMPLOYEES} \bowtie_{\text{Project=Code}} \text{PROJECTS}$$

A theta-join in which the condition of selection F is a conjunction of atoms of equality, each with an attribute of the first relation and one of the second, is called *equi-join*. The relation in Figure 3.19 was obtained by means of an equi-join.

From the practical point of view, the theta-join and the equi-join are very important. This is because most current database systems do not take advantage of attribute names in order to combine relations, and thus use the equi-join and theta-join rather than the natural join. We examine this concept more thoroughly when we discuss SQL queries in Chapter 4. In fact SQL queries mainly correspond to equi-joins, while the natural join was made available only in the most recent versions of SQL.

At the same time, we presented the natural join first because it allows the simple discussion of important issues, which can then be extended to the equi-join. For example, we refer to natural joins in the discussion of some issues related to normalization in Chapter 8.

Note also that the natural join can be simulated using renaming, equi-join and projection. Without going into too much detail, here is an example. Given two relations, $r_1(ABC)$ and $r_2(BCD)$, the natural join of r_1 and r_2 can be expressed by means of other operators in three steps:

- renaming the attributes so as to obtain relations on disjoint schemas: $\varrho_{B'C' \leftarrow BC}(r_2)$

- equi-joining such relations, with equality conditions on the renamed attributes: $r_1 \bowtie_{B=B' \wedge C=C'} (\varrho_{B'C' \leftarrow BC}(r_2))$

- concluding with a projection that eliminates all the 'duplicate' attributes (one for each pair involved in the equi-join):

$$\pi_{ABCD}(r_1 \bowtie_{B=B' \wedge C=C'} (\varrho_{B'C' \leftarrow BC}(r_2)))$$

3.1.6 Queries in relational algebra

In general, a query can be defined as a function that, when applied to database instances, produces relations. More precisely, given a schema $\mathbf{R}$ of a database, a query is a function that, for every instance $\mathbf{r}$ of $\mathbf{R}$, produces a relation on a given set of attributes X. The expressions in the various query languages (such as relational algebra) 'represent' or 'implement' queries: each expression defines a function. We indicate by means of $E(\mathbf{r})$ the *result* of the application of the expression E to the database $\mathbf{r}$.

In relational algebra, the queries on a database schema $\mathbf{R}$ are formulated by means of expressions whose atoms are (names of) relations in $\mathbf{R}$ (the 'variables'). We conclude the presentation of relational algebra by showing the formulation of some queries of increasing complexity, which refer to the schema containing the two relations:

EMPLOYEES(<u>Number</u>, Name, Age, Salary)
SUPERVISION(Head, <u>Employee</u>)

A database on such a schema is shown in Figure 3.20.

The first query is very simple, involving a single relation: *find the numbers, names and ages of employees earning more than 40 thousand*. In this case, using

EMPLOYEES

Number	Name	Age	Salary
101	Mary Smith	34	40
103	Mary Bianchi	23	35
104	Luigi Neri	38	61
105	Nico Bini	44	38
210	Marco Celli	49	60
231	Siro Bisi	50	60
252	Nico Bini	44	70
301	Steve Smith	34	70
375	Mary Smith	50	65

SUPERVISION

Head	Employee
210	101
210	103
210	104
231	105
301	210
301	231
375	252

Figure 3.20 A database giving examples of expressions

a selection, we can highlight only the tuples that satisfy the condition (salary above 40 thousand) and by means of a projection eliminate the unwanted attributes:

$$\pi_{Number,Name,Age}(\sigma_{Salary>40}(\text{EMPLOYEES})) \qquad (3.1)$$

The result of this expression, applied to the database in Figure 3.20, is shown in Figure 3.21.

Number	Name	Age
104	Luigi Neri	38
210	Marco Celli	49
231	Siro Bisi	50
252	Nico Bini	44
301	Steve Smith	34
375	Mary Smith	50

Figure 3.21 The result of the application of Expression 3.1 to the database in Figure 3.20.

The second query involves both the relations, in a very natural way: *find the registration numbers of the supervisors of the employees earning more than 40 thousand*:

$$\pi_{Head}(\text{SUPERVISION} \bowtie_{Employee=Number}(\sigma_{Salary>40}(\text{EMPLOYEES}))) \qquad (3.2)$$

The result is shown in Figure 3.22, referring again to the database in Figure 3.20.

Let us move on to some more complex examples. We begin by slightly changing the above query: *find the names and salaries of the supervisors of the employees earning more than 40 thousand*. Here, we can obviously use the preceding expression, but we must then produce, for each tuple of the result, the information requested on the supervisor, which must be extracted from

Head
210
301
375

Figure 3.22 The result of the application of Expression 3.2 to the database in Figure 3.20.

the relation EMPLOYEES. Each tuple of the result is constructed on the basis of three tuples, the first from EMPLOYEES (about an employee earning more than 40 thousand), the second from SUPERVISION (giving the number of the supervisor of the employee in question), and the third again from EMPLOYEES (with the information concerning the supervisor). The solution intuitively requires the join of the relation EMPLOYEES with the result of the preceding expression, but a warning is needed. In general, the supervisor and the employee are not the same, and thus the two tuples of EMPLOYEES that contribute to a tuple of the join are different. The join must therefore be preceded by a suitable renaming. The following is an example:

$$\pi_{NameH,SalaryH} \left(\varrho_{NumberH,NameH,SalaryH,AgeH \leftarrow Number,Name,Salary,Age} (\text{EMPLOYEES}) \right)$$
$$\bowtie_{NumberH=Head}$$
$$(\text{SUPERVISION} \bowtie_{Employee=Number} (\sigma_{Salary>40}(\text{EMPLOYEES})))) \quad (3.3)$$

The result is shown in Figure 3.23, again referring to the database in Figure 3.20.

NameH	SalaryH
Marco Celli	60
Steve Smith	70
Mary Smith	65

Figure 3.23 The result of the application of Expression 3.3 to the database in Figure 3.20.

The next query is a variation on the one above, requesting the comparison of two values of the same attribute, but from different tuples: *find the employees earning more than their respective supervisors, showing registration numbers, names and salaries of the employees and supervisors.* The expression is similar to the one above, and the need for renaming is also evident. (The result is shown in Figure 3.24.)

$$\pi_{Number,Name,Salary,NumberH,NameH,SalaryH}$$
$$(\sigma_{Salary>SalaryH}(\varrho_{NumberH,NameH,SalaryH,AgeH \leftarrow Number,Name,Salary,Age} (\text{EMPLOYEES}))$$
$$\bowtie_{NumberH=Head}(\text{SUPERVISION} \bowtie_{Employee=Number}(\text{EMPLOYEES})))) \quad (3.4)$$

Number	Name	Salary	NumberH	NameH	SalaryH
104	Luigi Neri	61	210	Marco Celli	60
252	Nico Bini	70	375	Mary Smith	65

Figure 3.24 The result of the application of Expression 3.4 to the database in Figure 3.20.

The last example requires even more care: *find the registration numbers and names of the supervisors whose employees all earn more than 40 thousand.* The query includes a sort of universal quantification, but relational algebra does not contain any constructs directly suited to this purpose. We can, however, proceed with a double negation, finding the supervisors none of whose employees earns 40 thousand or less. This query is possible in relational algebra, using the difference operator. We select all the supervisors except those who have an employee who earns 40 thousand or less. The expression is as follows:

$$\pi_{Number,Name}(\text{EMPLOYEES} \bowtie_{Number=Head}$$
$$(\pi_{Head}(\text{SUPERVISION}) -$$
$$\pi_{Head}(\text{SUPERVISION} \bowtie_{Employee=Number} (\sigma_{Salary\leq40}(\text{EMPLOYEES})))))) \qquad (3.5)$$

The result of this expression on the database in Figure 3.20 is shown in Figure 3.25.

Number	Name
301	Steve Smith
375	Mary Smith

Figure 3.25 The result of Expression 3.5 on the database shown in Figure 3.20.

3.1.7 Equivalence of algebraic expressions

Relational algebra, like many other formal languages, allows the formulation of expressions equivalent among themselves, that is, producing the same result. For example, the following equivalence is valid where x, y and z are real numbers:

$$x \times (y + z) \equiv x \times y + x \times z$$

For each value substituted for the three variables, the two expressions give the same result. In relational algebra, we can give a similar definition. A first notion of *equivalence* refers to the database schema:

- $E_1 \equiv_R E_2$ if $E_1(\mathbf{r}) = E_2(\mathbf{r})$, for every instance of $\mathbf{r}$ in $\mathbf{R}$.

  Absolute equivalence is a stronger property and is defined as follows:

- $E_1 \equiv E_2$ if $E_1 \equiv_R E_2$, for every schema $\mathbf{R}$.

The distinction between the two cases is due to the fact that the attributes of the operands are not specified in the expressions (particularly in the natural join operations). An example of absolute equivalence is the following:

$$\pi_{AB}(\sigma_{A>0}(R)) \equiv \sigma_{A>0}(\pi_{AB}(R))$$

while the following equivalence

$$\pi_{AB}(R_1) \bowtie \pi_{AC}(R_2) \equiv_R \pi_{ABC}(R_1 \bowtie R_2)$$

holds only if in the schema **R** the intersection between the sets of attributes of R_1 and R_2 is equal to A. In fact, if there were also other attributes, the join would operate only on A in the first expression and on A and such other attributes in the second, with different results in general.

The equivalence of expressions in algebra is particularly important in query optimization, which we discuss in Chapter 9. In fact, SQL queries (Chapter 4) are translated into relational algebra, and the *cost* is evaluated, cost being defined in terms of the size of the intermediate and final result. When there are different equivalent expressions, the one with the smallest cost is selected. In this context, *equivalence transformations* are used, that is, operations that substitute one expression for another equivalent one. In particular, we are interested in those transformations that are able to reduce the size of the intermediate relations or to prepare an expression for the application of one of the above transformations. Let us illustrate a first set of transformations.

1. Atomization of selections: a *conjunctive selection* can be substituted by a cascade of atomic selections:

$$\sigma_{F_1 \wedge F_2}(E) \equiv \sigma_{F_1}(\sigma_{F_2}(E))$$

   where E is any expression. This transformation allows the application of subsequent transformations that operate on selections with atomic conditions.

2. Cascading projections: a projection can be transformed into a cascade of projections that 'eliminate' attributes in various phases:

$$\pi_X(E) \equiv \pi_X(\pi_{XY}(E))$$

   if E is defined on a set of attributes that contain Y (and X). This too is a preliminary transformation that will be followed by others.

3. Anticipation of the selection with respect to the join (often described as 'pushing selections down'):

$$\sigma_F(E_1 \bowtie E_2) \equiv E_1 \bowtie \sigma_F(E_2)$$

   if the condition F refers only to attributes in the sub-expression E_2.

4. Anticipation of the projection with respect to the join ('pushing projections down'); let E_1 and E_2 be defined on X_1 and X_2, respectively; if $Y_2 \subset X_2$ and $Y_2 \supseteq X_1 \cap X_2$ (so the attributes in $X_2 - Y_2$ are not involved in the join), then the following holds:

$$\pi_{X_1 Y_2}(E_1 \bowtie E_2) \equiv E_1 \bowtie \pi_{Y_2}(E_2)$$

By combining this rule with that of cascading projections, we can obtain the following equivalence for theta-joins:

$$\pi_Y(E_1 \bowtie_F E_2) \equiv \pi_Y(\pi_{Y_1}(E_1) \bowtie_F \pi_{Y_2}(E_2))$$

where X_1 and X_2 represent the attributes of E_1 and E_2 respectively and J_1 and J_2 the respective subsets involved in the join condition F, and, finally:

○ $Y_1 = (X_1 \cap Y) \cup J_1$

○ $Y_2 = (X_2 \cap Y) \cup J_2$

On the basis of the equivalences above, we can eliminate from each relation all the attributes that do not appear in the final result and are not involved in the join.

5. Combination of a selection and a cartesian product to form a theta-join:

$$\sigma_F(E_1 \bowtie E_2) \equiv E_1 \bowtie_F E_2$$

Let us look at an example that clarifies the use of preliminary transformations and the important rule of anticipation of selections. Suppose we wish to find, by referring to the database in Figure 3.20, *the registration numbers of the supervisors of the employees younger than 30*. A first expression for this could be the specification of the cartesian product of the two relations (which have no attributes in common) followed by a selection and then a projection:

$$\pi_{Head}(\sigma_{Number=Employee \wedge Age<30}(\text{EMPLOYEES} \bowtie \text{SUPERVISION}))$$

By means of the previous rules, we can significantly improve the quality of this expression, which is very low indeed: it first computes a large cartesian product, although the final result contains only a few tuples. Using Rule 1, we break up the selection:

$$\pi_{Head}(\sigma_{Number=Employee}(\sigma_{Age<30}(\text{EMPLOYEES} \bowtie \text{SUPERVISION})))$$

and we can then merge the first selection with the cartesian product, and form an equi-join (Rule 5) and anticipate the second selection with respect to the join (Rule 3), obtaining:

$$\pi_{Head}(\sigma_{Age<30}(\text{EMPLOYEES}) \bowtie_{Number=Employee} \text{SUPERVISION})$$

Finally, we can eliminate from the first argument of the join (with a projection) the unnecessary attributes, using Rule 4:

$$\pi_{\text{Head}}(\pi_{\text{Number}}(\sigma_{\text{Age}<30}(\text{EMPLOYEES}))) \bowtie_{\text{Number=Employee}} \text{SUPERVISION})$$

Some other transformations can be useful, particularly other forms of anticipation of selections and projections.

6. Distribution of the selection with respect to the union:

$$\sigma_F(E_1 \cup E_2) \equiv \sigma_F(E_1) \cup \sigma_F(E_2)$$

7. Distribution of the selection with respect to the difference:

$$\sigma_F(E_1 - E_2) \equiv \sigma_F(E_1) - \sigma_F(E_2)$$

8. Distribution of the projection with respect to the union:

$$\pi_X(E_1 \cup E_2) \equiv \pi_X(E_1) \cup \pi_X(E_2)$$

It is worth noting that projection is not distributive with respect to difference, as we can verify by applying the expressions:

$$\pi_A(R_1 - R_2) \quad \text{and} \quad \pi_A(R_1) - \pi_A(R_2)$$

to two relations on AB that contain tuples equal on A and different on B.

Other interesting transformations are those based on correspondence between set operators and complex selections:

9. $\sigma_{F_1 \vee F_2}(R) \equiv \sigma_{F_1}(R) \cup \sigma_{F_2}(R)$

10. $\sigma_{F_1 \wedge F_2}(R) \equiv \sigma_{F_1}(R) \cap \sigma_{F_2}(R) \equiv \sigma_{F_1}(R) \bowtie \sigma_{F_2}(R)$

11. $\sigma_{F_1 \wedge \neg(F_2)}(R) \equiv \sigma_{F_1}(R) - \sigma_{F_2}(R)$

Then, there is the commutative and associative property of all the binary operators excluding difference and the distributive property of the join with respect to the union:

$$E \bowtie (E_1 \cup E_2) \equiv (E \bowtie E_1) \cup (E \bowtie E_2)$$

Finally, we should be aware that the presence of empty intermediate results (relations with zero tuples) makes it possible to simplify expressions in a natural way. Note that a join (or also a cartesian product) in which one of the operators is the empty relation, produces an empty result.

3.1.8 Algebra with null values

In the above sections, we have always taken for granted that the algebraic expressions were being applied to relations containing no null values. Having already stressed, in Section 2.1.5, the importance of null values in actual applications, we must at least touch upon the impact that they have on the languages discussed in this chapter. The discussion is dealt with further in Chapter 4, in the context of the SQL language.

Let us look at the relation in Figure 3.26 and the following selection:

$$\sigma_{Age>30}(\text{PEOPLE})$$

PEOPLE

Name	Age	Salary
Aldo	35	15
Andrea	27	21
Maria	NULL	42

Figure 3.26 A relation with null values.

Now, the first tuple of the relation must contribute to the result and the second must not, but what can we say about the third? Intuitively, the age value is a null of unknown type, in that the value exists for each person, and the null means that we ignore it. With respect to these queries, instead of the conventional two-valued logic (in which formulas are either true or false) a three-valued logic can be used. In this logic, a formula can be true or false or can assume a third, new truth value that we call *unknown* and represent by the symbol *U*. An atomic condition assumes this value when at least one of the terms of the comparison assumes the null value. Thus, referring to the case under discussion, the first tuple certainly belongs to the result (*true*), the second certainly does not belong (*false*) and the third perhaps belongs and perhaps does not (*unknown*). The selection produces as a result the tuples for which the formula is true.

The following are the truth tables of the logical connectives *not*, *and* and *or* extended in order to take the unknown value into account. The semantic basis of the three connectives is the idea that the unknown value is somewhere between true and false.

not	
F	T
U	U
T	F

and	T	U	F
T	T	U	F
U	U	U	F
F	F	F	F

or	T	U	F
T	T	T	T
U	T	U	U
F	T	U	F

We should point out that the three-valued logic for algebraic operators also presents some unsatisfactory properties. For example, let us consider the algebraic expression

$$\sigma_{Age>30}(\text{PEOPLE}) \cup \sigma_{Age\leq30}(\text{PEOPLE})$$

Logically, this expression should return precisely the PEOPLE relation, given that the age value is either higher than **30** (first sub-expression) or is not higher than **30** (second sub-expression). On the other hand, if the two sub-expressions are evaluated separately, the third tuple of the example (just like any other tuple with a null value for **Age**), has an unknown result for each sub-expression and thus for the union. Only by means of a global evaluation (definitely impractical in the case of complex expressions) can we arrive at the conclusion that such a tuple must certainly appear in the result. The same goes for the expression

$$\sigma_{Age>30 \lor Age \leq 30}(\text{PEOPLE})$$

in which the disjunction is evaluated according to the three-valued logic.

In practice the best method for overcoming the difficulties described above is to treat the null values from a purely syntactic point of view. This approach works in the same way for both two-valued logic and three-valued logic. Two new forms of atomic conditions of selection are introduced to verify whether a value is specified or null:

- A IS NULL assumes the value true on a tuple t if the value of t on A is null and false if it is not;

- A IS NOT NULL assumes the value true on a tuple t if the value of t on A comes from the domain of A and false if the value is null.

In this context, the expression

$$\sigma_{Age>30}(\text{PEOPLE})$$

returns the people whose age is known and over **30**, whereas to obtain those who are or could be over **30** (that is, those whose age is known and over **30** or not known), we can use the expression:

$$\sigma_{Age>30 \lor Age \text{ IS NULL}}(\text{PEOPLE})$$

Similarly, the expressions

$$\sigma_{Age>30}(\text{PEOPLE}) \cup \sigma_{Age \leq 30}(\text{PEOPLE})$$
$$\sigma_{Age>30 \lor Age \leq 30}(\text{PEOPLE})$$

do not return an entire relation, but only the tuples that have a value not null for **Age**. If we want the entire relation as the result, then we have to add an 'IS NULL' condition:

$$\sigma_{Age>30 \lor Age \leq 30 \lor Age \text{ IS NULL}}(\text{PEOPLE})$$

This approach, as we explain in Chapter 4, is used in the present version of SQL, which supports a three-valued logic, and is usable in earlier versions, which adopted a two-valued logic.

3.1.9 Views

In Chapter 1, we saw how it can be useful to make different representations of the same data available to users. In the relational model, this is achieved by means of *derived relations*, that is, relations whose content is defined in terms of the contents of other relations. In a relational database, there can thus exist *base* relations, whose content is autonomous and actually stored in the database, and derived relations, whose content is derived from the content of other relations. It is possible that a derived relation is defined in terms of other derived relations, on condition that an ordering exists among the derived relations, so that all derived relations can be expressed in terms of base relations.[1]

There are basically two types of derived relations:

- *materialized views:* derived relations that are actually stored in the database;

- *virtual relations* (also called *views*, without further qualification): relations defined by means of functions (expressions in the query language), not stored in the database, but useable in the queries as if they were.

Materialized views have the advantage of being immediately available for queries. Frequently, however, it is a heavy task to maintain their contents consistent with those of the relations from which they are derived, as any change to the base relations from which they depend has to be propagated to them. On the other hand, virtual relations must be recalculated for each query but produce no consistency problems. Roughly, we can say that materialized views are convenient when there are fewer updates than queries and the calculation of the view is complex.[2] It is difficult, however, to give general techniques for maintaining consistency between base relations and materialized views. For this reason, most commercial systems provide mechanisms for organizing only virtual relations, which from here on, with no risk of ambiguity, we call simply *views*.

Views are defined in relational systems by means of query language expressions. Then queries on views are resolved by substituting the definition of the view for the view itself, that is, by composing the original query with the view query. For example, consider a database on the relations:

$$R_1(ABC), R_2(DEF), R_3(GH)$$

with a view defined using a cartesian product followed by a selection

---

1. This condition is relaxed in the recent proposals for deductive databases, which allow the definition of *recursive views*. We discuss this issue briefly in Section 3.3.
2. We return to this subject in Chapter 12, in which we discuss active databases, and in Chapter 13, in which we discuss data warehouses.

$$R = \sigma_{A>D}(R_1 \bowtie R_2)$$

On this schema, the query

$$\sigma_{B=G}(R \bowtie R_3)$$

is executed by replacing R with its definition

$$\sigma_{B=G}(\sigma_{A>D}(R_1 \bowtie R_2) \bowtie R_3)$$

The use of views can be convenient for a variety of reasons.

- A user interested in only a portion of the database can avoid dealing with the irrelevant components. For example, in a database with two relations on the schemas

EMPLOYEES(Employee, Department)
MANAGERS(Department, Supervisor)

a user interested only in the employees and their respective supervisors could find his task facilitated by a view defined as follows:

$$\pi_{\text{Employee,Supervisor}}(\text{EMPLOYEES} \bowtie \text{MANAGERS})$$

- Very complex expressions can be defined using views, with particular advantages in the case of repeated sub-expressions.

- By means of access authorizations associated with views, we can introduce mechanisms for the protection of privacy; for instance, a user could be granted restricted access to the database through a specifically designed view; this application of views is discussed in Chapter 4.

- In the event of restructuring of a database, it can be convenient to define views corresponding to relations that are no longer present after the restructuring. In this way, applications written with reference to the earlier version of the schema can be used on the new one without the need for modifications. For example, if a schema $R(ABC)$ is replaced by two schemas $R_1(AB)$, $R_2(BC)$, we can define a view, $R = R_1 \bowtie R_2$ and leave intact the applications that refer to R. The results as we show in Chapter 8 confirm that, if B is a key for R_2, then the presence of the view is completely transparent.

As far as queries are concerned, views can be treated as if they were base relations. However, the same cannot be said for update operations. In fact, it is often not even possible to define a semantics for updating views. Given an update on a view, we would like to have exactly one set of updates to the base relations, such that the view, if computed after these changes to the base relations, appears as if the given update had been performed on it. Unfortunately, this is not generally possible. For example, let us look again at the view

$$\pi_{\text{Employee,Supervisor}}(\text{EMPLOYEES} \bowtie \text{MANAGERS})$$

Assume we want to insert a tuple into the view: we would like to have tuples to insert into the base relations that allow the generation of the new tuple in the view. But this is not possible, because the tuple in the view does not involve the **Department** attribute, and so we do not have a value for it, as needed in order to establish the correspondence between the two relations. In general, the problem of updating views is complex, and all systems have strong limitations regarding the updating of views.

We return to the subject of views and present further examples in Chapter 4, in which we show how views are defined and used in SQL.

3.2 Relational calculus

The term *relational calculus* refers to a family of query languages, based on first order predicate calculus. These are characterized by being *declarative*, meaning that the query is specified in terms of the property of the result, rather than the procedure to be followed to obtain it. By contrast, relational algebra is known as a *procedural* language, because its expressions specify (by means of the individual applications of the operators) the construction of the result step by step.

There are many versions of relational calculus and it is not possible to present them all here. We first illustrate the version that is nearest to predicate calculus, *domain relational calculus*, which presents the basic characteristics of these languages. We then discuss the limitations and modifications that make it of practical interest. We will therefore present *tuple calculus with range declarations*, which forms the basis for many of the constructs available for queries in SQL, which we look at in Chapter 4.

In keeping with the topics already discussed concerning the relational model, we use non-positional notation for relational calculus.

This section (on calculus) and the following one (on Datalog) can be omitted without impairing the understanding of the rest of the book.

It is not necessary to be acquainted with first order predicate calculus in order to read this section. We give now some comments that enable anyone with prior knowledge to grasp the relationship with first order predicate calculus; these comments may be omitted without compromising the understanding of subsequent concepts.

There are some simplifications and modifications in relational calculus, with respect to first order predicate calculus. First, in predicate calculus, we generally have predicate symbols (interpreted in the same way as relations) and function symbols (interpreted as functions). In relational calculus, the predicate symbols correspond to relations in the database (apart from other standard predicates such as equality and inequality) and there are no function symbols. (They are not necessary given the flat structure of the relations.)

Then, in predicate calculus both open formulas (those with free variables), and closed formulas (those whose variables are all bound and none free), are of interest. The second type have a truth value that, with respect to an interpretation, is fixed, while the first have a value that depends on the values substituted for the free variables. In relational calculus, only the open formulas are of interest. A query is defined by means of an open calculus formula and the result consists of tuples of values that satisfy the formula when substituted for free variables.

3.2.1 Domain relational calculus

Relational calculus expressions have this form:

$$\{A_1:x_1, \ldots, A_k:x_k \mid f\}$$

where:

- $A_1, \ldots, A_k$ are distinct attributes (which do not necessarily have to appear in the schema of the database on which the query is formulated);

- $x_1, \ldots, x_k$ are *variables* (which we will take to be distinct for the sake of convenience, even if this is not strictly necessary);

- f is a formula, according to the following rules:

  o There are two types of *atomic* formula:

    * $R(A_1:x_1, \ldots, A_p:x_p)$, where $R(A_1, \ldots, A_p)$ is a relational schema and $x_1, \ldots, x_p$ are variables;

    * $x\vartheta y$ or $x\vartheta c$, with x and y variables, c constant and ϑ *comparison operator* $(=, \neq, \leq, \geq, >, <)$.

  o If f_1 and f_2 are formulas, then $f_1 \vee f_2$, $f_1 \wedge f_2$, and $\neg f_1$ are formulas ($\vee$, $\wedge$, $\neg$ are the *logical connectives*); where necessary, in order to ensure that the precedences are unambiguous, brackets can be used;

  o If f is a formula and x a variable (which usually appears in f, even if not strictly necessary) then $\exists x(f)$ and $\forall x(f)$ are formulas ($\exists$ and $\forall$ are the *existential quantifier* and *universal quantifier*, respectively).

The list of pairs $A_1 : x_1, \ldots, A_k : x_k$ is called the *target list* because it defines the structure of the result, which is made up of the relation on $A_1, \ldots, A_k$ that contains the tuples whose values when substituted for $x_1, \ldots, x_k$ render the formula true. The formal definition of the truth value of a formula goes beyond the scope of this book and, at the same time, its meaning can be explained informally. Let us briefly follow the syntactic structure of formulas (the term 'value' here means 'an element of the domain', where we assume, for the sake of simplicity, that all attributes have the same domain):

- an atomic formula $R(A_1:x_1, \ldots, A_p:x_p)$ is true for values of $x_1, \ldots, x_p$ that form a tuple of R;

- an atomic formula $x \vartheta y$ is true for values of x and y such that the value of x stands in relation ϑ with the value of y; similarly for $x \vartheta c$;

- the meaning of connectives is the usual one;

- for the formulas built with quantifiers:

  - $\exists x(f)$ is true if there exists at least one value for x that makes f true;

  - $\forall x(f)$ is true if f is true for all possible values for x.

Let us now illustrate relational calculus by showing how it can be used to express the queries that we formulated in relational algebra in Section 3.1.6, over the schema:

EMPLOYEES(<u>Number</u>, Name, Age, Salary)

SUPERVISION(Head, <u>Employee</u>)

Let us begin with a very simple query: *find the registration numbers, names, ages and salaries of the employees earning more than 40 thousand,* which we can formulate in algebra with a selection:

$$\sigma_{\text{Salary}>40}(\text{EMPLOYEES}) \tag{3.6}$$

There is an equally simple formulation in relational calculus, with the expression:

$$\{\text{Number}:m, \text{Name}:n, \text{Age}:a, \text{Salary}:s \mid$$
$$\text{EMPLOYEES}(\text{Number}:m, \text{Name}:n, \text{Age}:a, \text{Salary}:s) \wedge s > 40\} \tag{3.7}$$

Note the presence of two conditions in the formula (connected by the logical operator *and*):

- the first, EMPLOYEES(Number:m, Name:n, Age:a, Salary:s), requires that the values substituted respectively for the variables m, n, a, s constitute a tuple of the relation EMPLOYEES;

- the second requires that the value of the variable s is greater than **40**.

The result is made up of the values of the four variables that originate from the tuples of EMPLOYEES for which the value of the salary is greater than 40 thousand.

A slightly more complex query is: *find the registration numbers, names and ages of the employees who earn more than 40 thousand.* This query requires a subset of the attributes of EMPLOYEES and thus in algebra can be formulated with a projection (Expression 3.1):

$$\pi_{\text{Number},\text{Name},\text{Age}}(\sigma_{\text{Salary}>40}(\text{EMPLOYEES}))$$

This query in calculus can be formulated in various ways. The most direct, if not the simplest, is based on the observation that what interests us are the values of **Number**, **Name** and **Age**, which form part of the tuples for which

Salary is greater than 40. That is, for which there exists a value of Salary, greater than 40, which allows the completion of a tuple of the relation EMPLOYEES. We can thus use an existential quantifier:

$$\{\text{Number}:m, \text{Name}:n, \text{Age}:a \mid$$
$$\exists s(\text{EMPLOYEES}(\text{Number}:m, \text{Name}:n, \text{Age}:a, \text{Salary}:s) \wedge s > 40)\} \qquad (3.8)$$

The use of the quantifier is not actually necessary, since by simply writing

$$\{\text{Number}:m, \text{Name}:n, \text{Age}:a \mid$$
$$\text{EMPLOYEES}(\text{Number}:m, \text{Name}:n, \text{Age}:a, \text{Salary}:s) \wedge s > 40\} \qquad (3.9)$$

we can obtain the same result.

The same structure can be extended to more complex queries, which in relational algebra we formulated using the join operator. We will need more atomic conditions, one for each relation involved, and we can use repeated variables to indicate the join conditions. For example, the query that requests *find the registration numbers of the supervisors of the employees who earn more than 40 thousand*, formulated in algebra by Expression 3.2:

$$\pi_{\text{Head}}(\text{SUPERVISION} \bowtie_{\text{Employee=Number}}(\sigma_{\text{Salary}>40}(\text{EMPLOYEES})))$$

can be formulated in calculus by:

$$\{\text{Head}:h \mid \text{EMPLOYEES}(\text{Number}:m, \text{Name}:n, \text{Age}:a, \text{Salary}:s) \wedge$$
$$\text{SUPERVISION}(\text{Employee}:m, \text{Head}:h) \wedge s > 40\} \qquad (3.10)$$

where the variable m, common to both atomic conditions, builds the same correspondence between tuples specified in the join. Here, also, we can use existential quantifiers for all the variables that do not appear in the target list. However, as in the case above, this is not necessary, and would complicate the formulation.

If the involvement of different tuples of the same relation is required in an expression, then it is sufficient to include more conditions on the same predicate in the formula, with different variables. Consider the query: *find the names and salaries of the supervisors of the employees earning more than 40 thousand*, expressed in algebra by Expression 3.3, which has a join of the relation with itself:

$$\pi_{\text{NameH},\text{SalaryH}} (\rho_{\text{NumberH},\text{NameH},\text{SalaryH},\text{AgeH}\leftarrow\text{Number},\text{Name},\text{Salary},\text{Age}} (\text{EMPLOYEES})$$
$$\bowtie_{\text{NumberH=Head}}$$
$$(\text{SUPERVISION} \bowtie_{\text{Employee=Number}} (\sigma_{\text{Salary}>40}(\text{EMPLOYEES}))))$$

This query is formulated in calculus by requiring, for each tuple of the result, the existence of three tuples: one relating to an employee earning more than 40 thousand, a second that indicates who is his supervisor, and the last (again in the EMPLOYEES relation) that gives detailed information on the supervisor:

$$\{\text{NameH}:nh,\ \text{SalaryH}:sh\ |$$
$$\text{EMPLOYEES}(\text{Number}:m,\ \text{Name}:n,\ \text{Age}:a,\ \text{Salary}:s) \wedge s > 40 \wedge$$
$$\text{SUPERVISION}(\text{Employee}:m,\ \text{Head}:h) \wedge$$
$$\text{EMPLOYEES}(\text{Number}:h,\ \text{Name}:nh,\ \text{Age}:ah,\ \text{Salary}:sh)\} \qquad (3.11)$$

Consider next the query: *find the employees earning more than their respective supervisors, showing registration number, name and salary of the employees and supervisors* (Expression 3.4 in algebra). This differs from the preceding one only in the necessity of comparing values of the same attribute originating from different tuples, which causes no particular problems:

$$\{\text{Number}:m,\ \text{Name}:n,\ \text{Salary}:s,\ \text{NumberH}:h,\ \text{NameH}:nh,\ \text{SalaryH}:sh\ |$$
$$\text{EMPLOYEES}(\text{Number}:m,\ \text{Name}:n,\ \text{Age}:a,\ \text{Salary}:s) \wedge$$
$$\text{SUPERVISION}(\text{Employee}:m,\ \text{Head}:h) \wedge$$
$$\text{EMPLOYEES}(\text{Number}:h,\ \text{Name}:nh,\ \text{Age}:ah,\ \text{Salary}:sh) \wedge s > sh\} \qquad (3.12)$$

The last example requires a more complex solution. We must *find the registration numbers and names of the supervisors whose employees all earn more than 40 thousand*. In algebra we used a difference (Expression 3.5) that generates the required set by taking into account all the supervisors except those who have at least one employee earning less than 40 thousand:

$$\pi_{\text{Number,Name}}(\text{EMPLOYEES} \bowtie_{\text{Number=Head}}$$
$$(\pi_{\text{Head}}(\text{SUPERVISION}) -$$
$$\pi_{\text{Head}}(\text{SUPERVISION} \bowtie_{\text{Employee=Number}} (\sigma_{\text{Salary}\leq 40}(\text{EMPLOYEES}))))) $$

In calculus, we must use a quantifier. By taking the same steps as for algebra, we can use a negated existential quantifier. We use many of these, one for each variable involved.

$$\{\text{Number}:h,\ \text{Name}:n\ |\ \text{EMPLOYEES}(\text{Number}:h,\ \text{Name}:n,\ \text{Age}:a,\ \text{Salary}:s) \wedge$$
$$\text{SUPERVISION}(\text{Employee}:m,\ \text{Head}:h) \wedge$$
$$\neg\exists m'(\exists n'(\exists a'(\exists s'(\text{EMPLOYEES}(\text{Number}:m',\ \text{Name}:n',\ \text{Age}:a',\ \text{Salary}:s') \wedge$$
$$\text{SUPERVISION}(\text{Employee}:m',\ \text{Head}:h) \wedge s' \leq 40))))\} \qquad (3.13)$$

As an alternative, we can use universal quantifiers:

$$\{\text{Number}:h,\ \text{Name}:n\ |\ \text{EMPLOYEES}(\text{Number}:h,\ \text{Name}:n,\ \text{Age}:a,\ \text{Salary}:s) \wedge$$
$$\text{SUPERVISION}(\text{Employee}:m,\ \text{Head}:h) \wedge$$
$$\forall m'(\forall n'(\forall a'(\forall s'(\neg(\text{EMPLOYEES}(\text{Number}:m',\ \text{Name}:n',\ \text{Age}:a',\ \text{Salary}:s') \wedge$$
$$\text{SUPERVISION}(\text{Employee}:m',\ \text{Head}:h)) \vee s' > 40))))\} \qquad (3.14)$$

This expression selects a supervisor h if for every quadruple of values m', n', a', s' relative to the employees of h, s' is greater than 40. The structure $\neg f \vee g$ corresponds to the condition 'If f then g' (in our case, if m' is an employee having h as a supervisor, then the salary of m' is greater than 40), given that it is true in all cases apart from the one in which f is true and g is false.

It is worth noting that variations of de Morgan laws valid for boolean algebra operators, such that:

$$\neg(f \wedge g) \equiv \neg(f) \vee \neg(g)$$

$$\neg(f \vee g) = \neg(f) \wedge \neg(g)$$

are also valid for quantifiers:

$$\exists x(f) = \neg(\forall x(\neg(f)))$$

$$\forall x(f) = \neg(\exists x(\neg(f)))$$

The two formulations shown for the last query can be obtained one from the other by means of these equivalences. Furthermore, in general, we can use a reduced form of calculus (but without losing expressive power), in which we have the negation, a single connective (for example, the conjunction) and a single quantifier (for example the existential, which is easier to understand).

3.2.2 Qualities and drawbacks of domain calculus

As we have shown in the examples, relational calculus presents some interesting aspects, particularly its declarative nature. There are, however, some defects and limitations, which are significant from the practical point of view.

First, note that calculus allows expressions that make very little sense. For example, the expression:

$$\{A_1 : x_1, A_2 : x_2 \mid R(A_1 : x_1) \wedge x_2 = x_2\}$$

produces as a result a relation on A_1 and A_2 made up of tuples whose values in A_1 appear in the relation R, and the value on A_2 is any value of the domain (since the condition $x_2 = x_2$ is always true). In particular, if the domain changes, for example, from the integers between 0 and 99 to the integers between 0 and 999, the answer to the query also changes. If the domain is infinite, then the answer is also infinite, which is undesirable. A similar observation can be made for the expression

$$\{A_1 : x_1 \mid \neg(R(A_1 : x_1))\}$$

the result of which contains the values of the domain not appearing in R.

It is useful to introduce the following concept here: an expression of a query language is *domain independent* if its result, on each instance of the database, does not vary if we change the domain on the basis of which the expression is evaluated. A language is *domain independent* if all its expressions are domain independent. The requirement of domain independence is clearly fundamental for real languages, because domain dependent expressions have no practical use and can produce extensive results.

Based on the expressions seen above, we can say that relational calculus is not domain independent. At the same time, it is easy to see that relational algebra is domain independent, because it constructs the results from the relations in the database, without ever referring to the domains of the attributes. So the values of the results all come from the instance to which the expression is applied.

If we say that two query languages are *equivalent* when for each expression in one there exists an equivalent expression in the other and vice versa, we can state that algebra and calculus are not equivalent. This is because calculus, unlike algebra, allows expressions that are domain dependent. However, if we limit our attention to the subset of relational calculus made up solely of expressions that are domain independent, then we get a language that is indeed equivalent to relational algebra. In fact:

- for every expression of relational calculus that is domain independent there exists an expression of relational algebra equivalent to it;

- for every expression of relational algebra there is an expression of relational calculus equivalent to it (and thus domain independent).

The proof of equivalence goes beyond the scope of this text, but we can mention its basic principles. There is a correspondence between selections and simple conditions, between projection and existential quantification, between join and conjunction, between union and disjunction and between difference and conjunction associated with negation. The universal quantifiers can be ignored in that they can be changed to existential quantifiers using de Morgan's laws.

In addition to the problem of domain dependence, relational calculus has another disadvantage, that of requiring numerous variables, often one for each attribute of each relation involved. Then, when quantifications are necessary the quantifiers are also multiplied. The only practical languages based at least in part on domain calculus, known as *Query-by-Example (QBE)*, use a graphic interface that frees the user from the need to specify tedious details. Appendix A, which deals with the Microsoft Access system, presents a version of QBE.

In order to overcome the limitations of domain calculus, a variant of relational calculus has been proposed, in which the variables denote tuples instead of single values. In this way, the number of variables is often significantly reduced, in that there is only a variable for each relation involved. This *tuple relational calculus* would however be equivalent to domain calculus, and thus also have the limitation of domain dependence. Therefore, we prefer to omit the presentation of this language. Instead we will move directly to a language that has the characteristics of tuple calculus, and at the same time overcomes the defect of domain dependence, by using the direct association of variables with relations of the database. The following section deals with this language.

3.2.3 Tuple calculus with range declarations

The expressions of *tuple calculus with range declarations* have the form

$$\{ \mathcal{T} \mid \mathcal{L} \mid f \}$$

where:

$\mathcal{L}$ is the *range list*, enumerating the free variables of the formula f, with the respective ranges of variability: in fact, $\mathcal{L}$ is a list of elements of type $x(R)$, with x variable and R relation name; if $x(R)$ is in the range list, then, when the expression is evaluated, the possible values for x are just the tuples in the relation R;

$\mathcal{T}$ is the *target list*, composed of elements of type $Y:x.Z$ (or simply $x.Z$, abbreviation for $Z:x.Z$), with x variable and Y and Z sequences of attributes (of equal length); the attributes in Z must appear in the schema of the relation that makes up the range of x. We can also write $x.*$, as abbreviation for $X:x.X$, where the range of the variable x is a relation on attributes X;

f is a formula with

- atoms of type $x.A\vartheta c$ or $x_1.A_1\vartheta x_2.A_2$, which compare, respectively, the value of x on the attribute A with the constant c and the value of x_1 on A_1 with that of x_2 on A_2;

- connectives as for domain calculus;

- quantifiers, which also associate ranges to the respective variables:

$$\exists x(R)(f) \quad \forall x(R)(f)$$

where, $\exists x(R)(f)$ means 'there is a tuple x in the relation R that satisfies the formula f' and $\forall x(R)(f)$ means 'every tuple x in R satisfies f'.

Range declarations in the range list and in the quantifications have an important role: while introducing a variable x, a range declaration $R(x)$ specifies that x can assume as values only the tuples of the relation R with which it is associated. Therefore this language has no need of atomic conditions such as those seen in domain calculus, which specify that a tuple belongs to a relation.

We show next how the various queries that we have already expressed in algebra and domain calculus can be formulated in this language.

The first query, which requests *registration numbers, names, ages and salaries of the employees earning more than 40 thousand*, becomes very concise and clear (compare with Expression 3.7):

$$\{e.* \mid e(\text{EMPLOYEES}) \mid e.\text{Salary} > 40\} \tag{3.15}$$

In order to produce only some of the attributes, *registration numbers, names and ages of the employees earning more than 40 thousand*

(Expression 3.1 in algebra and Expression 3.9 in domain calculus), it is sufficient to modify the target list:

$$\{e.(\text{Number, Name, Age}) \mid e(\text{EMPLOYEES}) \mid e.\text{Salary} > 40\} \qquad (3.16)$$

For queries involving more than one relation, more variables are necessary, specifying the conditions of correlation on the attributes. The query that requests *find the registration numbers of the supervisors of the employees earning more than 40 thousand* (Expression 3.2 in algebra and Expression 3.10 in domain calculus) can be formulated with:

$$\{s.\text{Head} \mid e(\text{EMPLOYEES}), s(\text{SUPERVISION}) \mid$$
$$e.\text{Number} = s.\text{Employee} \wedge e.\text{Salary} > 40\} \qquad (3.17)$$

Note how the formula allows for the conjunction of two atomic conditions, one that corresponds to the join condition ($e.\text{Number} = s.\text{Employee}$) and the other to the usual selection condition ($e.\text{Salary} > 40$).

In the case of expressions that correspond to the join of a relation with itself, there will be more variables with the same range. The query: *find names and salaries of supervisors of employees earning more than 40 thousand* (Expression 3.3 and Expression 3.11) can be formulated using the following expression:

$$\{\text{NameH, SalaryH} : e'.(\text{Name, Salary}) \mid$$
$$e'(\text{EMPLOYEES}), s(\text{SUPERVISION}), e(\text{EMPLOYEES}) \mid$$
$$e'.\text{Number} = s.\text{Head} \wedge s.\text{Employee} = e.\text{Number} \wedge$$
$$e.\text{Salary} > 40\} \qquad (3.18)$$

Similarly, we can *find the employees who earn more than their respective supervisors, showing registration number, name and salary of the employees and supervisors* (Expression 3.4 in algebra and Expression 3.12 in domain calculus):

$$\{e.(\text{Name, Number, Salary}), \text{NameH, NumberH, SalaryH} : e'.(\text{Name, Number, Salary}) \mid$$
$$e(\text{EMPLOYEES}), s(\text{SUPERVISION}), e'(\text{EMPLOYEES}) \mid$$
$$e.\text{Number} = s.\text{Employee} \wedge s.\text{Head} = e'.\text{Number} \wedge$$
$$e.\text{Salary} > e'.\text{Salary}\} \qquad (3.19)$$

Queries with quantifiers are much more concise and practical here than in domain calculus. The query that requests *find the registration number and name of the supervisors whose employees all earn more that 40 thousand* (Expression 3.5 in algebra and Expression 3.13 or Expression 3.14 in domain calculus) can be expressed with far fewer quantifiers and variables. Again, there are various options, based on the use of the two quantifiers and of negation. With universal quantifiers:

$$\{e.(\text{Number, Name}) \mid e(\text{EMPLOYEES}), s(\text{SUPERVISION}) \mid$$
$$e.\text{Number} = s.\text{Head} \wedge \forall e'(\text{EMPLOYEES})(\forall s'(\text{SUPERVISION})$$
$$(\neg(s.\text{Head} = s'.\text{Head} \wedge s'.\text{Employee} = e'.\text{Number}) \vee$$
$$e'.\text{Salary} > 40))\} \qquad (3.20)$$

With negated existential quantifiers:

$$\{e.(\text{Number, Name}) \mid e(\text{EMPLOYEES}), s(\text{SUPERVISION}) \mid$$
$$e.\text{Number} = s.\text{Head} \wedge \neg(\exists e'(\text{EMPLOYEES})(\exists s'(\text{SUPERVISION})$$
$$(s.\text{Head} = s'.\text{Head} \wedge s'.\text{Employee} = e'.\text{Number} \wedge$$
$$e'.\text{Salary} \leq 40)))\} \tag{3.21}$$

Unfortunately, it turns out that it is not possible in tuple calculus with range declarations to express all the queries that could be formulated in relational algebra (or in domain calculus). In particular, the queries that in algebra require the union operator, cannot be expressed in this version of calculus. Take, for example, the simple union of two relations on the same attributes: given $R_1(AB)$ and $R_2(AB)$, we wish to formulate the query that we would express in algebra by the union of R_1 and R_2. If the expression had two free variables, then every tuple of the result would have to correspond to a tuple of each of the relations. This is not necessary, because the union requires the tuples of the result to appear in at least one of the operands, not necessarily in both. If, on the other hand, the expression had a single free variable, this would have to refer to a single relation, without acquiring tuples from the other for the result. Therefore, the union cannot be expressed.

For this reason, SQL, as we will see in Chapter 4, allows for an explicit union construct, to express queries that would otherwise prove impossible. This is because the declarative aspects of SQL are based on tuple calculus with range declarations.

Note that if we allowed the definition of ranges made up of two or more relations, we would resolve the problem of simple unions. We could not however, formulate complex unions whose operands are sub-expressions not directly corresponding to relation schemas. For example, given two relations $R_1(ABC)$ and $R_2(BCD)$, the union of their projections on BC

$$\pi_{BC}(R_1) \cup \pi_{BC}(R_2)$$

could not be expressed even with this extension, because the two relations have different schemas, and thus a single variable cannot be associated with both.

We must stress that, while the union operator cannot be expressed in this version of calculus, the intersection and difference operators are expressible.

- Intersection requires the tuples of the result to belong to both the operands and thus the result can be constructed with reference to just one relation, with the additional condition that requires the existence of an equal tuple in the other relation; for example, the intersection:

$$\pi_{BC}(R_1) \cap \pi_{BC}(R_2)$$

can be expressed by:

$$\{x_1.BC \mid x_1(R_1) \mid \exists x_2(R_2)(x_1.B = x_2.B \wedge x_1.C = x_2.C)\}$$

- Similarly, the difference, which produces the tuples of an operand not contained in the other, can be specified by requesting precisely those tuples of the first argument that do not appear in the second. For example,

$$\pi_{BC}(R_1) - \pi_{BC}(R_2)$$

can be expressed by:

$$\{x_1.BC \mid x_1(R_1) \mid \neg \exists x_2(R_2)(x_1.B = x_2.B \wedge x_1.C = x_2.C)\}$$

3.3 Datalog

We conclude this chapter with a brief discussion of another database query language that has generated considerable interest in the scientific community since the mid-eighties. The basic concept on which the *Datalog* language is based is that of adapting the logic programming language *Prolog* for use with databases. We can illustrate neither Datalog nor Prolog in detail here, but we can mention the most interesting aspects, particularly from the point of view of a comparison with the other languages seen in this chapter.

In its basic form, Datalog is a simplified version of Prolog,[3] a language based on first order predicate calculus, but with a different approach from the relational calculus discussed above. There are two types of predicate in Datalog:

- *extensional* predicates, which correspond to relations in the database;

- *intensional* predicates, which essentially correspond to views (virtual relations), specified by means of logical rules.

Datalog rules have the form:

$$head \leftarrow body$$

where

- the *head* is an atomic formula of the form $R(A_1 : a_1, ..., A_p : a_p)$, similar to those used in domain relational calculus,[4] where each a_i, however, can be a constant or a variable;

- the *body* is a list of atomic formulas, of both forms allowed in domain calculus, that is, the form $R(...)$ and the comparison between variables or between a variable and a constant.

---

3. For those acquainted with Prolog, note that function symbols are not used in Datalog.
4. For the sake of continuity with previous sections, we use a non-positional notation for atomic formulas, while Datalog and Prolog usually have a positional notation. The substance of the language is, however, the same.

Rules define the 'content' of intensional predicates, as the tuples whose values satisfy the body. The following conditions are imposed:

- extensional predicates can appear only in the body of rules;

- if a variable appears in the head of a rule, then it must also appear in the body of the same rule;

- if a variable appears in a comparison atom, then it must also appear in an atom of the form $R(\ldots)$ in the same body.

The first condition ensures that there will be no attempt to redefine the relations stored in the database. The other two ensure a property similar (in this context) to domain independence as discussed with regard to relational calculus.

A basic characteristic of Datalog, which distinguishes it from the other languages we have seen up to now, is its use of *recursion*. It is possible for an intensional predicate to be defined in terms of itself (directly or indirectly). We will return to this aspect shortly.

Datalog queries are specified simply by means of atoms $R(A_1 : a_1, \ldots, A_p : a_p)$, usually preceded by a question mark '?', to underline precisely the fact that they are queries; however other syntactic conventions may be used. Queries produce as results the tuples of the relation R that can be obtained by suitable substitutions for the variables. For example, the query:

$$?\text{EMPLOYEES}(\text{Number}:m, \text{Name}:n, \text{Age}:30, \text{Salary}:s)$$

returns the employees who are thirty years old. To formulate more complex queries, we must use rules. For example, in order to *find the registration numbers of the supervisors of the employees who earn more than 40 thousand*, formulated in algebra by Expression 3.2 and in domain calculus by Expression 3.10, we define an intensional predicate SUPEROFRICH, with the rule:

$$
\begin{aligned}
\text{SUPEROFRICH}(\text{Head}:h) \leftarrow \\
\text{EMPLOYEES}(\text{Number}:m, \text{Name}:n, \text{Age}:a, \text{Salary}:s), \\
\text{SUPERVISION}(\text{Employee}:m, \text{Head}:h), s > 40
\end{aligned}
\tag{3.22}
$$

In order to evaluate a query of this nature, we must define the semantics of the rules. The basic concept is that the body of a rule is considered as the conjunction of the atoms that appear in it, and thus the rule can be evaluated in the same way as an expression of domain calculus. The body of the expression, substituting the commas with *and*, becomes the formula, and the head of the expression, apart from the name of the intensional predicate, becomes the target list. Expression 3.22 defines the intensional relation SUPEROFRICH as made up of the same tuples that appear in the result of

Expression 3.10 of calculus, which has precisely the structure described above:

$$\{ \text{Head}:h \mid \text{EMPLOYEES}(\text{Number}:m, \text{Name}:n, \text{Age}:a, \text{Salary}:s) \wedge$$
$$\text{SUPERVISION}(\text{Employee}:m, \text{Head}:h) \wedge s > 40 \}$$

Similarly, we can write rules (with auxiliary intensional predicates) for many of the queries we have looked at in preceding sections. In the absence of recursive definitions, the semantics of Datalog is therefore very simple, in the sense that the various intensional predicates can be calculated by means of expressions similar to calculus. However, using the definition given so far for Datalog, it is not possible to formulate all the queries that could be expressed in calculus (and in algebra). This is because there is no construct available corresponding to the universal quantifier (or to negation in the full sense of the term). It can be proven that non-recursive Datalog is equivalent to the domain independent subset of calculus without negations or universal quantifiers.

To furnish Datalog with the same expressive power as calculus, we must add to the basic structure the possibility of including in the body, not only atomic conditions, but also negations of atomic conditions (which we indicate by the symbol NOT).

Only in this way can we formulate the query that requests *find the registration numbers and names of the supervisors whose employees all earn more than 40 thousand* (Expression 3.13):

$$\{ \text{Number}:h, \text{Name}:n \mid \text{EMPLOYEES}(\text{Number}:h, \text{Name}:n, \text{Age}:a, \text{Salary}:s) \wedge$$
$$\text{SUPERVISION}(\text{Employee}:m, \text{Head}:h) \wedge$$
$$\neg \exists m'(\exists n'(\exists a'(\exists s'(\text{EMPLOYEES}(\text{Number}:m', \text{Name}:n', \text{Age}:a', \text{Salary}:s') \wedge$$
$$\text{SUPERVISION}(\text{Employee}:m', \text{Head}:h) \wedge s' \leq 40)))) \}$$

Let us proceed by defining a predicate for the supervisors who do not satisfy the condition:

$$\text{SUPEROFSOMENOTRICH}(\text{Head}:h) \leftarrow$$
$$\text{SUPERVISION}(\text{Employee}:m, \text{Head}:h),$$
$$\text{EMPLOYEES}(\text{Number}:m, \text{Name}:n, \text{Age}:a, \text{Salary}:s), s' \leq 40$$

We can use this predicate in the negated form:

$$\text{SUPEROFALLRICH}(\text{Number}:h, \text{Name}:n) \leftarrow$$
$$\text{EMPLOYEES}(\text{Number}:h, \text{Name}:n, \text{Age}:a, \text{Salary}:s)$$
$$\text{SUPERVISION}(\text{Employee}:m, \text{Head}:h),$$
$$\text{NOT SUPEROFSOMENOTRICH}(\text{Head}:h)$$

We could prove that non-recursive Datalog with negation is equivalent to the domain-independent subset of calculus.

Greater expressive power is obtained by using recursive rules. For example, referring again to the database with the relations EMPLOYEES and

SUPERVISION, we can define the intensional predicate SUPERIORS, which gives, for each employee, the supervisor, the supervisor's supervisor and so on, with no limits. For this we need two rules:

$$\text{SUPERIORS}(\text{Employee}:e,\ \text{SuperHead}:h) \leftarrow$$
$$\text{SUPERVISION}(\text{Employee}:e,\ \text{Head}:h)$$

$$\text{SUPERIORS}(\text{Employee}:e,\ \text{SuperHead}:h) \leftarrow$$
$$\text{SUPERVISION}(\text{Employee}:e,\ \text{Head}:h')$$
$$\text{SUPERIORS}(\text{Employee}:h',\ \text{SuperHead}:h)$$

The second rule is recursive, in that it defines the SUPERIORS relation in terms of itself. To evaluate this rule, we cannot proceed as we have done up to now, because a single evaluation of the body would not be sufficient to calculate the recursive predicate. There are various techniques for formally defining the semantics in this case, but they are well beyond the scope of this text. We will touch upon the simplest method, based on the technique known as *fixpoint*: the rules that define the intensional recursive predicate are evaluated many times until an iteration does not generate new results. In our case, the first iteration would generate a relation SUPERIORS equal to the extensional relation SUPERVISION, that is, containing the supervisors of the employees. The second step would add the supervisors of the supervisors, and so on. Obviously, queries of this nature cannot be formulated in relational algebra (or in calculus) because we would have no way of knowing how many times the join of the relation SUPERVISION with itself had to be specified.

As a final issue before concluding, we simply state the fact that certain recursive rules with negation are difficult to evaluate, because the fixpoint cannot be reached. This is why limits are imposed on the presence of negations in recursive rules. The reader should be aware that it is possible to identify a perfectly workable subset of recursive Datalog with negation that is much more expressive than calculus and relational algebra in that:

- for every expression of algebra there is an equivalent expression of Datalog with negation;

- there are recursive Datalog expressions for which there are no equivalent expressions in algebra and calculus.

3.4 Bibliography

Relational algebra was proposed by Codd [26] as an essential component of the model. Relational calculus and the close correspondence of the two families of languages were also proposed by Codd [28]. Deeper and more formal treatment of relational languages can be found in the books devoted to database theory: Ullman [88], Maier [58], Paredaens et al. [67], Atzeni and De Antonellis [3], Abiteboul, Hull and Vianu [1]. Datalog is discussed in depth by Ceri, Gottlob and Tanca [17], Ullman [88], Abiteboul, Hull and Vianu [1].

3.5 Exercises

Exercise 3.1 Study the database schema containing the relations:

FILMS(FilmNumber, Title, Director, Year, ProductionCost)
ARTISTS(ActorNumber, Surname, FirstName, Sex, BirthDate, Nationality)
ROLES(FilmNumber, ActorNumber, Character)

1. Produce a database on this schema for which the joins between the various relations are all complete.

2. Assuming two referential constraints between the relation ROLES and the other two, discuss possible cases of incomplete join.

3. Show a cartesian product that involves relations in this database.

4. Show a database for which one (or more) of the joins is (are) empty.

Exercise 3.2 With reference to the schema in Exercise 3.1, express the following queries in relational algebra, in domain calculus, in tuple calculus and in Datalog:

1. the titles of the films starring Henry Fonda;

2. the titles of the films in which the director is also an actor;

3. the actors who have played two characters in the same film; show the titles of the films, first name and surname of the actor and the two characters;

4. the titles of the films in which the actors are all of the same sex.

Exercise 3.3 Consider the database containing the following relations:

REPRESENTATIVE(Number, Surname, FirstName, Committee, County, Constituency)
CONSTITUENCIES(County, Number, Name)
COUNTIES(Code, Name, Region)
REGIONS(Code, Name)
COMMITTEES(Number, Name, President)

Formulate the following queries in relational algebra, in domain calculus and in tuple calculus;

1. find the name and surname of the presidents of the committees in which there is at least one representative from the county of Borsetshire;

2. find the name and surname of the members of the finance committee;

3. find the name, surname and constituency of the members of the finance committee;

4. find the name, surname, county and region of election of the delegates of the finance committee;

5. find the regions in which representatives having the same surname have been elected.

Exercise 3.4 Show how the formulation of the queries in Exercise 3.3 could be facilitated by the definition of views.

Exercise 3.5 Consider the database schema on the relations

COURSES(<u>Number</u>, Faculty, CourseTitle, Tutor)
STUDENTS(<u>Number</u>, Surname, FirstName, Faculty)
TUTORS(<u>Number</u>, Surname, FirstName)
EXAMS(<u>Student</u>, <u>Course</u>, Grade, Date)
STUDYPLAN(<u>Student</u>, <u>Course</u>, Year)

Formulate, in relational algebra, in domain calculus, in tuple calculus, and in Datalog, the queries that produce:

1. the students who have gained an 'A' in at least one exam, showing, for each of them, the first name, surname and the date of the first of such occasions;

2. for every course in the engineering faculty, the students who passed the exam during the last session;

3. the students who passed all the exams required by their respective study plans;

4. for every course in the literature faculty, the student (or students) who passed the exam with the highest grades;

5. the students whose study plans require them to attend lectures only in their own faculties;

6. first name and surname of the students who have taken an exam with a tutor having the same surname as the student.

Exercise 3.6 With reference to the following database schema:

CITIES(<u>Name</u>, Region, Population)
CROSSINGS(<u>City</u>, <u>River</u>)
RIVERS(<u>River</u>, Length)

formulate the following queries in relational algebra, domain calculus, tuple calculus and Datalog:

1. find the names, regions and populations for the cities that (i) have more than 50 thousand inhabitants and (ii) and are crossed by the Thames or the Mersey;

2. find the cities that are crossed by (at least) two rivers, giving the name of the city and that of the longest of the rivers.

Exercise 3.7 With reference to the following database schema:

$$\text{T\small{RIBUTARIES}}(\underline{\text{Tributary}}, \text{River})$$
$$\text{R\small{IVERS}}(\underline{\text{River}}, \text{Length})$$

formulate in Datalog, the query that finds all the tributaries, direct and indirect, of the Mississippi.

Exercise 3.8 Consider the relational schema consisting of the following relations:

$$\text{T\small{UTORS}}(\underline{\text{Number}}, \text{Surname}, \text{FirstName})$$
$$\text{C\small{OURSES}}(\underline{\text{Number}}, \text{CourseName}, \text{Tutor})$$
$$\text{S\small{TUDENTS}}(\underline{\text{Number}}, \text{Surname}, \text{FirstName})$$
$$\text{E\small{XAMS}}(\underline{\text{Student}}, \text{Course}, \text{Date}, \text{Grade})$$

With reference to this schema, formulate the expressions of algebra, tuple relational calculus and Datalog that produce:

1. the exams passed by the student named Detrouvelan–Delaney (supposing him to be the only one with such a surname), indicating, for each exam, the name of the course, the grade achieved and the name of the tutor;

2. the tutors who teach two courses (and not more than two), indicating the surname and first name of the tutor and the names of the two courses.

Exercise 3.9 Consider a relational schema containing the relations:

$$R_1(ABC), R_2(DG), R_3(EF)$$

Formulate in tuple and domain relational calculus, the query formulated in relational algebra with the following expression:

$$(R_3 \bowtie_{G=E} R_2) \cup \varrho_{DG \leftarrow AC}(\pi_{ACEF}(R_1 \bowtie_{B=F} R_3)))$$

Exercise 3.10 With reference to the schema in Exercise 3.9, formulate in relational algebra the queries specified in domain calculus by means of the following expressions:

$$\{H : g, B : b \mid R_1(A : a, B : b, C : c) \wedge R_2(D : c, G : g)\}$$

$$\{A : a, B : b \mid R_2(D : a, G : b) \wedge R_3(E : a, F : b)\}$$

$$\{A:a, B:b \mid R_1(A:a, B:b, C:c) \land \exists a'(R_1(A:a', B:b, C:c) \land a \neq a')\}$$

$$\{A:a, B:b \mid R_1(A:a, B:b, C:c) \land \forall a'(\neg R_1(A:a', B:b, C:c)) \lor a = a'\}$$

$$\{A:a, B:b \mid R_1(A:a, B:b, C:c) \land \neg \exists a'(R_1(A:a', B:b, C:c)) \land a \neq a'\}$$

Exercise 3.11 Consider the following algebraic expression:

$$\pi_{ADH}(\sigma_{(B=C)\land(E=F)\land(A>20)\land(G=10)}((R_1 \bowtie R_3) \bowtie R_2)$$

which refers to the schema

$$R_1(AB), R_2(CDE), R_3(FGH)$$

and transform it, with the goal of reducing the size of the intermediate results.

4
SQL

SQL is an acronym for Structured Query Language[1]. It was originally developed for the relational DBMS *System R*, created by the IBM Research Laboratory at San Jose in California during the late seventies. SQL has since been adopted by many other systems; it has been standardized and has become the reference language for relational databases.

SQL is not merely a query language. It contains the dual features of a *Data Definition Language*, DDL (with commands for the definition of a relational database schema) and a *Data Manipulation Language*, DML (with commands for the modification and querying of a database instance). In this chapter, we first introduce SQL as the definition language of a database schema (Section 4.1); then we describe the specification of queries (Section 4.2) and updates (Section 4.3). In Section 4.4 we describe some more advanced features of data definition, which require knowledge of the query language. In Section 4.5, we illustrate the commands for authorization control, and we conclude the chapter with a description of the interaction between SQL and traditional programming languages (Section 4.6).

Some advanced features of DBMSs, shown in Part III and Part IV, are also supported by SQL. We will defer the presentation of these aspects of the language until they can be introduced alongside the appropriate concepts. For this reason, we describe the SQL commands for the support of transactions and the definition of indices in Chapter 9, and the definition of active rules in Chapter 12.

Standardization of SQL   The widespread use of SQL is largely due to the vast amount of standardization work that has been devoted to it, carried out mainly within ANSI (the American National Standards Institute) and ISO (the Organization for International Standardization). Many vendors of relational systems have been able to take part in the decision-making process, rather

1. There are two different pronunciations of this acronym; the first enunciates the letters separately: S-Q-L, whereas the second pronounces it like the word 'sequel'. Sequel is the name by which the language was originally known.

than one vendor in particular having a dominant influence. This standardization work began in the early eighties and is continuing today. Thus, various versions of the language have emerged, each one an improvement on the previous one.

The first definition of a standard for SQL was promulgated in 1986 by ANSI. This first standard already contained many of the basics for query formulation, at the same time offering some (limited) support for schema definition and manipulation. The standard was then extended in 1989; the most significant addition to this version was the definition of referential integrity. This version is known as SQL-89.

A second version, for the most part compatible with the preceding one, but containing a large number of new features, was published in 1992, known as SQL-92 or SQL-2; we will use the name SQL-2. A new version of the standard, SQL-3, has recently been prepared and will also be called SQL-99. SQL-3 is completely compatible with SQL-2, but is still far from being widely adopted. For this reason, we will always refer to SQL-2 in this book, highlighting the new features that are not present in the earlier version. SQL-3 includes new capabilities resulting from recent research (among which are: active rules and triggers, recursive operations, aggregate operations, new types of data and object paradigm support). Some of these aspects are illustrated in the final part of the book, dealing with advanced aspects of databases.

Even without the new SQL-3 enhancements, SQL-2 is a rich and complex language, so much so that, some years after the appearance of the definition document, no commercial system yet makes available all the language features. To quantify the precise degree of compliance with the standard, three levels of complexity of the language constructs are defined. These are known respectively as *Entry SQL*, *Intermediate SQL* and *Full SQL*; the systems can be thus characterized according to the level that they support. Entry SQL is similar to SQL-89. It differs only in a few slight corrections that were introduced during the definition of SQL-2. Intermediate SQL contains characteristics that respond best to market requirements, and is offered by many of the recent versions of relational products. Full SQL contains advanced features that are progressively being added to the systems.

On the other hand, the systems frequently offer features that are not standardized. For example, active rules, or *triggers*, are present in several relational systems but not in SQL-2. In all these cases, the database vendors have chosen different syntaxes and have given different semantic interpretations to the same features. This is a problem for two reasons. Firstly, the need to choose, retrospectively, one from among the many solutions currently being implemented, compels the modification of systems already on the market and the rewriting of applications developed for them. Secondly, the existence of more than one proposal for the implementation of the same features is a serious obstacle to the standardization process. In fact, the definition of standards is a collective process that requires all the involved parties (vendors and sometimes representatives of users) to reach agreement.

If we look carefully at relational systems, we can see that each of them offers a different SQL; the differences emerge most dramatically when we compare their most recently developed features. Conversely, as regards the more consolidated aspects of the language, there is a strong adherence to the standard; this allows users to interact in standard SQL with systems that are completely different from each other, ranging from a single-user DBMS running on a PC, up to the DBMS on a mainframe storing the information base of a large organization.

A further important observation is that, in describing SQL, we assume that the user interacts directly with the SQL engine in order to define, update and query the database. With increasing frequency, systems offer interfaces that are easy to use and contain specific programs for the definition of schemas, updates, and queries. These programs use menus and graphical interfaces to generate the corresponding SQL instructions. This, however, does not diminish the importance of a knowledge of the *lingua franca* of database systems. This expertise is necessary for the development of all non-trivial database applications, regardless of the capability of the DBMS interface.

4.1 Data definition in SQL

In this section, we illustrate the use of SQL for the definition of database schemas. Before that, we need to illustrate the notation we intend to use for the syntax of the language statements. In general we will represent the terms of the language using a `typewriter-style font`, while the variable terms will be written in *italics*. Following usual conventions, we will use some special symbols:

- angular brackets ⟨ and ⟩ are used to enclose terms;

- square brackets [and] indicate that the enclosed term is optional, that is, it may not appear or appear only once;

- curly brackets { and } indicate that the enclosed term may not appear or may be repeated an arbitrary number of times;

- vertical bars indicate that one among the terms separated by the bars must appear.

Curved brackets (and) must always be taken as SQL keywords and not as grammar definition symbols.

4.1.1 Elementary domains

SQL provides six families of elementary domains, which can be used to define the domains associated with the attributes of the schema.

Character The domain `character` allows the representation of single characters or strings. The length of the strings of characters can be fixed or variable; for strings of variable length, the maximum length is indicated. A default character set is specified for each schema (e.g., Latin, Cyrillic, Greek, Kanji, etc.); when it is necessary to use more than one character set, we can specify it directly for each domain. The syntax is:

character [varying] [(*Length*)] [character set *CharSetName*]

To define a domain 'string of 20 characters' with this syntax, we can write `character (20)`, while a domain 'string of Greek letters of variable length, maximum length 1000', would be denoted as `character varying (1000) character set Greek`. If the length is not specified, the domain represents a single character. A varying string must specify its maximum length. SQL also allows the compact forms `char` and `varchar`, for `character` and `varying character` respectively.

Bit This domain, introduced in SQL-2, is used by attributes that can assume only the value 0 or the value 1. The domain `bit` is typically used to represent attributes, known as *flags*, which specify whether an object has or has not a certain property. SQL also allows a domain 'string of bits', for which the length is specified as a parameter. When no length is specified, the length of the string is set equal to one. The bit strings can be used for the concise representation of groups of properties. For bits, we can also define strings of variable length. The syntax is:

bit [varying] [(*Length*)]

To define a domain 'string of 5 bits' or 'string of bits of variable length and maximum length of 100' we can use the definitions `bit(5)` and `bit varying(100)`. The latter can be shortened to `varbit(100)`.

Exact numeric domains This family contains the domains that allow the representation of exact values, integer or with a fractional part (such as typical currency values). SQL makes available four different exact numeric domains:

* `numeric` [(*Precision* [, *Scale*])]

* `decimal` [(*Precision* [, *Scale*])]

* `integer`

* `smallint`

The domains `numeric` and `decimal` represent numbers with a *decimal base*. The parameter *Precision* specifies the number of significant digits; using a domain `decimal (4)` we can represent values between −9,999 and +9,999. Using the parameter *Scale* we can specify the scale of representation, that is, we can indicate how many digits should appear after the decimal point. If we want to include two decimal digits, we assign the value 2 to *Scale*. In order to specify the scale it is also necessary to specify the precision as defined above; thus with a domain numeric (6,3) we represent the values between −999.999 and +999.999. The difference between the domains numeric and decimal lies in the fact that the numeric domain has exactly the precision as indicated, while the precision of the decimal domain should be taken as a minimum requirement. Should the precision not be specified, the system uses a default implementation value. If the scale is not specified, it is assumed to be zero.

When the representation of fractions is not required, and an accurate control of the size of the decimal representation is not important, then it becomes possible to use the predefined domains integer and smallint. The degree of accuracy of these domains is not specified in the standard, but is left to the implementation.

Approximate numeric domains   To represent approximate real values (useful, for example, for representing physical quantities), SQL provides the following domains:

- float [(*Precision*)]

- double precision

- real

All these domains allow the description of real numbers by means of a floating point representation, in which each number corresponds to a pair of values: the mantissa and the exponent. The mantissa is a fractional value, while the exponent is an integer. The approximate value of the real number is obtained by multiplying the mantissa by the power of 10 specified by the exponent. For example, the notation 0.17E16 represents the value 1.7×10^{15}, and 0.4E-6 represents 4×10^{-7}. A given precision can be specified for the domain float, which represents the number of digits dedicated to the representation of the mantissa, while the precision of the exponent depends on the implementation. The domain double precision represents the numbers with a greater precision than the domain real.

Date and time   This family of domains and the next were introduced in SQL-2 in order to offer specific support to the management of temporal information, which is very important in many applications. They represent *instants* of time and comprise three forms:

- date

- time [(*Precision*)] [with time zone]

- timestamp [(*Precision*)] [with time zone]

Each of these domains can be structured in fields. The domain date allows the fields year, month and day, the domain time allows the fields hour, minute and second, and timestamp allows all the fields, from year to second. For both time and `timestamp` we can specify the precision, which represents the number of decimal places that must be used in the representation of fractions of a second. If the precision is not specified, `time` assumes a precision of zero (resolution to the second) and `timestamp` of 6 (temporal resolution to the microsecond). If the option `with time zone` is specified, then it becomes possible to access two fields, `timezone_hour` and `timezone_minute`. They represent the difference between local time and Universal Coordinated Time, formerly known as Greenwich Mean Time; thus `21:03:04+1:00` and `20:03:04+0:00` correspond to the same instant in time, but the first represents it in Middle European Time (differing from the base time zone by `+1:00`), the second in Universal Coordinated Time.

Temporal intervals   This family of domains allows the representation of intervals of time, such as, for example, the duration of an action. The syntax is:

$$\text{interval } FirstUnitOfTime \text{ [to } LastUnitOfTime\text{]}$$

FirstUnitOfTime and *LastUnitOfTime* define the units of measurement that must be used, from the greatest to the smallest. We can therefore define domains such as `interval year to month` to indicate that the length of the time interval must be measured by the number of years and the number of months. It has to be noted that the group of units of measurement is divided into two distinct groups: `year` and `month` on one hand, and the units from `day` to `second` on the other; this separation occurs because it is impossible to compare days and months exactly (given that a month can have between 28 and 31 days), making it infeasible to compare intervals of the two groups. The first unit that appears in the definition, whatever it may be, can be characterized by the precision, which represents the number of decimal digits used in the representation. When the smallest unit is the second, we can specify a precision that represents the number of decimal places to be used. If the second is the first (and therefore the only) unit, then the first parameter represents the number of significant decimal places and the second parameter would represent the number of decimal places of the fractional part. When the precision is not specified, it assumes the default value 2. Thus, `interval year(5) to month` allows the representation of intervals up to 99,999 years and 11 months, while `interval day(4) to second(6)` allows the representation of intervals up to 9,999 days, 23 hours 59 minutes and 59.999999 seconds, with a precision to a millionth of a second

4.1.2 Schema definition

SQL makes it possible to define a database schema as a collection of objects; each schema consists of a set of *domains, tables*,[2] *indices, assertions, views* and *privileges*, defined by the following syntax:

$$\textbf{create schema } [SchemaName] \text{ [[authorization] } Authorization]$$
$$\{SchemaElementDefinition\}$$

Authorization represents the name of the user who owns the schema. If the term is omitted, it is assumed that the user who issued the command is the owner. The name of the schema can be omitted and, in this case, the name of the owner is adopted as the name of the schema. After the `create schema` command, the user can define the schema components. It is not necessary for all the components to be defined at the same time as the schema is created: this can take place in several successive phases. Let us now look at tables and domains, postponing the other elements of the schema (assertions, views and privileges) until Section 4.4.

4.1.3 Table definition

An SQL table consists of an ordered set of attributes and of a (possibly empty) set of constraints. For example, the schema of a table DEPARTMENT is defined by means of the following SQL statement:

```
create table Department
(
    Name    char(20) primary key,
    Address char(50),
    City    char(20)
)
```

The above table has three attributes of character string domain; the attribute Name constitutes the primary key of the table.

The syntax for the definition of a table is:

```
create table TableName
(AttributeName Domain [DefaultValue] [Constraints]
    {, AttributeName Domain [DefaultValue] [Constraints]}
    [OtherConstraints]
)
```

Each table is defined by giving its name and the definition of its attributes; each attribute, in turn, has a name and domain and possibly a set of constraints, which must be satisfied by the attribute values. Once all the attributes have been defined, we can then define the constraints that involve more than one attribute of the table. A table is initially empty and the creator holds all the privileges regarding the table, that is, the rights to access and to modify the data.

4.1.4 User defined domains

In the definition of tables, beside the predefined domains we have illustrated in Section 4.1.1, it is possible to refer to domains that are explicitly defined by the user. Note that there is a close relationship between the definition of the domains of attributes and the definition of the types of variables in a

---

2. In this chapter we use the term *table* in place of relation and *row* in place of tuple, in keeping with SQL terms; in SQL, attributes are generally referred to as *columns*, but in this case we prefer to adhere to classical relational terminology.

high-level programming language (C, Pascal, etc.). In both cases the goal is the definition of the legal values for data. However, there are also important differences. On the one hand, the type constructors in SQL are much more limited than those in programming languages. On the other hand, however, SQL offers domain constraints, which have no counterpart in such languages. In SQL, new domains are specified using the predefined domains described in Section 4.1.1 by means of the create domain command.

```
create domain DomainName as ElementaryDomain
          [DefaultValue]
          [Constraints]
```

A domain is thus characterized by its own name, by an elementary domain (which can be predefined or previously user-defined), by a possible default value, and finally by a (possibly empty) set of constraints that represent the conditions that must be satisfied by legal domain values.

Unlike the type definition mechanisms of the various programming languages, SQL-2 does not provide domain constructors such as record or array (other than the possibility of defining strings of characters or bits). This constraint derives from the relational data model, which requires that all attributes have elementary domains.

The declaration of domains associates a domain name with a set of constraints. This becomes important when, for example, we need to repeat the same attribute definition in several tables. The definition of a domain enables its reuse and makes attribute definitions more easily modifiable. We can change just the domain definition (particularly the default and the constraints associated with it) and such a change is propagated to all the tables where it is used.

4.1.5 Default domain values

In the syntax for defining domains and tables, we note the presence of a term *DefaultValue*, associated with domains and attributes. This term specifies the value that the attribute must assume when a row is inserted into the table without a value being specified for the attribute itself. When a default value is not specified, the value *null* is assumed as default.

The syntax for the specification of default values is:

```
default ⟨GenericValue | user | null⟩
```

GenericValue represents a value that is compatible with the domain, provided as a constant or, more generally, defined as the result of the evaluation of an expression. The option user sets as default value the login name of the user who issues the command to update the table. When an attribute has a domain with a default value and is explicitly given a different default value, the default value associated with the attribute wins and becomes the effective default value.

For example, an attribute NumberOfChildren, which allows an integer as a value and which has the default value zero is defined by:

```
NumberOfChildren smallint default 0
```

If, during the insertion of a row, the value of the attribute is not specified, it is assigned the value zero.

4.1.6 Intra-relational constraints

In the definition of both domains and tables, we can define constraints, that is, properties that must be verified by every instance of the database. We introduced constraints in Section 2.2, making the distinction between intra-relational constraints (which involve a single relation) and inter-relational constraints (which take into account several relations). The most powerful construct for the specification of generic constraints, both inter-relational and intra-relational, is that of check, which, however, requires the specification of queries to the database. We deal with this later, in Section 4.4, once we have illustrated SQL queries. In this section, we will illustrate predefined intra-relational constraints.

The simplest intra-relational constraints are *not null*, *unique*, and *primary key*.

Not null   The null value is a special value, which indicates the absence of information. A null value can generally represent different situations as we discussed in Section 2.1.5.

However, SQL-2 does not allow the distinction among the various interpretations of the null value. Those applications that need to be able to distinguish among these various situations must resort to ad-hoc solutions, such as the introduction of other attributes.

The constraint not null indicates that the null value is not admissible as the attribute value. In this case, the attribute must always be specified, generally at the insertion stage. If, however, a default value other than null is associated with the attribute, then it becomes possible to carry out an insertion even without providing a value for the attribute, since the default value will be assigned to it automatically.

The constraint is specified by adding to the attribute definition the keywords not null:

```
Surname character(20) not null
```

Unique   A *unique* constraint is applied to an attribute (or a set of attributes) of a table and imposes the requirement that the attribute (or the set of attributes) is a (super)key. Thus, the constraint ensures that different rows do not possess the same values. An exception is made for the null value, which can appear in various rows without violating the constraint, since it is assumed that each null value represents an unknown actual value different from that of another null value.

This constraint can be defined in two ways. The first alternative can be used only when the constraint involves a single attribute. In this case, the specification of the attribute is followed by the keyword unique (similar to the specification of the *not null* constraint):

```
RegistrationNumber character(6) unique
```

The second alternative is necessary when we need to define the constraint on a set of attributes. In this case, after the definition of the attributes, we use the following clause:

```
unique (Attribute{, Attribute})
```

The following is an example of the use of this syntax:

```
FirstName character(20)    not null,
Surname   character(20)    not null,
unique (Surname, FirstName)
```

It should be noted that the above definition is very different from a definition such as the following:

```
FirstName character(20)    not null unique,
Surname   character(20)    not null unique
```

In the first case, the constraint imposes the condition that there can be no two rows that have both the same first name and the same surname. In the second (stricter) case, the constraint is violated if either the same first name or the same surname appears more that once.

Primary key   As we discussed in Section 2.2, it is usually important to specify a *primary key*, the most important identifier for a relation. Accordingly, SQL allows a *primary key* constraint to be specified only once for each table (while it is possible to use the constraints *unique* and *not null* an arbitrary number of times). Like the *unique* constraint, the *primary key* constraint can be directly defined on a single attribute, or it can be defined by listing the several attributes that make up the primary key. None of the attributes of a primary key can assume the null value; thus, the definition of *primary key* implies an implicit definition *not null* for all the attributes of the primary key.

For example, the following definition imposes the constraint that the pair of attributes FirstName and Surname constitute the primary key:

```
FirstName character(20),
Surname   character(20),
Dept      character(15),
Salary    numeric(9) default 0,
primary key (Surname,FirstName)
```

4.1.7 Inter-relational constraints

As we saw in Section 2.2, the most important inter-relational constraints are *referential integrity constraints*. In SQL, the appropriate construct to define them is the *foreign key* constraint.

This constraint creates a link between the values of the attribute(s) of a table and the values of the attribute(s) of another table. With respect to such a constraint, we call the involved tables *internal* and *external*. The constraint is that for every row of the internal table the value of a given attribute, if different from the null value, must be present among the values of a given attribute of the rows belonging to the external table. The only requirement that the syntax imposes is that the attribute referred to in the external table is subject to a *unique* constraint, that is, identifies the tuples of the external table. This attribute generally represents the *primary key* of the table, for which the *unique* constraint is guaranteed. Several attributes may be involved in the constraint, when the key for the external table consists of a set of attributes. In this case, the only difference is that it is necessary to compare tuples of values rather than single values.

The constraint can be defined in two ways, like the *unique* and *primary key* constraints. If there is only one attribute involved, it is possible to define it using the syntactic construct **references**, which indicates the external table and attribute. The more general definition, which is necessary when the link is represented by a set of attributes, uses the construct **foreign key**, syntactically placed after attribute definitions. This construct lists firstly the constrained attributes of the internal table involved in the link, followed by the name of the external table and the names of the referenced attributes. Let us give an example of the first use:

```
create table Employee
(
    RegNo      character(6) primary key,
    FirstName  character(20) not null,
    Surname    character(20) not null,
    Dept       character(15)
               references Department(DeptName),
    Salary     numeric(9) default 0,
    City       character(15),
    unique (Surname,FirstName)
)
```

The constraint specifies that the attribute **Dept** can assume only one of the values that the rows of the table DEPARTMENT possess for the attribute DeptName.

If we then need the attributes FirstName and Surname to appear in a table of personal records, we need to use the second alternative:

```
create table Employee
(
    RegNo      character(6)  primary key,
    FirstName  character(20) not null,
    Surname    character(20) not null,
    Dept       character(15)
               references Department(DeptName),
    Salary     numeric(9) default 0,
    City       character(15),
    unique (Surname,FirstName),
```

```
        foreign key(FirstName,Surname)
            references PersonalRecord(FirstName,Surname)
)
```

The correspondence between the local and external attributes reflects their order: the first attribute in the *foreign key* corresponds to the first attribute in the referenced table, and so on for the other attributes. In this case, FirstName and Surname of EMPLOYEE correspond respectively to FirstName and Surname of PERSONALRECORD.

In the case of all the constraints seen so far, when the system detects a violation generated by an update, the system just rejects the update, signalling the error to the user. With referential integrity constraints, SQL also allows the user to choose other actions to be taken when a violation is introduced.

We illustrate the point by means of an example. Consider the definition of the *foreign key* constraint on the attribute Dept in the table EMPLOYEE. The constraint can be violated by operating either on the rows of the internal table, EMPLOYEE, or on those of the external table, DEPARTMENT. There are only two ways to introduce violations by modifying the contents of the internal table: by inserting a new row or by changing the value of the referring attribute. No particular support is offered in the case of either of these violations; the operation will simply be rejected.

On the other hand, various options are offered for responding to violations generated by alterations to the external table. The reason for this asymmetry is due to the particular importance of the external table, which, from the application point of view, typically represents the principal table (or *master*). The internal table (or *slave*) must adapt itself to variations in the master. In fact, all actions will generate an intervention only on the internal table.

The operations on the external table that can produce violations are the update of values of the referenced attributes and the deletion of rows (in the example, deletion of rows in DEPARTMENT and update of the attribute DeptName). The type of reaction can differ according to the command that produced the violations.

In particular, for updates, it is possible to react in one of the following ways:

- cascade: the new value of the attribute of the external table is assigned to all the matching rows of the internal table;

- set null: the value null is assigned to the referring attribute in the internal table in place of the value modified in the external table;

- set default: the default value is assigned to the referring attribute in the internal table in place of the value modified in the external table;

- no action: the update is simply rejected, with no correcting action by the system.

For violations produced by the deletion of an element of the external table, the same set of reactions is available:

- cascade: all the rows of the internal table corresponding to the deleted row are also deleted;

- set null: the value null is assigned to the referring attribute in place of the value deleted from the external table;

- set default: the default value is assigned to the referring attribute in place of the value deleted from the external table;

- no action: the deletion is rejected.

We can specify different policies for different events (for example, using a cascade policy for updates and a set null policy for deletions).

The use of the cascade policy assumes that the rows of the internal table are tightly linked to the corresponding rows of the external table. Therefore, if modifications are made to the external table, the same modifications must be made to all the rows of the internal table. On the other hand, the other policies assume a weaker dependence between the rows of the two tables.

The reaction policy is specified immediately after the integrity constraint, according to the following syntax:

```
on <delete | update>
    <cascade | set null | set default | no action>
```

The following example shows a referential integrity constraint whose repair policies are set null for deletions and cascade for updates:

```
create table Employee
(
    RegNo      character(6),
    FirstName  character(20) not null,
    Surname    character(20) not null,
    Dept       character(15),
    Salary     numeric(9) default 0,
    City       character(15),
    primary key(RegNo),
    foreign key(Dept) references Department(DeptName)
            on delete set null
            on update cascade,
    unique (Surname,FirstName)
)
```

4.1.8 Schema updates

SQL provides primitives for the manipulation of database schemas, which enable the modification of previously introduced table definitions. The commands used for this purpose are alter and drop.

The alter command The alter command allows the modification of domains and schemas of tables. The command can assume various forms:

```
alter domain DomainName ⟨set default DefaultValue |
        drop default |
        add constraint ConstraintDef |
        drop constraint ConstraintName⟩
alter table TableName
        alter column AttributeName
                      ⟨set default DefaultValue | drop default⟩ |
        add constraint ConstraintDef |
        drop constraint Constraint |
        add column AttributeDef |
        drop column AttributeName ⟩
```

By using alter domain and alter table we can add and remove constraints and modify default values associated with domains and attributes; furthermore, we can add and remove attributes and constraints within the schema of a table. Note that when a new constraint is defined, it must be satisfied by the data already present in the database. If the database contains violations of the new constraint, the constraint definition will be rejected.

For example, the following command extends the schema of the table DEPARTMENT with an attribute NoOfOffices that makes it possible to represent the number of offices within the department:

```
alter table Department add column NoOfOffices numeric(4)
```

The drop command   While the alter command carries out modifications to the domains or schemas of the tables, the drop command allows the removal of components, whether they be schemas, domains, tables, views or assertions. Assertions are constraints that are not associated with any particular table; these will be presented in Section 4.4. The command has the syntax:

```
drop ⟨schema | domain | table | view | assertion⟩ ComponentName
     [restrict | cascade]
```

The restrict option specifies that the command must not be carried out if the component being deleted is not empty. Thus, a schema is not removed if it contains tables or other elements; a domain is not removed if it appears in a table definition; a table is not removed if it possesses rows or if it is present in a definition of a table or view; and, finally, a view is not removed if it is used in the definition of other views. The restrict option is the default.

With the cascade option, the component is removed together with the components depending on it. Thus, when a non-empty schema is removed, all the objects of which it is constructed are also eliminated. By removing a domain that appears in the definition of an attribute, the cascade option causes the name of the domain to be removed, but the attributes that were defined using that domain remain associated with the same basic domain definition. Consider, for example, the domain LongString, defined as char(100). If LongString is eliminated (by means of the command drop domain LongString cascade) all the attributes defined on that domain will directly assume the domain char(100). When a table is removed with the cascade option, all its rows are lost. If the table appeared in another definition of a table or view, these would also be removed. By eliminating a view that appears in other tables or views, these too are removed.

The `cascade` option usually generates a chain reaction. All the elements depending on an element that is eliminated are eliminated in their turn, until there are no remaining elements that contain, in their definitions, elements that have been eliminated. It is necessary to exercise extreme caution in the use of this option, since it is possible that, owing to some overlooked dependence, the command could have a different result from the one intended. Many systems make it possible to test the result of the `drop cascade` command, before it is actually executed.

4.1.9 Relational catalogues

Although only partly specified by the standard, each relational DBMS manages its own *data dictionary* (or rather the description of the tables present in the database) using a relational schema. The database therefore contains two types of table: those that contain the data and those that contain the *metadata*. This second group of tables constitutes the *catalogue* of the database.

This characteristic of relational system implementations is known as *reflexivity*. A DBMS typically manages the catalogue by using structures similar to those in which the database instance is stored. Thus, an object-oriented database, for example, will have a data dictionary that is defined on an object model (see Chapter 11). In this way, the database can use the same functions for the internal organization of metadata as are used for the management of the database instance.

The definition and modification commands of the database schema could, in theory, be replaced by manipulation commands that operate directly on the tables of the data dictionary, making superfluous the introduction of special commands for the definition of the schema. This is not done, however, for two reasons. The first is the absence of a standardization of the dictionary, which differs greatly from one product to the next. The second is the necessity of ensuring that the commands for the manipulation of schemas are clear and immediately recognizable, and furthermore syntactically distinguishable from the commands that modify the database instance.

The SQL-2 standard for the data dictionary is based on a two-tier description. The first level is that of DEFINITION_SCHEMA, made up of a collection of tables that contain the descriptions of all the structures in the database. The collection of tables appearing in the standard, however, is not used by any implementation, since the tables provide a description of only those aspects of a database covered by SQL-2. What is left out, in particular, is all the information concerning the storage structures, which, even if not present in the standard, form a fundamental part of a schema. The tables of the standard, therefore, form a template to which the systems are advised (but not obliged) to conform. The second component of the standard is the

INFORMATION_SCHEMA. This consists of a collection of views on the DEFINITION_SCHEMA. These views fully constitute part of the standard and form an interface for the data dictionary, which must be offered by the systems that want to be compatible with the standard. The INFORMATION_SCHEMA contains views such as DOMAINS, DOMAIN_CONSTRAINTS, TABLES, VIEWS, COLUMNS, up to a total of 23 views that describe the structure of the database.

Rather than describe the structure of these tables, we provide a simplified example of the contents of one of these views. In Figure 4.1 we can see the simplified contents of the COLUMNS view of the catalogue describing the tables EMPLOYEE and DEPARTMENT.

Table_Name	Column_Name	Ordinal_Position	Column_Default	Is_Nullable
Employee	RegNo	1	NULL	N
Employee	FirstName	2	NULL	N
Employee	Surname	3	NULL	N
Employee	Dept	4	NULL	Y
Employee	Salary	5	0	Y
Employee	City	6	NULL	Y
Department	DeptName	1	NULL	N
Department	Address	2	NULL	Y
Department	City	3	NULL	Y

Figure 4.1 Part of the contents of the view COLUMNS of the data dictionary.

In Figure 4.2 we see an example of the reflexivity of the data dictionary, with the description in COLUMNS of the view itself.

Table_Name	Column_Name	Ordinal_Position	Column_Default	Is_Nullable
Columns	Table_Name	1	NULL	N
Columns	Column_Name	2	NULL	N
Columns	Ordinal_Position	3	NULL	N
Columns	Column_Default	4	NULL	Y
Columns	Is_Nullable	5	Y	N

Figure 4.2 The reflexive description of COLUMNS.

4.2 SQL queries

The part of SQL dedicated to the expression of queries is included in the DML. However, the separation between the DDL and the DML is not rigid and part of the query definition syntax will also be used in the specification of certain advanced features of the schema (see Section 4.4).

4.2.1 The declarative nature of SQL

SQL expresses queries mainly in a declarative way, that is, by specifying the properties of retrieved data and not how to obtain it. In this respect, SQL follows the principles of relational calculus and contrasts with *procedural* query languages, such as relational algebra, in which a data retrieval procedure has to be specified in the query. The SQL query is passed for execution to the query optimizer. This is a DBMS component, which analyzes the query, selects a query execution strategy and formulates an equivalent query in the internal procedural language of the database management system. This procedural language is hidden from the user. In this way, whoever writes queries in SQL can ignore the translation and optimization aspects. The query optimizer will be discussed in Section 9.6. The enormous effort that has gone into the development of optimization techniques has made highly efficient query execution possible for most relational DBMSs.

There are generally many different ways to express a query in SQL: the programmer must make choices that are based not on efficiency but rather on characteristics such as readability and ease of modification of the query. In this way, SQL facilitates the programmer's work, making possible the description of abstract and high level queries.

4.2.2 Simple queries

Query operations in SQL are specified by means of the select statement. Let us first look at the essential structure of a select.

    select *TargetList*
    from *TableList*
    [where *Condition*]

The three parts that make up a select instruction are often called respectively the *target list*, the from clause, and the where clause. A more detailed description of the same syntax is as follows:

    select *AttrExpr* [[as] *Alias*] {, *AttrExpr* [[as] *Alias*]}
    from *Table* [[as] *Alias*] {, *Table* [[as] *Alias*]}
    [where *Condition*]

An SQL query considers the rows that belong to the cartesian product of the tables listed in the from clause, and selects those that satisfy the conditions expressed in the where clause. The result of the execution of an SQL query is a table, with a row for every row selected by the where clause, whose columns result from the evaluation of the expressions *AttrExpr* that appear in the target list. Each column can be re-named by means of the *Alias* that appears immediately after the expression. The tables can also be re-named using the *Alias*; the table alias is used either as a shorthand or as a variable, in a way that we will go into later.

Consider a database containing the tables EMPLOYEE(FirstName, Surname, Dept, Office, Salary, City) and DEPARTMENT(DeptName, Address, City).

EMPLOYEE	FirstName	Surname	Dept	Office	Salary	City
	Mary	Brown	Administration	10	45	London
	Charles	White	Production	20	36	Toulouse
	Gus	Green	Administration	20	40	Oxford
	Jackson	Neri	Distribution	16	45	Dover
	Charles	Brown	Planning	14	80	London
	Laurence	Chen	Planning	7	73	Worthing
	Pauline	Bradshaw	Administration	75	40	Brighton
	Alice	Jackson	Production	20	46	Toulouse

Figure 4.3   Contents of the EMPLOYEE table.

Query 1: Find the salary of the employees named Brown.

```
select Salary as Remuneration
from Employee
where Surname = 'Brown'
```

If there are no employees named Brown, the query returns an empty result. Otherwise, it returns a table with as many rows as there are employees with that surname. By applying the query to the table in Figure 4.3, we obtain the result shown in Figure 4.4: there are two employees named Brown and therefore the result contains two rows.

Remuneration
45
80

Figure 4.4   Result of Query 1.

Let us now continue the analysis of SQL queries, gradually introducing more complex constructs.

Target list   The target list specifies the elements of the schema of the resulting tables. The special character * (asterisk) can also appear in the target list, representing the selection of all the attributes of the tables listed in the from clause.

Query 2: Find all the information relating to employees named Brown. The result appears in Figure 4.5.

```
select *
from Employee
where Surname = 'Brown'
```

The target list can contain generic expressions on the values of the attributes of each selected row.

Query 3: Find the monthly salary of the employees named White. The result is shown in Figure 4.6.

FirstName	Surname	Dept	Office	Salary	City
Mary	Brown	Administration	10	45	London
Charles	Brown	Planning	14	80	London

Figure 4.5 Result of Query 2.

```
select Salary / 12 as MonthlySalary
from Employee
where Surname = 'White'
```

MonthlySalary
3.00

Figure 4.6 Result of Query 3.

From clause   When we need to formulate a query that involves rows belonging to more than one table, the argument of the from clause is given as a list of tables. The conditions in the where clause are applied to the cartesian product of these tables; a join can be specified by explicitly indicating comparisons between attributes of different tables.

Query 4: Find the names of the employees and the cities in which they work.

```
select Employee.FirstName, Employee.Surname, Department.City
from Employee, Department
where Employee.Dept = Department.DeptName
```

DEPARTMENT	DeptName	Address	City
	Administration	Bond Street	London
	Production	Rue Victor Hugo	Toulouse
	Distribution	Pond Road	Brighton
	Planning	Bond Street	London
	Research	Sunset Street	San José

Figure 4.7 Contents of the DEPARTMENT table.

Taking the contents of EMPLOYEE and DEPARTMENT respectively from Figure 4.3 and Figure 4.7, the result of the evaluation of Query 4 is the table shown in Figure 4.8.

In the above query we note the use of the *dot* operator to identify the tables from which attributes are extracted. For example, Employee.Dept denotes the Dept attribute of the table EMPLOYEE. This use is common in many programming languages, to identify the fields of a structured variable. It is necessary to use this notation when the tables listed in the from clause have attributes with the same name, in order to distinguish among the references to the homonym attributes. When there is no danger of ambiguity, because

FirstName	Surname	City
Mary	Brown	London
Charles	White	Toulouse
Gus	Green	London
Jackson	Neri	Brighton
Charles	Brown	London
Laurence	Chen	London
Pauline	Bradshaw	London
Alice	Jackson	Toulouse

Figure 4.8 Result of Query 4.

the attribute name appears in only one of the tables, we can specify the attribute without declaring the table to which it belongs.

Query 5: The only homonym attribute in the tables EMPLOYEE and DEPARTMENT is the attribute City. The preceding query can therefore be expressed as follows, by using an alias for table DEPARTMENT with the intention of abbreviating the reference to it:

```
select FirstName, Surname, D.City
from Employee, Department as D
where Dept = DeptName
```

Where clause   The condition in the where clause is a boolean expression constructed by combining simple predicates with the operators and, or and not. Each simple predicate uses the operators =, <>, <, >, <= and >= to build a comparison that has on one side an expression formed from the values of the attributes of the row and, on the other side, a constant value or another expression. The syntax gives precedence to the operator not in the evaluation, but does not introduce a precedence between the operators and and or. If we need to express a query that requires the use of both and and or, then we have to indicate the order of evaluation by using brackets.

Query 6: Find the first names and surnames of the employees who work in office number 20 of the Administration department.

```
select FirstName, Surname
from Employee
where Office = '20' and Dept = 'Administration'
```

The result in Figure 4.9 is obtained from the database in Figure 4.3.

FirstName	Surname
Gus	Green

Figure 4.9   Result of Query 6.

Query 7: Find the first names and surnames of the employees who work in either the Administration department or the Production department.

```
select FirstName, Surname
from Employee
where Dept = 'Administration' or
      Dept = 'Production'
```

By applying the query to the table in Figure 4.3, we obtain the result in Figure 4.10.

FirstName	Surname
Mary	Brown
Charles	White
Gus	Green
Pauline	Bradshaw
Alice	Jackson

Figure 4.10 Result of Query 7.

Query 8: Find the first names of the employees named 'Brown' who work in the Administration department or the Production department. The result is shown in Figure 4.11.

```
select FirstName
from Employee
where Surname = 'Brown' and
      (Dept = 'Administration' or
       Dept = 'Production')
```

FirstName
Mary

Figure 4.11 Result of Query 8.

As well as the usual predicates for relational comparisons, SQL provides an operator like for the comparison of strings. This operator performs pattern matching with partially specified strings, obtained by using the special characters _ (underscore) and % (percentage). The underscore represents an arbitrary character in the comparison, while the percent sign represents a string (possibly empty) of arbitrary characters. The comparison like 'ab%ba_' will thus be satisfied by any string of characters beginning with ab and having the pair of characters ba before the final position (for example, abcdedcbac or abbaf).

Query 9: Find the employees with surnames that have 'r' as the second letter and end in 'n'. The result is shown in Figure 4.12.

```
select *
from Employee
where Surname like '_r%n'
```

FirstName	Surname	Dept	Office	Salary	City
Mary	Brown	Administration	10	45	London
Charles	Brown	Planning	14	80	London
Gus	Green	Administration	20	40	Oxford

Figure 4.12 Result of Query 9.

Management of null values   As we saw in Section 2.1.5, a null value in an attribute can mean that a certain attribute is not applicable, or that the value is applicable but unknown, or even that we do not know which of the two situations applies.

For the selection of terms with null values, SQL supplies the is null predicate, the syntax of which is simply:

Attribute is [not] null

The predicate is null gives a true result only if the attribute has the value NULL. The is not null predicate produces the opposite result.

Null values have a particular impact on the evaluation of normal predicates. Consider a simple predicate for the comparison of the value of an attribute with a constant value:

Salary > 40

This predicate will be true for the rows in which the salary attribute is greater than 40. Bearing in mind what we said in Section 3.1.8, note that there are two different solutions for dealing with the situation in which the Salary attribute has the null value. The first solution, which was adopted by SQL-89, uses traditional two-valued logic and simply allows the predicate to be considered false. The second solution, on the other hand, is the one adopted by SQL-2. This uses a three-valued logic, in which a predicate returns the *unknown* value when any of the terms of the predicate has a null value. Note that the is null predicate is an exception, since it always returns either of the values true or false, never the unknown value.

The difference between the solutions based on two- or three-valued logic emerges only when complex expressions are evaluated. In some cases, the behaviour of the system when null values are present can be far from intuitive, particularly when complex predicates are constructed using negation or nested queries (introduced in Section 4.2.6).

Algebraic interpretation of SQL queries   We can construct a correspondence between SQL queries and the equivalent queries expressed in relational algebra.

Given a query in SQL in its simplest form:

```
select  T₁.Attribute₁₁,  ...,  Tₕ.Attributeₕₘ
from  Table₁ T₁,  ...,  Tableₙ Tₙ
where  Condition
```

we can use the following translation, where preliminary renamings (omitted here for simplicity) are applied to each TABLE$_i$ so that joins are indeed cartesian products:

$$\pi_{T_1.Attribute_{11},...,T_h Attribute_{hm}}(\sigma_{Condition}(TABLE_1 \bowtie ... \bowtie TABLE_n))$$

For more complex SQL queries, the conversion formula shown above is no longer directly applicable. We could, however, demonstrate a technique for translating an SQL query into an equivalent query in relational algebra.

The link between SQL and tuple calculus with range declarations is even stronger (Section 3.2.3).

Assuming that the aliases T_1, T_2, ..., T_h appear in the target list and that T_{h+1}, T_{h+2}, ..., T_n do not,[3] the generic statement select has a meaning that is equal to that of the following expressions of tuple calculus with range declarations:

$$\{t_1.\text{Attribute}_{11}, ..., t_h.\text{Attribute}_{hm}|$$
$$t_1(\text{TABLE}_1), ..., t_h(\text{TABLE}_h)$$
$$|\exists t_{h+1}(\text{TABLE}_{h+1}), (...,(\exists t_n(\text{TABLE}_n) (Condition')) ...)\}$$

where *Condition'* is the formula obtained from *Condition*, substituting the relational calculus notation into the SQL one. Note how each variable in calculus corresponds to a table alias. We will see that some uses of aliases in SQL make this similarity even more apparent.

It should be noted that these correspondences between SQL and the other languages do not hold any more if we consider some advanced features of SQL, such as the evaluation of aggregated operators (Section 4.2.3). Results of SQL queries and of algebraic or calculus expressions differ on duplicate tuples, as discussed below.

Duplicates   A significant difference between SQL and relational algebra and calculus is the management of duplicates. In algebra and calculus, a table is seen as a relation from the mathematical point of view, and thus as a set of elements (tuples) different from each other. In SQL a table can have many rows with the same values for all their attributes. These are known as *duplicates*.

For emulating the behaviour of relational algebra in SQL, it would be necessary to eliminate all the duplicates each time a projection operation is executed. However, the removal of duplicates is time consuming and often unnecessary, in that frequently the result contains no duplicates. For example, when the result includes a key for every table that appears in the from clause, the resulting table cannot contain identical rows. For this reason it was decided to allow the presence of duplicates in SQL, leaving it to the

---

3. Note that it is always possible to reorder the variables in such a way that this condition is satisfied.

person writing the query to specify when the removal of duplicates is necessary.

The elimination of duplicates is specified by the keyword `distinct`, placed immediately after the keyword `select`. The syntax also allows for the specification of the keyword `all` in place of `distinct`, indicating the requirement that the duplicates should be retained. The use of the word `all` is optional, in that the conservation of duplicates constitutes the default option.

Given the table PERSON(TaxCode, FirstName, Surname, City) (Figure 4.13), we wish to retrieve the cities in which the people named Brown live; we will show two examples, the first of which allows the presence of duplicates while the second uses the `distinct` option and therefore removes them.

PERSON	TaxCode	FirstName	Surname	City
	BRWMRA55B21T234J	Mary	Brown	Verona
	LBLCLR69T30H745Z	Charles	Leblanc	Paris
	BRWGNN41A31B344C	Giovanni	Brown	Verona
	BRWPRT75C12F205V	Pietro	Brown	Milan

Figure 4.13 The PERSON table.

Query 10: Find the cities of people named Brown:

```
select City
from Person
where Surname = 'Brown'
```

Query 11: Find the cities of people named Brown, with each city appearing only once:

```
select distinct City
from Person
where Surname = 'Brown'
```

By executing the two queries shown above on the table in Figure 4.13, we obtain the results shown in Figure 4.14.

City
Verona
Verona
Milan

City
Verona
Milan

Figure 4.14 The results of Query 10 and Query 11.

Inner and outer joins   An alternative syntax introduced in SQL-2 for the specification of joins makes it possible to distinguish between the conditions that represent join conditions and those that represent selections of rows. In this way we can also specify outer joins and other extensions.

The proposed syntax is as follows:

```
select AttrExpr [[as] Alias] {, AttrExpr[[as] Alias]}
from Table [[as] Alias]
     {[JoinType] join Table [[as] Alias] on JoinCondition}
[where OtherCondition]
```

Using this syntax, the join condition does not appear as the argument of the where clause, but instead is moved into the from clause, associated with the tables that are involved in the join.

The parameter *JoinType* specifies which type of join to use, and for this we can substitute the terms inner, right outer, left outer, or full outer (the term outer is optional). The inner join is the traditional theta-join of relational algebra.

Query 12: Query 5 can be rewritten using the syntax of the inner join in the following way:

```
select FirstName, Surname, D.City
from Employee inner join Department as D on Dept = DeptName
```

With the inner join between the two tables, the rows involved in the join are generally a subset of the rows of each table. It can happen that some rows are not included because there exists no corresponding row in the other table for which the condition is satisfied. This property often conflicts with the demands of applications that might need to retain the rows that would be eliminated by the join. In writing the application, we might prefer to use null values to represent the absence of information in the other table. As we have seen in Section 3.1.5, the outer join has precisely the task of executing a join while maintaining all the rows that appear in one or both the tables involved.

There are three different types of outer join: left, right and full. The left join gives the same result as the inner join, but includes the rows of the table that appears in the left of the join for which no corresponding rows exist in the right-hand table. The right join behaves symmetrically (keeps the rows of the right-hand table); finally, the full join gives the result of the inner join along with the rows excluded from both tables.

Consider the tables DRIVER and AUTOMOBILE shown in Figure 4.15.

Query 13: Find the drivers with their cars, including the drivers without cars:

```
select FirstName, Surname, Driver.DriverID, CarRegNo, Make, Model
from Driver left join Automobile on
     (Driver.DriverID = Automobile.DriverID)
```

The result is shown in Figure 4.16. Note the last row that shows a driver for whom there is no automobile.

Query 14: Find all the drivers and all the cars, showing the possible relationship between them:

DRIVER	FirstName	Surname	DriverID
	Mary	Brown	VR 2030020Y
	Charles	White	PZ 1012436B
	Marco	Neri	AP 4544442R

AUTOMOBILE	CarRegNo	Make	Model	DriverID
	ABC 123	BMW	323	VR 2030020Y
	DEF 456	BMW	Z3	VR 2030020Y
	GHI 789	Lancia	Delta	PZ 1012436B
	BBB 421	BMW	316	MI 2020030U

Figure 4.15 DRIVER and AUTOMOBILE tables

Firstname	Surname	DriverID	CarRegNo	Make	Model
Mary	Brown	VR 2030020Y	ABC 123	BMW	323
Mary	Brown	VR 2030020Y	DEF 456	BMW	Z3
Charles	White	PZ 1012436B	GHI 789	Lancia	Delta
Marco	Neri	AP 4544442R	NULL	NULL	NULL

Figure 4.16 Result of Query 13.

```
select FirstName, Surname, Driver.DriverID, CarRegNo, Make, Model
from Driver full join Automobile on
            (Driver.DriverID = Automobile.DriverID)
```

The query produces the table shown in Figure 4.17. Note the last row of the table, describing an automobile for which there is no corresponding element in DRIVER.

Firstname	Surname	DriverID	CarRegNo	Make	Model
Mary	Brown	VR 2030020Y	ABC 123	BMW	323
Mary	Brown	VR 2030020Y	DEF 456	BMW	Z3
Charles	White	PZ 1012436B	GHI 789	Lancia	Delta
Marco	Neri	AP 4544442R	NULL	NULL	NULL
NULL	NULL	NULL	BBB 421	BMW	316

Figure 4.17 Result of Query 14.

Some implementations of SQL specify the outer join in a non-standard way by adding a particular character or sequence of characters (for example * or (+)) to the attributes involved in the join condition. In this way we can formulate the outer join without using the syntax above. For example, Query 13 could be formulated in the following way:

Query 15:

```
select FirstName, Surname, Driver.DriverID, CarRegNo, Make, Model
from Driver, Automobile
where Driver.DriverID * = Automobile.DriverID
```

These solutions, being outside the SQL-2 standard, are not portable from one system to another.

A further feature of SQL-2 is the possibility of using the keyword natural before the join type. This makes it possible to define the natural join of relational algebra. Therefore, in the joining of two tables, we can use an implicit condition of equality on all the attributes having the same name (see Section 3.1.5). For example, Query 14 could be written as:

Query 16:

```
select FirstName, Surname, Driver.DriverID, CarRegNo, Make, Model
from Driver natural full join Automobile
```

In spite of the advantage of an increased compactness, the natural join is not normally available on commercial systems. One reason is that a query that uses a natural join can introduce risks to the applications, because its behaviour can change significantly as a result of small variations on the schema. Another reason is that the natural join makes it necessary to analyze completely the schema of the tables involved in order to understand the join condition. This is a disadvantage when writing and when reading the query, because in both situations it is necessary to do a careful comparison of the schemas of the joined tables in order to be sure of the behaviour of the query.

Use of variables   We have already seen how we can associate alternative names, called aliases, with the tables that appear in the from clause. The name is used to refer to the table in the context of the query. This feature can be used to avoid the necessity for writing out the full name of the table each time it is requested, as seen already in Query 5, and for other reasons.

In the first place, by using aliases we can refer more than once to the same table, in a way similar to the use of the renaming operator ρ of relational algebra. Each time an alias is introduced, we declare a variable of type table, which possesses as a value the contents of the table for which it is an alias. When a table appears only once in a query, there is no difference between interpreting the alias as a pseudonym or as a new variable. When a table appears more than once, however, it is essential to see aliases as new variables.

Query 17: Find all the employees who have the same surname (but different first names) of an employee belonging to the Production department.

```
select E1.FirstName, E1.Surname
from Employee E1, Employee E2
where E1.Surname = E2.Surname and
      E1.FirstName <> E2.FirstName and
      E2.Dept = 'Production'
```

This query compares each row of EMPLOYEE with all the rows of EMPLOYEE associated with the Production department. Note that in this query, each row whose **Dept** attribute has the value **Production** is also compared with itself, but the comparison of the row with itself will never be satisfied, in that the predicate of inequality on the attribute FirstName can never be true.

To illustrate the execution of this query, we can imagine that when we define the aliases, two different tables E1 and E2 are created, each containing all the rows of EMPLOYEE. Figure 4.18 shows the idea and the fact that there is a comparison of each row of E1 with each row of E2.

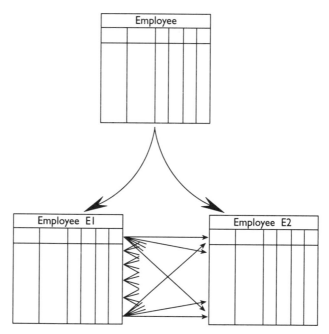

Figure 4.18 Description of the execution of Query 17.

The definition of aliases is also important for the specification of nested queries, as we will see in Section 4.2.6.

To demonstrate the correspondence between the renaming operator of relational algebra and the use of variables in SQL, we can use SQL to formulate the query shown in Section 3.1.6 (Expression 3.3). Suppose the table SUPERVISION(Head, Employee) describes the relationship between employees and supervisors.

Query 18: Find the names and salaries of the supervisors of the employees who earn more than 40 thousand.

```
select E1.Name as NameH, E1.Salary as SalaryH
from Employee E1, Supervision, Employee E2
where E1.Number = Supervision.Head and
      E2.Number = Supervision.Employee and
      E2.Salary > 40
```

Ordering Whereas a relation is made up of a non-ordered set of tuples, applications ·often require an ordering of the rows. Consider the case in which the user wants to know which are the highest salaries paid by the company. This needs a query that returns the employees' data ordered on the value of the Salary attribute.

SQL makes it possible to impose an order on the rows of the result of a query by means of the order by clause, with which the query is ended. The clause obeys the following syntax.

order by *OrderingAttribute* [asc | desc]
    {, *OrderingÃttribute* [asc | desc]}

In this way, the query specifies the attributes that must be used for the ordering. The rows are ordered according to the first attribute in the list. For rows that have the same value for this attribute, the values of the attributes that follow are taken into account, in sequence. The order on each attribute can be ascending or descending, and it is specified by means of the qualifiers asc or desc. If the qualifier is omitted, the ascending order is assumed.

Consider the database in Figure 4.15.

Query 19: Extract the content of the AUTOMOBILE table in descending order of make and model.

```
select *
from Automobile
order by Make desc, Model desc
```

The result is shown in Figure 4.19.

CarRegNo	Make	Model	DriverID
GHI 789	Lancia	Delta	PZ 1012436B
DEF 456	BMW	Z3	VR 2030020Y
ABC 123	BMW	323	VR 2030020Y
BBB 421	BMW	316	MI 20220030U

Figure 4.19 Result of Query 19.

4.2.3 Aggregate queries

Aggregate operators constitute one of the most important extensions of SQL in comparison with relational algebra.

In relational algebra, all the conditions are evaluated one tuple at a time: the condition is always a predicate that is evaluated on each tuple independently of all the others.

Often, however, it is necessary to evaluate properties that are dependent on sets of tuples. Suppose that we wish to find the number of employees in the Production department. The number of employees will correspond to the number of tuples in the relation EMPLOYEE having Production as the value of the attribute Dept. This number, however, is not a property possessed by one tuple in particular, and therefore the query is not expressible in relational algebra. In order to express it in SQL we use the aggregate operator count.

Query 20: Find the number of employees in the Production department:

```
select count(*)
from Employee
where Dept = 'Production'
```

The query is first executed in the normal manner, taking into account only the from and where clauses. The aggregate operator is then applied to the table containing the result of the query. In the example above, firstly a table is constructed containing all the rows of EMPLOYEE having Production as the value of the attribute Dept. Then, the aggregate operator is applied to the table, counting the number of rows that appear in it.

Standard SQL provides five aggregate operators; they are count, sum, max, min and avg.

The count operator uses the following syntax:

count (⟨* | [distinct | all] *AttributeList*⟩)

The first option (*) returns the number of rows. The distinct option returns the number of different values for the attributes in *AttributeList*. The all option returns the number of rows that possess values different from the null value for the attributes in *AttributeList*. If an attribute is specified without distinct or all, all is assumed as default.

Query 21: Find the number of different values on the attribute Salary for all the rows in EMPLOYEE:

```
select count(distinct Salary)
from Employee
```

Query 22: Find the number of rows of EMPLOYEE having a not null value on the attribute Salary:

```
select count (all Salary)
from Employee
```

Let us turn to the other four operators sum, max, min and avg. They allow as argument an attribute or expression, possibly preceded by one of the keywords, distinct or all. The aggregate functions sum and avg allow as argument only expressions that represent numeric values or intervals of time. The functions max and min require only that an order be defined in the expression, making them applicable also to character strings and instants of time.

⟨sum | max | min | avg⟩ ([distinct | all] *AttributeExpression*)

The operators apply to the rows that are selected by the where clause of the query, and have the following meanings:

• sum: returns the sum of the values possessed by the attribute expression;

• max and min: return respectively the maximum and minimum values;

- avg: returns the average of the values of the attribute expression.

The keywords distinct and all have the meaning already discussed: distinct ignores duplicates, while all leaves out only null values; the use of distinct or all with the max and min operators has no effect on the result.

The various implementations of SQL frequently offer a wider range of aggregate operators, providing statistical operators such as variance, standard deviation, median, etc.

Query 23: Find the sum of the salaries of the Administration department:

```
select sum(Salary)
from Employee
where Dept = 'Administration'
```

We can also evaluate several aggregate operations in a single query.

Query 24: Find the maximum, the average and the minimum salaries of all employees:

```
select max(Salary), avg(Salary), min(Salary)
from Employee
```

Aggregate evaluation may take place after an arbitrary query, such as the following one, which has a join.

Query 25: Find the maximum salary among the employees who work in a department based in London.

```
select max(Salary)
from Employee, Department
where Dept = DeptName and
      Department.City = 'London'
```

Note that the following version of the same query is not correct:

Query 26:

```
select FirstName, Surname, (max(Salary))
from Employee, Department
where Dept = DeptName and
      Department.City = 'London'
```

On an intuitive level, this query would select the highest value of the Salary attribute, and thus would automatically select the attributes FirstName and Surname of the corresponding employee. However, such semantics could not be generalized to the aggregate queries, for two reasons. In the first place, there is no guarantee that the operator will select a single element, given that there could be more than one row containing a particular salary. In the second place, written like this, the query could be applied to the operators max and min, but would have no meaning for the other aggregate operators. Therefore, the SQL syntax does not allow aggregate functions and attribute expressions (such as, for example, attribute names) within the same target list (except for queries with the group by clause, described in the next section).

4.2.4 Group by queries

We have described the aggregate operators as those that are applied to a set of rows. The examples that we have seen up to now operate on all the rows that are produced as the result of the query. It is often necessary to apply an aggregate operator more finely, to specific subsets of rows. To use the aggregate operator like this, SQL provides the group by clause, which makes it possible to specify how to divide the table up into subsets. The clause accepts as argument a set of attributes, and the query will operate separately on each set of rows that possess the same values for this set of attributes.

To understand the meaning of the group by clause better, let us analyze how an SQL query using the group by clause is executed.

Query 27: Find the sum of salaries of all the employees of the same department:

```
select Dept, sum(Salary)
from Employee
group by Dept
```

Suppose that the table contains the information shown in Figure 4.20.

EMPLOYEE	FirstName	Surname	Dept	Office	Salary	City
	Mary	Brown	Administration	10	45	London
	Charles	White	Production	20	36	Toulouse
	Gus	Green	Administration	20	40	Oxford
	Jackson	Neri	Distribution	16	45	Dover
	Charles	Brown	Planning	14	80	London
	Laurence	Chen	Planning	7	73	Worthing
	Pauline	Bradshaw	Administration	75	40	Brighton
	Alice	Jackson	Production	20	46	Toulouse

Figure 4.20 Contents of the EMPLOYEE table.

First, the query is considered as if the group by clause did not exist, selecting the attributes that appear either as the argument of group by or within an expression that is the argument of the aggregate operator. In the query we are looking at, it is as if the following query were executed:

```
select Dept, Salary
from Employee
```

The result is shown in Figure 4.21.

The resulting table is then analyzed, dividing the rows into subsets sharing the same value on the attributes that appear in the group by clause. In the example, the rows are grouped according to the same value of the attribute Dept (Figure 4.22).

Once the rows are partitioned into subsets, the aggregate operator is applied separately to each subset. The result of the query consists of a table

Dept	Salary
Administration	45
Production	36
Administration	40
Distribution	45
Planning	80
Planning	73
Administration	40
Production	46

Figure 4.21 Projection on the attributes **Dept** and **Salary** of the EMPLOYEE table.

Dept	Salary
Administration	45
Administration	40
Administration	40
Distribution	45
Planning	80
Planning	73
Production	36
Production	46

Figure 4.22 Regrouping according to the value of the **Dept** attribute.

with rows that contain the results of the evaluation of the aggregate operators, possibly alongside the values of the attributes used for the aggregation. In Figure 4.23 the final result of the query is shown, giving the sum of the salaries paid to the employees of the department, for each department.

Dept	Salary
Administration	125
Production	82
Distribution	45
Planning	153

Figure 4.23 Result of Query 27.

The SQL syntax imposes the restriction that, whenever the group by clause is used, the attributes that can appear in the select clause must be a subset of the attributes used in the group by clause. References to these attributes are possible because each tuple of the group will be characterized by the same values. The following example shows the reasons for this limitation:

Query 28:

```
select (Office)
from Employee
group by Dept
```

This query is incorrect, in that a number of values of the **Office** attribute will correspond to each value of the **Dept** attribute. Instead, after the grouping has been carried out, each sub-group of rows must correspond to a single row in the table resulting from the query.

On the other hand, this restriction can sometimes seem excessive, such as when we need to show the values of attributes that exhibit single values for given values of the grouping attributes. (We say that the attributes functionally depend on the grouping attributes; see Section 8.2 for a discussion of functional dependencies.)

Query 29:

```
select DeptName, count(*),(D.City)
from Employee E join Department D on (E.Dept = D.DeptName)
group by DeptName
```

This query should return the department name, the number of employees of each department, and the city in which the department is based. Given that the attribute **DeptName** is the key of **DEPARTMENT**, a particular value of **City** corresponds to each value of **DeptName**. The system could therefore provide a correct response, but SQL prohibits queries of this nature. In theory the language could be modified in such a way as to allow the identification of the attributes that are keys to the schemas of the tables, and highlight the attributes that could appear in the target list. In practice it was preferred to keep the language simple, possibly requiring that the query use a redundant group of attributes. The query can be correctly rewritten as follows:

Query 30:

```
select DeptName, count(*), D.City
from Employee E join Department D on (E.Dept = D.DeptName)
group by DeptName, D.City
```

Group predicates   We have seen how rows can be organized into subsets by means of the **group by** clause. It is sometimes possible that an application needs to consider only the subsets that satisfy certain conditions. If the conditions that must be satisfied by the subsets are verifiable at the single row level, then it is sufficient to use the appropriate predicates as the argument of the **where** clause. If, however, the conditions have to refer to values that are the result of aggregations, we have to use a new construct, the **having** clause.

The **having** clause describes the conditions that must be applied at the end of the execution of a query that uses the **group by** clause. Each subset of rows forms part of the result of the query only if the predicate argument of having is satisfied.

Query 31: Find which departments spend more than 100 thousand on salaries:

```
select Dept
from Employee
group by Dept
having sum(Salary) > 100
```

Applying the query to the table shown in Figure 4.20, we follow the steps described for group by queries. Once the rows have been grouped according to the value of the Dept attribute, the predicate argument of the having clause is evaluated. This selects the departments for which the sum of the values of the attribute Salary, for all the rows of the subset, is higher than 100. The result of the query is shown in Query 4.24.

Dept
Administration
Planning

Figure 4.24 Result of Query 31.

The syntax also allows for the definition of queries using the having clause, without a corresponding group by clause. In this case the entire set of rows is treated as a single group, but this has very limited application possibilities, because if the condition is not satisfied, the resulting table will be empty. Like the where clause, the having clause will also accept as argument a boolean expression of simple predicates. The simple predicates are generally comparisons between the result of the evaluation of an aggregate operator and a generic expression. The syntax also allows the presence of predicates on the attributes forming the argument of the group by, but it is preferable to collect all such simple conditions into the context of the where clause. To establish which predicates of a query that uses grouping are arguments of the where clause and which are arguments of the having clause, we establish only the following criterion: only the predicates containing aggregate operators should appear in the argument of the having clause.

Query 32: Find the departments in which the average salary of employees working in office number 20 is higher than 25 thousand:

```
select Dept
from Employee
where Office = '20'
group by Dept
having avg(Salary) > 25
```

The general concise form of an SQL query thus becomes:

SelectSQL ::=select *TargetList*
     from *TableList*
     [where *Condition*]
     [group by *GroupingAttributeList*]
     [having *AggregateCondition*]
     [order by *OrderingAttributeList*]

4.2.5 Set queries

SQL also provides set operators, similar to those we saw in relational algebra. The available operations are union (for which the operator is union), intersection (intersect) and difference (except or minus). Each has a meaning similar to the corresponding relational algebra operator.

Note that each query that uses the intersect and except operators can be expressed using other constructs of the language (generally using nested queries, which we will discuss in Section 4.2.6). On the other hand, for the same reasons discussed in Section 3.2.3 for relational calculus with range declarations, the union operator enhances the expressive power of SQL and allows the definition of queries that would otherwise be impossible.

The syntax for the use of the operators is as follows:

SelectSQL {⟨union | intersect | except⟩ [all] *SelectSQL*}

Set operators, unlike the rest of the language, assume the elimination of duplicates as a default. We can see two reasons for this. Firstly, the elimination of duplicates is much closer to the intuitive semantics of these operators. Secondly, their execution (particularly *difference* and *intersection*) requires a computation for which the additional cost of eliminating duplicates would be negligible. If we wish to adopt a different interpretation of the operators in the query, and we wish to use set operators that maintain the duplicates, it is sufficient to specify the all keyword when using the operator. In the following examples we will compare what happens in both cases. A further observation is that SQL does not require the schemas on which the operations are executed to be identical (unlike relational algebra), but only that the attributes have compatible domains. The correspondence between the attributes is not based on the name but on the position of the attributes. If the attributes have different names, the result normally uses the names of the first operand.

Query 33: Find the first names and surnames of the employees:

```
select FirstName as Name
from Employee
     union
select Surname
from Employee
```

The query first obtains the values of the attribute FirstName for the rows of EMPLOYEE. It then obtains the values of the attribute Surname for the same rows and finally constructs the table by uniting the two partial results. Given that the set operators eliminate the duplicates, there will be no repeated elements in the resulting table, in spite of the presence of duplicates in both the initial tables, and in spite of the presence of some identical values in both tables. Taking the initial data to be that of the table in Figure 4.20, the result of the evaluation of the query is shown in Figure 4.25.

Name
Mary
Charles
Gus
Jackson
Laurence
Pauline
Alice
Brown
White
Green
Neri
Chen
Bradshaw

Figure 4.25 Result of Query 33.

Query 34: Find the first names and the surnames of all the employees, except those belonging to the Administration department, keeping the duplicates:

```
select FirstName as Name
from Employee
where Dept <> 'Administration'
      union all
select Surname
from Employee
where Dept <> 'Administration'
```

In this case all the duplicates are retained. The result of the query, again based on the table in Figure 4.20, is shown in Figure 4.26.

Query 35: Find the surnames of employees that are also first names:

```
select FirstName as Name
from Employee
      intersect
select Surname
from Employee
```

From this query, we obtain the result in Figure 4.27.

Query 36: Find the first names of employees that are not also surnames:

```
select FirstName as Name
from Employee
      except
```

```
select Surname
from Employee
```

The result of this query is shown in Figure 4.28.

Name
Charles
Jackson
Charles
Laurence
Alice
White
Neri
Brown
Chen
Jackson

Figure 4.26 Result of Query 34.

Name
Jackson

Figure 4.27 Result of Query 35.

Name
Mary
Charles
Gus
Laurence
Pauline
Alice

Figure 4.28 Result of Query 36.

4.2.6 Nested queries

Up to now, we have looked at queries in which the argument of the where clause is based on compound conditions in which each predicate represents a simple comparison between two values. SQL also allows the use of predicates with a more complex structure, in which a value expression can be compared with the result of the execution of an SQL query. The query used for the comparison is defined directly in the internal predicate of the where clause and is known as a *nested query*.

The value expression to be used as the first operand in the comparison is most typically an attribute name. In this case, we are then confronted with the problem of heterogeneity in the terms of the comparison. On one side of the comparison we have the result of the execution of a query in SQL, generally a set of values, while on the other side we have the value of the attribute for the particular row. The solution offered by SQL consists of using the keywords all or any to extend the normal comparison operators (=, <>, <, >, <= and >=). The keyword any specifies that the row satisfies the condition if the comparison predicate of the attribute value for the row is true with at least one of the elements returned by the query. The keyword all specifies that the row satisfies the condition only if all the elements returned by the nested query make the comparison true. The syntax requires that the domain of the elements returned by the nested query is compatible with the attribute with which the comparison is made.

Query 37: Find the employees who work in departments in London:

```
select FirstName, Surname
from Employee
where Dept = any (select DeptName
                  from Department
                  where City = 'London')
```

The query selects the rows of EMPLOYEE for which the value of the attribute Dept is equal to at least one of the values of the DeptName attribute of the rows of DEPARTMENT with City equal to London.

This query can also be expressed using a join between the tables EMPLOYEE and DEPARTMENT, and, in fact, the optimizers are generally able to deal with the two different formulations of this query in the same way. The choice between one representation and the other can be influenced by the degree of readability of the solution. In cases as simple as these, there is no difference, but for more complex queries, the use of several nested queries can improve readability.

Let us consider a query that allows us to find the employees belonging to the Planning department who have the same first name as a member of the Production department. The query lends itself to both possible formulations: the first is more compact and uses variables.

Query 38:

```
select E1.FirstName, E1.Surname
from Employee E1, Employee E2
where E1.FirstName = E2.FirstName and
      E2.Dept = 'Production' and
      E1.Dept = 'Planning'
```

The second method uses a nested query, expressing the query without needing aliases:

Query 39:

```
select FirstName, Surname
from Employee
where Dept = 'Planning' and
      FirstName = any (select Firstname
```

```
                         from Employee
                         where Dept = 'Production')
```

We consider now a different query:

Query 40: Find the departments in which there is no one named Brown:

```
select DeptName
from Department
where DeptName <> all (select Dept
                       from Employee
                       where Surname = 'Brown')
```

The nested query selects the values of Dept for all the rows in which the surname is Brown. The condition is therefore satisfied by the rows of DEPARTMENT for which the value of the attribute DeptName is not among the values produced by the nested query. This query could not be expressed by means of a join. Note how this query could have been implemented in relational algebra using the following expression ($\pi_{\text{DeptName}}(\text{DEPARTMENT}) - \rho_{\text{DeptName} \leftarrow \text{Dept}} \pi_{\text{Dept}}(\sigma_{\text{Surname}='Brown'}(\text{EMPLOYEE}))$), and therefore could also have been expressed using the set operator except as follows:

Query 41:

```
select DeptName
from Department
      except
select Dept as DeptName
from Employee
where Surname = 'Brown'
```

SQL offers two special operators to represent set membership and its negation, in and not in. These are indeed shorthand for = any and <> all respectively. Examples of their use are given in the queries of the next section.

Finally we can observe how some queries that use the operators max and min could be expressed by means of nested queries.

Query 42: Find the department of the employee earning the highest salary (using the aggregate function max):

```
select Dept
from Employee
where Salary = any (select max(Salary)
                    from Employee)
```

Query 43: Find the department of the employee earning the highest salary (using only a nested query):

```
select Dept
from Employee
where Salary >= all (select Salary
                     from Employee)
```

The two queries are equivalent in that the maximum value is exactly the value that is greater than or equal to all the values of the same attribute in the other rows of the relation. In these cases, however, it is advisable to use the aggregate operator, as it gives a more readable result (and possibly it is executed more efficiently). It is also interesting to note that for the first nested query there is no difference between using the keywords any and all, since the query always returns a single row.

Complex nested queries A simple and intuitive interpretation for understanding nested queries lies in the assumption that the nested query is executed before the analysis of the rows of the external query. The result of the query can be saved in a temporary variable and the predicate of the external query can be evaluated by using the temporary result. What is more, this interpretation produces an efficient execution, since the nested query is processed only once. Consider again Query 40. The system can first carry out the nested query, which returns the value of the Dept attribute for all the employees named Brown. Once this is done, each department is then checked to see that the name is not included in the table produced, using the operator <> all.

Sometimes, however, the nested query refers to the context of the query in which it is enclosed; this generally happens by means of a variable defined within the external query and used in the internal query. Such a mechanism is often described as the 'transfer of bindings' from one context to another. This mechanism enhances the expressive power of SQL. In this case, the simple interpretation given before for nested queries is no longer valid. Instead, it is necessary to reconsider the standard interpretation of SQL queries, which first compute the cartesian product of the tables in the from clause and next evaluate the where clause on each row. The nested query is a component of the where clause and it must also be evaluated separately for every row produced by the consideration of the external query. Thus, the new interpretation is the following: for each row of the external query, we first evaluate the nested query, and then compute the row-level predicate of the external query. Such a process can be arbitrarily nested for an arbitrarily complex use of variables within the nested queries; however, the readability and declarative nature of the language are compromised. With regard to the visibility (or *scope*) of SQL variables, there is a restriction on the use of a variable: a variable can be used only within the query in which it is defined or within a query that is recursively nested in the query where it is defined. If a query contains nested queries at the same level (on distinct predicates), the variables introduced in the from clause of a query cannot be used in the context of another query. The following query, for example, is incorrect.

Query 44:

```
select *
from Employee
where Dept in (select DeptName
               from Department D1
               where DeptName = 'Production') or
```

```
              Dept in (select DeptName
                       from Department D2
                       where (D1.City)= D2.City )
```

We exemplify the meaning of complex nested queries together with the description of a new logical operator, **exists**. This operator allows a nested query as a parameter and returns the true value only if the query does not produce an empty result. This operator can be usefully employed only if there is a binding transfer between the external query and the nested query.

Consider a table PERSON(TaxCode, FirstName, Surname, City) describing people's tax records.

Query 45: Find all the homonyms, that is, persons who have the same first name and surname but different tax codes:

```
select *
from Person P
where exists (select *
              from Person P1
              where P1.FirstName = P.FirstName and
                    P1.Surname = P.Surname and
                    P1.TaxCode <> P.TaxCode )
```

The query searches the rows of the PERSON table for which there exists a further row in PERSON with the same FirstName and Surname, but a different TaxCode.

In this case, we cannot execute the nested query before evaluating the external query, given that the nested query is not properly defined until a value has been assigned to the variable P. It is necessary, instead, to evaluate the nested query for every single row produced within the external query. Thus, in the example, the rows of the variable P will first be examined one by one. For each of these rows, the nested query will be executed and it will return or not the empty result depending upon whether or not there are persons with the same name and surname. This query could also have been formulated with a join of the PERSON table with itself.

Consider now a different query.

Query 46: Find all persons who do not have homonyms:

```
select *
from Person P
where not exists (select *
                  from Person P1
                  where P1.FirstName = P.FirstName and
                        P1.Surname = P.Surname and
                        P1.TaxCode <> P.TaxCode )
```

The interpretation is similar to that of the preceding query, with the single difference that the predicate is satisfied if the nested query returns an empty result. This query could also have been implemented by a difference that subtracted from all the first names and surnames, those of the people sharing a first and second name, determined using a join.

Another way to formulate the same query uses the *tuple constructor*, represented by a pair of curved brackets that enclose the list of attributes.

Query 47: Find all the persons who do not have homonyms (using the tuple constructor):

```
select *
from Person P
where (FirstName, Surname) not in (select FirstName, Surname
                                   from Person P1
                                   where P1.TaxCode <> P.TaxCode)
```

Consider a database with a table SINGER(Name, Song) and a table SONGWRITER(Name, Song).

Query 48: Find the singers who have performed only their own songs:

```
select Name
from Singer
where Name not in (select Name
                   from Singer S
                   where Name not in
                        (select Name
                         from Songwriter
                         where Songwriter.Song = S.Song))
```

The external query has no link with the nested queries, and therefore can be initially suspended, waiting for the result of the first-level nested query. Such first-level query, however, presents a binding. Therefore, the query is executed by means of the following phases.

1. The nested query `select Name from Singer S` is applied to all the rows of the table `Singer`.

2. For each row, the most internal query is evaluated. This returns the names of the songwriters of the song titles appearing in the rows of S. Thus, if the name of the singer does not appear among the names of the songwriters (which therefore means that the singer is not the writer of the song he sings), then the name is selected.

3. Finally, the table that contains the names of the singers who have performed only their own songs (the more external query) is constructed. This query returns all the rows whose **Name** does not appear as result of the nested query.

The logic of this query execution is more evident when we consider that the query can be expressed in the same way by using the **except** operator:

Query 49:

```
select Name
from Singer
    except
select Name
from Singer S
```

```
where Name not in (select Name
                   from Songwriter
                   where Songwrite.Song = S.Song )
```

Commercial SQL systems do not always carry out the nested queries internally by scanning the external table and producing a query for every row of the relation. Instead, they try to process as many queries as possible in a set-oriented way, with the aim of handling a large quantity of data by means of as few operations as possible. Several optimizations are possible, such as retaining the results of the nested subqueries for multiple uses, and anticipating the evaluation of the parts of query predicates that are not nested. We will discuss optimization issues further in Section 9.6.

4.3 Data modification in SQL

The Data Manipulation Language of SQL includes commands for querying and modifying the database. The commands that allow the modification of the contents of a database are insert, delete and update. We will analyze the individual commands separately, although, as we shall see, they have similar forms.

4.3.1 Insertions

The command for inserting a row into the database offers alternative syntaxes:

insert into *TableName* [(*AttributeList*)] ⟨values (*ListOfValues*) | *SelectSQL*⟩

The first form allows the insertion of single rows into the tables. The argument of the values clause represents explicitly the values of the attributes of the single row. For example:

```
insert into Department(DeptName, City)
       values('Production', 'Toulouse')
```

The second form allows the addition of a set of rows, which are first retrieved from the database.

The following command inserts the results of the selection from the table PRODUCT of all the rows having London as the value of the attribute ProdArea, into the table LONDONPRODUCTS.

```
insert into LondonProducts
       (select Code, Description
        from Product
        where ProdArea = 'London')
```

The two forms have different applications. The first case is typically used in programs to fill in a table with data provided directly by the users. Each use of the insert command is generally associated with the filling of a form, that is, a friendly interface in which the user supplies values for various attributes. The second case inserts data into a table based on other information already present in the database.

If the values of some of the attributes of the table are not specified during an insertion, the default value is assigned to them, or failing this, the null value (Section 4.1.6). If the insertion of the null value violates a *not null* constraint defined on the attribute, the insertion will be rejected. Finally, note that the correspondence between the attributes of the table and the values to be inserted is dictated by the order in which the terms appear in the definition of the table. For this reason, the first element of the *ValuesList* (for the first form of the statement) or the first element of the target list (for the second form) must correspond to the first attribute that appears in *AttributeList* (or in the definition of the table if *AttributeList* is omitted), and so on for the other attributes.

4.3.2 Deletions

The delete command eliminates rows from the tables of the database, following this simple syntax:

    delete from *TableName* [where *Condition*]

When the condition forming the subject of the `where` clause is not specified, the command removes all the rows from the table, otherwise only the rows that satisfy the condition are deleted. In case there is a referential integrity constraint with a `cascade` policy in which the table is referenced, the cancellation of rows of the table can cause the cancellation of rows belonging to other tables. This can generate a chain reaction if these cancellations in their turn cause cancellation of rows in other tables.

    delete from Department
    where DeptName = 'Production'

The command deletes the row of DEPARTMENT having the name Production. (Since **DeptName** was declared as the primary key for the table, there can be only one row having that particular value.)

The condition has the same syntax as in the select statement, which means that nested queries referring to other tables can appear within it. A simple example is the command that deletes the departments without employees:

    delete from Department
            where DeptName not in (select Dept
                                    from Employee)

Note the difference between the `delete` command and the `drop` command described in Section 4.1.8. A command such as:

    delete from Department

deletes all the rows of the DEPARTMENT table, possibly also deleting all the rows of the tables that are linked by referential integrity constraints with the table, if the `cascade` policy is specified in the event of deletion. The schema of the database remains unchanged, however, and the command modifies only the database instance. The command:

```
drop table Department cascade
```

has the same effect as the command `delete`, but in this case the schema of the database is also modified, deleting the DEPARTMENT table from the schema, as well as all the views and tables that refer to it in their definitions. However, the command:

```
drop table Department restrict
```

fails if there are rows in the DEPARTMENT table.

4.3.3 Updates

The update command is slightly more complex.

```
update TableName
    set Attribute = ⟨Expression | SelectSQL | null | default⟩
    {, Attribute = ⟨Expression | SelectSQL | null | default⟩}
[where Condition]
```

The `update` command makes it possible to update one or more attributes of the rows of *TableName* that satisfy a possible *Condition*. If the condition does not appear, a true value is assumed as default, and the modification is carried out on all the rows. The new value to which the attribute is assigned, can be one of the following:

1. the result of the evaluation of an expression on the attributes of the table;

2. the result of an SQL query;

3. the null value; or,

4. the default value for the domain.

The command:

```
update Employee set Salary = Salary + 5
where RegNo = 'M2047'
```

operates on a single row, updating the salary of the employee number M2047 whereas the following example operates on a set of rows.

```
update Employee set Salary = Salary * 1.1
where Dept = 'Administration'
```

The command produces a 10% salary increase for all the employees who work in Administration. The assignment operator has the usual property, for which **Salary** on the right-hand side of the operator represents the old value, which is evaluated for every row to which the update must be applied. The result of the expression becomes the new value of the salary.

The set-oriented nature of SQL should be taken into account when writing update commands. Suppose we wish to modify the employees' salaries, increasing the salaries under 30 thousand by 10%, and the higher salaries by

15%. One way to update the database to reach this goal is to execute the following command:

```
update Employee set Salary = Salary * 1.1
where Salary <= 30

update Employee set Salary = Salary * 1.15
where Salary > 30
```

The problem with this solution is that if we consider an employee with an initial salary of 28 thousand, this will satisfy the first update command and the Salary attribute will be set equal to 30.8. At this point, however, the row also satisfies the conditions of the second update command, and thus the salary will be modified again. The final result is that for this row the total increase is 26.5%.

The problem originates because SQL is set-oriented. With a tuple-oriented language it would be possible to update the rows one by one and apply one or the other modification according to the value of the salary. In this particular case, the solution is to invert the order of execution of the two commands, first increasing the higher salaries and then the remaining ones. In more complex situations, the solution might require the introduction of intermediate updates, or a complete change of approach using a program in a high-level programming language, using cursors. This technique will be described in Section 4.6.

4.4 Other definitions of data in SQL

Having described how to formulate queries in SQL, we can complete the summary of the components of a schema. We will now describe the check clause, assertions and the primitives for the definition of views.

4.4.1 Generic integrity constraints

We have seen how SQL allows the specification of a certain set of constraints on the attributes and tables, satisfying the most important, but not all, of the application requirements. For the specification of further constraints, SQL-2 has introduced the check clause, with the following syntax:

check (*Condition*)

The conditions that can be used are those that can appear in the where clause of an SQL query. The condition must always be verified to maintain the correctness of the database. In this way it is possible to specify all the tuple constraints we discussed in Section 2.2.1, and even more, because the *Condition* can include references to other fields.

An effective demonstration of the power of the construct is to show how the predefined constraints can all be described by means of the check clause. For this, we can redefine the schema of the first version of the EMPLOYEE table given in Section 4.1.7:

```
create table Employee
(
    RegNo   character(6)
            check (RegNo is not null and
                   1 = (select count(*)
                        from Employee E
                        where RegNo = E.RegNo)),
    Surname character(20) check (Surname is not null),
    Name    character(20) check (Name is not null and
                                 1 = (select count(*)
                                      from Employee E
                                      where Name = E.Name
                                      and Surname = E.Surname)),
    Dept    character(15) check (Dept in
                                 (select DeptName
                                  from Department))
)
```

By comparing this specification with the one using predefined constraints, we can make a number of observations. First, the predefined constraints allow a more compact and readable representation; for example, the key constraint requires a fairly complex representation, which uses the aggregate operator count. Note also that using the check clause, we lose the possibility of assigning a policy of reaction to violations to the constraints. Finally, when the constraints are defined using the predefined constructs, the system can recognize them immediately and can verify them more efficiently.

To understand the power of the new check construct, we can, for example, describe a constraint that forces the employee to have a supervisor of his own department only if the registration number does not begin with the value 1. The above table definition can be extended with the following declaration:

```
Superior character(6)
check (RegNo like "1%" or
       Dept = (select Dept
               from Employee E
               where E.RegNo = Superior))
```

4.4.2 Assertions

Besides the check clause, we can define a further component of the schema of the database, assertions. Introduced in SQL-2, these represent constraints that are not associated with any row or table in particular, and belong to the schema.

Using assertions, we can express all the constraints that we have already specified when dealing with table definitions. But assertions also allow the expression of constraints that would not otherwise be expressible, such as constraints on more than one table or constraints that require that a table have a minimum cardinality. Assertions are named, and therefore they can be explicitly dropped by means of the drop instruction for schema updates (see Section 4.1.8).

The syntax for the definition of assertions is as follows:

```
create assertion AssertionName check (Condition)
```

An assertion can for example impose that in EMPLOYEE there is always at least one row present.

```
create assertion AlwaysOneEmployee
        check (1 <= (select count(*)
                     from Employee))
```

Every integrity constraint, either check or assertion, is associated with a check policy that indicates whether it is immediate or deferred. Immediate constraints are verified immediately after each modification of the database, while deferred constraints are verified only at the end of a series of operations, called a transaction. When an immediate constraint is not satisfied, it is because the specific data modification operation causing the violation was just executed and it can be 'undone'; this is called *partial rollback*. All the fixed format constraints, introduced in Section 4.1.6 (*not null, unique, primary key*) and Section 4.1.7 (*foreign key*), are immediately verified, and their violation causes a partial rollback. When instead a violation of a deferred constraint is detected at the end of a transaction, the data modification operation causing the violation is not known, and therefore the entire transaction has to be undone; this is called *rollback*. Transactions and rollbacks are discussed further in Chapter 9, on database technology. Due to the above mechanisms, the execution of a data manipulation instruction on a database instance that satisfies all the constraints will always produce a database instance that also satisfies all the constraints. We also say that they produce a 'consistent database state'. Consistency is defined in Section 9.1.

Within a program, we can change the attribute of a constraint, by setting it `immediate` or `deferred`; this is done by means of the commands `set constraints` [*ConstraintName*] `immediate` and `set constraints` [*Constraint-Name*] `deferred`.

4.4.3 Views

In Chapter 3 views were introduced as 'virtual' tables, whose contents depend on the contents of the other tables in the database. Views are defined in SQL by associating a name and a list of attributes with the result of the execution of a query. Other views can also appear within the query that defines the view. However, views cannot be mutually dependent, either immediately (defining a view in terms of itself), or transitively (defining a view V_1 using a view V_2, V_2 using V_3 and so on until V_n is defined by means of V_1),

A view is defined using the command:

```
create view ViewName [(AttributeList)] as SelectSQL
[with [local | cascaded] check option]
```

The SQL query and the schema of the view must have the same number of attributes. We can, for example, define a view ADMINEMPLOYEE that contains all the employees in the Administration department with a salary higher than 10 thousand.

```
create view AdminEmployee(RegNo, FirstName, Surname, Salary) as
select RegNo, FirstName, Surname, Salary
from Employee
where Dept ='Administration' and
      Salary > 10
```

We can now construct a view JUNIORADMINEMPLOYEE based on the ADMINEMPLOYEE view, which will contain the administrative employees with a salary between 10 thousand and 50 thousand:

```
create view JuniorAdminEmployee as
select *
from AdminEmployee
where Salary < 50
with check option
```

On certain views, we can carry out modification operations; these must be translated into the appropriate modification commands on the base tables on which the view depends. As we have already mentioned in Chapter 3, we cannot always find an unambiguous way of modifying the base table or tables. Difficulties are encountered, particularly when the view is defined by means of a join between more than one table. In standard SQL, a view can be updated only when a single row of each base table corresponds to a row in the view.

Commercial SQL systems generally consider that a view can be updated only if it is defined on a single table; some systems require that the attributes of the view should contain at least a primary key of the table. The check option clause can be used only in the context of views that can be updated. It specifies that update operations can be carried out only on rows belonging to the view, and after the update the rows must continue to belong to the view. This can happen, for example, if a value is assigned to an attribute of the view that makes one of the selection predicates false. When a view is defined in terms of other views, the local or cascaded option specifies whether the control over row removal must be made only at the (local) view or whether it must be propagated to all the views on which the view depends. The default option is cascaded.

Since the JUNIORADMINEMPLOYEE view has been defined using the check option, an attempt to assign a value of 8 thousand to the Salary attribute would not be accepted by the present definition of the view, but would be accepted if the check option were defined as local. A modification of the Salary attribute of a row of the view to allocate the value 60 thousand would not be accepted even with the local option.

4.4.4 Views in queries

Views can be used in SQL to formulate queries that it would otherwise be impossible to express. Using the definition of appropriate views, we can define queries in SQL that require a nesting of various aggregate operators, or that make a sophisticated use of the union operator. In general, views can be considered as a tool that increases the possibility of creating nested queries.

We wish to determine which department has the highest expenditure on salaries. In order to achieve this we define a view that will be used by Query 50.

```
create view SalaryBudget (Dept, SalaryTotal) as
select Dept, sum(Salary)
from Employee
group by Dept
```

Query 50: Find the department with the highest salary expenditure.

```
select Dept
from SalaryBudget
where SalaryTotal = (select max(SalaryTotal)
                          from SalaryBudget )
```

The definition of the view SALARYBUDGET builds a table in which there appears a row for every department. The attribute Dept corresponds to the attribute Dept of EMPLOYEE and contains the name of the department. The second attribute SalaryTotal contains, for each department, the sum of the salaries of all the employees of that department

Another way to formulate the same query is as follows:

Query 51:

```
select Dept
from Employee
group by Dept
having sum(Salary) >= all (select sum(Salary)
                                from Employee
                                group by Dept )
```

This solution is not recognized by all SQL systems, which may impose that the condition in the having clause must be a simple comparison with an attribute or a constant, and cannot use a nested query. We can give another example of the use of views to formulate complex queries.

```
create view DeptOffice(DeptName,NoOfOffices) as
select Dept, count(distinct Office)
from Employee
group by Dept
```

Query 52: Find the average number of offices per department:

```
select avg(NoOfOffices)
from DeptOffice
```

We could think of expressing the same query like this:

Query 53:

```
select (avg(count)(distinct Office))
from Employee
group by Dept
```

The query is, however, incorrect, because the SQL syntax does not allow the cascading of aggregate operators. The basic problem is that the evaluation of the two different operators happens at different levels of aggregation, whereas a single occurrence of the `group by` clause for every query is admissible.

4.5 Access control

The presence of data protection mechanisms takes on great importance in modern applications. One of the most important tasks of a database administrator is the choice and implementation of appropriate access control policies. SQL recognizes the importance of this aspect and a set of instructions is dedicated to this function.

SQL is designed so that every user is identifiable by the system in a way that is unambiguous. The user identification can exploit the capabilities of the operating system (so that each user of the system corresponds to a user of the database), or database users can be independent of system users. Most commercial systems offer an independent organization, each with its own identification procedure. In this way, more than one system user can correspond to a database user and vice versa.

4.5.1 Resources and privileges

The resources that are protected by the system are usually tables, but we can protect any of the system components, such as the attributes of a table, views and domains.

As a rule, the user who creates a resource is its owner and is authorized to carry out any operation upon it. A system in which only the owners of the resources were authorized to make use of them would be of limited use, as would a system in which all the users were able to use every resource in an arbitrary manner. SQL however, offers flexible organization mechanisms that allow the administrator to specify those resources to which the users may have access, and those that must be kept private. The system bases access control on a concept of privilege. The users possess *privileges* of access to the systems resources.

Every privilege is characterized by the following:

1. the resource to which it refers;

2. the user who grants the privilege;

3. the user who receives it;

4. the action that is allowed on the resource; and,

5. whether or not the privilege can be passed on to other users.

When a resource is created, the system automatically concedes all the privileges on that resource to its creator. In addition, there is a predefined user, _system, which represents the database administrator, who possesses all privileges on all resources.

The available privileges are as follows:

- insert: allows the insertion of a new object into the resource (this can be applied only to tables or views);

- update: allows the value of an object to be updated (this can be used on tables, views, and attributes);

- delete: allows the removal of an object from the resource (tables or views only);

- select: allows the user to read the resource, in order to use it within a query (used on tables, views and attributes);

- references: allows a reference to be made to a resource in the context of the definition of a table. It can be associated only with tables and specific attributes. With the references privilege (say on the table DEPARTMENT, property of Paolo), a user who is granted the privilege (say, Stefano) is able to define a *foreign key* constraint (for example, on his table EMPLOYEE) referencing the resource that is granted (for example, the key of DEPARTMENT). At this point, if Stefano specifies a no action policy on the referential integrity constraint, Paolo is prevented from cancelling or modifying rows of his own table DEPARTMENT, if such an update command renders the contents of EMPLOYEE incorrect. Thus, giving out a references privilege on a resource might limit the ability to modify that resource;

- usage: applies to domains, and allows them to be used, for example, in the definition of the schema of a table.

The privilege of carrying out a drop or an alter on an object cannot be granted, but remains the prerogative of the creator of the object itself. Privileges are conceded or remitted by means of the instructions grant and revoke.

4.5.2 Commands for granting and revoking privileges

The syntax of the grant command is as follows:

    grant *Privilege* on *Resource* to *Users* [with grant option]

The command allows the granting of *Privileges* on the *Resource* to the *Users*. For example, the command:

    grant select on Department to Stefano

grants to the user Stefano the select privilege on the DEPARTMENT table. The with grant option clause specifies whether the privilege of propagating the privilege to other users must also be granted. We can use the keywords all privileges in place of the distinct privileges. These identify all the privileges that the user can grant on a particular resource. Thus the command:

grant all privileges on Employee to Paolo, Riccardo

concedes to the users Paolo and Riccardo all the privileges on the EMPLOYEE table that can be granted by whoever executes the command.

The revoke command does the reverse, taking away privileges that a user had already been granted.

revoke *Privileges* on *Resource* from *Users* [restrict | cascade]

Among the privileges that can be revoked, apart from those that can appear as subject of the grant command, there is also the grant option privilege, which derives from the use of the clause with grant option.

The only user who can revoke privileges from another user is the user who granted the privileges in the first place; a revoke can take away all or a subset of the privileges that were originally granted. The default option restrict specifies that the command must not be carried out in case revoking this user's privilege causes a further revoking of privileges. This can happen when the user has received the privileges with the grant option and has propagated the privileges to other users. In a situation of this nature, the restrict option will cause an error to be signalled. With the cascade option, instead, the execution of the command is imperative; all the privileges that were propagated are revoked and all the elements of the database that were constructed by exploiting these privileges are removed. Note that in this case too, the cascade option can generate a chain reaction, in which for each element removed, all the objects that have some dependent relation to it are also removed. As in other such cases, it is necessary to be very careful that a simple command does not produce extensive and undesirable modifications on the database.

It is not only the revoke command that can produce chain reactions: the grant command can also produce similar effects. It can happen that a user has received a privilege on a table that has allowed him to create views that refer to this table, by means of, for example, the select privilege. If the user is granted further privileges on the table, then these privileges will be automatically extended to cover the views (and subsequently to views constructed on these views).

4.6 Use of SQL in programming languages

It is rare that access to information contained in a database happens as a result of personal interaction using SQL. In practice, by far the most typical use of a database happens by means of integrated applications built into the information system, while direct use of the SQL interpreter is reserved for a few expert users.

The use of special applications rather than the SQL interpreter to gain access to information is justified by a number of factors. Very often, access to the information is not required directly by a user but by a non-interactive (batch) application. Further, for interactive users, the access techniques are often simple and predictable. It is therefore useful to reduce the complexity of access to the database by constructing an application that provides a simplified interface for carrying out the task. Finally, the presentation of the data offered by the system might be unsuitable for the user's requirements, while a special application is free from constraints and can provide a representation adequate for the requirements.

There are many tools that can be used for the creation of database applications. A thriving market is that of the *fourth generation languages* (4GLs), highly sophisticated development tools that make it possible to develop complete database management applications with little effort. Most database vendors offer, together with the database manager, a set of tools for the development of applications. Moreover there is a rich supply of products that are not linked to any database in particular, all of which are able to manage a dialogue with the relational system by means of standard SQL. These tools make possible the effective definition of database schemas, and the construction of complex interfaces.

Another method for writing applications uses traditional high-level programming languages. We will concentrate our analysis on this method, because it is still of considerable importance, and because of the lack of uniformity among 4GLs.

4.6.1 Integration problems

In order to use SQL instructions within a procedural program, the SQL instructions must be *encapsulated* within the program. From the implementation point of view, it is necessary to provide the high-level language compiler with a preprocessor. This preprocessor is able to detect the calls to the DBMS services, and submit them to the DBMS query execution environment, which includes the query optimizer. This solution offers the usual advantages of portability and abstraction that already characterize the use of a standard language such as SQL. At execution, the program begins a dialogue with the database, sending the query directly to the system.

One particular problem lies in the fact that programming languages access the elements of a table by scanning the rows one by one, using what is known as a *tuple-oriented* approach. In contrast, SQL is a *set-oriented* language, which always acts upon entire tables and not upon single rows. Even the result of an SQL query is an entire table. These aspects cause the problem known as *impedance mismatch*.[4] We will talk further about this problem in Chapter 11, dedicated to object-oriented systems.

---

4. The term is derived from electrical engineering, which requires the entry and exit impedances of circuits connected to each other to be as similar as possible.

There are two possible solutions to this problem. The first consists of using a programming language that makes more powerful data constructs available and in particular is able to organize a 'set of rows' type structure in a natural way. This solution is gaining more interest due to the increasing spread of object-oriented programming languages, characterized by powerful type-definition mechanisms. However, most applications are written using languages that do not possess this capability. A further difficulty with this solution is the lack of a standard solution accepted by all systems, for example, by object-oriented and object-relational systems (see Chapter 11).

The second strategy, more commonly used, has been standardized and does not need a complicated extension of existing programming languages, although it is not as high-level and friendly to the programmer as one would like it to be. This solution is based on the use of *cursors*.

4.6.2 Cursors

A *cursor* is a mechanism that allows a program to access the rows of a table one at a time; the cursor is defined using a query. Let us look first at the syntax for the definition and use of cursors.

```
declare CursorName [scroll] cursor for SelectSQL
     [for ⟨read only | update [of Attribute {, Attribute}])]
```

The `declare cursor` command defines a cursor associated with a particular query on the database. The `scroll` option specifies whether we wish to allow the program to move freely on the result of the query. The final option `for update` specifies whether the cursor can be used for expressing an `update` command, possibly adding the specification of the attributes that will be updated.

```
open CursorName
```

The `open` command applies to a cursor; when invoked, the query is carried out and the query result can be accessed using the `fetch` command.

```
fetch [Position from] CursorName into FetchList
```

The `fetch` command takes a row from the cursor and returns its values into the variables of the program that appear in *FetchList*. The *FetchList* must include a variable for every element in the target list of the query, such that every element of the *FetchList* is type-compatible with the domains of the elements of the target list of the query. An important concept is that of *current row*, which represents the last row used by the fetch operation. The *Position* parameter is used to set the current row. It can assume the following values:

- `next` (the current row becomes the row that follows the current one);
- `first` (the first row of the query result);
- `last` (the last row);

- absolute *IntegerExpression* (the row that appears in the *i*-th position of the query result, where *i* is the result of the evaluation of the expression);

- relative *IntegerExpression* (the row that appears in the *i*-th position, starting from the current position).

These options can be used only on condition that the scroll option (which guarantees the possibility of free movement within the result of the query) was specified when the cursor was defined. If the scroll option is not specified, the only value available for the parameter is next; in this case, implementation is easier, as the rows of the result can be discarded immediately after being returned. This can be very useful for reducing response times, particularly when the query returns a large number of rows.

```
update TableName
    set Attribute = 〈Expression | null | default〉
    {, Attribute = 〈Expression | null | default〉}
    where current of CursorName
```

The update and delete commands allow modifications to be made to the database by means of cursors. The only extension required to the syntax of update and delete lies in the possibility of using in the where clause, the keywords current of *CursorName*, which indicates the current row (that must be updated or removed). The modification commands can be used only if the cursor gives access to an actual row of a table, and is not applicable when the query associated with the cursor requires a join between different tables.

```
close CursorName
```

The close command frees the cursor, i.e., communicates to the system that the result of the query is no longer needed. At this point, the resources dedicated to the cursor are released, particularly the memory space storing the result.

A simple example is as follows:

```
declare EmployeeCursor scroll cursor for
    select Surname, Firstname, Salary
    from Employee
    where Salary < 100 and Salary > 40
```

In this way, the cursor EmpoloyeeCursor is allocated to the query that makes it possible to obtain data relating to the employees who earn between 40 thousand and 100 thousand.

Let us now look at a simple example of a C program that uses cursors. The SQL commands are identified by the character '$' in the first column, and the variables of the program are distinguished by the fact that their names are preceded by the ':' (colon) character. The variables must be of a type compatible with the values that they will contain. A predefined variable, sqlcode, is used. It contains zero if the execution of the last command has been successful, and a non-zero error code otherwise. Its main use is to detect when the rows of a cursor have all been fetched.

```
        void DisplayDepartmentSalaries(char DeptName[])
        {
          char FirstName[20], Surname[20];
          long int Salary;

        $ declare DeptEmp cursor for
             select FirstName, Surname, Salary
             from Employee
             where Dept = :Deptname;
        $ open DeptEmp;
        $ fetch DeptEmp into :FirstName, :Surname, :Salary;
        printf("Department %s\n",DeptName);
        while (sqlcode == 0)
        {
          printf("Name of the employee: %s %s",FirstName,Surname);
          printf("Salary: %d\n",Salary);
        $ fetch DeptEmp into :FirstName, :Surname, :Salary;
        }

        $ close cursor DeptEmp;
        }
```

Certain queries whose results are guaranteed to consist of a single tuple, called *scalar* queries, have a simpler interface with the programming language; we do not need to define a cursor on them, but we can use the into clause. In this way, we can directly establish to which variables of the program the result of the query must be assigned. Let us examine how the syntax of the select instruction is extended:

> *SelectSQL* ::=select *TargetList* [into *VariableList*]
> from *TableList*
> [where *Condition*]
> [group by *GroupingAttributeList*]
> [having *AggregateCondition*]
> [order by *OrderingAttributeList*]

Here is an example:

```
        $ select Firstname, Surname into :EmpFName, :EmpSurname
          from Employee
          where Number = :EmpNumber
```

The values of the attributes FirstName and Surname of the employee whose registration number is contained in the variable EmpNumber will be copied into the variables EmpFName and EmpSurname.

4.6.3 Dynamic SQL

There are many situations in which it is necessary to allow the user to formulate arbitrary queries on the database.

If the queries have a predefined structure and the part that varies is merely the parameter used in the query, then we can construct the application by means of cursors, as illustrated in the examples in the previous section. There are other cases, however, in which it is necessary to manage queries that require more flexibility. These queries differ not only in the parameters used, but also in the structure of the queries and in the set of tables being accessed. The mechanisms for invoking SQL commands seen in the previous section will not work in this context, given that they require the structure of the queries to be predefined. This family of mechanisms is collectively known as *static* SQL. An alternative family of commands permit the use of *dynamic* SQL. These commands make it possible to construct a program that executes SQL commands constructed when the program is run. These commands, however, require special support from the system.

The greatest problem to be overcome is the transfer of parameters between the SQL command and the program, both incoming and outgoing. Given that the SQL command is arbitrary, the program has no way of recognizing at the time of compilation, which are the required input and output parameters of the command. This information is necessary for the program to be able to organize the query internally.

The use of dynamic SQL alters the mode of interaction with the system. In static SQL, the commands can be processed by a compiler, which analyzes the structure of the command and constructs a translation into the internal language of the system. In this way, commands do not need to be translated and optimized each time, but can be executed immediately. This brings considerable advantages in terms of performance. If, for example, a command is carried out repeatedly, with this solution the translation is made only once, whereas interacting with the engine each separate execution of the command would require its own phase of translation.

In dynamic SQL attempts are made to retain these advantages as much as possible, making available two different types of interaction. The query can be carried out immediately, meaning that the execution of the query follows immediately after the analysis, or, alternatively, the management of the query happens in two phases, analysis and execution.

Immediate execution command The execute immediate command requires the execution of an SQL statement, either directly stated or contained in a program variable of type string of characters.

```
execute immediate SQLStatement
```

The immediate method can be used only for statements that do not require parameters for either input or output. An example of the use of the command is as follows:

```
execute immediate
"delete from Department where Name = 'Administration'"
```

In a C program we could write:

```
SQLString =
        "delete from Department where name = 'Administration'";
...
$ execute immediate :SQLString
```

Instead, when a statement is executed more than once, or when the program must organize an exchange of input/output parameters with the query, we must distinguish between the two phases.

Preparation phase　The `prepare` command analyzes and optimizes an SQL statement and translates it into the internal procedural language of the DBMS.

```
prepare CommandName from SQLStatement
```

The SQL statement can contain input parameters, represented by a question mark. For example:

```
prepare :SQLStatement
        from "select City from Department where Name = ?"
```

In this case, the translation of the query corresponds to the variable `SQLStatement`, with an entry parameter that corresponds to the name of the department that must be selected by the query.

When a prepared SQL statement is no longer needed, we can free the memory occupied by the translated statement by using the `deallocate prepare` command, with the following syntax:

```
deallocate prepare CommandName
```

For example, to deallocate the previous statement, we could use:

```
deallocate prepare :SQLStatement
```

Execution phase　To invoke a statement elaborated by `prepare`, the `execute` command is used, with the following syntax:

```
execute CommandName [into TargetList] [using ParameterList]
```

The target list contains the list of parameters in which the result of the execution of the statement must be written. (This part is optional if the SQL command has no output parameters.) The list of parameters, on the other hand, specifies which values must be assumed by the variable parameters on the list. (This part can also be omitted if the SQL statement has no input parameters.)

Here is an example:

```
execute :SQLStatement into :city using :department
```

Suppose that the string `Production` is assigned to the variable `department`. The effect of this command is to carry out the query:

```
select City from Department where Name = 'Production'
```

and as a consequence to obtain the string `Toulouse` in the variable `city` as a result.

Use of cursors with dynamic SQL　The use of cursors with dynamic SQL is very similar to the use made of them with static SQL. There are only two differences. The first is that the query identifier is assigned to the cursor instead of to the query itself. The second is that the commands for use of the cursor allow the specification of the into and using clauses, which allow the specification of possible input and output parameters.

One example of the use of a dynamic cursor is as follows, in which we suppose that the query defined in the string SQLStatement allows an input parameter:

```
prepare :SQLStatement from :SQLString
declare PrgCursor cursor from :SQLStatement
open PrgCursor using :PrgVariable
```

4.6.4 Procedures

Standard SQL allows for the definition of procedures, also known as *stored procedures* because they are usually stored in the database as components of the schema. As with programming languages, procedures make it possible to associate a name with an SQL statement, with the possibility of specifying parameters to be used for communication to the procedure. The advantages are an increase in the clarity of the program, easier maintenance, and in many cases a noticeable increase in efficiency. Once the procedure has been defined, it is treated as part of the set of predefined SQL commands. As a first example, let us look at the following SQL procedure, which updates the name of the city of a department.

```
procedure AssignCity(:Dep char(20), :City char(20))
update Department
set City = :City
where Name = :Dep;
```

The procedure is invoked by giving a value to the parameters. The following example shows an invocation of the procedure within a C program, using two variables, DeptName and CityName:

```
$ AssignCity(:DeptName, :CityName);
```

Standard SQL-2 does not handle the writing of complex procedures, but is limited to the definition of procedures made up of a single SQL command. Many systems remove this limitation, driven by users' requirements.

The procedural extensions proposed by many systems differ widely among themselves. There are systems that allow only sequences of commands within a procedure, and others that allow the use of control structures, declarations of local variables and the invocation of external programs. In each case, the use of these functions is outside the scope of the SQL-2 standard and renders the SQL code thus generated non-portable. SQL-3 extends this aspect of the language and provides a rich syntax for the definition of procedures. In the meantime, if we decide to use the procedural extensions provided by a given system, we must also rewrite them in case there is a need to move the application to another environment.

The following example shows a (non-standard) procedure composed of a sequence of two SQL instructions. The procedure makes it possible to give to the attribute City the value of :NewCity, for all the rows of DEPARTMENT and EMPLOYEE in which the attribute is equal to :OldCity.

```
procedure ChangeAllCities(:NewCity char(20), :OldCity char(20))
begin
  update Department
  set City = :NewCity
  where City = :OldCity;
  update Employee
  set City = :NewCity
  where City = :OldCity;
end;
```

One of the extensions usually provided by current systems is the control structure *if-then-else*, which allows the expression of conditional executions and can be used to handle exceptional conditions. We show an example of a procedure that assigns to City of department :DeptName the value in :NewCity; if the department is not found, a row is inserted into DEPTERROR.

```
procedure ChangeCity(:DeptName char(20), :NewCity char(20))
begin
  if not exists(select *
                from Department
                where Name = :DeptName)
    insert into DeptError values(:DeptName)
  else
    update Department
    set City = :NewCity
    where Name = :DeptName;
  end if;
end;
```

As we have already indicated, there are commercial systems that offer powerful procedural extensions of SQL; these extensions are often able to make the language computationally complete, that is, to give it the same expressive power as a traditional programming language. The possibility exists therefore, of writing an entire application with this extended SQL. However, this is rarely the best solution, because generally the relational system is optimized only for data access. Finally, let us look at an example of a program written in PL/SQL, the extension of the relational system Oracle Server, to give an idea of the level of functionality offered by these systems. PL/SQL is described in Appendix C:

```
procedure Debit(ClientAccount char(5), Withdrawal integer) is
  OldAmount  integer;
  NewAmount  integer;
  Threshold  integer;
begin
  select Amount, OverDraft into OldAmount, Threshold
    from BankAccount
    where AccountNo = ClientAccount
    for update of Amount;
  NewAmount := OldAmount - Withdrawal;
  if NewAmount > OverDraft then
    update BankAccount set Amount = NewAmount
      where AccountNo = ClientAccount;
  else
    insert into OverDraftExceeded
```

```
       values(ClientAccount,Withdrawal,sysdate);
    end if;
  end Debit;
```

The example shows a procedure that subtracts `Withdrawal` from the account with the code `ClientAccount`, if there is enough money in the account. The procedure uses local variables (`OldAmount`, `NewAmount` and `Threshold`) and applies the control structure *if-then-else*.

4.7 Summarizing examples

1. Consider the following relational schema, which describes the schedule of a competition among national teams:

$$\text{STADIUM}(\underline{\text{Name}}, \text{City, Capacity})$$
$$\text{MATCH}(\underline{\text{StadiumName}}, \underline{\text{Date}}, \underline{\text{Time}}, \text{Country1, Country2})$$
$$\text{NATIONALITY}(\underline{\text{Country}}, \text{Continent, Category})$$

Express the following queries in SQL:

(a) Find the names of the stadiums in which no European teams will play.

SOLUTION:

```
select Name
from Stadium
where Name not in
  (select StadiumName
   from Match
   where (Country1 in
     (select Country
      from Nationality
      where Continent = 'Europe' ))
   or
     (Country2 in
      (select Country
       from Nationality
       where Continent = 'Europe' )))
```

(b) Express query (a) in relational algebra, calculus and Datalog.

SOLUTIONS:

i. Relational algebra:

$$\pi_{\text{Name}}(\text{STADIUM}) -$$
$$\rho_{\text{Name}\leftarrow\text{StadiumName}}\pi_{\text{StadiumName}}((\pi_{\text{Country}}$$
$$(\sigma_{\text{Continent}='Europe'}(\text{NATIONALITY})))$$
$$\bowtie_{\text{Country1}=\text{Country}\vee\text{Country2}=\text{Country}}$$
$$(\pi_{\text{StadiumName,Country1,Country2}}(\text{MATCH})))$$

ii. Relational calculus:

$$\{s.\text{Name} \mid s(\text{STADIUM})$$
$$\mid \neg(\exists m(\text{MATCH}) \, (\exists n(\text{NATIONALITY})$$

$$(m.\text{StadiumName} = s.\text{Name} \land$$
$$n.\text{Continent} = '\textit{Europe}' \land$$
$$(m.\text{Country1} = n.\text{Country} \lor m.\text{Country2} = n.\text{Country}))))\}$$

iii. Datalog:

STADIUMWITHEUROPE(StadiumName : n) ←
    MATCH(StadiumName : n, Date : d, Time : t,
        Country1 : $c1$, Country2 : $c2$),
    NATIONALITY(Country : $c1$, Continent : cn, Category : ct),
    cn = 'Europe'

STADIUMWITHEUROPE(StadiumName : n) ←
    MATCH(StadiumName : n, Date : d, Time : t,
        Country1 : $c1$, Country2 : $c2$),
    NATIONALITY(Country : $c2$, Continent : cn, Category : ct),
    cn = 'Europe'

?STADIUM(Name : n, City : c, Capacity : cp),
    NOT STADIUMWITHEUROPE(StadiumName : n)

(c) Extract the total capacity of the stadiums in which matches are played and that have a South American national team as the first team. (Note: to evaluate the total capacity, summarize the capacities allocated to each contest, even if many contests take place in the same stadium).

SOLUTION:

```
select sum(Capacity)
from Stadium join Match on Name = StadiumName
where Country1 in
    (select Country
     from Nationality
     where Continent = 'South America')
```

(d) Extract the city in which the Brazil team plays the most matches.

SOLUTIONS:

Here are two solutions.

i. With a specific view:

```
create view BrazilStad(StadiumName,NumberOfMatches) as
select StadiumName, count(*)
from Match
where Country1 = 'Brazil' or
      Country2 = 'Brazil'
group by StadiumName

select City
from Stadium
where Name in
    (select StadiumName
```

```
            from BrazilStad
            where NumberOfMatches =
                    (select max(NumberOfMatches)
                     from BrazilStad))
```

ii. With a more general view:

```
    create view Teams(StadiumName,Team,NumberOfMatches) as
        select StadiumName, Country, count(*)
        from Match, Nationality
        where (Country1 = Country or Country2 = Country)
        group by StadiumName, Country

    select City
    from Stadium
    where Name in
            (select StadiumName
             from Teams
             where Team = 'Brazil' and
                    NumberOfMatches =
                        (select max(NumberOfMatches)
                         from Teams
                         where Team = 'Brazil'))
```

2. Given the following relational schema:

$$\text{MOTORCYCLE}(\underline{\text{Number}}, \text{Make}, \text{Nationality}, \text{Tax})$$
$$\text{OWNER}(\underline{\text{Name}}, \underline{\text{Number}})$$

   write the following queries in SQL:

(a) Find the names of the owners of only Japanese motorcycles of at least
    two different makes

   SOLUTIONS:

   i. First solution:

```
    select Name
    from Owner join Motorcycle on Owner.Number = Motorcycle.Number
    where Name not in (select Name
                        from Owner join Motorcycle on
                            Owner.Number = Motorcycle.Number
                        where Nationality <> 'Japanese')
    group by Name
    having count(distinct Make) >= 2
```

   ii. Second solution:

```
    select P1.Name
    from Owner P1, Motorcycle M1, Owner P2, Motorcycle M2
    where P1.Name not in (select Name
                        from Owner join Motorcycle on
                            Owner.Number = Motorcycle.Number
                        where Nationality <> 'Japanese') and
        P1.Number = M1.Number and
        P2.Number = M2.Number and
        P1.Name = P2.Name and
        M1.Make <> M2.Make
```

(b) Formulate the query in relational algebra.

SOLUTION:

$$\pi_{Name}((\text{OWNER} \bowtie \text{MOTORCYCLE})$$
$$\bowtie_{Make \neq Make2 \wedge Name=Name2}$$
$$(\varrho_{Name2 \leftarrow Name}(\text{OWNER}) \bowtie \varrho_{Make2 \leftarrow Make}(\text{MOTORCYCLE}))) -$$
$$\pi_{Name}(\text{OWNER} \bowtie \sigma_{Nationality \neq 'Japanese'}\text{MOTORCYCLE})$$

(c) For each owner, highlight the tax he or she must pay for all the motorcycles owned, taking into account that if there is more than one owner for a motorcycle, the total tax will be equally divided among the owners.

SOLUTION:

```
create view IndTax(Number, Tax) as
    select Number, Tax/count(*)
    from Motorcycle join Owner
        on Motorcycle.Number = Owner.Number
    group by Number, Tax

select Name, sum(Tax)
from Owner join IndTax
    on Owner.Number = IndTax.Number
group by Name
```

4.8 Bibliography

SQL was first proposed by Chamberlin et al. [21] and [22]. The official description of standard SQL can be obtained from the international standards organization ISO. These documents are, indeed, very expensive and not easy to read. However, there are a great number of books on SQL-2, including those by Cannan and Otten [12], Date and Darwen [34], and Melton and Simon [61]. Eisenberg and Melton [36] discuss the standardization process in general and with specific reference to the database field. Melton [60] gives an overview of the main issues in SQL-3.

Most of the manuals accompanying commercial relational systems are very detailed and can provide a useful reference point. The manual of each system is also essential to know which SQL features have been implemented in that particular system.

4.9 Exercises

Exercise 4.1 Order the following domains according to the maximum value that can be represented, taking integer to have 32 bits for its representation and smallint 16 bit: numeric(12,4), decimal(10), decimal(9), integer, smallint, decimal(6,1).

Exercise 4.2 Define an attribute that allows the representation of strings of maximum length of 256 characters, on which no null values are admitted and with an 'unknown' default value.

Exercise 4.3 Give the SQL definitions of the tables

CrossCountrySkier(<u>Name</u>, Country, Age)
Competes(<u>SkierName</u>, <u>ContestName</u>, Placement)
Contest(<u>Name</u>, Place, Country, Length)

showing particularly the *foreign key* constraints of the Competes table.

Exercise 4.4 Give the SQL definitions of the tables

Author(<u>FirstName</u>, <u>Surname</u>, DateofBirth, Nationality)
Book(<u>BookTitle</u>, AuthorFirstName, AuthorSurname, Language)

For the *foreign key* constraint specify a `cascade` policy on deletions and `set null` on updates.

Exercise 4.5 Given the schema in Exercise 4.4, explain what can happen as a result of the execution of the following update commands:

```
delete from Author
    where Surname = 'Russell'
update Book set FirstName = 'Umberto'
    where Surname = 'Eco'
insert into Author(FirstName, Surname)
    values('Isaac', 'Asimov')
update Author set FirstName = 'Emile'
    where Surname = 'Zola'
```

Exercise 4.6 Given the definitions:

```
create domain Domain1 integer default 10
create table Table1(Attribute1 Domain1 default 5)
```

indicate what will happen as a result of these commands:

```
alter table Table1 alter column Attribute1 drop default
alter domain Domain1 drop default
drop domain Domain1
```

Exercise 4.7 Given the following schema:

Airport(<u>City</u>, Country, NumberOfRunways)
Flight(<u>FlightID</u>, <u>Day</u>, DepartCity, DepartTime, ArrCity, ArrTime, PlaneType)
Plane(<u>PlaneType</u>, NumberOfPassengers, Payload)

write the SQL queries with which we can find out:

1. The cities with airports for which the number of runways is not known.

2. The arrival and departure countries of flight AZ 274.

3. The types of aircraft used for flights leaving Boston.

4. The types of aircraft and the corresponding number of passengers for the types of aircraft used for flights leaving Boston. If the description of the aircraft is not available, give only the type.

5. The cities from which international flights leave.

6. The cities from which direct flights to Sydney leave, in alphabetical order.

7. The number of international flights that leave Paris on Thursdays.

8. The number of international flights that leave Canadian cities each week (to be done in two ways, one showing the airports without international flights and one not.)

9. The French cities from which more than twenty direct flights to Germany leave each week.

10. The Belgian airports that have only domestic flights. Show this query in four ways: (*i*) with set-theory operators, (*ii*) with a nested query with the not in operator, (*iii*) with a nested query with the not exists operator, (*iv*) with the outer join and the count operator. Express the query also in relational algebra.

11. The cities served by the type of aircraft able to carry the maximum number of passengers.

12. The maximum number of passengers who could arrive in a Greek airport from Norway on Thursday. If there are several flights, the total number of passengers must be found.

Exercise 4.8 Given the following schema:

CD(CDNumber, Title, Year, Price)
TRACK(CDNumber, PerformanceCode, TrackNo)
RECORDING(Performance, SongTitle, Year)
COMPOSER(CompName, SongTitle)
SINGER(SingerName, PerformanceCode)

write SQL queries that will find:

1. The people who have written and sung a particular song and whose names begin with 'D'.

2. The titles of the CDs that contain songs of which the year of recording is not known.

3. The tracks on the CDs with the serial number 78574. Provide these in numerical order, indicating the performers for the tracks having a singer.

4. The exclusive composers and singers. That is, composers who have never recorded a song and singers who have never written a song.

5. The singers on the CD that contains the largest number of songs.

6. The CDs on which all the songs are by a single singer and on which at least three recordings are from years preceding the release year of the CD.

7. The singers who have never recorded a song as soloists.

8. The singers who have never made a CD in which they appear as the only singers.

9. The singers who have always recorded songs as soloists.

Exercise 4.9 Give a sequence of update commands that alter the attribute Salary in the EMPLOYEE table, increasing by 10% the salaries below 30 thousand and decreasing by 5% those above 30 thousand.

Exercise 4.10 Define on the EMPLOYEE table the constraint that the 'Administration' department has fewer than 100 employees, with an average salary higher than 40 thousand.

Exercise 4.11 Define at schema level the constraint that the maximum salary of the employees of departments based in London is less than the salary of all the employees in the Directors department.

Exercise 4.12 Define a view that shows for each department the average value of the salaries higher than the average.

Exercise 4.13 Using the definition of a view, allow the user 'Fred' to access the contents of EMPLOYEE, excluding the Salary attribute.

Exercise 4.14 Describe the effect of the following instructions: which authorizations are present after each instruction? (Each row is preceded by the name of the person who issues the command.)

```
Stefano:   grant select on Table1 to Paolo, Riccardo
                                    with grant option
Paolo:     grant select on Table1 to Piero
Riccardo:  grant select on Table1 to Piero with grant option
Stefano:   revoke select on Table1 from Paolo cascade
Piero:     grant select on Table1 to Paolo
Stefano:   revoke select on Table1 from Riccardo cascade
```

Part II

Database design

5
Design techniques and models

In the preceding chapters we analyzed database models and languages, assuming in most cases the existence of the database with which the users were to interact. In this chapter, we will begin to deal with the issue of designing a database according to the users' requirements. Designing a database means defining its structure, characteristics and contents. As we might imagine, this is a process in which many delicate decisions must be taken. The use of the appropriate techniques is therefore essential for the creation of a high-quality product.

In this introductory chapter, we will begin to look at the problem of database design in general terms and suggest suitable methods for this job. In particular, in Section 5.1, we will give an overall picture of the background of information systems development and we will present a structured approach to the design process. In Section 5.2 we will illustrate the *Entity-Relationship* model, which provides the designer with a means for data representation, known as the *conceptual schema*, which is used during the first phase of database design. The design process is divided into three main phases: *conceptual design*, *logical design* and *physical design*. The first two will be presented in detail in the next two chapters. The third will be presented further on, in Section 9.7, once the technological concepts to which it refers have been introduced. This part of the book is completed with a chapter on *normalization*, an important technique for the analysis of database schemas.

5.1 The database design process

5.1.1 The life cycle of information systems

Database design is just one of the many activities in the development of an information system within an organization. It should therefore be presented within the wider context of the information system life cycle.

As shown in Figure 5.1, the life cycle of an information system generally consists of the following activities.

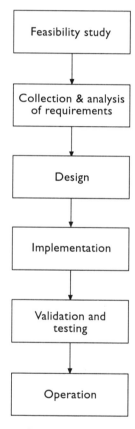

Figure 5.1 Life cycle of an information system.

- Feasibility study. This serves to define, as precisely as possible, the costs of the various possible solutions and to establish the priorities for the creation of the various components of the system.

- Collection and analysis of requirements. This consists of the definition and study of the properties and functionality of the information system. It requires interaction with the users in order to capture the application requirements; it produces a complete (informal) description of the data involved and of the operations to be carried out on it. The hardware and software requirements of the information system are also established.

- Design. This is generally divided into two tasks: *database design* and *operational design*. In the first, the necessary structure and organization of the data are established, and in the second, the characteristics of the application programs are defined. The two steps are complementary and can take place either simultaneously or consecutively. The descriptions of data and programs produced during this activity are formal and refer to specific models.

- Implementation. This consists of the creation of the information system according to the structure and the characteristics defined in the design activity. The database is constructed and populated and the programs are coded.

- Validation and testing. This is to check the correct functioning and quality of the information system. The tests should encompass, as far as possible, all possible operating conditions.

- Operation. This is the activity in which the information system becomes live, and, it is hoped, performs the tasks for which it was originally designed. Assuming there are no major errors to be repaired or changes to the functionality required, this activity requires only management and maintenance operations.

It should be stressed that the process is rarely strictly sequential, given that during one of the activities above it is often necessary to reconsider decisions made during an earlier one, thus forming a 'cycle'. Moreover, sometimes another activity is added, called *prototyping*, which consists of the use of specific software tools for the rapid creation of a simplified version of the information system, with which to test its functionality. The prototype can be shown to the users in order to verify that the high-level requirements of the information system were correctly collected and modelled. This activity is often the basis for the modification of the requirements and possibly the revision of the project.

The database constitutes only one of the components of an information system, which also includes application programs, user interfaces and other service programs. However, the central role that the data itself plays in an information system more than justifies an independent study of database design. For this reason, we deal with only those aspects of information system development that are closely of databases, focusing on data design and on the related activities of collection and analysis of the requirements. This process is in keeping with the *data-driven* approach to information system development, in which attention is concentrated on the data and its properties. With this approach, the database is designed first, followed by the applications that use it.

5.1.2 Methodologies for database design

In this part of the book, we follow a structured approach to database design that can be regarded as a 'design methodology'; as such, it is presented by means of:

- a *decomposition* of the entire design activity in successive steps, independent one from the other;

- a series of *strategies* to be followed in the various steps and some *criteria* from which to choose in the case of there being options;

- some *reference models* to describe the inputs and outputs of the various phases.

The properties that such a methodology must guarantee are principally:

- *generality* with regard to the application and the systems in play (and thus the possibility of use that is independent of the specific application and of the available systems);

- the *product quality* in terms of accuracy, completeness and efficiency;

- the *ease of use* both of the strategies and of the reference models.

Within the field of databases, a design methodology has been consolidated over the years, which satisfies all the properties described. This methodology is divided into three phases to be followed consecutively (see Figure 5.2). It is based on a simple but highly efficient engineering principle: that of cleanly separating the decisions relating to 'what' to represent in the database (first phase), from those relating to 'how' to do it (second and third phases).

- Conceptual design. The purpose of this is to represent the informal requirements of an application in terms of a formal and complete description, but independent of the criteria for representation used in database management systems. The product of this phase is called the *conceptual schema* and refers to a *conceptual data model*. As we mentioned in Section 1.3, conceptual models allow the description of the organization of data at a high level of abstraction, without taking into account the implementation aspects. In this phase, the designer must try to represent the *information content* of the database, without considering either the means by which this information will be implemented in the actual system, or the efficiency of the programs that make use of this information.

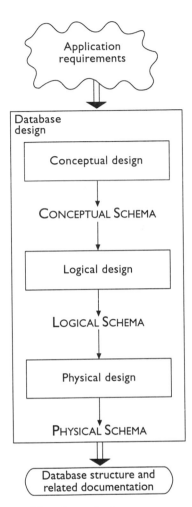

Figure 5.2 The phases of database design.

- Logical design. This consists of the translation of the conceptual schema defined in the preceding phase, into the data model adopted by the database management system available. The product of this phase is called the *logical schema* of the database and refers to a *logical data model*. As we have noted, a logical model represents data in a way that is still independent of the physical details, although the DBMS used for the implementation must be one that supports that data model. In this phase, the designer must also take into account some optimization criteria, based on the operations to be carried out on the data. Formal techniques for verification of the quality of the logical schema are often used. In the case of the relational data model, the most commonly used technique is that of *normalization*.

- Physical design. In this phase, the logical schema is completed with the details of the physical implementation (file organization and indexes) on a given DBMS. The product of this phase is called the *physical schema*, and refers to a *physical data model*. This model depends on the specific database management system chosen and takes into account the criteria for the physical organization of the data in that system.

Let us now look at how the application requirements are used in the various phases of design. We can distinguish between *data requirements*, concerning the content of the database, and *operational requirements*, concerning the use of the database by users or programs. In conceptual design, data requirements provide most of the information, whereas operational requirements are used only to verify that the conceptual schema is complete. (That is, it contains the information necessary to carry out all the operations that will be needed.) In logical design, on the other hand, the conceptual schema, given as input, summarizes the data requirements; whereas the operational requirements, together with the predicted application load, are used to obtain a logical schema, which allows for the efficient execution of such operations. Finally, in the physical design, the logical schema and the operational requirements are used to optimize the performance of the information system. In this phase, it is necessary to take into account the characteristics of the particular DBMS used.

The result of the design process of a database is not only the physical schema, but also the conceptual schema and the logical schema. The conceptual schema provides a high-level representation of the database, which can be very useful for documentation purposes. The logical schema provides a description of the contents of the database that, leaving aside the implementation aspects, is useful as a reference for writing queries and updates.

In Figure 5.3, we show the products of the various phases in the case of the design of a relational database based on the use of the best-known conceptual data model, the Entity-Relationship model. An Entity-Relationship schema can be represented by a diagram, which shows the database at conceptual level. This representation is then translated into a relational schema, made up of a collection of tables. Finally, the data is described from a physical point of view (type and size of the fields), and auxiliary structures, such as indexes, are specified for efficient access to data.

In the next chapters we will examine in detail the various activities of database design described in Figure 5.2 and with reference to the models used in Figure 5.3. Before we begin, we will present, in Section 5.2, the Entity-Relationship model, which is recognized as the standard conceptual data model for database design. Conceptual design, which we will discuss in the next chapter, is based on this model. During logical design we will use the relational data model, which, as we have seen in earlier chapters, is the most widely used by current DBMSs.

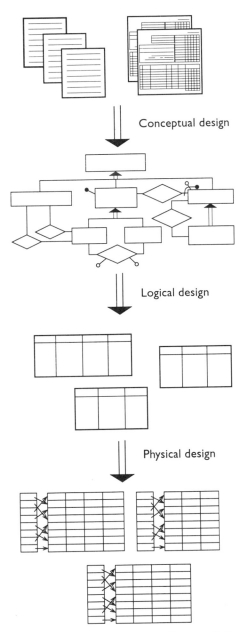

Figure 5.3 The products of the various phases of the design of a relational
database with the Entity-Relationship model.

5.2 The Entity-Relationship model

The Entity-Relationship (E-R) model is a *conceptual* data model, and as such
provides a series of *constructs* capable of describing the data requirements of
an application in a way that is easy to understand and is independent of the
criteria for the management and organization of data on the system. These

constructs are used to define schemas, which describe the organization and dictate which the legal *occurrences*[1] of data are, that is, the actual values that the database could hold at different times.

In the table in Figure 5.4 all the constructs that the E-R model provides are listed: note that, for every construct, there is a corresponding graphical

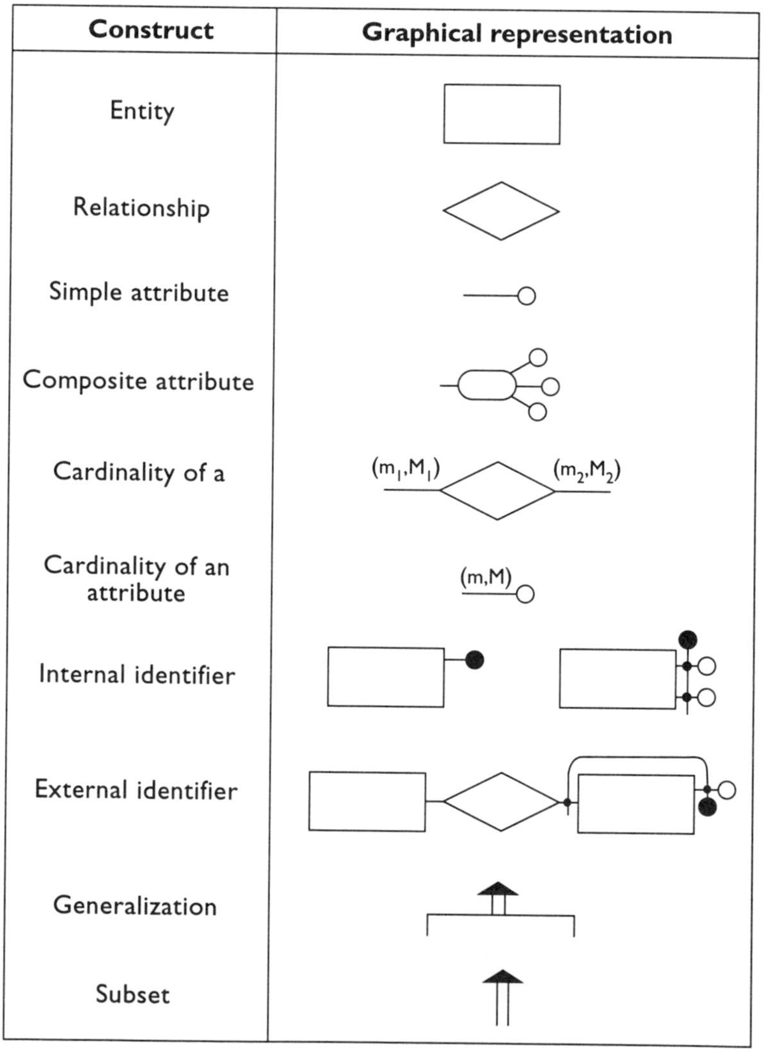

Construct	Graphical representation
Entity	
Relationship	
Simple attribute	
Composite attribute	
Cardinality of a	(m_1,M_1) (m_2,M_2)
Cardinality of an attribute	(m,M)
Internal identifier	
External identifier	
Generalization	
Subset	

Figure 5.4 The constructs of the E-R model and their graphical representation.

---

1. The term *instance* is generally used rather than *occurrence*, but we have preferred to use occurrence here in order to avoid confusion with the concept of instance (set of tuples) used in the relational model.

representation. As we shall see, this representation allows us to define an E-R schema diagrammatically.

5.2.1 The basic constructs of the model

We will begin by analyzing the main constructs of this model: the entities, the relationships and the attributes.

Entities These represent classes of objects (facts, things, people, for example) that have properties in common and an autonomous existence: CITY, DEPARTMENT, EMPLOYEE, PURCHASE and SALE are examples of entities in an application for a commercial organization. An occurrence of an entity is an object of the class that the entity represents. The cities of Stockholm, Helsinki, and Oslo are examples of occurrences of the entity CITY, and the employees Petersen and Johanssen are examples of occurrences of the EMPLOYEE entity. Note that an occurrence of an entity is not a value that identifies an object (for example, the surname of the employee or a social security number) but it is the object itself (the employee 'in the flesh'). An interesting consequence of this fact is that an occurrence of an entity has an existence (and an identity) independent of the properties associated with it. (In the case of an employee, the employee exists regardless of having a name, a surname, an age, etc.) In this respect, the E-R model shows a marked difference from the relational model in which, as we saw in Chapter 2, it is not possible to represent an object without knowing its properties. (An employee is represented by a tuple containing the name, surname, age, and other attributes.)

In a schema, every entity has a unique name and is graphically represented by means of a box containing the entity name. Figure 5.5 shows some entities.

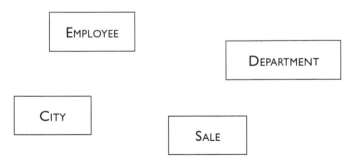

Figure 5.5 Examples of entity of the E-R model.

Relationships These represent logical links between two or more entities. RESIDENCE is an example of a relationship that can exist between the entities CITY and EMPLOYEE, whereas EXAM is example of a relationship that can exist between the entities STUDENT and COURSE. An occurrence of a relationship is an *n*-tuple (a pair in the most frequent case of the binary relationship) made up of occurrences of entities, one for each of the entities involved. The pair of objects made up of the employee named Johanssen and the city named Stockholm, or the pair of objects made from the employee named Petersen and the city named Oslo, are examples of occurrences in the relationship RESIDENCE. Examples of occurrences of the relationship EXAM between the entities STUDENT and COURSE are the pairs e_1, e_2, e_3, e_4, e_5 and e_6 shown in Figure 5.6, in which the occurrences of the entities involved are also shown.

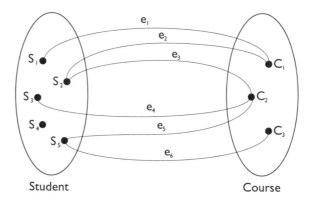

Figure 5.6 Example of occurrences of the EXAM relationship.

In an E-R schema, each relationship has a unique name and is graphically represented by means of a diamond, containing the name of the relationship, and by lines that connect the diamond with each component entity of the relationship. Figure 5.7 shows examples of schemas with relationships between entities. Note that there can be different relationships between the same entities, such as the relationships WORKPLACE and RESIDENCE between the entities EMPLOYEE and CITY. In the choice of names of relationships it is preferable to use nouns rather than verbs, so as not to imply or suggest a 'direction' in the relationship. For example, WORKPLACE is preferable to WORKSIN.

A very important aspect of relationships is that the set of occurrences of a relationship is, to all intents and purposes, a mathematical relation between the occurrences of the involved entities, as shown by Figure 5.6. A mathematical relation on two sets of entities is a subset of their cartesian product. This means that no n-tuples can be repeated among the occurrences of a relationship of the E-R model. This aspect has important consequences: for example, the relationship EXAM in Figure 5.7 does not have the capacity to report the fact that a certain student has taken the same exam more than once (because this would produce identical pairs). In this case, the exam should be represented by an entity on its own, linked to the entities STUDENT and COURSE by means of two binary relationships.

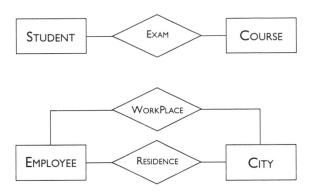

Figure 5.7 Examples of relationships in the E-R model.

Recursive relationships are also possible, that is, relationships between an entity and itself. For example, in Figure 5.8, the recursive relationship COLLEAGUE on the entity EMPLOYEE connects pairs of people who work together, while the relationship SUCCESSION on the entity SOVEREIGN allocates the next in line to each sovereign of a dynasty. Note that, unlike the first relationship, the relationship SUCCESSION is not symmetrical. In this case it is necessary to indicate the two roles that the entity involved plays in the relationship. This can be achieved by associating identifiers with the lines emanating from the recursive relationship (in this case, Successor and Predecessor).

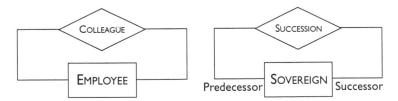

Figure 5.8 Examples of recursive relationships in the E-R model.

Finally, we can have relationships that involve more than two entities. An example is shown in Figure 5.9: an occurrence of the relationship SUPPLY describes the fact that a given supplier supplies a certain product to a department.

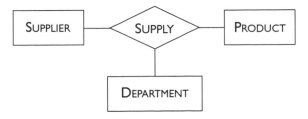

Figure 5.9 Example of a ternary relationship in the E-R model.

A possible set of occurrences of this relationship could establish that the firm Acme supplies printers to the sales department and calculators to the research department, while the firm Nakio supplies photocopiers to the sales department. A graphical representation of the possible occurrences of the SUPPLY relationship is shown in Figure 5.10 (triples s_1, s_2, s_3, and s_4). In the diagram, the occurrences of the entities involved are also shown.

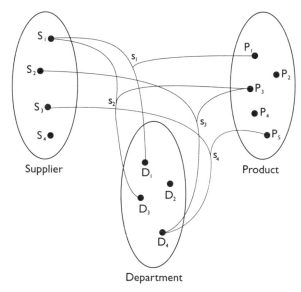

Figure 5.10 Example of occurrences of the SUPPLY relationship.

Attributes These describe the elementary properties of entities or relationships. For example, Surname, Salary and Age are possible attributes of the EMPLOYEE entity, while Date and Mark are possible attributes for the relationship EXAM between STUDENT and COURSE. An attribute associates with each occurrence of an entity (or relationship) a value belonging to a set known as the *domain of the attribute*. The domain contains the admissible values for the attribute. For example, the attribute Surname of the entity EMPLOYEE can have any 20-character string as a domain, while the Age attribute can have as a domain the integers between 18 and 65. Figure 5.11 shows how the attributes are represented graphically. Domains are not shown, as they are usually described in the associated documentation.

It can sometimes be convenient to group attributes of the same entity or relationship that have closely connected meanings or uses. The set of attributes obtained in this manner is called a *composite attribute*. We can, for example, group together the attributes Street, HouseNumber and PostCode in the PERSON entity to form the composite attribute Address. A graphical representation of a composite attribute is shown in Figure 5.12. Composite attributes can be very useful in practice as a means for summarizing several

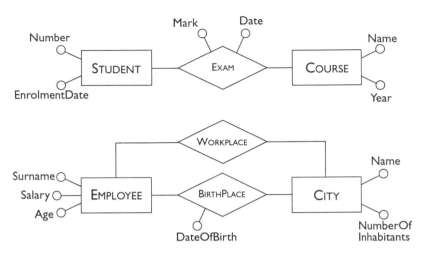

Figure 5.11 E-R schemas with relationships, entities and attributes.

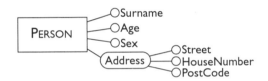

Figure 5.12 An example of an entity with a composite attribute.

related attributes, for example, all clinical exams of a patient, omitting their detailed description.

Schemas with basic constructs   The three constructs of the E-R model seen up to now already allow us to define schemas of a certain level of complexity. Consider for example the E-R schema shown in Figure 5.13. It represents some information concerning a firm with several branches. Beginning with the entity BRANCH and continuing in an anti-clockwise direction, we can see that each branch of the firm is situated in a city and has an individual address (attributes **City** and **Address**). A branch is organized into departments (COMPOSITION relationship), and each department has a name and a telephone number (DEPARTMENT entity and related attributes). The employees of the company belong to these departments, starting on a particular date (MEMBERSHIP relationship and **StartDate** attribute) and some employees manage such departments (MANAGEMENT relationship). For each employee, the surname, salary and age and an identification code are shown (EMPLOYEE entity and related attributes). The employees work on projects beginning on a certain date (PARTICIPATION relationship and **StartDate** attribute). Each project has a name, a budget and a release date (PROJECT entity and related attributes).

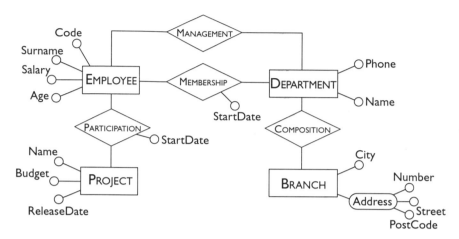

Figure 5.13 An Entity-Relationship schema.

5.2.2 Other constructs of the model

Let us now examine the remaining constructs of the E-R model: the *cardinality* of relationships and attributes, the *identifiers* and the *generalizations*. As we shall see, only the last is a 'new' construct. The others constitute *integrity constraints* on constructs we have already seen, that is, properties that must be satisfied by the occurrences of entities and relationships in order to be considered 'valid'.

Cardinality of relationships These are specified for each entity participating in a relationship and describe the maximum and minimum number of relationship occurrences in which an entity occurrence can participate. They state therefore, how many times in a relationship between entities an occurrence of one of these entities can be linked to occurrences of the other entities involved. For example, suppose that in a relationship ASSIGNMENT between the entities EMPLOYEE and TASK we specify for the first entity a minimum cardinality equal to one and a maximum cardinality equal to five. This means that we wish to indicate that an employee can participate in a minimum of one and a maximum of five occurrences of the ASSIGNMENT relationship. In other words, we wish to say that, in our application, at least one task must be assigned to an employee, but not more than five may be. Again, suppose that for the TASK entity we specify a minimum cardinality equal to zero and a maximum cardinality equal to 50. In this case we only impose the constraint that a task can appear in a maximum of 50 occurrences of the ASSIGNMENT relationship. Thus, a certain task could be assigned to no employees or to a number of employees less than or equal to 50. In an E-R schema, the minimum and maximum cardinalities of the participation of entities in relationships is specified in brackets, as shown in Figure 5.14.

In principle, it is possible to assign any non-negative integer to the cardinality of a relationship with the only constraint that the minimum cardinality must be less than or equal to the maximum cardinality. In most

Figure 5.14 Cardinality of a relationship in the E-R model.

cases, however, it is sufficient to use only three values: zero, one and the symbol 'N' (which is called 'many' and indicates generically an integer greater than one). In particular:

- for the minimum cardinality, zero or one; in the first case we say that the participation in the relationship is *optional*, in the second we say that the participation is *mandatory*;

- for the maximum cardinality, one or many (N); in the first case each occurrence of the entity is associated at most with a single occurrence of the relationship, while in the second case each occurrence of the entity is associated with an arbitrary number of occurrences of the relationship[2].

Let us reconsider Figure 5.6; it shows that the STUDENT entity participates in the EXAM relationship with a cardinality equal to (0,N). This means that there are students who do not participate in any occurrence of the relationship (student S_4), and others who participate in more than one occurrence of the relationship (for example, student S_2 who participates in e_2 and e_3).

In Figure 5.15, various cases of cardinality for relationships are shown. For example, the cardinality of the relationship RESIDENCE tells us that each person can be resident in one city and one only, while each city can have no resident, or many of them.

By observing the maximum cardinalities, it is possible to classify the binary relationships based on the type of correspondence that is established among the occurrences of the involved entities. The relationships having a maximum cardinality equal to one for both the entities involved, such as the SALE relationship in Figure 5.15, define a one-to-one correspondence between such entities and are therefore called *one-to-one relationships*. Similarly, relationships between an entity with maximum cardinality equal to one and another with maximum cardinality equal to N, such as the relationship RESIDENCE in Figure 5.15, are called *one-to-many relationships*. Finally, relationships having a maximum cardinality equal to N for both the entities involved, such as the relationship RESERVATION in Figure 5.15, are called *many-to-many relationships*.

---

2. In the case of a binary relationship, the participation of the entity with maximum cardinality set to one can be seen as a function (partial if the minimum cardinality is equal to zero) that associates with an occurrence of the entity a single occurrence (or none) of the other entity involved in the relationship.

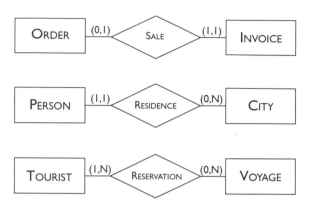

Figure 5.15 Examples of cardinality of relationships.

For minimum cardinality, on the other hand, note that the case of mandatory participation for all the entities involved is rare. This is because, when a new entity occurrence is added, very often the corresponding occurrences of the other entities linked to it are not yet known or even do not exist. For example, consider the first schema in Figure 5.15. When a new order is received, there exists as yet no invoice relating to it and therefore it is not possible to construct an occurrence for the SALE relationship that contains the new order.

In n-ary relationships, the entities involved almost always have a maximum cardinality that is equal to N. An example is provided by the ternary relationship SUPPLY in Figure 5.9: as we can see in Figure 5.10, there are examples of occurrences of each of the entities involved (S_1, P_3 and D_4) that appear in many occurrences of this relationship. When an entity is involved in an n-ary relationship with a maximum cardinality equal to one, it means that one of its occurrences can be linked to a single occurrence of the relationship, and thus to a single n-tuple of occurrences of the other entities involved in the relationship. This means that it is possible (and at times can seem more natural) to replace the n-ary relationship with n binary one-to-many relationships that link such an entity with the others. We will return to this subject in Chapter 8, which deals with normalization, where we give more precise criteria for analysis.

Cardinality of attributes   These can be specified for the attributes of entities (or relationships) and describe the minimum and maximum number of values of the attribute associated with each occurrence of an entity or a relationship. In most cases, the cardinality of an attribute is equal to $(1,1)$ and is omitted. In these cases, the attribute represents a function that associates a single value with each entity occurrence. The value of a certain attribute however can be null (under the same conditions as those introduced in Section 2.1.5 for the relation model), or there can exist various values of a certain attribute associated with an entity occurrence. These situations can be represented by allocating to the attribute a minimum cardinality equal to zero in the first case, and a cardinality equal to many (N) in the second. Figure 5.16 shows an example of an entity whose attributes have cardinality. Due to cardinalities, we know that a person has one and only one surname, can have a driving license (but if he or she has one, it is unique) and can have several cars, but also none.

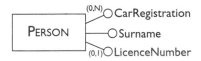

Figure 5.16 Example of entity attributes with cardinality.

In a similar way to the participation of entity occurrences to relationships, we say that an attribute with a minimum cardinality equal to zero is *optional* for the related entity (or relationship), while it is *mandatory* if the minimum cardinality is equal to one. Also, we say that an attribute is *multivalued* if its maximum cardinality is equal to N. As we discussed in Chapter 2, it can happen in many situations that certain information is not available, and therefore optional attributes are quite common. Multivalued attributes, on the other hand, should be used with great caution, because they represent situations that can be modelled, sometimes, with additional entities linked by one-to-many (or many-to-many) relationships to the entity to which they refer. To give an example, assume we have a multivalued attribute Qualifications for the PERSON entity in Figure 5.16, because a person can have many qualifications. The qualification is, however, a concept shared by many people: it can therefore be natural to model it with an entity QUALIFICATION linked to the PERSON entity by a many-to-many relationship. We will, however, leave this discussion until Section 6.2, in which we will give criteria for the choice of E-R construct most appropriate for the representation of a 'real-world' concept.

Identifiers   These are specified for each entity of a schema and describe the concepts (attributes and/or entities) of the schema that allow the unambiguous identification of the entity occurrences. In many cases, an identifier is formed by one or more attributes of the entity itself: in this case we talk about an *internal* identifier (also known as a *key*). For example, an internal identifier for the entity AUTOMOBILE with attributes Model, Registration, and Colour, will be the attribute Registration, assuming that there cannot exist two cars with the same registration number. In the same way, an internal identifier for the PERSON entity with attributes FirstName, Surname, Address, and DateOfBirth can be the set of the attributes FirstName, Surname and DateOfBirth. This assumes, of course, that in our application there are no two people sharing the same first name, surname and date of birth. In Figure 5.17 the symbols used to represent the internal identifiers in an E-R schema are shown. Note the different notation used to indicate internal identifiers made up of a single attribute and identifiers made up of several attributes.

Figure 5.17 Examples of internal and external identifiers.

Sometimes, however, the attributes of an entity are not sufficient to identify its occurrences unambiguously. Consider, for example, the entity STUDENT in Figure 5.18. At first glance, it can seem that the attribute Registration can be an identifier for such an entity, but this is not the case. The schema, in fact, describes students enrolled in various universities, and two students enrolled in different universities could have the same registration number. In this case, in order to identify a student unambiguously, we need the relevant university, as well as the registration number. Thus, a correct identifier for the STUDENT entity in this schema is made up of the attribute Registration and of the UNIVERSITY entity. This is called an *external* identifier. It should be observed that this identification is made possible by the mandatory one-to-many relationship between the entities UNIVERSITY and STUDENT, which associates every student with a single university. Thus, an entity E can be identified by other entities only if each such entity is involved in a relationship in which E participates with cardinality (1,1). The diagrammatic representation of an external identifier is shown in Figure 5.18.

Figure 5.18 Example of an external entity identifier.

Based on what we have said on the subject of identifiers, we can make some general observations:

- an identifier can involve one or more attributes, provided that each of them has (1,1) cardinality;

- an external identifier can involve one or more entities, provided that each of them is member of a relationship to which the entity to identify participates with cardinality equal to (1,1);

- an external identifier can involve an entity that is in its turn identified externally, as long as cycles are not generated;

- each entity must have one (internal or external) identifier, but can have more than one. Actually, if there is more than one identifier, then the attributes and entities involved in an identification can be optional (minimum cardinality equal to o).

At this point we can re-examine the schema shown in Figure 5.13, introducing cardinality and identifiers. The resulting schema is shown in Figure 5.19.

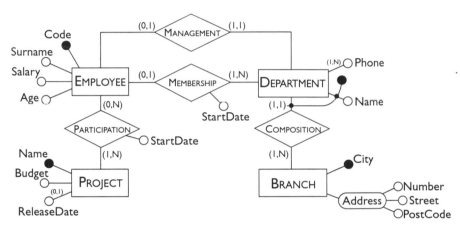

Figure 5.19 The schema shown in Figure 5.13 completed by identifiers and cardinality.

We can observe that the name of a city identifies a branch of the company. This means that there is only one branch in a city. A department, on the other hand, is identified by the name and by the branch of which it is part. (We can deduce from the cardinality that a branch has many departments but every department belongs to a single branch.) A department has at least one telephone number, but can have more than one. An employee (identified by a code) can belong to a single department (but it can happen that he or she belongs to no department, for example if new to the company) and can manage zero or one department. Further, each department has a sole manager, and one or more employees. Many employees (but at least one) work on each project (identified unambiguously by their names) and each employee works in general on many projects (but it is also possible that they work on no projects). Finally, the release date of a project need not be fixed.

Generalizations These represent logical links between an entity E, known as *parent* entity, and one or more entities $E_1, \ldots, E_n$, called *child* entities, of which E is more general, in the sense that it comprises them as a particular case. In this situation we say that E is a *generalization* of $E_1, \ldots, E_n$ and that the entities $E_1, \ldots, E_n$ are *specializations* of the E entity. For example, PERSON is a generalization of MAN and WOMAN, while PROFESSIONAL is a generalization of ENGINEER, DOCTOR and LAWYER. Conversely, MAN and WOMAN are specializations of PERSON.

Among the entities involved in a generalization the following properties are valid.

- Every occurrence of a child entity is also an occurrence of the parent entity. For example, an occurrence of LAWYER is also an occurrence of PROFESSIONAL.

- Every property of the parent entity (attributes, identifiers, relationships and other generalizations) is also a property of a child entity. For example, if the PERSON entity has attributes Surname and Age, then the entities MAN and WOMAN also possess these attributes. Furthermore, the identifier of PERSON is also a valid identifier for the entities MAN and WOMAN. This property of generalizations is known as *inheritance*.

Generalizations are represented graphically by means of arrows that join the child entities with the parent entity as shown in the examples in Figure 5.20. Observe that, for the child entities, the inherited properties are not explicitly represented.

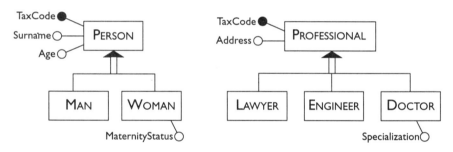

Figure 5.20 Examples of generalizations among entities.

Generalizations can be classified on the basis of two orthogonal properties:

- a generalization is *total* if every occurrence of the parent entity is also an occurrence of one of the child entities, otherwise it is *partial*;

- a generalization is *exclusive* if every occurrence of the parent entity is at most an occurrence of one of the child entities, otherwise it is *overlapping*.

The generalization, PERSON, of MAN and WOMAN in Figure 5.20 is, for example, total (the men and the women constitute 'all' the people) and exclusive (a person is either a man or a woman). The generalization, VEHICLE, of AUTOMOBILE and BICYCLE, is, on the other hand, partial and exclusive, because there are other types of vehicles (for example, motor bikes) that are neither cars nor bicycles. Finally, the generalization PERSON of STUDENT and EMPLOYEE is partial and overlapping, because there are students who are also employed.

This last example suggests that in reality, overlapping generalizations can be easily transformed into exclusive generalizations by adding one or more child entities, to represent the concepts that constitute the 'intersections' of the entities that overlap. In the case of students and employees, it is sufficient to add the entity EMPLOYEDSTUDENT in order to obtain an exclusive generalization. Thus, we assume from here on, without significant loss of generality, that generalizations are always exclusive.

Total generalizations are usually represented by drawing the arrow with a solid line (see the example in Figure 5.21).

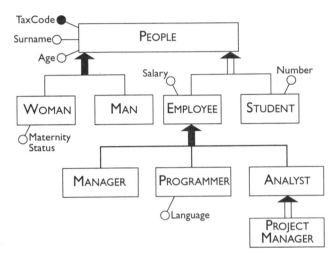

Figure 5.21 Hierarchy of generalizations between entities.

In general, an entity can be involved in many different generalizations. There can also be generalizations on more than one level: this is known as a generalization *hierarchy*. Finally, a generalization can have a single child entity: this is known as a *subset*. In Figure 5.21 a generalization hierarchy is shown. The relation that exists between the entities PROJECT MANAGER and ANALYST is an example of a subset.

5.2.3 Final overview of the E-R model

We have seen how the Entity-Relationship model provides the designers with some constructs for describing the data involved in an application, associated with a graphical representation that is easy to understand.

All the constructs of the E-R model are illustrated in the schema in Figure 5.22, which at the same time provides an example of an E-R schema and a simplified description of the E-R model itself. Let us now analyze this schema and consider this exploration as an exercise of 'reading an E-R schema'; this is an activity that we need to practice, as it is one that occurs frequently in the analysis and maintenance of existing information systems.

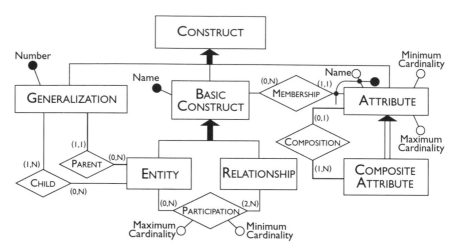

Figure 5.22 Description of the E-R model using the E-R model.

We can see that the model is made up of a series of constructs of which two are considered 'basic': the entity and the relationship. An entity can participate in zero or more relationships, whereas a relationship involves two or more entities. The participation of an entity in a relationship has a minimum and a maximum cardinality. The other constructs of the model are attributes and generalizations. An attribute has a name and a minimum and maximum cardinality, and belongs to a basic concept, that is, to an entity or a relationship. Due to the generalization, the relationship MEMBERSHIP is inherited by the children of the entity BASICCONSTRUCT. Composite attributes are a specialization of attributes and are made up of one or more attributes. According to the cardinalities, a generalization has exactly one parent entity and one (in the case of subsets) or more child entities. An entity can be parent or child of many generalizations (and also of none). Finally, note that a basic construct is identified unambiguously by its name (in fact, it is essential in a schema to avoid using the same name for different entities or relationships). Two attributes can have the same name if they belong to different relationships or entities as described by the external identification. (See for example the attribute Name in Figure 5.19.) Generalizations do not usually have a name and to identify them we assume that they are numbered.

There exist, finally, other constraints on the use of constructs that cannot be expressed in the schema. For example, a hierarchy of generalizations cannot contain cycles. Also, a minimum cardinality must be less than or equal to the related maximum cardinality. The problem of documentation of constraints that can not be expressed in the E-R model will be discussed more fully in the next section.

We will conclude the section with a consideration of a general nature. E-R schemas provide an abstract representation of the data involved in an application, and therefore they can be used for purposes other than database design. There are various examples of the possible use of conceptual schemas apart from design.

- E-R schemas can be used for documentation purposes, as non-specialists easily understand them.

- They can be used to describe the data of an information system already in existence (for example, to integrate it with other databases). In the case of a system made up of heterogeneous subsystems, there is the advantage that the E-R schema can represent the various components with an abstract language, which is therefore unifying.

- In the case of modification of the requirements of an application, E-R schemas can be used to understand which portion of the system must be changed and what modifications are to be carried out.

5.3 Documentation of E-R schemas

We have seen how the Entity-Relationship model provides highly expressive modelling tools that allow the easy and efficient description of very complex situations. An E-R schema, however, is rarely sufficient by itself to represent all the aspects of an application in detail. Firstly, in an E-R schema, only the names of the various concepts appear, and this can be insufficient to explain their meaning. If we look again at the example given in Figure 5.19, it might not be clear if the PROJECT entity refers to projects internal to the company or to external projects, in which the company is taking part.

Moreover, when a schema is particularly complex, it might not always be possible to represent all the properties of the various concepts, in a way that is comprehensible. With reference to the example in Figure 5.19, it would, for instance, be difficult to represent other attributes for EMPLOYEE, without reducing the readability of the schema. In general, representing large schemas graphically requires a certain ability in devising a readable layout; this is further discussed in Section 6.4.

Other limitations concern the expressive power of the E-R model. It is actually impossible in certain cases to represent some properties of data by means of the constructs that the E-R model provides. Look again at the example in Figure 5.19 and suppose that in our company an employee can be manager only of the department to which he belongs. This property cannot be directly expressed in the schema because it refers to two independent concepts (management and membership) described by two relationships, and there are no constructs in the model that allow the correlation of two relationships. Another example of properties that cannot be directly expressed by the constructs of the E-R model is the fact that an employee cannot have a salary higher than the manager of his or her department. Both the above properties correspond to integrity constraints on the data. In fact, while the E-R model is sufficiently expressive to represent data, it does not provide suitable means for the representation of complex constraints on data.

Thus, it is indispensable to provide every E-R schema with support documentation, which can facilitate the interpretation of the schema itself and describe properties of the data that cannot be expressed directly by the constructs of the model. In the next sections we will therefore describe structures and techniques for the documentation of an E-R schema. The concepts introduced should not be taken as new representation constructs, but simply as tools suitable for completion and enrichment of the description of the data in an application created using a conceptual model. They should therefore be considered as a support for the conceptual analysis and cannot be a substitute for it.

5.3.1 Business rules

Business rules are one of the tools used by information systems analysts to describe the properties of an application that cannot be directly expressed with a conceptual model. As suggested by their name, they allow the specification of 'rules' of the particular application domain that we are considering. Returning to the example given above, the fact that an employee cannot earn more than his or her own manager is actually a rule of the business.

The term business rule is often used with a broader meaning by analysts, to indicate any information that defines or constrains some aspect of an application. In particular a business rule can be:

1. the *description of a concept* relevant to the application, or rather the precise definition of an entity, an attribute or a relationship of the E-R model;

2. an *integrity constraint* on the data of the application, whether it be the documentation of a constraint expressed by means of some construct of the E-R model (for example, the cardinality of a relationship) or the description of a constraint that is not directly expressible using the constructs of the model;

3. a *derivation*, or rather a concept that can be obtained, by means of an inference or an arithmetical calculation, by other concepts of the schema (for example an attribute Cost whose value can be obtained from the sum of the attributes Net and Taxes).

For rules of the first type, it is clearly impossible to define a precise syntax, and in general, we have to use sentences in natural language. As we will describe in the following section, these rules are typically represented in the form of glossaries, grouping the descriptions as appropriate (for example, by entity, or by relationship).

The rules that describe integrity constraints and derivations, on the other hand, lend themselves more to formal definitions and rather complex syntax has been proposed for expressing them. Given, however, that there are no standards and that every formalization runs the risk of not being sufficiently expressive, we will continue to use definitions in natural language, taking care, however, to structure such definitions in the appropriate manner.

In particular, integrity constraints can always be expressed in the form of *assertions*, that is, statements that must always be satisfied in our database. For reasons of clarity and ease of creation, such statements must be 'atomic'. That is, they cannot be decomposed into phrases that constitute assertions in themselves. Furthermore, since they are used to document an E-R schema, assertions should be stated in a declarative manner, which should not suggest ways to satisfy them, because such suggestion would give insights on the implementation, but this is not relevant to conceptual representation. For this reason, a notation of the type **if** *<condition>* **then** *<action>* is not suitable to express business rules, when they document an E-R schema. An appropriate structure to state business rules in the form of assertions could be the following:

<concept> **must/must not** *<expression on concepts>*

where the concepts cited can correspond either to concepts of the E-R schema to which it refers, or to concepts that can be derived from them. For example, returning to the example given for the schema in Figure 5.19, business rules that express integrity constraints are:

(BR1)   *the manager of a department* **must** *belong to that department;*

(BR2)   *an employee* **must not** *have a salary greater than that of the manager of the department to which he or she belongs;*

(BR3)   *a department of the Rome branch* **must** *be managed by an employee with more than 10 years' employment with the company.*

Note how concepts such as 'department manager' and 'employee with more than 10 years' employment with the company' are not represented directly on the schema, but can nonetheless be retrieved from it.

Let us now consider the business rules that describe derivations. These rules can be expressed by specifying the operations (arithmetical or otherwise) that allow us to obtain the derived concept. A possible structure is thus:

<concept> **is obtained by** *<operations on concepts>*

For example, if, in our example, the entity DEPARTMENT has an attribute NumberOfEmployees, there could be a rule of the type:

(BR4)   *the number of employees in a department* **is obtained by** *counting the employees who belong to it*

We have said that business rules constitute a form of documentation of a conceptual schema. When the conceptual schema is translated into a database (logical and physical phases of design), non-descriptive business rules (that is, those that express constraints or derivations) should be implemented in some way to guarantee the consistency of the data with respect to the properties that they represent. It is possible to follow different approaches:

- using SQL to define the logical schema of a database, by means of predefined and generic constraints or SQL-2 assertions (as described in Chapter 4);

- using triggers or active rules (as we will explain in Chapter 12);

- with appropriate SQL manipulation statements invoked from within a program.

5.3.2 Documentation techniques

We have said that an E-R schema should be supplied with support documentation, to facilitate the interpretation of the schema itself and to describe properties of the data that cannot be expressed directly by the constructs of the model. We have seen furthermore, that this documentation can be expressed in terms of business rules. Let us now see in which form it is possible to produce this documentation, referring to an example.

The documentation of the various concepts represented in a schema, that is, the business rules of the descriptive type, can be easily organized as a *data dictionary*. This is made up of two tables: the first describes the entities of the schema with their names, an informal definition in natural language, the list of all the attributes (with possible descriptions associated with them) and the possible identifiers. The other table describes the relationships with their names, an informal description, the list of attributes (with possible descriptions) and the list of the entities involved, together with their participation cardinalities. An example of a data dictionary for the schema in Figure 5.19 is shown in Figure 5.23. Note how the dictionary can also be used to document some constraints on the data and thus other forms of business rules. As we have already indicated, the use of the data dictionary is particularly important when the schema is complex and it is laborious to specify all the attributes of entity and relationship directly on the schema.

As regards the other business rules, we can resort to another table, which lists the various rules, organized by type. Such rules can be expressed in the forms suggested in the section above, if possible referring explicitly to the concepts of the schema. Remember that it is important to represent all the rules that describe constraints not expressed in the schema, but it can sometimes be useful also to represent rules that document constraints already expressed in the schema. An example of documentation of this type for the schema in Figure 5.19 is shown in Figure 5.24.

Entity	Description	Attributes	Identifier
EMPLOYEE	Employee working in the company.	Code, Surname, Salary, Age	Code
PROJECT	Company project on which employees are working.	Name, Budget, ReleaseDate	Name
DEPARTMENT	Department of a company branch.	Phone, Name	Name, BRANCH
BRANCH	Company branch in a particular city.	City, Address (Number, Street and PostCode)	City

Relationship	Description	Entities involved	Attributes
MANAGEMENT	Associates a manager with a department.	Employee (0,1) Department (1,1)	
MEMBERSHIP	Associates an employee with a department.	Employee (0,1) Department (1,N)	StartDate
PARTICIPATION	Associates employees with projects.	Employee (0,N) Project (1,N)	StartDate
COMPOSITION	Associates a department with a branch.	Department (1,1) Branch (1,N)	

Figure 5.23 The data dictionary for the schema in Figure 5.19.

Constraints
(BR1)   The manager of a department must belong to that department.
(BR2)   An employee must not have a salary greater than that of the manager of the department to which he or she belongs.
(BR3)   A department of the Rome branch must be managed by an employee with more than 10 years' employment with the company.
(BR4)   An employee who does not belong to a particular department must not participate in any project.
Derivations
(BR5)   The budget for a project is obtained by multiplying the sum of the salaries of the employees who are working on it by 3.

Figure 5.24 Business rules of the schema in Figure 5.19.

5.4 Bibliography

There are many texts on information system development and, more in general, on software engineering, among which we mention Davis [35], Fairly [39], Senn [74] and Pressman [68]. The organization of the database design process in four phases (conceptual, logical, and physical design, preceded by requirement analysis) was proposed by Lum et al. [57] as the result of a workshop held in 1978. A detailed treatment of conceptual and logical design is offered by Batini, Ceri and Navathe [7]. Additional readings on database design include Mannila and Raiha [59], Teorey and Fry [85], Teorey [84], and Wiederhold [92]. Most of these books also include a detailed description of a version of the Entity-Relationship model. The E-R model is usually attributed to Chen [23], who presented a simplified version compared to that presented in this chapter, systematizing concepts already discussed in the literature. Many extensions were later proposed, the most important of which are included in our treatment. The generalization construct was introduced by Smith and Smith [82]. Tsichritzis and Lochovski [87] and Hull and King [48] present and compare several data modelling features.

Business rules have been discussed in depth by Fleming and von Halle [41].

5.5 Exercises

Exercise 5.1 Consider the E-R schema in Figure 5.25: the schema represents various properties of men and women.

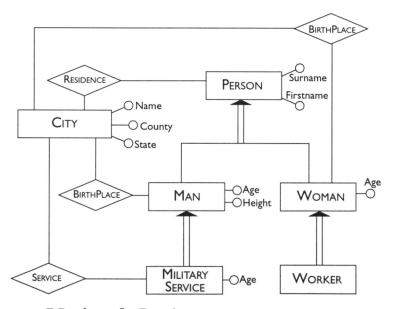

Figure 5.25 E-R schema for Exercise 5.1.

1. Correct the schema, taking into account the fundamental properties of the generalizations.

2. The schema represents only the female workers; modify the schema to represent all the workers, men and women.

3. Among the properties of cities, the **State** attribute can be seen also as an subproperty of the attribute **County**. Restructure the schema in this sense.

Exercise 5.2 Add the minimum and maximum cardinalities and the identifiers to the schema produced in Exercise 5.1. State whether there are integrity constraints on the schema that cannot be expressed by the Entity-Relationship model.

Exercise 5.3 Represent the following, using the constructs of the Entity-Relationship model.

1. In a zoological garden there are animals belonging to a species and having a certain age; each species is situated in a sector (having a name) of the zoo.

2. An automobile rental firm has a vehicle pool, in which each automobile has a registration number and a colour and belongs to one category; for each category, there is a rental tariff.

3. A company produces CDs with a code and a title; each CD has been recorded by one or more singers, each of whom has a name and an address and some of whom have a stage name.

Exercise 5.4 Complete the schemas produced in the exercise above with further information based on reasonable assumptions about each one.

Exercise 5.5 Show the following concepts, using, where appropriate, the generalization construct of the Entity-Relationship model. Indicate, in each case, the attributes of the various entities and the type of generalization, resolving the cases of overlapping.

1. The employees of a company are divided into managers, programmers, analysts, project leaders and secretaries. There are analysts who are also programmers. The project leader must be a manager. Each employee has a code, a name and a surname. Each category of employee has its own basic salary. Each employee, apart from the managers, has fixed working hours.

2. A French airline offers flights, each of which has a number that identifies the flight (for example Paris–Boston), a date (25 March 2000), a departure time (8:00) and an arrival time (12:00), a departure airport and a destination airport. There are national and international flights. The international flights can have one or more stopovers. For completed flights, information to be recorded is the actual time of departure and arrival (for example with reference to the flight given above, 8:05 and 12:07). For future flights, the number of seats available must be known.

3. An automobile company produces cars, motor cycles, lorries and tractors. The vehicles are identified by a chassis number and have a name (for example Punto), a cylinder capacity and a colour. The cars are sub-

divided according to size: compact (up to 2.5m in length) and family (over 2.5m); and according to engine capacity: small (up to 1200cc), medium (from 1200 to 2000cc) and large (over 2000cc). The motorcycles are divided into mopeds (cylinder capacity below 125cc) and roadsters (above 125cc). The lorries have a weight and can be articulated.

Exercise 5.6 Consider the Entity-Relationship schema in Figure 5.26. Describe in words the information it represents.

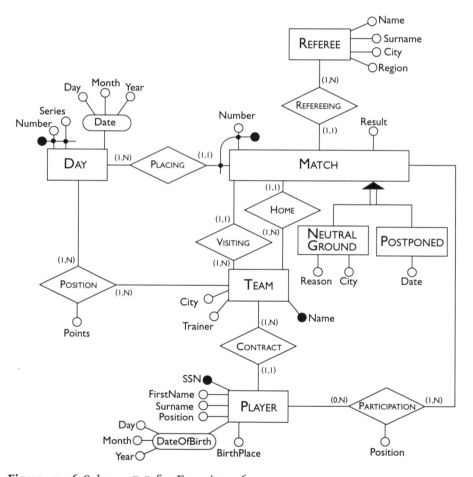

Figure 5.26 Schema E-R for Exercise 5.6.

Exercise 5.7 Translate into business rules the following properties of the data in the schema in Figure 5.26.

1. There can be no more than five players in a team who play in the same position.

2. A team earns 3 points if it wins, 1 if it draws, zero if it loses.

3. If a team plays a match at home, then it is the visiting team in the next match.

Produce the complete documentation for such a schema.

Exercise 5.8 Modify the Entity-Relationship schema in Figure 5.26 so as to describe also the past contracts between players and teams with the date of beginning and end of the contracts and the main position played by each player in each team. It is possible that a player can have different contracts with the same team in different periods. For current contracts we wish to know the date of commencement.

Exercise 5.9 In each of the following cases, reference is made to two or more entities defined in an Entity-Relationship schema and to a concept that involves them. Specify the schemas, defining the constructs (one or more relationships and, if necessary, further entities with the relative identifier) necessary to represent the concept, maintaining the entities indicated.

1. Entities: sport, country and surface. Concept: the fact that in one country a sport is practised on a certain surface (for example, tennis is played on grass in England and in Australia, on red shale in Italy and France, on Astroturf in the USA, Italy and France; soccer on grass in Italy, on grass and Astroturf in the USA, on grass in England).

2. Entities: scientist and department. Concept: the fact that the scientist has held seminars in the department. For every seminar, it is necessary to show the date, time and title, with the constraint that a scientist cannot hold more than one seminar in one day.

3. Entities: professional and company. Concept: the fact that the professional has been a consultant for the company. It is necessary to show the number of consulting sessions held by the professional for each company, with the total cost.

Exercise 5.10 Consider a ternary relationship involving the entities EMPLOYEE, PROJECT and CONSULTANT. Show in which of the following cases it is appropriate to substitute two or three binary relationships for such relationship. In the cases where it is possible, show how it is done.

1. Each employee is involved in zero or more projects and interacts with zero or more consultants. Each consultant is involved in zero or more projects and interacts with zero or more employees. Each project involves one or more employees and one or more consultants (who need not interact among themselves). An employee and a consultant collaborate in the field of a project if and only if they collaborate between themselves and are both involved in the project.

2. Each employee is involved in zero or more projects, in each of which they interact with one or more consultants (who can be different from project to project and who can in general be a subset of the consultants involved in the project). Each consultant is involved in zero or more projects in each of which he or she interacts with one or more employees (who can be different from project to project and who can in general be a subset of the employees involved in the projects). Each project involves one or more employee-consultant pairs.

3. Each employee is involved in zero or more projects. Each consultant is involved in zero or more projects. Each project involves one or more employees and one or more consultants. An employee and a consultant interact if and only if there is at least one project in which they are both involved.

6
Conceptual design

The conceptual design of a database consists of the construction of an Entity-Relationship schema, providing an optimal description of the user requirements. Even for simple applications, the schema can contain many concepts, correlated in a quite complex way. It follows that the construction of the final schema is, often, an incremental process. The conceptual schema is refined and enriched during a series of transformations and possibly corrections. In this chapter, we describe the strategies that can be followed during the development of a conceptual schema.

Before we begin to discuss these strategies, it is worth devoting some attention to the activity that precedes the actual design process itself: the collection and analysis of the requirements. This phase is not entirely separate from design, but often tends to overlap with it. The construction of an E-R schema begins well before the collection of requirements is completed and it can influence further collection activity.

The discussion of requirements collection and analysis is followed by a presentation of some general criteria for transforming informal requirements into Entity-Relationship constructs. We then move on to illustrate the most important design strategies and to analyze the qualities that a well-designed conceptual schema must possess. We close the chapter with a comprehensive method for conceptual design. To give a better explanation of the various aspects, we use a practical example, which refers to the design of an application for a training company.

6.1 Requirements collection and analysis

It must first be stated that the activities of requirements collection and analysis are difficult to standardize, because they depend greatly on the application. We will, however, discuss some practical rules that it is helpful to follow in this phase of the development of a database.

By *requirements collection* we mean the complete identification of the problems that the application must solve, and the features that should characterize such an application. By this, we mean both the static aspects (the data) and the dynamic aspects (the operations on the data). The requirements are first gathered into specifications that are generally expressed in natural language; therefore, they are often ambiguous and disorganized. The *requirements analysis* consists of the clarification and organization of the requirements specification. Obviously, we are dealing with activities that are closely related to one another: the task of analysis can begin as soon as the first requirements are known and can then proceed in step with the task of collection. Moreover, the need for further collection of requirements can be identified as the result of the analysis of previously obtained requirements. The requirements generally come from different sources, as follows.

- The *users of the application*. In this case, the information is acquired through interviews or by means of documents specifically written and exchanged for this purpose.

- All the *existing documentation* that has some connection with the problem: forms, internal rules, business procedures, laws and regulations, etc. In this case, gathering and selection are required. The user will usually help here, but the responsibility rests with the designer.

- *Possible earlier applications* that are to be replaced or that must interact in some way with the new application. The knowledge of these software packages (record formats, screen forms, algorithms, associated documentation) can provide us with important information that also relates to existing problems that must be resolved.

It should be stressed that, in the requirement acquisition process, an important role is played by the interactions with the users of the information system. During this interaction, the various users can provide different information, often complementary, but also at times contradictory. In general, the higher-level users have a view that is wider but less detailed. They can, however, direct the designer to the experts on individual problems.

As a rule, during the course of the interviews, it is a good idea to make continual checks on the consistency of the information being gathered. This can be done by means of practical examples or by asking for precise definitions and classifications. It is furthermore very important to try to identify which aspects are essential and which marginal, and to work towards further refinements.

As we mentioned earlier, the requirements specifications are often written in natural language, at least in the first draft. Natural language is, by nature, subject to ambiguity and misinterpretation. Therefore, we need to carry out an in-depth analysis of the specification document in order to remove any inaccuracies and ambiguous terms. To develop some practical rules for carrying out this task, consider this example. Imagine that we need to design a database for a training company and that we have gathered the data specifications shown in Figure 6.1. The data was gathered through interviews with the company personnel. Note that we have also acquired information on the expected data load.

	Training Company
1	*We wish to create a database for a company that runs training courses.*
2	*For this, we must store data about the trainees and the instructors. For*
3	*each course participant (about 5000), identified by a code, we want to*
4	*store the social security number, surname, age, sex, place of birth,*
5	*employer's name, address and telephone number, previous employers*
6	*(and period employed), the courses attended (there are about 200*
7	*courses) and the final assessment of each course. We need also to*
8	*represent the seminars that each participant is attending at present*
9	*and, for each day, the places and times the classes are held. Each course*
10	*has a code and a title and any course can be given any number of times.*
11	*Each time a particular course is given, we will call it an 'edition' of the*
12	*course. For each edition, we represent the start date, the end date, and*
13	*the number of participants. If a trainee is a self-employed professional,*
14	*we need to know his or her area of expertise, and, if appropriate, his or*
15	*her title. For somebody who works for a company, we store the level and*
16	*position held. For each instructor (about 300), we will show the*
17	*surname, age, place of birth, the edition of the course taught, those*
18	*taught in the past and the courses that the tutor is qualified to teach.*
19	*All the instructors' telephone numbers are also stored. An instructor*
20	*can be permanently employed by the training company or can be*
21	*freelance.*

Figure 6.1 Example of requirements expressed in natural language.

It is evident that such material contains a number of ambiguities and inaccuracies. For example, we have interchangeable use of *participants* or *trainees*, *tutors* or *instructors*, *courses* or *seminars*. We will now establish some rules for writing requirements specifications more precisely and without ambiguities.

- Choose the appropriate level of abstraction. It is wise to avoid terms that are too general or too specific since they can make a concept less clear. For example, in our case, the terms *period* (on line 6), *title* (line 15) and *assessment* (line 7) could be specified more precisely (for example, as *start date* and *end date*, *professional title* and *marks out of ten*).

- Standardize sentence structure. In specifying requirements, it is preferable always to use the same style. For example, 'for *<concept>* we hold *<properties>*'.

- Avoid complex phrases. Definitions should be kept clear and simple. For example, *employee* is preferable to *somebody who works for a company* (line 15).

- Identify synonyms and homonyms, and standardize terms. Synonyms are words that have the same meaning, for example, *tutor* (line 18) and *instructor* (line 16), *course participant* (line 3) and *trainee* (line 2); homonyms are words with more than one meaning, for example, *place*, meaning both town of birth (line 4) and classroom where the classes are held (line 9). These situations can cause ambiguities and must be clarified: for synonyms, single terms must be chosen, and for homonyms, different terms must be used.

- Make cross-references explicit. The absence of a reference between terms can make certain concepts ambiguous. For example, in line 5, it is not clear whether the terms *address* and *telephone number* are referring to the trainees or to their employers. Furthermore, in the phrase *somebody who works for* … (line 15), we must clarify to whom exactly we are referring (trainees, instructors?) in order to avoid confusion.

- Construct a glossary of terms. It is very useful, both for understanding and for accuracy of terms used, to build a glossary. For each term, the glossary contains a brief description, possible synonyms and reference to other terms contained in the glossary with which there is a logical link. A brief glossary for our application is shown in Figure 6.2.

Term	Description	Synonym	Links
Trainee	Participant in a course. Can be an employee or self-employed.	Participant	Course, Company
Instructor	Course tutor. Can be freelance.	Tutor	Course
Course	Course offered. Can have various editions.	Seminar	Instructor, Trainee
Company	Company by which participant is employed or has been employed.		Trainee

Figure 6.2 An example of a glossary of terms.

Once the various ambiguities and inaccuracies have been identified, they can be eliminated by substituting more appropriate terms for the incorrect ones. Where doubt remains, the user who provided the information must be re-interviewed, or the particular document must be consulted again.

Let us look at the main modifications to be made to our text. First, all the instances of *course participant* must be replaced by *trainee*. Then, as we have said, *place of birth* (lines 4 & 17) should be substituted by *town of birth*. Moreover, we have to make explicit that *address* and *telephone number* (line 5) refer to the employers of the trainees. The terms *period* (line 6) and *assessment* (line 7), must be replaced by *start date* and *end date* and *marks out of ten*, respectively. It must also be clear that a trainee does not attend *seminars* (line 8) but rather *editions of courses*. Also, the term *place* (line 9) must be replaced by *classroom*, *title* (line 15) by *professional title*, and *tutor* (line 18) by *instructor*. Finally, *title* of course (line 10) is a homonym of *professional title* of a trainee. In this case, we could replace *title* of course by *name* of course.

At this point, we can rewrite our specifications using the suggested modifications. It is very useful, in this phase, to break down the text into groups of homogenous phrases, referring to the same concept. In this way, we can begin to impose a structure on the data requirements as shown in Figure 6.3.

Of course, as well as the specification of the data itself, we also need to specify the operations to be executed on this data. For this, we must use the same terminology as that chosen for the data and we must find out how often the various operations will need to be carried out. As we shall see, this knowledge will be important in the logical design phase. For our application, the operations on the data could be as follows:

- **operation 1:** insert a new trainee including all his or her data (to be carried out approximately 40 times a day);

- **operation 2:** assign a trainee to an edition of a course (50 times a day);

- **operation 3:** insert a new instructor, including all his or her data and the courses he or she is qualified to teach (twice a day);

- **operation 4:** assign a qualified instructor to an edition of a course (15 times a day);

- **operation 5:** display all the information on the past editions of a course with title, class timetables and number of trainees (10 times a day);

- **operation 6:** display all the courses offered, with information on the instructors who are qualified to teach them (20 times a day);

- **operation 7:** for each instructor, find the trainees for all the courses he or she is teaching or has taught (5 times a week);

- **operation 8:** carry out a statistical analysis of all the trainees with all the information about them, about the editions of courses they have attended and the marks obtained (10 times a month).

Phrases of a general nature
We wish to create a database for a company that runs training courses. We wish to hold the data for the trainees and the instructors.

Phrases relating to the trainees
For each trainee (about 5000), identified by a code, we will hold the social security number, surname, age, sex, town of birth, current employer, previous employers (along with the start date and the end date of the period employed), the editions of the courses the trainee is attending at present and those he or she has attended in the past, with the final marks out of ten.

Phrases relating to the employers of the trainees
For each employer of a trainee we will hold the name, address and telephone number.

Phrases relating to the courses
For each course (about 200), we will hold the name and code. Each time a particular course is given, we will call it an 'edition' of the course. For each edition, we will hold the start date, the end date, and the number of participants. For the editions currently in progress, we will hold the dates, the classrooms and the times in which the classes are held.

Phrases relating to specific types of trainee
For a trainee who is a self-employed professional, we will hold the area of expertise and, if appropriate, the professional title. For a trainee who is an employee, we will hold the level and position held.

Phrases relating to the instructors
For each instructor (about 300), we will hold surname, age, town of birth, all telephone numbers, the edition of courses taught, those taught in the past and the courses the instructor is qualified to teach. The instructors can be permanently employed by the training company or can be freelance.

Figure 6.3 Example of structuring of requirements.

Once the structuring of the requirements is complete, we are ready to begin the first design phase. This step consists of the construction of a conceptual schema that describes all the specifications of the collected data.

6.2 General criteria for data representation

As an introduction to design techniques, we will establish some general criteria for the translation of informal specifications into Entity-Relationship constructs. It must be stressed that the same information can be modelled in many different ways. This is because two designers can have different perceptions of the same situation. We can however establish some general guidelines for the E-R model. It is recommended, overall, that the 'conceptual rules' of the model should be followed.

- *If a concept has significant properties and/or describes classes of objects with an autonomous existence, it is appropriate to represent it by an entity.* For example, referring to the specifications for the training company above, it makes sense to represent the concept of *instructor* with an entity, because it possesses various properties (surname, age, town of birth) and its existence is independent of the other concepts.

- *If a concept has a simple structure, and has no relevant properties associated with it, it is convenient to represent it by an attribute of another concept to which it refers.* For example, the concept of age can certainly be represented as an attribute of the trainee. In general, the concept of town could have significant properties. In our application, however, it is better to model it as an attribute, because, apart from the name, none of its other properties is of interest to us.

- *If the requirements contain a concept that provides a logical link between two (or more) entities, this concept can be represented by a relationship.* For example, in our application, the concept of attending a course can certainly be represented by a relationship between the entities that represent the *trainees* and the *editions of courses*. It must be stressed that this is valid only in the situation in which the concept does not, itself, have the characteristics of the entity. A typical example, which we have already mentioned in Section 5.2.1, is the concept of *exam* relating to students and courses. This concept can be represented by a relationship between student and course if the aspect of interest is, say, only the individual student marks. Suppose however, that we are also interested in the date, the location and the examining board, and, above all, that we wish to represent the fact that a student can take an exam more than once for the same course. In this case the exam must be represented by an entity linked by one-to-many relationships to the entities representing students and courses.

- *If one or more concepts are particular cases of another concept, it is convenient to represent them by means of a generalization.* In our application, it is obvious that the concepts of *professional* and *employee* constitute particular examples of the concept of *trainee* and it is therefore a good idea to define a generalization between the entities that represent these concepts.

These criteria are valid in general, and are thus independent of the chosen design strategy. In fact, for every strategy, it is eventually necessary to translate a specification into an E-R construct.

6.3 Design strategies

The development of a conceptual schema based on its specification must be considered to all intents and purposes an engineering process, and, as such, design strategies used in other disciplines can be applied to it. Let us examine these strategies with specific reference to the modelling of a database.

6.3.1 Top-down strategy

In this strategy, the conceptual schema is produced by means of a series of successive refinements, starting from an initial schema that describes all the requirements by means of a few highly abstract concepts. The schema is then gradually expanded by using appropriate modifications that increase the detail of the various concepts. This procedure is shown in Figure 6.4 where the various levels of refinement are shown. Each of these levels contains a schema that describes the same information with a different degree of detail. Thus, in a pure top-down strategy, all the concepts present in the final schema are present, in principle, at each level of refinement.

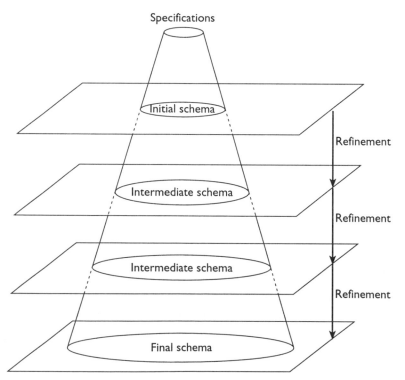

Figure 6.4 The top-down strategy.

Moving from one level to another, the schema is modified using some basic transformations called *top-down transformation primitives*. Major examples of top-down transformation primitives are shown in Figure 6.5. As we can see, these primitives operate on a single concept of the schema and transform it into a more complex structure, capable of describing the original concept in more detail.

Transformation	Initial concept	Result
T_1 From one entity to two entities and a relationship between them		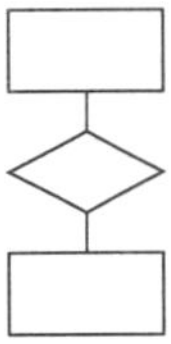
T_2 From one entity to a generalization	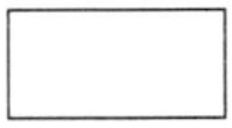	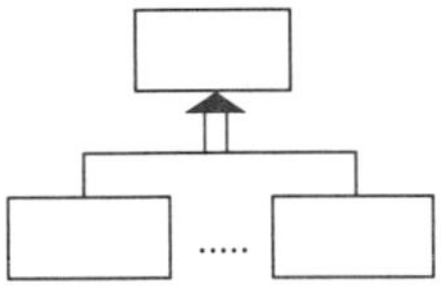
T_3 From one relationship to multiple relationships	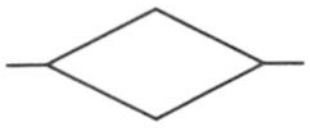	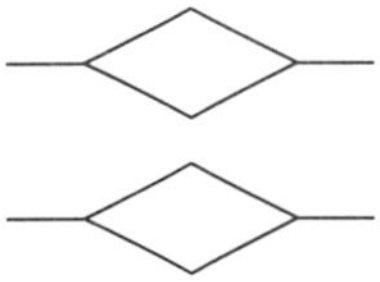
T_4 From one relationship to an entity with relationships	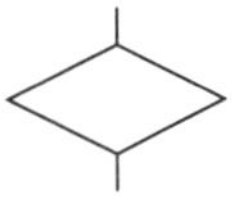	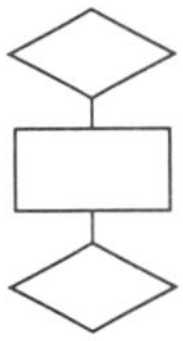
T_5 Adding attributes to an entity	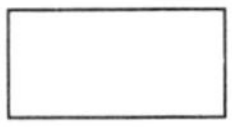	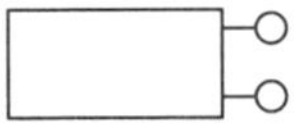
T_6 Adding attributes to a relationship		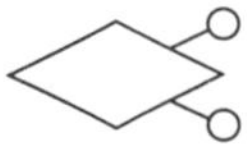

Figure 6.5 Top-down transformation primitives.

Transformation T_1: this is applied when an entity describes two different concepts logically linked to each other. For example, in the training company application, we could have begun with an entity COURSE. Then we realize that this is too abstract and that COURSETYPE (having a code and a title) should be distinct from COURSEEDITION (having a start date and an end date) and that these entities are linked by a relationship that we can call TYPE.

Transformation T_2: this is applied when an entity is made up of distinct subentities. In our application, this happens when we realize that among the trainees there are the distinct cases EMPLOYEE and PROFESSIONAL.

Transformation T_3: this is applied when a relationship describes two or more different concepts linking the same entities. For example, in the relationship TEACHING between instructors and courses, CURRENTTEACHING should be distinguished from PASTTEACHING.

Transformation T_4: this is applied when a relationship describes a concept having an autonomous existence. For example, if a relationship CONTRACT between an entity CONSULTANT and an entity COMPANY has many attributes, then it is better represented by an entity linked to the others by means of binary relationships.

Transformation T_5: this is applied for the addition of properties (attributes) to entities. This happens, for example, when we refine the entity TRAINEE by adding its attributes SocialSecurityNumber, Surname, Age, Sex, and TownOfBirth.

Transformation T_6: this is applied to add properties to relationships, in a similar way to transformation T_5.

The advantage of the top-down strategy is that the designer can start with a full representation of the requirements, even though some details are missing. Obviously, this is possible only if we possess a global view of all the relevant concepts. However, this is extremely difficult when dealing with complex cases.

6.3.2 Bottom-up strategy

In this strategy, the initial specifications are decomposed into smaller and smaller components, until each component describes an elementary fragment of the specifications. At this point, the various components are represented by simple conceptual schemas that can also consist of single concepts. The various schemas thus obtained are then amalgamated until a final conceptual schema is reached. This procedure is shown in Figure 6.6, which shows the decomposition of the requirements, the subsequent construction of the basic E-R schemas, and the final phase in which the elementary schemas are integrated. In contrast to the top-down strategy, the various concepts present in the final schema are progressively introduced.

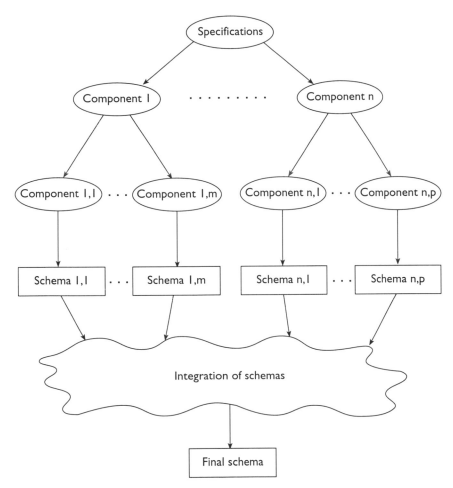

Figure 6.6 The bottom-up strategy.

In this case also, the final schema is obtained by means of some elementary transformations, here called *bottom-up transformation primitives*. In Figure 6.7, the main bottom-up transformation primitives are shown. As we can see, these primitives introduce into the schema new concepts that were not present previously and are capable of describing aspects of the application that have not been taken into account before.

Transformation T₁: this is applied when a class of objects with properties in common is identified in the specifications. For example, in the application for the training company, this can happen when we identify the entity COURSECLASS (held in a certain classroom at a certain time) from the course specification.

Transformation T₂: this is applied when a logical link between two entities is identified in the specifications. In our application, this can happen when

Transformation	Initial concept	Result
T_1 Generation of an entity		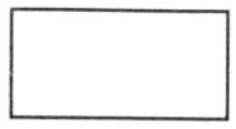
T_2 Generation of a relationship	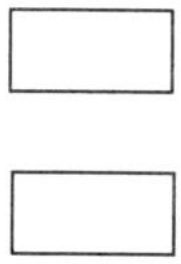	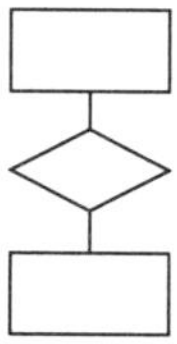
T_3 Generation of a generalization	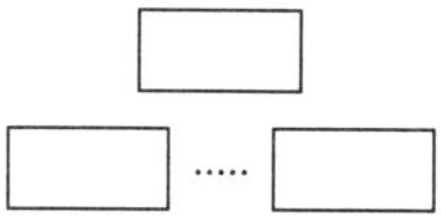	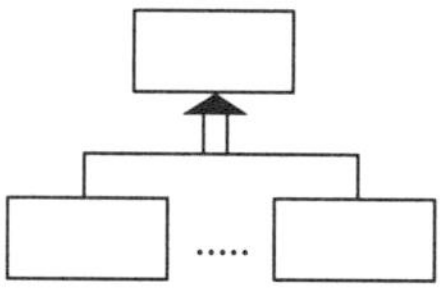
T_4 Aggregation of attributes on an entity		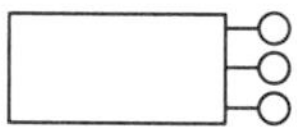
T_5 Aggregation of attributes on a relationship		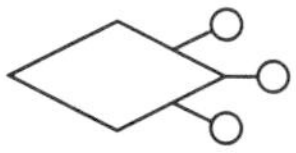

Figure 6.7 Bottom-up transformation primitives.

we identify the relationship QUALIFICATION between the entities INSTRUCTOR and COURSE.

Transformation T_3: this is applied when a generalization between entities is identified in the specification. For example, in our application this can happen when we understand that the entity INSTRUCTOR is a generalization of the entities PERMANENT and FREELANCE.

Transformation T_4: this is applied when we identify an entity that can be regarded as an aggregation of a series of attributes. For example, this happens in our application if we identify the entity TRAINEE from the properties SocialSecurityNumber, Surname, Age, Sex, and TownOfBirth.

Transformation T₅: this is applied in a way similar to transformation T_4, when a relationship is identified that can be regarded as an aggregation of attributes.

The advantage of the bottom-up strategy is that it allows the decomposition of a problem into simple components, which are often easily identified, and whose design can be handled by different designers if necessary. It therefore lends itself to work undertaken in groups or sub-divided within a group. On the other hand, its disadvantage is the fact that it requires the integration of many conceptual schemas, an operation that often presents difficulties.

6.3.3 Inside-out strategy

This strategy can be regarded as a particular type of bottom-up strategy. It begins with the identification of only a few important concepts and, based on these, the design proceeds, spreading outward 'radially'. That is, first the concepts nearest to the initial concepts are represented, and we then move towards those further away by means of 'navigation' through the specification.

An example of inside-out development of a conceptual schema is shown in Figure 6.8 with reference to an example seen in the previous chapter. In this

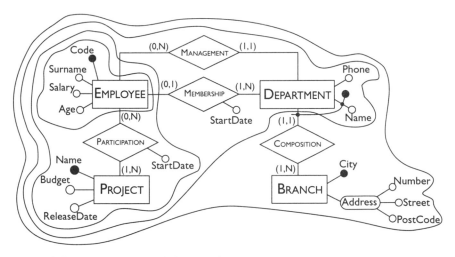

Figure 6.8 An example of the inside-out strategy.

diagram, the various areas indicate a possible chronological development of the schema.

Note that the entity EMPLOYEE was identified first, along with its attributes. On this basis, the employee participation in projects was then represented, together with the properties of the projects. Following this, the correlation between the employees and the company departments was analyzed, identifying the relationships MANAGEMENT and MEMBERSHIP and the entity DEPARTMENT. Finally, based on this last entity, the branches of the company were represented (BRANCH entity with its attributes), together with the fact that the various departments belong to the branches (COMPOSITION relationship).

This strategy has the advantage of not requiring integration steps. On the other hand, from time to time, it is necessary to examine all of the specification looking for concepts not yet represented and to describe these new concepts in detail.

6.3.4 Mixed strategy

As is often the case, it turns out that each of the strategies has both positive and negative aspects. Therefore, we can devise a mixed strategy that tries to combine the advantages of top-down strategy with those of bottom-up and inside-out. The designer decomposes the requirements into a number of components, as in the bottom-up strategy, but not to the extent where all the concepts are separated. At the same time he or she defines a *skeleton schema* containing, at the abstract level, the principal concepts of the application. This skeleton schema gives a unified, although synthetic, view of the whole design and favours the integration of the schemas developed separately.

For example in Figure 6.9, we show a possible skeleton schema for our training company application. From a simple inspection of the requirements

Figure 6.9 Skeleton schema for the training company.

in Figure 6.3, we can immediately identify three principal concepts that can be represented by entities: the trainees, the courses and the instructors. There are relationships between these entities that we can assume to be descriptions of the attendance of the trainees to the editions of courses and of the teaching activities undertaken by the instructors of the courses. At this point we can move on, examining separately these main concepts and can proceed with gradual refinements (thus following the top-down strategy) or extending the various components of the schema with concepts that are not yet represented (thus following the bottom-up strategy).

The mixed strategy is probably the most flexible of those we have seen, because it lends itself well to contrasting requirements: that of subdividing a complex problem into smaller ones and that of proceeding by gradual refinement. In fact, this strategy also encompasses the inside-out strategy, which as we have seen, is only a variation of the bottom-up strategy. It is actually quite natural, during the bottom-up development of a sub-component of the project, to proceed from the inside out in order to represent the parts of the specification of the database that are not yet represented. It must also be stated that, in almost all practical cases, the mixed strategy is the only one that can actually be adopted. In fact, it is often necessary to begin the design before all the data requirements are available, and of the data that is known, our knowledge of detail can vary.

6.4 Quality of a conceptual schema

A 'good' conceptual schema should possess a number of properties, which can be used to verify the *quality* of the schema itself. Let us analyze the most important of these properties, and see how we can check them during the conceptual design stage.

Correctness A conceptual schema is *correct* when it uses properly the constructs made available by the conceptual model. As with programming languages, the errors can be *syntactic* or *semantic*. The first relates to illegal use of a construct, as for example, in specifying a generalization between relationships rather than between entities. The second relates to the use of a construct that does not follow its definition. For example, the use of a relationship to describe the fact that an entity is a specialization of another. The correctness of a schema can be verified by inspection, comparing the concepts present in the schema with the requirements and with the definitions of the constructs of the conceptual model used.

Completeness A conceptual schema is *complete* when it includes concepts that represent all the data requirements and allow for the execution of all the operations included in the operational requirements. The completeness of a schema can be verified by checking that all the requirements on the data are represented by some concept present in the schema, and that all the concepts involved in an operation can be reached by 'navigating' across the schema.

Readability A conceptual schema is *readable* when it represents the requirements in a way that is natural and easy to understand. Therefore, the schema must be self-explanatory, for example, by choosing suitable names for concepts. Readability also depends on purely aesthetic criteria: the comprehension of a schema is made easier if we draw it with consistent dimensions for its components. Some suggestions for making the schema more readable are as follows:

- arrange the constructs on a grid, choosing as central elements those that have most links (relationships) with others;

- use only horizontal and vertical lines and try to keep intersections to a minimum;

- arrange parent entities above the respective child entities;

The readability of a schema can be verified by carrying out comprehension tests with the users.

Minimality A schema is *minimal* when all the specifications on the data are represented only once in the schema. A schema is therefore not minimal when there are *redundancies*, that is, concepts that can be derived from others. A typical source of redundancy in an E-R schema is the presence of cycles caused by the presence of relationships and/or generalizations. However, a redundancy is not always undesirable, but can be the result of precise design choices.[1] In any case, these situations need always to be documented. The minimality of a schema can be verified by inspection, checking whether there exist concepts that can be deleted from the schema without compromising its completeness.

In the next section we will see how the verification of the quality of a conceptual schema can be incorporated into a comprehensive method.

6.5 A comprehensive method for conceptual design

In this section, we will sum up all that we have said concerning conceptual database design. With regard to the design strategies we have seen, we should stress that in practice it is rare for a project to proceed always in a top-down or in a bottom-up manner. Independently of the chosen strategy, in reality there is always a need to modify the schema being constructed using both top-down transformations, which refine concepts already present, and bottom-up transformations, which add concepts not already present. We will therefore show a method for conceptual design with reference to the mixed strategy, which, as we have said, includes the others as special cases. The technique is made up of the following steps.

1. **Analysis of requirements**
   (a) Construct a glossary of terms.
   (b) Analyze the requirements and eliminate any ambiguities.
   (c) Arrange the requirements in groups.

2. **Basic step**
   (a) Identify the most relevant concepts and represent them in a skeleton schema.

3. **Decomposition step** (to be used if appropriate or necessary).
   (a) Decompose the requirements with reference to the concepts present in the skeleton schema.

4. **Iterative step:** to be repeated for all the schemas until every specification is represented.
   (a) Refine the concepts in the schema, based on the requirements.
   (b) Add new concepts to the schema to describe any parts of the requirements not yet represented.

---

1. We will discuss this point further when we deal with logical design.

5. **Integration step** (to be carried out if step 3 has been used).
   (a) Integrate the various subschemas into a general schema with reference to the skeleton schema.

6. **Quality analysis**
   (a) Verify the correctness of the schema and carry out any necessary restructuring.
   (b) Verify the completeness of the schema and carry out any necessary restructuring.
   (c) Verify the minimality, list the redundancies and if necessary restructure the schema.
   (d) Verify the readability of the schema and carry out any necessary restructuring.

Note that if Step 3 and Step 5 are omitted, and if in Step 4 only refinements are made, we have a pure top-down strategy. Conversely, if the basic step is not carried out and if in the iterative step only new concepts are added, we are using a pure bottom-up strategy. Finally, in the bottom-up transformations, we can proceed according to the inside-out strategy.

In the method shown, we have only briefly mentioned an important activity that accompanies every design phase: the documentation of the schemas. As we said in Section 5.3, this activity should also be suitably organized. Specifically, it is very useful to construct, in parallel to the development of a schema, a data dictionary that makes the interpretation of the various concepts easier. Furthermore, we can use business rules to describe the presence of redundancies or requirements of the application that we are not able to translate into constructs of the E-R model.

Finally, a few comments on the analysis of the quality of the design are needed. First, it must be stated that quality analysis should not be relegated to the end of the conceptual design: indeed this is a parallel activity, which should be carried out regularly during the development of a conceptual schema. Furthermore, it is very delicate, since it often requires restructuring to be carried out in order to remedy 'errors' made in previous phases. It is necessary to pay particular attention to concepts of the schema that have particular properties: for example, entities without attributes, groups of concepts that form cycles, over-complex generalization hierarchies or particularly tortuous portions of the schema. As we mentioned in Section 6.4, this analysis does not automatically mean the necessity for restructuring, but only a re-organization of the schema to make it more readable.

6.6 An example of conceptual design

Let us now look at a complete example of conceptual design, again with reference to our training company. We have already carried out the first stage of the method described above and we have shown a possible skeleton schema in Figure 6.9. With reference to this schema, we can, at this point, decide to analyze separately the specifications that relate to the trainees, the courses and the instructors, and to proceed inside-out for each of them.

We will now carry out the iterative step, dealing first with the trainees. Of these, two types are immediately identifiable: the *professionals* and the *employees*. These entities can be represented as a specialization of the TRAINEE entity: the resulting generalization is total. At this point, the *employers of the trainees* need to be represented. This can be done by introducing the entity EMPLOYER, which is linked by a relationship to the entity EMPLOYEE. If we analyze the requirements, we notice that we need to represent two distinct concepts: past and present employment. We will decide therefore, to sub-divide this relationship into two relationships: PASTEMPLOYMENT and PRESENTEMPLOYMENT. The first has a start date and an end date and is linked to the entity TRAINEE (because the professionals, too, could have a past employment); the second has only a start date and is linked to the entity EMPLOYEE. By adding the attributes to entities and relationships, the cardinalities to the relationships and the identifiers to the entities, we obtain the schema in Figure 6.10. Observe that the entity TRAINEE has two

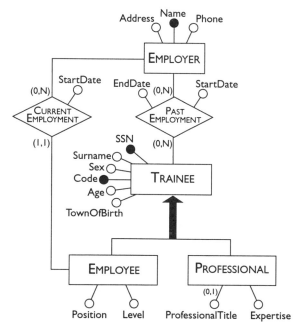

Figure 6.10 The refinement of a portion of the skeleton schema.

identifiers, the internal code given by the company and the social security number. Note also that the attribute ProfessionalTitle is optional, in that the specification states that this information can be missing.

For the instructors, we need to distinguish between those employed by the training company and those who work for the company on a freelance basis.

This can be done in a natural way with a total generalization of which INSTRUCTOR is the parent entity. We can then add the attributes Surname, Age, TownOfBirth, and Phone to the INSTRUCTOR entity. The last attribute is multi-valued because an instructor can have more than one telephone number and we wish to represent them all. Note that the available attributes provide no natural identifier for the INSTRUCTOR. Here, we can decide to use the social security number of the instructor, even if this information is not in the requirements. As an alternative, we could have introduced an internal code, used only for this purpose. The resulting subschema is shown in Figure 6.11.

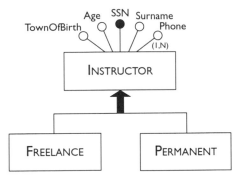

Figure 6.11 The refinement of another portion of the skeleton schema.

Let us move on to the analysis of the COURSE entity. First there are two distinct concepts that are linked: the abstract concept of course (which has a name and a code) and the edition of a course (which has a start date, an end date, and a number of trainees). We will represent these two concepts with distinct entities linked by the relationship TYPE. The classes of the course are then considered, which we can describe by an entity linked to the editions of the courses by a relationship COMPOSITION. We can then add the attributes, the cardinalities and the identifiers. With regard to classes, we assume that a class is identified by the classroom, the time and the date (it is not possible to have two different classes with the same day, classroom and time). For the editions of the course, on the other hand, we assume that two different editions of the same course cannot begin on the same day and thus an identifier for the COURSEEDITION is made up of the attribute StartDate and of the entity COURSE. The resulting subschema is shown in Figure 6.12.

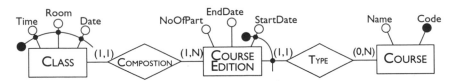

Figure 6.12 The refinement of another portion of the skeleton schema.

The final schema is obtained by the integration of the schemas obtained up to this point. We will begin with the schemas relating to the instructors and to the courses represented in Figure 6.11 and in Figure 6.12 respectively. In the skeleton schema, this link is represented by the TEACHING relationship. This needs to be refined; from the analysis of the requirements, it is not difficult to identify three types of different links between instructors and courses: the current teaching, the past teaching and the qualification to teach a course. We will represent these links by means of three relationships: the first two relate the entities INSTRUCTOR and COURSEEDITION (because an instructor teaches or has taught a specific edition of a course) while the third relates the INSTRUCTOR entity and the COURSE entity (because an instructor is qualified to teach a course in general). The schema obtained has now to be integrated with the portion relating to the trainees, shown in Figure 6.10. Looking at the skeleton schema we see that, in order to do this, we must first clarify the relationship that links courses and trainees. We can identify two cases: the current attendances and the past ones. Therefore, we define two relationships between the entity TRAINEE and the entity COURSEEDITION. For past attendances, we are interested in the final marks. These are represented by an attribute of the corresponding relationship. By adding the various cardinalities, we obtain the final schema shown in Figure 6.13.

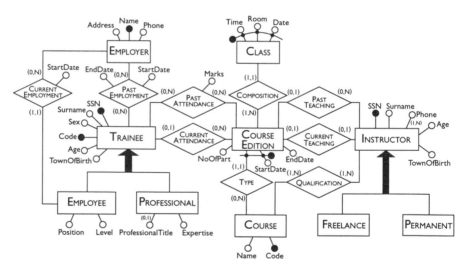

Figure 6.13 The final E-R schema for the training company.

Note that we have worked in this case by decomposing and then integrating. However, given that we are dealing with a relatively simple schema, we could also have worked directly on the skeleton schema, gradually refining it without integration steps.

At this point, we have to verify the properties of the schema thus obtained. In particular, the completeness is verified by going back over all the requirements and checking that all the data is represented and that the operations can be carried out. To give an example, consider operation 7, which asks for the trainees of all the courses taught by an instructor. The data needed for this operation can be retrieved using the schema in Figure 6.13 as follows: we start from the INSTRUCTOR entity, we then traverse the relationships CURRENTTEACHING and PASTTEACHING, the entity COURSEEDITION, and the relationships CURRENTATTENDANCE and PASTATTENDANCE, and we finally reach the entity TRAINEE. With regard to minimality, we note that there is a redundancy in the schema: the attribute NumberOfParticipants in the entity COURSEEDITION can be derived, for each edition, by counting the number of instances of the TRAINEE entity that are linked to this edition. We will postpone the discussion of whether to eliminate or maintain such a redundancy until the next design phase, where we deal with logical design.

Finally, we must remember that the schema must have appropriate documentation. It is particularly important to describe possible constraints not expressed directly by the schema, possibly in the form of business rules. For example, the fact that an instructor teaches (or may have taught) a course only if he or she is qualified to do so.

6.7 CASE tools for database design

Database design is a complex activity that is often difficult or impossible to carry out manually. The process can be made easier by using general-purpose editing programs with graphical interfaces for creating tables and diagrams. There are, however, software packages expressly designed for the creation and development of databases. These systems belong to the class of CASE (Computer Aided Software Engineering) tools and provide support for the main phases of the development of a database (conceptual, logical and physical design).

The functionalities vary widely from one package to another, but there are some basic features that are present in a more or less extensive form in all systems:

- a *graphical interface* with which it is possible to manipulate E-R schemas diagrammatically;

- a *data dictionary,* which stores information on the various components of the schema (entities, attributes, relationships, integrity constraints, etc.);

- a series of *integrated tools,* which carry out, either automatically or through interaction with the user, specific design tasks (automatic layout of diagrams, verification of correctness and completeness, quality analysis of a schema, automatic production of DDL code for the creation of a database, etc.).

Many systems are integrated directly with database management systems. Other systems also provide support for requirements analysis. Still others provide libraries of predefined generic projects that can be used as a starting point for a new project.

With specific regard to conceptual design, it is generally possible to follow the strategies suggested in the sections above, even when these systems are used. Many of them make it possible to use a top-down strategy, allowing the partial specification of concepts of the schema and the gradual refinement of them. For example, we can define an entity without specifying attributes or identifiers. There are still other systems that allow views over a schema to be defined and manipulated separately, automatically propagating to the schema modifications made on the view, thus proceeding in a bottom-up manner.

Figure 6.14 shows a conceptual schema managed by one of the most popular tools, ER-Win.

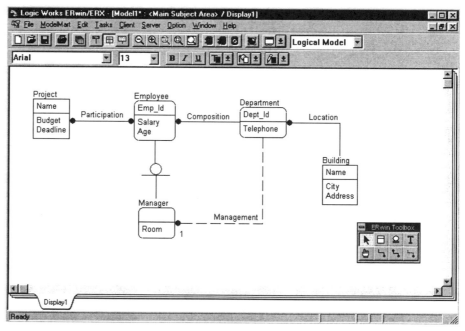

Figure 6.14 Conceptual design using a CASE tool.

Note that the notation used to describe the constructs of the E-R model is different from that used in this chapter. In particular the attributes are directly represented within the entity, separating the identifiers from the other attributes. The lines represent relationships and particular symbols on the lines are used to express cardinality constraints. Generalizations are represented by lines separated by a special symbol (relationship between EMPLOYEE and MANAGER). This representation does not allow the specification of attributes for relationships.

This example shows a well-known problem that must be confronted when using a CASE tool for database design: there are standardizations neither of the notations used, nor of the conceptual model, and each system substantially adopts a specific version of the E-R model. There are, for example, systems that manage generalizations of only a certain type, others that do not manage them at all, still others that manage only binary relationships. Furthermore, in practice, all the products use different notations to represent the same constructs. Thus, considerable effort is often required on the part of the designer to adapt his or her own personal knowledge of models and techniques to the characteristics of the chosen product.

6.8 Bibliography

Conceptual data design is dealt with in detail in the books by Batini, Ceri and Navathe [7] and by Teorey [84]. Batini, Ceri and Navathe also discuss the problem of the integration of schemas. We also mention two interesting texts reporting on the DATAID project, which has developed many aspects of database design, by Albano, De Antonellis and Di Leva [2] and Ceri [14]. Our description of the activities of collection and analysis of requirements is based on the results of this project.

An in-depth review written by David Reiner on CASE tools for database design is given in Chapter 15 of Batini, Ceri and Navathe [7].

6.9 Exercises

Exercise 6.1 We wish to automate the management of loans in a library. The specification of the application, acquired through an interview with the librarian, is shown in Figure 6.15. Analyze the specifications, filter the

The Library
A reader who uses the library has an identity card on which is written his or her code, name and address. The user makes requests for the loan of books catalogued in the library. Each book has a title and a list of authors and there can be many copies of any book. Each book in the library is identified by a code. Following a request, the archive of available books is first consulted (that is, those not out on loan at present). If the book is available, we look for the book on the shelves. Once the book is found it is given to the reader. The text is then classified as one on loan. When the reader has finished, the book is returned, put back on the shelves and re-classified as available. For each loan the times and dates of taking out and returning are recorded.

Figure 6.15 The library specification for Exercise 6.1.

ambiguities and then group them according to type. Pay particular attention to the difference between the concept of book and copy of book.

Identify the logical links between the various groups of specifications thus obtained.

Exercise 6.2 Represent the specifications of the previous exercise using an E-R model schema.

Exercise 6.3 Define an Entity-Relationship schema that describes the data of an application relating to a chain of automobile workshops. We are interested in:

• the workshops, with name (identifying), address and telephone number;

• the automobiles, with registration number (identifying), and model (a string of characters with no further structure) and owner;

• the customers (automobile owners), with social security number, surname, first name and telephone; each client can be the owner of more than one automobile;

• the maintenance work carried out in a workshop, with a number (unique in a particular workshop), start date and end date, parts replaced (with quantities) and number of hours labour;

• the spare parts available with code, name and unit cost.

Show the cardinalities of the relationships and (at least) one identifier for each entity.

Exercise 6.4 Define an E-R schema that describes the data of an application relating to the electoral roll of the city of WhoKnowsWhere, with citizens and families. The following are stored:

• information on the citizens born in the area and on those resident in the area; each citizen is identified by a social security number, and has surname, first name, sex and date of birth; furthermore:

  ○ for anyone born in the area, the birth registration number is also stored;

  ○ for anyone born in another area, the city and state of birth are stored.

• information on resident families, each of which has one and one only head of the family and zero or more other members; for each of them, the relationship to the head of the family is recorded (spouse, child, parent or other); each resident citizen belongs to one and one family only; all the members of a family have the same residence (street, street number, apartment number).

Try to use the inside-out strategy. At the end, verify the quality of the schema obtained.

Exercise 6.5 Analyze the specifications relating to matches of a soccer tournament shown in Figure 6.16 and construct a glossary of terms.

Soccer Tournament
For each match, we store the series and the day on which it takes place, which match it is (e.g. first match, second match etc.) the date with day, month, year, the teams involved in the match with the name of the city for the team and the trainer, and finally for each team whether played at home. We store the name and the surname of each player in each team with his date of birth and main position. We store, for each day, how many points each team has and we also store, for each match, the players of each team who played and in which position each player played (the positions can change from one game to another). For each match, we store the referee, with first name, surname, city and region of birth. The matches played as scheduled must be distinguished from those postponed. For a postponed match, we store the date in which it is actually played. We also identify the matches played in a city other than that of the home team; for each of these, we store the city in which it took place, as well as the reason for the variation of venue. For each player, we are interested in the city of birth.

Figure 6.16 Specifications for Exercise 6.5.

Exercise 6.6 Having organized the specifications of Exercise 6.5 into groups of similar type, show them using an Entity Relationship model, using a top-down strategy starting from an initial skeleton schema. Note that the schema in Figure 5.26 represents a possible solution to this exercise.

Exercise 6.7 Try to represent again the specifications in Figure 6.16 with an Entity-Relationship schema, using a bottom-up strategy this time. Construct separate fragments of the schema that describe the various homogenous components of the specification and then proceed with the integration of the various schemas. Compare the result with the schema obtained from Exercise 6.6.

Exercise 6.8 We wish to carry out a reverse engineering operation. That is, given a relational database, we wish to construct its conceptual representation using the E-R model. The database is for an application concerning trains and railway stations and is made up of the following relations:

- STATION(<u>Code</u>, Name, City) with a referential constraint between the attribute City and the CITY relation;

- CITY(<u>Code</u>, Name, Region);

- ROUTE(<u>From</u>, <u>To</u>, Distance), with referential constraints between the attributes From and the relation STATION and between the attribute To and the relation STATION; this relation contains all and only the pairs of stations connected directly by a route (that is without intermediate stations);

- TRAINTIMETABLE(<u>Number</u>, From, To, DepartureTime, ArrivalTime) with referential constraints between the attributes From and the relation STATION and between the attribute To, and the relation STATION;

- TRAINROUTE(<u>TrainNumber</u>, <u>From</u>, <u>To</u>) with referential constraints between the attribute TrainNumber and the relation TRAINTIMETABLE and between the attributes From and To and the relation STATION;

- STOPTIME(<u>TrainNumber</u>, <u>Station</u>, Arrival, Departure) with referential constraints between the attribute TrainNumber and the relation TRAINTIMETABLE and between the attribute Station and the relation STATION;

- ACTUALTRAIN(<u>TrainNumber</u>, <u>Date</u>, DepartureTime, ArrivalTime) with a referential constraint between the attribute TrainNumber and the TRAINTIMETABLE relation;

- ACTUALSTOP(<u>TrainNumber</u>, <u>Date</u>, <u>Station</u>, Arrival, Departure) with a referential constraint between the two attributes TrainNumber and Station and the STOPTIME relation.

Indicate possible redundancies.

Exercise 6.9 Define an E-R schema that describes the data of an application for a hospital ward. We are interested in:

- each patient, with social security number, first name, surname and date of birth;

- the admission of each patient, with admission date (an identifier for each admission of a patient) and the doctor in charge of the case; as well as, for a discharge, the date of discharge and the reason (cure, transfer, etc.), and, for a patient in the ward at present, the contact number of a relative (which we can assume is simply a string);

- each doctor, with registration number, surname, first name, specialization and graduation date;

- each examination, with the date, time, doctors present, medicines prescribed (with dosages) and the illnesses diagnosed – each examination is identified by the patient involved and by the date and time;

- for each medicine, the identification code, the name and cost;

- for each illness, an identifying code, a name and a description.

Exercise 6.10 Define an Entity-Relationship schema that describes the data for an application for the management of apartment blocks, according to the following specifications:

- each apartment block has a name (which identifies it) and an address, and has one or more buildings, each of which contains a number of apartments;

- if the apartment block has more than one building, each of them has a code (e.g. building 'A') which identifies it together with the name of the block;

- each apartment is identified, in its respective block, by the building (if many exist) and by a number (the apartment number) and has a rental charge;

- each apartment has an owner and a tenant; for both of them, we are interested in the name, surname, social security number; for the owners we want to store also their addresses and telephone numbers; each person can be the owner of many apartments but can be the tenant of one apartment only.

7

Logical design

The aim of logical design is to construct a logical schema that correctly and efficiently represents all of the information described by an Entity-Relationship schema produced during the conceptual design phase. This is not just a simple translation from one model to another for two reasons. First, there is not a close correspondence between the models involved because not all the constructs of the Entity-Relationship model can be translated naturally into the relational model. For example, while an entity can easily be represented by a relation, there are various options for the generalizations. Secondly, the aim of conceptual design is to represent the data accurately and naturally from a high-level, computer-independent point of view. Logical design is instead the basis for the actual implementation of the application, and must take into account, as far as possible, the performance of the final product. The schema must therefore be restructured in such a way as to make the execution of the projected operations as efficient as possible. In sum, we must plan a task that is not only a *translation* (from the conceptual model to the logical) but also a *reorganization*. Since the reorganization can for the most part be dealt with independently of the logical model, it is usually helpful to divide the logical design into two steps, as shown in Figure 7.1.

- **Restructuring of the Entity-Relationship schema,** which is independent of the chosen logical model and is based on criteria for the optimization of the schema and the simplification of the following step.

- **Translation into the logical model,** which refers to a specific logical model (in our case, the relational model) and can include a further optimization, based on the features of the logical model itself.

The input for the first step is the conceptual schema produced in the preceding phase and the estimated *database load*, in terms of the amount of data and the operational requirements. The result obtained is a restructured E-R schema, which is no longer a conceptual schema in the strict sense of the

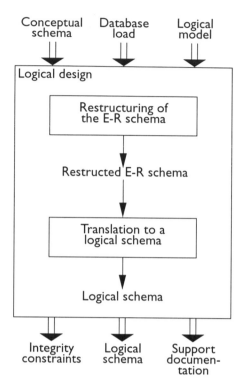

Figure 7.1 Logical database design.

term, in that it constitutes a representation of the data that takes into account implementation aspects.

This schema and the chosen logical model constitute the input of the second step, which produces the logical schema of our database. In this step, we can also carry out quality controls on the schema and, possibly, further optimizations based on the characteristics of the logical model. An analysis technique used for the relational model (called *normalization*) will be presented separately in the next chapter. The final logical schema, the integrity constraints defined on it and the relevant documentation, constitute the final product of logical design.

In the remainder of this chapter, we will present the two steps that make up the logical design of a database. We will first discuss the techniques that can be used to analyze the efficiency of a database by referring to its conceptual schema.

7.1 Performance analysis on E-R schemas

An E-R schema can be modified to optimize some *performance indicators*. We use the term indicator, because the efficiency of a database cannot be precisely evaluated with reference to a conceptual schema. The reason is that the actual behaviour is also dependent on physical aspects that are not pertinent to a conceptual representation. It is possible, however, to carry out evaluations of the two parameters that influence the performance of any software system. These are:

- **cost of an operation:** this is evaluated in terms of the number of occurrences of entities and relationships that are visited to execute an operation on the database; this is a coarse measure and it will sometimes be necessary to refer to more detailed criteria;

- **storage requirement:** this is evaluated in terms of number of bytes necessary to store the data described by the schema.

In order to study these parameters, we need the following information.

- **Volume of data.** That is:

  o number of occurrences of each entity and relationship of the schema;

  o size of each attribute.

- **Operation characteristics.** That is:

  o type of operation (interactive or batch);

  o frequency (average number of executions in a certain time span);

  o data involved (entities and/or relationships).

To give a practical example, we will look at an already familiar schema, which is shown again for convenience, in Figure 7.2.

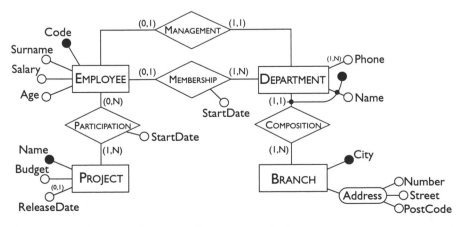

Figure 7.2 An E-R schema on the personnel of a company.

Typical operations for this schema can be:

- **operation 1:** assign an employee to a project;

- **operation 2:** find the data for an employee, for the department in which he or she works and for the projects in which he or she is involved;

- **operation 3:** find the data for all the employees of a certain department;

- **operation 4:** for each branch, find its departments with the surnames of the managers and the list of the employees in each department.

Although the operations above might look oversimplifying with respect to the actual database load, we can note that database operations follow the so-called 'eighty-twenty rule'. This rule states that eighty percent of the load is generated by twenty percent of the operations. This fact allows us to concentrate only on some operations and still give an adequate indication of the workloads for the subsequent analysis.

The volume of data and the general characteristics of the operations can be described by using tables such as those in Figure 7.3. In the *table of volumes*,

Table of volumes

Concept	Type	Volume
Branch	E	10
Department	E	80
Employee	E	2000
Project	E	500
Composition	R	80
Membership	R	1900
Management	R	80
Participation	R	6000

Table of operations

Operation	Type	Frequency
Op 1	I	50 per day
Op 2	I	100 per day
Op 3	I	10 per day
Op 4	B	2 per week

Figure 7.3 Examples of volume table and operations table.

all the concepts of the schema are shown (entities and relationships) with their estimated volumes. In the *table of operations* we show, for each operation, the expected frequency and a symbol that indicates whether the operation is interactive (I) or batch (B). Note that, in the volumes table, the number of occurrences of a relationship depends on two parameters. These are (i) the volume of the entities involved in the relationship and (ii) the number of times an occurrence of these entities participates on average in an occurrence of the relationship. The latter depends in turn on the cardinalities of the relationship. For example, the number of occurrences of the COMPOSITION relationship is equal to the number of departments, since the cardinalities dictate that each department belongs to one and only one branch. On the other hand, the number of occurrences of the relationship MEMBERSHIP is little less than the number of employees, since few employees belong to no department. Finally, if an employee is involved on average in three projects, we have 2000 × 3 = 6000 occurrences for the relationship PARTICIPATION (and thus 6000 ÷ 500 = 12 employees on average for each project).

For each operation we can, moreover, describe the data involved by means of a *navigation schema* that consists of the fragment of the E-R schema relevant to the operation. On this schema, it is useful to draw the 'logical path' that must be followed to access the required information. An example of a navigation schema is proposed in Figure 7.4 with reference to operation 2. To obtain the required information, we begin with the EMPLOYEE entity and

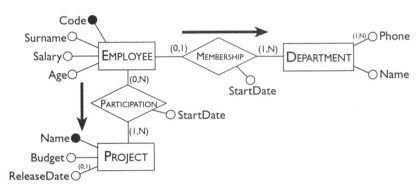

Figure 7.4   Example of a navigation schema.

we gain access to his department by means of the MEMBERSHIP relationship, and to the projects in which he is involved by means of the PARTICIPATION relationship.

Once this information is available, we can estimate the cost of an operation on the database by counting the number of accesses to occurrences of entities and relationships necessary to carry out the operation. Look again at operation 2. According to the navigation schema, we must first access an occurrence of the EMPLOYEE entity in order then to access an occurrence of the MEMBERSHIP relationship and, by this means, to an occurrence of the DEPARTMENT entity. Following this, to obtain the data of the projects on which he or she is working, we must access on average three occurrences of the PARTICIPATION relationship (because we have said that on average an employee works on three projects). Then, through this, we access on average three occurrences of the PROJECT entity. All this can be summed up in a *table of accesses* such as that shown in Figure 7.5. In the last column of this table, the type of access is shown: R for read access, and W for write access. It is necessary to make this distinction because, as we shall see in Chapter 9, write operations are generally more onerous than read ones.

In the next section, we will see how these simple analysis tools can be used to make decisions during the restructuring of E-R schemas.

Table of accesses

Concept	Type	Accesses	Type
Employee	Entity	1	R
Employment	Relation	1	R
Department	Entity	1	R
Participation	Relation	3	R
Project	Entity	3	R

Figure 7.5 Table of accesses for operation 2.

7.2 Restructuring of E-R schemas

The restructuring step of an E-R schema can be sub-divided into a series of tasks to be carried out in sequence (see Figure 7.6).

• **Analysis of redundancies** decides whether to delete or retain possible redundancies present in the schema.

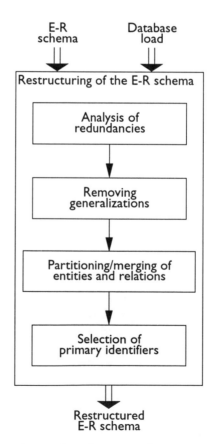

Figure 7.6 Restructuring tasks of an E-R schema.

- **Removing generalizations** replaces all the generalizations in the schema by other constructs.

- **Partitioning and merging of entities and relationships** decides whether is it convenient to partition concepts in the schema into more than one concept or to merge several separate concepts into a single one.

- **Selection of primary identifiers** chooses an identifier for those entities that have more than one.

Later in the section, we will examine separately the various restructuring tasks using practical examples.

7.2.1 Analysis of redundancies

A redundancy in a conceptual schema corresponds to a piece of information that can be derived (that is, obtained by a series of retrieval operations) from other data. An Entity-Relationship schema can contain various forms of redundancy. The most frequent examples are as follows.

- Attributes whose value can be derived, for each occurrence of an entity (or a relationship), from values of other attributes of the same occurrence. For example, the first schema in Figure 7.7 consists of an entity INVOICE in which one of the attributes can be deduced from the others by means of arithmetic operations.

- Attributes that can be derived from attributes of other entities (or relationships), usually by means of aggregate functions. An example of such a redundancy is present in the second schema in Figure 7.7. In this schema, the attribute TotalAmount of the PURCHASE entity is a derived one. It can be computed from the values of the attribute Price of the PRODUCT entity, by summing the prices of the products of which a purchase is made up, as specified by the COMPOSITION relationship.

- Attributes that can be derived from operations of counting occurrences. For example, in the third schema in Figure 7.7, the attribute NumberOfInhabitants of a town can be derived by counting the occurrences of the relationship RESIDENCE in which the town participates. This is actually a variant of the previous example, which is discussed separately, as it occurs frequently.

- Relationships that can be derived from other relationships in the presence of cycles. The last schema in Figure 7.7 contains an example of this type of redundancy: the TEACHING relationship between students and lecturers can be derived from the relationships ATTENDANCE and ASSIGNMENT. It must be clearly stated that the presence of cycles does not necessarily generate redundancies. If, for example, instead of the TEACHING relationship, this schema had contained a relationship SUPERVISION

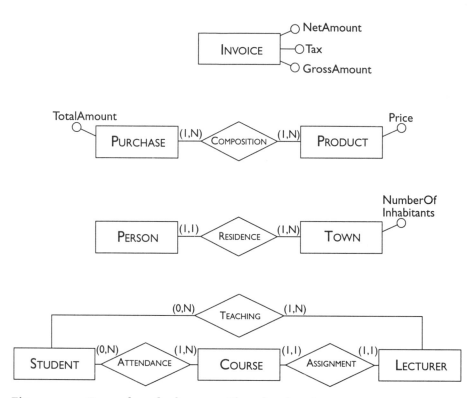

Figure 7.7 Examples of schemas with redundancies.

representing the link between students and supervisors then the schema would not have been redundant.

The presence of a derived piece of information in a database presents an advantage and some disadvantages. The advantage is a reduction in the number of accesses necessary to obtain the derived information. The disadvantages are a larger storage requirement (which is, however, a negligible cost) and the necessity for carrying out additional operations in order to keep the derived data up to date. The decision to maintain or delete a redundancy is made by comparing the cost of operations that involve the redundant information and the storage needed, in the case of presence or absence of redundancy.

Using a practical example, let us look at how the evaluation tools described above can be used to make a decision of this type. Consider the schema about people and towns in Figure 7.7 and imagine that it refers to a regional electoral roll application for which the following main operations are defined:

- **operation 1**: add a new person with the person's town of residence.

- **operation 2**: print all the data of a town (including the number of inhabitants).

Let us suppose, moreover, that for this application, the load is that shown in Figure 7.8.

Table of volumes

Concept	Type	Volume
Town	E	200
Person	E	1000000
Residence	R	1000000

Table of operations

Operation	Type	Frequency
Op 1	I	500 per day
Op 2	I	2 per day

Figure 7.8 Tables of volumes and operations for the schema in Figure 7.7.

Let us first try to evaluate the indicators of performance in the case of presence of redundancy (attribute NumberOfInhabitants in the TOWN entity).

Assume that the number of inhabitants of a town requires four bytes. We can see that the redundant data requires $4 \times 200 = 800$ bytes, that is, less than one Kbyte of additional storage. Let us now move on to estimating the cost of the operations. As described in the access tables in Figure 7.9, operation 1 requires the following. A write access to the PERSON entity (to add a new

Table of accesses in presence of redundancy

Operation 1			
Concept	Type	Acc.	Type
Person	E	1	W
Residence	R	1	W
Town	E	1	R
Town	E	1	W

Operation 2			
Concept	Type	Acc.	Type
Town	E	1	R

Table of accesses in absence of redundancy

Operation 1			
Conceto	Type	Acc.	Type
Person	E	1	W
Residence	R	1	W

Operation 2			
Concept	Type	Acc.	Type
Town	E	1	R
Residence	R	5000	R

Figure 7.9 Tables of accesses for the schema on electoral roll data in Figure 7.7.

person), a write access to the RESIDENCE relationship (to add a new person-town pair) and finally a read access (to find the relevant town) and another write access to the TOWN entity (to update the number of inhabitants of that occurrence). This is all repeated 500 times per day, for a total of 1500 write accesses and 500 read accesses. The cost of operation 2 is almost negligible, as it requires a single read access to the TOWN entity to be repeated twice a day. Supposing a write access to cost twice as much as a read access, we have a total of 3500 accesses a day when there is redundant data.

Let us now consider what happens when there is no redundant data.

For operation 1 we need a write access to the PERSON entity and a write access to the RESIDENCE relationship for a total of 1000 write accesses per day. (There is no need to access the TOWN entity since there is no derived information). For operation 2 however, we need a read access to the TOWN entity (to obtain the data for the town), which we can neglect, and 5000 read accesses to the RESIDENCE relationship on average, (obtained by dividing the number of people by the number of towns) to calculate the number of inhabitants of this town. This gives a total of 10000 read accesses per day. Counting twice the write accesses, we have a total of 12000 accesses per day when there is no redundant data. Thus, approximately 8500 accesses more per day are required where there is no redundant data in order to save a mere Kbyte. This depends on the fact that the read accesses needed to compute the derived data are much more than the write accesses needed to keep the derived data up to date.

It is obvious that, in this case, it worth maintaining the redundant data.

7.2.2 Removing generalizations

The relational model does not allow the direct representation of generalizations of the E-R model. We need, therefore, to transform these constructs into other constructs that are easier to translate. As we shall see later in Section 7.4.2, the E-R constructs for which the translation into the relational model is easy are entities and relationships.

To represent a generalization using entities and relationships there are essentially three possible options. We will demonstrate these by referring to the generic E-R schema in Figure 7.10.

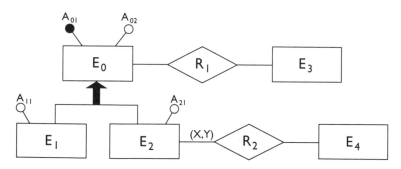

Figure 7.10 Example of a schema with generalization.

The possible outcomes are shown in Figure 7.11 and are obtained by means of the following restructurings.

1. **Collapse the child entities into the parent entity.** The entities E_1 and E_2 are deleted and their properties are added to the parent entity E_0. To this entity, a further attribute Atype is added, which serves to distinguish the 'type' (E_1 or E_2) of an occurrence of E_0. For example, a generalization

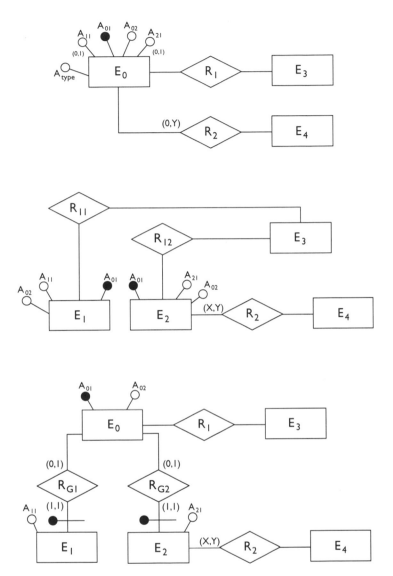

Figure 7.11 Possible restructurings of the schema in Figure 7.10.

between the parent entity PERSON and the child entities MAN and WOMAN can be collapsed into the entity PERSON by adding to it the attribute Sex. Note that the attributes A_{11} and A_{21} can assume null values (because they are inapplicable) for some occurrences of E_0. In addition, the relationship R_2 will have a minimum cardinality equal to zero for the E_0 entity (because the occurrences of E_2 are only a subset of the occurrences of E_0).

2. **Collapse the parent entity into the child entities.** The parent entity E_0 is deleted and, for the property of inheritance, its attributes, its identifier and the relationships to which this entity was involved, are added to both the child entities E_1 and E_2. The relationships R_{11} and R_{12}

represent respectively the restriction of the relationship R_1 on the occurrences of the entities E_1 and E_2. Consider, for example, a generalization between the entities PERSON, having Surname and Age as attributes and SSN (Social Security Number) as an identifier, and the entities MAN and WOMAN. If this is restructured in this way, then the attributes Surname and Age and the identifier SSN are added to both the entities MAN and WOMAN.

3. **Substitution of the generalization with relationships.** The generalization is transformed into two one-to-one relationships that link the parent entity with the child entities E_1 and E_2. There are no transfers of attributes or relationship and the entities E_1 and E_2 are identified externally by the entity E_0. Additional constraints hold in the new schema: each occurrence of E_0 cannot participate in both R_{G1} and R_{G2}; moreover, if the generalization is complete, each occurrence of E_0 must participate in exactly one of R_{G1} and R_{G2}.

The choice among the various options can be made in a manner similar to that used for derived data. That is, by considering the advantages and disadvantages of each of the possible choices in terms of storage needed and cost of the operations involved. We can, however, establish some general rules.

- Option 1 is convenient when the operations involve the occurrences and the attributes of E_0, E_1 and E_2 more or less in the same way. In this case, even if we waste storage for the presence of null values, the choice assures fewer accesses compared to the others in which the occurrences and the attributes are distributed among the various entities.

- Option 2 is possible only if the generalization is total, otherwise the occurrences of E_1 that are occurrences of neither E_1 nor E_2 would not be represented. It is useful when there are operations that refer only to occurrences of E_1 or of E_2, and so they make distinctions between these entities. In this case, storage is saved compared to Option 1, because, in principle, the attributes never assume null values. Further, there is a reduction of accesses compared to Option 3, because it is not necessary to visit E_0 in order to access some attributes of E_1 and E_2.

- Option 3 is useful when the generalization is not total and the operations refer to either occurrences and attributes of E_1 (E_2) or of E_0, and therefore make distinctions between child and parent entities. In this case, we can save storage compared to Option 1 because of the absence of null values, but there is an increase of the number of accesses to keep the occurrences consistent.

There is an important aspect that must be clarified about the above. For the restructuring of the generalizations, the simple counting of instances and accesses is not always sufficient for choosing the best possible option. Given these factors, it would seem that Option 3 would hardly ever be suitable, as it usually requires more accesses in order to carry out operations on the data. This restructuring, however, has the great advantage of generating entities with fewer attributes. As we shall see, this translates into logical and then physical structures of small dimensions for which a physical access allows the retrieval of a greater amount of data (tuples) at once. Therefore, in some critical cases, a more refined analysis needs to be carried out. This might take into account other factors, such as the quantity of data that can be retrieved by means of a single access to secondary storage. These aspects will be discussed in more detail in Chapter 9.

The options presented are not the only ones allowed, but it is possible to carry out restructurings that combine them. An example is given in Figure 7.12, which consists in another possible transformation of the schema given in Figure 7.10. In this case, based on considerations similar to those

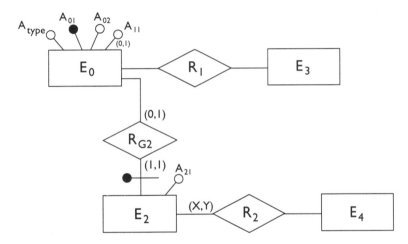

Figure 7.12 Possible restructuring of the schema in Figure 7.10.

discussed above, it was decided to incorporate E_0 and E_1 and to leave the entity E_2 separate from the others. The attribute A_{type} was added to distinguish the occurrences of E_0 from those of E_1.

Finally, regarding generalizations on more than one level, we can proceed in a similar way, analyzing a generalization at a time, starting from the bottom of the entire hierarchy. Based on the above, various configurations are possible, which can be obtained by combining the basic restructurings on the various levels of the hierarchy.

7.2.3 Partitioning and merging of entities and relationships

Entities and relationships of an E-R schema can be partitioned or merged to improve the efficiency of operations, using the following principle. Accesses are reduced by separating attributes of the same concept that are accessed by different operations and by merging attributes of different concepts that are accessed by the same operations. The same criteria as those discussed for redundancies are valid in making a decision about this type of restructuring.

Partitioning of entities   An example of entity partitioning is shown in Figure 7.13: the EMPLOYEE entity is substituted by two entities, linked by a

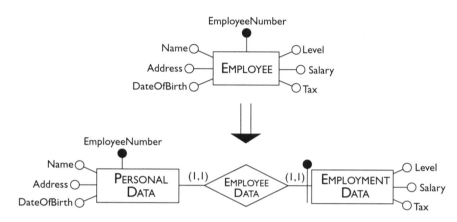

Figure 7.13 Example of partitioning of entities.

one-to-one relationship. One of them describes personal information of an employee. The other describes information about the employment of an employee. This restructuring is useful if the operations that frequently involve the original entity require, for an employee, either only information of a personal nature or only information relating to his or her employment.

This is an example of *vertical* partitioning of an entity, in the sense that the concept is sub-divided according to its attributes. It is also possible, however, to carry out *horizontal* partitioning in which the sub-division works on the occurrences of entities. For example, there could be some operations that relate only to the analysts and others that operate only on the salespeople. In this case, too, it could be useful to partition the EMPLOYEE entity into two distinct entities, ANALYST and SALESPERSON having the same attributes as the original entity. Note that horizontal partitioning corresponds to the introduction of hierarchies at the logical level.

Horizontal partitioning has the side effect of having to duplicate the relationships in which the original entity participated. This phenomenon can have negative effects on the performance of the database. On the other hand, vertical partitioning generates entities with fewer attributes. They can therefore be translated into physical structures from which we can retrieve a great deal of data with a single access. Partitioning operations will be further discussed in Chapter 10, when dealing with the fragmentation of distributed databases.

Deletion of multi-valued attributes One type of partitioning that should be discussed separately deals with the deletion of multi-valued attributes. This restructuring is necessary because, as with generalizations, the relational model does not allow the direct representation of these attributes.

The restructuring required is quite simple and is illustrated in Figure 7.14.

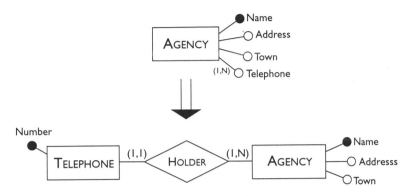

Figure 7.14 Example of deletion of multi-value attributes.

The AGENCY entity, is separated into two entities: an entity having name and attributes as the original entity, apart from the multi-valued attribute **Telephone**, and a new TELEPHONE entity, with the attribute **Number**. These entities are linked by a one-to-many relationship. Obviously, if the attribute had also been optional, then the minimum cardinality for the AGENCY entity in the resulting schema would have been zero.

Merging of entities Merging is the reverse operation of partitioning. An example of merging of entities is shown in Figure 7.15 in which the PERSON and APARTMENT entities, linked by a one-to-one relationship OWNER, are merged into a single entity having the attributes of both. This restructuring

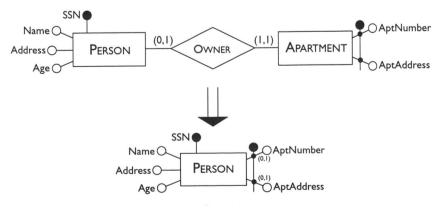

Figure 7.15 Example of merging of entities.

can be suggested by the fact that the most frequent operations on the PERSON entity always require data relating to the apartment that the person possesses. Thus, we wish to avoid the accesses necessary to retrieve this data by means of the OWNER relationship. A side-effect of this restructuring is the possible presence of null values because, according to the cardinalities, there are people who do not own apartments. Therefore, there are no values for them for the attributes APTADDRESS and APTNUMBER.

Merging is generally carried out on one-to-one relationships, rarely on one-to-many relationships and hardly ever on many-to-many relationships. This is because merging of entities linked by a one-to-many relationship or a many-to-many relationship generates redundancies. In particular, it is easy to verify that redundancies can appear in non-key attributes of the entity that participates in the original relationship with a maximum cardinality equal to N. We will come back to illustrate this point in Chapter 8.

Other types of partitioning and merging Partitioning and merging operations can also be applied to relationships. This can be done for two reasons. Firstly, in order to separate occurrences of a relationship that are always accessed separately. Secondly, to merge two (or more) relationships between the same entities into a single relationship, when their occurrences are always accessed together. An example of partitioning of relationship is given in Figure 7.16 in which the current players of a basketball team are distinguished from past players.

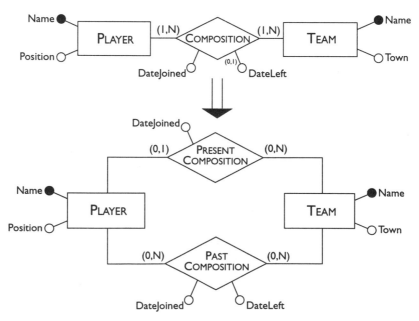

Figure 7.16 Example of partitioning of a relationship.

We should mention that the decisions about partitioning and merging can be postponed until the physical design phase. Many of today's database management systems allow the specification of *clusters* of logical structures, that is, grouping of tables, carried out at the physical level. Clusters allow rapid access to data distributed throughout different logical structures.

7.2.4 Selection of primary identifiers

The choice of an identifier for each entity is essential to the translation into the relational model, because of the major role keys play in a value-based data model, as we discussed in Chapter 2. Furthermore, database management systems require the specification of a *primary key* on which auxiliary structures for fast access to data, known as *indices*, are automatically constructed. Indices are discussed in more detail in Section 9.5.5. Thus, where there are entities for which many identifiers (or none) have been specified, it is necessary to decide which attributes constitute the primary identifier.

The criteria for this decision are as follows.

- Attributes with null values cannot form primary identifiers. These attributes do not guarantee access to all the occurrences of the corresponding entity, as we pointed out while discussing keys for the relational model.

- One or few attributes are preferable to many attributes. This ensures that the indices are of limited size, less storage is needed for the creation of logical links among the various relations, and join operations are facilitated.

- For the same reason, an internal identifier with few attributes is preferable to an external one, possibly involving many entities. This is because external identifiers are translated into keys comprising the identifiers of the entities involved in the external identification. Thus, keys with many attributes would be generated.

- An identifier that is used by many operations to access the occurrences of an entity is preferable to others. In this way, these operations can be executed efficiently, since they can take advantage of the indices automatically built by the DBMS.

At this stage, if none of the candidate identifiers satisfies the above requirements, it is possible to introduce a further attribute to the entity. This attribute will hold special values (often called *codes*) generated solely for the purpose of identifying occurrences of the entity.

It is advisable to keep track of the identifiers that are not selected as primary but that are used by some operations for access to data. As we will discuss in Chapter 9, for these identifiers we can explicitly define efficient access structures, generally known as *secondary indices*. Secondary indices can be used to access data as an alternative to those generated automatically on the primary identifiers.

7.3 Translation into the relational model

The second step of logical design corresponds to a translation between different data models. Starting from an E-R schema, an *equivalent* relational schema is constructed. By equivalent, we mean a schema capable of representing the same information. According to the restructuring made on the E-R schema in the first step of logical design, it is sufficient to consider a simplified version of the E-R model. In this version, a schema contains no generalizations or multi-valued attributes and has only primary identifiers.

We will deal with the translation problem systematically, beginning with the fundamental case, that of entities linked by many-to-many relationships. This example demonstrates the general principle on which the whole translation technique is based.

7.3.1 Entities and many-to-many relationships

Consider the schema in Figure 7.17.

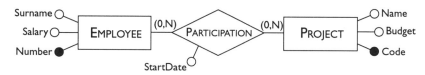

Figure 7.17 An E-R schema with a many-to-many relationship.

Its natural translation into the relational model allows the following:

- for each entity, a relation with the same name, having as attributes the same attributes as the entity and having its identifier as key;

- for the relationship, a relation with the same name, having as attributes the attributes of the relationship and the identifiers of the entities involved; these identifiers, taken together, form the key of the relation.

If the original attributes of entities or relationships are optional, then the corresponding attributes of relations can assume null values.

The relational schema obtained is thus as follows:

EMPLOYEE(<u>Number</u>, Surname, Salary)
PROJECT(<u>Code</u>, Name, Budget)
PARTICIPATION(<u>Number</u>, <u>Code</u>, StartDate)

To make the meaning of the schema clearer it is helpful to do some renaming. For example, in our case we can clarify the contents of the PARTICIPATION relation by defining it as follows:

PARTICIPATION(<u>Employee</u>, <u>Project</u>, StartDate)

The domain of the **Employee** attribute is a set of employee numbers and that of the **Project** attribute is a set of project codes. There are referential constraints between these attributes and the EMPLOYEE relation and the PROJECT relation respectively.

Renaming is essential in some cases. For example, when we have recursive relationships such as that in Figure 7.18.

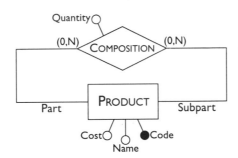

Figure 7.18 E-R schema with recursive relationship.

This schema is translated into two relations:

PRODUCT(<u>Code</u>, Name, Cost)
COMPOSITION(<u>Part</u>, <u>Subpart</u>, Quantity)

In this schema, both the attributes **Part** and **Subpart** have product codes as domain. There is in fact a referential constraint between each of them and the PRODUCT relation.

The translation of a relationship involving more than two entities is similar to the translation of a binary relationship. For example, consider the schema with a ternary relationship in Figure 7.19.

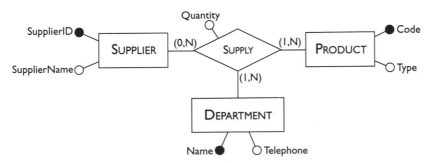

Figure 7.19 E-R schema with ternary relationship.

This schema is translated into the following four relations:

$$\text{SUPPLIER}(\underline{\text{SupplierID}}, \text{SupplierName})$$
$$\text{PRODUCT}(\underline{\text{Code}}, \text{Type})$$
$$\text{DEPARTMENT}(\underline{\text{Name}}, \text{Telephone})$$
$$\text{SUPPLY}(\underline{\text{Supplier}}, \underline{\text{Product}}, \underline{\text{Department}}, \text{Quantity})$$

There are referential constraints for the schema thus obtained between the attributes Supplier, Product, and Department of the SUPPLY relation and, respectively, the SUPPLIER relation, the PRODUCT relation, and the DEPARTMENT relation.

In this last type of translation, we need to verify whether the identifiers of the entities, taken together, do not constitute a key but, instead, a redundant *superkey* for the relation that represents the relationship of the E-R schema. This can happen, for example, in the case of the schema in Figure 7.19, if there is a sole supplier who supplies a given product to a given department. Note that the cardinality is still valid, since this supplier can supply many products to this or other departments. In this case, the key to the SUPPLY relation would be made up of the attributes Product and Department only, because, given a product and a department, the supplier is unambiguously determined.

7.3.2 One-to-many relationships

Consider the schema with a one-to-many relationship in Figure 7.20.

Figure 7.20 E-R schema with one-to-many relationships.

According to the rule seen for many-to-many relationships, the translation of this schema would be as follows:

$$\text{PLAYER}(\underline{\text{Surname}}, \underline{\text{DateofBirth}}, \text{Position})$$
$$\text{TEAM}(\underline{\text{Name}}, \text{Town}, \text{TeamColours})$$
$$\text{CONTRACT}(\underline{\text{PlayerSurname}}, \underline{\text{PlayerDateOfBirth}}, \text{Team}, \text{Salary})$$

Note that in the CONTRACT relation, the key consists of only the identifier of PLAYER because the cardinalities of the relationship tell us that each player has a contract with a single team. At this point, the relations PLAYER and CONTRACT have the same key (the surname and the date of birth of a player) and we can therefore merge them in a single relation with no risk of redundancy. This is because there is a one-to-one correspondence between the respective instances. Thus, for the schema in Figure 7.20, the following translation is preferable, in which the PLAYER relation represents both the entity and the relationship of the original E-R schema:

$$\text{PLAYER}(\underline{\text{Surname}}, \underline{\text{DateofBirth}}, \text{Position}, \text{Team}, \text{Salary})$$
$$\text{TEAM}(\underline{\text{Name}}, \text{Town}, \text{TeamColours})$$

In this schema, there is obviously the referential constraint between the attribute Team of the PLAYER relation and the TEAM relation.

Note that the participation of the PLAYER entity is mandatory. If it were optional (it is possible to have players who have no contract with a team), then both of the translations with three relations and with two relations would be valid. Even if in the second translation we have fewer relations, it is in fact possible to have null values in the PLAYER relation on the attributes Team and Salary. Conversely, in the first translation, this cannot happen.

We mentioned in Section 5.2.2, that n-ary relationships are usually many-to-many. However, when an entity participates with a maximum cardinality of one, we can save a relation, as happens with the translation of one-to-many binary relationships. The entity that participates in the relationship with maximum cardinality of one, is translated into a relation that includes the identifiers of the other entities involved in the relationship (as well as possible attributes of the relationship itself). There is, therefore, no longer any need to represent the original relationship with a separate relation. For example, assume that the PRODUCT entity participated in the relationship in Figure 7.19 with a minimum and maximum cardinality of one. This means that, for each product there is a sole supplier who supplies it and a sole department that is supplied. Then the schema is translated as follows.

$$\text{SUPPLIER}(\underline{\text{SupplierID}}, \text{SupplierName})$$
$$\text{DEPARTMENT}(\underline{\text{Name}}, \text{Telephone})$$
$$\text{PRODUCT}(\underline{\text{Code}}, \text{Type}, \text{Supplier}, \text{Department}, \text{Quantity})$$

Here there are referential constraints between the attribute Supplier of the PRODUCT relation and the SUPPLIER relation, and between the attribute Department of the PRODUCT relation and the DEPARTMENT relation.

7.3.3 Entities with external identifiers

Entities with external identifiers give rise to relations having keys that contain the identifier of the 'identifying' entities. Consider, for example, the E-R schema shown in Figure 7.21.

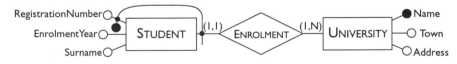

Figure 7.21 E-R schema with external identifier.

The corresponding relational schema is as follows:

STUDENT(<u>RegistrationNumber</u>, <u>University</u>, Surname, EnrolmentYear)
UNIVERSITY(<u>Name</u>, Town, Address)

in which there is a referential constraint between the attribute University of the STUDENT relation and the UNIVERSITY relation.

As we can see, by representing the external identifier, we also represent the relationship between the two entities. Remember that entities identified externally always participate in the relationship with a minimum and maximum cardinality of one. This type of translation is valid independently of the cardinality with which the other entities participate in the relationship.

7.3.4 One-to-one relationships

For one-to-one relationships, there are generally many possibilities for translation. We will begin with one-to-one relationships with mandatory participation for both the entities, such as that in the schema in Figure 7.22.

Figure 7.22 E-R schema with one-to-one relationships.

There are two symmetrical and equally valid possibilities for this type of relationship:

HEAD(<u>Number</u>, Name, Salary, Department, StartDate)
DEPARTMENT(<u>Name</u>, Telephone, Branch)

With the referential constraint between the attribute Department of the HEAD relation and the DEPARTMENT relation, or:

HEAD(<u>Number</u>, Name, Salary)
DEPARTMENT(<u>Name</u>, Telephone, Branch, Head, StartDate)

for which there is the referential constraint between the attribute Head of the DEPARTMENT relation and the HEAD relation.

Since there is a one-to-one correspondence between the occurrences of the two entities, a further option would seem possible in which we have a single relation containing all the attributes in the schema. This option should be discarded, however, because we must not forget that the schema that we are translating is the result of a process in which precise choices were made regarding the merging and the partitioning of entities. This means that, if the restructured E-R schema has two entities linked by a one-to-one relation, we found it convenient to keep the two concepts separate. It is therefore not appropriate to merge them during the translation into the relational model.

Let us now consider the case of a one-to-one relationship with optional participation for one of the entities, such as that in the schema in Figure 7.23.

Figure 7.23 E-R schema with one-to-one relationship

In this case we have one preferable option:

EMPLOYEE(<u>Number</u>, Name, Salary)
DEPARTMENT(<u>Name</u>, Telephone, Branch, Head, StartDate)

for which there is the referential constraint between the attribute **Head** of the DEPARTMENT relation and the EMPLOYEE relation. This option is preferable to the one in which the relationship is represented in the EMPLOYEE relation through the name of the department managed, because, for this attribute, we could have null values.

Finally, consider the case in which both the entities have optional participation. For example, assume that, in the schema in Figure 7.23, there can be departments with no head (and thus the minimum cardinality of the DEPARTMENT entity is equal to zero). In this case, there is a further possibility that allows for three separate relations:

EMPLOYEE(<u>Number</u>, Name, Salary)
DEPARTMENT(<u>Name</u>, Telephone, Branch)
MANAGEMENT(<u>Head</u>, Department, StartDate)

Note that the key of the MANAGEMENT relation could be the attribute **Department** as well. Here, we have referential constraints between the attributes **Head** and **Department** of the MANAGEMENT relation and the EMPLOYEE and DEPARTMENT relations, respectively.

This solution has an advantage of never having null values on the attributes that implement the relationship. On the other hand, we need an extra relation, with a consequent increase of the complexity of the database. Therefore, the three-relation solution is to be considered only if the number of occurrences of the relationship is very low compared to the occurrences of the entities involved in the relationship. In this case, there is the advantage of avoiding the presence of many null values.

7.3.5 Translation of a complex schema

To see how to proceed in a complex case, we will carry out a complete example of a translation based on the schema shown in Figure 7.24.

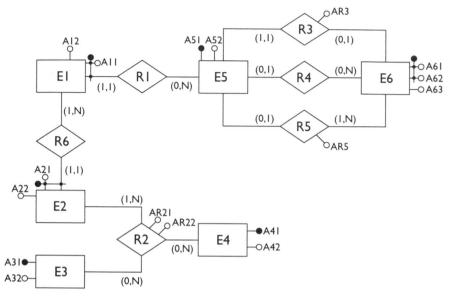

Figure 7.24 An E-R schema for translation.

In the first phase, we translate each entity into a relation. The translation of the entities with internal identifiers is immediate:

$$E3(\underline{A31}, A32)$$
$$E4(\underline{A41}, A42)$$
$$E5(\underline{A51}, A52)$$
$$E6(\underline{A61}, \underline{A62}, A63)$$

Now we translate the entities with external identifiers. We obtain the following relations:

$$E1(\underline{A11}, \underline{A51}, A12)$$
$$E2(\underline{A21}, \underline{A11}, \underline{A51}, A22)$$

Note how E2 takes the attribute A11 and (transitively) the attribute A51, which, together with A21, identifies E1. Some referential constraints are defined for the relations produced (for example, there is a referential constraint between the attribute A51 of E1 and E5).

We now move on to the translation of relationships. Relationships R1 and R6 have already been translated because of the external identification of E2 and E1 respectively. We assume we have decided to obtain a minimum number of relations in the final schema and we will try therefore to merge relations where possible. We obtain the following modifications to be carried out on the initial relations:

• in order to translate R3, we introduce, with appropriate renaming, the attributes that identify E6, among those of E5, as well as the attribute AR3 of R3. Thus, we introduce A61R3, A62R3 and AR3 in E5;

- similarly for R4, we introduce A61R4 and A62R4 in E5;

- similarly for R5, we introduce A61R5, A62R5 and AR5 in E5.

Note that the renaming is indispensable in order to be able to distinguish between the uses of the same attributes to represent different relationships (for example, A61R3, which represents R3, and A61R4, which represents R4). Finally, we translate the only many-to-many relationship:

$$R2(\underline{A21}, \underline{A11}, \underline{A51}, \underline{A31}, \underline{A41}, AR21, AR22)$$

The relational schema obtained is therefore as follows:

$$E1(\underline{A11}, \underline{A51}, A12)$$
$$E2(\underline{A21}, \underline{A11}, \underline{A51}, A22)$$
$$E3(\underline{A31}, A32)$$
$$E4(\underline{A41}, A42)$$
$$E5(\underline{A51}, A52, A61R3, A62R3, AR3, A61R4, A62R4, A61R5, A62R5, AR5)$$
$$E6(\underline{A61}, \underline{A62}, A63)$$
$$R2(\underline{A21}, \underline{A11}, \underline{A51}, \underline{A31}, \underline{A41}, AR21, AR22)$$

Let us note that we have obtained relations (E2 and R2) with keys composed of many attributes. In such cases one could decide to introduce simple keys (codes) either at this stage or earlier in the restructuring step as discussed in Section 7.2.4.

7.3.6 Summary tables

The translations we have seen are summarized in Figure 7.25 and Figure 7.26. For each type of configuration of E-R schema, a description of the case and the possible translations are supplied.

In these tables, the symbols X and Y indicate any one of the allowed cardinalities. The asterisks indicate the possibility of having null values on the related attributes and the broken underline indicates an alternative key to the one indicated by a solid underline.

7.3.7 Documentation of logical schemas

As with conceptual design, the result of logical design does not consist merely of a simple database schema but also of the documentation associated with it. First, much of the documentation of the conceptual schema produced in the logical design phase can be inherited by the logical schema. In particular, if the names of the concepts of the E-R schema are reused to construct the relational schema, the business rules defined previously can also be used for the documentation of this last. This documentation must be completed with the referential constraints introduced by the translation.

In this context, we can adopt a simple graphical notation for the representation of both the relations and the referential constraints existing between the various relations. An example of this notation is given in

Type	Initial schema	Possible translation
Binary many-to-many relationship	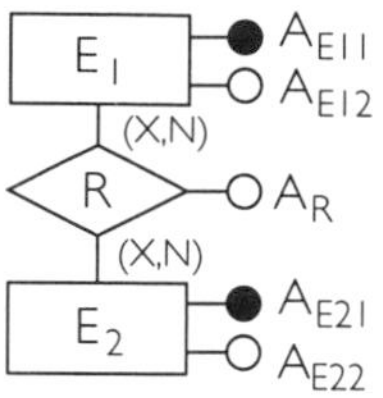	$E_1(\underline{A_{E11}}, A_{E12})$ $E_2(\underline{A_{E21}}, A_{E22})$ $R(\underline{A_{E11}}, \underline{A_{E21}}, A_R)$
Ternary many-to-many relationship	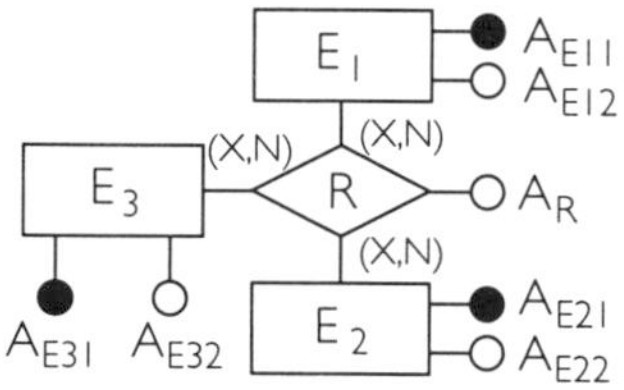	$E_1(\underline{A_{E11}}, A_{E12})$ $E_2(\underline{A_{E21}}, A_{E22})$ $E_3(\underline{A_{E31}}, A_{E32})$ $R(\underline{A_{E11}}, \underline{A_{E21}}, \underline{A_{E31}}, A_R)$
One-to-many relationship with mandatory participation	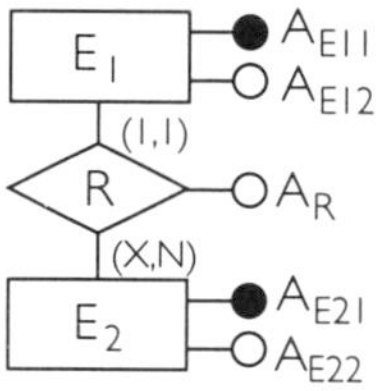	$E_1(\underline{A_{E11}}, A_{E12}, A_{E21}, A_R)$ $E_2(\underline{A_{E21}}, A_{E22})$
One-to-many relationship with optional participation	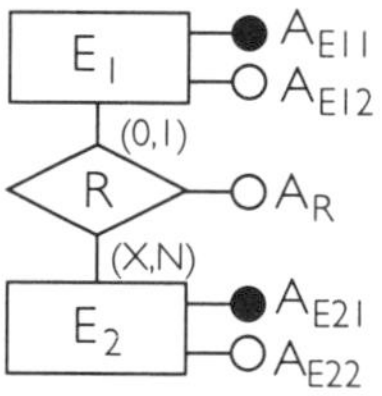	$E_1(\underline{A_{E11}}, A_{E12})$ $E_2(\underline{A_{E21}}, A_{E22})$ $R(\underline{A_{E11}}, A_{E21}, A_R)$ Alternatively: $E_1(\underline{A_{E11}}, A_{E21}, A_{E21}^{*}, A_R^{*})$ $E_2(\underline{A_{E21}}, A_{E22})$
Relationship with external identifiers	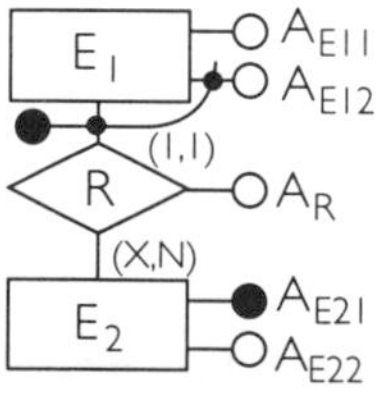	$E_1(\underline{A_{E12}}, \underline{A_{E21}}, A_{E11}, A_R)$ $E_2(\underline{A_{E21}}, A_{E22})$

Figure 7.25 Translations from the E-R model to the relational.

Figure 7.27, with reference to the translation of the schema in Figure 7.17. In this representation keys of relations appear in bold face, arrows describe referential constraints and the presence of asterisks on the attributes denotes the possibility of having null values on them.

In this way, we can keep track of the relationships of the original E-R schema. This is useful to identify easily, the *join paths*, that is, the join

Type	Initial schema	Possible translation
One-to-one relationship with mandatory participation for both entities	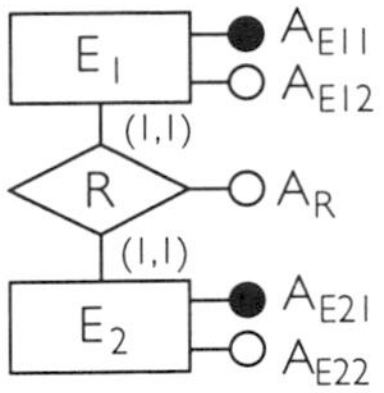 E_1 $\bullet A_{E11}$ $\circ A_{E12}$ $(1,1)$ R $\circ A_R$ $(1,1)$ E_2 $\bullet A_{E21}$ $\circ A_{E22}$	$E_1(\underline{A_{E11}}, A_{E12}, A_{E21}, A_R)$ $E_2(\underline{A_{E21}}, A_{E22})$ Alternatively: $E_2(\underline{A_{E21}}, A_{E22}, A_{E11}, A_R)$ $E_1(\underline{A_{E11}}, A_{E12})$
One-to-one relationship with optional participation for one entity	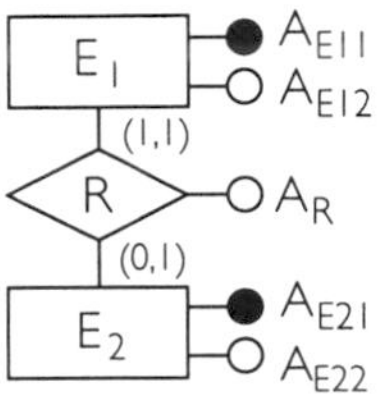 E_1 $\bullet A_{E11}$ $\circ A_{E12}$ $(1,1)$ R $\circ A_R$ $(0,1)$ E_2 $\bullet A_{E21}$ $\circ A_{E22}$	$E_1(\underline{A_{E11}}, A_{E12}, A_{E21}, A_R)$ $E_2(\underline{A_{E21}}, A_{E22})$
One-to-one relationship with optional participation for both entities	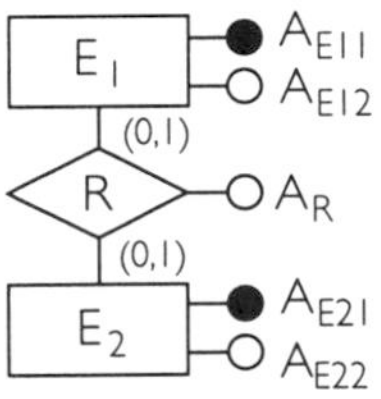 E_1 $\bullet A_{E11}$ $\circ A_{E12}$ $(0,1)$ R $\circ A_R$ $(0,1)$ E_2 $\bullet A_{E21}$ $\circ A_{E22}$	$E_1(\underline{A_{E11}}, A_{E21})$ $E_2(\underline{A_{E21}}, A_{E22}, A_{E11}^*, A_R^*)$ Alternatively: $E_1(\underline{A_{E11}}, A_{E12}, A_{E21}^*, A_R^*)$ $E_2(\underline{A_{E21}}, A_{E22})$ Alternatively: $E_1(\underline{A_{E11}}, A_{E12})$ $E_2(\underline{A_{E21}}, A_{E22})$ $R(\underline{A_{E11}}, A_{E21}, A_R)$

Figure 7.26 Translations from the E-R model to the relational.

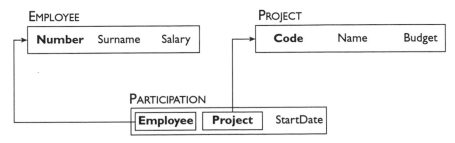

Figure 7.27 Graphical representation of a translation of the schema in Figure 7.17.

operations necessary to reconstruct the information represented by the original relationship. Thus, in the case in the example, the projects in which the employees participate can be retrieved by means of the PARTICIPATION relation.

Another example of the use of this notation is given in Figure 7.28, with reference to the translation of the schema in Figure 7.20.

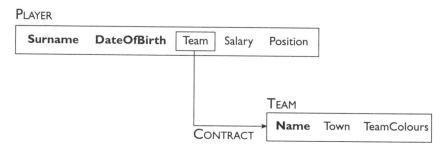

Figure 7.28 Graphical representation of a translation of the schema in Figure 7.20.

Note that this method also allows us to represent explicitly the relationships of the original E-R schema, to which, in the equivalent relational schema, no relation corresponds (the CONTRACT relationship in the example in question).

As a final example, Figure 7.29 shows the representation of the relational schema obtained in Section 7.3.5. Now, the logical links between the various relations can be easily identified.

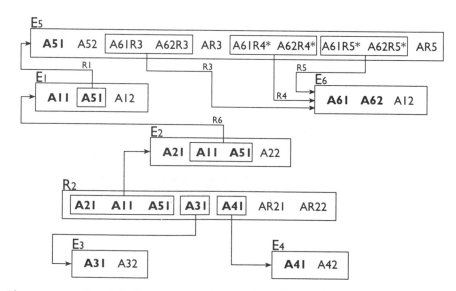

Figure 7.29 Graphical representation of the relational schema obtained in Section 7.3.5.

In Appendix A, we will see that a variant of the graphical formalism shown is actually adopted by the Access database management system, both to represent relational schemas and to express join operations.

7.4 An example of logical design

Let us return to the example in the preceding chapter regarding the training company. The conceptual schema is shown again, for convenience, in Figure 7.30.

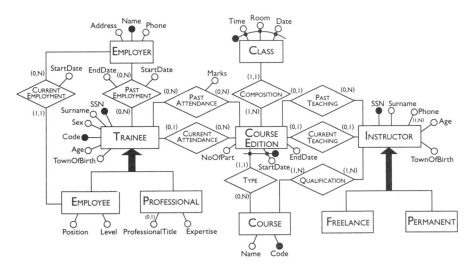

Figure 7.30 The E-R schema of a training company.

The following operations were planned on the data described by this schema:

- **operation 1:** insert a new trainee indicating all his or her data;

- **operation 2:** assign a trainee to an edition of a course;

- **operation 3:** insert a new instructor indicating all his or her data and the courses he or she is qualified to teach;

- **operation 4:** assign a qualified instructor to an edition of a course;

- **operation 5:** display all the information on the past editions of a course with title, class timetables and number of trainees;

- **operation 6:** display all the courses offered, with information on the instructors who are qualified to teach them;

- **operation 7:** for each instructor, find the trainees for all the courses he or she is teaching or has taught;

- **operation 8**: carry out a statistical analysis of all the trainees with all the information on them, on the edition of courses they have attended and on the marks obtained.

7.4.1 Restructuring phase

The database load is shown in Figure 7.31. We will now carry out the various restructuring tasks. The various transformations are shown together in the final schema in Section 7.33.

Table of volumes

Concept	Type	Volume
Class	E	8000
CourseEdition	E	1000
Course	E	200
Instructor	E	300
Freelance	E	250
Permanent	E	50
Trainee	E	5000
Employee	E	4000
Professional	E	1000
Employer	E	8000
PastAttendance	R	10000
CurrentAttendance	R	500
Composition	R	8000
Type	R	1000
PastTeaching	R	900
CurrentTeaching	R	100
Qualification	R	500
CurrentEmployment	R	4000
PastEmployment	R	10000

Table of operations

Operation	Type	Frequency
Op 1	I	40 per day
Op 2	I	50 per day
Op 3	I	2 per day
Op 4	I	15 per day
Op 5	I	10 per day
Op 6	I	20 per day
Op 7	I	5 per day
Op 8	B	10 per month

Figure 7.31 Tables of volumes and operations for the schema in Figure 7.30.

Analysis of redundancies   There is only one redundant piece of data in the schema: the attribute NumberOfParticipants in COURSEEDITION, which can be derived from the relationships CURRENTATTENDANCE and PASTATTENDANCE. The storage requirement is $4 \times 1000 = 4000$ bytes, having assumed that four bytes are necessary for every occurrence of COURSEEDITION to store the number of participants. The operations involved with this information are 2, 5 and 8. The last of these can be left out because it deals with an infrequent operation that is carried out in batch mode. We will therefore evaluate the cost of operations 2 and 5 in the cases of the presence or absence of redundant data. We can deduce from the table of volumes that each edition of the course has, on average, eight classes and 10 participants. From this data we can easily derive the access tables shown in Figure 7.32.

Accesses with redundancy

Operation 2			
Concept	Cnstr	Acc	Type
Trainee	E	I	R
CurrentAtt'nce	R	I	W
CourseEdition	E	I	R
CourseEdition	E	I	W

Operation 5			
Concept	Cnstr	Acc	Type
CourseEdition	E	I	R
Type	R	I	R
Course	E	I	R
Composition	R	8	R
Class	E	8	R

Accesses without redundancy

Operation 2			
Concept	Cnstr	Acc	Type
Trainee	E	I	R
CurrentAtt'nce	R	I	W

Operation 5			
Concept	Cnstr	Acc	Type
CourseEdition	E	I	R
Type	R	I	R
Course	E	I	R
Composition	R	8	R
Class	E	8	R
PastAttendance	R	10	R

Figure 7.32 Access table for the schema in Figure 7.30.

From the access tables we obtain:

- with redundancy: for operation 2 we have $2 \times 50 = 100$ read accesses and as many again in write accesses per day, while, for operation 5, we have $19 \times 10 = 190$ read accesses per day for a total of 490 accesses per day (having given double weight to the write accesses);

- without redundancy: for operation 2 we have 50 read accesses per day and as many again in write accesses per day, while, for operation 5, we have $29 \times 10 = 290$ read accesses per day, for a total of 440 accesses per day (having given double weight to write accesses).

Thus, when the redundancy is present, we have disadvantages both in terms of storage and access time. We will therefore delete the attribute NumberOfParticipants from the entity COURSEEDITION.

Removing generalizations There are two generalizations in the schema: that relating to the instructors and that relating to the trainees. For the instructors, it can be noted that the relevant operations, that is, 3, 4, 6 and 7, make no distinction between freelance instructors and those employed on a permanent basis by the company. Furthermore, the corresponding entities have no specific attributes for them. Therefore, we decide to delete the child entities of the generalization and add an attribute Type to the INSTRUCTOR entity. This attribute has a domain made up of the symbols F (for freelance) and P (for permanent).

For the trainees, we observe that in this case too, the operations involving this data (operations 1, 2 and 8) make no substantial difference between the various types of occurrence. We can see, however, from the schema that professionals and employees both have specific attributes. We should, therefore, leave the entities EMPLOYEE and PROFESSIONAL, adding two one-to-one relationships between these entities and the TRAINEE entity. In this way, we can avoid having attributes with possible null values on the parent entity of the generalization and we can reduce the dimension of the relations. The result of the restructuring can be seen in the schema in Figure 7.33.

Partitioning and merging of concepts From the analysis of data and operations, many potential restructurings of this type can be identified. The first relates to the COURSEEDITION entity. We can see that operation 5 relates only to the past editions and that the relationships PASTTEACHING and PASTATTENDANCE refer only to these editions of the course. Thus, in order to make the above operation more efficient, we could decompose the entity horizontally to distinguish the current editions from the past ones. The disadvantage of this choice, however, is that the relationships COMPOSITION and TYPE would be duplicated. Furthermore, operations 7 and 8 do not make great distinctions between current editions and past ones and would be more expensive, because they would require visits to two distinct entities. Therefore, we will not partition this entity.

Two other possible restructurings that we could consider are the merging of the relationships PASTTEACHING and PRESENTTEACHING and the similar relationships PASTATTENDANCE and PRESENTATTENDANCE. In both cases, we are dealing with two similar concepts between which some operations make no difference (7 and 8). The merging of these relationships would produce another advantage: it would no longer be necessary to transfer occurrences from one relationship to another at the end of a course edition. A negative factor is the presence of the attribute Mark, which does not apply to the current editions and could thus produce null values. For the rest, the table of volumes tells us that the estimated number of occurrences of the CURRENTATTENDANCE relationship is 500. Therefore, supposing that we need four bytes to store the marks, the waste of storage would be only two Kbytes. We can decide therefore to merge the two pairs of relationships as described in Figure 7.33. We must add a constraint that is not expressible by the schema, which requires that an instructor cannot teach more than one edition of a course in any one period. Similarly, a participant cannot attend more than one edition of a course at a particular time.

Finally, we need to remove the multi-valued attribute Telephone from the INSTRUCTOR entity. To do this we must introduce a new entity TELEPHONE linked by a one-to-many relationship with the INSTRUCTOR entity, from which the attribute will be removed.

It is interesting to note that some decisions made in this phase reverse, in some way, decisions made during the conceptual design phase. This is not surprising however: the aim of conceptual design is merely to represent the requirements in the best way possible, without considering the efficiency of the application. In logical design we must instead try to optimize the performance and re-examining earlier decisions is inevitable.

Selection of primary identifiers Only the TRAINEE entity presents two identifiers: the social security number and the internal code. It is far preferable to chose the second. A social security number can require several bytes while an internal code, which serves to distinguish 5000 occurrences (see volume table) requires no more than two bytes.

There is another pragmatic consideration to be made regarding identifiers, to do with the COURSEEDITION entity. This entity is identified by the StartDate attribute and by the COURSE entity. This gives a composite identifier that, in a relational representation, must be used to implement two relationships (ATTENDANCE and TEACHING). We can see, however, that each course has a code and that the average number of editions of a course is five. This means that it is sufficient to add a small integer to the course code to have an identifier for the course editions. This operation can be carried out efficiently and accurately during the creation of a new edition. It follows that it is convenient to define a new identifier for the editions of the courses that replaces the preceding external identifier. This is an example of analysis and restructuring that is not in any of the general categories we have seen, but in practice can be encountered.

This is the end of the restructuring phase of the original E-R schema. The resulting schema is shown in Figure 7.33.

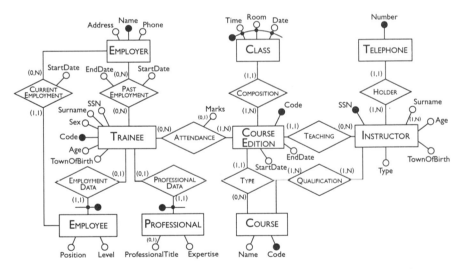

Figure 7.33 The E-R schema of Figure 7.30 after the restructuring phase.

7.4.2 Translation into the relational model

By following the translation techniques described in this chapter, the E-R schema in Figure 7.33 can be translated into the following relational schema.

COURSEEDITION(<u>Code</u>, StartDate, EndDate, Course, Instructor)
CLASS(<u>Time</u>, <u>Room</u>, <u>Date</u>, Edition)
INSTRUCTOR(<u>SSN</u>, Surname, Age, TownOfBirth, Type)

TELEPHONE(<u>Number</u>, Instructor)
COURSE(<u>Code</u>, Name)
QUALIFICATION (<u>Course</u>, <u>Instructor</u>)
TRAINEE (<u>Code</u>, SSN, Surname, Age, TownOfBirth, Sex)
ATTENDANCE(<u>Trainee</u>, <u>Edition</u>, Marks*)
EMPLOYER(<u>Name</u>, Address, Telephone)
PASTEMPLOYMENT(<u>Trainee</u>, <u>Employer</u>, StartDate, EndDate)
PROFESSIONAL(<u>Trainee</u>, Expertise, ProfessionalTitle*)
EMPLOYEE(<u>Trainee</u>, Level, Position, Employer, StartDate)

The logical schema will naturally be completed by a support document that describes, among other things, all the referential constraints that exist between the various relations. This can be done using the graphical notation introduced in Section 7.3.7.

7.5 Logical design using CASE tools

The logical design phase is generally supported by all the CASE tools for database development available on the market. In particular, since the translation to the relational model is based on precise criteria, it is carried out by these systems almost automatically. On the other hand, the restructuring step, which precedes the actual translation, is difficult to automate and the various products provide little or no support for it. For example, some systems automatically translate all the generalizations according to just one of the methods described in Section 7.2.2. We have seen, however, that the restructuring of an E-R schema is a fundamental activity of the design for an important reason. Namely, it can provide solutions to efficiency problems that should be resolved before carrying out the translation and that are not relevant to conceptual design. The designer should therefore take care to handle this aspect without putting too much confidence into the tool available.

An example of the output of the translation step using a database design tool is shown in Figure 7.34. The example refers to the conceptual schema of Figure 6.14. The resulting schema is shown in graphical form, which represents the relational tables together with the relationships of the original schema. Note how the many-to-many relationship between EMPLOYEE and PROJECT has been translated into a relation. Also, note how new attributes have been added to the relations originating from entities to represent the one-to-many and one-to-one relationships. In the figure, the SQL code also appears, generated automatically by the system. It allows the designer to define the database using a specific database management system. Some systems allow direct connection with a DBMS and can construct the corresponding database automatically. Other systems provide tools to carry out the reverse operation: reconstructing a conceptual schema based on an existing relational schema. This operation is called reverse engineering and

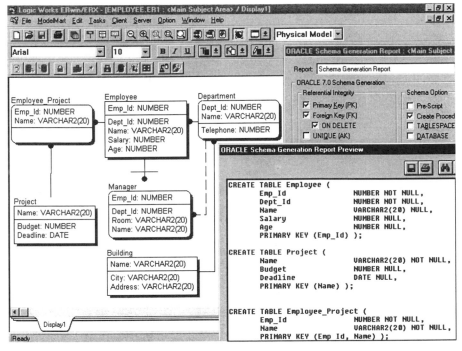

Figure 7.34 Logical design with a CASE tool.

is particularly useful for the analysis of a legacy system, possibly oriented towards a migration to a new database management system.

7.6 Bibliography

Logical design is covered in detail in the books by Batini, Ceri and Navathe [7], Teorey [84] and Teorey and Fry [85]. The problem of translating an E-R schema into the relational model is discussed in the original paper by Chen [23] and in a paper by Teorey, Yang and Fry [86], which considers a detailed list of cases.

7.7 Exercises

Exercise 7.1 Consider the E-R schema in Exercise 6.4. Make hypotheses on the volume of data and on the operations possible on this data and, based on these hypotheses, carry out the necessary restructuring of the schema. Then carry out the translation to the relational model.

Exercise 7.2 Translate the E-R schema on the personnel of a company (shown again for convenience in Figure 7.35) into a schema of the relational model.

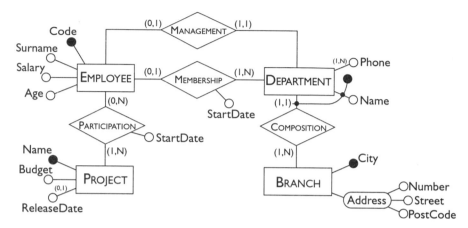

Figure 7.35 An E-R schema on the personnel of a company.

Exercise 7.3 Translate the E-R schema obtained in Exercise 6.6 into a relational schema.

Exercise 7.4 Define a relational schema corresponding to the E-R schema obtained in Exercise 6.10. For the restructuring phase, indicate the possible options and choose one, making assumptions on the quantitative parameters. Assume that the database relates to certain apartment blocks, having on average five buildings each, and that each building has on average twenty apartments. The main operations are the registration of a tenant (50 per year per block) and recording the payment of rent.

Exercise 7.5 Translate the E-R schema of Figure 7.36 into a relational database schema. For each relation indicate the key and, for each attribute, specify if null values can occur (supposing that the attributes of the E-R schema do not admit null values).

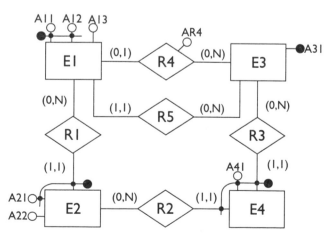

Figure 7.36 An E-R schema to translate.

Exercise 7.6 Take the E-R schema in Figure 7.37. Restructure the schema, deleting the generalizations, supposing the most important operations are as follows, each carried out 10 times per day:

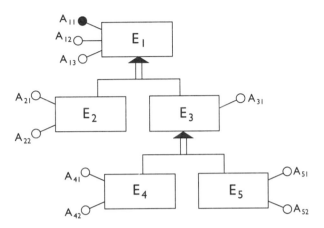

Figure 7.37 An E-R schema with generalizations.

- **operation 1:** read access to attributes A_{21}, A_{22}, A_{11}, A_{12}, A_{13} for all the occurrences of entity E_2;

- **operation 2:** read access to attributes A_{41}, A_{42}, A_{31}, A_{11}, A_{12}, A_{13} for all the occurrences entity E_4;

- **operation 3:** read access to attributes A_{51}, A_{52}, A_{31}, A_{11}, A_{13} for all the occurrences entity E_5.

Exercise 7.7 Consider the conceptual schema in Figure 7.38, which describes bank account data. Observe that a client can have more than one account and that a single account can belong to many clients.
Suppose that on this data, the following main operations are defined:

- **operation 1:** open an account for a client;

- **operation 2:** read the total balance for a client;

- **operation 3:** read the balance for an account;

- **operation 4:** withdraw money from an account by means of a transaction at the bank counter;

- **operation 5:** deposit money into an account by means of a transaction at a bank counter;

- **operation 6:** show the last 10 transactions for an account;

- **operation 7:** register an external transaction for an account;

- **operation 8:** prepare the monthly statement of an account;

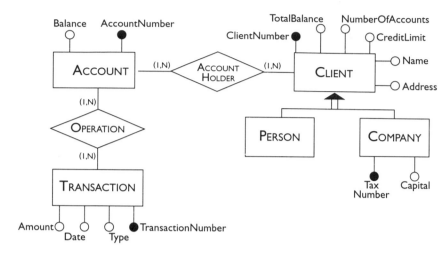

Figure 7.38 An E-R schema to translate.

- **operation 9:** find the number of accounts held by a client;

- **operation 10:** show the transactions for the last three months of accounts of each client with a negative balance.

Finally, suppose that in the operation stage, the database load for this application is that shown in Figure 7.39.

Volumes

Concept	Type	Volume
Client	E	15000
Account	E	20000
Transaction	E	600000
Person	E	14000
Company	E	1000
AccountHolder	R	30000
Operation	R	800000

Operations

Operation	Type	Frequency
Op 1	I	100 per day
Op 2	I	500 per day
Op 3	I	1000 per day
Op 4	I	2000 per day
Op 5	I	1000 per day
Op 6	I	200 per day
Op 7	B	1500 per day
Op 8	B	1 per month
Op 9	I	75 per day
Op 10	I	20 per day

Figure 7.39 Volumes and operations tables for the schema in Figure 7.38.

Carry out the logical design phase on the E-R schema, taking into account the data provided. In the restructuring phase, keep in mind the fact that there are two redundancies on the schema: the attribute TotalBalance and NumberOfAccounts in the entity CLIENT. These can be derived from the relationship ACCOUNTHOLDER and from the ACCOUNT entity.

8
Normalization

In this chapter, we will study some properties, known as *normal forms*, which we can use to evaluate the quality of a relational database. We will see that when a relation does not satisfy a normal form, then it presents redundancies and produces undesirable behaviour during update operations. This principle can be used to carry out quality analysis on relational databases and so constitutes a useful tool for database design. For the schemas that do not satisfy a normal form, we can apply a procedure known as *normalization*. Normalization allows the non-normalized schemas to be transformed into new schemas for which the satisfaction of a normal form is guaranteed.

There are two important points to be clarified. First, the design techniques seen in the preceding chapters usually allow us to obtain schemas that satisfy a normal form. In this framework, normalization theory constitutes a useful verification tool, which indicates amendments, but cannot substitute for the wider range of analysis and design techniques described in Chapter 5. Second, normalization theory has been developed in the context of the relational model and for this reason, it provides means and techniques for the analysis of the outcomes of logical design. We will see, however, that the same techniques can be used, with minor variations, on Entity-Relationship schemas. Normalization can also be used earlier, for example, during the quality analysis step of the conceptual design.

We will deal with this subject in stages, first discussing the problems (redundancies and anomalies) that can be verified in a relational schema, and then deriving systematic techniques for analysis and normalization. We will discuss later the same principles with reference to the Entity-Relationship model.

8.1 Redundancies and anomalies

We will use an example to illustrate the basic principles. Consider the relation in Figure 8.1. The key is made up of the attributes **Employee** and

Employee	Salary	Project	Budget	Function
Brown	20	Mars	2	technician
Green	35	Jupiter	15	designer
Green	35	Venus	15	designer
Hoskins	55	Venus	15	manager
Hoskins	55	Jupiter	15	consultant
Hoskins	55	Mars	2	consultant
Moore	48	Mars	2	manager
Moore	48	Venus	15	designer
Kemp	48	Venus	15	designer
Kemp	48	Jupiter	15	manager

Figure 8.1 Example of a relation with anomalies.

Project. We can also easily verify that the relation satisfies the following properties:

1. the salary of each employee is unique and depends only on the employee; it is independent of the projects on which the employee is working;

2. the budget of each project is unique and depends only on the project; it is independent of the employees who are working on it.

These facts have certain consequences for the contents of the relation and for the operations that can be carried out on it. We will limit our discussion to the first property, leaving the analysis of the second as an exercise.

• The value of the salary of each employee is repeated in all the tuples relating to it: therefore there is a *redundancy*; if, for example, an employee participates in 20 projects, his or her salary will be repeated 20 times.

• If the salary of an employee changes, we have to modify the value in all the corresponding tuples. This inconvenient process, which makes it necessary to carry out many modifications simultaneously, is known as *update anomaly*.

• If an employee stops working on all the projects but does not leave the company, all the corresponding tuples are deleted and so, even the basic information, name and salary, which is not related to projects, is lost. This would require us to keep a tuple with a null value for the attribute

Project, but, since Project is part of the key, this is not allowed, as we saw in Chapter 2. This problem is known as the *deletion anomaly*.

- Similarly, if we have information on a new employee, we cannot insert it until the employee is assigned to a project. This is known as the *insertion anomaly*.

An intuitive explanation for the presence of these undesirable phenomena can be as follows. We have used a single relation to represent items of information of different types. In particular, in this relation the following are represented: employees with their salaries, projects with their budgets and participation of the employees in the projects with their functions.

In general, we can arrive at the following conclusions, which highlight the defects presented by a relation whose tuples each include various items of information, representing independent real-world concepts.

- Items of information often need to be repeated, that is, to appear in different tuples.

- If some information is repeated redundantly, the updating must be repeated for each occurrence of the repeated data. Now, the relational languages, such as SQL, all allow the specification of multiple updates using a single command. However, this resolves the problem only from the point of view of the programmer and not from that of the system. The reason is that all the tuples involved in the update must be modified and thus it is necessary to access each one of them physically.

- Problems can occur with the deletion of a tuple in the case where just one item of information it expresses is no longer valid. The cancellation can cause the deletion of all the information in question, even the portion that is still valid.

- The insertion of a single item of information in a relation is not possible without values for the entire set of items making up a complete tuple (or at least its primary key).

8.2 Functional dependencies

To systematically study the principles introduced informally above, it is necessary to use a specific notion, *functional dependency*. This is a particular integrity constraint for the relational model, which, as the name suggests, describes functional relationships among the attributes of a relation.

Let us look again at the relation in Figure 8.1. We have seen that the salary of each employee is unique and thus each time a certain employee appears in a tuple, the value of his or her salary always remains the same. We can thus say that the value of the attribute Salary functionally depends on the value of the Employee attribute. That is, a function exists that associates with each Employee value in the relation, a single value for the Salary attribute. A similar argument can be made for the relationship between the attributes Project and Budget because the value of the budget functionally depends on the value of the project.

We can formalize this principle as follows. Given a relation r on a schema $R(X)$ and two non-empty subsets Y and Z of the attributes X, we say that there is a functional dependency on r between Y and Z, if, for each pair of tuples t_1 and t_2 of r having the same values on the attributes Y, t_1 and t_2 also have the same values of the Z attributes.

A functional dependency between the attributes Y and Z is generally indicated by the notation $Y \rightarrow Z$ and, as with other integrity constraints, is associated with a schema: a valid relation on that schema has to satisfy this functional dependency. Given a functional dependency $Y \rightarrow Z$, we will call Y the *left hand side* and that Z the *right hand side* of the dependency. Returning to our example, we can thus say that on the relation in Figure 8.1 there are the functional dependencies:

$$\text{Employee} \rightarrow \text{Salary}$$
$$\text{Project} \rightarrow \text{Budget}$$

There are some observations to be made on functional dependencies. The first is as follows: based on the given definition, we can state that, in our relation, this functional dependency is also satisfied:

$$\text{Employee Project} \rightarrow \text{Project}$$

That is, two tuples with the same values on each of the attributes Employee and Project have the same value on the attribute Project, which is one of them. This is a 'trivial' functional dependency because it asserts an obvious property of the relation. Functional dependencies should instead be used to describe significant properties of the application that we are representing. We then say that a functional dependency $Y \rightarrow Z$ is *non-trivial* if no attribute in Z appears among the attributes of Y.

Note that a 'hybrid' functional dependency of the type

$$\text{Project} \rightarrow \text{Project Budget}$$

which contains a trivial property (a project depends on itself), can be made non-trivial by deleting from the right hand side of the dependency, all the attributes that also appear in the left hand side. It is easy, in fact, to demonstrate that if the functional dependency $Y \rightarrow Z$ is valid, then the functional dependency $Y \rightarrow W$ is also valid, where W is a subset of Z. From here on, we will refer only to functional dependencies that are non-trivial, often omitting the adjective for brevity.

A second observation on functional dependencies concerns their link with the key constraint. If we take a key K of a relation r, we can easily verify that there is a functional dependency between K and any other attribute of r. This is because, by the definition of key constraint, there cannot exist two tuples with the same values on K. Referring to our example, we have said that the attributes Employee and Project form a key. We can then affirm that, for example, the functional dependency Employee Project $\rightarrow$ Function is valid. In particular, there will be a functional dependency between the key of a relation and all the other attributes of the schema of the relation. In our case we have:

Employee Project $\rightarrow$ Salary Budget Function

We can therefore conclude by saying that the functional dependency constraint generalizes the key constraint. More precisely, we can say that a functional dependency $Y \rightarrow Z$ on a schema $R(X)$ degenerates into the key constraint if the union of Y and Z is equal to X. In this case, Y is a (super)key for the $R(X)$ schema.

8.3 Boyce–Codd normal form

8.3.1 Definition of Boyce–Codd normal form

In this section, we will formalize the ideas illustrated in Section 8.1, in the light of what we have said on functional dependencies. Let us start by observing that, in our example, the two properties causing anomalies correspond exactly to attributes involved in functional dependencies:

- the property 'the salary of each employee is unique and depends only on the employee, independently of the project on which he or she is working' can be formalized by means of the functional dependency Employee $\rightarrow$ Salary;

- the property 'the budget of each project is unique and depends only on the project, independently of the employees who are working on it' corresponds to the functional dependency Project $\rightarrow$ Budget.

Furthermore, it is appropriate to note that the Function attribute indicates, for each tuple, the role played by the employee in the project. This role is unique, for each employee-project pair. We can model this property too using a functional dependency:

- The property 'in each project, each of the employees involved can carry out only one function' corresponds to the functional dependency Employee Project $\rightarrow$ Function. As we have mentioned in the previous section, this is also a consequence of the fact that the attributes Employee and Project form the key of the relation.

We saw in Section 8.1, how the first two properties (and thus the corresponding functional dependencies) generate undesirable redundancies and anomalies. The third dependency is different. It never generates redundancies because, having Employee and Project as a key, the relation cannot contain two tuples with the same values of these attributes (and thus of the Function attribute). Also, from a conceptual point of view, we can say that it cannot generate anomalies, because each employee has a salary (and one only) and each project has a budget (and one only), and thus for each employee-project pair we can have unique values for all the other attributes of the relation. In some cases, such values might not be available. In these cases, since they are not part of the key, we would simply replace them with null values without any problem. We can thus conclude that the dependencies:

$$\text{Employee} \to \text{Salary}$$
$$\text{Project} \to \text{Budget}$$

cause anomalies, whereas the dependency

$$\text{Employee Project} \to \text{Function}$$

does not. The difference, as we have mentioned, is that Employee Project is a superkey of the relation. All the reasoning that we have developed with reference to this specific example, is more general. Indeed: redundancies and anomalies are caused by the functional dependencies $X \to Y$ that allow the presence of many equal tuples on the attributes in X. That is, from the functional dependencies $X \to Y$ such that X does not contain a key.

We will formalize this idea by introducing the notion of Boyce–Codd normal form (BCNF), which takes the name from its inventors. A relation r is in *Boyce–Codd normal form* if for every (non-trivial) functional dependency $X \to Y$ defined on it, X contains a key K of r. That is, X is a superkey for r.

Anomalies and redundancies, as discussed above, do not appear in databases with relations in Boyce–Codd normal form, because the independent pieces of information are separate, one per relation.

8.3.2 Decomposition into Boyce–Codd normal form

Given a relation that does not satisfy Boyce–Codd normal form, we can often replace it with one or more normalized relations using a process called *normalization*. This process is based on a simple criterion: if a relation represents many real-world concepts, then it is decomposed into smaller relations, one for each concept.

Let us show the normalization process by means of an example. We can eliminate redundancies and anomalies for the relation in Figure 8.1 if we replace it with the three relations in Figure 8.2, obtained by projections on the sets of attributes corresponding respectively to the three items of information mentioned above. The three relations are in Boyce–Codd normal form. Note that we have constructed three relations so that each dependency corresponds to a different relation, the key of which is actually the left hand side of the same dependency. In this way, the satisfaction of the Boyce–Codd normal form is guaranteed, by the definition of this normal form itself.

Employee	Salary
Brown	20
Green	35
Hoskins	55
Moore	48
Kemp	48

Project	Budget
Mars	2
Jupiter	15
Venus	15

Employee	Project	Function
Brown	Mars	technician
Green	Jupiter	designer
Green	Venus	designer
Hoskins	Venus	manager
Hoskins	Jupiter	consultant
Hoskins	Mars	consultant
Moore	Mars	manager
Moore	Venus	designer
Kemp	Venus	designer
Kemp	Jupiter	manager

Figure 8.2 Decomposition of the relation in Figure 8.1.

In the example, the separation of the dependencies (and thus of the properties represented by them) is facilitated by the structure of the dependency itself, 'naturally' separated and independent of the others. In many cases, the decomposition can be carried out by producing as many relations as there are functional dependencies (or rather, the functional dependencies with different left hand sides). Unfortunately, some dependencies are found to be complex: it might be unnecessary (or impossible) to base the decomposition on all the dependencies and it can be difficult to identify the ones on which we must base the decomposition. We will clarify this point by looking at a simple example.

It is easy to verify that the relation in Figure 8.3 satisfies the dependencies Employee → Category and Category → Salary. By proceeding in the way described above, we could easily obtain a database with two relations, both in Boyce–Codd normal form. On the other hand, for the same relation, we could have identified both the functional dependencies Category → Salary and Employee → Category Salary (rather than Employee → Category). Note that this dependency describes the situation with more or less the same accuracy. In this case however, we would have had no hints on how to generate a decomposition into Boyce–Codd normal form, because obviously the dependency Employee → Category Salary covers all the attributes and thus does not suggest any decomposed relation. This simple example shows that the identification of dependencies can cause difficulties with decomposition.

We can imagine what could happen when the relation has many attributes and several functional dependencies are defined on it.

Employee	Category	Salary
Hoskins	3	30
Green	3	30
Brown	4	50
Moore	4	50
Kemp	5	72

Figure 8.3 A relation with various functional dependencies.

A complete study of normalization would require, as a prerequisite, a detailed examination of the properties of functional dependency. The complete development of these concepts goes beyond the scope of this book. Given the importance of the subject, however, we intend to give an informal description of some of the most important aspects.

It should be noted, moreover, that we study normal forms mainly as auxiliary quality control tools for relations and not as a design technique. The design techniques discussed in preceding chapters are intended for the generation of relations (in the logical design phase) based on entities and relationships that appear in the conceptual schema (produced during the conceptual design phase). The conceptual design phase serves to identify the fundamental concepts of the application to model, separating them into distinct entities or relationships. Since the translation is then carried out considering each entity and each relationship separately, it is evident that if the conceptual design is carried out correctly, the relational schema produced during the logical design phase will be already normalized.

In this context, normalization theory is in any case useful as a verification tool for the products of both conceptual and logical design. We will re-examine this subject in more detail in Section 8.6.

8.4 Decomposition properties

In this section, we examine the concept of decomposition in more detail. We explain how not all decompositions are desirable and identify some essential properties that must be satisfied by a 'good' decomposition.

8.4.1 Lossless decomposition

In order to discuss the first property, let us examine the relation in Figure 8.4. This relation satisfies the functional dependencies:

$$\text{Employee} \rightarrow \text{Branch}$$
$$\text{Project} \rightarrow \text{Branch}$$

that specify the fact that each employee works at a single branch and that each project is developed at a single branch. Observe that each employee can work on more than one project even if, based on functional dependencies, they must all be projects allocated to the branch to which he or she belongs.

Employee	Project	Branch
Brown	Mars	Chicago
Green	Jupiter	Birmingham
Green	Venus	Birmingham
Hoskins	Saturn	Birmingham
Hoskins	Venus	Birmingham

Figure 8.4   A relation to illustrate the lossless decomposition.

Proceeding in the same way as before, that is, separating on the basis of dependencies, we will find it suitable to decompose the relation into two parts:

• a relation on the attributes **Employee** and **Branch**, corresponding to the dependency **Employee** → **Branch**;

• a second relation on the attributes **Project** and **Branch**, corresponding to the functional dependency **Project** → **Branch**.

The instance in Figure 8.4 would be decomposed into the two relations in Figure 8.5 by projecting on the involved attributes.

Employee	Branch
Brown	Chicago
Green	Birmingham
Hoskins	Birmingham

Project	Branch
Mars	Chicago
Jupiter	Birmingham
Saturn	Birmingham
Venus	Birmingham

Figure 8.5   Relations obtained by projection of the relation in Figure 8.4.

Let us examine the two relations in detail. In particular, consider how it would be possible to reconstruct information on the participation of the employees in the projects. The only possibility is to use the attribute **Branch**, which is the only attribute common to the two relations: we can thus link an employee to a project if the project is developed at the branch where the employee works. Unfortunately, however, in this case we are not able to reconstruct exactly the information in the original relation: for example the employee called Green works in Birmingham and the Saturn project is being developed in Birmingham, but in fact Green does not actually work on that project.

We can generalize the observation by noting that the reconstruction of the original relation must be carried out through a natural join of the two projections. Unfortunately, the natural join of the two relations in Figure 8.5 produces the relation in Figure 8.6, which is different from the relation in Figure 8.4. The relation in Figure 8.6 contains all the tuples of the original

Employee	Project	Branch
Brown	Mars	Chicago
Green	Jupiter	Birmingham
Green	Venus	Birmingham
Hoskins	Saturn	Birmingham
Hoskins	Venus	Birmingham
Green	Saturn	Birmingham
Hoskins	Jupiter	Birmingham

Figure 8.6   The result of the join of the relations in Figure 8.5.

relation (Figure 8.4) as well as other tuples (the last two in the table). The situation in the example corresponds to the general situation: given a relation r on a set of attributes X, if X_1 and X_2 are two subsets of X the union of which is equal to X itself, then the join of the two relations obtained by projecting r on X_1 and X_2, respectively, is a relation that contains all the tuples of r, plus possible others, which we can call 'spurious'. Let us say that the decomposition of r on X_1 and X_2 is *lossless* if the join of the projections of r on X_1 and X_2 is equal to r itself (that is, not containing spurious tuples). It is clearly desirable, or rather an indispensable requirement, that a decomposition carried out for the purpose of normalization is lossless.

We can identify a condition that guarantees the lossless decomposition of a relation, as follows. Let r be a relation on X and let X_1 and X_2 be subsets of X such that $X_1 \cup X_2 = X$. Furthermore, let $X_0 = X_1 \cap X_2$. If r satisfies the functional dependency $X_0 \rightarrow X_1$ or the functional dependency $X_0 \rightarrow X_2$, then the decomposition of r on X_1 and X_2 is lossless.

In other words, we can say that r has a lossless decomposition on two relations if the set of attributes common to the two relations is a key for at least one of the decomposed relations. In the example, we can see that the intersection of the sets of attributes on which we have carried out the two projections is made up of the **Branch** attribute, which is not the left hand side of any functional dependency.

We can justify the condition in the following manner, with reference to a relation r on the attributes ABC and to its projections on AB and AC. Let us suppose that r satisfies $A \rightarrow C$. Then, A is key for the projection of r on AC and thus in this there are not two different tuples with the same values of A. The join constructs tuples based on the tuples in the two projections. Let us consider a generic tuple $t = (a, b, c)$ in the result of the join. We show that t

belongs to r, so proving the equality of the two relations: t is obtained from $t_1 = (a, b)$ in the projection of r on AB, and $t_2 = (a, c)$ in the projection of r on AC. Thus, by definition of the projection operator, there must be two tuples in r, t_1' with values a and b on AB, and t_2' with values a and c on AC. Since r satisfies $A \rightarrow C$, there is a single value of C in r associated with the value a on A: given that (a, c) appears in the projection, this value is exactly c. Thus the value of t_1' on C is c and thus t_1' (which belongs to r) has values a, b and c, and thus coincides with t, which therefore belongs to r, as we intended to show.

It is appropriate to note briefly how the condition stated is sufficient but not strictly necessary to ensure a lossless decomposition: there are relations that satisfy neither of the two dependencies, but at the same time they have a lossless decomposition. For example, the relation in Figure 8.6 (obtained as the join of the projections) has a lossless decomposition on the two sets **Employee Branch** and **Project Branch**. On the other hand, the condition given ensures that all the relations that satisfy a given set of dependencies have a lossless decomposition, and this is a useful result: each time we decompose a relation into two parts, if the set of common attributes is a key for one of the two relations, then all the valid instances of the relation have a lossless decomposition.

8.4.2 Preservation of dependencies

To introduce the second property, we can re-examine the relation in Figure 8.4. We still wish to remove the anomalies, so we could think about exploiting only the dependency **Employee** $\rightarrow$ **Branch**, in order to obtain a lossless decomposition. We then have two relations, one on the attributes **Employee** and **Branch** and the other on the attributes **Employee** and **Project**. The instance in Figure 8.4 would be thus decomposed into the relations in Figure 8.7.

Employee	Branch
Brown	Chicago
Green	Birmingham
Hoskins	Birmingham

Employee	Project
Brown	Mars
Green	Jupiter
Green	Venus
Hoskins	Saturn
Hoskins	Venus

Figure 8.7 Another decomposition of the relation in Figure 8.4.

The join of the two relations in Figure 8.7 produces the relation in Figure 8.4, for which we can say that the original relation has a lossless decomposition on **Employee Branch** and **Employee Project**. This is confirmed by the fact that **Employee** is the key for the first relation. Unfortunately, the decomposition in Figure 8.7 produces another problem, as follows. Suppose we wish to insert a new tuple that specifies the participation of the employee named Armstrong, who works in Birmingham, on the Mars project. In the original relation, that is, the one in Figure 8.4, an update of this kind would be immediately identified as illegal, because it would cause a violation of the Project → Branch dependency. On the decomposed relations however, it is not possible to reveal any violation of dependency. On the relation over Employee and Project, it is actually not possible to define any functional dependency and thus there can be no violations to show, while the tuple with the values Armstrong and Birmingham satisfies the dependency Employee → Branch. We can therefore note how it is not possible to carry out any verification on the dependency Project → Branch, because the two attributes Project and Branch have been separated: one into one relation and one into the other.

We can conclude that, in each decomposition, each of the functional dependencies of the original schema should involve attributes that appear all together in one of the decomposed schemas. In this way, it is possible to ensure, on the decomposed schema, the satisfaction of the same constraints as the original schema. We can say that a decomposition that satisfies this property *preserves the dependencies* of the original schema.

8.4.3 Qualities of decompositions

To summarize the points discussed above, we can state that decompositions should always satisfy the properties of *lossless decomposition* and *dependency preservation*.

- Lossless decomposition ensures that the information in the original relation can be accurately reconstructed, that is, reconstructed without spurious information, based on the information represented in the decomposed relations. In this case, by querying the decomposed relations, we obtain the same results that we would obtain by querying the original relation.

- Dependency preservation ensures that the decomposed relations have the same capacity to represent the integrity constraints as the original relations and thus to reveal illegal updates: each allowed update (respectively, illegal) on the original relation corresponds to an allowed update (respectively, illegal) on the decomposed relations. Obviously, we can have further updates on the single decomposed relations, which have no counterpart in the original relation. Such updates are impossible on non-normalized relations where they are sources of anomalies.

As a result, from here on we will consider only decompositions that satisfy these two properties. Given a schema that violates a normal form, the normalization activity is thus aimed at obtaining a decomposition that is lossless, preserves the dependencies and contains relations in normal form. Note how the decomposition discussed in Section 8.1 shows all three qualities.

8.5 Third normal form

8.5.1 Definition of third normal form

In most cases, the aim of obtaining a good decomposition into Boyce–Codd normal form can be achieved. Sometimes, however, this is not possible, as we can see from an example. Look at the relation in Figure 8.8.

Manager	Project	Branch
Brown	Mars	Chicago
Green	Jupiter	Birmingham
Green	Mars	Birmingham
Hoskins	Saturn	Birmingham
Hoskins	Venus	Birmingham

Figure 8.8 A relation to show a decomposition with problems.

We can assume that the following dependencies are defined:

- Manager → Branch: each manager works at a particular branch;

- Project Branch → Manager: each project has more managers who are responsible for it, but in different branches, and each manager can be responsible for more than one project; however, for each branch, a project has only one manager responsible for it.

The relation is not in Boyce–Codd normal form because the left hand side of the Manager → Branch dependency is not a superkey. At the same time, we can note how no good decomposition of this relation is possible; the dependency Project Branch → Manager involves all the attributes and thus no decomposition is able to preserve it. The example shows us that schemas exist that violate Boyce–Codd normal form and for which there is no decomposition that preserves the dependencies. We can therefore state that sometimes, 'Boyce–Codd normal form cannot be achieved'. In such cases, we can however establish a less restrictive condition, which allows situations such as the one described above, but does not allow further sources of redundancy and anomaly.

This condition defines a new normal form: we will say that a relation r is in *third normal form* if, for each (non-trivial) functional dependency $X \rightarrow Y$ defined on it, at least one of the following is verified:

- X contains a key K of r;

- each attribute in Y is contained in at least one key of r.

Returning to our example, we can easily verify that, even if the schema does not satisfy the Boyce–Codd normal form, it satisfies the third normal form. The Project Branch → Manager dependency has as its left hand side a key for the relation, while **Manager** → **Branch** has a unique attribute for the right hand side, which is part of the **Project Branch** key. Note that the relations show a form of redundancy: each time a manager appears in a tuple, the branch for which he or she works is repeated. This redundancy is 'tolerated' however, by the third normal form, because intuitively, a decomposition that eliminated such redundancy and at the same time preserved all the dependencies would not be possible.

The third normal form is less restrictive than the Boyce–Codd normal form and for this reason does not offer the same guarantees of quality for a relation; it has the advantage however, of always being achievable.

The name of this normal form suggests the existence of other normal forms, which we will deal with briefly. The *first normal form* simply establishes a condition that is at the basis of the relational model itself: the attributes of a relation are defined on atomic values and not on complex values, whether sets or relations. We will see in Chapter 11 how this constraint is relaxed in other database models. The *second normal form* is a weak variation of the third, which allows functional dependencies such as that between **Category** and **Salary** of the relation in Figure 8.3. Note that this dependency satisfies neither of the conditions of the third normal form. There are indeed other normal forms that refer to other integrity constraints. None of these normal forms is used significantly in current applications since the third normal form and the Boyce–Codd normal form already provide the right compromise between simplicity and the quality of results.

8.5.2 Decomposition into third normal form

Decomposition into third normal form can proceed as suggested for the Boyce–Codd normal form. A relation that does not satisfy the third normal form is decomposed into relations obtained by projections on the attributes corresponding to the functional dependencies. The only condition to guarantee in this process is of always maintaining a relation that contains a key to the original relation. We can see this by referring to the relation in Figure 8.9, for which we have a single functional dependency, **Employee** → **Salary**.

Employee	Project	Salary
Brown	Mars	50
Green	Jupiter	30
Green	Venus	30
Hoskins	Saturn	40
Hoskins	Venus	40

Figure 8.9 A relation for the discussion of decomposition into third normal form.

A decomposition in the relation on the attributes **Employee Salary** and in another on the sole attribute **Project** would violate the property of lossless decomposition, essentially because neither of the two relations contains a key for the original relation. To guarantee this property, we must define the second relation on the attributes **Employee Project**, which actually forms a key for the original relation. We insist however on the fact that the success of a decomposition depends for the most part on the dependencies we have identified.

To conclude, we return to the example in Figure 8.1 and note that the relation does not satisfy even the third normal form. Proceeding as suggested, we can still obtain the decomposition shown in Figure 8.2, which, we saw, is also in Boyce–Codd normal form. This is a result that is valid in a wide range of cases: a decomposition with the intent of obtaining the third normal form often produces schemas in Boyce–Codd normal form. In particular, we can show that if a relation has only one key (as in this case) then the two normal forms coincide. That is, a relation with only one key is in third normal form if and only if it is in Boyce–Codd normal form.

8.5.3 Other normalization techniques

Referring to Figure 8.8, we will look at further ideas about normal forms. By examining the specifications more closely, we see that we could have described this part of the application in a more suitable manner by introducing a further attribute **Division**, which separates the single branches according to their managers. The relation is shown in Figure 8.10.

Manager	Project	Branch	Division
Brown	Mars	Chicago	1
Green	Jupiter	Birmingham	1
Green	Mars	Birmingham	1
Hoskins	Saturn	Birmingham	2
Hoskins	Venus	Birmingham	2

Figure 8.10 A restructuring of the relation in Figure 8.8.

The dependencies can be defined as follows:

- **Manager** → **Branch Division**: each manager works at one branch and manages one division;

- **Branch Division** → **Manager**: for each branch and division there is a single manager;

- **Project Branch** → **Division**: for each branch, a project is allocated to a single division and has a sole manager responsible; the functional dependency **Project Branch** → **Manager** can indeed be reconstructed.

For this schema, there is a good decomposition, as shown in Figure 8.11:

- the decomposition is lossless, because the common attributes Branch and Division form a key for the first relation;

- the dependencies are preserved, because for each dependency there is a decomposed relation that contains all the attributes involved;

- both the relations are in Boyce–Codd normal form, because for all the dependencies the left hand side is made up of a key.

Manager	Branch	Division
Brown	Chicago	1
Green	Birmingham	1
Hoskins	Birmingham	2

Project	Branch	Division
Mars	Chicago	1
Jupiter	Birmingham	1
Mars	Birmingham	1
Saturn	Birmingham	2
Venus	Birmingham	2

Figure 8.11 A good decomposition of the relation in Figure 8.10.

We can therefore conclude by stating that, often, the difficulty of achieving Boyce–Codd normal form could be due to an insufficiently accurate analysis of the application.

8.6 Database design and normalization

The theory of normalization, even if studied in simplified form, can be used as a basis for quality control operations on schemas, in both the conceptual and logical design phases. We will briefly comment on its use in logical design, and then illustrate the adaptation of the principles to the Entity-Relationship model and thus to conceptual design.

A design is sometimes incomplete, and so a revision of the relations obtained during the logical design phase can identify places where the conceptual schema can be refined. The verification of the design is often relatively easy. This is because the identification of the functional dependencies and the keys must be carried out within the context of a single relation, which is derived from an entity or a relationship already analyzed in the conceptual design phase. In this context, the structure of dependencies is generally rather simple and it is thus possible to identify directly the decomposition necessary to obtain a normal form. For example, the relation in Figure 8.3 would be produced only if, during the conceptual design phase, we do not realize that category and employee are independent concepts. By identifying the existence of functional dependencies, it is therefore possible to remedy errors.

8.6.1 Verification of normalization on entities

The ideas on which normalization is based can also be used during the conceptual design phase for the quality control of each element of the conceptual schema. It is possible to consider each entity or relationship as if it were a relation. In particular, the relation that corresponds to an entity has attributes that correspond exactly to the attributes of the entity. For an entity with an external identifier, further attributes are necessary to include the entities that participate in the identification. In practice, it is sufficient to consider the functional dependencies that exist among the attributes of the entity and to verify that each of them has the identifier as left hand side (or contains it). For example, let us consider (see Figure 8.12) an entity PRODUCT, with attributes Code, ProductName, Supplier, Address, SupplierCode. Supplier is the name of the supplier of a product, for which the Address and the SupplierCode are important.

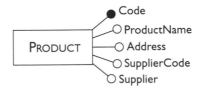

Figure 8.12 An entity to undergo a verification of normalization.

In identifying the dependencies for this entity, we can note that various suppliers can exist with the same surname or the same address, while all the properties of each supplier are identified by its SupplierCode. Therefore, the dependency SupplierCode → Supplier Address exists. Furthermore, all the attributes are functionally dependent on the Code attribute, which correctly constitutes the identifier of the entity. Once a code has been fixed, the product and the supplier are unambiguously determined, with their properties. Since the only identifier of the entity is made up of the sole attribute Code, we can conclude that the entity violates the third normal form. This is because the dependency SupplierCode → Supplier Address has a left hand side that does not contain the identifier and a right hand side made up of attributes that are not part of the key. In these cases, the test of normalization indicates that the conceptual schema is not accurate and suggests the decomposition of the entity itself.

The decomposition can take place, as we saw earlier, with direct reference to the dependencies, or more simply, by reasoning on the concepts represented by the entities and the functional dependencies. In the example, we understood that the concept of supplier is independent of that of product and has associated properties (code, surname and address). Thus, based on the arguments developed about conceptual design, we can say that it is appropriate to model the concept of supplier by means of a separate entity.

This entity has **SupplierCode** as the identifier and **Name** and **Address** as further attributes.

Since the concepts of product and supplier appear together in the same entity in the original schema, it is evident that if we separate them into two entities it is appropriate that these entities be connected. That is, there is a relationship that links them. We can reason about the cardinalities of this relationship as follows. Since there is a functional dependency from **Code** to **SupplierCode**, we are sure that each product has at most one supplier. Thus, the participation of the entity PRODUCT in the relationship must have a maximum cardinality of one. Since there is no dependency from **SupplierCode** to **Code**, we have an unlimited maximum cardinality (N) for the participation of the entity SUPPLIER in the relationship. For the minimum cardinalities, we can reason intuitively. For example, assume that for each product the supplier must always be known, while we can also have suppliers that (at the moment) do not supply any product. The cardinalities are those in Figure 8.13.

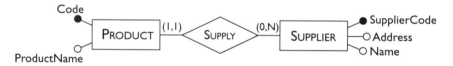

Figure 8.13 The result of the decomposition of an entity.

We can verify that the decomposition obtained satisfies the two fundamental properties. It is a lossless decomposition, because on the basis of the one-to-many relationship it is possible to reconstruct the values of the attributes of the original entity. It preserves the dependencies, because each of the dependencies is embedded in one of the entities or it can be reconstructed from them. For example, the dependency between the product codes and the supplier names can be reconstructed based on the SUPPLY relationship and the dependency SupplierCode → Name.

8.6.2 Verification of normalization on relationships

Concerning relationships, the reasoning is even simpler. The set of occurrences of each relationship is a relation, and thus it is possible to apply the normalization techniques directly. However, the domains on which the relation is defined are the sets of occurrences of the entities involved. Consequently, to verify that a normal form is satisfied, we must identify the existing functional dependencies among the entities involved. Since it is easy to show that each binary relation is in third normal form (and also in Boyce–Codd normal form), the verification of normalization is carried out only on the *n*-ary relationships, that is, on those which involve at least three entities.

Consider for example, the relationship THESIS, in Figure 8.14, which involves the entities STUDENT, PROFESSOR, DEGREEPROGRAMME and DEPARTMENT. It describes the fact that students, enrolled on degree programmes, write theses in departments under the supervision of professors.

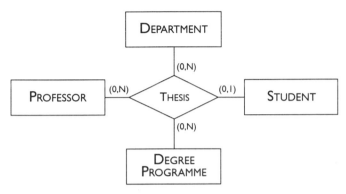

Figure 8.14 A relationship for which normalization is to be verified.

We can arrive at the following conclusions:

- each student is enrolled on a degree programme;

- each student writes a thesis under the supervision of a single professor (who is not necessarily related to the degree programme);

- each professor belongs to a single department and the students under his or her supervision write their theses under the care of that department.

Let us suppose that for the purposes of the thesis, the professor's department is not relevant to the degree programme on which the student is enrolled. We can then say that the properties of the application are completely described by the following three functional dependencies:

$$\text{STUDENT} \rightarrow \text{DEGREEPROGRAMME}$$
$$\text{STUDENT} \rightarrow \text{PROFESSOR}$$
$$\text{PROFESSOR} \rightarrow \text{DEPARTMENT}$$

The (unique) key of the relation is STUDENT: given a student, the degree programme, the professor and the department are unambiguously identified. Consequently, the third functional dependency causes a violation of the third normal form. The affiliation of a professor to a department is a concept independent of the existence of students who write theses with the professor. Reasoning as before, we can conclude that the relationship presents undesirable aspects and that it should be decomposed, separating the functional dependencies with different left hand sides. In this way, we can obtain the schema in Figure 8.15, which contains two relationships, both in third normal form (and in Boyce–Codd normal form). Here also, we have a lossless decomposition with preservation of dependencies.

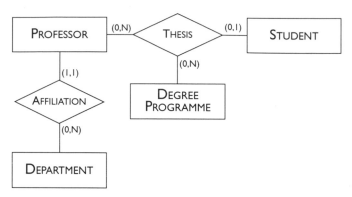

Figure 8.15 The result of the decomposition of a relationship.

8.6.3 Further decomposition of relationships

On the schema in Figure 8.15, we can make some further observations. These observations go beyond the theory of normalization in its strictest sense, but remain within the field of analysis and verification of conceptual schemas by means of formal tools, in the specific case of functional dependencies. The relationship THESIS is in third normal form, because its key is made up of the STUDENT entity, and the only dependencies that exist on it are those that have this entity as left hand side, namely, STUDENT → PROFESSOR and STUDENT → DEGREEPROGRAMME. On the other hand, the properties described by the two dependencies are independent of each other. Not all students are writing theses and so not all of them have supervisors. From the normalization point of view, this situation does not present problems, because we assume that the relations can contain null values, provided that they are not in the key. Thus, it is reasonable to accept dependencies with the same left hand sides. However, at the conceptual modelling level, we must distinguish among the various concepts. Moreover, there is no concept of 'null values in a relationship', nor would there be any sense in introducing one. Using the dependencies, we can therefore conclude that it would be appropriate to decompose the relationship further, obtaining two relationships, one for each of the two concepts. Figure 8.16 shows the decomposed schema. The decomposition is acceptable in this case also, because it preserves the dependencies and is lossless.

If we generalize the argument developed above, we conclude that it is appropriate to decompose the *n*-ary relationships on which there is a dependency whose right hand side contains more than one entity. Since it is rare to encounter relationships that involve more than three entities, we can say that it is usually convenient to decompose any ternary relationship if it has a functional dependency whose left hand side consists of one entity and the right hand side consists of the other two.

In some cases however, the decomposition can be inconvenient. For example, if the two entities in the right hand side of the dependency are closely linked to each other or if there exist other dependencies that would

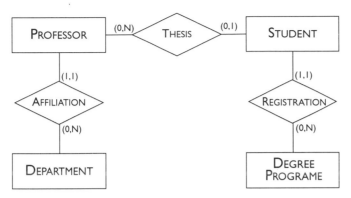

Figure 8.16 The result of a further decomposition of a relationship.

not be preserved in the decomposition, such as, if we are interested only in students who are already writing their theses. Thus, for each of them, we have a degree programme and a professor who is supervising his or her thesis.

8.6.4 Further restructurings of conceptual schemas

The case discussed in Section 8.4, of a relation for which there can be no good decomposition into Boyce–Codd normal form, can also be examined in the context of conceptual design. For example, consider the schema in Section 8.17 and assume that this schema satisfies the functional dependencies discussed in Section 8.4.

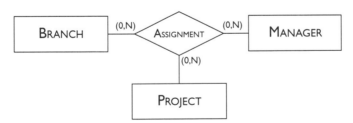

Figure 8.17 A relationship that is difficult to decompose.

We can see that the relationship is not in Boyce–Codd normal form and cannot be usefully decomposed. At this stage we can identify the possibility of introducing the concept of division by means of a new entity, as shown in the schema in Section 8.18, which replaces the ternary relationship.

This entity separates the individual branches, as indicated by its external identifier. Moreover, the cardinality constraints tell us that each division of a branch has a manager and several projects associated with it. From this conceptual schema it is possible to obtain the relational schema in Figure 8.11.

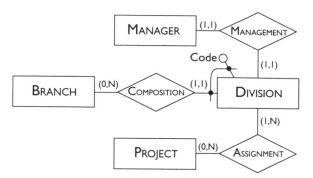

Figure 8.18 A restructuring of the schema in Section 8.17.

8.7 Bibliography

The basic notions on normalization, with the definition of third normal form, were proposed by Codd [27]. The theory of normalization can be studied in depth in the texts on database theory, such as those by Maier [58], Ullman [88], and Atzeni and De Antonellis [3]. They also give an in-depth and formal study of various aspects related to functional dependencies.

8.8 Exercises

Exercise 8.1 Consider the relation in Figure 8.19 and identify the functional dependencies of the corresponding application. Identify possible redundancies and anomalies in the relation.

Tutor	Department	Faculty	HeadOfDept	Course
Thomson	Maths	Engineering	Jackson	Statistics
Thomson	Maths	Engineering	Jackson	Number theory
Robinson	Physics	Engineering	Jackson	Statistics
Robinson	Physics	Science	Johnson	Statistics
MacKay	Physics	Science	Johnson	Relativity

Figure 8.19 Relation for Exercise 8.1.

Exercise 8.2 Identify the key(s) and functional dependencies of the relation shown in Exercise 8.1 and then identify a decomposition into Boyce–Codd normal form.

Exercise 8.3 Consider the relation shown in Figure 8.20, which represents information on the products of a carpentry firm and their components. The following are given: the type of component of a product (attribute Type), the quantity of the component necessary for a certain product (attribute Quantity), the unit price of the component of a certain product (attribute PriceOfC), the supplier of the component (attribute Supplier) and the total price of the single product (attribute PriceOfP). Identify the functional dependencies and the key(s) for this relation.

Product	Component	Type	Quantity	PriceOfC	Supplier	PriceOfP
Bookcase	Wood	Walnut	5	10.00	Smith	400
Bookcase	Screw	B212	200	0.10	Brown	400
Bookcase	Glass	Crystal	3	5.00	Jones	400
Seat	Wood	Oak	5	15.00	Smith	300
Seat	Screw	B212	250	0.10	Brown	300
Seat	Screw	B412	150	0.30	Brown	300
Desk	Wood	Walnut	10	8.00	Quasimodo	250
Desk	Handle	H621	10	20.00	Brown	250
Table	Wood	Walnut	4	10.00	Smith	200

Figure 8.20 A relation containing data for a carpentry firm.

Exercise 8.4 With reference to the relation in Figure 8.20 consider the following update operations:

- insertion of a new product;

- deletion of a product;

- addition of a component in a product;

- modification of the price of a product.

Discuss the types of anomaly that can be caused by these operations.

Exercise 8.5 Consider again the relation in Figure 8.20. Describe the redundancies present and identify a decomposition of the relation that removes these redundancies. Show the schema thus obtained. Then verify that it is possible to reconstruct the original table from this schema.

Exercise 8.6 Consider the schema of the relation in Figure 8.21. Its key is made up of the attributes Title and CopyNo, and on this relation we have the dependency Title $\rightarrow$ Author Genre. Verify whether the schema is in third normal form, and if not, decompose it appropriately. Verify whether the decomposition also satisfies the Boyce–Codd normal form.

Exercise 8.7 Consider the Entity-Relation schema in Figure 8.22. The following properties are valid:

- a player can play for only one team (or none);

- a trainer can train only one team (or none);

- a team belongs to one and only one city.

Title	Author	Genre	CopyNo	Shelf
Decameron	Boccaccio	Stories	I	A75
Rubàiyàt	Omar Khayyàm	Poem	I	A90
Rubàiyàt	Omar Khayyàm	Poem	2	A90
Le Bourgeois Gentilhomme	Molière	Play	I	A90
Le Bourgeois Gentilhomme	Molière	Play	2	A22
Washington Square	James	Novel	I	B20
Richard III	Shakespeare	Play	I	B10

Figure 8.21 Relation for Exercise 8.6.

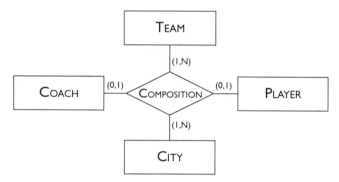

Figure 8.22 A relationship whose normalization is to be verified.

Verify whether the schema satisfies the Boyce–Codd normal form and if not, restructure it into a new schema so that it satisfies this normal form.

Exercise 8.8 Consider the relation in Figure 8.23 and the following possible decompositions:

- Department, Surname in one relation and Surname, FirstName, Address in the other;

- Department, Surname, FirstName in one relation and FirstName, Address in the other;

- Department, Surname, FirstName in one relation and Surname, FirstName, Address in the other.

Department	Surname	FirstName	Address
Sales	Eastland	Fred	6 High Street
Purchasing	Eastland	Fred	6 High Street
Accounts	Watson	Ethel	27 Acacia Avenue
Personnel	Eastland	Sydney	27 Acacia Avenue

Figure 8.23 Relation for Exercise 8.8.

With reference both to the specific instance and to the possible instances on the same schema, identify which of these decompositions are lossless.

Exercise 8.9 Reconsider the relation in Figure 8.23. Verify whether the following decompositions preserve the dependencies:

- a relation on Department, Surname and FirstName and the other on Surname and Address;

- a relation on Department, Surname and FirstName and the other on Surname, FirstName and Address;

- a relation on Department and Address and the other on Department, Surname and FirstName.

Part III

Database technology

9

Technology of a database server

This chapter concentrates on the technological aspects of database servers, that is, of systems dedicated to data management. While up to now we have concentrated on the external functionality of database management systems, we will now look at the internal mechanisms that make such functionality possible. There are various important reasons for looking 'inside' a DBMS.

- Firstly, database administrators are often required to make decisions about configurations or execution parameters that influence the behaviour of the system, and such decisions require an understanding of the underlying technology.

- Secondly, although the mechanisms described below are often encapsulated within database products, many of these mechanisms can be extracted from the DBMS and made available in the form of 'services'. Knowledge of these services is essential in order to decide on the best configuration of an application.

The following components are present in a data management server:

- The *optimizer* decides the best strategies for data access, that is, the ones that guarantee the fastest query response. This component receives a query, from which it performs a lexical, syntactic and semantic analysis, to identify possible errors. It then transforms the correct queries into an internal form, similar to the relational algebra seen in Chapter 3, and selects the best strategy for access to the data.

- The *access methods manager*, known as the *relational storage system* (RSS) in a relational DBMS, has the task of carrying out the physical accesses to data, according to the strategy defined by the optimizer.

- The *buffer manager* is responsible for the management of actual transfers of the pages of the database from the secondary storage devices to the main memory. This component manages large areas of the main memory allocated to the DBMS and is often shared among the various applications.

- The *reliability control system* deals with the preservation of the contents of the database in case of failures.

- The *concurrency control system* regulates the simultaneous accesses to the database and ensures that the interference among applications does not cause a loss of consistency.

This division of a server into five modules does not always correspond to the actual configuration of a system, but is ideal as a model for the study of the mechanisms. We will deal with the five components, proceeding from the lowest to the highest levels of functionality, and in doing so will construct an abstract machine for data management.

We will first introduce the concept of *transaction*, which is fundamental to the understanding of the requirements that the DBMS technology must meet. We will then discuss concurrency control, buffer management, and reliability control. Finally, we will deal with physical access structures and query optimization. At the end of this construction, it will be possible to understand how the five sub-systems are integrated into the architecture of a centralized server.

We will postpone the description of the techniques for the interaction of multiple servers in a distributed or parallel architecture to the next chapter. For the sake of consistency, we will refer to relational technology, although a large part of the discussion is applicable both to pre-relational systems and to object-oriented systems.

9.1 Definition of transactions

A *transaction* identifies an elementary unit of work carried out by an application, to which we wish to allocate particular characteristics of reliability and isolation. A system that makes available mechanisms for the definition and execution of transactions is called a *transaction processing system*.

A transaction can be defined syntactically: each transaction, irrespective of the language in which it is written, is enclosed within two commands: begin transaction (abbreviated to bot) and end transaction (abbreviated to eot). Within the transaction code, two particular instructions can appear, commit work and rollback work, to which we will make frequent reference using the two terms *commit* and *abort*, which indicate the action associated with the respective instructions.

The effect of these two commands is crucial for the outcome of the transaction. The transaction will be completed successfully only following a commit command, while no tangible effect will be shown on the database as the result of an abort command. From the expressive power aspect, note that the `rollback work` instruction is very powerful, in that through this the database user can cancel the effects of the work carried out during the transaction, irrespective of its complexity.

An example of transaction is given in the following code:

```
begin transaction
x := x - 10;
y := y + 10;
commit work;
end transaction
```

We can interpret the above transaction as a bank operation to transfer a sum from account x to account y. The transaction code shown in the example provides an abstract description of the transaction, which in reality corresponds to a much more complex section of code, and which could be written, for example, in SQL.

A transaction is described as *well-formed* if it fulfils the following conditions: it begins its execution with `begin transaction`, ends with `end transaction`, and includes in every possible execution only one of the two commands, `commit work` or `rollback work`. Further, no update or modification operations are carried out following the execution of the `commit work` or `rollback work` command. In some transactional interfaces, a pair of commands `end transaction` and `begin transaction` are immediately and implicitly carried out after each commit or abort, to render well-formed all the transactional computations. From now on, we will assume that all the programs for the modification of the contents of a database are well-formed.

9.1.1 ACID properties of transactions

Transactions must possess particular properties: *atomicity*, *consistency*, *isolation* and *durability*. Since the initials of these terms give rise to the acronym ACID, these are often referred to as the *acid properties* of transactions.

Atomicity   Atomicity represents the fact that a transaction is an *indivisible* unit of execution. Either all the effects of a transaction are made visible, or the transaction must have no effect on the database, with an 'all or nothing' approach. In practice, it is not possible to leave the database in an intermediate state arrived at during the processing of the transaction.

Atomicity has significant consequences on the operational level. If during the execution of the operations, an error appears and one of the operations of the transaction cannot be completed, then the system must be able to recreate the situation at the start of the transaction. This means *undoing* the work carried out by those instructions up to that time. Conversely, after the execution of the commit command, the system must ensure that the transaction leaves the database in its final state. As we shall see, this can mean that the system must *redo* the work carried out. The correct execution of the commit fixes the atomic (and thus indivisible) event in which the transaction is successfully completed. Before executing the commit, any failure will cause the elimination of all the effects of the transaction, whose original state is recreated.

When the `rollback work` command is carried out, the situation is similar to a *suicide* decided independently within the transaction. Conversely, the system can decide that the transaction cannot be successfully completed and *kills* the transaction. Finally, various transactions can be *killed* following a failure in the system. In both situations (suicide or homicide), the mechanisms that create the abort of a transaction use the same data structures and sometimes the same algorithms. In general, we expect the applications to be well written and for this reason most transactions are successfully completed and end with a commit command. In only a few sporadic cases due to failures or unforeseen situations do the transactions terminate with an abort command.

Consistency   Consistency demands that the carrying out of the transaction does not violate any of the integrity constraints defined on the database. When a transaction violates a constraint, the system intervenes to cancel the transaction or to correct the violation of the constraint.

The verification of constraints of *immediate* type can be made during the transaction execution: a constraint violation removes the effects of the specific instruction that causes the violation of the constraint, without necessarily causing the transactions to be aborted. By contrast, the verification of integrity constraints of the *deferred* type must be carried out at the end of the transaction, after the user has requested a commit. Note that in this second case, if the constraint is violated, a commit instruction cannot be successfully completed, and the effects of the transaction are cancelled *in extremis*. That is, just before producing and showing the final state of the database, given that this state would be inconsistent.

Isolation   Isolation demands that the execution of a transaction is independent of the simultaneous execution of other transactions. In particular, it requires that the parallel execution of a set of transactions gives the result that the same transactions would obtain by carrying them out singly. The goal of isolation is also to make the result of each transaction independent of all the others. It must thus prevent the execution of a rollback of a transaction from causing the rollback of other transactions, possibly generating a chain reaction.

Durability   Durability, on the other hand, demands that the effect of a transaction that has correctly executed a commit is not lost. In practice, a database must guarantee that no piece of data is lost for any reason. To understand the importance of durability, consider the use of databases that support financial applications, such as banks and systems for stock trading.

9.1.2 Transactions and system modules

Atomicity and durability are guaranteed by the reliability control system. Isolation is guaranteed by the concurrency control system. Finally, consistency is guaranteed by DDL compilers, which introduce appropriate consistency controls in the data and appropriate procedures for their verification, which are then carried out by the transactions.

In conclusion, note that the definition of transaction given in this section is different from the concept of transaction that a user could have. For the system, a transaction is a unit of execution characterized by ACID properties. For the user, a transaction is any interaction with the system, characterized by the production of an initial input of data, which is followed by a response from the system. Often the two notions coincide, but at other times, a system transaction contains various user transactions, or a user transaction contains various system transactions.

9.2 Concurrency control

A DBMS must often serve many applications, and respond to requests from many users. The application load of a DBMS can be measured using the *number of transactions per second* (abbreviated to *tps*) managed by the DBMS to satisfy the needs of applications. Typical systems, for example banks or financial information systems, must respond to loads of tens to hundreds of tps. The booking systems of large airlines or credit card management must reach thousands of tps. For this reason, it is essential that the transactions of a DBMS be carried out simultaneously. It is unthinkable that the transactions could be carried out in sequence. Only the concurrency of transactions allows for the efficient operation of a DBMS, maximizing the number of transactions carried out per second and minimizing their response times.

9.2.1 Architecture of concurrency control

The concurrency control system refers to the lowest level in the architecture of a DBMS, relative to the *input/output operations*, which carry out the transfer of blocks from the secondary memory to the main memory and vice-versa. Consider read and write actions. Each read operation consists of the transfer of a block from the secondary memory to the main memory, and each write operation consists of the opposite transfer. Traditionally, blocks are called *pages* once they are loaded into the memory. The read and write operations are managed by a module of the system generally known as the *scheduler*, which determines whether the requests can be satisfied. This situation is illustrated in Figure 9.1.

In this section we will give an abstract description of the database in terms of objects x, y, z. Using these symbolic names, we refer to numeric data (to which we will apply simple arithmetic operations), but in reality reading and writing them requires the reading and writing of the whole page on which the data is to be found.

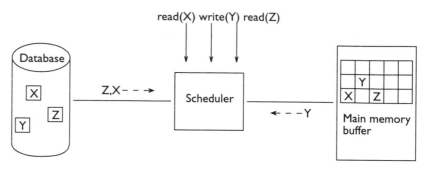

Figure 9.1   Architecture of the concurrency control system.

9.2.2 Anomalies of concurrent transactions

The simultaneous execution of various transactions can cause problems, termed *anomalies*; their presence causes the need of a concurrency control system. Let us look at three typical cases.

Update loss   Let us suppose that we have two identical transactions that operate on the same object of the database.

$$t_1: r(x), x = x + 1, w(x)$$
$$t_2: r(x), x = x + 1, w(x)$$

Here, $r(x)$ represents the reading of the generic object x and $w(x)$ represents the writing of the same object. A change in value of the object x is done by an application program. Let us suppose that the initial value of x is 2. If we carry out the two transactions t_1 and t_2 in sequence, at the end x will have the value 4. Let us now analyze a possible concurrent execution of the two transactions, which highlights the sequence of the actions. We will assume that each action happens instantly.

Transaction t_1	Transaction t_2
bot	
$r_1(x)$	
$x = x + 1$	
	bot
	$r_2(x)$
	$x = x + 1$
	$w_2(x)$
	commit
$w_1(x)$	
commit	

In this case, the final value of x is 3, because both the transactions read 2 as the initial value of x. This anomaly is called a *lost update*, because the effects of the transaction t_2 (the first to write the new value for x) are lost.

Dirty read   Consider now the case in which the first transaction is aborted:

Transaction t_1 Transaction t_2

bot
$r_1(x)$
$x = x + 1$
$w_1(x)$

                                     bot
                                     $r_2(x)$
                                     $x = x + 1$
                                     $w_2(x)$
                                     commit

abort

The final value of x at the end of the execution is 4, but it should be 3. The critical aspect of this execution is the reading of the transaction t_2, which sees an intermediate state generated by the transaction t_1. The transaction t_2, however, should not have seen this state, because it is produced by the transaction t_1, which subsequently carries out an abort. This anomaly is known as *dirty read*, as a piece of data is read that represents an intermediate state in the processing of a transaction. Note that the only way to restore consistency following the abort of t_1 would be to impose the abort of t_2 and, therefore, of all the transactions that would have read data modified by t_2. This situation, known as the 'domino effect', is extremely hard to manage.

Inconsistent read   Let us suppose now that the t_1 transaction carries out only read operations, but that it repeats the read of the x data in successive instants, as described in the following execution:

Transaction t_1 Transaction t_2
bot
$r_1(x)$

                                       bot
                                     $r_2(x)$
                                     $x = x + 1$
                                     $w_2(x)$
                                     commit

$r_1(x)$
commit

In this case, x assumes the value 2 after the first read operation and the value 3 after the second read operation. Instead, it is convenient that a transaction that accesses the database twice finds exactly the same value for each piece of data read, and is not affected by the other transaction.

Ghost update   Consider a database with three objects, x, y and z, which satisfy an integrity constraint, such that $x + y + z = 1000$; assume that we carry out the following transactions:

Transaction t_1	Transaction t_2
bot	
$r_1(x)$	
	bot
	$r_2(y)$
$r_1(y)$	
	$y = y - 100$
	$r_2(z)$
	$z = z + 100$
	$w_2(y)$
	$w_2(z)$
	commit
$r_1(z)$	
$s = x + y + z$	
commit	

The transaction t_2 does not alter the sum of the values and thus does not violate the integrity constraint. However, at the end of the evaluation of t_1 the variable s, which contains the sum of x, y and z, takes the value 1100. In other words, the transaction t_1 observes only some of the effects of the transaction t_2, and thus observes a state that does not satisfy the integrity constraints. This anomaly is called a *ghost update*.

9.2.3 Concurrency control theory

We will now give a careful analysis of the problems posed by the concurrent execution of transactions. For this, we must define a formal model of a transaction. We define a transaction as a sequence of read or write actions. We assume that each transaction has a unique, system-assigned transaction identifier. In comparison with the four examples of anomaly illustrated above, this model omits any reference to the manipulation operations performed on the data by the transaction. As far as the theory of concurrency control is concerned, each transaction is a syntactical object, of which only the input/output actions are known.

Let us assume that all the transactions are initiated by the begin transaction command and terminated by end transaction, which, however, will also be omitted. Furthermore, the concurrency control system accepts or refuses concurrent executions during the evolution of the transactions, without knowing their final outcome (commit or abort). For example, a transaction t_1 is represented by the sequence:

$$t_1: \quad r_1(x)\ r_1(y)\ w_1(x)\ w_1(y)$$

We assume that normally no transaction reads or writes the same object more than once.

Given that the transactions happen concurrently, the input and output operations are requested by various transactions at successive times. A *schedule* represents the sequence of input/output operations presented by concurrent transactions. A schedule S_1 is thus a sequence of the type:

$$S_1 : \quad r_1(x) \, r_2(z) \, w_1(x) \, w_2(z) \, \ldots$$

where $r_1(x)$ represents the reading of the object x carried out by the transaction t_1, and $w_2(z)$ the writing of the object z carried out by transaction t_2. The operations appear in the schedule following the chronological order in which they were carried out in the database.

The task of concurrency control is to accept some schedules and refuse others. For example, the system must avoid the anomalies shown in the section above. This is carried out by a *scheduler*, the task of which is to keep track of all the operations performed on the database by the transactions, and to accept or reject the operations that are requested by the transactions.

We will begin by assuming that the transactions that appear in schedules have a result (commit or abort) known in advance. In this way, we can ignore the transactions that produce an abort, removing all their actions from the schedule, and concentrating only on the transactions that produce a commit. Such a schedule is known as a *commit-projection* of the actual execution of the input/output operations, since it contains only the actions of transactions that produce a commit. This assumption simplifies the theory of concurrency control, but is unacceptable in practice, because the scheduler must decide whether or not to accept the actions of a transaction independently of their final result, which cannot be known beforehand. For example, this assumption makes it impossible to deal with 'dirty reads' described above, which are generated when the transaction results in an abort. Thus, we must abandon this assumption when we move from the theory of concurrency control to practical concurrency control methods.

We now need to determine the conditions of the schedules that guarantee the correct execution of the corresponding transactions. For this purpose, we define as *serial* a schedule in which the actions of all the transactions appear in sequence, without being mixed up with instructions from other transactions. The schedule S_2 is a serial schedule in which the transactions t_0, t_1 and t_2 are executed in sequence.

$$S_2 : \quad r_0(x) \, r_0(y) \, w_0(x) \, r_1(y) \, r_1(x) \, w_1(y) \, r_2(x) \, r_2(y) \, r_2(z) \, w_2(z)$$

The execution of the commit-projection of a given schedule S_i is correct when it produces the same result as some serial schedule S_j of the same transactions. In this case, we say that S_i is *serializable*. We must still clarify, however, what we mean by 'producing the same result'. To this end, various successive notions of equivalence between schedules are introduced. Each notion allows the identification of a more or less wide-ranging class of acceptable schedules, at the cost, however, of a rather complex test for equivalence. First, we will introduce *view-equivalence*, then the *conflict-equivalence*, then *two-phase locking*, and finally *timestamp-based* concurrency control.

View-Equivalence The notion of *view-equivalence* requires, as preliminary definitions, the notions of the *reads-from* relation and of the *final writes*. A read operation $r_i(x)$ *reads-from* a write $w_j(x)$ in a schedule S when $w_j(x)$ precedes $r_i(x)$ in S and there is no other write operation $w_k(x)$ included between the two operations $r_i(x)$ and $w_j(x)$ in S. A write operation $w_i(x)$ in a schedule S is called a *final write* if it is the last write of the object x to appear in S.

Two schedules are called *view-equivalent* $(S_i \approx_V S_j)$ if they possess the same reads-from relation and the same final writes. A schedule is called *view-serializable* if it is view-equivalent to some serial schedule. The set of view-serializable schedules is called VSR.

Consider the schedules S_3, S_4, S_5, S_6. S_3 is view-equivalent to the serial schedule S_4 (thus, it is view-serializable). S_5 is not view-equivalent to S_4, but it is view-equivalent to the serial schedule S_6, and thus this also is view-serializable.

$$S_3: \quad w_0(x) \; r_2(x) \; r_1(x) \; w_2(x) \; w_2(z)$$
$$S_4: \quad w_0(x) \; r_1(x) \; r_2(x) \; w_2(x) \; w_2(z)$$
$$S_5: \quad w_0(x) \; r_1(x) \; w_1(x) \; r_2(x) \; w_1(z)$$
$$S_6: \quad w_0(x) \; r_1(x) \; w_1(x) \; w_1(z) \; r_2(x)$$

Note that the following schedules, corresponding to anomalies of update loss, inconsistent reads and ghost updates, are not view-serializable:

$$S_7: \quad r_1(x) \; r_2(x) \; w_2(x) \; w_1(x)$$
$$S_8: \quad r_1(x) \; r_2(x) \; w_2(x) \; r_1(x)$$
$$S_9: \quad r_1(x) \; r_1(y) \; r_2(z) \; r_2(y) \; w_2(y) \; w_2(z) \; r_1(z)$$

The view-equivalence of two given schedules can be decided by an algorithm that has polynomial complexity. Such an algorithm simply scans the two schedules and checks that the reads-from relations and the final writes are identical. Therefore, the concept of view-equivalence can be used to compare two different schedules. However, to determine whether a schedule is view-serializable requires us to test whether it is view-equivalent to any serial schedule; this is an NP-complete problem[1]. This complexity is due to the need to compare the given schedule with all the serial schedules that can be obtained by permuting, in every way possible, the order of the transactions that are present in the schedule. Therefore, this notion of

---

1. The efficiency of algorithms is characterized by their *computational complexity*; it expresses the total amount of elementary computation required by the algorithm as a function of the size of the data set to which the algorithm is applied. Many algorithms have polynomial complexity, that is, a complexity that can be expressed as a polynomial function of the data set size; these problems are known as tractable. Linear complexity is a special case of polynomial complexity. NP-complete problems are a class of problems for which there is no known solution algorithm with a polynomial complexity, and as such they are regarded as intractable.

equivalence cannot be used to decide on serializability with enough efficiency. It is thus preferable to define a more restricted condition of equivalence, which does not cover all the cases of view-equivalence between schedules, but which is usable in practice, being less complex.

Conflict-equivalence A more practical notion of equivalence requires the definition of conflict. We say that the action a_i is in *conflict* with a_j $(i \neq j)$, if both operate on the same object and at least one of them is a write. There can exist *read-write* conflicts (*rw* or *wr*) and *write-write* conflicts (*ww*).

We say that the schedule S_i is *conflict-equivalent* to the schedule S_j ($S_i \approx_C S_j$) if the two schedules present the same operations and each pair of operations in conflict is in the same order in both the schedules. A schedule is therefore *conflict-serializable* if there is a serial schedule that is conflict-equivalent to it. The set of conflict-serializable schedules is called CSR.

It is possible to prove that the class of CSR schedules is properly included in that of the VSR schedules. There are thus schedules that belong to VSR but not to CSR, while all the CSR schedules belong to VSR. Thus conflict serializability is a sufficient but not necessary condition for view-serializability.

Figure 9.2 illustrates the conflict-serializable schedule S_{10} with its conflicts in evidence; next, it shows the serial schedule S_{11}, which is conflict-equivalent to S_{10}.

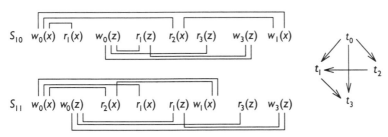

Figure 9.2 A schedule S_{10} conflict-equivalent to a serial schedule S_{11}.

It is possible to determine whether a schedule is conflict-serializable by means of the *conflict graph*. The graph is constructed with a node for each transaction and an arc from t_i to t_j if there is at least one conflict between an action a_i and an action a_j such that a_i precedes a_j (see Figure 9.2). It can be proved that the schedule is in CSR if and only if the graph is acyclic. The analysis of cyclicity of a graph has a linear complexity with respect to the size of the graph itself.

In spite of the linear complexity, conflict serializability is still too laborious in practice. For example, consider a system with 100 tps and transactions with access to 10 pages and lasting on average 5 seconds. In each instant, it will be necessary to organize graphs with 500 nodes and record the 5000 accesses of the 500 active transactions. Further, this graph continues to modify itself dynamically, making decisions very laborious for the scheduler.

The technique is unacceptable in a distributed database context, given that, as we shall see, the graph must be reconstructed based on arcs that are recognized by the different servers of the distributed system. Thus, conflict equivalence, too, cannot be used in practice.

Two-phase locking   The concurrency control mechanisms used by almost all commercial DBMSs is called *locking*; it overcomes the limitations discussed above. Locking is based on a very simple principle: all the read and write operations must be protected by means of the execution of three different primitives: *r_lock*, *w_lock* and *unlock*. The scheduler (also known as the *lock manager*) receives a sequence of execution requests for these primitives by the transactions, and their outcome is determined by a simple inspection of an adequate data structure, at a negligible computational cost.

During the execution of read and write operations the following constraints must be satisfied:

1. Each read operation should be preceded by an *r_lock* and followed by an *unlock*. The lock in this case is called *shared*, because more than one lock of this type can be active on one piece of data at one time.

2. Each write operation must be preceded by a *w_lock* and followed by an *unlock*. The lock in this case is known as *exclusive*, because no other locks (exclusive or shared) can exist on the same piece of data.

When a transaction follows these rules it is called *well formed with regard to locking*. Note that the lock operation of a resource can happen much earlier than a read or write action on that resource. In some systems, a single lock primitive is available, which does not distinguish between read and write, and thus behaves like an exclusive lock. If a transaction must read and then write a resource, the transaction can request only an exclusive lock, or it can start with a shared lock and can then move from a shared lock to an exclusive lock, 'increasing' the level of lock; this process requires a specialized lock primitive, and is called *lock escalation*.

In general, transactions are automatically well-formed with regard to locking, because the appropriate lock and unlock requests are automatically issued by transactions when they need to read or write pages. The lock manager receives the lock requests from the transactions and can either grant or deny the lock, based on the locks previously granted to the other transactions. When a lock request is granted, we say that the corresponding resource is acquired by the requesting transaction. At the time of unlock, the resource is released. When a lock request is not granted, the requesting transaction is put in a waiting state. The waiting ends when the resource is unlocked and becomes available. The locks already granted are stored in a *lock table*, managed by the lock manager.

Each lock request received by the lock manager is characterized only by the identifiers of the transaction making the request, and by the resource for which the request is carried out. The policy followed by the lock manager to grant locks is represented in the conflict table in Figure 9.3, in which the rows identify the requests and the columns the current state of the resource requested. The first value of the cell shows the result of the request and the second value in the cell shows the state that will be assumed by the resource after the execution of the primitive.

Request	Resource state		
	free	r_locked	w_locked
r_lock	OK / r_locked	OK / r_locked	No / w_locked
w_lock	OK / w_locked	No / r_locked	No / w_locked
unlock	error	OK / depends	OK / free

Figure 9.3 Conflict table for the locking method.

The three **No** entries present in the table represent the conflicts that can appear when a read or write is requested on an object already locked for writing, or a write on an object already locked for reading. In practice, only when an object is locked for reading is it possible to give a positive response to another request for a read lock, as shown by the **OK** entry. In the case of *unlock* of a resource locked by a shared lock, the resource becomes *free* when there are no other read transactions operating on it, otherwise, the resource remains locked. For this reason, the corresponding cell of the matrix of conflicts has the **depends** value. To keep track of the number of readers we introduce a counter, which increases at each request for *r_lock* granted, and decreases at each *unlock*.

The locking mechanism seen so far ensures that the writing actions are exclusive, while reading actions can occur concurrently. This is the traditional control of readers and writers, normally presented in the context of operating systems. In order to guarantee, however, that the transactions form a serializable schedule, we must impose the following restriction on the ordering of the lock requests. The restriction is known as *two-phase locking* (2PL).

Two-phase locking (2PL): A transaction, after having released a lock, cannot acquire other locks.

As a consequence of this principle, two different phases can be distinguished during the execution of the transaction. During the first phase, locks on resources are acquired (*growing phase*); during the second phase, the acquired locks are released (*shrinking phase*). The transfer of an *r_lock* to a *w_lock* constitutes an increase in the level of lock on the resource, which can thus appear only in the growing phase of the transaction. Figure 9.4 shows a graphic representation of the requested behaviour of the two-phase locking protocol. The *x*-axis represents time and the *y*-axis represents the number of resources obtained by a transaction during its execution.

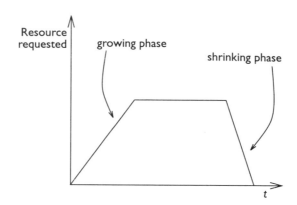

Figure 9.4 Representation of the resources allocated to a transaction with a two-phase locking protocol.

Consider a system in which the transactions are well-formed with regard to locking, with a lock manager that respects the policy described in the conflict table of Figure 9.3, and in which the transactions follow the two-phase locking principles. Such a system is characterized by the serializability of its transactions. The 2PL class contains the schedules that satisfy these conditions.

We will now give an informal proof of the fact that if a schedule satisfies 2PL then it is conflict serializable. In other words, 2PL is contained in CSR. Assume, by way of contradiction, that a schedule S satisfies 2PL and is not in CSR. If the schedule does not belong to CSR, this means that the conflict graph among the transactions contains a cycle $t_1, t_2, \ldots, t_n, t_1$. If there is a conflict between t_1 and t_2, it means that there is a resource on which both the transactions operate in conflict. For the transaction t_2 to proceed, it is necessary that transaction t_1 releases its lock on the resource. On the other hand, if we observe the conflict between t_n and t_1, it means that there is a resource on which both the transactions operate in conflict. For the transaction t_1 to proceed, it is necessary for the transaction t_1 to acquire the lock on the resource, released by t_n. Thus, the transaction t_1 cannot be two-phased. It releases a resource before acquiring another.

It is easier to prove that the 2PL and CSR classes are not equivalent, and thus that 2PL is strictly included in CSR. To do this, it is sufficient to show an example of a schedule that is not in 2PL but is in CSR, such as:

$$S_{12}: \quad r_1(x)\ w_1(x)\ r_2(x)\ w_2(x)\ r_3(y)\ w_1(y)$$

In this schedule, the t_1 transaction must release an exclusive lock on the resource x and then request an exclusive lock on the resource y; therefore, it cannot be produced by a two-phase locking scheduler. Conversely, the schedule is conflict-serializable relative to the sequence t_3, t_1, t_2.

Finally, let us look at how two-phase locking resolves the problem of the ghost updates. Consider the example introduced in Section 9.2.2. We will represent the same sequence of accesses that introduced a ghost update, and show that 2PL resolves the problem. Figure 9.5 describes for each resource its

t_1	t_2	x	y	z
bot		free	free	free
$r\_lock_1(x)$		1:read		
$r_1(x)$				
	bot			
	$w\_lock_2(y)$		2:write	
	$r_2(y)$			
$r\_lock_1(y)$			1:wait	
	$y = y - 100$			
	$w\_lock_2(z)$			2:write
	$r_2(z)$			
	$z = z + 100$			
	$w_2(y)$			
	$w_2(z)$			
	commit			
	$unlock_2(y)$		1:read	
$r_1(y)$				
$r\_lock_1(z)$				1:wait
	$unlock_2(z)$			1:read
$r_1(z)$				
	eot			
$s = x + y + z$				
commit				
$unlock_1(x)$		free		
$unlock_1(y)$			free	
$unlock_1(z)$				free
eot				

Figure 9.5 Prevention of the occurrence of a ghost update by means of two-phase locking.

free state, read-locked from the i-th transaction (i : read) or write-locked from the i-th transaction (i : write). We will also illustrate the negative result of a lock request from the i-th transaction, left in a waiting state (i : wait). Note that, as a result of 2PL, the lock request of t_1 relative to the resources z and x are put in waiting, and the transaction t_1 can proceed only when these resources are unlocked by t_2. At the end of the transaction, the variable s contains the correct value of the sum $x + y + z$.

Remember at this point the hypothesis of using a commit-projection. To remove it, it is necessary to introduce a further constraint on the 2PL protocol, thereby introducing the so-called *strict* 2PL:

Strict two-phase locking: the locks on a transaction can be released only after having carried out the commit/abort operations.

With this constraint, the locks are released only at the end of the transaction, after which each item of data has arrived at its final state. This version of 2PL is the one used by commercial DBMSs. By using strict 2PL the anomaly of dirty reads, shown in Section 9.2.2, does not occur. The example in Figure 9.5 uses strict 2PL, in that the release actions of the lock follow the commit action, explicitly required by the schedule.

Concurrency control based on timestamps We will conclude the overview of concurrency control theory by introducing a method that is easy to manage, but is less efficient than two-phase locking. This method makes use of a *timestamp*, that is, of an identifier that defines a total ordering of temporal events within a system. In centralized systems, the timestamp is generated by reading the value of the system clock at the time at which the event happened. The concurrency control with timestamps (*TS method*) is carried out as follows:

- every transaction is assigned a timestamp that represents the time at which the transaction begins.

- a schedule is accepted only if it reflects the serial ordering of the transactions based on the value of the timestamp of each transaction.

This method of concurrency control, perhaps the simplest of all from the point of view of its construction, serializes transactions on the basis of the order in which they acquire their timestamps. Each object x has two indicators, $RTM(x)$ and $WTM(x)$, which are the highest timestamps of the transactions that carried out respectively read and write operations on x. The scheduler receives requests for access to objects of the type *read(x, ts)* or *write(x, ts)*, where *ts* represents the timestamp of the requesting transaction. The scheduler accepts or rejects the requests according to the following policies:

- *read(x, ts)*: if $ts < WTM(x)$ then the request is rejected and the transaction is killed, otherwise the request is accepted and $RTM(x)$ is set equal to the greater of $RTM(x)$ and *ts*.

- *write(x, ts)*: if $ts < WTM(x)$ or $ts < RTM(x)$ then the request is rejected and the transaction is killed, otherwise the request is accepted and $WTM(x)$ is set equal to *ts*.

In practice, no transaction can read or write an item of data written by a transaction with a greater timestamp, and cannot write on an item of data that has already been read by a transaction with a greater timestamp.

Let us look at an example. Suppose that $RTM(x)$ is equal to 7 and $WTM(x)$ equals 5 (that is, the object x was read by the transaction with highest timestamp 7 and written by the transaction with highest timestamp 5).

Below, we will describe the scheduler's reply to the read and write requests received:

Request	Response	New values
$read(x, 6)$	OK	
$read(x, 8)$	OK	$RTM(x) = 8$
$read(x, 9)$	OK	$RTM(x) = 9$
$write(x, 8)$	NO	t_8 killed
$write(x, 11)$	OK	$WTM(x) = 11$
$read(x, 10)$	NO	t_{10} killed

The TS method causes the forced abort of a large number of transactions. Furthermore, this version of the method is correct only under the hypothesis of use of a commit-projection. To remove this hypothesis we must 'buffer' the writes, that is, store them in memory and transcribe them to the secondary memory only after the commit. This means that other transactions wanting to read the data stored in the buffer and waiting for commit are also made to wait until the commit of the writing transaction. This has the effect of introducing wait mechanisms similar to those of locking.

Multiversion concurrency control An interesting modification of this method on the theoretical level is the use of *multiversions*. This consists of keeping many copies of the objects of the database, one for each transaction that modifies it. Each time that a transaction writes an object, the old value is not discarded, but a new copy is created, with a corresponding $WTM_N(x)$. We have, however, a sole global $RTM(x)$. Thus at any time, $N \geq 1$ copies of each object x are active. By this method, the read requests are never refused, but are directed to the correct version of the data according to the timestamp of the requesting transaction. The copies are discarded when they are no longer useful, in that there are no read transactions interested in their values. The rules of behaviour become;

- $read(x, ts)$: a read is always accepted. The copy x_k is selected for reading such that: if $ts > WTM_N(x)$, then $k = N$, otherwise k is taken such that $WTM_k(x) < ts < WTM_{k+1}(x)$.

- $write(x, ts)$: if $ts < RTM(x)$ the request is refused, otherwise a new version of the item of data is added (N increased by one) with $WTM_N(x) = ts$.

The idea of adopting many versions, introduced theoretically within the context of timestamp-based methods, has also been extended to other methods, including two-phase locking. An interesting use of the versions is obtained by limiting the maximum number of copies to two, that is, keeping an earlier and a later copy of each update during write operations. The read transactions which are synchronized before the write transaction can access the earlier copy.

Comparison of VSR, CSR, 2PL and TS Figure 9.6 illustrates the taxonomy of the methods VSR, CSR, 2PL and TS. Observe that the VSR class is the most general: it strictly includes CSR, which in its turn includes both the 2PL class and the TS class. 2PL and TS in their turn present a non-empty intersection, but neither of them includes the other. This last characteristic can be easily verified, by constructing a schedule that is in TS but not in 2PL, or in 2PL but not in TS, or finally in 2PL and in TS.

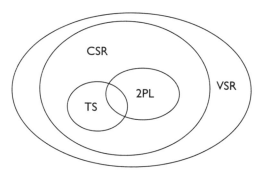

Figure 9.6 Taxonomy of the classes of schedule accepted by the methods VSR, CSR, 2PL and TS.

First, we will show that there can exist schedules that are in TS but not in 2PL. Consider the schedule S_{13}, in which the indices of transactions are interpreted as timestamps:

$$S_{13}: \quad r_1(x)\ w_2(x)\ r_3(x)\ r_1(y)\ w_2(y)\ r_1(v)\ w_3(v)\ r_4(v)\ w_4(y)\ w_5(y)$$

The corresponding graph of conflicts, illustrated in Figure 9.7, shows the absence of cycles; thus, the schedule belongs to CSR. The serial ordering of the transactions that is conflict-equivalent to S_{13} is $t_1\ t_2\ t_3\ t_4\ t_5$. The schedule is not 2PL because t_2 first releases x (so that it is read by t_3) and then acquires y (released by t_1); but is actually in TS since, on each object, the transactions operate in the order defined by their timestamps.

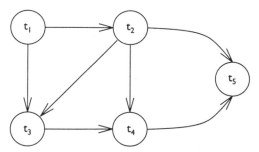

Figure 9.7 Conflict graph for the schedule S_{13}.

A schedule that is both in TS and in 2PL is the simple schedule $r_1(x)\ w_1(x)$ $r_2(x)\ w_2(x)$. On the other hand, the schedule $r_2(x)\ w_2(x)\ r_1(x)\ w_1(z)$, in which transaction t_2 acquires the timestamp after transaction t_1 but presents itself first to the object x, does not belong to TS but to 2PL.

Let us compare 2PL and TS, the two techniques that can be used in practice. Some significant differences emerge.

- In 2PL, the transactions are put in waiting. In TS they are killed and then restarted.

- The serialization order in 2PL is imposed by conflicts, while in TS it is imposed by the timestamps.

- The necessity of waiting for the commit of the transaction before showing its final state causes a lengthening of the locking time in 2PL (the transfer from 2PL to strict 2PL) and the creation of waiting conditions in TS.

- The 2PL method can give rise to deadlocks, which we will see in the next section.

- The restart used by TS costs more that the waiting time imposed by 2PL.

If we analyze the choices made by commercial systems, we can observe that almost all commercial DBMSs use strict 2PL. Therefore we devote the next section to the discussion of a few more aspects and problems arising in the use of locks.

9.2.4 Lock management

The lock manager is a component of the DBMS, used by all the processes that access the database. The lock manager provides for these processes an interface that is based on the three procedures r_lock, w_lock and unlock, generally characterized by the following parameters:

```
r_lock(T, x, errcode, timeout)
w_lock(T, x, errcode, timeout)
unlock(T, x)
```

T represents the identifier for the transaction; x the element for which the lock is requested or released; errcode represents a value returned by the lock manager, and is equal to zero whenever the request is satisfied, while it assumes a non-zero value whenever the request is not satisfied; timeout represents the maximum interval that the calling procedure is prepared to wait to obtain the lock on the resource.

When a process requests a resource and the request can be satisfied, the lock manager records the change of status of the resource in its internal table and immediately returns the control to the process. In this case, the delay introduced by the lock manager on the execution time of the transaction is very small.

However, when the request cannot be satisfied immediately, the system inserts the requesting process into a queue associated with that resource. This causes an arbitrarily long waiting time, and thus the process associated with the transaction is suspended. As soon as a resource is released, the lock manager checks whether there are processes waiting for the resource; if so, it grants the resource to the first process in the queue. The efficiency of the lock manager thus depends on the probability that the request for a transaction will conflict with other transactions.

When a timeout is released and the request is not satisfied, the requesting transaction can carry out a rollback, which will generally be followed by a restart of the same transaction. Alternatively, it can decide to continue, repeating the request for a lock, and keeping all the locks that were previously acquired.

The lock tables are accessed frequently. For this reason, the lock manager keeps the information in the main memory, so as to minimize the access times. The tables have the following structure: two status bits, which are allocated to each object to represent the three possible states, and a counter that represents the number of processes reading that object.

Hierarchical locking   Up to now we have discussed the locking of generic resources and objects of the database, in that the theoretical principles on which 2PL is based are independent of the type of objects to which the method is applied. In many real systems, however, it is possible to specify the lock on different levels. This is known as *lock granularity*. For example, it is possible to lock entire tables, or parts of them (called *fragments*, see Section 10.2.3), or tuples, or even fields of single tuples. Figure 9.8 illustrates the hierarchy of resources that make up a database.

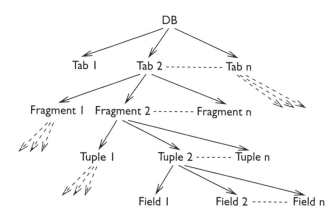

Figure 9.8   The hierarchy of resources.

To introduce different levels of lock granularity, an extension of the protocol of traditional lock is introduced, called *hierarchical locking*. This technique allows the transactions to lock items at given levels of the hierarchy. Thus it is possible for a transaction to obtain a lock for the entire database (as can be needed when we wish to make a copy of the entire database), or for a specific tuple or field.

The technique provides a richer set of primitives for lock requests; we rename read and write locks as follows:

- XL: exclusive lock, corresponds to the write-lock of the 2PL protocol;

- SL: shared lock, corresponds to the read-lock of the 2PL protocol.

The following three locks are specific to this technique:

- ISL: intention shared lock. This expresses the intention of locking in a shared manner one of the nodes that descend from the current node;

- IXL: intention exclusive lock. This expresses the intention of exclusively locking one of the nodes descending from the current node;

- SIXL: shared intention-exclusive lock. This locks the current node in a shared mode and expresses the intention of exclusively locking one of the nodes descending from the current node.

If, for example, we wish to place a write lock on a tuple of the table, and the hierarchy is that shown in Figure 9.8, then we must first request an IXL on the database level. When the request is satisfied, we can request an IXL for the relation and the fragment in which the desired tuple lies. When these locks are granted, we can request an XL for the particular tuple. Then when the transaction is ended, it will have to release the locks in reverse order to that in which they were granted, ascending the hierarchy one step at a time.

Here is a more formal description of the rules that must be followed by the protocol.

1. Locks are requested beginning at the root and moving down the tree.

2. Locks are released starting at the node locked by the smallest granularity and moving up the tree.

3. In order to request an SL or ISL on a node, a transaction must already hold an ISL or IXL lock on the parent node.

4. In order to request an IXL, XL, or SIXL on a node, a transaction must already hold an SIXL or IXL lock on the parent node.

5. The rules of compatibility used by the lock manager to decide whether to accept the lock request, based on the status of the node and on the type of request, are shown in Figure 9.9.

The choice of level of lock is left to the designer of the applications or to the database administrator, based on the characteristics of the transactions. Transactions that carry out 'localized' modifications, having access to a limited set of objects, use a fine granularity. Transactions that carry out accesses to large quantities of data use a coarser granularity. The choice must be careful, as the use of too coarse a granularity can cause limitations to the parallelism (it increases the probability of the occurrence of a conflict), while

Request	Resource state				
	ISL	IXL	SL	SIXL	XL
ISL	OK	OK	OK	OK	No
IXL	OK	OK	No	No	No
SL	OK	No	OK	No	No
SIXL	OK	No	No	No	No
XL	No	No	No	No	No

Figure 9.9 Compatibility among the lock functions in the presence of hierarchies.

the use of too fine a granularity means that a large number of locks must be requested one at a time, causing a great deal of work for the lock manager and exposing it to the risk of failure after the acquisition of many resources.

Lock functions offered by SQL-2   In SQL-2 it is possible to define each transaction as read only or read write. The default case is read write. Read only transactions cannot modify the contents of the database (with the primitives insert, delete and update) or modify the contents of the schema (with the primitives create, drop and alter). Thus, they request only shared locks.

Furthermore, it is possible to indicate the level of isolation for each transaction, choosing among four possibilities: serializable, repeatable read, read committed, and read uncommitted. The default case is serializable; this level guarantees the maximum requirements of isolation. The three successive levels correspond to reduced requirements on the isolation of read operations. This simplifies the concurrency control for the transaction and ensures an increase in performance, but exposes it to possible inconsistencies. Note that in each case, the write requests the use of exclusive locks and of the protocol of strict 2PL.

To understand the difference between serializable and repeatable read, we must discuss a further problem caused by concurrency. Let us consider a transaction that evaluates an aggregate value from the set of all the elements that satisfy a selection predicate. For example, the average grade of first-year students. Consider the case in which the aggregate value is evaluated twice, and between the first and second evaluations a new first-year student is inserted. In this case, the two average values read by the transaction could be different. This anomaly is not recognized by the concurrency control as defined in Section 9.2.3. The first read operation is not in conflict with the insertion operation, thus the two transactions are recognized as serializable, with the insertion transaction that precedes the read transaction.

In reality, the transactions are in conflict. To prevent the anomaly, it is necessary for the first transaction to impose a lock, which prevents any other transaction from modifying the data that satisfies the selection predicate. This new lock is called a *predicate lock* and can be created in the relational systems using mechanisms that lock particular data structures, which are known as indexes, and which will be introduced in Section 9.7. The serializable level allows for the use of predicate locks and thus also avoids this anomaly, while the repeatable read level does not introduce them and thus guarantees the level of isolation that is obtained by strict 2PL. Note that the term repeatable read is misleading, in that really the two readings of aggregate data discussed above can, when repeated, give different values.

Finally, let us look at the cases of read committed and read uncommitted. In both cases, the 2PL protocol is not used, and thus the serializability is not guaranteed. In the first case, the readings of data corresponding to an intermediate (uncommitted) state of a transaction are excluded, thus avoiding the anomaly of dirty read described in Section 9.2.2. This effect is obtained by a read lock request, which will, however, be immediately released after having been obtained. In the second case, no locks at all are used for read operations, thus even dirty reads are accepted.

The most developed systems make all four levels of isolation available to the programmer. It is up to the application programmer to choose which level to use. For the applications for which the accuracy of the data read is essential (for example, financial applications), the highest level will be chosen. Where the accuracy is not important (for example, statistical evaluations in which approximate values are acceptable), lower levels will be chosen.

9.2.5 Deadlock management

Locking can generate a serious problem, *deadlock*, when we have concurrent transactions, each of which holds and waits for resources held by others. Suppose that we have a transaction t_1, which performs the sequence of operations $r(x)$, $w(y)$, and a second transaction t_2, which performs the sequence of operations $r(y)$, $w(x)$. If the two-phase lock protocol is used, the following schedule can occur:

$$r\_lock_1(x),\ r\_lock_2(y),\ read_1(x),\ read_2(y)\ w\_lock_1(y),\ w\_lock_2(x)$$

At this point, neither of the two transactions can proceed and the system is locked. The deadlock occurs because t_1 is waiting for the object y, which is blocked by t_2, and in its turn, t_2 is waiting for the object x, which is locked by t_1. This situation is characteristic of all the systems in which mechanisms of locks on resources are used.

Let us evaluate the probability of such an event happening. Consider a table that consists of n different tuples, with identical access probability. The probability of a conflict between two transactions that make a single access is $1/n$; the probability of a deadlock of length 2, is equal to the probability of a second conflict of the same two transactions, and thus is equal to $1/n^2$. We will ignore the case of deadlocks generated by longer chains, because in this case the deadlock probability decreases exponentially with the increase of the length of the chain. Limiting ourselves to the case of deadlocks caused by pairs of transactions, the probability of conflict increases in a linear manner with the global number k of transactions present in the system. Further, it increases quadratically with the average number m of resources to which each transaction has access. The actual probability of the occurrence of deadlock is slightly higher than the simple statistical analysis above would lead us to believe, due to the dependencies that exist among data. (When a transaction has access to a given data item, it is more likely that it accesses other items that are semantically related.) In conclusion, we can assume that the probability of a deadlock in transactional systems is low, but not negligible. This consideration is confirmed by experiment.

Three techniques are commonly used to resolve the problem of deadlock:

1. timeout;

2. deadlock detection;

3. deadlock prevention.

Use of timeout   Avoiding deadlocks by means of timeouts is very simple. The transaction remains in waiting for a resource for a pre-set time. If this time expires and the resource has not yet been granted, then the lock request is given a negative response. In this way, a transaction in deadlock is in any case removed from the waiting condition, and presumably aborted. Because of its simplicity, this technique is preferred by commercial DBMSs.

The choice of timeout values depends on the following trade-off. On one hand, a timeout that is too high tends to resolve deadlocks late, after the transactions involved in the lock have spent a long time in waiting. On the other hand, a timeout that is too low runs the risk of defining as deadlock situations in which a transaction is waiting for a resource without causing an actual deadlock. This might needlessly kill a transaction and waste the work already carried out by the transaction.

Deadlock prevention   Different techniques can be used to prevent the occurrence of a deadlock. One simple but impractical technique is based on requesting locks on all the resources necessary to the transaction at once. Unfortunately, this technique cannot be used because transactions do not normally know beforehand the resources to which they require access.

Another technique for the prevention of deadlock is to cause the transactions to acquire a timestamp. The technique consists of allowing the transaction t_i to wait for a resource acquired by t_j only if there is a determined relation of precedence between the timestamps of t_i and t_j (for example, $i < j$). In this way, about 50% of the requests that generate a conflict can wait in a queue, while in the remaining 50% of cases a transaction must be killed.

There are various options for choosing the transaction to kill. Let us first separate them into *pre-emptive* policies, and *non-pre-emptive* policies. A policy is pre-emptive if it resolves the conflict by killing the transaction that possesses the resource (to release the resource, which can thus be granted to another transaction). In the opposite case, the policy is non-pre-emptive, and a transaction can be killed only in the act of making a new request.

One policy can be that of killing the transaction that is making a request when it has done less work than the transaction holding the lock. A problem with this policy is that a transaction accessing many objects that are often used by other transactions would be often in conflict, and being the one that has done least work, it would repeatedly be killed. In this situation there are no deadlocks, but there is a potential for starvation. To resolve the problem we must guarantee that each transaction cannot be killed an unlimited number of times. A solution that is often adopted is to maintain the same timestamp when a transaction is aborted and restarted, at the same time giving increasing priority to 'older' transactions. In this way, the problem of starvation is solved.

This technique is never used in commercial DBMSs, as the probability of killing a transaction is about half of the probability of a conflict, while the probability of a deadlock is much lower that the probability of a conflict.

Deadlock detection   This technique requires controlling the contents of the lock tables, as often as necessary in order to reveal possible block situations. The control can be carried out at predefined intervals, or when the timeout of a transaction occurs. The discovery of a deadlock requires the analysis of the waiting conditions among the various transactions, and in determining whether there is a cycle. The search for cycles in a graph, especially if carried out periodically, is practically feasible. For this reason, some commercial DBMSs use this technique, which will be described in more detail in Section 10.3.2, in the context of distributed systems.

9.3 Buffer management

The efficient management of main memory buffers is an essential aspect of database systems. The *buffer* is a large area of the main memory pre-allocated to the DBMS and shared among the various transactions. Recent years have seen memory costs fall, with the consequent allocation of larger and larger memory buffers to the DBMSs; in certain cases the entire DBMS can be copied and managed in the main memory.

9.3.1 Architecture of the buffer manager

The buffer manager deals with the loading and unloading of pages of the main memory to the secondary memory. It provides primitives for access to the pages present in the buffer, called *fix*, *use*, *unfix*, *flush* and *force*. It then simultaneously creates input/output operations in response to these primitives, so long as the shared access to the data is allowed by the scheduler (generally a lock manager). The architecture of the subsystem is illustrated in Figure 9.10.

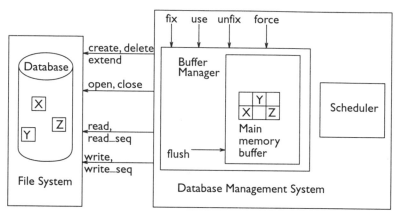

Figure 9.10 Architecture of the buffer manager.

The buffer is organized in pages, which are either equal to or a multiple of the size of the input/output blocks used by the operating system for reading from and writing to secondary memory. The size of pages ranges from a few Kbytes to about a hundred Kbytes. When a page of the secondary memory is present in the buffer, the DBMS can carry out its reading and writing operations directly on it. Given that the access times to main memory are in the order of six orders of magnitude faster than access times to secondary memory, it is clear that having access to the pages of the buffer represents an important increase of performance.

The policies of buffer management are similar to those of main memory management from the point of view of the operating systems, and they obey the same principle, called data locality, based on which the currently referenced data has a greater probability of being referenced in the future. In addition, a well-known empirical law says that only 20% of data is typically accessed by 80% of applications. This law means that generally the buffers contain the pages on which most of the accesses are made.

The buffer manager supports a *directory*, which describes the current contents of the buffer. For each page loaded, it indicates the physical file and the corresponding block number. Note that, as the size of the buffer increases, the importance of managing this directory efficiently also increases.

9.3.2 Primitives for buffer management

The operations supported by the buffer manager to organize the loading and unloading of pages are the following.

- The *fix* primitive is used to request the access to a page and to load it into the buffer. At the end of the operation, the page is loaded and *valid*, that is, allocated to an active transaction; a pointer to the page is returned to the transaction. The execution of the primitive requires read operations from the secondary memory only when the chosen page is not already resident in the buffer.

- The *use* primitive is used by the transaction to gain access to the page previously loaded in the memory, confirming its allocation in the buffer and its status as a valid page.

- The *unfix* primitive indicates to the buffer manager that the transaction has terminated the use of the page, which is no longer valid.

- The *force* primitive synchronously transfers a page from the buffer manager to the secondary memory. The requesting transaction remains suspended until the end of the execution of the primitive, which consists of physical write operations to the secondary memory.

In practice, the primitives *fix* and *use* allow the loading into the buffer and the reading of data, and the primitive *force* is used by the transactions to write data in the secondary memory. Furthermore, the *flush* primitive is used by the buffer manager itself to transfer to the secondary memory the pages that are no longer valid and remain inactive for a long time, either during the *fix* operation relating to other pages, or asynchronously and independently of the active transactions. Asynchronous transfers happen when the buffer manager is not occupied by other operations such as *fix* or *force*. They make pages of the buffer available, which become free and can be immediately used by successive *fix* operations. In summary, the writing of pages of the buffer into the secondary memory can be synchronous, commanded by the transactions, or asynchronous, commanded by the buffer manager and independent from the transactions.

The *fix* primitive operates as follows.

1. First it searches for the required page among those already present in the memory, after the *unfix* of other transactions. If the search has a positive result, the operation is concluded and the address of the page is granted to the requesting transaction. Due to the principle of locality, this happens quite often.

2. Otherwise, a page in the buffer is chosen for loading the secondary memory page into it. If a free page exists, it is selected. Otherwise, the page is selected from among those that are not free; that page is called *victim*. As we further discuss next, the selection can consider only non-valid pages (and fail if no page is available), or else consider also valid pages allocated to other transactions (and in such case it never fails). If a page that is not free is chosen, it must in any case be rewritten in the secondary memory, invoking the *flush* operation.

9.3.3 Buffer management policies

We will now describe two pairs of alternative policies for buffer management.

- The *steal* policy, used during the execution of the *fix* operation, allows the buffer manager to select an active page allocated to another transaction as a victim, while a *no-steal* policy excludes this possibility. Note that with the steal policy, the pages of active transactions can be written in the secondary memory by the buffer manager before the end of the transaction. In particular, we might have to rewrite the initial value of the page when the transaction carries out an abort.

- The *force* policy requires that all the active pages of a transaction are transcribed in the secondary memory when the transaction performs a commit. The *no-force* policy entrusts the writing of the pages of a transaction to the asynchronous mechanisms of the buffer manager. This latter makes it possible for the write to come well after the end of the transaction, because of *flush* operations or when a page is a chosen victim.

The no-steal/no-force pair of policies is preferred by the DBMSs, as the no-steal policy is the easiest to carry out and the no-force policy guarantees the higher efficiency. We will return to this subject in the next section, which deals with reliability.

There is also the possibility of 'anticipating' the loading and unloading times of the pages, by means of *pre-fetching* and *pre-flushing* policies. The former means loading the pages before the actual request by the transaction, when the pattern of access to the pages of the database is known in advance. The latter means unloading the pages before the time when a page is chosen as a victim.

9.3.4 Relationship between buffer manager and file system

The file system is a module made available by the operating system. The DBMS uses its functionality. However, contrary to appearances, the relationship between the functions delegated to the file system and those handled directly by the DBMS is not simple. There was a long period in which the functionality offered by the operating systems could not guarantee availability, reliability or efficiency, for which reason the DBMSs had to implement their own input/output functions. Today, DBMSs use the file system but create their own abstraction of the files, in order to ensure the efficiency (by means of the buffers) and robustness (by means of the reliability system). It is quite possible that in the future this functionality will migrate towards the operating system, 'exporting' the functionality of the database beyond the DBMS. There follows a brief description of the functionality of the file system, which serves to create links between this subject and operating systems. Listed below are the functions traditionally offered by the file system and exploited by the DBMS.

- The creation (`create`) and removal (`delete`) of a file. In general, at the time of creation an initial number (minimum) of blocks is allocated to a file, which can be dynamically extended (`extend`).

- The opening (`open`) and closing (`close`) of a file, necessary to load the information that describes the file in appropriate main memory structures. The opening of a file normally allocates a numerical identifier (`fileid`) to the name of the file (`filename`).

- The primitive `read(fileid, block, buffer)` for the direct access to a block of a file, identified by the first two parameters, which is transcribed in the page of the buffer indicated using the third parameter.

- The primitive `read_seq(fileid, f-block, count, f-buffer)` for sequential access to a fixed number (`count`) of blocks of a file, identifying the first block of the file by means of the second parameter and the first page of the buffer by means of the last parameter.

- The dual primitives `write` and `write_seq`, characterized by exactly the same parameters as the corresponding read primitives.

Furthermore, other primitives allow for the structuring of the secondary memory by introducing directories, to which the files are allocated. The file system is responsible for knowing the structure of the secondary memory in directories and the current situation of secondary memory use. It must identify which blocks are free and which are allocated to files, to be able to respond to the primitives.

9.4 Reliability control system

The architecture described up to now allows for the concurrent and efficient reading and writing of blocks of the secondary memory. At this point, we must concern ourselves with reliability, one of the main goals in database management. The reliability control system ensures two fundamental properties of transactions, defined in Section 9.1.1: atomicity and durability. The system is responsible for the writing of the *log*; a permanent archive, which registers the various actions, carried out by the DBMS. As we shall see, each write action on the database is protected by means of an action on the log, so that it is possible to 'undo' the actions following malfunctions or failures preceding the commit, or 'redo' these actions whenever their success is uncertain and the transactions have performed a commit.

To give an indication of the role of the log, we can make use of two metaphors, one mythological and the other based on a popular fable. The log can be likened to 'Arianna's thread', used by Theseus to find his way out of the Minotaur's palace. In this case, by rewinding the log, Theseus can 'undo' the path he has taken. A similar role is given by Hansel and Gretel to the crumbs of bread left along the way through the forest, but in the Grimm's fairy tale the crumbs were eaten by the birds, and Hansel and Gretel were lost in the forest. This analogy shows that, in order to be able to carry out its role effectively, the log must be sufficiently durable.

9.4.1 Architecture of the reliability control system

The reliability control system (see Figure 9.11) is responsible for executing the transactional commands: begin transaction, commit work, rollback work, abbreviated where necessary to B:begin, C:commit, A:abort, and for executing the primitives for recovery after malfunctions. These primitives are known respectively as *warm restart* and *cold restart*. Further, the reliability control system receives requests for reading and writing pages, which are transferred to the buffer manager, and generates other requests for reading and writing of pages necessary to ensure durability and resistance to failure. Finally, the system prepares the data required for doing recoveries after failures, in particular, by creating *checkpoints* and *dumps*.

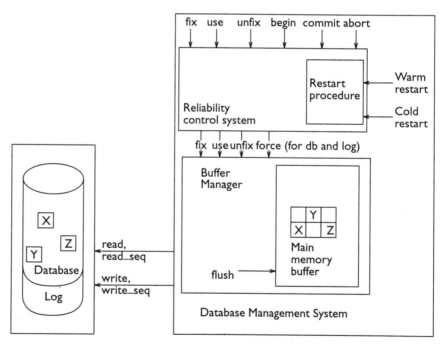

Figure 9.11 Architecture of the reliability control system.

Stable memory To be able to operate, the reliability control system must make use of a *stable memory*, that is, a memory that is failure-resistant. Stable memory is an abstraction, in that no memory can have zero probability of failure. However, mechanisms of replication and robust writing protocols can bring such a probability close to zero. The mechanisms of reliability control are defined as if the stable memory were immune to failure. A failure of the stable memory would be considered *catastrophic* and we assume it to be impossible, at least in this section.

The stable memory is organized in different ways, depending upon the specific requirements of an application. In some applications, it is assumed that a tape unit is stable. In other cases, it is assumed that a pair of devices are stable, for example, a tape unit and a disk storing the same information. A typical organization of a stable memory uses, in place of a single disk unit, two disk units referred to as 'mirrored'. The two disks contain exactly the same information and are written with a 'careful writing' operation, which is held to be successful only if the information is recorded on both the disks. In this way, the stable information is also 'in line' (available on a direct access device).

9.4.2 Log organization

The log is a sequential file managed by the reliability control system, written in the stable memory. The actions carried out by the various transactions are recorded in the log, in chronological order. For this reason, the log has a top block, the last one to be allocated to the log. The records in the log are written sequentially to the top block; when it is full, another block is allocated to the log, and becomes the top block.

There are two types of log record.

- *Transaction records* describe the activities carried out by each transaction, in chronological order. For this reason, each transaction inserts a begin record in the log, followed by various records related to actions carried out (insert, delete, update), followed by a record of either commit or abort. Figure 9.12 shows the sequence of records present in a log. The records for the transaction t_1 are highlighted, in a log that is also written by other transactions. The t_1 transaction carries out two updates before successfully completing with a commit.

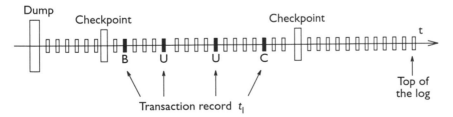

Figure 9.12 Description of a log.

- *System records* indicate the carrying out of the operations dump (rare) and checkpoint (more frequent), which we will illustrate in more detail later. Figure 9.12 highlights the presence of a dump record and of various checkpoint records in the log.

Structure of log records Listed below are the log records that are written to describe the action of a transaction t_1.

- The begin, commit and abort records contain the type of record and the identifier t of the transaction.

- The update records contain the identifier t of the transaction, the identifier O of the object on which the update takes place, and then two values BS and AS, which describe respectively the value of the object O before the modification (the *before state*) and after the modification (the *after state*). In this section we will assume for the sake of simplicity that AS and BS contain complete copies of the modified pages, but in practice, this information is much more compact.

- The insert and delete records are similar to those of update; in the insert record there is no before state, while in the delete records there is no after state.

From here on we will use the symbols $B(T)$, $A(T)$ and $C(T)$ to denote begin, abort and commit records and $U(T, O, BS, AS)$, $I(T, O, AS)$ and $D(T, O, BS)$ to denote update, insert and delete records.

Undo and redo The log records make it possible to undo and redo the respective actions on the database.

- The *undo* primitive: to undo an action on an object O it is sufficient to copy the value BS into the object O. The insert is undone by deleting the object O.

- The *redo* primitive: to redo an action on an object O it is sufficient to copy the value AS into the object O. The delete will be redone by deleting the object O.

Given that the primitives *undo* and *redo* are defined by means of a copy action, this counts as an essential property, known as the *idempotence* of *undo* and *redo*, for which the carrying out of an arbitrary number of undos and redos of the same action is equivalent to the carrying out of such actions only once. In fact:

$$undo(undo(A)) = undo(A) \qquad redo(redo(A)) = redo(A)$$

The property is very important because, as we shall see, there could be errors during the recovery operations, which cause the repetition of *undo* and *redo*.

Checkpoint and dump A *checkpoint* is an operation that is carried out periodically, with the objective of recording which transactions are active and of updating secondary memory relative to all completed transactions. During the execution of the checkpoint, all the pages written by transactions that have already carried out the commit or abort are transferred from the buffer into secondary memory. These operations are carried out by the buffer manager, which executes suitable *flush* operations. After having initiated a checkpoint, no commit operations are accepted by the active transactions. The checkpoint ends by synchronously writing (*forcing*) a checkpoint record, which contains the identifiers of the active transactions. In this way, we are sure that the effects of the transactions that have carried out a commit are permanently recorded in the database. At the same time, the transactions listed in the checkpoint have not yet performed a commit or an abort. This schema can be optimized by DBMSs for improving performance without violating the basic checkpointing principles described above.

A *dump* is a complete copy of the database, which is normally created when the system is not operative. The copy is stored in the stable memory, typically on tape, and is called *backup*. At the conclusion of the *dump* operation, a dump *record* is written in the log, which signals the presence of a copy made at a given time and identifies the file or device where the dump took place. After this, the system can return to its normal function.

Hereafter, we will use the symbols *DUMP* to denote the dump record and $CK(T_1, T_2, ..., T_n)$ to denote a checkpoint record, where $T_1, T_2, ..., T_n$ denote the identifiers of the active transactions at the time of the checkpoint.

9.4.3 Transaction management

During the normal functioning of the transactions, the reliability control system must follow two rules, which define the minimum requirements that allow the accurate recovery of the database in case of failures.

- The *WAL* rule (write-ahead log) imposes the constraint that the before-state parts of the log records are written in the log (that is, in the stable memory) before carrying out the corresponding operation on the database. This rule makes it possible to undo the writing already done in the secondary memory by a transaction that has not yet carried out a commit. That is, for each update, the preceding value written is made available in a reliable manner.

- The *Commit-Precedence rule* imposes the constraint that the after-state parts of the log records are written in the log (that is, in the stable memory) before carrying out the commit. This rule makes it possible to redo the writing already decided by a transaction that has carried out the commit, whose modified pages have not yet been transferred from the buffer manager to the secondary memory.

In practice, even if the rules refer separately to the before–state and after-state of the log records, in many cases both of the components of the log record are written together. For this reason, a simplified version of WAL imposes the constraint that the *log records are written before the corresponding records in the database*, while a simplified version of the commit-precedence rule imposes the constraint that the *log records are written before the execution of the commit operation*.

The atomic outcome of a transaction is established at the time when it writes the commit record in the log synchronously, using the *force* primitive. Before this event, a failure is followed by the *undo* of the actions, so reconstructing the original state of the database. After this event, a failure is followed by the *redo* of the actions carried out to reconstruct the final state of the transaction. The writing of an abort record in the log atomically defines the decision to abort the transaction, either produced by the 'suicide' of the transaction or imposed by the system. Given, however, that it does not modify the decisions of the reliability control system, the abort record can be simply written asynchronously into the top block of the log, which is contained in the buffer. This block can be rewritten to the log with a *flush* operation, or with a *force* operation caused by another transaction.

Joint writing of log and database The WAL and Commit-Precedence rules impose the following protocols for the writing of the log and of the database, described in Figure 9.13. Let us suppose that the actions carried out by the transactions are updates (they could also be inserts or deletes). We distinguish three schemas:

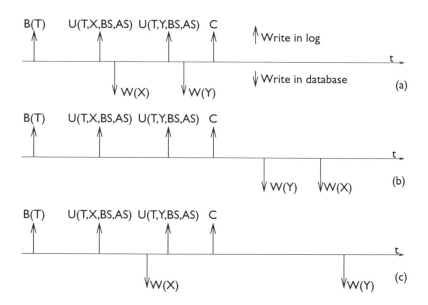

Figure 9.13 Description of protocol for the joint writing of log and database.

- In the first schema, illustrated in Figure 9.13.a, the transaction first writes the record $B(T)$, then carries out its update actions by writing first the log records and then the pages of the database, which thus changes from the value BS to the value AS. These pages are written (either with *flush* primitives or with explicit requests for *force*) from the buffer manager to secondary memory before the commit, which is always implemented with a synchronous writing (*force*) in the log. In this way, at the commit, all the pages of the database modified by the transaction are already written in the secondary memory. This schema does not require *redo* operations.

• In the second schema, illustrated in Figure 9.13b, the writing of log records precedes that of the actions on the database, which, however, happen only after the decision to commit and the consequent synchronous writing of the commit record in the log. This schema does not require *undo* operations.

• The third schema, more general and commonly used, is illustrated in Figure 9.13.c. According to this schema, the writing in the database, once protected by the appropriate writing on the log, can happen at any time with regard to the writing of the commit record in the log. This schema allows the buffer manager to optimize the *flush* operations; however, it requires both *undo* and *redo*.

Note that all three protocols respect the two rules (WAL and Commit-Precedence) and write the commit record synchronously. They differ only regarding the time in which the pages of the database are written.

We have seen which actions must be carried out in the log in order to support failure recovery. These actions have a cost, comparable to the cost of updating the database. The use of the above protocols represents a sensitive overloading of the system, but cannot be avoided because of the need for 'acid' properties of the transactions. Log operations can be optimized, for example by writing several log records in the same page, or by writing them on the page in which the commit record of the transaction will be written, and then using only one *force* operation. Other optimization techniques allow a group-commit of transactions: various commit records are placed on the same page of the log and written with a single *force*, expected by all the requesting transactions. Finally, a transaction system with a high number of transactions per second (tps) can also resort to parallel schemas for the writing of the log.

9.4.4 Failure management

Before studying the mechanisms for failure management, it is appropriate to classify the types of failures that can occur in a DBMS. Failures are divided into two categories.

• **System failures** These are failures caused by software bugs, for example of the operating system, or by interruptions of the functioning of the devices, due, for example, to loss of power. This can cause a loss of the contents of the main memory (and thus all the buffers), although maintaining the contents of the secondary memory (and thus of the database and the log).

- **Device failures**   These are failures of secondary memory devices (for example, disk head crashes), which cause the loss of secondary memory contents. Given our assumption that the log is written in the stable memory, these failures should affect only the database content; device failures causing the loss of the contents of the log are therefore classified as catastrophic events, for which there is no remedy.

The ideal failure model is called *fail-stop*. When the system identifies a failure, whether of the system or of a device, it imposes a complete halt of transactions, followed by a restart of the system (*boot*). This is known as a *warm restart* in case of system failure and *cold restart* in case of device failure. At the end of the restart procedure, the system can again be used by the transactions. The buffer is empty and can begin to reload pages from the database or from the log. The model of behaviour is illustrated in Figure 9.14.

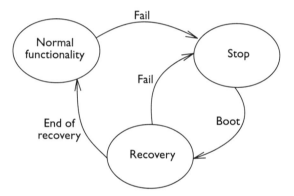

Figure 9.14 Fail-stop model of the functioning of a DBMS.

With this model, the failure is an instantaneous event that happens at a certain time in the operation of the database. Let us look at the objectives of the restart process. There are potentially active transactions at the time of failure. That is, we do not know whether they have completed their actions on the database (as the buffer manager has lost all useful information). These are classified into two categories, based on information present in the log. Some of them have committed, and for these it is necessary to redo the actions in order to guarantee durability. Others have not committed, and for these it is necessary to undo the actions, as the database must be left in its state before the execution of the transaction. Note that it would be possible, in order to simplify the restart protocols, to add another record to the log, known as the **end** record, written when the transcription operation (*flush*) of all the pages of a transaction is terminated. This allows the identification of a third class of transaction, for which it is not necessary either to undo or to redo the actions. However, in general, the **end** record is not used by DBMSs, so as not to complicate the management of transactions. From here on we will assume a fail-stop failure model and the absence of an **end** record.

Warm restart   The warm restart is divided into four successive phases.

1. The last block of the log is accessed, that is, the one that was at the top at the time of failure, and the log is traced back until the most recent checkpoint record.

2. Decisions are made about which transactions must be redone or undone. Two sets are constructed, called *UNDO* and *REDO*, containing transaction identifiers. The *UNDO* set is initially equal to the active transactions at the checkpoint; the *REDO* set is initially empty. The log is then traced forward, adding to the *UNDO* set all the transactions for which there is a begin record, and moving from the *UNDO* set to the *REDO* set all the identifiers of the transactions for which a commit is present. At the end of this phase, the *UNDO* and *REDO* sets contain respectively all the identifiers of the transactions to undo or redo.

3. The log is traced back undoing all the transactions in the *UNDO* set, until the first action of the 'oldest' transaction in the two sets, *UNDO* and *REDO*, is found. Note that this action could precede the checkpoint record in the log.

4. Finally, in the fourth phase, the *redo* actions are applied, in the order in which they are recorded in the log. In this way, the behaviour of the original transactions is replicated exactly.

This mechanism ensures atomicity and durability of the transactions. As far as atomicity is concerned, it guarantees that the transactions in progress at the time of failure leave the database either in the initial state or in the final one. Concerning durability, we know that the pages in the buffer relating to transactions completed but not yet transcribed to the secondary memory are actually completed by a write to the secondary memory. Note that each 'uncertain' transaction that is present in the last checkpoint record or started after the last checkpoint, is either undone or redone. It is undone if its last record written in the log is a transaction or an abort record, and redone if its last record written in the log is a commit record.

Let us look at an example of the application of the protocol. Suppose that in the log the following actions are recorded: $B(T_1)$, $B(T_2)$, $U(T_2, O_1, B_1, A_1)$, $I(T_1, O_2, A_2)$, $B(T_3)$, $C(T_1)$, $B(T_4)$, $U(T_3, O_2, B_3, A_3)$, $U(T_4, O_3, B_4, A_4)$, $CK(T_2, T_3, T_4)$, $C(T_4)$, $B(T_5)$, $U(T_3, O_3, B_5, A_5)$, $U(T_5, O_4, B_6, A_6)$, $D(T_3, O_5, B_7)$, $A(T_3)$, $C(T_5)$, $I(T_2, O_6, A_8)$. Following this, a failure occurs.

The protocol operates as follows.

1. The checkpoint record is accessed; $UNDO = \{T_2, T_3, T_4\}$, $REDO = \{\}$.

2. Then the log record is traced forward, and the *UNDO* and *REDO* sets are updated:

    (a) $C(T_4)$: $UNDO = \{T_2, T_3\}$, $REDO = \{T_4\}$

(b) $B(T_5)$: UNDO $= \{T_2, T_3, T_5\}$, REDO $= \{T_4\}$

(c) $C(T_5)$: UNDO $= \{T_2, T_3\}$, REDO $= \{T_4, T_5\}$

3. Following this, the log is traced back to the action $U(T_2, O_1, B_1, A_1)$ executing the following sequence of *undo* operations:

(a) Delete (O_6)

(b) Re-insert $(O_5 = B_7)$

(c) $O_3 = B_5$

(d) $O_2 = B_3$

(e) $O_1 = B_1$

4. Finally, the *redo* operations are carried out:

(a) $O_3 = A_4$ (note: $A_4 = B_5$!)

(b) $O_4 = A_6$

Cold restart   The cold restart responds to a failure that causes damage to a part of the database. It is divided into three successive phases.

1. During the first phase, the *dump* is accessed and the damaged parts are selectively copied from the database. The most recent dump record in the log is then accessed.

2. The log is traced forward. The actions on the database and the commit or abort actions are applied as appropriate to the damaged parts of the database. The situation preceding the failure is thus restored.

3. Finally, a warm restart is carried out.

   This schema reconstructs all the work relating to the damaged part of the database, and therefore guarantees the durability and atomicity that existed at the time of the failure. The second phase of the algorithm can be optimized, for example by carrying out only the actions of successfully committed transactions.

9.5 Physical access structures

Physical access structures are used for the efficient storage and manipulation of data within the DBMS. In general, each DBMS has a limited number of types of access structure available. For example, in relational systems, indexes are defined by the designer using DDL instructions. Access structures can also be found outside DBMSs, for example, they may be coded within applications that do not use a DBMS. In this section, we will consider sequential, hash-based, and tree-based data structures.

9.5.1 Architecture of the access manager

The *access manager* is responsible for transforming an access plan, produced by the optimizer, into an appropriate sequence of accesses to the pages of the database. The access manager supports *access methods*, that is, software modules providing data access and manipulation primitives for each physical access structure; access methods can select the block of a specific file that must be loaded into the memory, passing this information to the buffer manager. For example, sequentially organized data can be scanned by reading the first block and then the successive blocks, until the last.

The access methods also know the *organization of the tuples on the pages*, and thus they support primitives for the reading and manipulation (insertion, update, deletion) of tuples within pages; for instance, they can return the value of an attribute from all the tuples that are stored in a given page.

An architecture that includes these access methods is shown in Figure 9.15. The diagram shows a reference architecture without entering into details of the primitives offered by each access method. Below, we will first look at how the tuples are organized on the page, and we can then examine in detail the most important access methods.

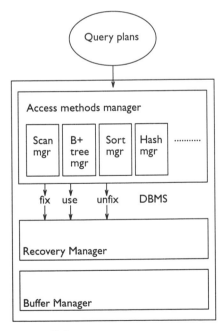

Figure 9.15 Architecture of the access manager.

9.5.2 Organization of tuples within pages

Although each access method can have its own page organization, some access methods (sequential and hash-based) have characteristics in common, which we highlight in the following discussion. On each page, there is both useful information and control information. The useful information is the actual application-specific data; the control information allows access to the useful information. We will look at them in detail with reference to Figure 9.16.

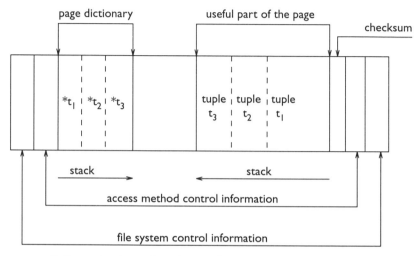

Figure 9.16 Organization of tuples within pages.

- Each page, as it coincides with a block of secondary memory, has an initial part (*block header*) and a final part (*block trailer*) containing control information used by the file system.

- Each page, as it belongs to an access structure, has an initial part (*page header*) and a final part (*page trailer*) containing control information about the access method. This information will typically contain the identifier of the object (table, index, data dictionary, etc.) contained on the page, pointers to successive or preceding pages in the data structure, number of items of useful elementary data (tuples) contained on the page, and quantity of available memory (adjacent or non-adjacent) available on the page.

- Each page has its *page dictionary*, which contains pointers to each item of useful elementary data contained in the page and a useful part, which contains the data. In general, the page dictionary and the useful data grow as opposing stacks, leaving free memory in the space between the two stacks.

- Finally, each page contains a *checksum*, to verify that the information in it is valid.

Some page managers do not allow the separation of a tuple on more than one page, and in this case, the maximum size of a tuple is limited to the maximum space available on a page. Most page managers, on the other hand, allow the distribution of tuples over several pages.

Furthermore, in some cases all the tuples have the same size. In this way, the page structure is simplified, but there is a risk of wasting space on the page. As we shall see, some access methods are characterized by tuples of fixed size. If the tuples can be of different lengths, the page dictionary contains an indication of the offset of each tuple relative to the beginning of the useful part and of each value of the various fields present in the tuple relative to the beginning of the tuple itself. Finally, in some cases it is possible to have tuples belonging to different relations on the same page.

The primitives offered by the page manager are the following.

- *Insertion and update of a tuple*, which does not require a reorganization of the page if there is sufficient space to manage the extra bytes introduced. Otherwise, the operations must be preceded by a reorganization of the page, which has limited cost when it takes place in the main memory, but could sometimes need access to other blocks or the allocation of new blocks.

- *Deletion of a tuple*, which is always possible and is often carried out without reorganizing the information on the page (that is, without reducing the stack relative to the useful part, but simply marking the tuple as 'invalid').

- *Access to a particular tuple*, identified by means of the value of the key or based on its offset, present in the dictionary.

- Access to a field of a particular tuple, identified according to the offset and to the length of the field itself, after identifying the tuple by means of its key or its offset (as described above).

Note that tree structures have a different page organization, which will be illustrated in Section 9.5.5.

9.5.3 Sequential structures

We will now move on to analyze the way in which the pages are linked to each other in data structures, starting with sequential organization. The sequential structures are characterized by a sequential arrangement of tuples in the secondary memory. The file is made up of various blocks of memory, and the tuples are inserted into the blocks according to a sequence. Depending on the application, the sequence can belong to one of a variety of types:

- in an *entry-sequenced* organization, the sequence of the tuples is dictated by their order of entry;

- in an *array* organization, the tuples are arranged as in an array, and their positions depend on the values of an index (or indexes);

- in a *sequentially ordered* organization, the sequence of the tuples depends on the value assumed in each tuple by a field that controls the ordering, known as a *key field*.

Let us look at some further characteristics of each of the above organizations.

Entry-sequenced sequential structure An entry-sequenced sequential structure is optimal for the carrying out of sequential reading and writing operations. Given that the tuples are not in any pre-established order, the most typical method for gaining access to their contents is by means of a sequential *scan*. This organization uses all the blocks available for files and all the spaces within the blocks, and thus the scan is particularly efficient.

The initial operations for the loading and insertion of data happen at the end of the file and in sequence. This is also highly efficient, as it is enough to use a pointer on the last tuple to be able to carry out the operation. More problems are caused by the update or delete operations. Given that the tuples are arranged one after another in sequence, each update that represents an increase of the size of the tuple cannot be easily managed 'in place'. In addition, each deletion causes a potential waste of memory, because it is typically implemented by leaving space unused.

Array sequential structure An array sequential structure is possible only when the tuples are of fixed length. In this case, a number n of adjacent blocks are allocated and each block is given a number m of available slots for tuples, giving rise to an array of $n \times m$ slots overall. Each tuple is given a numeric value i, which functions as an index (that is, the tuple is placed in the i-th position of the array). For the initial loading of the file, the indices are obtained simply by increasing a counter. However, insertions and deletions are possible. The deletions create free slots; the insertions may be carried out within the free slots or at the end of the file. Typical primitives guaranteed by this organization are as follows. Firstly, there is `read-ind` (reading of the tuple corresponding to a determined index value). Next, there are, `insert-at`, `insert-near` and `insert-at-end` (insertion in a specific free slot, or in the first successive free slot, or finally at the end of the file). Finally, there are the intuitive `update-ind` and `delete-ind`.

Ordered sequential structure Sequential ordering allocates to each tuple a position based on the value of the key field. This structure, although classic and well understood, has recently fallen out of use, as its management costs are high. It is based on the concept of giving a physical ordering to the tuples that reflects the lexical ordering of the values present in the key field. Thus, it favours those transactions that require access to the tuples of a table based on the key.

Historically, ordered sequential structures were used on sequential devices (tapes). They were constructed by batch processes, which were responsible for putting the records in order based on the key, and loading them in sequence into a file, called the *main file*. The modifications were collected in *differential files*, also ordered according to the key value, and periodically processed by batch processes, which were responsible for merging the main file and the differential file, obtaining a new version of the main file. Obviously, a periodic merge is unacceptable in the present DBMS technology.

Having rejected this technique, let us look instead at which options are still possible for the management of a sequentially ordered file. The main problem with this structure is the necessity for inserting new tuples (or changing them, when the change brings about an increase in the space needed), as these modifications represent a reordering of the tuples already present. The cancellations can be created in situ, making the corresponding positions in the memory invalid (and unused). To avoid these reorderings, the following techniques are available.

- We can leave a certain number of slots free at the time of first loading. This will allow us to retain the sequential organization using 'local reordering' operations.

- We can integrate the sequentially ordered files with an *overflow file*, dedicated to the management of new tuples, which require extra space. The blocks of the overflow file are linked among themselves in an *overflow chain*. Each chain starts from a block of the sequentially ordered file. Thus, the sequential searches must be intertwined with the analysis of the overflow blocks. This technique is also used for hash-based structures, described below.

9.5.4 Hash-based structures

Hash-based structures ensure an *associative* access to data, in which it is possible to make efficient access to data, based on the value of a *key* field. Keys of hash-based and tree structures have nothing to do with primary keys of the relational model; they can be composed of an arbitrary number of attributes of a given table. A hash-based structure is created by allocating a number B of blocks to a file, often adjacent. Efficient functioning is obtained by making the file larger than necessary, and thus not filling all the blocks. This access method makes use of a hashing function, which, once applied to the key, returns a value between zero and $B-1$. This value is interpreted as the position of the block in the file.

The structure is ideal where the application needs to access the tuple that contains a specific key value. The address produced by the hashing function is passed to the buffer manager and gives direct access to the block thus identified. Similarly, the writing of a tuple that contains a determined key value is carried out in that block. Thus, in the absence of collisions (which we will describe below), this access method allows the reading and writing of tuples (provided that the value of the access key is known) using a single operation of input/output to localize the block relevant to the operation.

The primitive that allows the transformation of a key value into a block number has the format: hash(fileid,Key):Blockid. It receives the name of the file and the key value as parameters, and returns a block number. The corresponding function offered by the system consists of two parts.

- A first operation, known as *folding*, transforms the key values so that they become positive integer values, uniformly distributed over a large range. An example of folding consists of separating the key into various sections, each four bytes long, and then computing the exclusive OR (XOR) of the bits of all the sections. This produces four bytes, to be interpreted as a positive binary number between zero and $2^{32} - 1$.

- The successive hashing operation transforms the positive binary number into a number between zero and $B - 1$. For example, a simple hashing function is obtained by the 'modulo B' division. A more complex function requires raising 2 to the power of the number obtained after the folding. $\text{Log}_2 B$ bits of this number are then taken and interpreted as an internal positive binary number, which is used as the block number.

This technique works better if the file is made larger than necessary. More precisely, if T represents the number of tuples expected for the file and F the average number of tuples stored in each page, then a good choice for B is given by $T/(0.8 \times F)$, thereby using only 80% of the available space for storing tuples. This choice is justified by statistical considerations, which are beyond the scope of this text.

The main problem of structures managed by hashing is that of collisions, that is, situations in which the same block number is returned by the function, based on two different values of the key. Each page can contain a maximum of F tuples. However, when the value of F is exceeded, it is then necessary to resort to a different technique to allocate and retrieve the tuples that find their blocks occupied. We will try, first, to quantify the probability of such an event. If the tuples are uniformly distributed, the probability $p(t)$ that an arbitrary page receives t tuples is equal to the probability that the hashing function produces exactly t identical values and $T - t$ different values; $p(t)$ is given by the following formula:

$$p(t) = \binom{T}{t} \times \left(\frac{1}{B}\right)^t \times \left(1 - \frac{1}{B}\right)^{(T-t)} \quad \text{where } \binom{T}{t} \text{ denotes the binomial coefficient}$$

The probability p of having more than F collisions is equal to:

$$p = 1 - \sum_{i=0}^{F} p(i)$$

When an excessive number of collisions appears and the page capacity is exhausted, the solution is the construction of the overflow chain. These chains originate in the blocks in which an excessive number of collisions appear. The table in Figure 9.17 shows the average length of the overflow chain as a function of the ratio $T/(F \times B)$ and of the average number F of tuples per page. Obviously, the presence of overflow chains slows the search time, as it is necessary to request an input/output operation for each block in the chain. In particular, a search has a positive result when the requested tuple is found, and a negative result at the end of the scan of the overflow chain. An insertion will take place in the first slot available, sometimes at the end of the chain.

	F				
	1	2	3	5	10
.5	0.500	0.177	0.087	0.031	0.005
.6	0.750	0.293	0.158	0.066	0.015
.7	1.167	0.494	0.286	0.136	0.042
.8	2.000	0.903	0.554	0.289	0.110
.9	4.495	2.146	1.377	0.777	0.345

(left column label: $\dfrac{T}{F \times B}$)

Figure 9.17 The average length of the overflow chain following too many collisions.

In conclusion, note that hashing is the most efficient technique for gaining access to data based on queries with equality predicates, but is extremely inefficient for queries with interval predicates, that is, queries that require access to intervals of values

9.5.5 Tree structures

Tree structures, called *B-trees* or *B+ trees*, are most frequently used in relational DBMSs. They allow associative access, that is, access based on a value of a *key*, without necessarily placing constraints on the physical location of the tuples in specific positions in the file. A key may correspond to several attributes, but for simplicity we will consider keys corresponding to one attribute. Note that the primary key of the relational model and the key used by a tree structure are different concepts. The first refers to an abstract property of the schema and the second to a property of the physical implementation of the database.

When a user specifies in DDL an index relating to an attribute or a list of attributes of a table, the system generates appropriate tree structures for physical data management. Each tree structure is characterized by a root node, a number of intermediate nodes, and a number of leaf nodes. Each node coincides with a page or block at the file system and buffer manager levels. The links between the nodes are established by pointers, which link the blocks between themselves. In general, each node has a large number of descendants, the exact number depending on the block size; each node may have tens or even hundreds of descendants. This allows the construction of trees with a limited number of *levels*, in which the majority of pages are occupied by leaf nodes. Another important requirement for the successful functioning of these data structures is that the trees be balanced; when a tree is perfectly *balanced*, the lengths of the paths from the root node to the leaf nodes are all equal. In this case, the access times to the information contained in the tree are almost constant.

Node contents and search techniques   The typical structure of each intermediate node of a tree (including the root) is shown in Figure 9.18. Each node contains F keys (in lexicographic order) and $F + 1$ pointers. Each key K_j, $1 \leq j \leq F$, is followed by a pointer P_j; K_1 is preceded by a pointer P_0. Each pointer addresses a sub-tree:

- the pointer P_0 addresses the sub-tree that contains the information about the keys with values less than K_1;

- the pointer P_F addresses the sub-tree that contains the information about the keys with values greater than or equal to K_F;

- each intermediate pointer P_j, $0 < j < F$, addresses a sub-tree that contains all the information about the keys K included in the interval $K_j \leq K < K_{j+1}$.

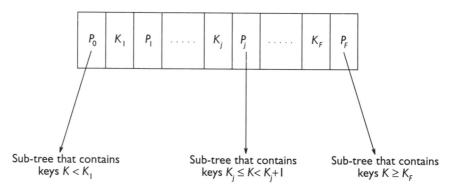

Figure 9.18 Information contained in a node (page) of a B+ tree.

The value $F + 1$ is called the *fan-out* of the tree. F depends on the size of the page and on the amount of space occupied by the key values and pointer values in the 'useful part' of a page.

The typical search primitive made available by the tree manager allows associative access to the tuple or tuples that contain a certain key value V. The search mechanism consists of following pointers starting from the root. At each intermediate node:

- if $V < K_1$ follow the pointer P_0;

- if $V \geq K_F$ follow the pointer P_F;

- otherwise, follow the pointer P_j such that $K_j \leq V < K_{j+1}$.

The search continues in this way to the leaf nodes of the tree, which can be organized in two ways.

- In the first case, the leaf node contains the entire tuple. The data structure obtained in this case is called *key-sequenced*. In it, the position of a tuple is determined by the value assumed by its key field. However, as we shall see, it is quite simple to insert or cancel tuples in this structure. The position is not produced by an algorithm (as in the case of the relative sequential structure or hashing), but can vary dynamically.

- In the second case, each leaf node contains pointers to the blocks of the database that contain tuples with specified key values. The data structure that is obtained in this case is called *indirect*. The tuples can be anywhere in the file, and thus this mechanism makes it possible to access tuples allocated by means of any other 'primary' mechanism (for example, entry-sequenced, hash-based, or key-sequenced).

In some cases, the index structure is not complete. That is, not all the key values are included in the index. In this case, the index is called *sparse*. A sparse index can be constructed only on a sequentially ordered structure, using indexes to locate a key value close to the value being sought, and then to carry out a sequential-type search.

A key-sequenced structure is generally preferred for the creation of the so-called *primary index* of each table, that is, the one that is usually defined on the primary key. The leaves generally contain a number of tuples less than F because the size of a tuple is generally larger than the sum of the dimensions of a key and a pointer. However, in this case, the leaf nodes do not contain pointers to data pages.

Indirect structures are preferred in order to create the secondary indexes, which can be either *unique* or *multiple*. In the first case, only one tuple is associated with each index key. In the second case, various tuples can correspond to each index key; each tuple is reached by means of a different pointer placed in suitably organized leaf nodes.

The insertion and cancellation of tuples also produce updates to the tree structure, which must reflect the situation generated by a variation in the values of the key-field. An insertion does not cause problems when it is possible to insert the new key value into a leaf of the tree, whose page has a free slot. In this case, the index remains unchanged, and the new key value is found by simply applying the search algorithm. When the page of the leaf has no available space, however, a split operation is necessary. The split divides the information already present in the leaf plus the new information into two equal parts, allocating two leaf nodes in place of one. This operation requires a modification of the arrangement of the pointers, shown in Figure 9.19.a. Note that a split causes an increment in the number of pointers on the next (higher) level in the tree. In this way, it can again exceed the capacity of a page, causing a further split. In practice, the split can continue to happen in this way as far back as the tree root. In extreme cases, it can cause the addition of one level to the tree. A deletion can always be carried out in situ. The slot previously occupied by the deleted tuple is simply shown as empty. There are two other problems, however.

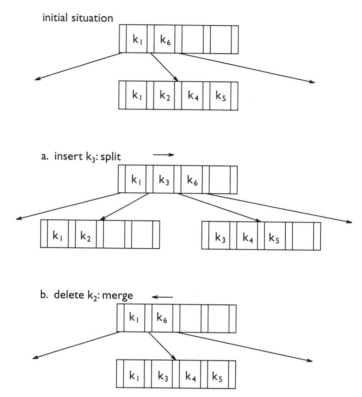

Figure 9.19 Split and merge operations on a B+ tree structure.

- When the deletion involves one of the key values present in the internal nodes of the tree, it is appropriate (even if not strictly necessary) to recover the successive key value from the database and put it in place of the deleted key value. In this way, all the key values present in the B+ tree also belong to the database.

- When the deletion leaves two adjacent pages at leaf level underused, this allows all the information present in them to be concentrated into a single page. Therefore a merge operation should be carried out. This is the opposite of the split operation, and collects all the information of the two pages into a single page. This operation requires a modification of the arrangement of the pointers, shown in Figure 9.19.b. Note that a merge causes a decrease in the number of pointers at a higher level of the tree, and thus can cause a further merge. In practice, as in the case of a split, the merge can continue upwards until it reaches the tree root, where it may cause a reduction in the depth of the tree.

The modification of the value of a key field is treated as the deletion of its initial value followed by the insertion of a new value. Hence, it is dealt with by a sequence of a deletion and an insert, as discussed above.

The careful use of the split and merge operations makes it possible to maintain the average occupancy of each node higher than 50%. Furthermore, even if the tree is initially balanced, differences in the pathway lengths can appear, making it necessary to re-balance the tree. A perfectly balanced tree gives the highest retrieval efficiency. The re-balancing of the tree is an operation that is typically decided by the database administrator, when the tree efficiency becomes too low.

Difference between B and B+ trees   It now only remains to clarify the distinction between B and B+ trees. In B+ trees, the leaf nodes are linked by a chain, which connects them in the order imposed by the key, as illustrated in Figure 9.20. This chain allows the efficient execution even of queries with a selection predicate that is satisfied by an interval of values. In this case, it is sufficient to access the first value of the interval (using a normal search), then scan sequentially the leaf nodes of the tree up to a key value greater than the second value of the interval. In the key-sequenced case, the response will consist of all the tuples found by this type of search, while in the indirect case it will be necessary to access all the tuples using the pointers thus selected. In particular, this data structure also makes possible an ordered scan, based on the key values, of the entire file, which is quite efficient. This versatility makes the B+ structure widely used in DBMSs.

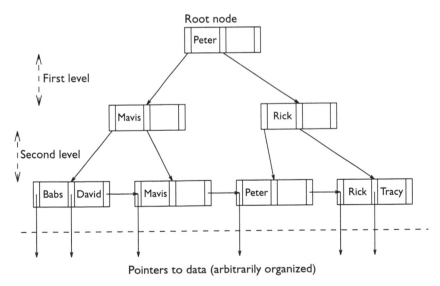

Figure 9.20 Example of B+ tree.

In B trees, there is no provision for the sequential connection of leaf nodes. In this case, intermediate nodes use two pointers for each key value K_i. One of the two pointers is used to point directly to the block that contains the tuple corresponding to K_i, interrupting the search. The other pointer is used to continue the search in the sub-tree that includes the key values greater than K_i and less than $K_i + 1$, as shown in Figure 9.21. The first pointer P_0 highlights the sub-tree corresponding to key values less than K_1, while the last pointer P_F highlights the sub-tree corresponding to key values greater than K_F. This technique saves space in the pages of the index and at the same time allows the termination of the search when a given key value is found on intermediate nodes, without having to go through each level.

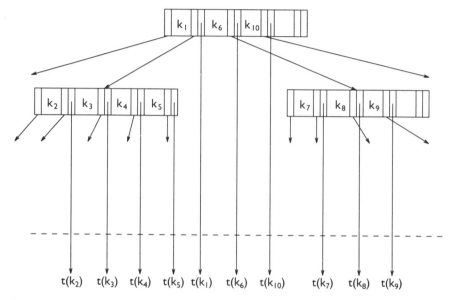

Figure 9.21 Example of a B tree.

The efficiency of traversal of a B or B+ tree by a given transaction, from the root to given leaves, is normally satisfactory, because the pages that store the first levels of the tree often remain in the buffer due to other transactions. Fortunately, the transactions are normally limited to reading these pages, and by means of locking, it is possible to gain access to them in a shared manner. Optimization of the occupied space occurs by means of the compression of key values. This can be done, for example, by maintaining only their prefixes in the high levels of the tree and only their suffixes in the low levels of the tree, where the final part of the search is carried out.

9.6 Query optimization

The optimizer is an important and classic module in the architecture of a database. It receives a query written in SQL. The query is initially analyzed to identify any possible lexical, syntactic or semantic errors, which are indicated to the user for correction. During this phase, the system accesses the data dictionary to allow semantic checks. The data dictionary also supplies statistical information concerning the size of the tables. Once accepted, the query is translated into an internal, algebraic form. At this point, the actual optimization begins. It consists of the following phases.

- First, an algebraic optimization is carried out. This consists of the execution of all the algebraic transformations that are always convenient, such as the 'push' of selections and projections, as described in Section 3.1.7. This logical optimization happens independently of the system's cost model.

- Following this, there is an optimization that depends on both the type of data access methods supported by the underlying level, and the cost model used. For this phase, although general optimization principles are well defined, each system presents its own particular characteristics.

- Finally, code is generated using the physical data access methods provided by the DBMS. Thus, an access program is obtained in 'object' or 'internal' format, which uses the data structures provided by the system.

The process of optimization of a query is illustrated in Figure 9.22. Note that, unlike all the other system modules described in this chapter, the optimizer is a module that acts at compilation time. Often, the query is compiled once and carried out many times ('compile and store' approach). In this case, the code is produced and stored in the database, together with an indication of the dependencies of the code on the particular versions of tables and indexes of the database, present in the data dictionary. In this way, if the database changes significantly for the query (for example, because an index has been added), the compilation of the query is invalidated and repeated. Sometimes, however, a query is compiled and carried out immediately ('compile and go' approach), without being stored.

Hereafter, we will concentrate on the central phase of this process, looking at cost-based optimization. Given that this part of the optimization depends specifically on the storage structures and on the cost model used by the DBMS, we can give only a qualitative and approximate description. We assume at this point that the algebraic optimization has produced an optimized description of the query, in which all the obvious algebraic transformations have been carried out. The result of this work represents each SQL query in a tree structure, in which the leaf nodes represent tables and the intermediate nodes represent operations of relational algebra.

9.6.1 Relation profiles

Each commercial DBMS possesses quantitative information about the characteristics of the tables, called *relation profiles*, which are stored in the data dictionary. The profiles contain some of the following information:

- the cardinality CARD(T) (number of tuples) of each table T;

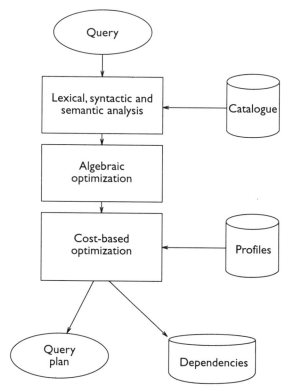

Figure 9.22 Compilation of a query.

- the dimension in bytes, $\text{SIZE}(T)$, of each tuple of T;

- the dimension in bytes, $\text{SIZE}(A_j, T)$, of each attribute A_j in T;

- the number of distinct values, $\text{VAL}(A_j, T)$, of each attribute A_j in T;

- the minimum and maximum values, $\text{MIN}(A_j, T)$ and $\text{MAX}(A_j, T)$, of each attribute A_j in T.

The profiles are calculated on the basis of the data actually stored in the tables, by activating appropriate system primitives (for example, the update statistics command). It is the task of the database administrator to activate these commands periodically. Normally, the possibility of keeping the profiles updated during the normal execution of transactions is excluded, because this option is too expensive. In general, it is sufficient that the profiles contain approximate values, given that the statistical models applied to them are in any case approximate.

Cost-based optimization requires the formulation of hypothesis on the size of the intermediate results produced by the evaluation of algebraic operations with a statistical approach. For example, let us look at the profiles of the main algebraic operations; selection, projection and join.

Formulas of profiles of selections   The profile of a table T' produced by a selection $T' = \sigma_{A_i=v}(T)$ is obtained using the following formulas, the justification for which is left as an exercise:

1. $\text{CARD}(T') = (1/\text{VAL}(A_i)) \times \text{CARD}(T)$;

2. $\text{SIZE}(T') = \text{SIZE}(T)$;

3. $\text{VAL}(A_i, T') = 1$;

4. $\text{VAL}(A_j, T') = col(\text{CARD}(T), \text{VAL}(A_j, T), \text{CARD}(T'))$, for $j \neq i$;[2]

5. $\text{MAX}(A_i, T') = \text{MIN}(A_i, T') = v$;

6. $\text{MAX}(A_j, T')$ and $\text{MIN}(A_j, T')$ maintain the same values as $\text{MAX}(A_j, T)$ and $\text{MIN}(A_j, T)$, for $j \neq i$.

Formulas of profiles of projections   The profile of a table T' produced by a projection $T' = \pi_L(T)$, where L is the set of attributes A_1, A_2, ..., A_n, is obtained using the following formulas:

1. $\text{CARD}(T') = \text{MIN}(\text{CARD}(T), \prod_{i=1}^{n}\text{VAL}(A_i, T))$;

2. $\text{SIZE}(T') = \sum_{i=1}^{n}\text{SIZE}(A_i(T))$;

3. $\text{VAL}(A_i, T')$, $\text{MAX}(A_i, T')$, $\text{MIN}(A_i, T')$ maintain the same values as $\text{VAL}(A_i, T)$, $\text{MAX}(A_i, T)$ and $\text{MIN}(A_i, T)$.

Formulas of profiles of joins   The profile of a table T^J produced by an equi-join $T^J = T' \bowtie_{A=B} T''$, assuming that A and B have identical domains and in particular $\text{VAL}(A, T') = \text{VAL}(B, T'')$.

1. $\text{CARD}(T^J) = (1/\text{VAL}(A_i, T')) \times \text{CARD}(T') \times \text{CARD}(T'')$;

2. $\text{SIZE}(T^J) = \text{SIZE}(T') + \text{SIZE}(T'')$;

3. $\text{VAL}(A_i, T^J)$, $\text{MAX}(A_i, T^J)$, $\text{MIN}(A_i T^J)$ maintain the same values as in their respective relations, before executing the join.

The above formulas show the limits of this type of statistical analysis. For example, all the formulas assume a uniform distribution of data in the tables and an absence of correlation among the various conditions present in a query. Note that often the formulas assign to the result of an operation parameters identical to those of their operands (for example, as regards the minimum and maximum values of a certain attribute), because it is not

---

2. The formula $col(n, m, k)$ relating to $\text{VAL}(A_j)$, calculates the number of distinct colours present in k objects extracted, starting from n objects of m distinct colours, homogeneously distributed. Each colour represents one of the different values present in attribute A_j. This formula allows the following approximation:
   (a) $col(n, m, k) = k$ if $k \leq m/2$
   (b) $col(n, m, k) = (k + m)/3$ if $m/2 \leq k \leq 2m$
   (c) $col(n, m, k) = m$ if $k \geq 2m$.

possible to make a better prediction. However, this statistical analysis enables us to establish, although approximately, the dimensions of the intermediate results (for example, an estimate of the number of occupied pages); this quantitative data is in any case sufficient to carry out the optimization.

9.6.2 Internal representation of queries

The representation that the optimizer gives to a query takes into account the physical structure used to implement the tables, as well as the indexes available on them. For this reason, the internal representation of a query uses trees whose leaves correspond to the physical data structures available for table storage and whose intermediate nodes represent data access operations that are supported on the physical structures. Typically, the operations supported by the relational DBMSs include sequential scans, orderings, indexed accesses and various types of join.

Scan operation A scan operation performs a sequential access to all the tuples of a table, at the same time executing various operations of an algebraic or extra-algebraic nature:

- projection of a set of attributes;

- selection on a simple predicate (of type: $A_i = v$);

- sort (ordering) of the tuples of a table based on the values assumed by the attributes present in an ordered set of attributes;

- insertions, deletions, and modifications of the tuples when they are accessed during the scan.

During a scan, a pointer to the current tuple is always maintained; the scan is carried out by means of the following primitives:

- The primitive *open* initializes the scan.

- The primitive *next* lets the scan proceed, advancing the pointer to the current tuple.

- The primitive *read* reads the current tuple.

- The primitives *modify* and *delete* act on the current tuple, modifying the contents or deleting them.

- The primitive *insert* inserts a new tuple into the current position.

- The primitive *close* concludes the scan.

Sort operation The problem of ordering data structures is a classic one of algorithm theory. Various methods make it possible to obtain optimal performances in ordering the data contained in the main memory, typically represented by means of a record array. The techniques for ordering data used by DBMSs exploit these algorithms, which we will not describe further. However, a DBMS must resolve a second problem, to do with the loading of data in the buffer. At times, it is not possible to load all the data in the buffer, because of the excessive quantity of data and therefore the impossibility of allocating a large enough number of buffers to the operation. In that case, portions of the data must be separately ordered and then merged, using the available buffer space.

Indexed access Indexes, created using tree structures, are created by the database administrator to favour the associative access of queries that include simple predicates (of the type $A_i = V$) or interval predicates (of the type $V_1 \leq A_i \leq V_2$). In this case, we say that a predicate of the query is *supported* by the index.

In general, if the query presents only one supported predicate, it is convenient to use the corresponding index. When a query presents a conjunction of supported predicates, the DBMS chooses the most selective one (that is, the predicate that is satisfied by fewest tuples) for the primary access via index. The other predicates are evaluated in main memory, once the pages that satisfy the first predicate are loaded in the buffer. When, on the other hand, the query presents a disjunction of predicates, it is sufficient that one of them be not supported to impose the use of a complete scan. If instead all the predicates of a disjunctive expression are supported, we can use either the corresponding indexes or a scan. If indexes are used, however, it is necessary to be careful to eliminate the duplicates of those tuples that are found using more than one index.

Note that the use of indexes requires multiple accesses for each retrieved tuple. When the query is not very selective, a simple scan can be more efficient than using an index.

Join methods The join is considered the most costly operation for a DBMS, as there is a risk of an explosion of the number of tuples of the result. Defining the method and order of the join operations has a central role in the global optimization of queries. For this reason it is not surprising that DBMS technology has produced various methods for join evaluation. Only recently, with the increase in interest in aggregate operations, similar algorithms and quantitative approaches have been dedicated to aggregate operations and grouping. Below, we will look at three techniques for join evaluation, called *nested-loop*, *merge-scan* and *hashed*.

• **Nested-loop** In a nested-loop join, one table is defined as *external* and one as *internal* (see Figure 9.23). A scan is opened on the external table. For each tuple found by the scan, the value of the join attribute is collected, and then the matching tuples of the internal tables are searched for. The matching is most efficient if there is an index on the join attribute of the internal table, which could be created ad-hoc. Otherwise, it is necessary to open a scan on the internal table for every value of the join of the external table. The name 'nested-loop' is given to this technique because it suggests an 'embedded' scan in the internal table. Note that this technique has different costs depending on the tables selected as internal and external.

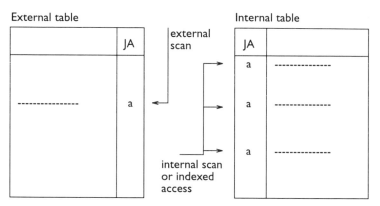

Figure 9.23 Join technique with nested-loop.

• **Merge-scan**   The technique requires that both the tables be ordered according to the join attributes (see Figure 9.24). Then, two coordinated scans are opened on them, which run through the tuples in parallel, as in a merge over ordered lists. The scans are carefully carried out, to guarantee that all the copies of tuples with identical values of the join attributes give rise to a resulting tuple.

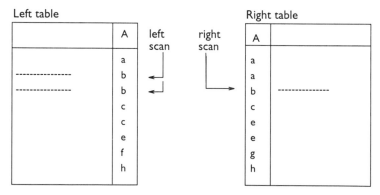

Figure 9.24 Join techniques with merge scan.

• **Hash join**   This method requires that a hashing function h on the join attributes be used to store both tables (see Figure 9.25). Supposing that the function h makes the values of the domain of this attribute correspond to B partitions on each table, the tuples with the same values in the join attribute will be placed in partitions with identical partition number. Thus, it will be possible to find all the tuples resulting from the join by carrying out B simple joins between the partitions with equal partition numbers, as shown in Figure 9.25. Various versions of this method allow the optimization of performance using a careful construction of the hash functions and careful management of the main memory buffers.

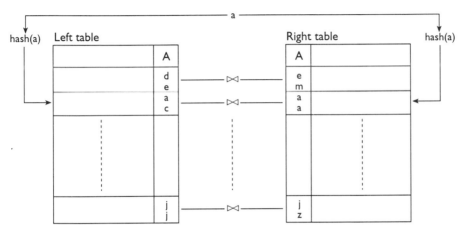

Figure 9.25 Join technique with hashing.

The three techniques are based on the combined use of scanning, hashing, and ordering. It is clear that each strategy has a cost that depends on the 'initial conditions' to which the join method is applied. For this reason, the execution cost of any of these techniques cannot be evaluated on its own, but must be evaluated as a function of the choices that precede or follow it.

9.6.3 Cost-based optimization

Finally, let us look at how global optimization works. The problem appears difficult on a computational level, because various degrees of optimization are possible.

- We need to select which data access operations to execute. In particular, as far as the first data access is concerned, it is sometimes necessary to choose between a scan and an indexed access.

- We need to select the order in which the operations are to be carried out (for example, the order of the various joins present in a query).

- When a system offers various options for the execution of an operation, we need to select which option to allocate to each operation (for example, choosing the join method).

- When the query or the method of execution requires ordering, we need to define the level of the plan on which to execute the ordering operation.

Further options appear in selecting a plan within a distributed context. Confronted with a problem of such complexity, the optimizers generally make use of approximate cost formulas. These construct a *decision tree*, in which each node corresponds to the choice of a particular option from among those listed above. Obviously, the size of such a tree increases exponentially according to the number of options present. Each leaf node of the tree corresponds to a specific *execution plan* of the query described by the choices that are found on the path from the root to the leaf node. Thus, the problem of optimization can be formulated as a search of the leaf node in the decision tree characterized by the lowest cost.

Figure 9.26 shows the execution of a conjunctive query (that is, using only selections, projections and joins) with three tables and two joins, in which the optimizer must decide only the order and the join method to use. There are three possible orderings of the joins and four possible ways to carry out the join operations, giving rise to 48 options. This simple example is indicative of the complexity of the problem in its most general terms.

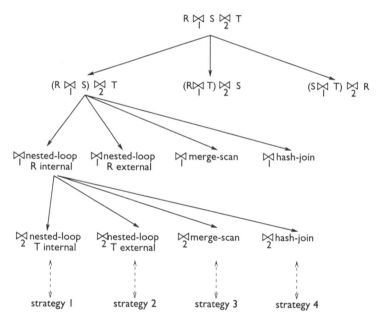

Figure 9.26 Execution options in a conjunctive query.

The problem is typically resolved using cost formulas that allocate a cost in terms of input/output operations and of CPU instructions necessary to evaluate each operation that appears as a node of the tree. In this way, it is possible to allocate a cost to a leaf node:

$$C_{total} = C_{I/O} \times n_{I/O} + C_{cpu} \times n_{cpu}$$

Where $C_{I/O}$, C_{cpu} are known parameters and $n_{I/O}$, n_{cpu} are global values that indicate the number of input/output operations and of CPU instructions necessary to evaluate the cost of the query. The cost is obtained from the sum of all the accumulated costs due to all the operations that make up a plan. The search for optimal solutions is typically done by discarding the solutions of those sub-trees whose partial cost is higher than the cost of the global strategy. This is done using a technique of operations research, called branch and bound, for the exact or approximate elimination of sub-trees.

Intermediate results are often stored in the buffers and discarded immediately after their production, exploiting the *pipelining* of the operations. Pipelining is the process of running through the entire tree of operations for each of the tuples extracted, rather than carrying out each operation completely on all the tuples. Sometimes however, it is necessary to rewrite the results of the intermediate operations in the secondary memory. In this case, the cost of rewriting the intermediate results becomes part of the cost of a strategy.

The optimizers are generally satisfied by obtaining 'good' solutions, that is, solutions whose cost is near that of the optimal solution. In particular, 'good solutions' are suggested with a 'compile and go' approach. There is no sense in finding the optimal solution by a method that takes a long time, when it is possible to find a 'good' solution in a shorter time and carry out the strategy in a total time (inclusive of optimization time) that is lower than that of the optimal solution.

9.7 Physical database design

After discussing the physical access structures and query optimization techniques, we can return to the problem of database design, which was discussed in Part II. The final phase in the process of database design is the physical design. This phase produces the physical schema of the database, made up of the definitions of the relations and of the physical access structures used, with the related parameters. Physical design takes as input the logical schema of the database and the predictions for the application load, and depends on the characteristics of the chosen DBMS.

The activity of physical database design can be very complex, because apart from the choices of the physical structures, we need to define many parameters: firstly, the setting of the initial dimensions of the physical files and the possibility of their dynamic expansion; then, the allocation of buffer space to the DBMS; finally, the choice of allocating within the same pages data from multiple data sets (for example, related tuples from two different tables). Some systems offer tens of parameters, the values of which can be important for the performance of the applications. Usually these parameters have default values, which are assumed by the system when they are not explicitly specified.

Most of the choices to be made during physical design depend on the specific DBMS used, so the treatment here is necessarily incomplete. We will give only a few suggestions, which can be considered sufficient for databases of average size, and with not particularly complex workloads. We will assume that the DBMS allows only for non-ordered files, with the possibility of defining indexes. In this context, physical design can be reduced to the activity of identifying indexes to be defined on each relation.

In order to get our bearings in the choice of indexes, we should remember that, as we said in Section 9.6, the most delicate operations in a relational database are those of selection and join. Each of the two operations can be carried out efficiently if we define indexes that allow direct access to the fields involved.

Consider, for example, a database on two relations: EMPLOYEE, with the attributes RegistrationNumber (the key), Surname, FirstName and Department; and DEPARTMENT, with the attributes Code (the key), Name and Director.

Assume that we wish to carry out a selection on the attribute RegistrationNumber in the EMPLOYEE relation (a search for an employee given the registration number). If the relation has an index for this attribute, we can proceed with a direct access, which is very efficient, otherwise we must carry out a scan, with a cost proportional to the size of the file. The same applies to a search based on the employee's surname. Note that if an index is defined on an attribute, only the searches based on this attribute can benefit from it. If the relation has an index on RegistrationNumber, and not on Surname, the selections on RegistrationNumber can be carried out efficiently while those on Surname will remain inefficient.

An equi-join between the two relations links each employee with the corresponding department; with an index on the key Code of the DEPARTMENT relation, the join can be carried out efficiently using the nested-loop method. The EMPLOYEE relation is scanned sequentially and for each employee, a direct access is carried out on the DEPARTMENT relation, based on the index. If the index is not defined, the access to the DEPARTMENT relation is inefficient, and the entire join becomes much more expensive.

It is important to remember that most of the joins that appear in our applications are equi-joins and for at least one of the two relations, the fields involved form a key, as in the example just shown. At the same time, note that the key of a relation is usually involved in selection or join operations (or both). For this reason, it is a good idea to define, on each relation, an index corresponding to the primary key. Most DBMSs construct this index automatically. Additional indexes can be defined on other fields on which selection operations are defined or on which an ordering is requested (because an index orders the records logically, lowering the cost of ordering).

With the indexes thus defined, we can test the behaviour of our application. If the performance is unsatisfactory, we can add other indexes, proceeding very carefully, however, as the addition of an index can cause an increase in the load facing the update operations. At times, moreover, the behaviour of the system is unpredictable, and the addition of indexes does not alter the strategy of optimization of main queries. It is good practice, after the addition of an index, to check that the queries use it. There is often a command show plan, which describes the access strategy chosen by the DBMS. For this reason, the choice of indexes in physical relational database design is often carried out empirically, with a trial-and-error approach. More generally, the tuning activity of physical design often makes it possible to improve the performance of the database

9.7.1 Definition of indexes in SQL

To conclude this brief view of physical design, we will look at the commands available in relational systems for the creation and cancellation of indexes. These commands are not part of standard SQL, for two reasons. Firstly, no agreement has been reached within the standardization committee, and secondly, indexes are regarded as an aspect closely linked to the implementation of the system, and are thus inappropriate to standardize. However, the syntax that we will demonstrate is used in the best-known commercial systems.

The syntax of the command for the creation of an index is

    create [unique] index *IndexName* on *TableName*(*AttributeList*)

With this command, we create an index called *IndexName* in the table *TableName*, operating on the attributes listed in *AttributeList*. The order in which the attributes appear in the list is important, as the keys of the index are ordered on the values of the attributes, starting from the first one. The use of the word unique specifies that no two tuples in the table may have the same value in the key attributes. To eliminate an index, the drop index command is used, characterized by a simple syntax:

    drop index *IndexName*

This command can be useful when the application context changes and a certain index is no longer used. It is also useful when the advantage obtained in terms of response times for certain queries does not compensate for the extra work required by the index, in order to keep it consistent with updates to the table.

To give an example of the use of commands seen above, we can specify an index on the EMPLOYEE table, which allows efficient access to data of the employee, given the surname and town:

    create index TownNameIndex on Employee(Surname, Town)

To eliminate the index, we use the command:

    drop index TownNameIndex

9.8 Bibliography

The subjects presented in this chapter are discussed both in general texts on databases and in more specific books. The main reference for most of the topics of the chapter is the comprehensive book by Gray and Reuter [46]. For the presentation of concurrency control we have followed an organization very close to that of Vossen [90]. Concurrency control and reliability are handled by Bernstein, Hadzilacos and Goodman [8]. The organization of reliability control and of the quantitative optimization of queries (in particular concerning profiles) is discussed in detail by Ceri and Pelagatti [18]. A good introduction to the design of physical structures and their dimensioning is given by Shasha [75]. The concept of transaction introduced in this chapter was recently extended by introducing more complex transactional models, such as nested or long-lived transactions; a good reference is the book edited by Elmagarmid [37].

9.9 Exercises

Exercise 9.1 Indicate whether the following schedules can produce anomalies; the symbols c_i and a_i indicate the result (commit or abort) of the transaction.

1. $r_1(x)$, $w_1(x)$, $r_2(x)$, $w_2(y)$, a_1, c_2

2. $r_1(x)$, $w_1(x)$, $r_2(y)$, $w_2(y)$, a_1, c_2

3. $r_1(x)$, $r_2(x)$, $r_2(y)$, $w_2(y)$, $r_1(z)$, a_1, c_2

4. $r_1(x)$, $r_2(x)$, $w_2(x)$, $w_1(x)$, c_1, c_2

5. $r_1(x)$, $r_2(x)$, $w_2(x)$, $r_1(y)$, c_1, c_2

6. $r_1(x)$, $w_1(x)$, $r_2(x)$, $w_2(x)$, c_1, c_2

Exercise 9.2 Indicate whether the following schedules are VSR:

1. $r_1(x)$, $r_2(y)$, $w_1(y)$, $r_2(x)$, $w_2(x)$

2. $r_1(x)$, $r_2(y)$, $w_1(x)$, $w_1(y)$, $r_2(x)$, $w_2(x)$

3. $r_1(x)$, $r_1(y)$, $r_2(y)$, $w_2(z)$, $w_1(z)$, $w_3(z)$, $w_3(x)$

4. $r_1(y)$, $r_1(y)$, $w_2(z)$, $w_1(z)$, $w_3(z)$, $w_3(x)$, $w_1(x)$

Exercise 9.3 Classify the following schedules (as: Non-VSR, VSR, CSR). In the case of a schedule that is both VSR and CSR, indicate all the serial schedules equivalent to them.

1. $r_1(x)$, $w_1(x)$, $r_2(z)$, $r_1(y)$, $w_1(y)$, $r_2(x)$, $w_2(x)$, $w_2(z)$

2. $r_1(x)$, $w_1(x)$, $w_3(x)$, $r_2(y)$, $r_3(y)$, $w_3(y)$, $w_1(y)$, $r_2(x)$

3. $r_1(x)$, $r_2(x)$, $w_2(x)$, $r_3(x)$, $r_4(z)$, $w_1(x)$, $w_3(y)$, $w_3(x)$, $w_1(y)$, $w_5(x)$, $w_1(z)$, $w_5(y)$, $r_5(z)$

4. $r_1(x)$, $r_3(y)$, $w_1(y)$, $w_4(x)$, $w_1(t)$, $w_5(x)$, $r_2(z)$, $r_3(z)$, $w_2(z)$, $w_5(z)$, $r_4(t)$, $r_5(t)$

5. $r_1(x)$, $r_2(x)$, $w_2(x)$, $r_3(x)$, $r_4(z)$, $w_1(x)$, $r_3(y)$, $r_3(x)$, $w_1(y)$, $w_5(x)$, $w_1(z)$, $r_5(y)$, $r_5(z)$

6. $r_1(x)$, $r_1(t)$, $r_3(z)$, $r_4(z)$, $w_2(z)$, $r_4(x)$, $r_3(x)$, $w_4(x)$, $w_4(y)$, $w_3(y)$, $w_1(y)$, $w_2(t)$

7. $r_1(x)$, $r_4(x)$, $w_4(x)$, $r_1(y)$, $r_4(z)$, $w_4(z)$, $w_3(y)$, $w_3(z)$, $w_1(t)$, $w_2(z)$, $w_2(t)$

Exercise 9.4 If the above schedules are presented to a scheduler that uses two-phase locking, which transactions would be placed in waiting? (Note that once a transaction is placed in waiting, its successive actions are not considered.)

Exercise 9.5 Define the data structure necessary for the management of locking, for a non-hierarchical model with read repeatability. Implement in a programming language of your choice the functions lock_r, lock_w and unlock. Assume that an abstract data type 'queue' is available with the appropriate functions for the insertion of an element into a queue and for extracting the first element of the queue.

Exercise 9.6 With reference to the exercise above, add a timeout mechanism. Assume that we have available functions for getting the current system time and for extracting a specific element from a queue.

Exercise 9.7 If the schedules described in Exercise 9.3 were presented to a timestamp-based scheduler, which transactions would be aborted?

Exercise 9.8 Consider both single-version and multi-version concurrency control based on timestamp for an object X. Initially $\text{WTM}(X) = 5$, $\text{RTM}(X) = 7$. Indicate the actions of the scheduler in response to the following input:

$r(x, 8)$, $r(x, 17)$, $w(x, 16)$, $w(x, 18)$, $w(x, 23)$, $w(x, 29)$, $r(x, 20)$, $r(x, 30)$, $r(x, 25)$

Exercise 9.9 Define the data structures necessary for buffer management. Implement in a programming language of your choice the functions *fix*, *use* and *unfix*. Assume we have available the file system functions described in Section 9.3.4.

Exercise 9.10 Describe the warm restart, indicating the progressive building of the sets *UNDO* and *REDO* and the recovery actions, given the following situation on the log:

DUMP, $\text{B}(T_1)$, $\text{B}(T_2)$, $\text{B}(T_3)$, $\text{I}(T_1, O_1, A_1)$, $\text{D}(T_2, O_2, R_2)$, $\text{B}(T_4)$, $\text{U}(T_4, O_3, B_3, A_3)$, $\text{U}(T_1, O_4, B_4, A_4)$, $\text{C}(T_2)$, $\text{CK}(T_1, T_3, T_4)$, $\text{B}(T_5)$, $\text{B}(T_6)$, $\text{U}(T_5, O_5, B_5, A_5)$, $\text{A}(T_3)$, $\text{CK}(T_1, T_4, T_5, T_6)$, $\text{B}(T_7)$, $\text{A}(T_4)$, $\text{U}(T_7, O_6, B_6, A_6)$, $\text{U}(T_6, O_3, B_7, A_7)$, $\text{B}(T_8)$, $\text{A}(T_7)$, failure

Exercise 9.11 Assume that in the above situation a device failure involves the objects O_1, O_2 and O_3. Describe the cold restart.

Exercise 9.12 Consider a hash structure for storing tuples whose key field contains the following names:

Green, Lovano, Osby, Peterson, Pullen, Scofield, Allen, Haden, Harris, McCann, Mann, Brown, Newmann, Ponty, Cobbham, Coleman, Mingus, Lloyd, Tyner, Hutcherson, Green, Fortune, Coltrane, Shepp.

1. Suggest a hashing function with $B = 8$ and $F = 4$.

2. Supposing $B = 40$ and $F = 1$, what is the probability of conflict? And with $B = 20$ and $F = 2$?

3. With $F = 5$ and $B = 7$, what is the approximate average length of the overflow chain?

Exercise 9.13 Consider a B+ tree structure for storing tuples whose key field contains the data listed in the above exercise.

1. Describe a balanced B+ tree structure with $F = 2$, which contains the listed data.

2. Introduce a data item that causes the split of a node at leaf level, and show what happens at leaf level and at the level above.

3. Introduce a data item that causes a merge of a node at leaf level, and show what happens at leaf level and at the level above.

4. Show a sequence of insertions that causes the split of the root and the lengthening of the tree.

5. Describe a B tree structure, with $F = 3$, that contains the given data.

Exercise 9.14 Consider the database made up of the following relations:

PRODUCTION(<u>ProdNumber</u>, PartType, Model, Quan, Machine)
ORDERDETAIL (<u>OrderNumber</u>, <u>ProdNumber</u>)
ORDER(<u>OrderNumber</u>, Client, Amount)
COMMISSION(<u>OrderNumber</u>, Seller, Amount)

Assume the following profiles

CARD(PRODUCTION) = 200,000	SIZE(PRODUCTION) = 41
CARD(ORDERDETAIL) = 50,000	SIZE(ORDERDETAIL) = 15
CARD(ORDER) = 10,000	SIZE(ORDER) = 45
CARD(COMMISSION) = 5,000	SIZE(COMMISSION) = 35

$$\text{SIZE(ProdNumber)} = 10 \qquad \text{VAL(ProdNumber)} = 200{,}000$$
$$\text{SIZE(PartType)} = 1 \qquad \text{VAL(PartType)} = 4$$
$$\text{SIZE(Model)} = 10 \qquad \text{VAL(Model)} = 400$$
$$\text{SIZE(Quan)} = 10 \qquad \text{VAL(Quan)} = 100$$
$$\text{SIZE(Machine)} = 10 \qquad \text{VAL(Machine)} = 50$$
$$\text{SIZE(OrderNumber)} = 5 \qquad \text{VAL(OrderNumber)} = 10{,}000$$
$$\text{SIZE(Client)} = 30 \qquad \text{VAL(Client)} = 400$$
$$\text{SIZE(Amount)} = 10 \qquad \text{VAL(Amount)} = 5{,}000$$
$$\text{SIZE(Seller)} = 20 \qquad \text{VAL(Seller)} = 25$$

Describe the algebraic optimization and the computation of the profiles of the intermediate results for the following queries, which need to be initially expressed in SQL and then translated into relational algebra:

1. Find the available quantity of the product 77Y6878.

2. Find the machines used for the production of the parts sold to the client Brown.

3. Find the clients who have bought from the seller White a box model 3478.

For the last two queries, which require the joining of three tables, indicate the ordering between joins that seem most convenient based on the size of the tables. Then describe the decision tree for the second query allowing for a choice of only two join methods.

Exercise 9.15 List the conditions (dimensions of the tables, presence of indexes or of sequential organizations or of hashing) that make the join operation more or less convenient using the nested-loop, merge-scan and hash methods. For some of these conditions, suggest cost formulas that take into account the number of input/output operation as a function of the average costs of the access operations involved (scans, ordering, index-based accesses).

10
Distributed architectures

Distribution is an ingredient of almost any modern application of database systems. This chapter defines the various types of distributed architectures, and then deals with each of them separately.

The simplest and most widespread distributed architecture uses the *client-server* paradigm. This architecture is based on separating the role of server from the role of client. The server contains the core functions of the DBMS engine and is executed on a computer with suitable main and secondary memory. The client runs on a different computer, which is dedicated to the user interface and hosts the user's productivity software (for example, e-mail and word processing). The network connects the server and client computers.

Distributed databases present an entirely different set of problems. A distributed database is characterized by the presence of at least two database servers, which can carry out local transactions independently from each other. However, in many cases the servers must interact, thus supporting distributed transactions. This interaction takes place on increasingly complex levels. We will see that the greatest problem is presented by the difficulty of guaranteeing the ACID properties of distributed transactions (as defined in Section 9.1.1), especially when the transactions carry out write operations on two or more servers. To manage these situations, a *two-phase commit* protocol is introduced; this is one of the most interesting protocols in the data distribution context, as it takes into account the interaction of aspects of distribution, atomicity and durability. We will also look at another typical protocol that describes *deadlock detection* in a distributed context.

Another type of database architecture uses parallelism to improve performance. The *parallel databases* are characterized by the use of multiprocessor machines and multiple data management devices, with various interconnection functions. There is a clear distinction between distributed databases and parallel databases. In a distributed database, each server has its own identity and stores data that is 'functionally' associated with that server. In a parallel database the data is allocated to each device and controlled by each processor in a way that responds only to efficiency criteria. For this reason, parallelism introduces a series of problems that are quite different from those of distribution.

The most recent architectures for databases have gradually become specialized with regard to the dominant applications, presenting two distinct components. One component is dedicated to 'on line' data management, to guarantee the modification of data in real time, and the other is responsible for 'decision support', being used to carry out complex data analyses. Thus, two types of hardware/software architecture have emerged:

- Some systems are aimed at optimized management and reliable transactions, performing *On-Line Transaction Processing*, OLTP. These systems are made to manage hundreds or even thousands of transactions per second, arriving from clients all over the network.

- Other systems are aimed at data analysis, performing *On-Line Analytical Processing*, OLAP. To do this, they must export the data from the OLTP systems, where data is generated, and import them into *data warehouses*. (See Chapter 13.)

Data management servers can typically support both OLTP, managing high transaction loads, and OLAP, for the efficient execution of complex queries. The reason for both functions being present is because the separation of OLTP and OLAP is very recent and many application environments do not yet separate the two functions. However, the separation of OLTP and OLAP allows for the specialization, better organization, and optimal sizing of the servers. In this chapter, we will dwell on the technology common to both OLTP and OLAP, while Chapter 13 will be dedicated to OLAP describing the programming paradigms and use of the data warehouse.

A service technology has recently emerged for the creation of distributed applications, particularly in the presence of separated environments for OLTP and OLAP: that of *data replication*. This term denotes the capacity to construct copies of data, exporting them from one node to another in a distributed system, to maximize the availability of data and to increase reliability.

In an overall technological view characterized by the necessity for interactions between different products, the problems of portability and of interoperability assume even more importance.

- *Portability* denotes the possibility of transporting programs from one environment to another (and it is thus a typical property of *compilation time*).

- *Interoperability* denotes the ability of interacting between heterogeneous systems (and it is thus a typical property of *execution time*).

In order to obtain portability and interoperability, *standards* are very important. In particular, portability depends on language standards (primarily SQL), while interoperability depends on the standards concerning data access protocols. In this chapter, we will describe the standard *Open Database Connectivity* (*ODBC*), for making heterogeneous databases communicate among themselves. We will also examine *X-OPEN Distributed Transaction Processing* (*DTP*), a standardized version of the two-phase commit protocol that ensures the possibility of making different DBMS systems interact in the same ACID transaction.

10.1 Client-server architecture

The client-server paradigm is a model of interaction between software processes, where interacting processes are sub-divided among *clients* (which require services) and *servers* (which offer services). Client-server interaction thus requires a precise definition of a *service interface*, which lists the services offered by the server. The client process is typically dedicated to the final user; it carries out an active role, in that it autonomously generates requests for services. The server process on the other hand is reactive. It carries out a computation only as a result of a request on the part of any client. Normally, a client process can request in sequence some (few) services from various server processes, while each server process responds to (many) requests from many client processes. In this section, we will hypothesize that each client sends all the requests to a single server, and that these requests are identified as belonging to the same transaction, initiated at the first request made by the client. We will deal with the interaction of a client with various servers in the next section.

It is not necessary for server and client processes to be allocated different machines. The distinction between client and server processes is an excellent paradigm for the construction of software independently of the allocation of processes. However, in data management, allocation of client and server processes to distinct computers is now widespread.

There are various reasons for the use of the client-server architecture for databases.

- The functions of client and server are well identified in the database context. They give rise to a convenient separation of design and management activities. The application programmer has the responsibility for writing and managing the software for making the client respond to specific demands. The database administrator (DBA) has responsibility for data design and management on the server, which is shared among various clients. The DBA must organize the database to guarantee optimal services to all the client processes.

- Apart from the functional breakdown of processes and tasks, the use of different computers for client and server in the database is particularly convenient. The computer dedicated to the client must be suitable for interaction with the user. It is often a personal computer, provided with productivity tools (electronic mail, word processing, spreadsheets, Internet access, and workflow management). Among these tools, often masked by a 'user-friendly interface', some applications request the use of a database. The power of the computer dedicated to the server depends on the services that it must offer. It must have a large main memory (to support buffer management) and a high capacity disk (for storing the entire database).

- The SQL language, used in all relational databases, offers an ideal programming paradigm for the identification of the 'service interface'. The SQL queries are formulated by the client and sent to the server. The results of the query are calculated by the server and returned to the client. The query can be expressed at the client side as an invocation of a predefined remote service, or can be sent at execution time as a string of characters. The server processes the queries, extracting the query result from the database content, and packaging the result of the query. Furthermore, it carries out any database update as expressed in the query. Thus, on the network, only the information useful to the client will travel, and this represents a tiny fraction of the information extracted from the secondary memory. In addition, the standardization, portability and interoperability of the SQL language allows the construction of client applications that involve different server systems.

The client-server architecture can adapt itself both to statically-compiled queries and to queries with dynamic SQL. With a static process ('compile and

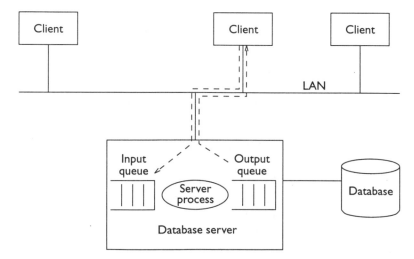

Figure 10.1   Client-server architecture.

store'), the queries are presented to the server once and are then recalled many times. Using a dynamic process, ('compile and go'), the queries are transmitted in the form of strings of characters that are compiled and processed by the server. In both cases, the optimizer and the access methods lie with the server, which thus includes all the mechanisms illustrated in the preceding chapter.

With the static process, a server normally stores a parametric query; at execution time, the client assigns values to some entry parameters and then calls the execution of the query, typically using a procedure. Often, the server that manages such requests is *multi-threaded*. From the point of view of the operating system, it behaves like a single process that works dynamically on behalf of different transactions. Each unit of execution of the server process for a given transaction is called a *thread*. This organization, shown in Figure 10.1, allows the management of servers as permanently active processes that control an *input queue* for client requests and an *output queue* for the query results. The use of a multi-threaded model is more convenient than the allocation of a dedicated process to each request, because it saves process allocation and de-allocation times. The servers can manage the queues directly or by means of other processes, called *dispatchers*, whose task is to distribute the requests to the servers and return the responses to the clients. In some cases, the dispatchers can dynamically define the number of active server processes as a function of the number of requests received. In this case, we say that a *server class* is available. The server class contains an arbitrary number of server processes indistinguishable one from another. This phenomenon is similar to the management of a supermarket, where the number of open checkouts varies dynamically depending on the number of customers present.

The architecture illustrated up to now is called a *two-tier* architecture because it encompasses a client, with functions both of user interface and of application management, and a server dedicated to data management. Recently an alternative architecture has become popular, called *three-tier* architecture, in which a second server is present, known as the *application server*, responsible for the management of the application logic common to many clients. In this architecture, the client is named *thin-client*; it is responsible only for the interface with the final user. The client sends requests to the application server, which communicates with the data management server using the techniques illustrated above. This architecture is becoming widespread with the growth of the Internet, because it allows the creation of clients using a simple browser (see Chapter 14).

10.2 Distributed databases

We have seen that in a client-server architecture, a transaction involves at most one server. When more than one server is involved, we talk of *distributed databases*. In this section, we will deal with distributed databases from the functional point of view, looking at how a user can specify distributed queries. In the next section, we will concentrate on the technological aspects and we will look at how we need to extend the server technology so as to allow their use in a distributed database.

10.2.1 Applications of distributed databases

The reasons for the development of distributed solutions in data management are pragmatic. They respond to the demand for the data management architecture to conform to the needs of the enterprises in which data is produced and used, because these enterprises are structurally distributed. Distributed data management is in contrast to the centralized data processing organization typical of large computing centres, which was dominant until the mid-eighties. It allows the distribution of data processing and control to the environment where it is generated and largely used. On the technological level, we have recently witnessed the gradual replacement of centralized systems by distributed systems, justified by many reasons; among them are greater flexibility, modularity and resistance to failures. Distributed systems can be configured by the progressive addition and modification of components, with a much greater flexibility and modularity than those systems based on the use of centralized resources (mainframes). Although they are more vulnerable to failures due to their structural complexity, they are actually capable of so-called 'graceful degradation', that is, of responding to failures with a reduction in performance but without a total failure.

A first classification of distributed databases considers the type of DBMS and network used. When all the servers use the same DBMS, the database is known as *homogenous*; otherwise, it is called *heterogeneous*. A distributed database can use a *local area network* (LAN) or a *wide area network* (WAN). This classification introduces a corresponding classification of application solutions.

Obviously homogenous systems on LANs correspond to solutions that are technologically simpler and more widespread, present in a large number of application contexts. They include data management applications developed within a small company, or inside a single building or office. More complex homogenous applications have become indispensable in contemporary society. For example, distributed homogenous systems serve many financial applications (including the management of bank accounts); these are created both on LANs and on WANs depending on the distribution of the bank's branches in the territory.

The heterogeneous solution is also widely used. For example, many integrated inter-divisional information systems present in companies are heterogeneous (perhaps more from necessity than from choice). Each part of the company often develops its own software independently for its own applications and in particular independently chooses the software for data management. Then, at management level, it is discovered that the company sectors must interact, but at this point the resulting information system is heterogeneous. This company evolution justifies the use of *open architectures*, that is, of systems that can interact regardless of their heterogeneity. They are in contrast with the *proprietary architectures*, in which hardware and software are provided by a sole supplier, and are capable of guaranteeing compatibility only within a family of products.

Airline booking systems are often distributed over many nodes linked by WANs. Communication among different systems could be necessary, for instance, in order to put together a journey of many stages involving more than one airline; this requires the use of complex protocols based upon the interaction of heterogeneous systems on WANs. Another example of widespread use, which falls into the context of WANs for heterogeneous systems, is that of inter-banking systems. These allow the execution of financial operations that involve many banks, in which each bank is in turn the owner of a distributed database, on a local or wide area network. The table in Figure 10.2 shows the typical application of distributed databases described up to now, classifying them according to the type of DBMS and network.

Type of DBMS	Network type	
	LAN	WAN
Homogeneous	Data management and financial applications	Travel management and financial applications
Heterogeneous	Inter-divisional information systems	Integrated banking and inter-banking systems

Figure 10.2   Examples of typical applications of distributed databases showing the type of DBMS and network.

10.2.2 Local independence and co-operation

From an abstract point of view, a distributed database can be considered as a unique collection of data. Database servers guarantee the application programs access to these resources, offering the user exactly the same type of interaction as that obtained by a centralized system. It is, however, important to note that in a distributed database each server has its own capacity to manage applications independently. Guaranteeing the independence of each server is one of the main objectives of distributed databases.

The reason for having a distributed database is not that of maximizing the interaction and the necessity of transmitting data via networks. On the contrary, the planning of data distribution and allocation should be done in such a way that the largest number possible of applications should operate independently on a single server, to avoid the large execution costs that are typical of distributed applications.

10.2.3 Data fragmentation and allocation

Data fragmentation is a technique for data organization that allows efficient data distribution and processing. This technique is applicable only if data distribution follows a well understood pattern, which is taken into account during the design of the distributed database.

Let us consider a relation R. Its fragmentation consists of determining a certain number of fragments R_i, obtained by applying algebraic operations to R. Depending on the operation used, the fragmentation can be of two types, horizontal or vertical.

- In horizontal fragmentation, the fragments R_i are groups of tuples having the same schema as the relation R. Each horizontal fragment can be interpreted as the result of a selection applied to the relation R.

- In vertical fragmentation, the fragments R_i each have a schema obtained as a subset of the schema of R. Each vertical fragment can be interpreted as the result of a projection applied to the relation R.

The fragmentation is correct if the following properties are valid:

- *Completeness:* each data item of R must be present in one of its fragments R_i.

- *Restorability:* the content of R must be restorable from its fragments.

Horizontal fragments are normally disjoint, that is, they have no tuples in common. Conversely, vertical fragments include the primary key defined for R, to guarantee the restorability; in this way they constitute a lossless decomposition of R (as discussed in Chapter 8). Note that fragments are formally defined using operations on the relations. In other words, fragmentation expresses *logical* properties of data.

Let us look at an example of horizontal and vertical fragmentation. Consider the relation:

EMPLOYEE (Empnum, Name, Deptnum, Salary, Taxes)

The horizontal fragmentation is obtained by subdividing the tuples of EMPLOYEE into many fragments by selection operations:

$$\text{EMPLOYEE1} = \sigma_{Empnum \leq 3} \text{ EMPLOYEE}$$
$$\text{EMPLOYEE2} = \sigma_{Empnum > 3} \text{ EMPLOYEE}$$

- The reconstruction of the relation based on its fragments requires a union operation:

$$\text{EMPLOYEE} = \text{EMPLOYEE1} \cup \text{EMPLOYEE2}$$

The vertical fragmentation is obtained by subdividing the tuples of EMPLOYEE into many fragments by projection operations that include in each fragment the primary key of the relation:

$$\text{EMPLOYEE1} = \pi_{\text{EmpNum,Name}}(\text{EMPLOYEE})$$
$$\text{EMPLOYEE2} = \pi_{\text{EmpNum,DeptName,Salary,Tax}}(\text{EMPLOYEE})$$

The reconstruction of the relation based on its fragments requires an equi-join operation with equal key-values (natural join).

$$\text{EMPLOYEE} = \text{EMPLOYEE1} \bowtie \text{EMPLOYEE2}$$

The two examples of horizontal and vertical fragmentation described above are illustrated in Figure 10.3, Figure 10.4 and Figure 10.5.

EmpNum	Name	DeptNum	Salary	Tax
1	Robert	Production	3.7	1.2
2	Greg	Administration	3.5	1.1
3	Anne	Production	5.3	2.1
4	Charles	Marketing	3.5	1.1
5	Alfred	Administration	3.7	1.2
6	Paolo	Planning	8.3	3.5
7	George	Marketing	4.2	1.4

Figure 10.3 Table used in the examples of fragmentation.

EmpNum	Name	DeptNum	Salary	Tax
1	Robert	Production	3.7	1.2
2	Greg	Administration	3.5	1.1
3	Anne	Production	5.3	2.1

First horizontal fragment

EmpNum	Name	DeptNum	Salary	Tax
4	Charles	Marketing	3.5	1.1
5	Alfred	Administration	3.7	1.2
6	Paolo	Planning	8.3	3.5
7	George	Marketing	4.2	1.4

Second horizontal fragment

Figure 10.4 Example of horizontal fragmentation.

Each fragment R_i corresponds to a different physical file and is allocated to a different server. Thus, the relation is present in a virtual mode (like a view), while the fragments are actually stored. The *allocation schema* describes the mapping of full relations or of fragments of relations to the servers that store them, allowing the transfer from a logical description to a physical description of data. This mapping can be:

- *non-redundant*, when each fragment or relation is allocated to a single server;

EmpNum	Name
1	Robert
2	Greg
3	Anne
4	Charles
5	Alfred
6	Paolo
7	George

First vertical fragment

EmpNum	DipNum	Salary	Tax
1	Production	3.7	1.2
2	Administration	3.5	1.1
3	Production	5.3	2.1
4	Marketing	3.5	1.1
5	Administration	3.7	1.2
6	Planning	8.3	3.5
7	Marketing	4.2	1.4

Second vertical fragment

Figure 10.5 Example of vertical fragmentation.

- *redundant*, when a fragment or relation is allocated to more than one server.

10.2.4 Transparency levels

The distinction between fragmentation and allocation allows us to identify various levels of transparency in the applications. These vary from an abstract view of data, independent of the distribution, to a concrete view, dependent on its physical allocation. There are three significant levels of transparency: transparency of fragmentation, of allocation and of language. In addition, a system could have a total absence of transparency, when there is no common language for access to data present in the various servers. In this case, the programmer must address each server with a specific SQL 'dialect'.

Let us look at an example of these four levels of transparency. Consider the table that describes the suppliers for a firm:

SUPPLIER(<u>SNum</u>, Name, City)

Fragmented horizontally into two fragments for the cities of London and Manchester, the only cities in which the company operates:

$$\text{SUPPLIER1} = \sigma_{City='London'}(\text{SUPPLIER})$$
$$\text{SUPPLIER2} = \sigma_{City='Manchester'}(\text{SUPPLIER})$$

Manchester uses a replicated database, as the second fragment is allocated on two nodes *Manchester1* and *Manchester2*. Thus, the allocation of fragments is:

SUPPLIER1@company.London.uk
SUPPLIER2@company.Manchester1.uk
SUPPLIER2@company.Manchester2.uk

Let us then consider the simple application that requires a number of suppliers and returns their names. We can write this application in SQL at the various levels of transparency.

- *Fragmentation transparency:* on this level, the programmer should not worry about whether or not the database is distributed or fragmented. The query is identical to that which would be written for a non-fragmented relation.

```
procedure Query1(:snum, :name);
    select Name into :name
    from Supplier
    where SNum = :snum;
end procedure
```

- *Allocation transparency:* on this level, the programmer knows the structure of the fragments, but does not have to indicate their allocation. In particular, if the system allows replicated fragments (as in our example), the programmer does not have to indicate which copy is chosen for access (this additional property is called *replication transparency*). The following program examines the fragments in sequence. We assume that the parameter :empty assumes the value true if the first SQL query does not find a value.

```
procedure Query2(:snum, :name);
    select Name into :name
    from Supplier1
    where SNum = :snum;
if :empty then
    select Name into :name
    from Supplier2
    where SNum = :snum;
end procedure;
```

- *Language transparency:* at this level the programmer must indicate in the query both the structure of the fragments and their allocation. For example, a choice must be made to access the fragment stored in the node *Manchester1*. This level is the lowest at which fragmentation can be addressed by using a single query language in which to express the query.

```
procedure Query3(:snum, :name);
    select Name into :name
    from Supplier1@company.London.uk
    where SNum = :snum;
if :empty then
    select Name into :name
    from Supplier2@company.Manchester1.uk
    where SNum = :snum;
end procedure;
```

- *Absence of transparency:* In this case, each DBMS accepts its own SQL 'dialect', because the system is heterogeneous and the DBMSs do not support a standard of common interoperability. As in the earlier case, the programmer must indicate explicitly the fragments and their allocation in the system.

Note that the last two levels characterize the queries that are actually carried out by the servers. Queries expressed at a higher level of transparency are transformed during the optimization phase, by introducing into their specifications the choice of particular fragments and their allocation to specific nodes. Such transformation is done by the distributed query optimizer, a subsystem that is aware of data fragmentation and allocation.

This application can be made more efficient by using parallelism: instead of submitting the two requests in sequence, they can be processed in parallel, thus saving on the global response time. Note, however, that in this specific example, parallel processing requires the computation of two queries (one of which is empty), while the sequential processing is interrupted if the first query is successful, thereby saving some computation. We will deal further with parallelism in Section 10.7.

A different strategy is shown in the following program, which uses the information about the city of the supplier in order to direct the query towards the right server. The query operates at the level of *allocation transparency*. Note that this solution introduces an element of rigidity: if in future the fragmentation should change, the code would be rewritten.

```
procedure Query4(:snum, :name, :city);
case :city of
    "London":
    select Name into :name
    from Supplier1
    where SNum = :snum;
    "Manchester":
    select Name into :name
    from Supplier2
    where SNum = :snum;
end procedure;
```

10.2.5 Classification of transactions

A classification schema of transactions based on the composition of the SQL statements that make up a transaction was suggested by IBM and later adopted by various other vendors. In this schema, each client refers to a sole DBMS and the distribution of the transaction becomes the task of the DBMS. The client can obviously address local transactions to the DBMS, that is, transactions made up of queries where the tables are all allocated to that DBMS. It can then address non-local transactions, which involve data stored on other DBMSs. These transactions can be more or less complex.

- *Remote requests* are read-only transactions made up of an arbitrary number of select queries, addressed to a single remote DBMS.

- *Remote transactions* are transactions made up of any number of SQL commands (select, insert, delete, update) directed to a single remote DBMS.

- *Distributed transactions* are transactions made up of any number of SQL commands (select, insert, delete, update) directed to an arbitrary number of remote DBMSs, such that each SQL command refers to data that is stored on a single DBMS.

- *Distributed requests* are arbitrary transactions, made up of an arbitrary number of SQL commands, in which each SQL command can refer to data distributed on any DBMS. Note that all the queries at fragmentation transparency level are classifiable as distributed requests.

This classification is important because it identifies progressive levels of complexity in the interaction between DBMSs. In the first case, the remote DBMS can only be queried. In the second case we can execute update operations, but each transaction writes on a sole DBMS. In the third case we can include update operations on more than one node, but each SQL query is addresses to a specific DBMS. In the last case, the SQL query must be distributed to more than one node. As we shall see, the third case requires the use of the two-phase commit protocol and the fourth case requires, in addition, the availability of an optimizer for distributed queries.

A typical example of a transaction is the transfer between two accounts, described by the relation:

ACCOUNT(AccNum, Name, Total)

We can assume that the relation is fragmented so that all the accounts with account numbers lower than 10000 are allocated on the first fragment and all the accounts above this number are allocated to the second fragment. A transfer of 100,000 from the account number 3154 to account number 14878 thus consists of two operations, one for each fragment. This is an example of a distributed transaction written at the allocation transparency level.

```
begin transaction
    update Account1
    set Total = Total - 100000
    where AccNum = 3154;

    update Account2
    set Total = Total + 100000
    where AccNum = 14878;
    commit work;
end transaction
```

The holders of accounts numbered 3154 and 14878 (and obviously the bank) wish the transaction to be carried out accurately on both nodes. Alternatively, it is acceptable that neither of the two modifications is executed. It is an unacceptable violation of atomicity that one of the modifications is executed while the other is not.

10.3 Technology of distributed databases

In the above sections, we have seen some characteristics of applications of distributed databases. We will now look at how to create these applications.

First, we will address the problem of understanding how the database technology must be extended to take into account data distribution. We will see that some subsystems are not affected by the introduction of distribution, while other subsystems are deeply affected. Data distribution does not influence two of the four ACID properties of transactions, consistency and durability.

- *Consistency* of transactions does not depend on the distribution of data, because the integrity constraints describe only the local properties of a DBMS. This is more than anything else a limit of the actual DBMS technology, in that integrity constraints could easily refer to distributed data, but in fact there are no mechanisms that allow their specification or verification.

- In a similar way, *durability* is not a problem that depends on the data distribution, because each system guarantees durability in the case of local device failures by using local recovery mechanisms (logs, checkpoints, and dumps).

On the other hand, other subsystems require major enhancements in order to cope with distributed database technology. We will first look at query optimization, then at concurrency control and finally at reliability control.

10.3.1 Distributed query optimization

Distributed query optimization is required only when a DBMS receives a distributed request, in which data allocated to more than one DBMS is required for the same query. The DBMS that is queried is responsible for the so-called 'global optimization'. It decides on the breakdown of the query into many sub-queries, each addressed to a specific DBMS. A strategy of distributed execution consists of the co-ordinated execution of various programs on various DBMSs and in the exchange of data among them, which is necessary when the results of a sub-query are used as subjects for another sub-query.

The global optimizer decides the most convenient plan by examining a decision tree, as discussed in Section 9.6. Among the cost factors of a distributed query, there is also the quantity of data transmitted on the network.

As with centralized systems, the optimizer selects the order of operations and their method of execution. In addition, it defines the execution strategy of the operations whose data are allocated to distinct nodes, defining a data transmission strategy and the allocation of results. When the data is redundant, it is also necessary to select the particular copy used. As with centralized optimizers, we can allocate a cost to a leaf node representing the global cost of a query processing strategy. This time we require the contribution of three components (extending the formula presented in Section 9.6.3):

$$C_{total} = C_{I/O} \times n_{I/O} + C_{cpu} \times n_{cpu} + C_{tr} \times n_{tr}$$

The two new elements n_{tr} and C_{tr} measure, respectively, the quantity of data transmitted on the network and the unit cost of transmission, and these are added to the processing and input/output costs described in Section 9.6. The importance of this third factor has changed over time. Originally, the transmission cost was the most significant factor, and optimization of distributed queries was based entirely on the reduction of transmission costs. This simplification of the problem is no longer justified, given that the transmission rate of data is, especially on LANs, comparable to that of input/output devices.

The submission of a query by a client starts all the processes necessary for the execution of the query in the various servers. The execution of access methods happens locally within each DBMS.

10.3.2 Concurrency control

Concurrency control in a distributed environment causes theoretical difficulties. However, in practice, we will see that two-phase locking and timestamping methods are still valid in a distributed context.

We begin by stating the problem. In a distributed system, a transaction t_i can carry out various sub-transactions t_{ij}, where the second subscript denotes the node of the system on which the sub-transaction works. For example, a distributed transaction t_i, which works on two objects x and y allocated on the nodes 1 and 2, appears, from the point of view of its concurrent accesses, as follows:

$$t_1: \quad r_{11}(x) \; w_{11}(x) \; r_{12}(y) \; w_{12}(y)$$

Note that the local serializability within the schedulers is not sufficient guarantee of serializability. Let us suppose that there is a second transaction t_2, which also operates on data x and y, but accesses them in reverse order:

$$t_2: \quad r_{22}(y) \; w_{22}(y) \; r_{21}(x) \; w_{21}(x)$$

It is possible that the two transactions operate on nodes 1 and 2, presenting two schedules S_1 and S_2 as follows:

$$S_1: \quad r_{11}(x) \; w_{11}(x) \; r_{21}(x) \; w_{21}(x)$$

$$S_2: \quad r_{22}(y) \; w_{22}(y) \; r_{12}(y) \; w_{12}(y)$$

These two schedules are locally serializable. However, when we observe their global conflict graph, defined as in Section 9.2.3, we discover a cycle between t_1 and t_2, in that:

- on node 1, t_1 precedes t_2 and is in conflict with t_2;

- on node 2, t_2 precedes t_1 and is in conflict with t_1.

Thus the two executions are not conflict-serializable (CSR). It is easy to construct applications in which two transactions t_1 and t_2 that act in the way described by the schedules S_1 and S_2 cause loss of updates or ghost updates.

Global serializability   The global serializability of distributed transactions over the nodes of a distributed database requires the existence of a unique *serial schedule S* equivalent to all the local schedules S_i produced at each node. This means that, for each node i, the projection $S[i]$ of S, containing only the actions that happen on that node, must be equivalent to the schedule S_i. This property is difficult to verify when using schedulers that directly apply view-equivalence or conflict-equivalence, but can be immediately verified whenever the strict two-phase locking or the timestamping method is used. The following properties are valid.

- If each scheduler of a distributed database uses the two-phase locking method on each node, and carries out the commit action atomically at a time when all the sub-transactions at the various nodes have acquired all the resources, then the resulting schedules are globally conflict-serializable.

- If distributed transactions each acquire a single timestamp and use these timestamps in their requests to all the schedulers that use concurrency control based on timestamp, the resulting schedules are globally serial, based on the order imposed by the timestamps.

The above two properties have great practical relevance, because as a consequence the methods of two-phase locking and timestamping can be applied unaltered to distributed databases. In particular, the synchronization of the commit action in the various nodes, which is required by two-phase locking, is imposed by the atomicity of the transaction (see the two-phase commit protocol in Section 10.4).

Lamport method for assigning timestamps   To guarantee the effective function of timestamp-based concurrency control, each transaction must acquire a timestamp that corresponds to the time at which the distributed transaction will be synchronized with the other transactions. We can use the *Lamport method* for assigning timestamps that reflect the precedence among events in a distributed system. Using this method, a timestamp is a number characterized by two groups of digits. The least significant digits identify the node at which the event occurs; the most significant digits identify the events that happen at that node. The most significant digits can be obtained from a local counter, which is incremented at each event; in this way, each event has a different timestamp. In addition, each time two nodes communicate by exchanging a message, the timestamps become synchronized: given that the sending event precedes the receiving event, the receiving event must have a timestamp greater than the timestamp of the sending event. This may require the increasing of the local counter on the receiving node.

Figure 10.6 describes a certain number of events on three nodes of a distributed system, and shows n assignments of timestamps obtained using the Lamport method. Note that each event is characterized by a distinct timestamp and that the timestamp reflects the order of events produced by the exchange of messages, denoted by broken arrows.

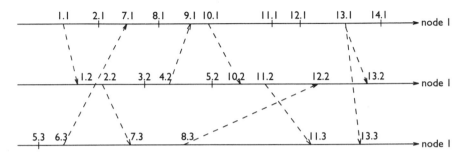

Figure 10.6 Example of assignment of timestamps using the Lamport method.

Distributed deadlock detection   Finally, we come to the problem of distributed deadlocks, that is, deadlocks between distributed transactions. Resolving them is more complex, as they can be due to circular waiting situations that happen on two or more nodes. Obviously, the simple solution of timeout is valid no matter what the context in which the deadlocks are created, and thus it is used in most systems. There is however, an elegant and rather efficient algorithm that resolves the deadlocks. It is described below and is a characteristic example of an asynchronous and distributed protocol, implemented in a distributed version of IBM DB2.

Imagine a distributed database model in which the transactions are broken down into sub-transactions. In this context, it is possible that the sub-transactions are activated synchronously, and in this case when the sub-transaction t_{11} activates the sub-transaction t_{12} (for example, using a *remote procedure call*, that is, a synchronous call to a procedure that is remotely executed), t_{11} waits for the termination of t_{12}. Thus, this model allows for two distinct types of waiting. Firstly, two sub-transactions of the same transaction can be in waiting in the distinct DBMSs as one waits for the termination of the other. Secondly, two different sub-transactions on the same DBMS can wait as one blocks a data item to which the other one requires access.

An example of distributed deadlock is shown in Figure 10.7. The deadlock is due to the following wait conditions:

1. t_{11} waits for t_{12}, activated by a remote procedure call (*rpc*);

2. t_{12} waits for a resource locked by t_{22};

3. t_{22} waits for t_{21}, activated using a remote procedure call;

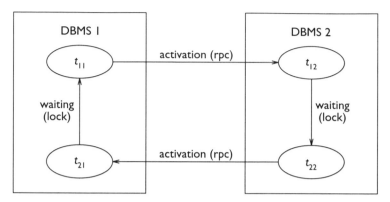

Figure 10.7 Example of a distributed deadlock.

4. finally, t_{21} waits for a resource locked by t_{11}.

The waiting conditions visible to each DBMS can be characterized using precedence conditions. On DBMS 1, we know that t_{21} is activated by a remote DBMS and is waiting for t_{11}, which in its turn has activated a sub-transaction on a remote DBMS. Thus we have:

$$EXT \rightarrow t_{21} \rightarrow t_{11} \rightarrow EXT$$

Symmetrically, on DBMS 2 we have the precedences:

$$EXT \rightarrow t_{12} \rightarrow t_{22} \rightarrow EXT$$

Now consider any waiting condition in which a sub-transaction t_i, activated by a remote DBMS, also waits because of the lock situation for another transaction t_j, which in its turn waits for a remote sub-transaction. The waiting condition is summarized using a *wait sequence*:

$$(1) \quad EXT \rightarrow t_i \rightarrow t_j \rightarrow EXT$$

The algorithm for distributed deadlock detection is periodically activated on the various DBMSs of the system. When it is activated, it analyzes the wait conditions on its DBMS and communicates the wait sequences to other instances of the same algorithm. To avoid the situation in which the same deadlock is discovered more than once, the algorithm allows for a message (1), containing wait sequences, to be sent only 'ahead'. That is, it is sent towards the DBMS where the sub-transaction for which t_j is waiting is activated. Further, the message is sent only if, for example, $i > j$ and i and j are the identifiers of the transactions.

The algorithm is activated periodically and works as follows:

1. The messages containing wait sequences arriving from other remote DBMSs are read and the information present in the messages is combined with the local wait conditions, building a wait graph. Each transaction is represented on the graph by a single node, independently of the number

of sub-transactions of which it is composed. The nodes corresponding to remote transactions are added to the local wait graph.

2. A local deadlock search is carried out. Deadlock situations are resolved by forcing the abort of one of the transactions involved in the deadlock.

3. The wait sequences are then computed and sent to the remote DBMSs 'ahead', according to the rule described above. At the end of the transmission, the algorithm is deactivated.

Figure 10.8 shows the application of this algorithm to a distributed database.

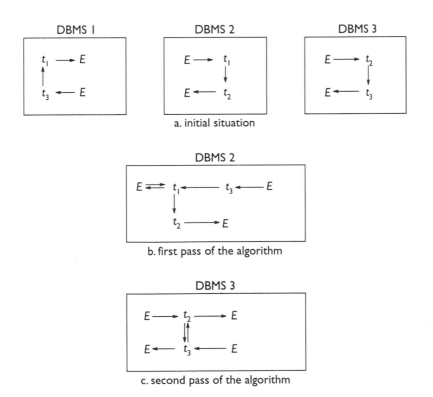

a. initial situation

b. first pass of the algorithm

c. second pass of the algorithm

Figure 10.8 Example of a distributed deadlock detection.

We assume an initial wait condition characterized by these wait sequences:

$$S_1 : EXT \rightarrow t_3 \rightarrow t_1 \rightarrow EXT$$

$$S_2 : EXT \rightarrow t_1 \rightarrow t_2 \rightarrow EXT$$

$$S_3 : EXT \rightarrow t_2 \rightarrow t_3 \rightarrow EXT$$

In these conditions, given that the wait sequences must be exchanged 'ahead', only DBMS 1 can transmit its wait sequence to DBMS 2, where the sub-transaction activated by t_1 is being carried out. Figure 10.8b illustrates the situation that is verified by DBMS 2 after having received the wait condition S_1. Thus a new wait condition appears:

$$S_4 : \quad EXT \rightarrow t_3 \rightarrow t_2 \rightarrow EXT$$

This wait condition is sent to DBMS 3, where the sub-transaction activated by t_2 is being carried out. Figure 10.8c shows the situation that is generated in DBMS 3 after receiving the wait condition S_4. Finally, the deadlock consisting of the pair t_2, t_3 is recognized (note that the original deadlock also involved t_1). One of the two transactions is chosen for the rollback, which involves all of its sub-transactions on all the nodes, and the deadlock is resolved.

10.3.3 Failures in distributed systems

To conclude our analysis of ACID properties for distributed transactions, we still need to deal with atomicity. To guarantee atomicity it is necessary that all the nodes that participate in a transaction reach the same decision regarding the transaction (commit or abort). Thus, it is necessary to follow particular protocols, known as *commit protocols*, which allow a transaction to reach the correct commit or abort decision.

Unfortunately, atomicity is difficult to guarantee, due to many possible causes of failures that may occur in a distributed system; we turn our attention to a classification of failures, before focusing on commit protocols in the next section.

A distributed system is subject to node failures, which may occur on any node of the system; these may be soft or hard, as discussed in Section 9.4.4. In addition to node failures, *message losses* can occur, which leave the execution in an uncertain situation. To guarantee the progress of a protocol, each protocol message is followed by an acknowledgement message (*ack*). However, the loss of either one of the two messages (the first one or the ack) leaves the sender uncertain about whether the message has been received. Since messages can be lost, the commit protocol imposes a limited time on the reception of each ack message; once the time is expired, the sender decides to proceed anyway with the protocol. In this case, it is possible that the timeout expires even when there is no real message loss. Simply, it could happen that one of the two computers exchanging the messages is overloaded and thus is too slow to process those messages.

A third kind of failure occurs when some communication links of the computer network can be interrupted. In this case, in addition to message losses, another phenomenon may occur: the *network partitioning* in two sub-networks that have no communication between each other. This failure can cause further problems, as a transaction can be simultaneously active in more than one sub-network.

In summary, the causes of failure in distributed systems amount to node failures, message losses, or network partitionings; they can jeopardize the atomicity of distributed transactions. We will now devote our attention to the two-phase commit protocol.

10.4 Two-phase commit protocol

The two-phase commit protocol is similar in essence to a marriage, in that the decision of two parties is received and registered by a third party, who ratifies the marriage. In order for the marriage to take place, both participants must express their wish to marry. The celebrant, during the first phase, receives the desire to marry, expressed separately by the two parties in order to give notice in a second phase that the marriage has taken place. In this context, the servers – who represent the participants to the marriage – are called *resource managers* (RM). The celebrant (or coordinator) is allocated to a process, called the *transaction manager* (TM). The number of participants at the marriage is not limited to two, but is arbitrary.

The two-phase commit protocol takes place by means of a rapid exchange of messages between TM and RM. To make the protocol failure resistant, RM and TM write some new records in their logs.

10.4.1 New log records

New log records are written during the two-phase commit protocol by extending the log records shown in Section 9.4.2. Both TM and RM are provided with their own logs. The TM writes additional log records.

- The **prepare** record contains the identity of all the RM processes (that is, their identifiers of nodes and processes). Continuing with the marriage analogy, this record corresponds to the announcements that are written before the marriage.

- The **global commit** or **global abort** record describes the global decision. Anticipating the protocol, we note that the time at which the TM writes in its log the **global commit** or **global abort** record, it reaches the final decision. A global commit decision consists of bringing the entire transaction to a successful (that is, atomic and durable) termination on all the nodes on which it works. A global abort decision consists of leaving the initial database state unaltered on all the nodes at which the transaction operates.

- The **complete** record is written at the end of the two-phase commit protocol.

The RM process represents a sub-transaction. As in the centralized context, each RM writes a **begin** record, followed by various records of **insert**, **delete**, and **update** that represent the operations carried out by sub-transactions. As regards the two-phase commit protocol, there is a single new record on the RM.

- The **ready** record indicates the irrevocable availability to participate in the two-phase commit protocol, thereby contributing to a decision to commit. The identifier (process identifier and node identifier) of the TM is also written on this record.

Note that the participant, once the **ready** record is written, loses all independence of decision making. The final result of the transaction will be decided by the TM. Furthermore, a participant can write the **ready** record only when it is in a 'recoverable state'. This means that it must use appropriate locks to block all the resources to which it has access and it must follow the WAL and commit-precedence rules, as defined in Section 9.4.3, in the management of its log.

10.4.2 Basic protocol

In the absence of failure, the two-phase commit protocol consists of a rapid sequence of writes on the log and of exchange of messages between the TM and the RMs. In communication with the RMs, the TM can use *broadcast* mechanisms that transmit the same message to many nodes. It must then be able to collect responses arriving from various nodes. Otherwise, the TM uses a serial communication with each of the RMs.

The *first phase* of the protocol is as follows.

1. The TM writes the **prepare** record in its log and sends a **prepare** message to inform all the RMs of the start of the protocol. A timeout is then set by the TM indicating the maximum time allocated to the completion of the first phase. The timeout will expire in the case of an excessive delay in the receipt of the reply message from some of the RMs.

2. The RMs that are in a recoverable state await for the **prepare** message. As soon as the **prepare** message arrives, they write on their own logs the **ready** record and transmit to the TM a **ready** message, which indicates the positive choice of commit participation. If an RM is not in a recoverable state, because a transaction failure has taken place, it sends a **not-ready** message and ends the protocol. Any RM can at any time autonomously abort a sub-transaction, by undoing the effects and ending the protocol before it begins. As we shall see, the global effect of this situation on the transaction is a global abort.

3. The TM collects the reply messages from the RMs. If it receives a positive message from all the RMs, it writes a **global commit** record on its log. If, however, one or more negative messages are received or the timeout expires without the TM receiving all the messages, the TM writes a **global abort** record on the log.

The *second phase* of the protocol is as follows.

1. The TM transmits its global decision to the RMs. It then sets a second timeout, which will be activated in the case of an excessive delay in the receipt of responses from the RMs.

2. The RMs that are ready await the decision message. As soon as the message arrives, they write the commit or abort record on their own logs. Then they send an acknowledgement to the TM. At this point, the implementation of the commit or abort proceeds on each server as described in the preceding chapter. In particular, the pages modified by the transaction are written to the database by the buffer manager.

3. The TM collects all the ack messages from the RMs involved in the second phase. If the timeout expires without the TM having received all the acks, the TM sets another timeout and repeats the transmission to all the RMs from which it has not received an ack. This sequence is repeated until all the RMs respond by sending their acks. When all the acks have arrived, the TM writes the complete record on its log.

To summarize, a communication failure between TM and RM during the first phase provokes a global abort, while a communication failure between TM and RM during the second phase provokes a repetition of the transmissions, until a communication between the TM and all the RMs is re-established. In this way, the final result of the transaction is communicated to all the RMs in a ready condition. The protocol is shown in Figure 10.9, which describes the exchange of messages and writes on the logs of the TM and one of the RMs.

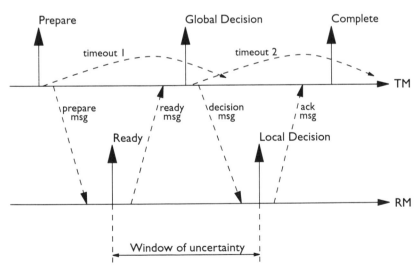

Figure 10.9 Two-phase commit protocol.

An RM in a ready state loses its autonomy and awaits the decision of the TM. This situation is particularly dangerous, as a failure of the TM during the protocol leaves each RM process in an uncertain state. In this state, the resources acquired by an RM process (using lock mechanisms) are blocked. Thus, it runs the risk of blocking large portions of the database for long periods. The interval that passes between the writing on the participant's log of the **ready** record and the writing of the **commit** or **abort** record is called the *window of uncertainty*. The protocol is designed to keep this interval to a minimum.

The entire group of actions carried out by the processes of *client, server* and TM is described in Figure 10.10 for a specific RM (but obviously, there must be at least two RMs). The client sends a task to be executed by the RM and waits for it to be completed. It then sends, either in sequence or in parallel, other tasks to be executed by other servers. Note that in the model in Figure 10.10 the client acts as coordinator of the distributed execution. Alternatively, the client can direct its request to a single RM and this last can send requests to other RM processes, carrying out the role of coordinator of the distributed execution. In both cases, the client or the RM process coordinator waits for all the RMs to finish their tasks, and then activates the two-phase commit protocol, interacting with the TM. At this point, all the RMs are waiting to participate in the commit, receiving the first **prepare** message. The commit protocol happens very rapidly, as both the RM and the TM simply write the records in the log and send messages, thereby minimizing the window of uncertainty.

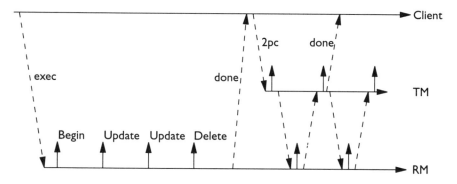

Figure 10.10 Two-phase commit protocol in the context of a transaction.

In a large number of applications, the processes of client, RM and TM establish their connections once, when processes are initialized, and then reuse them many times, for various transactions. They use permanent communication mechanisms, called *sessions*, which guarantee an efficient and robust transmission environment for distributed transactions. The concept of sessions refers to the communication protocols between processes and is beyond the scope of this text.

10.4.3 Recovery protocols

Let us now look at the possible causes of error that can affect the execution of the two-phase commit protocol, and at the recovery actions that take place in each case.

Failure of a participant   The failure of a participant causes the loss of the contents of the buffers and can thus leave the database in an inconsistent state. As in Section 9.4.4, the state of those participants that are 'uncertain' can be deduced from reading the contents of the log, which is supposed to be stored in the stable memory. The *warm restart* protocol, as discussed in Section 9.4.4, tells us how to behave in two cases. In both cases, whether a transaction is distributed or centralized is irrelevant:

- when the last record written in the log is a record that describes an action or an abort record, the actions are *undone*;

- when the last record written in the log is a commit, the actions are *redone*.

Thus, the only additional case, introduced by the 2PC protocol, concerns those transactions in which the last record written in the log is a ready. In this case, the participant is *in doubt* about the result of the transaction. Note that the transaction could have committed as a consequence of the positive indication given by the participant, or could have aborted due to a negative indication given by some other participant or to the expiring of the timeout of phase one. During the warm restart protocol, the identifier of the transactions in doubt are collected in a set (called *ready* set). For each of these transactions, we have to request the final result of the transaction to TMs. This can happen as a result of a direct (*remote recovery*) request from the RM node to the TM nodes. Alternatively, the information can be transferred to the TMs from the RM, as a repetition of the second phase of the protocol or following an explicit request to carry out the RM recovery (as in the X-OPEN protocol, which will be described below).

Coordinator failure   The failure of the coordinator happens during the transmission of messages and can cause their loss. It is possible to use the log to retrieve the information on the state of the protocol, but the log will not provide information on which messages have been correctly sent. The state of the TM is characterized by the following three cases.

- When the last record in the log is a prepare, the failure of the TM might have placed some RMs in a blocked situation. Their recovery, by the TM, usually happens by deciding on a global abort, writing this record in the log, and then carrying out the second phase of the protocol. Alternatively, the TM can also repeat the first phase, hoping that all the RMs are still waiting in a ready condition, in order then to decide on a global commit. Note that this alternative requires the RM to respond a ready message while being in the ready state.

- When the last record in the log is a global decision, the failure of the TM might have caused a situation in which some RMs have been correctly informed of the decision and others have been left in a blocked state. In this case, the TM must repeat the second phase, redistributing the decision to all the RMs.

- When the last record in the log is a `complete`, the failure of the coordinator has no effect on the transaction.

Note that the repetition of the second phase can cause a participant to receive the same decision about the same transaction many times. In this case, the participant can simply ignore the decision, but must in any case respond with an ack, to complete the recovery process.

Message loss and network partitioning   Finally, let us analyze the cases of message loss and of network partitioning.

- The loss of a `prepare` message and the loss of the succeeding `ready` messages are not distinguishable by the TM. In both cases, the timeout of the first phase expires and a global abort decision is made.

- The loss of a `decision` message or of the succeeding `ack` message are also indistinguishable. In both cases, the timeout of the second phase expires and the second phase is repeated.

- A *network partitioning* does not cause further problems, in that the transaction will be successful only if the TM and all the RMs belong to the same partition during the critical phases of the protocol

10.4.4 Protocol optimization

The protocol we have seen is laborious. Up to now, we have assumed that all the writings in the log were *synchronous* (that is, carried out using a *force* operation) to guarantee durability. Some variations of the protocol allow the avoidance of the synchronous writing of some log records, based on the use of default choices on the result of the transaction in case of failure of the TM. Thus, the TM can, in the absence of information about some participants, indicate by default that these participants have made a decision to commit or abort.

Two variants of the protocol are constructed. They are called *presumed commit* or *presumed abort*. We will describe below the protocol of presumed abort, which is adopted by most commercial DBMSs.

Presumed abort protocol   The presumed abort protocol is based on the following rule:

- when a TM receives a remote recovery request from an in doubt RM and the TM does not know the outcome of that transaction, the TM returns a global abort decision as default to the RM.

As a consequence of the above rule, we can avoid some synchronous writes of records in the TM log. In particular, the *force* of `prepare` and global abort records can be avoided. In the case of loss of these records caused by a failure of the TM, the TM following the default behaviour would give an identical response during the recovery of the transaction. Furthermore, the `complete` record is not critical for the algorithm; in some systems, it is omitted, and in general its loss causes the repetition of the second phase. In conclusion, only the records `ready` and `commit`, in the RM log, and `global commit`, in the TM log, must be written synchronously, and must be written using the *force* primitive. These records can be written using group operations, as indicated in Section 9.4.3, in order to improve performance.

'Read-only' optimization   A further optimization of the two-phase commit protocol appears when a participant is found to have carried out read operations but no write operations. In this case, the participant must not influence the outcome of the transaction, and must remain disinterested in the 2PC protocol. Note that the participants whose *read-only* role was known beforehand could be excluded from the protocol even earlier. The optimization of the protocol of a participant found to be 'read-only' consists of responding `read-only` to the `prepare` message arriving from the coordinator. The participant at this point does not carry out any write operation on the log and suspends the execution of the protocol after sending the message. Having received the `read-only` reply, the coordinator ignores the participant in the second phase of the protocol.

10.4.5 Other commit protocols

The main problem of the two-phase commit protocol is the possibility that an RM remains blocked because of the failure of the TM. To avoid this problem, other protocols have been developed, with three or four phases. They make it possible to avoid the blocking by introducing a greater complexity of execution. We will briefly touch upon three and four phase protocols.

The four-phase commit protocol   The four-phase commit protocol was created by *Tandem*, a provider of hardware-software solutions for data management based on the use of replicated resources to obtain reliability. In this area, the TM process is also replicated by a backup process, located on a different node. At each phase of the protocol, the TM first informs the backup of its decisions and then communicates with the RMs, as shown in Figure 10.11. In this way, the backup knows the exact state of the transaction and can replace the TM in case of failure of the TM. When a backup becomes TM, it first activates another backup, to which it communicates the information about its state, and then continues the execution of the transaction.

The three-phase commit protocol   The three-phase commit protocol has been defined but not successfully implemented. The basic idea is to introduce a third phase in the standard protocol, as shown in Figure 10.12. Note that a participant is in `pre-commit` state only if all the other participants are ready, and so are in a recoverable state. The addition of a phase in the protocol allows the reaction to a failure of the TM by electing one of the participants as the substitute for the TM. This new coordinator can decide the result of the transaction by looking at its log.

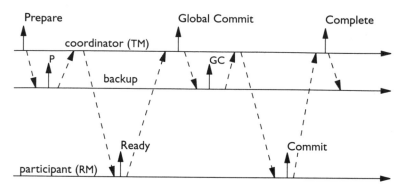

Figure 10.11 Four-phase commit protocol.

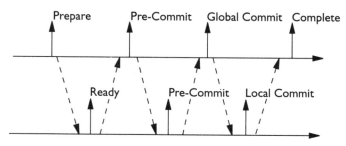

Figure 10.12 Three-phase commit protocol.

- If the new coordinator finds a **ready** in its log, it knows that none of the other participants in the protocol can have gone beyond the **pre-commit** condition, and thus can make the decision to abort. Thus the new coordinator registers a global abort decision and communicates it to the other participants.

- If the new coordinator finds a **pre-commit** in its log, it knows that the other participants are at least in the ready state, and thus can make the decision to commit. Thus, the participant registers a global commit decision and communicates it to the other participants.

The three-phase commit protocol has, however, serious inconveniences, which in practice make it unusable. In the first place, it lengthens the window of uncertainty, and thus makes blocking more probable. In the second place, the atomicity can be lost whenever a network partitioning occurs and two or more participants are chosen as coordinators to end the protocol (one in each partition). To resolve the problem, we must also be sure that the commit or abort decision is made by a sufficient number of participants to guarantee that a different decision could not be made in another partition. This is done using mechanisms based on the use of votes and quorums, which go beyond the scope of this textbook.

10.5 Interoperability

Interoperability is the main problem in the development of heterogeneous applications for distributed databases. The term denotes the capacity for interaction, and requires the availability of functions of adaptability and conversion, which make it possible to exchange information between systems, networks and applications, even when heterogeneous. Interoperability is made possible by means of standard protocols such as those for the exchange of files (ftp), electronic mail (SMTP/MIME), and so on. With reference to databases, interoperability is guaranteed by the adoption of suitable standards.

In this section we will look at ODBC, a standard to guarantee remote access (but not the two-phase commit protocol), and X-OPEN DTP, a standard specifically focused on the commit protocol. In this way, we will set down the technological premises for the creation of a cooperative architecture between heterogeneous databases, which will be discussed in the next section. In Chapter 11, we will also look at the CORBA standard, which is concerned with interoperability in the context of generic object-oriented applications.

10.5.1 Open Database Connectivity (ODBC)

The standard *Open Database Connectivity* (ODBC) is an application interface proposed by Microsoft in 1991 for the construction of heterogeneous applications. It is supported by most relational products. Using the ODBC interface, an applications written in SQL can have access to remote data. The language supported by ODBC is a particularly 'restricted' SQL, characterized by a minimal set of instructions, defined in 1991 within the SQL Access Group (SAG), a group of about 50 large users of DBMSs.

In the ODBC architecture, the link between an application and a server requires the use of a *driver*, a library that is dynamically connected to the applications. The driver masks the differences of interaction due not only to the DBMS, but also to the operating system and to the network protocol used. The driver thus masks all the problems of heterogeneity (not only those imposed by the DBMS), and facilitates the writing of applications. In order to guarantee the compatibility with the ODBC standard, each DBMS supplier must guarantee drivers that allow for the use of that DBMS within the environment of a specific network and with a specific operating system. For example, the trio (*Sybase, Windows/NT, Novell*) identifies a specific driver.

Access to a remote database using ODBC requires the cooperation of four system components (see Figure 10.13).

- The *application* issues the SQL queries, in a way that is independent of the communication protocol, the DBMS server, and the operating system of the node where the DBMS is installed; all these features are masked by drivers.

- The *driver manager* is responsible for loading the drivers at the request of

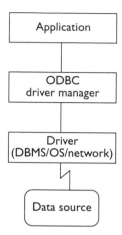

Figure 10.13 Architecture of ODBC.

the application. This software is supplied by Microsoft and also guarantees some functions for converting the names of data items used by the application into names used by the DBMS. These functions guarantee the correct operation of the driver.

- The *drivers* are responsible for carrying out ODBC functions. Thus, they can execute SQL queries, possibly translating them to adapt to the syntax and semantics of specific products. Drivers are also responsible for returning results to applications, using buffering mechanisms.

- The data source is the remote DBMS system, which carries out the functions transmitted by the client.

In ODBC it is possible to request transactional commands commit-work and rollback-work, which ensure the atomicity of the transactions. These instructions must however be addressed specifically to one DBMS server, because ODBC does not directly support the two-phase commit protocol. In addition, the error codes are standardized to allow the control of error conditions at the time of execution. SQL queries can be specified in a static way, or can be included in strings that are generated and executed dynamically as discussed in Section 4.6.3. In this case, the execution is subject to compilation errors when the SQL code contained in the strings is incorrect.

10.5.2 X-OPEN Distributed Transaction Processing (DTP)

X-OPEN Distributed Transaction Processing (DTP) is a protocol that guarantees the interoperability of transactional computations on DBMSs of different suppliers. X-OPEN DTP assumes the presence of one client, several RMs and one TM, which interact as described in Figure 10.10 (already discussed). The protocol consists of two interfaces:

- the interface between client and TM, called *TM-interface*;

- the interface between TM and each RM, called *XA-interface*.

In order to guarantee that their servers are accessible to the TMs, the vendors of DBMSs must guarantee the availability of the XA-interface. For this reason, in addition to a proprietary version of the two-phase commit protocol (used to create homogenous applications) various relational DBMSs support an implementation of the XA-interface (used to create heterogeneous transactional applications). The X-OPEN standard is adopted by various products specializing in transaction management, such as *Encina* (a product of the Transarc company) and *Tuxedo* (from Unix Systems, originally AT&T), which provide the TM component.

The main characteristics of the X-OPEN DTP standard are as follows.

- The standard allows for totally passive RMs. All the protocol control is concentrated in the TM, which activates the RM functions, made available in the form of a library of remotely callable primitives.

- The protocol uses the two-phase commit protocol with the presumed abort and read-only optimizations described above.

- The protocol supports *heuristic decisions*, which in the presence of failures allow the evolution of a transaction under the control of the operator. These heuristic decisions can cause a loss of atomicity, and in this case, the protocol guarantees that the client processes are notified.

The TM-interface is made up of the following procedures:

- tm_init and tm_exit, to initiate and terminate the client-TM dialogue.

- tm_open, to open a session with the TM. The session allows the establishment of a stable support for the client-TM-RM communications, which can be used by multiple transactions. The session is closed at the beginning of the request for the primitive tm_term from the client.

- tm_begin, to begin a transaction.

- tm_commit, to request a global commit.

The XA-interface is made up of the following procedures:

- xa_open and xa_close, to open and close a session between TM and a given RM; the TM issues several xa_open requests with all the RMs participating in transactions, after the establishment of a session with the client;

- xa_start and xa_end, to activate and complete a new RM transaction;

- xa_precom, to request that the RM carry out the first phase of the commit protocol; the RM process can respond positively to the call only if it is in a recoverable state;

- `xa_commit` and `xa_abort`, to communicate the global decision about the transaction;

- `xa_recover`, to initiate a recovery procedure, which is made necessary after the possible failure of a process (TM of RM);

- `xa_forget`, to allow an RM to forget transactions decided in a heuristic manner.

A typical interaction among client, TM and RM is shown in Figure 10.14.

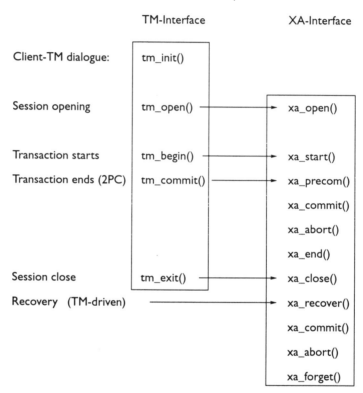

Figure 10.14 Interactions among client, TM and server with the X-OPEN DTP protocol.

When an RM is blocked because of the failure of the TM, an operator can impose a heuristic decision (generally the abort), thus allowing the release of the resources. The recovery procedure is guided by the TM, which calls the RM immediately after its successful restart from the failure. At this point, the RM process consults its log and indicates three sets of transactions:

- transactions *in doubt*;

- transactions decided by a *heuristic commit*;

- transactions decided by a *heuristic abort*.

The TM process communicates to the transactions in doubt their actual result (commit or abort) and uses its log to verify whether the heuristic decisions are in conflict with those communicated to the client. If this happens, it notifies the client, informing it of the inconsistency. The resolution of inconsistencies due to erroneous heuristic decisions is application-specific. In any case, the transactions decided heuristically are then forgotten by the RM, following a primitive of `xa_forget`, sent by the TM.

10.6 Co-operation among pre-existing systems

The rapid development of information technology provides possibilities for the integration among pre-existing information systems. This can happen for different reasons, which range from the simple demand for integration of components developed separately within the same organization, to the co-operation or fusion of different companies and organizations.

In this context, we must distinguish between interoperability and *co-operation*. The latter consists of the capacity of the applications of a system to make use of application services made available by other systems, possibly managed by different organizations. Obviously, the application servers also use interoperability services.

Co-operation is sometimes centred on processes; the systems offer one another services, by exchanging messages, information or documents, or by triggering activities, without making remote data explicitly visible. We will concentrate instead on *data-centred co-operation*, in which the data is naturally distributed, heterogeneous and autonomous, and accessible from remote locations according to some co-operation agreement.

In general, each system should continue to satisfy local user requests, even when carrying out global functions at the same time.

Autonomy, heterogeneity and distribution often cause major difficulties for the development of co-operative systems. They are sometimes seen as obstacles, to be removed by means of appropriate standardization initiatives and rationalization activities. Among these activities, the integration of databases is sometimes attempted; but such integration is quite difficult. Often the demands of each of the system components vary with time and therefore, over-ambitious integration and standardization objectives are destined to fail, or to generate very laborious alignment processes. In this context, the 'ideal' model, a highly integrated database, which can be queried transparently and efficiently, is impossible to develop and manage, and in any case is usually too expensive.

There can be many forms of co-operation centred on data. They differ in levels of transparency, complexity of the operations managed and level of currency of data.

- The *transparency level*, as discussed in Section 10.2.3, measures how the distribution and heterogeneity of the data are masked, and thus how the set of involved databases appear from the outside as a single database.

- The *complexity of distributed operations* is a measure of the degree of co-ordination necessary to carry out operations on the co-operating databases.

- The *currency level* indicates whether the data being accessed is up-to-date or not. In particular, in a co-operating system there are two possible situations: (a) direct access to up-to-date remote data; (b) access to derived data, often managed by a system that is more easily accessible, but whose content is typically not up-to-date.

Based on the above criteria, we can identify three architectures, which represent the three options for guaranteeing data-based co-operation.

A first category is that of *multi-database systems*, shown in Figure 10.15. In these systems, each of the participating databases continues to be used by its respective users (programs or end users). The single systems are also accessed by modules, called *mediators*, which transform and filter the accesses, showing only the portion of database that must be exported, and makes it available to a *global manager*, which carries out the integration. This architecture presents an integrated view to the users, 'as if the database were a single entity'. It thus provides a high level of transparency. The currency is also high, because data is accessed directly. At the same time, the complexity is also high; in general, data cannot be modified by means of mediators, because the local management of modifications at each source system is preferable.

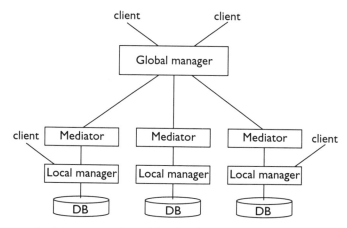

Figure 10.15 Architecture of a multi-database system.

A second category of systems uses *replicated data* to guarantee read only access to secondary copies of the information provided externally. An example of a system that falls into this category is shown in Figure 10.16: the only difference from the one in Figure 10.15 is the presence of the data warehouse. The *data warehouse* contains data extracted from various heterogeneous distributed systems and offers a global view of data. These systems also guarantee a high level of transparency, but have a reduced degree of currency. They support complex read-only queries, while updates are not relevant, since it is not possible to update the data sources through the data warehouse. We will look further into this concept in Chapter 13.

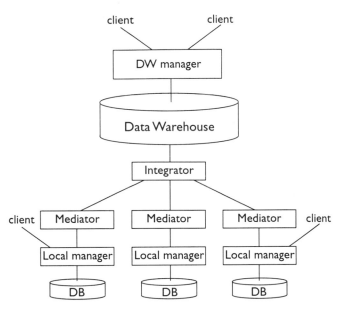

Figure 10.16 Architecture for data warehouse systems.

Finally, a third typical architecture is that of *local information systems with external data access*, as shown in Figure 10.17. The substantial difference from earlier cases lies in the fact that in this architecture, data integration is carried out explicitly by the application (that is, the client). For this reason, the architecture has a low degree of transparency and complexity, with a degree of currency that depends on specific demands. In the example, three sources are integrated: an external database, a local database and a data warehouse, which in turn uses three sources of information.

10.7 Parallelism

Parallelism is an important component of database technology. Having witnessed the failure of special architectures for databases (the so-called *database machines*) during the eighties, parallelism was developed during the nineties along with the spread of standard multiprocessor architectures, that is, architectures that are not specifically dedicated to databases. From the architectural point of view, parallelism is possible with multiprocessor architectures both with and without shared memory. Obviously these have different technical solutions, but in this section we will concentrate on the aspects more specifically linked to data management without dwelling on the technological differences of multiprocessor architectures.

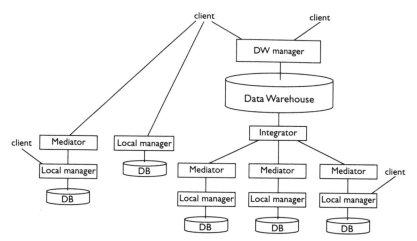

Figure 10.17 Architecture with external data access.

The reason for the success of parallelism in databases is that the computations carried out on a database lend themselves to being carried out in parallel with great efficiency. For example, a complete scan of a large database can be executed using n scans, each on a portion of the database. If the database is stored on n different disks managed by n different processors, the response time will be approximately $1/n$ of the time required for a serial search. In general, data management operations are quite repetitive in nature, and therefore they are suitable for being carried out in parallel, thereby reducing the time to process a query.

10.7.1 Inter-query and intra-query parallelism

Parallelism is introduced in databases for a specific purpose, that is, to guarantee better performance. There are two types of parallelism:

- Parallelism is called *inter-query* when it carries out different queries in parallel. In this case, the load imposed on the DBMS is typically characterized by many very simple transactions, which arrive frequently (up to thousands of transactions per second). As was indicated at the beginning of this chapter, this parallelism is particularly useful when the DBMS manages on-line transactions (an OTLP system).

- Parallelism is known as *intra-query* when it carries out part of the same query in parallel. In this case, the load on the DBMS is characterized by a few extremely complex queries, and thus it is appropriate to subdivide each query into various partial sub-queries, to be entrusted to various processors. This parallelism is particularly useful when the DBMS manages transactions for the analysis of data (an OLAP system).

In both cases, parallelism allows each processor to be allocated a part of the load. In inter-query parallelism, characterized by a heavy transaction load but by a limited number of services offered, parallelism is introduced by multiplying the number of servers and allocating an optimal number of requests to each server. In many cases, the queries are collected by a *dispatcher* process, whose sole task is to redirect each query to one of the servers. For example, the dispatcher might equalize the load on the servers, or it might direct each query to the server that can gain the most efficient access to the data involved in the query.

Intra-query parallelism is characterized by complex queries, which involve many operators and are evaluated on large amounts of data. In general, a well-defined set of processes is applied in order to answer the same query in parallel; queries are carried out one after another, using the entire multi-processor system for each query. In order to take advantage of intra-query parallelism, the optimizer must decompose the query into sub-queries and add the provisions for co-ordination and synchronization between them. The sub-queries can be limited to the distributed execution of specific operations (for example: scan, sort, join) or each can be more complex, carrying out a chain of operations.

10.7.2 Parallelism and data fragmentation

Parallelism is normally associated with data fragmentation: the fragments are distributed among many processors and allocated to distinct secondary memory devices. For example, consider a database for the management of bank accounts, characterized by the following relations:

ACCOUNT(<u>AccNum</u>, Name, Balance)
TRANSACTION(<u>AccNum</u>, <u>Date</u>, <u>SerialNumber</u>, TransactionType, Amount)

Suppose that the tables are fragmented based on predefined intervals of account number, and each fragment is assigned to a processor. This fragmentation can be *static*, that is, permanent, or *dynamic*, that is, created to respond to a specific query. In the second case, which applies to complex OLAP queries, it is necessary to include, in the cost of the query, the initial distribution of the data on the different secondary memory devices of the parallel system.

A typical OTLP query is the request for the balance of a specific account holder:

```
procedure Query5(:acc-num, :total);
    select Balance into :total
    from Account
    where AccNum = :acc-num;
end procedure
```

A typical OLAP query is the request for the account holders who have carried out transactions for total amounts above 100,000 during 1998.

```
procedure Query6();
    select AccNum, sum(Amount)
    from Account join Transaction on
```

```
          Account.AccNum = Transaction.AccNum
     where Date >= 1.1.1998 and Date < 1.1.1999
     group by AccNum
     having sum(Amount) > 100000
end procedure;
```

In general, the OLTP queries can be directed towards specific fragments depending on their selection predicates. OLAP queries, on the other hand, are carried out on all of the fragments in parallel.

Note that the proposed fragmentation and allocation of data about accounts and transactions allows the execution of *distributed joins* among fragments, that is, the join of pairs of fragments corresponding to the same account number interval. The join between the matching fragments can be carried out in parallel; the parallel execution of *n* joins on fragments of dimension $(1/n)$ is obviously preferable to the execution of a single join that involves the entire table. For this reason, the execution of distributed joins is essential for intra-query parallelism. In general, when the initial fragmentation does not allow the distributed execution of the joins present in the query, data is dynamically redistributed to support distributed joins.

10.7.3 Speed-up and scale-up

The effects of parallelism are typically described by two curves, called speed-up and scale-up.

The *speed-up* curve characterizes only inter-query parallelism and measures the increase of services, measured in *tps* (transactions per second), against the increase in the number of processors. Figure 10.18 illustrates an ideal situation in which the services increase almost linearly against the increase in processors. OLTP systems guarantee services very close to the ideal, and many vendors are capable of showing almost linear speed-up curves.

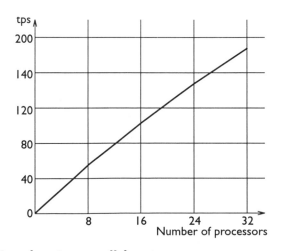

Figure 10.18 Speed-up in a parallel system.

The *scale-up* curve characterizes both inter-query parallelism and intra-query parallelism, and measures the average cost of a single transaction against the increase of the number of processors. Figure 10.19 illustrates an ideal situation, in which the average costs remain almost constant with an increase in processors. In this case, we say that the system 'scales' in an ideal way. In OLTP systems the increase in processors permits the management of a greater number of transactions per second and so responds to an increased transaction load. In OLAP systems, the increase in processors allows an increase in data, which occurs when the data warehouse grows. Both the OLTP systems and the OLAP systems guarantee services that are very close to the ideal, and many constructors are able to show almost constant scale-up curves.

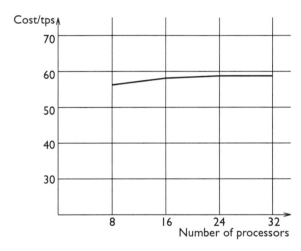

Figure 10.19 Scale-up in a parallel system.

10.7.4 Transaction benchmarks

Speed-up and scale-up curves have introduced the general problem of a comparative evaluation of DBMS performances, whether centralized, distributed or parallel. Measuring the services offered by a DBMS requires the existence of specific and precise objectives for transactions and for the loading conditions in which the measures operate. These specifications are called *benchmarks*. After a long competition among various bodies for the proposal of a standard, the standardization activities of TPC (Transaction Processing Performance Council) became accepted. This is a committee of about thirty suppliers of DBMSs and transaction systems.

Within the TPC consortium, three main benchmarks have been defined, called TPC-A, TPC-B and TPC-C, adapted respectively for OLTP applications, mixed applications and OLAP applications. Each benchmark is divided into various cases according to whether it refers to a mainframe-based architecture, or to a client-server architecture, or to a parallel architecture. The following parameters are included in the specifications of a benchmark:

- the transaction code; for example, in the TPC-A, a typical transaction on bank accounts is characterized by direct updates to a few records per table, with a few well-defined tables that describe money transfers, historical data and data regarding the bank's branches;

- the size of the database and the method used for generating data;

- the distribution of the arrivals of transactions, which characterizes the transaction load in terms of *tps*;

- the techniques for measuring and auditing the validity of the benchmarks.

10.8 Replicated databases

Data replication is an essential service for the creation of many distributed applications. This service is guaranteed by specific products, called *data replicators*, which allow the creation of copies of tables or of subsets of tables in a generic distributed context.

The main function of a data replicator is to maintain the consistency among copies. In general, there is one *main copy* and various *secondary copies*, and updates are propagated from the main copy to the secondary copies in an asynchronous way (that is, without using the two-phase commit protocol). Propagation can be *incremental*, when it is based on the use of variations; these are sent from the main copy to the secondary copy. Alternatively, the entire secondary copy is periodically completely re-created from the entire main copy. The data replicator does this transparently, without altering the applications that operate on the main copy.

The use of replication makes a system less sensitive to failure. For example, if a main copy is not available due to failure of the corresponding system, it is at least possible to gain access to one of its copies. A typical distributed architecture with replicated data is shown in Figure 10.20. This architecture was introduced for the management of financial applications in which the possible non-availability of the system could cause serious economic loss. The architecture allows for the presence of two sites. Each site manages the entire database; half of which is the main copy and the other half the secondary copy. The transactions are sent to the main copy and then redirected to the secondary copy. Each 'access point' to the system is connected to both sites. In the case of a failure that involves only one site, the system is capable of commuting almost instantly all the transactions onto the other site, which is powerful enough to sustain the entire load. When the problem is resolved, the replication manager restores the data transparently and then resets the two sites to normal operations.

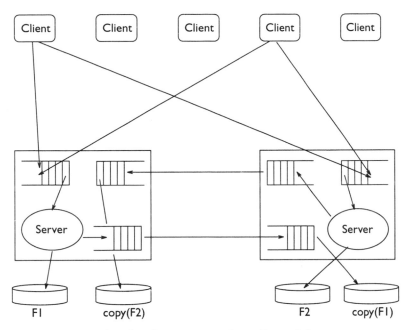

Figure 10.20 Example of architecture with replicated data.

As we have seen in the introduction of the concept of stable memory (in Section 9.4.1), redundancy is one of the methods for guaranteeing the durability of the information in the case of failure. There are some particularly critical information systems that use replication of data as a sophisticated form of backup. For example, the information systems of some Californian banks, located in a seismic area, have all their data replicated in an identical system, located in a different region. In this case, the copy-system is not normally able to hold the application load, but it is kept up to date by replicating on it the transactions that are committed at the main site.

Replication, fragmentation and distribution of data can be combined. For example, the information system describing production of the various components of a Tandem hardware architecture was created, towards the mid-eighties, by incorporating these three technologies. Tandem had about ten factories in various parts of the world, each responsible for the production of a specific part of the architecture of a computer (keyboards, screens, cpu-cases, and so on). The 'bill-of-materials' of the available parts in the company was modelled using an appropriate set of tables. These tables were fragmented to reflect the physical distribution of the construction process of the components, and then allocated to the nodes; each node was co-located with a factory. Fragments were allocated in a redundant way. The main copy of each fragment was on the node responsible for the production process of the hardware components described in that fragment, and then secondary copies of each fragment were stored at all the other nodes. The replication manager acted periodically, by collecting a batch of modifications on a given fragment and applying them asynchronously to all the other fragments.

Using this configuration, shown in Figure 10.21, the modifications were always directed to the main copy, but all queries could be performed locally, although on data that was not perfectly aligned.

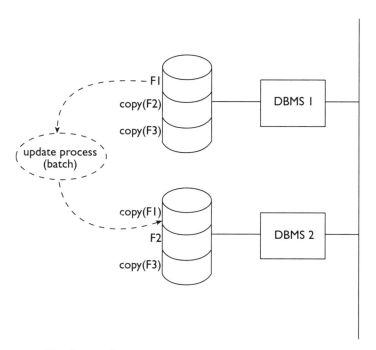

Figure 10.21 Tandem information system.

10.8.1 New functions of replication managers

Some products for data replication also support *symmetrical replication*, in which the modifications can be carried out on any copy, with a 'peer-to-peer' situation among the copies. In this case, clearly, it is possible to introduce conflicts, in that two copies of the same information are managed in a concurrent way *without* concurrency control. Therefore, all the anomalies described in Section 9.2.2 can appear in this context. To control this phenomenon, techniques are developed capable of revealing the anomalies after their occurrence and signalling them to a manager of the database, to deal with the inconsistencies in a way that depends on the specific application.

This problem has become more significant in the context of *mobile* distributed systems, in which the connection with the database can be broken. This happens when salespersons can connect to the database in order to download the availability of merchandise and upload the orders received. The salespersons use laptop computers as client machines. In this case, a salesperson can be disconnected from the database for many hours, accepting transactions on the laptop copy. This copy is 'reconciled' with the main copy when the salesperson reconnects to it, at the end of the sale activity.

10.9 Bibliography

This chapter also refers to the texts by Gray and Reuter [46] and Ceri and Pelagatti [18], mentioned in the previous chapter. Distributed databases are described in the more recent textbook by Ozsu and Valduriez [66]. The applications of distributed databases are described by Gray and Anderton [44]; the two-phase commit algorithms, and in particular their optimizations, the standardization in X-OPEN and their use within the field of commercial systems, are widely described by Samaras et al. [72]; distributed detection of deadlocks is described by Obermarck [62] and Lamport clocks are defined by Lamport [54]. The aspects relating to the co-operation of databases can be studied more widely in the texts by Brodie and Stonebraker [11] and Kim [52] and in the articles by Bernstein [9] and Sheth and Larson [76].

10.10 Exercises

Exercise 10.1 Consider the database:

PRODUCTION(<u>SerialNumber</u>, PartType, Model, Quantity, Machine)
PICKUP(<u>SerialNumber</u>, <u>Lot</u>, Client, SalesPerson, Amount)
CLIENT(<u>Name</u>, City, Address)
SALESPERSON(<u>Name</u>, City, Address)

Assume four production centres located in Dublin, San José, Zurich, and Taiwan and three sales points, located in San José, Zurich and Taiwan. Each production centre is responsible for one type of part; the parts are *CPU*, *Keyboard*, *Screen* and *Cable*. Suppose also three sales points, located in San José, Zurich and Taiwan. Suppose that the sales are distributed by geographic location; thus, Zurich clients are served only by salespeople in Zurich (assume that the sales point in Zurich also serves Dublin). Assume that each geographic area has its own database (that is, databases are available in Dublin, San José, Zurich, and Taiwan). Design the horizontal fragmentation of the tables PRODUCTION, PICKUP, CLIENT and SALESPERSON. Express the following queries on transparency levels of fragmentation, allocation and language:

1. Determine the available quantity of the product 77Y6878.

2. Determine the clients who have bought a lot from the retailer Wong, who has an office in Taiwan.

3. Determine the machines used for the production of the parts type **Keyboard** sold to the client Brown.

4. Modify the address of the retailer Brown, who is moving from '27 Church St.' in Dublin to '43 Pak Hoi St.' in Taiwan.

5. Calculate the sum of the amounts of the orders received in San José, Zurich, and Taiwan (note that the aggregate functions are also distributable).

Making any necessary assumptions about the use of the DBMS in Zurich, write a remote request, a remote transaction, a distributed transaction and a distributed request.

Exercise 10.2 Assign the timestamps to the events described in Figure 10.22 with the Lamport method, and indicate which events are pseudo-simultaneous (events at different nodes that cannot be ordered).

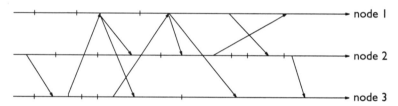

Figure 10.22 Event description for Exercise 10.2.

Exercise 10.3 Given the wait conditions shown in Figure 10.23, look for deadlocks with the distributed deadlock detection algorithm; assume two different hypotheses of wait conditions for node 4.

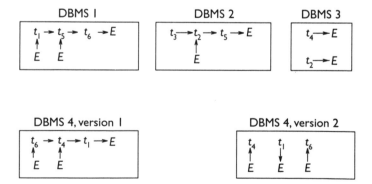

Figure 10.23 Wait conditions for Exercise 10.3.

Exercise 10.4 Describe how the warm restart protocol (of Chapter 9) is modified, by taking into account the fact that some sub-transactions can be in a ready state.

Exercise 10.5 Apply the warm restart protocol after the failure of a node, assuming a two-phase commit protocol, having the following input (where $R(t_i)$ indicates the presence of a **ready** record):

- $B(T_1)$, $B(T_2)$, $B(T_3)$, $I(T_1, O_1, A_1)$, $D(T_2, O_2, B_2)$, $B(T_4)$, $R(T_1)$, $U(T_4, O_3, B_3, A_3)$, $C(T_1)$, $CK(T_2, T_3, T_4)$, $B(T_5)$, $B(T_6)$, $U(T_5, O_5, B_5, A_5)$, $R(T_5)$, $B(T_7)$, $U(T_7, O_6, B_6, A_6)$, $B(T_8)$, $U(T_6, O_1, B_7, A_7)$, $A(T_7)$, $R(T_6)$, failure

Exercise 10.6 Describe the warm restart protocol after the failure of a node, assuming a three-phase commit protocol, having the following input (where $PC(t_i)$ indicates the presence of a **pre-commit** record):

- $B(T_1)$, $B(T_2)$, $B(T_3)$, $I(T_1, O_1, A_1)$, $D(T_2, O_2, B_2)$, $B(T_4)$, $R(T_1)$, $U(T_4, O_3, B_3, A_3)$, $PC(T_1)$, $C(T_1)$, $CK(T_2, T_3, T_4)$, $B(T_5)$, $B(T_6)$, $U(T_5, O_5, B_5, A_5)$, $R(T_5)$, $B(T_7)$, $U(T_7, O_6, B_6, A_6)$, $U(T_6, O_3, B_7, A_7)$, $B(T_8)$, $PC(T_5)$, $A(T_7)$, $R(T_6)$, failure

Exercise 10.7 Given a distributed system with eight nodes, assign a quorum necessary to decide commit and a quorum necessary to decide abort to maximize the probability of reaching a commit decision whenever there are four partitions with two nodes each.

Exercise 10.8 On the same database schema as in Exercise 10.1, describe an execution schema for the following queries that maximize the inter-query parallelism:

1. extract the sum of the production quantities, grouped according to type and model of parts;

2. extract the average value of parts sold by the salespeople, grouped according to type and model of parts.

Exercise 10.9 Describe an example of replicated database behaviour that produces a data inconsistency.

Exercise 10.10 Describe an example of symmetrical replication that produces a data inconsistency.

Part IV

Database evolution

11
Object databases

Object databases integrate database technology with the object-oriented paradigm. Object orientation was originally introduced within the field of programming languages and has become very popular as a paradigm for the organization and design of software systems. Object databases were originally developed in the mid eighties, in response to application demands for which the relational model was found to be inadequate.

In object databases, each entity of the real world is represented by an object. Classical examples of objects are:

- electronic components, designed using a *Computer Aided Design* (CAD) system;

- mechanical components, designed using a *Computer Aided Manufacturing* (CAM) system;

- specifications and programs, managed in a *Computer Aided Software Engineering* (CASE) environment;

- multimedia documents, which includes texts, images and sound, managed by multimedia document managers;

- spatial or geographic data, such as geometric figures or maps, managed by Geographic Information Systems (GIS).

These kinds of objects differ greatly from each other and are managed by specialized applications and systems. A common requirement of all of these applications is that of organizing the data as complex and unitary objects. This demand is not satisfied by the relational model, in which each 'real world object' is distributed among a number of tables. To view the object in its entirety requires the execution of complex queries that reconstruct the various components of an object from tables in the database, by using joins. Object databases represent real world objects by means of data objects with complex structure and with rich semantic relationships. These are modelled by means of constructs similar to those used for conceptual design, introduced in Chapter 5. The most relevant features introduced by object databases are:

- the use of inheritance, overloading, and late binding, as defined in the context of object-oriented programming languages;

- the integration of data with the operations (or 'methods') that are used for accessing and modifying objects.

These operations 'encapsulate' objects by providing predefined procedures for their manipulation. Operations respond to specific application demands, hiding a lot of complexity within their algorithms. For example, consider the operations for the three-dimensional representation of geometric objects.

There are two approaches for the introduction of objects into databases. Object-Oriented Database Systems (OODBMSs) have taken the revolutionary approach, extending the DBMSs based on the characteristics of object-oriented programming languages. Object-Relational Database Systems (ORDBMSs) have on the other hand assumed the evolutionary approach, by integrating the object concept into the relational model. It should be noted that the two approaches, which appeared to be in sharp conflict at the beginning of the nineties, have recently turned out to be convergent.

In this chapter, we will first deal with OODBMSs, introducing the typical components of the object models: type constructors, classes, methods, generalization hierarchies and mechanisms for the redefinition and refinement of methods. To describe these components, we will use the O2 system as a reference OODBMS. O2 was created in France by O2 Technology, and is currently a product of Ardent Software. We will then introduce the standards ODL (Object Data Language) and OQL (Object Query Language) for the definition and querying of OODBMSs, developed within the *Object Database Management Group* (ODMG).

We will then describe ORDBMSs, introducing the data model for SQL-3 (which is based on the classical notions of type, relation, hierarchy and function) and some elements of the SQL-3 query language. We will then give a brief description of multimedia databases, illustrating some of the characteristics necessary for the management of multimedia objects within the database, including an overview of Geographic Information Systems (GIS). We will conclude the chapter with a look at the main technological extensions needed for data management using object-oriented organization. In particular, we will discuss interoperability in the wider context of the standards CORBA and IDL, introduced by the *Object Management Group* (OMG).

11.1 Object-Oriented databases (OODBMSs)

In comparison to the relative simplicity of the relational model, object-oriented databases significantly extend the expressive power of the data model. The data model exhibits many of the characteristics of the Entity-Relationship model, seen in Chapter 5. In displaying the characteristics of the model, we use the syntax of a specific system (O2); this is required because the reference standards of ODMG do not cover some aspects (for example the implementation of methods) that are important for the understanding of the OODBMS approach.

11.1.1 Types

In an object database, types allow the definition of the properties of the objects. In particular, types define both static properties (which describe the structure of the objects) and dynamic properties (which describe the behaviour of the objects, by defining the operations, or 'methods', applicable to objects).

We will begin with the *static* part of types; the *dynamic* nature of types will be discussed in Section 11.1.3. The static part of types is constructed using *type constructors* and an extensive set of *atomic data types*, which include the classic data types present in programming languages: for example, integers, reals, boolean, and strings. Some systems allow the definition of enumeration types, the values of which are explicitly listed by the user. Atomic types include object identifiers (OID) which will be introduced later in the chapter. Most systems support the null value (sometimes indicated as nil) in all the atomic types. As in the relational model, nil is a *polymorphic* value, that is, belonging to many types.

Each type definition associates a name to a type. For example: Address:string is a type definition, which associates the name 'Address' to the string atomic type.

Complex data types   Type constructors allow the definition of types called *complex data types*, which dictate the structure of the instances (called *complex objects*) of an object database. A recursive definition of complex data types (based on type constructors) is as follows. Let us fix a set of atomic data types.

- The *record* constructor allows the definition of types whose instances are tuples of (complex) values of possibly different types. If $T_1,...,T_n$ are type names and $A_1,...,A_n$ are distinct labels, which we will call *attributes*, $T = record\text{-}of(A_1 : T_1,...,A_n : T_n)$ is a *record* type.

- *Set*, *bag* and *list* constructors allow the definition of types whose instances are collections of (complex) values of the same type. Sets are non-ordered collections without duplicates, bags are non-ordered collections allowing duplicates, and lists are ordered collections, possibly with duplicates. If T_1 is a type, then $T = set\text{-}of(T_1)$ is a *set* type, $T = bag\text{-}of(T_1)$ is a *bag* type and $T = list\text{-}of(T_1)$ is a *list* type.

Given a complex type T, an *object of data type T* is an instance of T. Type constructors are *orthogonal*, that is, they can be applied arbitrarily, resulting in objects of arbitrary complexity. However, as is customary in many object systems, we assume that a data type definition always has the record constructor at the top level. Thus, given an object x of type $T = record\text{-}of$ $(A_1:T_1,\ldots,A_n:T_n)$, we can say that the values for the attributes $A_1,\ldots A_n$ are the *properties* of x. The use of type constructors guarantees the *structural complexity* of objects; in particular, if a real-world object is complex, type constructors allow one to model its data structure accurately. Some object databases, however, do not support all constructors, and in any case, it is not generally convenient to construct excessively complex types, because it then becomes difficult to access the type components using programming and query languages.

Let us look at an example of definition of a type for the complex object AUTOMOBILE, characterized by various properties: RegistrationNumber, Model, Manufacturer, Colour, Price, MechanicalParts. Some of these properties have a complex structure of their own.

```
Automobile: record-of(
            RegistrationNumber: string,
            Model: string,
            Manufacturer: record-of(
                            Name: string,
                            President: string,
                            Factories: set-of(
                                        record-of(
                                        Name: string,
                                        City: string,
                                        NoOfEmployees: integer))),
            Colour: string,
            Price: integer,
            MechanicalParts: record-of(
                            Motor: string,
                            ShockAbsorber: string))
```

Given this type definition, we can show some typical values that are compatible with the definition. In the following example, records are contained within square brackets and sets in curved brackets:

```
V1: ["MI67T891", "Uno", ["Fiat", "Agnelli", {["Mirafiori",
    "Torino", 10000], ["Trattori", "Modena", 1000]}),
    "blue", 7000, ["1100CV", "Monroe"]]
```

Given a value of type record, we can gain access to its components using the classic dot notation, which can be applied recursively. For example:

```
V1.Colour = "blue"
V1.Manufacturer.President = "Agnelli"
V1.MechanicalParts.ShockAbsorber = "Monroe"
```

Objects and values   The above example demonstrates how we can satisfy the demand for allocating an arbitrarily complex structure to a single object. Thus, an automobile (or an integrated circuit) is described in a more detailed and unitary manner than it would be by using, for example, the relational model. However, this example also illustrates the limitations of a description based on 'values': for each automobile, made, say, by Fiat, the description of the manufacturer is repeated. Now, the manufacturer, in its turn, is made up of various data, including the name of the president and the locations of the factories. Such a description obviously introduces redundancy and goes against the normalization principles, discussed in Chapter 8.

In order to obviate this problem, we introduce object identifiers (OID). The structural part of an object is made up of a pair (*OID, Value*). The value is an instance of the object's type; we call it the 'state' of an object. OIDs provide the unambiguous identification of every object in the database, and allow the construction of references between objects. In the actual systems, OIDs are automatically assigned at object creation and are generally not visible to the users. An object can include explicit references to other objects: this can be implemented at schema level by allowing, in a data type definition, the notation $*T$, which denotes OIDs of objects of type T. If a property of an object has type $*T$, then we say it is *object-valued*.

The following definition introduces references to objects:

```
Automobile: record-of(RegistrationNumber: string,
                      Model: string,
                      Manufacturer: *Manufacturer,
                      Colour: string,
                      Price: integer,
                      MechanicalParts: record-of(
                                       Motor: string,
                                       ShockAbsorber: string)
Manufacturer: record-of(Name: string,
                        President: string,
                        Factories: set-of(*Factory))
Factory: record-of(Name: string,
                   City: string,
                   NoOfEmployees: integer)
```

A set of instances of the new type definitions is as follows:

```
01:  <OID1, ["MI67T891", "Uno", OID2, "blue", 7000,
            ["1100CV", "Monroe"]]
02:  <OID2, ["Fiat", "Agnelli", {OID3, OID4}]>
03:  <OID3, ["Mirafiori", "Turin", 10000]>
04:  <OID4, ["Trattori", "Modena", 1000]>
```

The example shows that object-valued properties allow references between objects (from an automobile to its manufacturer, from the manufacturer to its factory) and the sharing of objects by other objects (the same manufacturer is referenced by various automobiles). For example:

- the value 01.manufacturer is the OID of the object 02;

- the value 01.manufacturer.president is the string Agnelli.

Identity and equality The use of the OID also guarantees the possibility that two distinct objects have the same state and differ only in the OID (for example, two automobiles with the same properties); this possibility is not allowed by the relational model.

Two objects 01 and 02 are *identical* when they have the same OID (and obviously also the same state); in addition to identity, in the object-oriented model, there are two notions of equality:

- *superficial equality* (==) requires that two objects have the same state;

- *deep equality* (===) requires that two objects have identical 'reachable' values obtained by recursively substituting, at each object reference, the objects that can be reached using the OIDs for the OIDs themselves.

Note that the state of an object includes the OIDs of object-valued properties, and thus superficial equality implies deep equality. Note also that the construction of reachable values for testing deep equality could build very large objects. It could include all of the objects in the database and could even be endless in the presence of cyclic references. In general, many OODBMS systems offer an operator to verify the superficial equality of two objects, while deep equality must be programmed, for specific types, using suitable equality predicates on their reachable values.

For example, consider the following type definitions and the following objects:

```
T1: record-of(A: integer, B: *T2)
T2: record-of(C: character, D: *T3)
T3: record-of(E: integer)

O1: <OID1, [120, OID4]> of type T1
O2: <OID2, [120, OID4]> of type T1
O3: <OID3, [120, OID5]> of type T1
O4: <OID4, ["a", OID6]> of type T2
O5: <OID5, ["a", OID7]> of type T2
O6: <OID6, [15]> of type T3
O7: <OID7, [15]> of type T3
```

In this case:

- the superficial equalities are: 01==02, 06==07;

- the deep equalities are: 01===02, 01===03, 02===03, 04===05, 06===07.

The condition for defining deep equality of objects X and Y of type T1 can be programmed as follows: X.A=Y.A and X.B.C=Y.B.C and X.B.D.E=Y.B.D.E.

11.1.2 Classes

A class performs the function of an object container, to and from which objects can be dynamically added and removed. Objects belonging to the same class are homogeneous, that is, they have the same type. In the DDL, type definitions are typically given as a part of the class definitions. In general, the class definition is separated into two parts.

- The *interface* describes the type of the objects belonging to the class, which includes the signatures of all its methods; each signature consists of a list of the name and type of each parameter of the method.

Parameters, used in input to or in output from the method, enable the invocation of the method from within a program.

- The *implementation* describes the implementation of methods and, sometimes, the data structure used for the storage of objects.

The interface describes only the operations applicable to objects, while implementation hides the coding of operations. However, in object databases the values of objects are often visible using some user interfaces other than methods (for example, using the query language). Thus, OODBMSs do not give a rigorous interpretation to encapsulation. (The strict observance of encapsulation would force each access to an object to occur by means of a method.) We concentrate on the interface and will look at the description of implementation in the next section, dedicated to methods.

The distinction between types and classes is one of the most controversial arguments in the programming language field and in object databases. In our data model, types are abstractions that allow the description of both the state and the behaviour, while classes describe both the extensional representation of objects, and the implementation of methods relating to a type. The type describes abstract properties, while class describes the implementation of these abstract properties using data structures and programs. We have thus presented a data model in which:

- types and classes are distinct concepts;

- each class is associated to a single type;

- the concept of class describes both the implementation and the extension of a type.

The relationship among values, types and classes is shown in Figure 11.1. Each object has a value, which belongs to a type. Each object belongs to a class, which has a type.

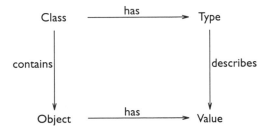

Figure 11.1 Relationship between values, objects, types and classes.

More complex object-oriented data models use the concept of class solely for defining the implementation of methods. They then introduce a third concept, that of extension, which allows the insertion of objects of the same type and class into different collections (or 'extents') and to give different names to these collections (for example, the type *citizen* could correspond to a same class but to different collections, called *Londoner* and *Florentine*). In this case, the three concepts of type, class and extension would be present. On the other hand, some OODBMSs do not distinguish types or classes, in that they unite the two concepts and give the type the role of defining extensions and implementations of methods.

For example, let us look at how in O2 the definition of class syntactically includes the type definition. Note the use of class names in the type definition, which are implicitly interpreted as references:

```
add class Automobile
    type tuple(RegistrationNumber: string,
            Model: string,
            Maker: Manufacturer,
            Colour: string,
            Price: integer,
            MechanicalParts: tuple(Motor: string,
                                ShockAbsorber: string))

add class Manufacturer
    type tuple(Name: string,
            President: Person,
            Factories: set(Factory))

add class Factory
    type tuple(Name: string,
            City: string,
            NoOfEmployees: integer)

add class Person
    type tuple(Name: string,
            Address: string,
            TaxCode: string)
```

The class structure can be represented graphically, highlighting the links between classes corresponding to object-valued properties. Figure 11.2 shows the four classes introduced up to now, inserted into a schema that includes other classes and a generalization hierarchy, to be discussed later.

11.1.3 Methods

Methods are used to manipulate the objects of an OODBMS. Their presence is the main innovative element in an OODBMS when compared to a relational database. A method has a *signature*, which describes the parameters of the method and includes all the information that allows its invocation, and an *implementation*, which contains the method code. Often the implementation of methods is written in an object-oriented programming language, such as Smalltalk or C++. The signature of the method is one of the components of the class definition.

In general, each method is associated with a specific object class. In this case, the method has a specific object class as *target*. There are, however, systems that allow *multi-target* methods, which are applied to an arbitrary

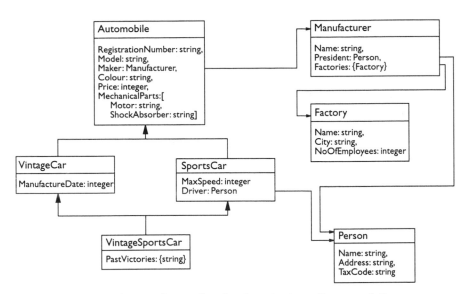

Figure 11.2 Database schema for the description of automobiles.

number of objects without favouring one in any specific manner. In this case, their definition is given separately from the class definition. We will assume, furthermore, that each method has an arbitrary number of *input parameters* and a single *output parameter*. These assumptions are valid for the O2 system (but not in standard OQL, described in Section 11.2).

The methods present in an OODBMS can be classified into four categories:

- *constructors* are used to construct objects based on their input parameters;

- *destructors* are used to cancel objects and possible other objects linked to them;

- *transformers* change the contents of the state of the objects;

- *accessors* are used to access portions of the object's state.

Other methods cannot be classified on the basis of this schema, and respond to specific application demands. In many systems, a distinction is made between *public* and *private* methods. Public methods can be called from any application program, while private methods can be called only from within other methods of the same class. Based on this distinction, objects are encapsulated to the maximum when it is possible to access them only by means of public methods.

In the DDL, signatures of methods may be introduced as part of the class definition; alternatively, each method can be autonomously introduced by a specific definition, in which the class target is nominated. This second option allows an incremental definition of the schema, and will be used later. The init method is a constructor; it builds part of the state of a newly created object of the class AUTOMOBILE. It receives as input parameters some values that should be assigned as the initial state of an object, and returns the object itself as output parameter. In the example, the method is applied to an object of the class AUTOMOBILE, which can be considered as an implicitly defined input parameter. Let us look at the definition of a signature (add method instruction) and of implementation (body instruction) in O2.

```
add method init(RegistrationNumber_par: string,
                Model_par: string,
                Colour_par: string,
                Price_par: integer): Automobile
                                in class Automobile is public
```

```
body init(RegistrationNumber_par: string,
          Model_par: string,
          Colour_par: string,
          Price_par: integer):
          Automobile in class Automobile
co2{self -> RegistrationNumber = RegistrationNumber_par;
    self -> Model = Model_par;
    self -> Colour = Colour_par;
    self -> Price = Price_par;
    return(self); }$
```

Note that the implementation of methods is written in CO2, an extension of C, which allows direct and transparent access to the objects stored in the database. Syntactically, the implementations are enclosed in a block initially delimited by a keyword co2 and terminated by the symbol $. These symbols invoke an appropriate pre-processor at execution time. The variable self, introduced implicitly in the implementation, denotes the object of the class target to which the method is applied. With a different terminology, the invocation of a method on a given object is denoted as sending a *message* to that object; self denotes the *receiving* object, that is, the object that should receive the message. The dot notation, introduced in Section 11.1.1, is used in CO2 as a C access mechanisms.

The invocation of the method init, in a program written in CO2, is as follows:

```
execute co2 {
  o2 Automobile X;
  X = new(Automobile);
  [X init("MI56T778", "Panda", "blue", 12000)]; }$
```

The first instruction of the program defines a variable o2 named X and of type Automobile. The second instruction creates an object of the class AUTOMOBILE, using the invocation of the new method. The polymorphic method new is available within all classes for the creation of new objects and their insertion into the class. Finally, the third instruction applies the method init to that object, giving an initial value to some of its properties. Note that in the method call we indicate the target object and the name of the method, followed by a list of the actual values of the input parameters. At the end of the execution of the method, the object on which the method itself is invoked is returned as an output parameter.

The method `Increase` in the class Automobile is a transformer. It increases the price by a certain amount. The amount is the only parameter of the method.

```
add method Increase(Amount: integer)
    in class Automobile is public

body Increase(Amount: integer) in class Automobile
    co2{ self -> Price += Amount;}$
```

The next example shows the nested invocation of the init and `Increase` methods, which are possible as the init method returns the target object as output parameter:[1]

```
execute co2 {
    o2 Automobile X;
    [[X init("MI56T778", "Panda", "blue", 12000)]
        Increase(2500)];}$
```

To end this section, we summarize the properties of objects. Each object has an OID, a *state* and a *behaviour*. The OID guarantees the unambiguous identification of the object in the database, and allows the construction of references between objects. The state of an object is the set of values assumed by its properties at a particular time. Finally, the behaviour of an object is defined by the methods that can be applied to the object itself, and predefines its evolution with time.

Impedance mismatch   These examples show an important characteristic of object-oriented databases: programs can manipulate persistent objects using instructions of a programming language. It is said that object-oriented databases resolve the *impedance mismatch,* introduced in Section 4.6.1, which characterizes relational query languages. The mismatch consist of the difference between operating upon scalar variables one at a time, as programming languages do, and processing sets of tuples, as in SQL. In effect, this mismatch requires the use of mechanisms such as cursors for scanning the results of a query one by one; but cursors, as illustrated in Section 4.6.2, are very rigid and not very user-friendly. In contrast, in the programming of OODBMSs, the programming language for writing methods acts upon persistent objects one by one, in the same way as it acts with the temporary variables of the program. In most cases, the program manipulates temporary and persistent objects in exactly the same way. In this case, it is said that persistence is an orthogonal characteristic, of which the programmer is unaware.

Historically, in object-oriented databases, much importance was given to this aspect, favouring the use of programming with *imperative style* in access to data. More recently, however, a demand has emerged for adding a query language to OODBs, for accessing objects based on their contents. As we shall

---

1. Note that the example is not very meaningful, as it first creates and then modifies the Price property, causing its immediate increase.

see in Section 11.2.2, OQL offers a query language for object-oriented databases, comparable to SQL.

Criteria for designing methods   One of the main advantages of object-oriented programming is the possibility of reusing the various system components. If the methods are carefully designed, most of the application code is defined only once, is included in the methods, and is used by various applications.

Some criteria help the designer in the design of methods to guarantee their maximum reusability. OMT is a popular object-oriented software design methodology, described by Rumbaugh et al. [71] which makes the following suggestions.

1. Methods must be brief. Informally, their code must not extend beyond more than two pages of text. Longer methods should be decomposed.

2. Methods should be *coherent* (that is, developing a single function) and *consistent* (that is, using consistent notations; for example, a common style for introducing variable names).

3. Methods should not internally confuse *policies* with *implementations*. Separating them increases the possibility of sharing the implementations among different policies.

4. Methods should *anticipate requirements* for future applications: rather than limiting themselves to carrying out the minimal requests for current applications, they should be more wide-ranging and deal with more general cases.

5. Methods should be *independent*. They should use information defined locally or accepted as parameters, avoiding the use of global variables.

6. *Inheritance* should be exploited as much as possible. The most commonly used methods should be defined in the super-classes and reused in the sub-classes. We will develop this concept in the next section.

11.1.4 Generalization hierarchies

The possibility of establishing generalization hierarchies between classes is probably the most important abstraction in object-oriented languages and databases. A generalization hierarchy defines the relationships between a super-class and its sub-classes. Generalization hierarchies between classes are very similar to the generalization hierarchies between entities, which we looked at in the Entity-Relationship model (Chapter 6). They guarantee the *semantic complexity* of objects. In a generalization hierarchy:

• all the objects of the sub-class belong automatically to the super-classes;

• all the properties and methods of the super-classes are *inherited* by the sub-classes;

- it is possible to introduce new properties and new methods into the description of sub-classes.

It is possible to redefine the implementation of a method without modifying its interface, to obtain various implementations of the same method, which can be called uniformly on objects of different types belonging to the hierarchy. The system uses the more specific implementation based on the type of the object. We will deal with this aspect in Section 11.1.6. It is also possible, even if it causes a few complications, to *refine* the state and the behaviour (that is, change the definition of some of the inherited attributes and methods in the subclasses, making them more specific). We will deal with this aspect in Section 11.1.7.

Generalizations have transitive properties. Thus if C_1 is a sub-class of C_2 and C_2 is a sub-class of C_3, then C_1 is also a sub-class of C_3. The relation of sub-class must be acyclic.

Due to inheritance, the definition of sub-classes can be limited to introducing new attributes and methods, while the attributes and methods defined for the super-class are automatically inherited by the sub-classes. For example, we define the sub-class SPORTSCAR and VINTAGECAR of the class AUTOMOBILE in O2:

```
add class SportsCar
    inherits Automobile
    type tuple(MaxSpeed: integer,
            Driver: Person)

add class VintageCar
    inherits Automobile
    type tuple(ManufactureDate: integer)
```

By virtue of inheritance, the class VINTAGECAR inherits the properties and the methods defined for AUTOMOBILE (for example, the attributes Model and Colour and the methods init and Increase). We can thus invoke the init method on an object of the class VINTAGECAR:

```
execute co2 {
    o2 VintageCar X;
    X = new(VintageCar);
    [X init("MI56543", "Ferrari", "red", 300000)];
    X -> ManufactureDate = 1957; }$
```

When a method m can be called in a class C_1, the implementation of m could be undefined in the class C_1. In this case, there must be an implementation of m in some super-class C_2 of C_1; this implementation of m is executed. When there are two super-classes C_2 and C_3 of the class C_1 that possess an implementation of m, the implementation of the lowest class in the hierarchy is chosen; this is also the most specific implementation relative to the class C_1.

Migrations between classes In the presence of generalization hierarchies, some OODBMSs allow objects to migrate from one level of the hierarchy to another. In other OODBMSs, objects remain for their entire existence in the class where they were created. The operation by which an object migrates from a super-class to a sub-class is called *specialization*. Due to a migration, the state of the object is generally modified, adding new properties. The inverse of specialization is called *generalization*, and allows an object to migrate from a sub-class to a super-class. The state in general loses some of its properties.

For example, an object of the AUTOMOBILE class can be specialized, becoming an instance of the class VINTAGECAR, at a certain point of its existence. On the other hand, an object of the SPORTSCAR class to which the generalization operation is applied, ceases to be an instance of that class, remaining, however, in the AUTOMOBILE class.

There is a distinction between being an *instance* or a *member* of a class. An object is an instance of a class only if it is the most specialized class for the object in the environment of a generalization hierarchy. The instances of a class are automatically members of its super-classes. In some OODBMSs, each object can be instances of many classes, that is, can belong to two or more distinct more specialized classes, which cannot be compared between themselves from the hierarchy point of view. In other OODBMSs, each object must be the instance of only one class. In our example, an object of the AUTOMOBILE class can be instances of the two classes if it is specialized into both classes SPORTSCAR and VINTAGECAR.

Multiple inheritance   In some systems, it is possible for a class to inherit from more than one super-class. This situation is called multiple inheritance. For example, we can define the class VINTAGESPORTSCAR with the following definition:

```
add class VintageSportsCar
    inherits SportsCar, VintageCar
    type tuple(PastVictories: set(string))
```

Note that this hierarchy of classes defines a situation illustrated in Figure 11.3, in which:

- the instances of the class VINTAGESPORTSCAR are automatically members of the classes AUTOMOBILE, SPORTSCAR and VINTAGECAR;

- some instances of the classes SPORTSCAR and VINTAGECAR are not in the class VINTAGESPORTSCAR; they are automatically members of the class AUTOMOBILE;

- finally, there are instances of the AUTOMOBILE class that are not in either SPORTSCAR or VINTAGECAR.

Note finally that whenever the system allows objects to be instances of two classes, SPORTSCAR and VINTAGECAR, at the same time (as the most specialized classes), they can exist in the database without being in the VINTAGESPORTSCAR class. The belonging of an object to a class is not

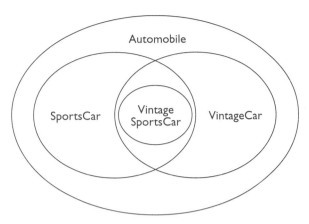

Figure 11.3   Representation of objects belonging to the classes
AUTOMOBILE, SPORTSCAR, VINTAGECAR and VINTAGESPORTSCAR.

automatic, and requires an explicit insertion operation of that object into the class.

Conflicts   Instances of classes with multiple inheritance or objects that are instances of more that one class can be the source of *name conflicts* whenever two or more super-classes have attributes or methods with the same name. In this case, we must define the policies for conflict resolution, to make the mechanisms of inheritance unambiguous. We list some of the possible solutions.

- Reveal the conflict at the time of definition of the classes and do not accept the definitions as correct. This solution has the disadvantage of imposing a rethink of already consolidated parts of the schema. The problem is eliminated only by changing the names of the attributes and/ or methods that cause the conflict.

- Define the mechanisms to make the choice unambiguous. For example, by using an ordering between classes defined beforehand, or by applying a method to an object in the context of a given target, which is explicitly defined in the method call, thus solving the conflict.

- Redefine the properties and methods locally, as described in the next section. The local redefinition eliminates the conflict.

11.1.5 Persistence

The objects defined in a program can be persistent or temporary. Temporary objects cease to exist at the end of the execution of a program, while persistent objects are inserted into the persistent storage space of the OODB. In general, an object becomes persistent by means of the following mechanisms.

- By *insertion into a persistent class*. In this case, the primitive new generates a persistent object, as described in some examples of this section.

- By *reachability* based on another persistent object. For example, if we have two objects of the types **Automobile** and **Manufacturer** in which the first refers to the second and then the first is inserted into a persistent class, then the second also becomes persistent. In this way, the state of an object that can be reconstructed recursively by means of references is persistent.

- By *denomination*, that is, by giving a name to an object (called a *handle*), which can be used to find it in a later invocation of the program. For example, in O2, we can declare a variable and then to give it a name, making the corresponding object persistent:

```
X SportsCar;
add name Ferrari_Testa_Rossa: X
```

Not all of these mechanisms for making objects persistent are supported in all OODBMSs. In some systems, persistence is defined at class level, that is, by distinguishing between persistent classes and temporary classes. The persistent or temporary nature of objects is defined when the object is inserted into the class. Persistence by means of reachability guarantees referential integrity of the OODB, that is, the automatic maintenance of referential integrity constraints between classes that are similar to the referential integrity constraints between tables, discussed in Section 2.2.4. This type of persistence however, brings some difficulties into the deletion of the object from the OODB. In practice, an object can be deleted from the system only when it can no longer be reached by denomination or referenced by other persistent objects. Deletion is performed by a specific subsystem called the 'garbage collector'.

11.1.6 Redefinition of methods

Once a hierarchy has been introduced, we can redefine methods of the subclasses. This technique is called *overriding* of methods and is extremely useful for guaranteeing the specialization of methods for subclasses, while at the same time presenting a uniform methods interface. The classic example that is used to show the advantages of redefinition is the display method, which is used to show an object on the screen. Let us suppose the existence of a generic OBJECT class, from which all the other classes inherit. In this class, we define the interface of the display method, having the target object as its only input parameter, and a fictitious implementation. The method is then redefined within all the other classes that inherit from OBJECT. We have, for example, the classes OWNER, HOUSE, PLAN, SALESCONDITIONS, relating to the activities of selling a house. Within each class, the display method is implemented differently. For example, display applied to the house retrieves and then shows a photograph of the house; for the plan, it shows a floor plan of the house; for owner and sale conditions, it shows a schema with the appropriate information. We can thus write code that, given a set S of heterogeneous objects, calls the function display for it in a compact way, for example:

```
for X in S do display(X)
```

Obviously, the choice of which implementation to invoke depends on the type of the object to which the method is applied. In particular, if the type of object is not known at compilation time (for example, because the objects can be specified during the transaction, or it can migrate between the classes), this choice must happen at execution time. This characteristic is called *late binding*. The system must be able to link dynamically, at execution time, a specific implementation of the method with the rest of the application program.

As an effect of redefinition, we can have various versions of the same method with identical interfaces (and in particular, identical method names). This phenomenon is called *overloading* of names of methods.

Let us look at an example of the overriding and overloading of methods. Consider data management for the design of software systems. In this case, we will introduce a generalization hierarchy with the generic class FILE and the sub-classes SOURCE and DOCUMENTATION. These classes are characterized by attributes introduced locally. The initialization method is able to initialize the objects based on their types.

```
add class File
type tuple(Name: string,
           Creator: User,
           Date: date)
method init(Name_par: string) is public

add class Source inherits File
type tuple(Manager: User)

add class Documentation inherits File
type tuple (ValidationDate: Date)

body init(Name_par: string) in class File is public
co2 { self -> Name = Name_par;
      self -> Creator = @ThisUser;
      self -> Date =@Today; }$

body init(Name_par: string) in class Source is public
co2 {[self init@File(Name_par)];
      self -> Manager = @ThisUser; }$

body init(Name_par: string) in class Documentation is public
co2 {[self init@File(Name_par)];
      self -> ValidationDate = @EndOfPeriod; }$
```

Note that the init method, defined in the FILE class, is reused in the two sub-classes. The operator @ is used to call the init method as implemented in a different class, thus enabling the reuse of defined methods in generic classes in the implementation of methods in more specific classes.

Note also that the use of the global variables @ThisUser, @Today and @EndOfPeriod (also recognized by an initial @) is acceptable in the context of the implementations of methods. Using the above method definition, we can initialize an object corresponding to a file independently of where it belongs in the class hierarchy. In the following code, it is necessary simply to replace the term CLASS by any of the three class names introduced in the example.

```
execute co2{
    o2 Class X;
    X = new(Class);
    [X init("myprog")]; }$
```

11.1.7 Refinement of properties and methods

The redefinition mechanisms seen in the previous paragraph do not modify the methods interface. However, it is also possible to refine properties and methods by modifying the interface, by introducing the notion of sub-typing.

Sub-typing is a relation between types. Intuitively, T_1 is a sub-type of T_2 if the possible values of type T_1 are more specific than the possible values of T_2. For example, if T_2 is an enumerated type, T_1 can be defined as a subset of values of T_2. Each type is a sub-type of itself, and in the O2 system, in which the classes are also interpreted as types, if T_1 is a sub-class of T_2, it is also a sub-type of T_2.

An important case is that of record: given a type record $T_1 = [A_1 : T_1,...,A_m : T_m]$, another record type T_2 is a sub-type of T_1 if it has the structure $T_2 = [A_1 : T'_1,...,A_m : T'_m, A_{m+1} : T'_{m+1},...,A_n : T'_n]$, with T'_i sub-type of T_i for $1 \le i \le m$ and with $n \ge m$. The sub-types can thus have other attributes that make them more specific, while the types T'_i of attributes A_i can be sub-types of T_i.

Having introduced the notion of sub-type, we can illustrate their use in the redefinition with refinement both of the properties and of the methods.

- Consider the definition of a class C_2, which inherits from C_1, and a generic property $A : T$ of C_1, where A is an attribute of type T. The *covariance of the properties* consists of giving the property A in C_2, which is redefined, a sub-type T' of T.

- Consider the definition of a class C_2, which inherits from C_1 a generic method m characterized by a certain number of input parameters, of type T_i, and one output parameter of type T. The *covariance of the output parameter* consists of giving the method m', which is redefined in C_2, a sub-type T' of T. As regards input parameters:

  ○ the *covariance* of an *input parameter* of m with type T_i in C_1, consists of giving to that parameter, which is redefined in C_2, a sub-type T'_i of T_i;

o the *contravariance of an input parameter* of *m* with type T_i in C_1 consists of giving to that parameter, which is redefined in C_2, a type T_i' such that T_i is a sub-type of T_i'.

The covariance of properties and of input parameters of methods, adopted by most object-oriented systems (including O2), is the most intuitive and useful notion in the specialization of properties and methods. However, the covariance of input parameters of methods may generate programs which cannot be statically checked for what concerns the correspondence between formal and actual parameters in method calls. This is illustrated by the following example.

Let us examine the mechanisms of redefinition. We adapt the previous example by adding two classes, USER and PROGRAMMER, whose structure is not relevant.

```
add class User ...
ass class Programmer inherits User ...

add class File
type tuple(Name: string,
           Creator: User,
           Date: date)
method init(Name_par: string, User_par: User): File is public

add class Source inherits File
type tuple(Creator: Programmer)
method init(Name_par: string, User_par: Programmer): Source
    is public

body init(Name_par: string, User_par: User): File
    in class File is public
co2 {[self -> Name = Name_par;
     self -> Creator = User_par;
     self -> Date = @Today;
     return(self); }$

body init(Name_par: string, User_par: Programmer): Source
    in class Source is public
co2 {[self init@File(name_par, user_par)];
     return(self)]; }$
```

Observe that in the redefinition of the SOURCE class, the property **Creator** is redefined: the creator is no longer a generic user, but rather a programmer. This is an example of *covariant definition of property*, which can be useful from an application point of view, if we wish to impose the condition that only the programmers can create source files.

The init method is called with an input parameter, which indicates who the user is, and must be correctly typed: the initialization of a generic FILE should receive as input parameter a generic user, but the initialization of a SOURCE must receive as input parameter a programmer. This is an example of *covariant redefinition of input parameters*. It is impossible to check at compilation time whether the invocation of the method is correct when objects can migrate dynamically from the USER class to the PROGRAMMER class and vice versa.

Finally, the output parameter of the method is also redefined, in that when it is invoked in a sub-class it returns a more specific type. This is an example of *covariant redefinition of the output parameter*, which poses no problems of type checking.

11.1.8 The object-oriented database manifesto

To conclude this section on OODBMSs, let us remember their main characteristics, as they are defined in the 'object-oriented database manifesto', an article that first introduced a certain order into the definition of characteristics of OODBMSs. Based on this article, the properties of an OODBMS are classified into mandatory and optional factors. The first ones include the following 13 properties.

1. *Structural complexity*, that is, the capacity for defining complex types using orthogonal type constructors.

2. *Object identity*, that is, the possibility of unambiguously identifying an object based on its OID.

3. *Encapsulation*, that is, the capacity for encapsulating an object within an interface that defines the public methods applicable to the object, the only ones capable of modifying the state. In the OODB world, however, normally the data structure is 'exposed'. That is, it is made public, to allow data manipulation by means of query languages.

4. *Types* and/or *classes*. The two concepts must both be present; the former concept represents a verification mechanism for the accuracy of programs at compilation time; the latter represents a mechanism that collects the object extensions and defines their implementation. Conversely, it is not necessary that there be two different ways to express types and classes, and thus it is possible to express one concept in the context of the other.

5. *Class* and/or *type hierarchies*, that is, the capacity to give semantic complexity to the OODB by organizing the classes (using generalization hierarchies) and by giving them more specific types (using type hierarchies).

6. *Overriding, overloading* and *late binding*, which make it possible for each object the execution of the method most specific to it, determined at execution time.

7. *Computational completeness* of the language in which methods are expressed.

8. *Extensibility*, that is, the capacity for defining new types based on user requirements.

9. *Durability*, that is, the capacity to support persistent data.

10. *Efficiency* in the management of secondary memory access.

11. *Concurrency*, that is, the capacity to manage concurrent accesses.

12. *Reliability*, that is, the capacity to react to failure.

13. *Declarativeness*, that is, the presence of a high-level query language.

Some further optional characteristics, which are considered interesting and useful but not essential in an OODBMS, include: multiple inheritance, the possibility of type checking of a program at compilation time, data distribution, management of long or embedded transactions, and the presence of explicit mechanisms for version management.

11.2 The ODMG standard for object-oriented databases

The *Object Database Management Group* is a committee in which the main constructors of OODMBSs are represented. The committee was brought together towards the end of the eighties, when it appeared evident that the lack of a model and a standard query language in OODBMSs was a common element of weakness in a market that is increasingly demanding portable solutions. The ODMG committee thus proposed a data model with a definition language (ODL), a query language (OQL), and mechanisms for the definition of methods in languages such as C++ and Smalltalk. These standards aim at achieving interoperability among the multiple systems of different suppliers.

11.2.1 Object Definition Language: ODL

In this section, we will describe the data model ODMG-93 and the ODL (Object Definition Language) for the definition of object schemas. In the ODMG-93 model there can be many classes for each type, each class containing a different implementation of the type. ODL describes types (and not classes) and is independent of the programming language chosen for the implementation of the classes. In ODL, the references between types are called relationships and are bi-directional: for each link between one type and another, an inverse link is defined. In this way, ODL offers a vision of the object-oriented schemas very close to those of the Entity-Relationship schemas. An ODMG-93 schema is shown in Figure 11.4.

Using the ODL syntax, let us look at a part of the example on automobile management, which was introduced above:

```
interface Automobile
  {extent Automobiles
  key RegistrationNumber}
  {attribute string RegistrationNumber;
  attribute string Model;
  attribute string Colour;
```

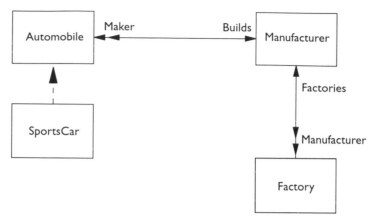

Figure 11.4 Object-oriented database schema for the description of cars according to the ODMG-93 model.

```
attribute integer Price
attribute structure MechanicalParts
                    {string Motor,
                     string ShockAbsorber};
relationship <Manufacturer> Maker
    inverse Manufacturer::Builds;}

interface Manufacturer
  {attribute string Name;
   attribute string President;
   relationship set<Automobile> Builds
       inverse Automobile::Maker;
   relationship set<Factory> Factories
       inverse Factory::Manufacturer;}

interface Factory
  {attribute string Name;
   attribute string City;
   attribute integer NoOfEmployees;
   relationship <Manufacturer> Manufacturer
       inverse Manufacturer::Factories}
```

Note that the first section of the interface, which is optional, describes the properties of types. This section is present only in the type AUTOMOBILE; the clause extent introduces the name of the container of objects of type AUTOMOBILE, and the clause key, as in the relational model, lists the attributes that identify the objects belonging to the type extensions. Note that the importance of keys in an OODB is minor in comparison with a relational database, as the identification is provided by the object identifiers.

We next show the ODL syntax for introducing sub-classes with the example of the definition of SPORTSCAR.

```
interface SportsCar: Automobile
  {attribute integer MaxSpeed}
```

In ODL, it is possible to define only method interfaces within type definition. Methods' implementation is carried out using a programming language. The standard defines two *bindings* towards the languages C++ and Smalltalk, for defining both the class structure and the implementations of methods. Within the Automobile class, the interfaces of methods init and Increase are defined in ODL as follows:

```
interface Automobile
{...
Automobile init (in string RegistrationNumber_par,
                 in string Model_par,
                 in string Colour_par,
                 in integer Price_par);
    void Increase (in integer Amount) raises(ExcessivePrice);
}
```

The methods in general have multiple input parameters, and can return zero or more output parameters. In ODL, each parameter is characterized by the keywords in, out, or inout (when a dual role is carried out). In addition, a method can be characterized by a main output parameter, returned by the method. The void clause in one of the two examples indicates the absence of the main parameter. The raises clause indicates the presence of an *exception*, which is raised whenever the price evaluated by the method is excessive.

The two examples of definition in O2 and ODL show quite different styles and syntaxes, but also show many common concepts.

11.2.2 Object Query Language: OQL

The OQL language, originally developed for O2, was adapted by the ODMG, with various modifications, and is currently considered the standard query language for OODBMSs. OQL is an extension of SQL, even if the similarities between the two languages are more apparent than real, and largely depend on the use of the same keywords. OQL, like SQL, is a pure query language. It does not include, for example, control structures. However, from OQL it is possible to invoke methods, which increase its expressive power. Currently, OQL does not include primitives for modifying the state of the objects contained in the database, as these modifications can be obtained by using methods. We must remember that, if the system guarantees a 'strong encapsulation', the only modifications of the state of the objects should happen by means of the use of its public methods.

Below, we will look at some typical queries in OQL, which give an idea of the expressive power of the language, without attempting to deal with all of its characteristics. The examples of the use of OQL given in this section refer to the database described in Figure 11.2, partly defined in O2 in Section 11.1.2 and Section 11.1.4.

The first example of the use of this language is the following query, which retrieves the registration numbers of the red cars:

```
select distinct x.RegistrationNumber
from x in Automobile
where x.Colour = "red"
```

This query returns an object of the type set(string). The keyword distinct, as in SQL, is used to eliminate duplicates; in this query it could be omitted if we assume that all the cars have distinct registration values. Note the use of the variable x, introduced in the from clause and declared on the AUTOMOBILE class.

The property of inheritance allows the invocation of properties defined within the generic super-classes. Thus, the query that retrieves the registration numbers of the red cars that won the 1954 Italian Grand Prix is simply:

```
select x.RegistrationNumber
from x in VintageSportsCar
where x.Colour = "red"
and "Italian GP 1954" in x.PastVictories
```

In the selection predicate, the operator in is used, as the type of the attribute **PastVictories** is a set of strings. Note that in this case the result is an object of type bag(string), although registration numbers typically have no duplicates.

Complex expressions A characteristic that makes OQL more powerful than SQL is the facility of using complex expressions (path expressions) in any expression where an object property may appear. For example, the next query retrieves the registration numbers of the vintage cars built at Maranello and driven by Fangio:

```
select x.RegistrationNumber
from x in VintageSportsCar
where x.Driver.Name = "Fangio"
and "Maranello" in x.Maker.Factories.Name
```

Given the schema in Figure 11.2, it is possible to ask whether there exist people who are both drivers and manufacturers of the same sports cars:

```
select x.Driver.Name
from x in VintageSportsCar
where x.Driver = x.Manufacturer.President
```

The result has the type bag(string); in this case there can be several different drivers with the same name. Note that the above query requires the *identity* of the person who is both a driver and president of the firm of manufacturers. Conversely, the following query also retrieves pairs of *homonymous* persons, that is, it requires *equality* of their names, and thus it is an incorrect formulation of the previous query:

```
select x.Driver.Name
from x in VintageSportsCar
where x.Driver.Name = x.Manufacturer.President.Name
```

Complex OQL path expressions can be broken down by introducing several variables in the from clause, and at the same time adding predicative expressions that link these variables. This programming style in OQL is similar to the use of joins in SQL. For example, the query that extracts the

Ferrari sports cars that were constructed at Maranello and have a maximum speed of over 250 Km/h can be expressed using three variables and two predicates. The variables are, respectively, on SPORTSCAR, MANUFACTURER and FACTORY. The predicates link the variables two by two – and are thus used in the same way as a join in SQL:

```
select a.RegistrationNumber
from a in SportsCar, c in Manufacturer, s in Factory
where c = a.Manufacturer and s in c.Factories
    and s.City = "Maranello" and c.Name = "Ferrari"
    and a.MaxSpeed > 250
```

Construction and use of complex objects In OQL it is possible to introduce structural complexity in all the clauses of a query. The following query extracts two attributes, whose type in OQL is constructed by means of a record: retrieve distinct models and colours of the sports cars that won the 1986 Le Mans 24 Hours:

```
select distinct struct(Model: x.Model, Colour: x.Colour)
from x in VintageSportsCar
where "LeMans86" in x.PastVictories
```

The type of the result is set(record(string, string)).

The following example introduces structural complexity in the select clause, by adding an OQL sub-query into it. The query retrieves the names of the manufacturers who sell sports cars at a price higher than 200000; for each of them, it lists the city and number of employees of the factories.

```
select distinct struct(
                Name: x.Maker.name,
                Fact: (select struct (Cit: y.City,
                                      Emp: y.NoOfEmployees)
                      from y in Factory
                      where y in x.maker.Factories))
from x in SportsCar
where x.Price > 200000
```

Note that in the evaluation of the query, the variable x is associated to those sports cars that satisfy the selection condition on prices, and y is associated with those factories that are related to the selected sports cars. The type of the result is set(record(string,bag(record(string,integer)))).

We can examine the use of an OQL sub-query within the from clause, for the query that extracts the number of models of cars built by manufacturers that have a global total of employees, in all factories, higher than 4500.

```
select count(select distinct x.Model
            from x in
              (select y
               from y in Automobile, z in Manufacturer
               where z = y.Maker
               and sum(z.Factories.NoOfEmployees) > 4500))
```

In this case, the aggregate function count is evaluated in the target list (on a set without duplicates) and the function sum is evaluated in the where clause of the most internal query (on a set). In general, the aggregate functions count, min, max, avg, and sum can be applied to sets, bags or lists.

Groupings and orderings   Finally, we will show some examples of the use of grouping and ordering, which are provided in OQL. For example, the following query retrieves the list of registration numbers in the class of cars:

```
sort x in Automobile by x.RegistrationNumber
```

The next query has the same expressive power as an SQL query with grouping. It extracts the number of cars grouped according to their manufacturers. Note the keyword partition, which denotes each partition obtained using the group by clause.

```
group a in Automobile
by (constr: a.Maker)
with (AutoNumber: count(select x
                        from x in partition))
```

The result is an object consisting of a set of tuples, which list, for each value of Maker in AUTOMOBILE, the set of AUTOMOBILE objects with that value (denoted through their OID) and the cardinality of that set. The type of the result is therefore set(struct(string,set(OID),integer)).

Finally, grouping can happen according to *partition predicates*. For example, the next query classifies the sports cars into low, medium and high according to the price:

```
group a in SportsCars
by (Low:    a.Price <   50000,
    Medium: a.Price >=  50000 and
            a.Price  < 100000,
    High:   a.Price >= 100000)
```

Supposing that n partitions are defined (n equals 3 in the example), the result has a particular structure. It is a set of records with $n + 1$ attributes. The first n attributes are boolean and assume in each record a single value *true* (corresponding to the value assumed by the partition) and $n - 1$ false values. The attribute $n + 1$ is a set containing the objects which are part of each partition. Thus the type of the result is set(struct(boolean, boolean, boolean, set(OID))>.

It is possible to apply a further aggregate function to this result, for instance to count the number of elements present in each partition, as follows:

```
select struct(Low: x.Low, Medium: x.Medium, High: x.High,
              Total: count(x.partition))
from x in
    (group a in SportsCar
     by (Low:    a.Price <   50000,
         Medium: a.Price >=  50000 and
                 a.Price  < 100000,
         High:   a.Price >= 100000))
```

11.3 Object-Relational databases (ORDBMSs)

Object-Relational databases (ORDBMSs) are an evolution of relational databases. These systems introduce compatible extensions of the classic notion of a table of SQL-2, and they allow the expression of most of the OODBMS concepts. In this section, we will show SQL-3, the language that is used to guarantee such compatible extensions. Then we will show the difference between SQL-3 and 'pure' object-oriented databases (OODBMSs) illustrated up to now. As we have already observed, the distance between OODBMSs and ORDBMSs is diminishing, especially in the data model. In the course of this section, we will first introduce the SQL-3 data model and will then show some characteristics of the SQL-3 query language.

11.3.1 SQL-3 data model

The data model used by ORDBMSs is also called the 'SQL-3 Data Model', as it is defined by the Data Definition Language (DDL) of SQL-3; it is compatible with the relational data model, as defined in SQL-2. Thus, in the SQL-3 model it is possible to define SQL-2 tables, such as for example the classic table for PERSON, with SQL-2 integrity constraints:

```
create table Person
    Name varchar(30) not null,
    Residence varchar(30),
    TaxCode char(16) primary key)
```

However, the approach suggested in the ORDBMSs is first to define a type for the tuples, to make it reusable. In any type definition, it is possible to use complex type constructors, which significantly extend the notion of domain present in SQL-2. Availability of type constructors is the first significant difference from classic relational databases.

Tuple types In the SQL-3 data model it is possible to use both *tuple types* (row types) and *abstract types*, which will be defined later. The first are used essentially for the construction of tuple structures for insertion into the tables. Thus, the previous definition can be split in the following two definitions:

```
create row type PersType(
    Name varchar(30) not null,
    Residence varchar(30),
    TaxCode char(16) primary key)

create table Person of type PersType
```

In this example, the type PersType can also be used in other tables. It is thus possible to define:

```
create table Industrial of type PersType
create table Driver of type PersType
```

Note that objects and classes in OODBMSs correspond to tuples and tables in ORDBMSs. In the context of ORDMBSs, the terms object and tuple are interchangeable.

As in OODBMS, it is possible to use type constructors orthogonally to construct arbitrarily complex types. It is further possible to use references from one type to another type, and thus create shared objects in the database. Let us return to the example in Section 11.1 and illustrate the definition of the corresponding tuple types, other than PersType. Note the use of the setof constructor (as a constructor of sets) and ref (to denote a reference to one type from another).

```
create row type FactoryType(
    Name varchar(25),
    City varchar(7),
    NoOfEmployees integer)

create row type ManufacturerType(
    ConstrId ref(ManufacturerType),
    Name varchar(25),
    President ref(PersType),
    Factories setof(FactoryType))

create row type CarTypeParts(
    Motor char(10),
    ShockAbsorber char(5))

create row type AutoType(
    RegistrationNumber char(10) primary key,
    Model varchar(30),
    Maker ref(ManufacturerType),
    MechanicalParts CarTypeParts)
```

Note that the types FactoryType and CarTypeParts are used within the types ManufacturerType and AutoType without introducing the construct ref, and thus without the introduction of independent objects. In this way, we construct tables that include sub-tables (at schema level) and objects that include as components sub-objects (at instance level), by guaranteeing an arbitrary structural complexity.

Note also that in the definition of the tuple type ManufacturerType, the attribute ManufacturerId is a reference to ManufacturerType itself, that is, to the type that is currently being defined. In this case, ManufacturerId carries out the role of OID; the values for ManufacturerId are system-generated but they can be used in the queries in the same way as any other attribute and can carry out the role of key. If this reference mechanism is not explicitly used in the type definition, then the system generates one OID for each object, but OIDs cannot be accessed in the queries. Note moreover, that this use of identifiers can cause the presence of dangling tuples. Whenever references to OIDs are explicitly cancelled or modified by the queries, the system guarantees the referential integrity only of those references that are not explicitly modifiable by the users.

At this point, we can create tables for the concepts AUTOMOBILE and

MANUFACTURER, which are included in the schema together with tables, PRESIDENT and DRIVER, already created.

```
create table Automobile of type AutoType

create table Manufacturer of type ManufacturerType
values for ManufacturerId are system generated
scope for President is Industrial
```

Note that the scope clause limits the possible values present in the attribute President, of the type PersType, to be a reference to the tuples belonging to the INDUSTRIAL table. If this clause were omitted, the values of the attribute President could be generic objects of the type PersType, present in any table that uses this type.

Hierarchies In SQL-3, we can define type and table hierarchies. Type hierarchies are used for extending previously defined types by adding new properties to them. For example, we can construct a tuple type VintageCarType by adding the attribute ManufactureYear, as follows:

```
create row type VintageCarType(
    ManufactureYear integer)
    under AutoType
```

Table hierarchies are analogous to class hierarchies discussed in Section 11.1.4. Thus, all sub-tables have as type a sub-type of the table from which they inherit. In addition, for each object (tuple) present in a sub-table there must exist an object (tuple) in the tables at all of the hierarchically higher levels.

The definition of VINTAGECAR as a sub-table of AUTOMOBILE, which requires an under clause in the context of the creation of the sub-table, can happen in two ways. It is possible to refer to the sub-type defined previously, as follows:

```
create table VintageCar of type VintageCarType under Automobile
```

Alternatively, we can define independently the type of VINTAGECAR in the context of type of AUTOMOBILE, assumed implicitly, as follows:

```
create table VintageCar(
    ManufactureYear integer)
    under Automobile
```

The only difference consists of the fact that VintageCarType is a reusable type in the first case and non-reusable, because not named, in the second case.

Abstract types and functions As well as tuple types, we can define generic abstract types, which can be used as components in the construction of tuple types. We can also provide the abstract types with a set of functions, which can be defined in SQL-3 or in an external programming language. The functions carry out the same role as the methods, discussed in Section 11.1.3, and in particular include standard forms for the *constructor, accessors* to the various attributes, and *transformers*. We can deny access privileges on the methods, obtaining the effect of encapsulating the data.

Let us look at the definition of the abstract data type CarTypeParts, which also includes the functions equals and greater than to express, respectively, equality and comparison between two parts.

```
create type CarTypeParts(
    Motor char(10),
    Power integer,
    Cylinders integer,

    equals EqualPower,
    greater than GreaterPower)
```

The functions defined in this way can be expressed in SQL-3 or in an external programming language. In any case, their definition requires the definition of a *signature* (which, as in Section 11.1.3, identifies the input and output parameters) and then their *implementation*. For the signature, a functional notation is used, in which there is only one output parameter, and the input parameters are enclosed within brackets. Each input parameter has a name and a type. The output parameter has no name and can be omitted; if the function has an output type, this is indicated after the returns clause.

Below, we will look at the two functions introduced above for the type CarTypeParts. The two implementations are self-explanatory, in that they are limited to a boolean expression constructed using the values of the attributes of the two parameters. We use a dot notation to extract the attribute of a table referenced by a variable, as in SQL-2. Note that, based on the arbitrary definitions given, two cars can be simultaneously either equal or ordered by the comparison; this example shows that the meaning of the functions is really dependent on the code of the method.

```
create function EqualPower(:p1 CarTypeParts,
                           :p2 CarTypeParts)
    returns boolean;
    returns (:p1.Power = :p2.Power)

create function GreaterPower(:p1 CarTypeParts,
                             :p2 CarTypeParts)
    returns boolean;
    returns ((:p1.Power > :p2.Power) or
        ((:p1.Power = :p2.Power) and
        (:p1.Cylinders > :p2.Cylinders)))
```

Finally, let us look at how reference is made in SQL-3 to an external implementation, using a specific programming language.

```
create function EqualPower(:p1 CarTypeParts,
                           :p2 CarTypeParts)
    returns boolean as external name Myfile language C;
```

11.3.2 SQL-3 query language

The query language SQL-3 is compatible with SQL-2. Thus, we can define 'standard' relational queries on the 'standard' tables. For example, the following query is written in SQL-2 and compatible with SQL-3:

```
select Name
from Person
where TaxCode = 'TRE SFN 56D23 S541S'
```

Below, we will look briefly at two new features of SQL-3, called *deferencing* and *double dot notation*, which allow access either to related objects or to component sub-objects. We will also look at the operations for *nesting* and *unnesting*, which enable the modification of complex object structures.

Deferencing Navigation among the references between types in SQL-3 requires the deferencing operator. This operator allows access from a source object *x* to an object *y* referenced in *x* as an object-valued property *A* in the following way: `x -> A`. The following example shows the use of the deferencing operator to access the value of the attribute Name of the object of the INDUSTRIAL table from objects of the MANUFACTURER table. In particular, it accesses those objects that satisfy the predicate Name = 'Fiat'.

```
select President -> Name
from Manufacturer
where Name = 'Fiat'
```

In SQL-3 the attributes of types OID can be used explicitly in queries, and in particular can be compared by the equality operator with the references to tuples of the same type. The above query can thus be expressed as follows:

```
select Name
from Manufacturer, Industrial
where Manufacturer.Name = 'Fiat'
    and Manufacturer.President = Industrial.ManufacturerId
```

The query constructs a join between the tables MANUFACTURER and INDUSTRIAL, in which the attribute President of the first table is compared with the identifier of the second table.

Double dot notation SQL-3 does not use the deferencing operation for accessing sub-components, but rather it introduces a new *double dot* operator. If an object *x* contains a sub-object *y* with attribute *A*, access to *A* happens by means of the expression `x..A`. The following example illustrates the use of double dot to access the Motor attribute of the sub-object MechanicalParts of cars. Note also the use of deferencing for access from an automobile to its manufacturer and from the manufacturer to the name of its president.

```
select Maker -> President -> Name
from Automobile
where MechanicalParts..Motor = 'XV154'
```

Nesting and unnesting We have seen that the SQL-3 model allows the construction of arbitrarily complex data from the structural point of view. The SQL-3 query language allows the building of query results that have different structures with respect to those supported in the schema, by means of the two operations of nesting and unnesting.

Unnesting (or flattening) is carried out by simply extracting a 'flat' relational structure by omitting some of the original type constructors (such as setof). For example, the next query shows the extraction of the pairs of names, manufacturer and cities of automobile developers. Flattening is obtained by assigning a structured attribute to a variable.

```
select C.Name, S.City
from Manufacturer as C, C.Factory as S
```

In contrast, *nesting* is created by using the group by operator, which constructs (as in SQL-2 and OQL) partitions of equal value on the grouping attribute. In SQL-3, it is possible to extract the set of values present in a partition, and this causes the construction of a nested result.

```
select City, set(Name)
from Manufacturer
group by City
```

11.3.3 The third generation database manifesto

To conclude this section on ORDBMSs, we must remember the 'third generation database manifesto', an article that represents the ORDBMS 'reply' to the OODBMS manifesto. The article defines the third generation database as a natural evolution of relational databases, which in their turn had replaced hierarchical databases and network databases, that is, the 'first generation' of DBMSs. The demand for a 'change of generation' is due to the necessity for supporting complex data and functions within the DBMS.

The article begins with three basic assumptions: third generation systems must be able to manage complex objects and rules, be compatible with second generation systems (that is, pure relational databases) and be open to interaction with other systems. In particular, the second assumption relating to the compatibility between second and third generations sets this manifesto against that of the OODBMS manifesto. The article then presents a series of proposals, many of which agree with those mentioned in the OODBMS manifesto. We can list the most important ones.

1. A third generation DBMS must have a rich type system, which must include orthogonal constructors for arrays, sequences, records and sets.

2. A third generation DBMS must allow generalization hierarchies among types, possibly also with multiple inheritance.

3. Functions (including procedures and methods) are useful characteristics, especially when accompanied by encapsulation.

4. It makes sense for a system to allocate OIDs to single objects if a primary

key is not available among the attributes defined by the user. Otherwise, it is better to resort to key attributes for the identification of objects.

5. Active rules (triggers) and passive rules (integrity constraints) will become an essential component of third generation DBMSs.

6. Independently of how much this is desirable, SQL is the reference language for DBMSs (it is a 'communication language for intergalactic dataspeak').

Discussing the merits of the third generation manifesto, written in 1990, is difficult. Nevertheless, we can at least state that the last 'prophecy' has been confirmed in the last decade relating to SQL. In spite of the success of OQL, SQL remains clearly the most widespread language in commercial databases.

11.4 Multimedia databases

In recent years, there has been an increasing demand for the management, along with alphanumeric data, of other data, that represents documents, images, video and audio, and which are generically known as 'multimedia data'. By 'multimedia database' we mean a system with the capacity to store, query and show multimedia data. In this chapter, we discuss specific aspects of multimedia data management, by regarding multimedia data as particular types of data, whose efficient management requires specific abstractions. However, multimedia data can also be managed by relational databases.

11.4.1 Types of multimedia data

We will begin with an analysis of the characteristics of the main types of multimedia data: images, audio, video, documents and annotations.

Images The demand for the storage of images within objects, often described by associated alphanumeric information, is increasingly widespread. Databases of images are used in the clinical field, where for example, each patient's X-rays are stored along with the patient's clinical records; police departments all over the world exchange detailed reports of wanted criminals, which contain images of their faces; estate agencies and realtors illustrate the houses on sale using photos; descriptions of tourist resorts include pictures. The main difficulty in the management of images is the high number of bits necessary for their storage in binary form. To reduce this number, standard formats are used. These include GIF, JPEG, TIFF and PNG which allow image representation in compressed form.

Audio Audio data can contain conversations, music and other sounds (for example 'audio clips', which are associated with the use of commands on the personal computer). An audio signal is typically segmented into small temporal *frames* within which the signal is presented more or less uniformly, that is, characterized by more or less constant amplitude and frequency. A large number of frames are required, however, to segment an audio recording in a way that guarantees good reproduction: for ten minutes of audio, up to 100,000 frames can be required. Thus, storage of audio recordings also requires use of compression techniques.

Video   Videos are collections of images (or frames) shown one after another by a reproduction device. A video can illustrate an historic event, a lesson, animals in action in their natural habitat, and so on. If the storage of images causes storage problems, videos exacerbate the problem, considering that a 60-minute video can contain more than 100,000 frames. There are several standards for video management (MPEG-1, MPEG-2, MPEG-4), which use different levels of compression. For example, MPEG-1 is of insufficient quality to guarantee television reproduction, MPEG-2 makes this possible by increasing the video quality (but also requires a greater number of bits) and MPEG-4 further improves the quality, allowing high-definition television reproduction.

Documents   Documents are made up of text and images, presented using a precise format. For example, the page of a newspaper, or the home page of the authors of this book, or a business letter written on headed paper and signed by the author, are examples of documents. The so-called 'digital libraries' are intended to store millions of books and other documents, and to make them available on the Internet. For the construction of documents, mark-up languages such as HTML, XML or SGML can be used (see Chapter 14).

Annotations   Finally, annotations are items of free text, sometimes even hand-written, which are added to other multimedia data for specific purposes (usually for the convenience of the writer, or for linking one document to another). Each annotation has personal characteristics, so in the management of annotations the user assumes a controlling role. Thus, the user decides, for example, whether annotations are to be accessible to other users or kept private.

11.4.2 Queries on multimedia data

While the coding of multimedia data is a general problem, the ability to query large amounts of multimedia data is a more specific problem of multimedia databases. In this section, we will look at some classic examples of querying applied to multimedia data, dealing more with their formulation than with the description of techniques for computing the result.

For example, a query to an archive of images can aim at the extraction of images with certain characteristics. We might need to find all the lung x-rays showing signs of bronchial pneumonia; or the individuals who most resemble the identikit picture transmitted by the police investigating a bank robbery; or all the Renaissance paintings of Madonna and Child stored in the Louvre. If the search for an image based on its characteristics already seems hard, it is even more difficult to extract audio signals or videos based on particular patterns. For example, suppose we want to find all the music of Wagner in which the same theme occurs, or the video sequences in which there appear goals scored by the Brazilian national soccer team. In these cases, the pattern must be reconstructed by operating on multiple frames or temporal windows. In all of the above cases, the query must initially exploit the structural information associated with multimedia data, in order to extract a few multimedia objects. After this, it will be necessary to evaluate, for each extracted object, its 'similarity' to the criteria requested.

In general, it is possible to select a multimedia object only in probabilistic terms. It will therefore be possible to present the result of a query starting from data that has the highest probability of satisfying the request, by setting a given probability threshold. Adaptive techniques allow the user to guide the search.

11.4.3 Document search

The most frequently occurring case of query on multimedia data is the extraction of documents that contain particular textual information. In this case, it is possible to use well-known and efficient techniques of *information retrieval*. To get an idea of the efficiency of such methods, it is sufficient to consider the quality of the 'search engines' on the Web, which find sites based on a few keywords. (For example, all the Web sites that contain the word 'Ferrari').

Information retrieval queries are typically composed by means of keywords, related by boolean operators. Text matching techniques are based on the capacity to extract useful information from a text in order to decide whether it is relevant to a query. This information is reduced to an optimized representation of the main keywords present in the text, with an associated indication of their frequency of occurrence. To construct this information for a generic text, it is necessary to operate as follows.

- Exclude irrelevant words from the text (articles, conjunctions, prepositions, etc.), which appear frequently but are not essential. These are known as 'stop words.'

- Reduce similar words to a single keyword (also known as 'stemming'). For example, the words 'inhabits', 'habitation', 'inhabited', 'inhabitant' are all linked to the unique concept of 'inhabit' and can thus be replaced by it.

- Allocate its own frequency to each keyword, defined as the ratio between the number of occurrences of the word and the total number of words present in the text.

At this point, the search for texts that satisfy a user query is reduced to the search for a text in which the keywords proposed by the user appear, in a combination compatible with the user request, with highest frequency. To define the efficiency of the search better, two measures are defined: *precision* and *recall*. Let us suppose that for each document, we know a-priori whether it is relevant, that is, whether it should be part of the result of the query or not. Then:

- *precision* indicates the number of relevant documents extracted as a percentage of the total extracted documents;

- *recall* indicates the number of relevant documents extracted as a percentage of the total documents in the database.

A good search algorithm must try to take account of both these factors. Firstly, it must offer a good degree of precision, to present documents that are highly relevant. Secondly, it needs a good recall, to reduce the risk of omitting the documents that are most relevant to the user.

Several techniques can be used for describing textual documents. Documents can be represented by using matrices, in which the rows and columns of the matrix represent respectively the documents and the keywords, and each element of the matrix represents the frequency of the keyword within the document.

Alternatively, we can represent the correspondence between keywords and documents by using inverted indexes. The indexes are organized as trees, containing at their intermediate nodes the keywords as illustrated in Section 9.5.5; leaves of the tree contain the identifiers of the documents corresponding to each keyword. Using these data structures, it is easy to extract the identifiers of documents that satisfy boolean conditions on keywords. For example, the intersection of two keywords is obtained simply by making an intersection of the sets of document identifiers. This is done by running through the index twice, with the two keywords selected by the user.

Other data structures first highlight the keywords of high frequency. For example, the signature of a document is a compact representation of the n keywords that appear in a document with highest frequency. Matching techniques are used for extracting the documents that respond to a given query by looking only at their signature; the signature can also be used to decide whether two documents are similar.

11.4.4 Representation of spatial data

Spatial data is used for describing the information present in a space of n dimensions, for example a geographical map (two-dimensional) or the project for a building under construction (three-dimensional). Spatial data management is a very specific application, which has recently acquired great importance. For this reason, it is often carried out by dedicated systems, called *Geographic Information Systems* (GIS).

The main problem of spatial data management is the selection of a data structure that allows the response to queries about the arrangement of data in the space. For example: extracting all the points of a map that are within a given distance from a particular point on the map; determining all the regions that are near to a given region; or determining the points of a map that are found along a line, and could represent the cities found along the course of a river. Obviously, GISs can describe not only the arrangement of data in the space, but also the characteristics of each point, line or region of the space. For example, points that describe cities have other information, as well as their own geographical co-ordinates, such as the population and the height above sea-level. Regions are characterized, for example, by the prevalent type of agriculture, or by the average monthly rainfall per unit surface. Lines can represent rivers, roads or railways. Using GISs, it will be possible to express queries in which spatial aspects are involved. The efficient management of spatial data requires the information to be organized using special data structures, which allow efficient execution of the queries. In particular, various types of tree structures allow the management of collections of points (for example, the cities in a geographical map) and they respond efficiently to queries of the following type: 'Extract all the cities that are less than a certain distance from a determined point.' Each point is represented by a tree node. Each node includes its co-ordinates X and Y, an item of information specific to the node and the pointers to the nodes of the successors.

In *2-d tree* organization (see Figure 11.5), each node has at most two

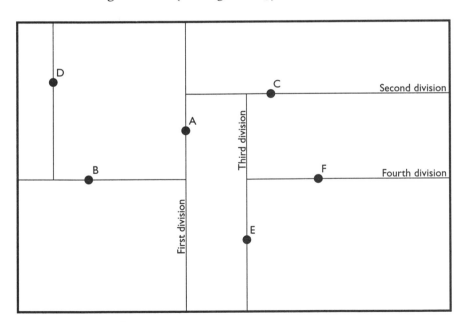

Figure 11.5 A 2-d tree.

successors. In this organization, the root node represents an entire geographic zone, and each node sub-divides the geographic zone represented by it into two zones using a line, which goes through the point whose co-ordinates are stored with the node. The line is horizontal or vertical according to whether the node is at an even or uneven distance in relation to the root. In Figure 11.5, A is the root node, B and C its descendents, E the descendent of C, F the descendent of E and D the descendent of B. Looking at the bottom right corner of the figure, A divides the figure vertically, C horizontally, E vertically and F horizontally.

In *quadtree* organization (see Figure 11.6), each node sub-divides the

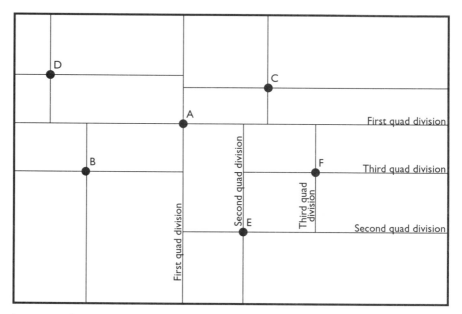

Figure 11.6   A quadtree.

geographical zone that it represents into four zones, using two lines, horizontal and vertical, which pass through the point itself. Thus, each node has four successors, which represent the four quadrants. In Figure 11.6, A is the root node, B, C, D and E are its descendents, and F is a descendent of E. Each point subdivides the figure into four zones.

Various commercial systems are specifically dedicated to the management of spatial data. The best known is ARC/INFO, which has a subsystem for the management of spatial data and can be integrated with the main relational databases. The Open GIS (OGIS) Committee is currently standardizing the format for the exchange of spatial data, to allow interoperability between the various GIS products.

11.5 Technological extensions for object-oriented databases

Object-oriented databases use database management systems technology, described in Chapter 9 and Chapter 10, but introduce some rather important technological extensions.

11.5.1 Representation of data and identifiers

The first problem is presented by the representation of complex objects in secondary memory, that is, in the *object servers*. To store a hierarchy of classes using files there are two approaches.

- The *horizontal* approach consists of storing each object adjacently. In particular, all the instances of a same class are stored within the same file. Thus, we would have, for the example in Figure 11.2, a file for each of the classes AUTOMOBILE, SPORTSCAR, VINTAGECAR, and VINTAGESPORTSCAR. Using this approach, access to a single object is particularly efficient. Conversely, the selection of objects based on their general properties is very laborious (for example, access to a generic automobile based on the attribute Colour requires access to four files).

- The *vertical* approach consists of storing the same properties adjacently, breaking an object down into its components. This approach is also called 'normalized' in that it could be directly applied to the relational model. In this case, we again have a file for each of the four classes mentioned. However, the file automobile contains information about all the objects that are instances or members of the AUTOMOBILE class. The objects are reconstructed based on references between their components, so that to collect all the information about objects of the class VINTAGESPORTSCAR requires access to four files.

These solutions are similar to the various options of translation from the Entity-Relationship model to the relational model that we discussed for logical database design (see Chapter 7). The horizontal solution is more consistent with the object paradigm because it manages each object in a unitary manner. However, it presents problems when an object can be an instance of more than one class. It is possible to choose an intermediate solution as well, when this is suggested by the demands of a particular application.

The vertical solution can also be used for managing structural complexity (due to the use of type constructors). In this case, however, references between sub-objects must be created at the time of partitioning an object and cannot reuse the object identifiers allocated to the entire objects. In addition, system-generated identifiers or counters must be used for managing the extensions of sets, bags, and lists.

Documents and multimedia data are typically represented as binary objects (*binary long objects* or *blobs*) and stored in specific files (one for each binary object).

A characteristic problem of OODBMSs is the representation of OIDs, for which two solutions are given.

- Use of a *physical address*, that is, including the physical allocation (block) of the object in the secondary memory. The obvious advantage is the speed of access. The disadvantage is the difficulty in moving an object to a different physical location, which can be managed using an indirect address, leaving a pointer to the new location in the page on which the object was initially stored.

- Use of a *surrogate*, that is, a value that is allocated unambiguously to an object using an algorithm (for example by allocating progressive numbers to objects, generated by a counter). An index or a hashing mechanism is then used to produce the physical address of each object out of the surrogate, thereby guaranteeing that objects can be accessed efficiently. In general, surrogates are unique in the context of specific extents, such as all the objects of a given class or at a given node of a distributed database. It is then necessary to generate surrogates by using distinct counters for each extent, and then add to the OID the indication of the extent to which the object belongs. OIDs can be large: in many distributed system implementations based on the standard CORBA, which we will see later, they can be as large as 64 bytes.

11.5.2 Complex indexes

In object systems, it is important to allow efficient access to path expressions, for efficient execution of queries and programs. To this end, *complex indexes* are developed for object-oriented databases.

Suppose that, for the database in Figure 11.2, a CITY class can be reached from the FACTORY class, using the Name attribute. Consider a complex path expression:

    X.Maker.Factories.City.Name

To carry out a query or a program that uses this path, we must find automobiles which are linked to cities with given values, such as 'London', 'Boston', etc., by going along the paths connecting CITY to AUTOMOBILE in the schema. In this way, we find the objects of the class AUTOMOBILE that satisfy the predicate:

    X.Maker.Factories.City.Name = 'London'

Complex indexes that can be defined in an OODBMS are of different types.

- A *multi-index* organization guarantees the presence of an index for each property used along the path expression. Thus, proceeding backwards:
  - an index from the strings corresponding to names of cities to the objects in CITY;
  - an index from the objects in CITY to the objects in FACTORY;
  - an index from the objects in FACTORY to the objects in MANUFACTURER;
  - an index from the objects in MANUFACTURER to the objects in AUTOMOBILE.

The use of the four indexes recalls the nested-loop method for the execution of joins (Section 9.6.2).

- A *nested index* directly connects the values that appear at one end of the chain to the objects that are at the other end of the chain. Thus, from the constant value 'London' one immediately makes access to all the objects of the class AUTOMOBILE that satisfy the predicate.

- Finally, an *index path expression* allows us to navigate from the values that appear at the end of the path to the objects of all the classes that appear along the path. Thus, from a city name it is possible to navigate backwards to CITY objects, FACTORY objects, MANUFACTURER objects or AUTOMOBILE objects.

Indexes introduced in this way are created with B+ trees of a particular structure. In managing these trees, we must take into account the creation and cancellation of intermediate objects, which can change the structure of the indexes.

11.5.3 Client-server architecture

In object-oriented databases too, objects are stored on servers dedicated to data management. As object-oriented database applications were developed in the nineties, object-oriented systems adopted the client-server architecture from their early development. However, especially in OODBMS, the paradigm for interaction between the client and the server is different, because clients execute application programs written in an imperative language. Thus, in OODBMSs, query languages such as SQL are replaced by imperative programming. We recall from Section 10.1 that the client-server separation of work induced by the use of SQL is one of the main reasons for the success of client-server architectures within the context of relational systems.

This paradigm change brings a different sub-division of tasks in client-server architecture, peculiar to object-oriented databases, in which the client system *imports* entire objects. In this way, the application programs can be carried out directly in the client system buffers. Imagine for example an engineering application, in which the user designs a mechanical component or a chip. Once the entire object is loaded on the workstation, the user no longer interacts with the object server for the duration of the design session. If, on the other hand, the objects remained in the server buffer during the design session, there would be laborious interactions between client and server, possibly causing overloading of the input/output channels and of the network.

In order to facilitate the input/output of objects, many systems use the same representation in the main memory as the objects existing in the secondary memory, and thus transfer from the servers to the client entire pages of memory. A typical optimization that takes place at the time of loading of objects from the secondary memory to the main memory buffers is the conversion of OIDs. The OIDs are changed from (complex) pointers to secondary memory into (simple) pointers to main memory. This operation takes the name *pointer swizzling*, and is justified by the greater efficiency and compactness of the main memory addresses compared to those of the secondary memory. In general, the pointer is *rewritten* exactly above the OID, leaving the page structure unaltered. To optimize the conversion process, the conversion from OID to main memory pointer can be at the first time when an application really uses the pointer. At the time of reloading of the objects in the secondary memory, it is necessary to carry out the reverse conversion. Suitable data structures on the client maintain the correspondence between pointers in the main memory and the original OID value.

11.5.4 Transactions

On a transactional level, object-oriented databases offer, in addition to the classic ACID transaction properties, also less restrictive mechanisms, which facilitate the co-operation among users. Let us look briefly at the requirements of some of these mechanisms.

* In concurrency control, *check-out* operations are normally defined. These allow the loading of entire objects to the workstation on which a user is operating, at the same time allowing other users to access the object on the database. In this way, the user may work on an object for long work sessions, at the same time allowing other users to have access to the object present on the server. Obviously, the dual operation of *check-in*, in which the object is returned to the server, requires the co-operation with the other users, who must be informed of the changes to the object.

* Another method for guaranteeing concurrent co-operative processes is based on the use of *versions*, that is, various copies of the same object at different times. In this case, it is also possible to define relations between objects that represent the evolution constraints between different versions. This problem is particularly critical in the context of CASE tools, in which it is necessary to allow for and to document the evolution of software and to guarantee that various versions constitute a unique logical unit (for example, with respect to the process of compilation and linking).

* In some applications, *long transactions* can be expected. An example is the transaction that occurs between the check-in and check-out of an object, which can be transferred to a design workstation for days at a time; yet, from the viewpoint of the other users, the changes constitute a unique, long transaction.

* Finally, transactions can be composed of *nested transactions*. This approach, which can also be developed for relational systems, occurs when a client process must create a unique task by communicating with various distinct servers that do not allow the use of global transactions. In this case, the global atomicity is obtained by means of co-ordination

between several, low-level, acid transactions. The most typical example is the organization of a trip, which might require access to a hotel booking system, a car hire company and the booking systems of various airlines. Each insertion or cancellation operation on one of the DBMSs is managed like an ACID transaction. Now, consider the case where it is impossible to book one of the resources, but this is revealed only after the booking of many of the others. Then, the cancellation of the booking already confirmed takes place through *compensating transactions*, activated by the co-ordinator of the complex transaction. The global atomicity is guaranteed when all compensation activities terminate. Co-ordination of activities is under the responsibility of a complex transaction manager.

11.5.5 Distribution and interoperability: CORBA

The object-oriented programming paradigm is suggested for the construction of distributed and heterogeneous software systems. The modularity inherent in the separation between interface and implementation guarantees a level of transparency that can also hide the data distribution.

CORBA (Common Object Request Broker Architecture) is an emerging architecture for the management of distributed objects, proposed by the Object Management Group (OMG) in 1991 (version 1.1), and then updated in 1995 (version 2.0). The main objective of CORBA is to guarantee interoperability of distributed objects, which client processes can access by invoking their methods. The clients do not need to know the location of objects or the language in which the methods are implemented; it is sufficient to know their interfaces. Object interfaces are defined by means of an *interface definition language*, IDL. IDL uses the same syntactic conventions as C++ and does not place any particular emphasis on data management. Nonetheless, it is compatible with ODL, the language proposed by ODMG for the standardization of OODBMS interfaces, which we saw in Section 11.2.1. The descriptive power of IDL is strictly included in the descriptive power of ODL.

The CORBA architecture consists of three elements.

- The *client* sends requests about objects. The interfaces for using the objects written in IDL are available to the client in the form of libraries. It is possible to have both static interfaces (precompiled), called *stubs*, which define a fixed way in which the clients invoke the services, or dynamic interfaces, which allow an invocation of services at execution time. The clients can also access services provided by request managers, described below.

- The *request manager* or *object request broker* (ORB) receives the request for objects by the clients and is responsible for identifying the objects in a distributed system. The ORB prepares the implementation of the objects to receive requests and to manage communications; after a client request it transfers control to the object adaptors or directly to the implementation of the objects. In case of error, the ORB transmits exceptions to the clients. The ORB also offers services to clients and object implementation, described below.

- The *object adaptor* offers services for access to object implementations, including the activation and de-activation of objects and of their implementation, and the recording of new implementations.

- *Object implementation* provides object semantics, using given data structures and method implementations. These are accessible using a *skeleton* written in IDL. An implementation can, in turn, require services made available by the object adaptor or the ORB.

Figure 11.7 illustrates the interactions among clients, request managers, adaptors and object implementations, according to CORBA architecture. Note that the modules with rounded corners refer to applications (clients and object implementations), while all the other modules are part of the CORBA architecture. The dynamic invocation libraries and the stubs of static descriptions are linked to the client codes, while the IDL skeletons are linked to the object implementation codes. The ORB service interface is identical for all the ORB implementations, while each type of object has a given stub and a skeleton. Finally, there can be various object adaptors, each presenting the same object from a different viewpoint. The main advantage of this architecture is the ability of clients to connect to remote objects without knowing the details about their location and implementation. Clients interact with ORBs provided by different vendors and are not sensitive to object evolution as long as objects do not change their interfaces; of course,

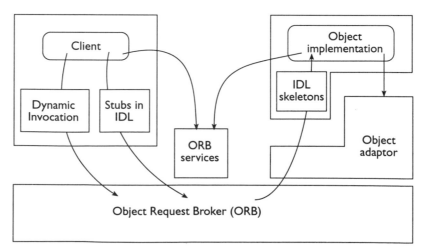

Figure 11.7   Interaction among the four components of a CORBA architecture.

implementations must continue to provide the correct application semantics. Another advantage of invocation of methods in CORBA is that IDL supports generalization hierarchies, and thus makes it possible for object methods to be inherited.

In version 2.0 of the standard, a series of services has been defined, the creation of which is still proceeding. We list a few of the most important services.

- *Object services* guarantee object functions, including durability, transactions, concurrency control, privacy, time management and notification of events. These services are presented as components described in IDL and extend the functionality of ORB systems.

- *Common facilities* define rules for the use of objects. They specialize in four application domains. The domains are:

  o user interfaces;

  o information management (including mechanisms for the management and exchange of documents);

  o system management (including installation, configuration and repair of distributed objects);

  o task management, to support the co-ordination of tasks (workflow) and the organization of task-performing agents.

OMG is continuously asking for new services to be proposed and then developed, through a mechanism of public dissemination. From the transaction point of view, CORBA adheres to the X-OPEN DTP standard, described in Section 10.5.2. Clients become transactional by invoking appropriate methods that are part of a transactional service added to CORBA 2.0, which includes the start and the termination of the transactions. These methods guarantee the ACID properties of the transactions and manage the logs and locks as described in Chapter 9 and Chapter 10.

11.6 Bibliography

Various texts are specifically dedicated to object-oriented databases, including the books by Bertino and Martino [10], Cattel [13] and Loomis [56]. The book edited by Bancilhon, Delobel, and Kanellakis [6], contains various articles on the O2 system. The first article contains the *Manifesto of object-oriented databases* mentioned in the text. The standard ODMG-93 and the ODL and OQL languages are described Cattel [13], while the CORBA architecture is described in various OMG publications, including Siegel [77]. A global view of relational and object-oriented databases is offered by Stonebraker [79], while the *Manifesto on third generation databases* is published as Stonebraker et al. [81]. Multimedia databases are described in the book by Subrahmanian [83]. A classic text on spatial data structures is that by Samet [73].

11.7 Exercises

Exercise 11.1 Define a class GEOMETRICFIGURE and three subclasses SQUARE, CIRCLE and RECTANGLE. Define a method Area, the implementation of which in GEOMETRICFIGURE returns the value zero, while in the sub-classes it is evaluated as a function of the properties of the given sub-classes. Show the invocation of the method by a program that scans a list of geometric figures of an arbitrary nature.

Exercise 11.2 Define a data dictionary of an object-oriented database. Suggest the introduction of classes and hierarchies concerning various concepts of an object-oriented schema, classes, atomic types, types structured using various constructors, generalization hierarchies and methods with their input/output parameters. Populate the data dictionary with data that describes part of the schema dealing with the management of automobiles, described in Figure 11.2. Then think of a query that allows, for example, the extraction of a list of the classes and methods with covariant redefinition of the output parameters.

Exercise 11.3 Consider the following schema of an O2 object-oriented database:

```
add class City
    type tuple(Name: string,
               Nation: string,
               Monuments: set(Monuments),
               Hotels: list(Hotel));

add class Hotel
    type tuple(Name: string,
               Address: tuple(Street: string,
                              City: City,
                              Number: integer,
                              PostCode: string);
               Stars: integer,
               Features: list(string));

add class Place
    type tuple(Name: string,
               Photograph: Bitmap,
               Address: tuple(Street: string,
                              City: City,
                              Number: integer,
                              PostCode: string);
               ThingsToSee: set(TouristService));

add class Monument inherits Place
    type tuple(ConstructionDate: date,
               ClosingDays: list(string),
               AdmissionPrice: integer,
               Architect: Person);
```

```
add class TouristService
    type tuple(Name: string,
               Places: set(Place),
               Cost: integer);

add class Theatre inherits Monument
    type tuple(ShowDays: list(date))

add class TheatreShow
    type tuple(Title: string,
               Place: Theatre,
               Character: Person,
               Rehearsals: set(date));

add class Concert inherits TheatreShow
    type tuple(Characters: Director,
               Orchestra: set(Musicians));

add class Person
    type tuple(Name: string,
               TaxCode: string,
               Nationality: string);

add class Director inherits Person
    type tuple(Appointment: Theatre);

add class Musician inherits Person
    type tuple(Instruments: set(string));
```

1. Graphically describe the above schema as illustrated in Figure 11.2.

2. Define the initialization methods of the classes PLACE, MONUMENT and THEATRE, reusing the methods while descending along the generalization hierarchy.

3. Which property of the schema is redefined in a covariant way?

4. Define the signature of the initialization method of a theatre show and then refine the signature in a covariant way in the input parameters whenever the show is a concert.

5. Give an example of invocation of the method defined above, in which it is not possible to verify its accuracy at the time of compilation.

Exercise 11.4 Describe the schema of the object-oriented database of Exercise 11.3 using the standard ODMG-93. Describe it graphically using the method illustrated in Figure 11.4.

Exercise 11.5 With reference to the object-oriented database schema in Exercise 11.3, write the following queries in OQL:

1. Extract the names of the four star hotels in Como.

2. Extract the names and costs of tourist services offered in Paris.

3. Extract the names of the five star hotels in the cities in which concerts conducted by Muti are planned.

4. Extract the names of the monuments in Paris created by Italian architects.

5. Extract the tourist services on offer partly in Paris and partly in another city.

6. Extract the names of the artistic directors of a theatre where no concerts are presented.

7. Extract the title of the concert, conductor, musicians and instruments used by each musician in the concerts of 12-2-99 in Milan.

8. Extract the cities having more than 10 monuments and fewer than five hotels.

9. Extract the names of the French architects who are also musicians.

10. Extract the total number of concerts conducted by Muti in either Italian or French theatres.

11. Extract the total number of concerts given in each Italian theatre.

12. Classify the monuments in Paris according to the date of construction. Use the classifications: 'Renaissance' (from 1450 to 1550), 'Baroque' (from 1550 to 1800), 'Imperial' (from 1800 to 1900), 'Modern' (from 1900 to today), and count the number of elements in each class.

Exercise 11.6 Use the SQL-3 syntax to describe the object model presented in Exercise 11.3 (represent O2 lists as sets).

Exercise 11.7 Considering the SQL-3 database schema introduced in the previous exercise, express the following queries in SQL-3.

1. Retrieve the names of the cities having 'Liechtenstein' as nation.

2. Retrieve the names of the musicians playing in the concerts directed by Karajan.

3. Retrieve the names of the monuments in London constructed in the 17th Century and closed on Mondays.

4. Retrieve the names of the directors who perform at theatres different from those to which they are affiliated.

5. Retrieve, for each theatre, the titles of all of the concerts that are planned for the year 2000.

Exercise 11.8 Build a 2d-tree and quadtree representation of the sequence of bi-dimensional points: A(5,4), B(3,3) C(6,2), D(2,2), E(4,6), F(1,1), G(7,5).

How many intermediate nodes appear, in the two representations, between A and F and between A and G?

Exercise 11.9 With reference to the object-oriented database schema of Exercise 11.3, indicate a choice of complex indexes for the efficient management of the path expressions that are most used by the queries of Exercise 11.5.

12
Active databases

An active database system is a DBMS that supports an integrated subsystem for the definition and management of production rules (active rules). The rules follow the *event-condition-action* paradigm: each rule reacts to some events, evaluates a condition and, based on the truth value of the condition, might carry out an action. The execution of the rules happens under the control of an autonomous subsystem, known as the *rule engine*, which keeps track of the events that have occurred and schedules the rules for execution. Thus, an active database system can execute either transactions, which are explicitly initiated by the users, or rules, which are under the control of the system. We say that the resulting system exhibits a *reactive behaviour*, which differs from the typical passive behaviour of a DBMS without active rules.

When a DBMS is active, the part of the application that is normally encoded by programs can also be expressed by means of active rules. As we shall see, active rules can, for example, manage integrity constraints, calculate derived data and manage exceptions, as well as pursue business objectives. This phenomenon adds a new dimension to the independence of the database, called *knowledge independence*: knowledge of a reactive type is removed from the application programs and coded in the form of active rules. Knowledge independence introduces an important advantage, because rules are defined with the DDL and are part of the schema, and therefore they are shared by all the applications, instead of being replicated in all the application programs. Modifications to the reactive behaviour can be managed by simply changing the active rules, without the need to modify the applications.

Many prototype systems, both relational and object-oriented, provide active rules that are particularly expressive and powerful. In this chapter, we will concentrate on active databases supported by relational DBMSs; almost all relational systems support simple active rules, called *triggers*, and therefore can be considered active databases in their own right. In this chapter we will use the terms 'active rule' and 'trigger' as synonymous.

Unfortunately, there is no consolidated standard proposal for triggers, as they were not defined in SQL-2. Thus, first we will give a general description, which can be adapted easily enough to any relational system. Next, we will describe the syntax and semantics of two specific relational systems, Oracle and DB2. Covering DB2 is particularly useful because the SQL-3 standard for active rules includes a standardization of triggers that uses the same solutions as DB2. We will complete this chapter with a discussion on properties of active databases and with an illustration of their applications.

12.1 Trigger behaviour in a relational system

The creation of triggers is part of the *data definition language* (DDL). Triggers can be dynamically created and dropped; in some systems they can also be dynamically activated and deactivated. Triggers are based on the event-condition-action (ECA) paradigm:

- the events are data manipulation primitives in SQL (insert, delete, update);

- the condition (which can sometimes be omitted) is a boolean predicate, expressed in SQL;

- the action is a sequence of generic SQL primitives, sometimes enriched by an integrated programming language available within the environment of a specific product (for example, PL/SQL in Oracle).

Triggers respond to events relating to a given table, called the trigger's *target*.

The ECA paradigm behaves in a simple and intuitive way: *when* the event is verified, *if* the condition is satisfied, *then* the action is carried out. It is said that a trigger is *activated* by the event, is *considered* during the verification of its condition and is *executed* if the condition is true, and therefore the action part is carried out. However, there are significant differences in the ways in that systems define the activation, consideration and execution of triggers.

Relational triggers have two levels of granularity, called *row-level* and *statement-level*. In the first case, activation takes place for each tuple involved in the operation; we say that the system has a tuple-oriented behaviour. In the second case, activation takes place only once for each SQL primitive, referring to all the tuples invoked by the primitive, with a set-oriented behaviour. Furthermore, triggers can have *immediate* or *deferred* functionality. The evaluation of immediate triggers normally happens immediately after the events that activated them (*after* option). Less often, the evaluation of immediate triggers logically precedes the event to which it refers (*before* option). The deferred evaluation of triggers happens at the end of the transaction, following a commit-work command.

Triggers can activate themselves one after another. This happens when the action of a trigger is also the event of another trigger. In this case, it is said that the triggers are *cascading*. Triggers can also activate themselves one after another indefinitely, generating a computation that does not terminate. We will address this problem in Section 12.5.

12.2 Definition and use of triggers in Oracle

We will look first at the syntactic characteristics of the command to create triggers, and will then demonstrate their behaviour using a typical application.

12.2.1 Trigger syntax in Oracle

The syntax for the creation of triggers in Oracle is as follows:

```
create trigger TriggerName
        Mode Event {, Event}
        on TargetTable
        [[referencing Reference]
          for each row
            [when SQLPredicate]]
        PL/SQLBlock
```

The *Mode* is before or after, the *Event* is insert, delete, or update; update may be followed by attribute names of the target table. The referencing clause allows the introduction of variable names, for referring to the old and new values of the row that is changed, with one or both of the following clauses:

```
old as OldVariable
| new as NewVariable
```

We will now discuss the various characteristics in detail. Each trigger controls any combination of the three DML update primitives (insert, delete, and update) on the target table. The granularity of triggers is determined by the optional clause for each row, which is present in the case of row-level granularity, while it is omitted in the case of statement-level granularity. The condition (*SQLPredicate*) can be present only in the triggers with row-level granularity and consists of a simple predicate on the current tuple. Triggers with statement-level granularity, however, may substitute condition predicates with the control structures of the action part. The action, both with row and statement-level granularity, is written in PL/SQL, which extends SQL by adding the typical constructs of a programming language (as shown in Appendix C). The action part cannot contain DDL instructions or transactional commands.

References to the before (old) and after (new) states of the row that is modified are possible only if a trigger is row-level. In the case of insert only the after state is defined, and in the case of delete only the before state is defined. The old and new variables are implicitly available to indicate, respectively, the old and new state of a tuple. Variable names other than old and new can be introduced by the referencing clause.

12.2.2 Behaviour of triggers in Oracle

Triggers in Oracle are immediate and allow for both the before and after options on both row- and statement-level granularity. Thus, combining the two granularities and the two functions, four combinations are obtained for each event:

```
before row
before statement
after row
after statment
```

The execution of an insert, delete or update statement in SQL is interwoven with the execution of the triggers that are activated by them, according to the following algorithm:

1. The before statement-level triggers are considered and possibly executed.

2. For each tuple of the target table involved in the statement:

   (a) the before row-level triggers are considered and possibly executed.
   (b) the statement is applied to the tuple, and then the integrity checks relative to the tuple are carried out.
   (c) the after row-level triggers are considered and possibly executed.

3. The integrity checks for the entire table are carried out.

4. The after statement-level triggers are considered and possibly executed.

If an error occurs during the evaluation or one trigger, then all the modifications carried out as a consequence of the SQL primitive that activates the trigger execution are undone. Oracle thus guarantees a *partial rollback* of the primitive and of all the actions caused by the triggers. Early versions of Oracle imposed a limit of one trigger per kind (before/after row/statement); recent versions have abolished these limitations, without, however, indicating how to prioritize triggers of the same kind that are activated by the same event.

The actions carried out by the triggers can cause the activation of other triggers. In this case, the execution of the current trigger is suspended and the other activated triggers are considered, by recursively applying the algorithm illustrated above. The highest number of triggers in *cascade* (that is, activated in sequence according to this schema) is 32. Once this level is reached, the system assumes that an infinite execution has occurred and suspends the execution, raising a specific exception.

12.2.3 Example of execution

We illustrate triggers in Oracle by showing them at work on a classical warehouse management problem. The Reorder trigger, illustrated below, is used to generate a new order automatically, by entering a tuple in the PENDINGORDERS table, whenever the available quantity, QtyAvbl, of a particular part of the WAREHOUSE table falls below a specific reorder level (QtyLimit):

```
create trigger Reorder
after update of QtyAvbl on Warehouse
when (new.QtyAvbl < new.QtyLimit)
for each row
    declare
        X number;
    begin
        select count(*) into X
        from PendingOrders
        where Part = new.Part;
        if X = 0
        then
            insert into PendingOrders
            values (new.Part, new.QtyReord, sysdate);
        end if;
    end;
```

This trigger has a row-level granularity and is considered immediately after each modification of the attribute QtyAvbl. The condition is evaluated row by row, comparing the values of the attributes QtyAvbl and QtyLimit; it is true if the available quantity falls below the limit. The action is a program written in PL/SQL. In the program, a numeric variable X is initially declared; it stores the number of orders already placed for the part being considered. We assume that PENDINGORDERS is emptied when the corresponding parts are delivered to the warehouse; at each time, only one order should be present for each part. Thus, if X is not zero, no new order is issued. If instead X is zero, an order is generated by inserting a tuple into the table PENDINGORDERS. The order contains the part numbers, the reorder quantity QtyReord (assumed to be fixed) and the current date. The values of the tuples that refer to the execution of the trigger are accessed by use of the correlation variable new. Assume that the initial content of the WAREHOUSE table is as shown in Figure 12.1.

WAREHOUSE	Part	QtyAvbl	QtyLimit	QtyReord
	1	200	150	100
	2	780	500	200
	3	450	400	120

Figure 12.1 Initial state of the WAREHOUSE table.

Consider then the following transaction activated on 10/10/1999:

```
T1: update Warehouse
    set QtyAvbl = QtyAvbl - 70
    where Part = 1
```

This transaction causes the activation, consideration and execution of the Reorder trigger, causing the insertion into the PENDINGORDERS table of the tuple (1, 100, 10/10/1999). Suppose that next the following transaction is carried out:

```
T2: update Warehouse
    set QtyAvbl = QtyAvbl - 60
    where Part <= 3
```

The trigger is thus considered for all parts, and the condition is verified for parts 1 and 3. However, the action on part 1 has no effect, because we assume that PENDINGORDERS still contains the tuple relating to part 1. Thus, the execution of the trigger causes the insertion into PENDINGORDERS of the single tuple (3, 120, 10/10/1999), relating to part 3.

12.3 Definition and use of triggers in DB2

In this section we will first look at the syntactic characteristics of the create trigger command, and will then discuss its behaviour and an application example.

12.3.1 Trigger syntax in DB2

Each trigger in DB2 is activated by a single event, which can be any data modification primitive in SQL. As in Oracle, triggers are activated immediately, before or after the event to which they refer, and have both row and statement-level granularity. The syntax of the creation instruction for triggers is as follows:

```
create trigger TriggerName
    Mode Event on TargetTable
    [referencing Reference]
    for each Level
    [when (SQLPredicate)]
    SQLProceduralStatement
```

where the *Mode* is before or after, the *Event* is insert, delete, or update (update may be followed by attributes of the target table), and the *Level* is row or statement. The referencing clause allows the introduction of variable names. If the level is row, the variables refer to the tuple that is changed; they are defined by the clauses:

```
old as OldTupleVar
| new as NewTupleVar
```

If the level is statement, then the variables refer to the table that is changed, with the clauses:

```
old_table as OldTableVar
| new_table as NewTableVar
```

As in Oracle, variables old, new, old_table and new_table are implicitly available, while the referencing clause enables the introduction of different variables. In the case of insertion, only the new or new_table variables are defined; in the case of deletion, only the old and old_table variables are defined.

12.3.2 Behaviour of triggers in DB2

In DB2, triggers activated before an event, the *before-triggers*, are used only to determine errors and to modify the values assigned to the new variables. These cannot contain DML commands that cause a modification of the state of the database, and thus cannot activate other triggers. The system guarantees a behaviour in which the side-effects of the before-triggers become visible before the execution of the SQL primitive that activates them. The before-triggers can thus require the prior evaluation of the new values produced by the SQL primitive, which are stored in temporary data structures.

Various triggers on different levels of granularity can refer to the same event. These are considered in an order managed by the system, which takes into account their time of creation. Row-level and statement-level triggers can be ordered arbitrarily (while in Oracle the relative ordering between triggers of different granularity is fixed, as illustrated by the algorithm in Section 12.2.2). If an action of a trigger with row-level granularity contains many SQL primitives, they are all carried out for one tuple before moving on to the next.

DB2 manuals describe precisely how the evaluation of triggers is carried out with reference to integrity constraints, in particular the referential ones, which are associated with a compensation action. Following a primitive S, the consideration and execution of the before-triggers are first carried out, and can cause modifications to the new variables. Then, the actions that are required for referential integrity are carried out. These actions can cause the activation of many triggers, which are added to the after-trigger activated by S. Finally, the system considers and executes all the activated triggers, based on their system-defined priorities. When the execution of these triggers contains SQL statements that may cause the activation of other triggers, the state of execution of the rule scheduling algorithm is saved and the system reacts by considering the triggers that were subsequently activated, thus initiating a recursive evaluation. At the end, the state of execution of the rule scheduling algorithm is restored, and the execution of the trigger that was suspended is resumed.

12.3.3 Example of execution

Consider a database containing the tables PART, DISTRIBUTOR, and AUDIT. The PART table has as its primary key the attribute, PartNum; it has also three other attributes, Supplier, City and Cost. A referential integrity constraint is present in the table PART and refers to the DISTRIBUTOR table:

```
foreign key (Supplier)
      references Distributor
      on delete set null
```

Let us consider the following triggers:

- SoleSupplier is a before-trigger that prevents the modification of the

Supplier attribute unless it is changed to the null value. In all the other cases, this gives an exception that forces a rollback of the primitive.

- AuditPart is an after-trigger that records in the AUDIT table the number of tuples modified in the PART table.

```
create trigger SoleSupplier
before update of Supplier on Part
referencing new as N
for each row
when (N.Supplier is not null)
    signal sqlstate '70005' ('Cannot change supplier')

create trigger AuditPart
after update on Part
referencing old_table as OT
for each statement
insert into Audit
    values(user, current-date, (select count(*) from OT))
```

For example, the removal from the DISTRIBUTOR table of all the suppliers located in Penang causes the violation of the referential integrity constraint. At this point, the management policy for violations of the constraint causes the modification to the null value of all the tuples of the PART table that remain dangling after the deletion. This activates the two triggers SoleSupplier and AuditPart. The first is a before-trigger, which is thus considered first. Its evaluation, tuple by tuple, happens logically before the modification, but it has available the N value, which describes the variation. Thus, this value is found to be NULL, and the condition is found to be false. Finally, the AuditPart trigger is activated, inserting into the table AUDIT a single tuple containing the user code, the current data and the number of modified tuples.

12.4 Advanced features of active rules

Building on the basic characteristics of relational triggers, seen above, some advanced systems and prototypes of active database systems have various characteristics that increase the expressive power of active rules. Their advanced features are as follows.

Temporal and user-defined events With regard to events, these can include *temporal* or *user-defined* events. The first ones allow the expression of time-dependent events such as, for example, 'every Friday evening' or 'at 17:30 on 20/6/1999'. User defined events are explicitly named and then raised by users' programs. For instance, a 'high-water' user-defined event could be defined and then raised by an application; the raising would activate a rule that reacts to the event.

Event expressions The activation of triggers can depend not only on a single event, but also on a set of events with a simple disjunctive interpretation. Activation can also depend on generic *boolean expressions of* *events*, constructed according to more complex operators, such as precedence among events and the conjunction of events.

Instead-of mode   As well as the `before` and `after` modes, there is also another mode, called `instead of`. When the condition of the corresponding rule is true, the action is carried out in place of the activation event. However, rules with `instead` `of` modes may give rather complex and unintuitive semantics (such as: 'when updating the salary of X, instead update the salary of Y'); therefore, this clause is not present in most systems.

Detached consideration and execution   The consideration and/or execution of rules can be *detached*. In this case, the consideration or execution would take place in the context of another transaction, which can be completely independent or can be co-ordinated with the transaction in which the event is verified, using mechanisms of reciprocal dependence.

Priorities   The conflicts between rules activated by the same event can be resolved by *explicit priorities*, defined directly by the user when the rule is created. They can be expressed either as a partial ordering (using precedence relations between rules), or as a total ordering (using numeric priorities). The explicit priorities substitute priority mechanisms implicitly present in the systems.

Rule sets   Rules can be organized in *sets* and each rule set can be separately *activated* and *deactivated*.

12.5 Properties of active rules

It is not difficult to design each individual active rule, once its event, condition and action are clearly identified. However, understanding the collective behaviour of active rules is more complex, because their interaction is often subtle. For this reason, the main problem in the design of active databases lies in understanding the behaviour of complex sets of rules. The main properties of these rules are termination, confluence and identical observable behaviour.

- A set of rules guarantees *termination* when, for each transaction that may activate the execution of rules, this execution produces a final state in a finite number of steps.

- A set of rules guarantees *confluence* when, for each transaction that may activate the execution of rules, the execution terminates producing a unique final state, which does not depend on the order of execution of rules.

- A set of rules guarantees an *identical observable behaviour* when, for each transaction that may activate the execution of rules, this execution is confluent and all the visible actions carried out by the rule are identical and produced in the same order.

These properties are not of equal importance or desirability. In particular, termination is an essential property; we must avoid a situation in which transactions, activated by the user, cause infinite executions normally revealed by the raising of an exception when the maximum number of recursively executed rules is exceeded. Note that infinite executions are due to rules written by the database administrator, and the user would have great difficulty in understanding the situation and finding a remedy. On the other hand, confluence and identical observable behaviour might not be essential, especially in the presence of various equally acceptable solutions of the same problem.

The process of *rule analysis* allows the verification of whether the properties requested are valid for a particular set of rules. In particular, an essential tool for verifying the termination of a set of rules is the *activation graph*, which represents interactions among rules. The graph is created by adding a node for each rule and an arc from a rule R_1 to a rule R_2 when the action of R_1 contains a DML primitive that is also one of the events of R_2. A necessary condition for non-termination is the presence of cycles in the activation graph: only in this case we can have an infinite sequence of execution of rules. An example of an activation graph is shown in Figure 12.2.

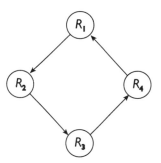

Figure 12.2 Cyclic activation graph.

Systems with many active rules are often cyclic. However, only a few cycles actually correspond to critical situations. In fact, cyclicity is a necessary but not sufficient condition for non-termination. Most cycles are indeed 'innocuous', as they describe an acceptable mutual interaction between rules.

Let us consider, for example, the rule SalaryControl (written in DB2), which creates a 'conservative' policy of salary control. It reduces the salary of all the employees when the average salary goes beyond a certain level:

```
create trigger SalaryControl
after update of Salary on Employee
then update Employee
      set Salary = 0.9 * Salary
      where (select avg(Salary) from Employee) > 100
```

The activation graph for this rule has only one node and a ring; thus, it presents a cycle, which indicates the possibility that the rule is re-activated by itself. On the other hand, whatever the initial transaction, the execution of the rule eventually terminates, as the rule progressively reduces the salaries until they are again within the established level. At this point, the condition is false. However, a slightly different rule, which gives a rise of salary rather than decreasing it, presents termination problems:

```
create trigger SalaryControl2
after update of Salary on Employee
then update Employee
      set Salary = 1.1 * Salary
      where (select avg(Salary) from Employee) > 100
```

The activation graph associated with this rule does not change. However, if the rule is executed once, it will be executed an infinite number of times, causing non-termination, as the operation carried out by the rule is unable to make its condition false.

This example shows that the cycles give only 'indications' of possible causes of non-termination. A detailed analysis of cycles, which can be partly automated, can give rise to the conclusion that a cycle is innocuous, or instead to suggest modifications to rules that guarantee its termination.

12.6 Applications of active databases

Active rules respond to several application needs. Many classic applications of active rules are *internal* to the database: the active rule manager works as a subsystem of the DBMS to implement some of its functions. In this case, triggers are generated by the system and are thus not visible to the users. The typical characteristic of internal applications is the possibility of giving a *declarative specification* of the functions, from which to derive the active rules. The main functions that can be entrusted to active rules of an internal type include the management of integrity constraints of a predefined structure, the calculation of derived data, and the management of replicated data. Other functions include version management, privacy management, data security enforcement and event logging.

Other rules, classified as *external*, express knowledge specific to the application, which are beyond predefined and rigid schemas. These rules are also called *business rules* as they express the strategies of a company for carrying out its primary functions (see also Chapter 5 and Chapter 6). In the case of business rules, there are no fixed techniques for the derivation of rules based on specifications. Consequently, each problem must be confronted separately. Below, we will look briefly at referential integrity and then we show some business rules.

12.6.1 Referential integrity management

The management of integrity constraints using active rules requires first that the constraint be expressed in the form of an SQL predicate. The predicate will correspond to the *condition* part of one or more active rules associated with the constraint; note, however, that the predicate must be negated in the rule, so that the consideration yields a truth value when the constraint is actually violated. After this, the designer will concentrate on the events that can cause a violation of the constraint. They contribute to the *event* parts of active rules. Finally, the designer will have to decide which action to carry out following the violation of the constraint. For example, the action could be to force the partial rollback of the primitive that has caused the violation, or could carry out a *repair action*, which corrects the violation of the constraint. This is how the action part of the active rule is constructed.

We illustrate this general approach to integrity maintenance with active rules by means of the classical referential integrity constraint. Note, however, that most systems manage referential integrity by means of ad hoc methods.

We look again at the simple referential integrity constraint discussed in Section 4.1.7. Given the tables EMPLOYEE and DEPARTMENT, the constraint indicates that the Dept attribute of EMPLOYEE is a *foreign key*, referencing the attribute DeptName of DEPARTMENT. The referential integrity specification is given by means of the following clause, inserted into the definition of the EMPLOYEE table:

```
foreign key(Dept) references Department(DeptName)
    on delete set null,
    on update cascade
```

We may consider the *foreign key* clause as a declarative specification of both the condition of the constraint and of the repair actions that must be performed to restore the database consistency. The operations that can violate this constraint are:

- insert into EMPLOYEE;

- delete from DEPARTMENT;

- update to EMPLOYEE.Dept;

- update to DEPARTMENT.DeptName.

The constraint can be expressed as an assertion for the table EMPLOYEE, which imposes for each employee the existence of a department to which the employee belongs:

```
exists (select * from Department
        where DeptName = Employee.Dept)
```

Note that this assertion indicates a property that must be true for all employees, but in an active rule, we are interested in capturing the situations that violate the constraint. We will therefore use the negation of the assertion illustrated above as the basis for building the condition to be included within the active rules:

```
not exists (select * from Department
            where DeptName = Employee.Dept)
```

The constraint can also be expressed as an assertion, already presented in negative form, for the table, DEPARTMENT. In this case, the constraint is violated if there is an employee without a department:

```
exists (select * from Employee
        where Dept not in
                (select Deptname from Department))
```

We then need to construct four active rules. Two react to each insertion in EMPLOYEE or modification of the Dept attribute, cancelling the effect of the operations if they violate the constraint. Remember that, according to the definition of referential integrity, violations caused by operations on the internal table have to cause a rejection of the operation. The other two rules react to each deletion from DEPARTMENT or update of the Dept attribute, and implement the policies specified with the constraint.

The first rule is coded by the following trigger in DB2:

```
create trigger DeptRef1
after insert on Employee
for each row
when (not exists
     (select * from Department
      where DeptName = New.Dept))
signal sqlstate '70006' ('employee without department');
```

The second rule is the same except for the event:

```
create trigger DeptRef2
after update of Dept on Employee
for each row
when (not exists
     (select * from Department
      where DeptName = New.Dept))
signal sqlstate '70006' ('employee without department');
```

The third rule reacts to the cancellation of a tuple of DEPARTMENT, imposing a null value on the attribute Dept of the tuples involved:

```
create trigger DeptRef3
after delete on Department
for each row
when (exists
     (select * from Employee
      where Dept = Old.Deptname))
update Employee
    set Dept = null
    where Dept = Old.Deptname
```

Note that the condition is simpler than that shown above. It identifies as critical those employees whose departments coincide with a department removed by the delete operation. In fact, the condition could even be omitted, as the action is performed on all and only the tuples that satisfy the condition.

The fourth rule reacts to modification of the attribute DeptName of DEPARTMENT, reproducing on EMPLOYEE the same modification on the Dept attribute as in the DEPARTMENT table:

```
create trigger DeptRef4
after update of Department on Deptname
for each row
when (exists
      (select * from Employee
       where DeptName = Old.DeptName))
update Employee
    set Dept = New.Deptname
    where Dept = Old.Deptname
```

Note that in this case, too, the condition is optimized and could even be omitted.

12.6.2 Business rules

Business rules express the strategies of a company in pursuing its objectives. Examples are the rules that describe the buying and selling of stocks based on the fluctuations in the market, rules for the management of a transport network or of energy, or rules for the management of a warehouse based on the variations of available quantities of each part (see Section 12.2.3). Some of these rules are simple *alerters*, which limit themselves to the action part and emit messages and warnings, leaving the users to manage abnormal situations.

Business rules have already been introduced in Section 5.3.1 to express schema constraints. Remember that these were classified as integrity or derivation rules. Integrity rules are predicates that express conditions that must be true. In commercial DBMSs, they can be programmed using the check clause or using *assertions*. However, many DBMSs introduce restrictions on the predicate that are expressible using these clauses, thus limiting their effective usability. Furthermore, the use of SQL-2 constraints goes together with adopting the reaction policies present in the standard (or supported by DBMSs), while the desired reaction is often different. Therefore, active rules (which are supported by most relational DBMSs) can be used for the specification and implementation of 'generic' constraints and 'arbitrary' reactions.

Let us look at how we can program the business rule BR2 introduced in Section 5.3.1, using an active rule. The business rule is repeated here: (BR2) *an employee must not have a salary greater than that of the manager of the department to which he or she belongs.*

Let us use the tables EMPLOYEE and DEPARTMENT, where EmpNum is the primary key of EMPLOYEE and DeptNum is the primary key of DEPARTMENT; EMPLOYEE has the attributes Mgr, Salary, and DeptNum, and DEPARTMENT has the attribute Director. The operations that can violate the constraint are the update of the salary of the employees in their double role as employee and manager, and the insertion of a new employee. Let us suppose that among these, the critical modification to be monitored is the increase in the salary awarded to an employee. Let us also suppose that the reaction policy is to block the update, and to signal this behaviour. These choices correspond to the following trigger, written using the DB2 syntax:

```
create trigger ExcessiveSalary
after update on Salary of Employee
for each row
when New.Salary > select Salary
                  from Employee
                  where EmpNum in
                        (select Director
                         from Department
                         where DeptNum = New.DeptNum)
then signal sqlstate '70005' ('Salary too high')
```

The rules concerning warehouse management or the handling of suppliers, illustrated in Section 12.2.3 and Section 12.3.3, can be considered as other examples of application-specific business rules.

Business rules are particularly advantageous when they express the reactive policies at schema level (and are thus valid for all applications) because they allow an unambiguous and centralized specification. This allows the property of *knowledge independence*, discussed in the introductory section to this chapter.

12.7 Bibliography

The book by Widom and Ceri [91], contains a thorough description of active database research prototypes, as well as a general introduction to commercial systems and applications. The book includes chapters dedicated to several research prototypes: Postgres, Ariel, Starburst, A-RDL, Chimera, Hipac, and Ode; two chapters also discuss commercial systems and applications. Furthermore, one of the six parts of Zaniolo et al. [94] is dedicated to active databases. A description of the triggers available in Oracle Server is discussed in their manuals: [65] and [64]. Triggers in IBM DB2 are described by Cochrane, Pirahesh, and Mattos [25], as well as in the book by Chamberlin [20] that gives a complete description of the DB2 system. The possibility of giving a declarative specification and then deriving the active rules was introduced by Ceri and Widom [19]. A methodology for design of databases that makes much use of active rules and also of object-oriented services is described in the book by Ceri and Fraternali [15].

12.8 Exercises

Exercise 12.1 Given the relational schema:

EMPLOYEE(<u>Name</u>, Salary, DeptNum)
DEPARTMENT(<u>DeptNum</u>, ManagerName)

define the following active rules in Oracle and DB2.

1. A rule that deletes all the employees belonging to a department when that department is deleted.

2. A rule that reacts to the deletion of the employee who is manager in a department by deleting that department and all its employees.

3. A rule that, each time that salary of an employee becomes higher than that of his or her manager, makes that salary equal to that of the manager.

4. A rule that, each time the salaries are modified, verifies that there are no departments in which the average salary increases more that three percent, and in this case cancels the modification.

5. A rule that, each time that the salaries are modified, verifies their average and if it is higher than 50 thousand, deletes all the employees whose salaries have been modified and are higher than 80 thousand.

Exercise 12.2 Referring to the active database system in Exercise 12.1, consider a database state with eight employees: Glenna, Mary, Tom, Bob, Andrew, Gary, Sandro and Clara, in which:

• Glenna is manager of department 1;

• Mary is manager of department 2, in which Tom and Andrew work;

• Gary is manager of department 3, in which Sandro and Clara work;

• Bob is manager of department 4.

Describe a SQL transaction that deletes the employee Glenna and then modifies some of the employees' salaries, thus activating rules 3–5. Describe the behaviour of triggers after these modifications; describe the state of the database after each statement and rule execution and at the end of the transaction.

Exercise 12.3 Discuss the properties of termination, confluence and observable determination for the rules of Exercise 12.1.

Exercise 12.4 Given the relational schema:

STUDENT(<u>Name</u>, Subject, Supervisor)
PROFESSOR(<u>Name</u>, Subject)
COURSE(<u>Title</u>, Professor)
EXAM(<u>StudentName</u>, <u>CourseTitle</u>)

Describe the triggers that manager the following integrity constraints (business rules):

1. Each student must work in the same area as his or her supervisor.

2. Each student must have taken at least three courses in the subject of his or her supervisor.

3. Each student must have taken the exam for the course taught by his or her supervisor.

13
Data analysis

Database technology, as illustrated in Chapter 9 and Chapter 10, was developed for supporting efficient and reliable on-line data management. Using *On Line Transaction Processing* (OLTP) technology, companies collect large amounts of data that enable their everyday operations. For example, banks collect data about their clients' transactions, and large supermarket chains collect data about their daily sales. This data could be useful to the companies not only on an operational level, but also for management, planning and decision support. For example, it could be possible to determine which of the financial products offered by a bank are the most successful, or observe the variations in sales of the various products in relation to the various promotions to evaluate their effectiveness. In practice, past and present data allows an analysis process essential for planning the future undertakings of the business.

For many decades, technological developments have neglected data analysis. It was thought that query languages were sufficient for both operational activity and for data analysis. Indeed, SQL allows the specification of complex queries, and thus offers some useful characteristics for data analysis (such as data aggregation). However, data analysis languages must be suitable for users who are not computer experts, and SQL is not sufficiently user-friendly for them. Moreover, it is extremely difficult to optimize data management so that it simultaneously satisfies the demands of analysis and operational applications; thus, the latter have generally prevailed over the former.

At the beginning of the nineties, parallel to the development of networks and data distribution products, a new architecture became popular, characterized by the *separation of environments*: alongside the traditional OLTP systems, other systems were developed, dedicated to *On-line Analytical Processing* (OLAP). This term states that data analysis happens on-line, that is, by means of interactive tools. The main element of OLAP architecture is the *data warehouse*, which carries out the same role as the database for OLTP architectures. New languages and paradigms were developed in order to facilitate data analysis by the OLAP clients. In this architecture, shown in Figure 13.1, OLTP systems carry out the role of data sources, providing data for the OLAP environment.

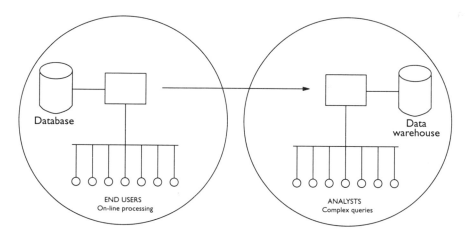

Figure 13.1 Separation between the OLTP and OLAP environments.

While the OLTP systems are normally shared by a high number of end users (mentioned in the first chapter), OLAP systems are characterized by the presence of few users (the 'analysts'), who perform strategic business functions and carry out decision support activities. In most cases, data analysis is carried out by a group of specialists who perform studies commissioned by their directors, in direct contact with the business management of their company. Sometimes, data analysis tools are used by managers themselves. There is a need, therefore, to provide the OLAP tools with user-friendly interfaces, to allow immediate and efficient decision-making, without the need for intermediaries.

While OLTP systems describe the 'current state' of an application, the data present in the warehouse can be historic; in many cases, full histories are stored, to describe data changes over a period. The data import mechanisms are usually asynchronous and periodical, so as not to overload the 'data sources', especially in the case of OLTP systems with particularly critical performances. Misalignments between data at OLTP sources and the data warehouse are generally acceptable for many data analysis applications, since analysis can still be carried out if data is not fully up-to-date.

Another important problem in the management of a warehouse is that of *data quality*. Often, the simple gathering of data in the warehouse does not allow significant analysis, as the data often contains many inaccuracies, errors and omissions. Finally, data warehouses support *data mining*, that is, the search for hidden information in the data.

In this chapter, we will first describe the architecture of a data warehouse, illustrating how it is decomposed into modules. We will then deal with the structure of the data warehouse and the new operations introduced into the data warehouse to facilitate data analysis. We will conclude the chapter with a brief description of the main data mining problems and techniques.

13.1 Data warehouse architecture

As illustrated in Figure 13.2, a data warehouse (DW) contains data that is extracted from one or more systems, called *data sources*. These include a large range of systems, including relational and object-oriented DBMSs, but also pre-relational DBMSs or file-based data organizations (*legacy systems*). For the extraction of data from heterogeneous sources and legacy systems, the techniques discussed in Section 10.6 are used.

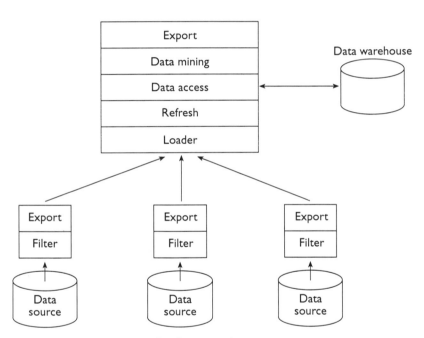

Figure 13.2 Architecture of a data warehouse.

The architecture of a DW contains the following components, which do not necessarily all have to be present. The first two components operate on the data source.

- The *filter* component checks data accuracy before its insertion into the warehouse. The filters can eliminate data that is clearly incorrect based on integrity constraints and rules relating to single *data sources*. They can also reveal, and sometimes correct, inconsistencies in the data extracted from multiple data sources. In this way, they perform data cleaning; this is essential to ensure a satisfactory level of data quality. It is important to proceed cautiously in the construction of warehouses, verifying data quality on small samples before carrying out a global loading.

- The *export* component is used for extracting data from the data sources. The process of extraction is normally incremental: the export component builds the collection of all the changes to the data source, which are next imported by the DW.

The next five components operate on the data warehouse.

- The *loader* is responsible for the initial loading of data into the DW. This component prepares the data for operational use, carrying out both ordering and aggregation operations and constructing the DW data structures. Typically, loader operations are carried out in batches when the DW is not used for analysis (for instance, at night). If the DW uses parallelism (illustrated in Section 10.7), this module also takes care of initial fragmentation of data. In some applications, characterized by a limited quantity of data, this module is invoked for loading the entire contents of the DW after each change to the data sources. More often, the DW data is incrementally updated by the refresh component, which is discussed next.

- The *refresh* component updates the contents of the DW by incrementally propagating to it the updates of the data sources. Changes in the data source are captured by means of two techniques: *data shipping* and *transaction shipping*. The first one uses triggers (see Chapter 12) installed in the data source, which, transparent to the applications, records deletions, insertions, and modifications in suitable *variation files*. Modifications are often treated as pairs of insertions and deletions. The second technique uses the transaction log (see Section 9.4.2) to construct the variation files. In both cases, the variation files are transmitted to the DW and then used to *refresh* the DW; old values are typically marked as historic data, but not deleted.

- The *data access* component is responsible for carrying out operations of data analysis. In the DW, this module efficiently computes complex relational queries, with joins, orderings, and complex aggregations. It also computes DW-specific new operations, such as *roll up*, *drill down* and *data cube*, which will be illustrated in Section 13.3. This module is paired with client systems that offer user-friendly interfaces, suitable for the data analysis specialist.

- The *data mining* component allows the execution of complex research on information 'hidden' within the data, using the techniques discussed in Section 13.5.

- The *export* component is used for exporting the data present in a warehouse to other DWs, thus creating a hierarchical architecture.

In addition, DWs are often provided with modules that support their design and management:

- A CASE environment for supporting DW design, similar to the tools illustrated in Chapter 7.

- The *data dictionary*, which describes the contents of the DW, useful for understanding which data analysis can be carried out. In practice, this component provides the users with a glossary, similar to the one described in Chapter 5.

We close this section about the DW architecture with some considerations regarding data quality. Data quality is an essential element for the success of a DW. If the stored data contains errors, the resulting analysis will necessarily produce erroneous results, and the use of the DW could at this point be counter-productive. Unfortunately, various factors prejudice data quality.

When source data has no integrity constraints, for example because it is managed by pre-relational technology, the quantity of *dirty data* is very high. Typical estimates indicate that erroneous data in commercial applications fluctuates between 5 and 30 percent of the total.

To obtain high levels of quality we must use filters, expressing a large number of integrity rules and either correcting or eliminating the data that does not satisfy these rules. More generally, the quality of a data source is improved by carefully observing the data production process, and ensuring that verification and correction of the data is carried out during data production.

13.2 Schemas for data warehouses

The construction of a company DW, which describes all the data present in a company, is an ambitious aim, often quite difficult to achieve. For this reason, the prevalent approach is to construct the DW by concentrating separately on simple subsets of company data (known as departmental data), for which the analytical aim is clear. Each simplified schema of departmental data takes the name *data mart*. Each data mart is organized according to a simple structure, called the *multidimensional schema* or, more simply, the *star schema*. The first term implies the presence of multiple dimensions of analysis; the second indicates the 'star' structure of the data mart schema once interpreted using the classic Entity-Relationship model.

13.2.1 Star schema

The star schema has a very simple structure, shown in Figure 13.3 using the Entity-Relationship model. A central entity represents the *facts* on which the analysis is focused. Various entities arranged in rays around it represent the *dimensions* of the analysis. Various one-to-many relationships connect each occurrence of fact to exactly one occurrence of each of the dimensions.

The schema in Figure 13.3 represents the management of a supermarket chain. The entity at the centre of the star represents the sales, that is, the

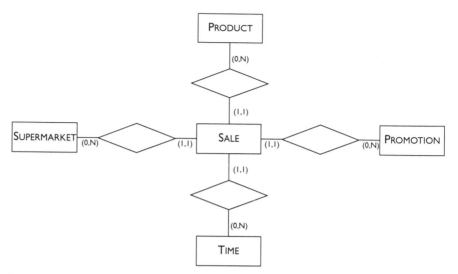

Figure 13.3   Data mart for a supermarket chain.

facts of interest; the dimensions represent the products sold, the supermarkets, the promotions and the times of each sale.

The schema in Figure 13.4 represents the management of payments by an insurance company. The entity at the centre of the star represents payments relating to those claims that are honoured by the company; the dimensions represent the insurance policies, the clients, the times and the types of problems that cause the claim.

The schema in Figure 13.5 represents the management of therapies in a group of hospitals. The entity at the centre of the star represents the

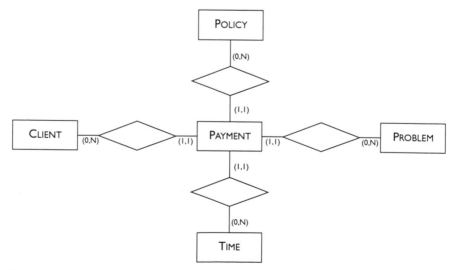

Figure 13.4   Data mart for an insurance company.

therapies; dimensions represent the illnesses, the patients, the doctors in charge and the hospitals to which the patients are admitted.

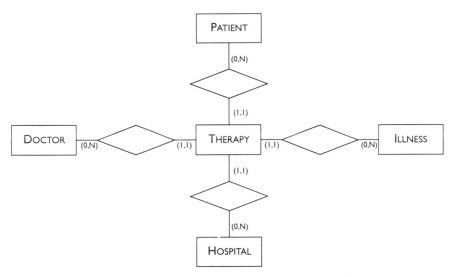

Figure 13.5 Data mart for a medical information system.

As shown in the three data marts, the main characteristic of the star schema is the use of a regular structure, independent of the problem under consideration. Obviously, the number of dimensions can be different, but at least two dimensions are needed (because, otherwise, the model degenerates into a simple one-to-many hierarchy). A high number of dimensions is also inadvisable, because data analysis can then become too complex.

13.2.2 Star schema for a supermarket chain

Let us look more closely at the data mart for the management of a supermarket chain, showing the relational schema corresponding to the E-R schema. By applying the translation techniques presented in Chapter 7, we translate one-to-many relationships by giving to the central entity an identifier composed of the set of the identifiers of each dimension. Thus, each tuple of the SALE relation has four codes, **ProdCode**, **MarketCode**, **PromoCode** and **TimeCode**, which, taken together, form a primary key. We can thus better describe an elementary sale as the set of all the sales that are carried out in a unit of time, relating to a product, acquired with a promotion and in a particular supermarket. Each occurrence of sale is thus in its turn an item of aggregated data. The non-key attributes are the quantity sold (**Qty**) and the amount of revenues (**Revenue**). We assume that each sale is for one and one only promotion, and we deal with the sales of products having no promotions by relating it to a 'dummy' occurrence of promotion.

Let us now look at the attributes for the four dimensions.

- The products are identified by the code (ProdCode) and have as attributes Name, Category, Subcategory, Brand, Weight, and Supplier.

- The supermarkets are identified by the code (MarketCode) and have as attributes Name, City, Region, Zone, Size, and Layout of the supermarket (e.g., on one floor or on two floors, and so on).

- The promotions are identified by the code (PromoCode) and have as attributes Name, Type, discount Percentage, FlagCoupon, (which indicates the presence of coupons in newspapers), StartDate and EndDate of the promotions, Cost and advertising Agency.

- Time is identified by the code (TimeCode) and has attributes that describe the day of sale within the week (DayWk: Sunday to Saturday), of the month (DayMonth: 1 to 31) and the year (DayYear: 1 to 365), then the week within the month (WeekMonth) and the year (WeekYear), then the month within the year (MonthYear), the Season, the PreholidayFlag, which indicates whether the sale happens on a day before a holiday and finally the HolidayFlag, which indicates whether the sale happens during a holiday.

Dimensions, in general, present redundancies (due to the lack of normalization, see Chapter 8) and derived data. For example, in the time dimension, from the day of the year and a calendar we can derive the values of all the other time-related attributes. Similarly, if a city appears several times in the SUPERMARKET relation, its region and zone are repeated. Redundancy is introduced to facilitate as much as possible the data analysis operations and to make them more efficient; for example, to allow the selection of all the sales that happen in April or on a Monday before a holiday.

The E-R schema is translated, using the techniques discussed in Chapter 7, into a logical relational schema, arranged as follows:

SALE(<u>ProdCode</u>, <u>MarketCode</u>, <u>PromoCode</u>, <u>TimeCode</u>, Qty, Revenue)
PRODUCT(<u>ProdCode</u>, Name, Category, SubCategory, Brand, Weight, Supplier)
MARKET(<u>MarketCode</u>, Name, City, Region, Zone, Size, Layout)
PROMOTION(<u>PromoCode</u>, Name, Type, Percentage, FlagCoupon, StartDate,
EndDate, Cost, Agency)
TIME(<u>TimeCode</u>, DayWeek, DayMonth, DayYear, WeekMonth, WeekYear,
MonthYear, Season, PreholidayFlag, HolidayFlag)

The fact relation is in Boyce–Codd normal form (see Chapter 8), in that each attribute that is not a key depends functionally on the sole key of the relation. On the other hand, as we have discussed above, dimensions are generally non-normalized relations. Finally, there are four referential integrity constraints between each of the attributes that make up the key of the fact table and the dimension tables. Each of the four codes that make up the key of the fact table is an external key, referencing to the dimension table which has it as primary key.

13.2.3 Snowflake schema

The *snowflake schema* is an evolution of the simple star schema in which the dimensions are structured hierarchically. The schema is introduced to take into account the presence of non-normalized dimensions. Figure 13.6 illustrates the data mart for the management of supermarkets, represented by the snowflake schema. While the dimensions of the promotions are unchanged, the other dimensions are organized hierarchically:

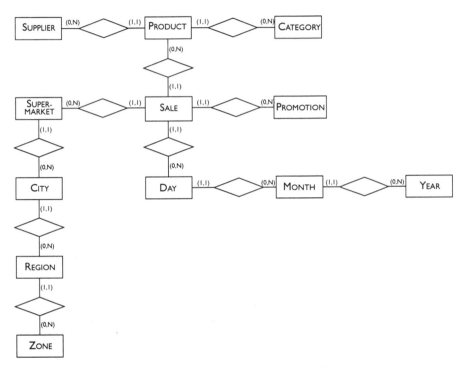

Figure 13.6 Snowflake schema for a supermarket chain.

- The dimensions of supermarkets are structured according to the hierarchy ZONE, REGION, CITY, SUPERMARKET. Each zone includes many regions, each region includes many cities, and each city has one or more supermarkets.

- The PRODUCT dimension is represented by a hierarchy with two new entities, the SUPPLIER and the CATEGORY of the product.

- The time dimension is structured according to the hierarchy DAY, MONTH, and YEAR.

Attributes of the star schema are distributed to the various entities of the snowflake schema, thus eliminating (or reducing) the sources of redundancy.

All the relationships described in Figure 13.6 are one-to-many, as each occurrence is connected to one and one only occurrence of the levels immediately above it.

The main advantage of the star schema is its simplicity, which, as we will see in the next section, allows the creation of only very simple interfaces for the formulation of queries. The snowflake schema represents the hierarchies explicitly, thus reducing redundancies and anomalies, but it is slightly more complex. However, easy-to-use interfaces are also available with this schema in order to support the preparation of queries. Below, we will assume the use of the star schema, leaving the reader to deal with the generalization in the case of the snowflake schema.

13.3 Operations for data analysis

We now illustrate the interfaces for the formulation of queries and introduce some operations to increase the expressive power of query languages.

13.3.1 Query formulation interfaces

Conducting data analysis for a given data mart, organized according to the star schema, requires first the extraction of a subset of facts and dimensions, based on the needs of the particular data analysis activity. These data extractions follow a standard paradigm: dimensions are used to select the data and to group it, while aggregate functions are usually applied to facts. It is thus possible to construct predefined modules for data retrieval from the DW, in which predefined choices are offered for the selection, aggregation and evaluation of aggregate functions.

Figure 13.7 shows a data retrieval interface for the data mart in Section 13.2.2. As regards the dimensions, three attributes are pre-selected: the name of the promotion, the name of the product, and the month of sale. For each fact, the quantities of sales are selected. The value 'Supersaver' is inserted into the lower part of the module. Supersaver identifies this particular promotion, thus indicating the interest in the sales obtained through it. Similarly, the value intervals 'pasta' and 'oil' (for products) and 'February' to 'April' are selected. The last row of the data extraction interface defines the structure of the result, which should include the dimensions PRODUCT (including the selected values 'pasta' and 'oil') and TIME (ranging between 'February' and 'April') and the total quantity of sales.

PROMOTION.Name	PRODUCT.Name	TIME.Month	Qty	Schema
Three for two	Wine	Jan...Dec		
Coupon 15%	Pasta			Options
SuperSaver	Oil			
SuperSaver	Pasta...Oil	Feb...Apr		Condition
	PRODUCT.Name	TIME.Month	sum	View

Figure 13.7 Interface for the formulation of an OLAP query.

This interface corresponds to an SQL query with a predefined structure, which is completed by the choices introduced by the user. In the query there are join clauses (which connect the table of facts to the dimensions), selection clauses (which extract the relevant data), grouping, ordering, and aggregation clauses:

```
select D1.C1, ... Dn.Cn, Aggr1(F.C1), ... Aggrn(F.Cn)
from Fact as F, Dimension1 as D1, ... DimensionN as Dn
where join-condition(F, D1)
  and ...
  and join-condition(F, Dn)
  and selection-condition
group by D1.C1, ... Dn.Cn
order by D1.C1, ... Dn.Cn
```

In the specific case, the query constructed according to the user choices is as follows:

```
select Time.Month, Product.Name, sum(Qty)
from Sale, Time, Product
where Sale.TimeCode = Time.TimeCode
  and Sale.ProductCode = Product.ProductCode
  and Sale.PromoCode = Promotion.PromoCode
  and (Product.Name = 'Pasta' or Product.Name = 'Oil')
  and Time.Month between 'Feb' and 'Apr'
  and Promotion.Name = 'SuperSaver'
group by Time.Month, Product.Name
order by Time.Month, Product.Name
```

The query result can be presented on the OLAP client in matrix or in graph form. In matrix form, dimensions correspond to the rows and columns, and facts correspond to the cells, as in a spreadsheet (Figure 13.8).

	Feb	Mar	Apr
Oil	5K	5K	7K
Pasta	45K	50K	51K

Figure 13.8 Result of the OLAP query.

This data representation is quite widely used by the analysis tools, as it enables spreadsheet operations upon the query results. Classical bar graphs or pie charts can be used to visualize data; for example, bar graphs may use different colours to represent different types of product at different times. In the following, we will keep a relational representation, and we will concentrate only on the total quantity of pasta sold (Figure 13.9).

13.3.2 Drill-down and roll-up

The spreadsheet analogy is not limited to the presentation of data. In fact, we have two additional data manipulation primitives that originate from two typical spreadsheet operations: *drill-down* and *roll-up*.

Time.Month	Product.Name	sum(Qty)
Feb	Pasta	45K
Mar	Pasta	50K
Apr	Pasta	51K

Figure 13.9 Subset of the result of the OLAP query.

Drill-down allows the addition of a dimension of analysis, thus dis-aggregating the data. For example, a user could be interested in adding the distribution of the quantity sold in the sales zones, carrying out the drill-down operation on **Zone**. Supposing that the attribute Zone assumes the values 'North', 'Centre' and 'South', we obtain the table shown in Figure 13.17.

Time.Month	Product.Name	Zone	sum(Qty)
Feb	Pasta	North	18K
Feb	Pasta	Centre	15K
Feb	Pasta	South	12K
Mar	Pasta	North	18K
Mar	Pasta	Centre	18K
Mar	Pasta	South	14K
Apr	Pasta	North	18K
Apr	Pasta	Centre	17K
Apr	Pasta	South	16K

Figure 13.10 Drill-down of the table represented in Figure 13.9.

Roll-up allows instead the elimination of an analysis dimension, re-aggregating the data. For example, a user might decide that sub-dividing by zone is more useful than sub-dividing by monthly sales. This result is obtained by carrying out the roll-up operation on **Month**, obtaining the result shown in Figure 13.18.

Product.Name	Zone	sum(Qty)
Pasta	North	54K
Pasta	Centre	50K
Pasta	South	42K

Figure 13.11 Roll-up of the table represented in Figure 13.10.

By alternating roll-up and drill-down operations, the analyst can better highlight the dimensions that have greater influence over the phenomena represented by the facts. Note that the roll-up operation can be carried out by operating on the results of the query, while the drill-down operation requires in general a reformulation and re-evaluation of the query, as it requires the addition of columns to the query result.

13.3.3 Data cube

The recurring use of aggregations suggested the introduction of a very powerful operator, known as the *data cube*, to carry out all the possible aggregations present in a table extracted for analysis. We will describe the operator using an example. Let us suppose that the DW contains the following table, which describes car sales. We will show the sole tuples relating to the red Ferraris or red Porsches sold between 1998 and 1999 (Figure 13.12).

Make	Year	Colour	Sales
Ferrari	1998	Red	50
Ferrari	1999	Red	85
Porsche	1998	Red	80

Figure 13.12 View on a SALE summary table.

The data cube is constructed by adding the clause with cube to a query that contains a group by clause. For example, consider the following query:

```
select Make, Year, Colour, sum(Sales)
from Sales
where (Make = 'Ferrari' or Make = 'Porsche')
  and Colour = 'Red'
  and Year between 1998 and 1999
group by Make, Year, Colour
with cube
```

This query extracts all the aggregates constructed by grouping in a combined way the tuples according to the three dimensions of analysis (Make, Year and Colour). The aggregation is represented by the polymorphic value ALL, which (like NULL) is present in all the domains and corresponds to all the possible values present in the domain (Figure 13.13).

A spatial representation of the data cube structure is shown in Figure 13.14. The diagram shows a cartesian space constructed on three axes, corresponding to the domains of three attributes. In this simple example, the domain Make assumes the values 'Ferrari' and 'Porsche', the domain Year assumes the values 1998 and 1999, and the domain Colour assumes the value 'Red'. The points in the space represent the tuples of Figure 13.12. Note that not all the points are normally present in the DW. In our example, three out of four are present. The three cartesian planes represent the aggregations of one dimension, the cartesian axes represent the aggregations of two dimensions and the origin of the cartesian axes represents the aggregation of all three dimensions. Obviously, a conceptually similar cartesian

Make	Year	Colour	sum(Sales)
Ferrari	1998	Red	50
Ferrari	1999	Red	85
Ferrari	1998	ALL	50
Ferrari	1999	ALL	85
Ferrari	ALL	Red	135
Ferrari	ALL	ALL	135
Porsche	1998	Red	80
Porsche	1998	ALL	80
Porsche	ALL	Red	80
Porsche	ALL	ALL	80
ALL	1998	Red	130
ALL	1999	Red	85
ALL	ALL	Red	215
ALL	1998	ALL	130
ALL	1999	ALL	85
ALL	ALL	ALL	215

Figure 13.13 Data cube of the table represented in Figure 13.12.

representation in space of n dimensions is possible in the case of data cube with an arbitrary number of grouping attributes.

The complexity of the evaluation of the data cube increases exponentially with the increase of the number of attributes that are grouped. A different extension of SQL builds progressive aggregations rather than building all possible aggregations; thus, the complexity of the evaluation of this operation increases only in a linear fashion with the increase of the number

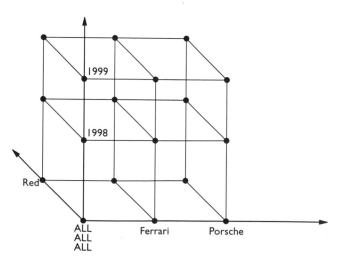

Figure 13.14 Spatial representation of the data cube of Figure 13.13.

of grouping attributes. This extension requires the with roll up clause, which replaces the with cube clause, as illustrated in the following example:

```
select Make, Year, Colour, sum(Sales)
from Sales
where (Make = 'Ferrari' or Make = 'Porsche')
  and Colour = 'Red'
  and Year between 1998 and 1999
group by Make, Year, Colour
with roll up
```

The result of the evaluation of this query is shown in Figure 13.5.

Make	Year	Colour	sum(Sales)
Ferrari	1998	Red	50
Ferrari	1999	Red	85
Porsche	1998	Red	80
Ferrari	1998	ALL	50
Ferrari	1999	ALL	85
Porsche	1998	ALL	80
Ferrari	ALL	ALL	135
Porsche	ALL	ALL	80
ALL	ALL	ALL	215

Figure 13.15 Roll-up of the table represented in Figure 13.12.

Note the progression of the aggregations, from right to left, and note that the result has fewer tuples than the result of the data cube operation.

The with cube and with roll up queries are present in many relational DBMSs and do not necessarily require the presence of a DW. In any case, an interpretation of the two queries according to the star model is always possible, as the attributes of the group by clause carry out the role of dimensions, while the remaining attributes of the select clause describe the aggregate operations applied to facts.

13.4 Development of the data warehouse

There are two alternative approaches to the development of a DW.

- The first approach consists of the use of relational technology, suitably adapted and extended. The data is stored using tables, but the analysis operations are carried out efficiently using special data structures. This type of system is called ROLAP (Relational OLAP).

- The second, more radical, approach consists of storing data directly in multi dimensional form, using vector data structures. This type of system is called MOLAP (Multi-dimensional OLAP).

The MOLAP solution is adopted by a large number of specialized products in the management of data marts. The ROLAP solution is used by large relational vendors. These add OLAP-specific solutions to all the technological experience of relational DBMSs, and thus it is very probable that ROLAP will prevail in the medium or long term.

In each case, the ROLAP and MOLAP technologies use innovative solutions for data access, in particular regarding the use of special indexes and view materialization (explained below). These solutions take into account the fact that the DW is essentially used for read operations and initial or progressive loading of data, while modifications and cancellations are rare. Large DWs also use parallelism, with appropriate fragmentation and allocation of data, to make the queries more efficient. Below, we will concentrate only on ROLAP technology.

13.4.1 Bitmap and join indexes

Bitmap indexes allow the efficient creation of conjunctions and disjunctions in selection conditions, or algebraic operations of union and intersection. These are based on the idea of representing each tuple as an element of a bit vector. The length of the vector equals the cardinality of the table. While the root and the intermediate nodes of a bitmap index remain unchanged (as with the indexes with B or B+ trees described in Chapter 9), the leaves of the indexes contain a vector for each value of the index. The bits in the vector are set to one for the tuples that contain that value and to zero otherwise.

Let us suppose for example that we wish to make use of a bitmap index on the attributes **Name** and **Agency** of the PROMOTION table, described in Section 13.2.2. To identify the tuple corresponding to the predicate `Name = 'SuperSaver'` and `Agency = 'PromoPlus'` we need only access the two vectors corresponding to the constants 'SuperSaver' and 'PromoPlus' separately, using indexes, extract them, and use an *and* bit by bit. The resulting vector will contain a one for the tuples that satisfy the condition, which are thus identified. Similar operations on bits allow the management of disjunctions.

Obviously, a bitmap index is difficult to manage if the table undergoes modifications. It is convenient to construct it during the data load operation, for a given cardinality of the table.

Join indexes allow the efficient execution of joins between the dimension tables and the fact tables. They extract those facts that satisfy conditions imposed by the dimensions. The join indexes are constructed on the dimension keys; their leaves, instead of pointing to tuples of dimensions, point to the tuples of the fact tables that contain those key values.

Referring again to the data mart described in Section 13.2.2, a join index on the attribute **PromoCode** will contain in its leaves references to the tuples of the facts corresponding to each promotion. It is also possible to construct join indexes on sets of keys of different dimensions, for example on **PromoCode** and **ProdCode**.

As always in the case of physical design (see Chapter 9), the use of bitmap and join indexes is subject to a cost–benefit analysis. The costs are essentially due to the necessity for constructing and storing indexes permanently, and the benefits are related to the actual use by the DW system for the resolution of queries.

13.4.2 View materialization

Many queries to the DW require repeated laborious aggregations and syntheses. In this case, it is convenient to evaluate views that express the aggregated data, and store them permanently. This technique is called *view materialization*. For example, in the data mart relating to the management of the supermarkets, a materialized view could contain the sales data aggregated by product, or the monthly sales of each store. The queries about these aggregations would be directly carried out on the materialized view, instead of in the DW.

The choice of views to be materialized is quite a complex problem, which requires the knowledge of typical queries used in data marts and their frequency of execution. In general, a view is convenient when it can sensibly reduce the execution time of several frequently used queries.

As seen in Chapter 3, each view depends on a set of base tables. The materialization is very convenient in an environment such as the DW, in which the base tables are not continuously modified. When the tables are reloaded or incrementally modified, however, we must update the views, propagating the effects of the modifications on the base tables to them. As mentioned in Chapter 12, data derivation is a typical internal application of the active rules, which indeed can be used to incrementally update materialized views.

13.5 Data mining

The term *data mining* is used to characterize search techniques used on information hidden within the data of a DW. Data mining is used for market research, for example the identification of items bought together or in sequence so as to optimize the allocation of goods on the shelves of a store or the selective mailing of advertising material. Another application is behavioural analysis, for example the search for frauds and the illicit use of credit cards. Another application is the prediction of future costs based on historical series, for example, concerning medical treatments. Data mining is an interdisciplinary subject, which uses not only data management technology, but also statistics – for the definition of the quality of the observations – and artificial intelligence – in the process of discovering general knowledge out of data. Recently, data mining has acquired significant popularity and has guaranteed a competitive advantage for many commercial businesses, which have been able to improve their management and marketing policies.

13.5.1 The data mining process

The objective of data mining is the extraction of useful information from large sets of data. This task is carried out repetitively and adaptively, initiating a progressive extraction of knowledge, which is divided into four phases.

1. *Comprehension of the domain:* it is impossible to extract useful information if a good understanding of the application domain in which it operates is not developed beforehand.

2. *Preparation of the data set:* this step requires the identification of a subset of data of the DW on which to carry out the data mining. It also requires the encoding of data to make it suitable input to the data mining algorithm.

3. *Discovery of patterns:* this consists of the application of techniques of data mining on the data set extracted earlier, in order to discover repetitive patterns in the data. Later in the chapter, we will concentrate our attention especially on the techniques used in this step.

4. *Evaluation of patterns:* this consists of drawing implications from the discovered patterns, evaluating which experiments to carry out next and which hypothesis to formulate, or which consequences to draw in the process of knowledge discovery.

The data mining process has an impact when it allows operational decisions to be made, for example, modifying the allocation policies of the merchandise in the large store or changing the credit concession policies.

13.5.2 Data mining problems

Although each application has specific features, there are various general problems that have been identified with a regular, recurrent structure; these problems can be formalized and then solved by a suite of data mining algorithms. Usually, data mining algorithms are characterized by good scalability, that is, they guarantee good efficiency characteristics when applied to large data sets. Below, we will look at three classic problems: the discovery of association rules, discretization and classification.

Discovery or association rules Association rules discover regular patterns within large data sets, such as the presence of two items within a group of tuples. The classic example, called *basket analysis*, is the search for goods that are frequently purchased together. A table that describes purchase transactions in a large store is shown in Figure 13.16. Each tuple represents the purchase of specific merchandise. The transaction code for the purchase is present in all the tuples and is used to group together all the tuples in a purchase. Rules discover situations in which the presence of an item in a transaction is linked to the presence of another item with a high probability.

Transaction	Date	Goods	Qty	Price
1	17/12/98	ski-pants	1	140
1	17/12/98	boots	1	180
2	18/12/98	T-shirt	1	25
2	18/12/98	jacket	1	300
2	18/12/98	boots	1	70
3	18/12/98	jacket	1	300
4	19/12/98	jacket	1	300
4	19/12/98	T-shirt	3	25

Figure 13.16 Database for basket analysis.

More correctly, an association rule consists of a premise and a consequence. Both premise and consequence can be single items or groups of items. For example, the rule *skis → ski poles* indicates that the purchase of skis (premise) is often accompanied by the purchase of ski poles (consequence). A famous rule about supermarket sales, which is not obvious at first sight, indicates a connection between nappies (diapers) and beer. The rule can be explained by considering the fact that nappies are often bought by fathers (this purchase is both simple and voluminous, hence mothers are willing to delegate it), but many fathers are also typically attracted by beer. This rule has caused the increase in supermarket profit by simply moving the beer to the nappies department.

We can measure the quality of association rules precisely. Let us suppose that a group of tuples constitutes an observation; we can say that an observation satisfies the premise (consequence) of a rule if it contains at least one tuple for each of the items. We can than define the properties of support and confidence.

- *Support:* this is the fraction of observations that satisfy both the premise and the consequence of a rule.

- *Confidence:* this is the fraction of observations that satisfy the consequence among those observations that satisfy the premise.

Intuitively, the support measures the importance of a rule (how often premise and consequence are present) while confidence measures its reliability (how often, given the premise, the consequence is also present). The problem of data mining concerning the discovery of association rules is thus enunciated as: *find all the association rules with support and confidence higher than specified values.*

For example, Figure 13.17 shows the associative rules with support and confidence higher than or equal to 0.25. If, on the other hand, we were interested only in the rules that have both support and confidence higher than 0.4, we would only extract the rules *jacket → T-shirt* and *T-shirt → jacket*.

Premise	Consequence	Support	Confidence
ski-pants	boots	0.25	1
boots	ski-pants	0.25	0.5
T-shirt	boots	0.25	0.5
T-shirt	jacket	0.5	1
boots	T-shirt	0.25	0.5
boots	jacket	0.25	0.5
jacket	T-shirt	0.5	0.66
jacket	boots	0.25	0.33
{T-shirt, boots}	jacket	0.25	1
{T-shirt, jacket}	boots	0.25	0.5
{boots, jacket}	T-shirt	0.25	1

Figure 13.17 Association rules for the basket analysis database.

Variations on this problem, obtained using different data extractions but essentially the same search algorithm, allow many other queries to be answered. For example, the finding of merchandise sold together and with the same promotion, or of merchandise sold in the summer but not in the winter, or of merchandise sold together only when arranged together. Variations on the problem that require a different algorithm allow the study of time-dependent sales series, for example, the merchandise sold in sequence to the same client. A typical finding is a high number of purchases of video recorders shortly after the purchases of televisions. These rules are of obvious use in organizing promotional campaigns for mail order sales.

Association rules and the search for patterns allow the study of various problems beyond that of basket analysis. For example, in medicine, we can indicate which antibiotic resistances are simultaneously present in an antibiogram, or that diabetes can cause a loss of sight ten years after the onset of the disease.

Discretization This is a typical step in the preparation of data, which allows the representation of a continuous interval of values using a few discrete values, selected to make the phenomenon easier to see. For example, blood pressure values can be discretized simply by the three classes 'high', 'average' and 'low', and this operation can successively allow the correlation of discrete blood pressure values with the ingestion of a drug.

Classification This aims at the cataloguing of a phenomenon in a predefined class. The phenomenon is usually presented in the form of an elementary observation record (tuple). The *classifier* is an algorithm that carries out the classification. It is constructed automatically using a *training set* of data that consists of a set of already classified phenomena; then it is used for the classification of generic phenomena. Typically, the classifiers are presented as decision trees. In these trees the nodes are labelled by conditions that allow the making of decisions. The condition refers to the attributes of the relation that stores the phenomenon. When the phenomena are described by a large number of attributes, the classifiers also take responsibility for the selection of few significant attributes, separating them from the irrelevant ones.

Suppose we want to classify the policies of an insurance company, attributing to each one a high or low risk. Starting with a collection of observations that describe policies, the classifier initially determines that the sole significant attributes for definition of the risk of a policy are the age of the driver and the type of vehicle. It then constructs a decision tree, as shown in Figure 13.18. A high risk is attributed to all drivers below the age of 23, or to drivers of sports cars and trucks.

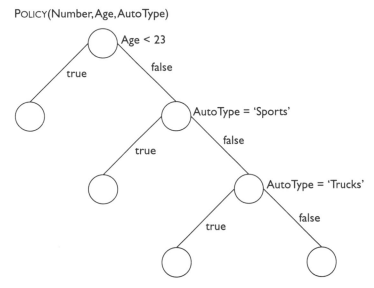

Figure 13.18 Classifier to identify risk policies.

13.5.3 Data mining perspectives

Data mining has been developed recently and is a result of various application demands. It is interdisciplinary, using large thematic areas of databases, artificial intelligence and statistics. It is a modern discipline, still in the early stages of development, but evolving very rapidly.

Observing the actual development of the discipline, some issues emerge. In the first place, it seems necessary and urgent that it is systematized, to allow the various problems of data mining to be viewed together. Up to now, they have been considered separately by researchers and managed using specific systems for each specific problem. We expect to see, in the near future, the definition of standard paradigms for the formulation of data mining problems and of general techniques for their resolution.

It is then necessary to deal with the management of large data sets. The current algorithms of data mining are not yet able to guarantee high scalability in the face of very large databases. The problem can be approached using sampling techniques, which consist of carrying out data mining on reduced – but significant – samples of the database.

Finally, we need to know the extent to which the data mining tools can be generic, that is, application-independent. In many cases, problems can be solved only if one takes into account the characteristics of the problems when proposing solutions. Aside from the general tools, which resolve the problems described in the section and few other problems of a general nature, there are also a very high number of problem-specific data mining tools. These last have the undoubted advantage of knowing about the application domain and can thus complete the data mining process more easily, especially concerning the interpretation of results; however, they are less generic and reusable.

13.6 Bibliography

In spite of the fact that the multi-dimensional data model was defined towards the end of the seventies, the first OLAP systems emerged only at the beginning of the nineties. A definition of the characteristics of OLAP and a list of rules that the OLAP systems must satisfy is given by Codd [31]. Although the sector was developed only a few years ago, many books describe design techniques for DWs. They include Inmon [49] and Kimball [53]. The data cube operator is introduced by Gray et al. [45].

The literature on data mining is still very recent. A systematic presentation of the problems of the sector can be found in the book edited by Fayyad et al. [40], which is a collection of various articles. Among them, we recommend the introductory article by Fayyad, Piatetsky-Shapiro and Smyth, and the one on association rules by Agrawal, Mannila and others.

13.7 Exercises

Exercise 13.1 Complete the data mart projects illustrated in Figure 13.4 and Figure 13.5, identifying the attributes of facts and dimensions.

Exercise 13.2 Design the data marts illustrated in Figure 13.4 and Figure 13.5, identifying the hierarchies among the dimensions.

Exercise 13.3 Refer to the data mart for the management of supermarkets, described in Section 13.2.2. Design an interactive interface for extraction of the data about classes of products sold in the various weeks of the year in stores located in large cities. Write the SQL query that corresponds to the proposed interface.

Exercise 13.4 Describe roll-up and drill-down operations relating to the result of the query posed in the preceding exercise.

Exercise 13.5 Describe the use of the with cube and with roll up clauses in conjunction with the query posed in Exercise 13.3.

Exercise 13.6 Indicate a selection of bitmap indexes, join indexes and materialized views for the data mart described in Section 13.2.2.

Exercise 13.7 Design a data mart for the management of university exams. Use as facts the results of the exams taken by the students. Use as dimensions the following:

1. time;

2. the location of the exam (supposing the faculty to be organized over more than one site);

3. the lecturers involved;

4. the characteristics of the students (for example, the data concerning pre-university school records, grades achieved in the university admission exam, and the chosen degree course).

Create both the star schema and the snowflake schema, and give their translation in relational form. Then express some interfaces for analysis simulating the execution of the roll up and drill down instructions. Finally, indicate a choice of bitmap indexes, join indexes and materialized views.

Exercise 13.8 Design one or more data marts for railway management. Use as facts the total number of daily passengers for each tariff on each train and on each section of the network. As dimensions, use the tariffs, the geographical position of the cities on the network, the composition of the train, the network maintenance and the daily delays.

Create one or more star schemas and give their translation in relational form.

Exercise 13.9 Consider the database in Figure 13.19. Extract the association rules with support and confidence higher or equal to 20 per cent. Then indicate which rules are extracted if a support higher than 50 percent is requested.

Exercise 13.10 Discretize the prices of the database in Exercise 13.9 into three values (low, average and high). Transform the data so that for each transaction a single tuple indicates the presence of at least one sale for each class. Then construct the association rules that indicate the simultaneous presence in the same transaction of sales belonging to different price classes. Finally, interpret the results.

Transaction	Date	Goods	Qty	Price
1	17/12/98	ski-pants	1	140
1	17/12/98	boots	1	180
2	18/12/98	ski-pole	1	20
2	18/12/98	T-shirt	1	25
2	18/12/98	jacket	1	200
2	18/12/98	boots	1	70
3	18/12/98	jacket	1	200
4	19/12/98	jacket	1	200
4	19/12/98	T-shirt	3	25
5	20/12/98	T-shirt	1	25
5	20/12/98	jacket	1	200
5	20/12/98	tie	1	25

Figure 13.19 Database for Exercise 13.9.

Exercise 13.11 Describe a database of car sales with the descriptions of the automobiles (sports cars, saloons, estates, etc.), the cost and cylinder capacity of the automobiles (discretized in classes), and the age and salary of the buyers (also discretized into classes). Then form hypotheses on the structure of a classifier showing the propensities of the purchase of cars by different categories of person.

14

Databases and the World Wide Web

The evolution of the Internet is one of the most important phenomena in information technology. The users are rapidly increasing in number and variety, from companies with high-speed networks to individuals with slow modem connections. Companies often arrange private networks that make use of the same protocols and tools developed and used on the Internet. These are called *intranets* and are sometimes connected to the Internet. A major technology on both Internet and intranets is the *World Wide Web* (WWW), often called simply the *Web*; the Web has introduced a new paradigm for both the dissemination and the acquisition of information, which is easy to use, flexible and economical.

The Web was originally an interface for access to distributed documents. It is now a platform for information systems of all types, having in common only the fact of being accessible, directly or indirectly, through generic tools, called *browsers*. Systems of this type are often called *Web Information Systems* (WIS); coupled to DBMSs, they are able to support and provide access to large amounts of data. For this reason, the inclusion of Web-based technology for data management is essential in a database textbook.

At the same time, WISs also present specific problems. In the first place, the type of supported information is highly heterogeneous. Since the beginning, the Web has been used to manage textual and multimedia information (images, audio, video). In contrast, traditional information systems mainly manage data that can be represented by means of simple data structures: sets of tuples with atomic values. In summary, the structure of the information managed through the Web is more complex and less structured and regular than that used in databases.

Another distinguishing feature of WISs is that they typically offer greater flexibility to the user in the interaction with the system: interaction is driven by the interest of the user rather than following pre-designed patterns. In contrast, users have limited opportunity for changing the data content. For instance, in electronic commerce, users can manipulate only the content of their private 'baskets', containing the sale details of the purchased goods, but cannot alter the content of the Web data describing offers.

Furthermore, the interaction between a Web browser and a source of information makes use of tools that are different from those used in traditional systems. Although the substantial standardization of browsers makes the interfaces fairly uniform, their characteristics can vary, depending on the device being used for accessing the Web. Think of the differences that can exist between the capabilities available on a powerful workstation with a big screen on a high-speed intranet and that of a portable computer with a small screen and a mobile telephone connection.

In addition, applications are offered to a very large community, all the Internet users. Therefore, the goals to be taken into account are much wider and more diverse than in traditional information systems.

For all these reasons, a rethinking of the WIS development process itself is required. This will apply both to the components explicitly developed and to those to be integrated into them.

In this chapter, we will look at the interaction between the techniques of databases and those of the Web. After recalling the fundamental concepts of the Internet and the Web, we will illustrate the evolution of WIS applications and the main categories into which they can be classified. In the two following sections we will deal with the aspects that are most relevant to databases. First, we address the problems concerning modelling and design of Web sites, by focusing on those Web sites in which data plays an important role. We call them *data-intensive Web sites* and we believe that their importance will increase significantly in the near future. Finally, we will deal with the technology for integrating Web sites and databases.

14.1 The Internet and the World Wide Web

We now give a brief overview of those aspects of the Internet and the World Wide Web that are a prerequisite for the rest of the chapter.

14.1.1 The Internet

The Internet can be defined as a federation of networks that communicate by means of the same set of protocols, those of the TCP/IP (*Transmission Control Protocol/ Internet Protocol*) family. Usually, a node of the Internet is part of a local network, which interconnects workstations or personal computers located within a small area. Local networks communicate with each other within network hierarchies, for example the network of a university, the network of all the universities in a country, an overall national network and so on.

Each node (computer) on the Internet has an *IP address*, which uniquely identifies it; IP addresses consist of four numbers, for example 131.175.21.1. Usually, a machine on the Internet also has a symbolic name, made up of identifiers separated by dots, which can be used instead of the IP address. For example, the symbolic name `morgana.elet.polimi.it` can be used to refer to the above IP address.

Through the address structure, the federal network organization becomes transparent, as the user (person or program) can refer to any node with a known address. From the logical point of view, each Internet node can connect directly with any other node. Communication takes place by means of a layered organization, which involves various protocols, including the already-mentioned TCP/IP, whose details go beyond the scope of this text. A fundamental characteristic of all the applications that operate on the Internet (and more generally on any other network that uses the TCP/IP protocols) is the adoption of the client-server paradigm, which we discussed in Section 10.1. The clients manage the interaction with the user and the servers carry out the requested operations, providing the clients with appropriate responses. Servers offer a set of predefined functions (in particular, Web services), based on standard protocols (such as HTTP), which in turn use the services provided by TCP/IP.

14.1.2 The World Wide Web

Let us introduce the World Wide Web through a series of steps. A *hypertext* is a document with a non-sequential structure, made up of various parts, related by means of links. The components can be directly accessed by following the links, without the rigidity of the sequential physical structure. To give a first example, let us illustrate how the content of a book could be organized by means of a hypertext, with a hierarchical structure (see Figure 14.1). The root contains a general description (for example the preface) and allows access to succeeding chapters, each of which is still organized with a possible brief introduction and links to its sections. In the course of the text, there can be references to one point or another (as in a traditional book there are references to pages or sections) or to a bibliography.

The concept of hypertext can be generalized in various ways. In the first place, we have spoken of a single document, while the same technique can be used to correlate many documents, originated by different people at different times. From the conceptual point of view, there is no difference between the internal links of a document and those to other documents. Furthermore, the documents can be not only textual but also of other types, such as images, video or audio. In this case, we refer to a *multimedia hypertext*, often abbreviated to *hypermedia*. Finally, as we are referring to the Internet, the set of documents that make up the hypermedia can be distributed over many nodes (see the schema in Figure 14.2). To summarize,

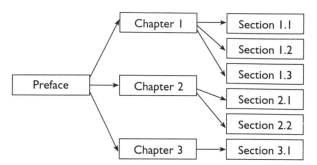

Figure 14.1 Hypertext with a hierarchical structure.

we can say that the World Wide Web is a *distributed multimedia hypertext* with *independent* components, as it connects documents of various types produced and maintained by different subjects over the Internet.

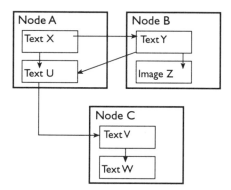

Figure 14.2 A distributed multimedia hypertext.

Not only does the Web allow access to static documents as described above, but it also offers the opportunity to launch programs that dynamically generate new pages. Thus, the generation of a given page can be based on contents extracted from a database.

The major technological components of the Web, which allow implementation of the ideas that we have described above, are briefly addressed below. They are the HTML (*HyperText Mark-up Language*) language, the URL (*Uniform Resource Locator*) concept for referencing resources, and the HTTP (*HyperText Transfer Protocol*) communication protocol.

14.1.3 HTML

The documents that make up the hypertext structure of the Web are written in HTML; HTML allows the formatting of documents and the description of hypertext links. We will not dwell on the details of HTML, but will highlight some important aspects.

HTML documents can be displayed by means of Web browsers (such as *Netscape Navigator* and *Microsoft Internet Explorer*), which can access local documents (behaving like a word processor in read-only mode) or documents located at remote sites. As regards formatting, it is important to underline that HTML describes the logical characteristics of a document and not the physical ones. For example, it can specify that a phrase must be emphasized, but not how the emphasis is created. This characteristic is very important, because the same document can be viewed by different clients, each with a different viewing device and browser. With modern browsers, the emphasis might be a change of font or a change of colour, whereas on a textual browser on an old-fashioned monochromatic terminal, it might be blinking.

As stated above, a fundamental feature of hypertexts is the possibility of creating links, connecting different documents or also different parts of the same document. The links are specified by associating a URL with a portion of text (or with an image), called an *anchor*. The URL specifies the resource (for example, the document or program) to which the anchor refers. The simplest form of URL consists of the specification of a local file. The text that forms an anchor is usually displayed underlined. When the user selects an anchor (by means of a mouse click), the browser requests the service corresponding to the URL. For example, an anchor with text `Charles Jones` and URL `charlie.html` causes the display of the string `Charles Jones` underlined; a click on that string opens the file `charlie.html` in the same directory.

A more general format for a URL is:

$$[Protocol://][Server/]Resource$$

where:

- the *Protocol* is one of those available on the Internet, for example HTTP (which we will look at below), FTP (for the remote transfer of files), Telnet (for terminal emulation) or an electronic mail protocol;

- the *Server* is usually specified by means of the symbolic name, but an IP address could be used as well;

- the *Resource* is in many cases a directory path followed by a file name, but can include parameters or can be an electronic mail address.

An example of a URL that uses the HTTP protocol to retrieve the file with the name `index.html` from the directory `vldb2001` of the server `www.dia.uniroma3.it` is:

<code>http://www.dia.uniroma3.it/vldb2001/index.html</code>

HTML also allows the creation of pages in which the users can insert values of parameters, to be sent to the server. These pages use the *form* construct, which provides fields where users may insert data. An *action* is associated with a form, specifying the URL of the program that must be executed when the form itself is completed (and 'submitted' to the Web server). The data specified by the user is transmitted to the program as parameters or as input data. The page can be used for providing content to be stored in the WIS (for example, by inserting tuples in a database), or for retrieving content, or for a mix of the two.

14.1.4 HTTP

The World Wide Web is operated by *HTTP servers* (also called *Web servers*), system programs that offer their services to browsers via HTTP, which in turn uses TCP (and then IP) at the lower level. HTTP consists of four phases.

1. *Opening the connection:* the browser (which has the role of client) contacts the HTTP server, at the address and with the protocol indicated in the URL, in order to verify the accuracy and availability. In particular, a TCP connection is requested;

2. *Establishment of the connection:* the server (if available) accepts the connection and sends a confirmation;

3. *Request:* the client sends a message to the server, with the request for a service, the details of the resource invoked and possible parameters for that invocation;

4. *Reply:* the server communicates whether the request can be satisfied and, if so, the results; at the same time, the server terminates the connection, without retaining any information to be used in subsequent connections.

It is important to underline the fact that the HTTP protocol has no memory (it is *stateless*). Thus, when a client issues several HTTP requests to the same server, the server itself is not able to maintain information about the operations already carried out on behalf of the same client and of their results. This choice is motivated by the simplicity of the protocol, which manages each request separately without keeping records of the context. Clearly, this represents a limitation of the protocol, because it becomes difficult to carry out procedures that require multiple interactions, such as those necessary for database transactions. We will briefly look at how we can overcome this limitation in Section 14.4.

14.1.5 Gateways

Web servers can invoke programs and pass parameters to them, such as the data input by the user in a form. Let us look at the basic concept, which we will develop in Section 14.4 with reference to database access. A *gateway* is any program called by a Web server. It can be a compiled program written in a high-level language, such as C, C++, or Java, or in interpretable languages such as Perl or Tcl (used for operations on strings), or even in scripting languages for operating system shells. As the name suggests, a gateway allows the establishment of a connection between the Web and another environment. A gateway is invoked by using a URL similar to those used for accessing an HTML file with the HTTP protocol. It thus specifies the name of the file, possibly preceded by the http:// string and by the specifications of the server and the directory. Parameters can be specified by appending them to the URL.

The communication mechanism between Web servers and gateways is called *Common Gateway Interface* (CGI) and is shown in Figure 14.3. It is divided as follows.

Figure 14.3   The CGI communication mechanism.

1. The user requests the URL by clicking on an anchor, or by sending a form. In both cases, parameters can be transmitted to the HTTP server. There are various techniques for the transmission of parameters, but we omit the details.

2. The server launches the gateway (also called a *CGI program*), according to the CGI protocol, and transmits the parameters.

3. The gateway is executed, with the parameters received, and possibly interacts with other resources, for example, a database.

4. The gateway returns the results to the Web server.

5. The Web server transmits the results to the client.

From our perspective, the most typical use of the CGI protocol is for interfacing a DBMS; in this case, the CGI program contains queries or updates to the database. We will return to this topic in Section 14.4.

14.2 Information systems on the Web

We said at the beginning of this chapter that the Web is a general interface for access to information systems of all types. We predict that in the near future it will become the standard interface, or at least the prevalent one. Certainly, the number of information systems on the Web (WIS) and their capability will increase rapidly. In order to prepare for a discussion on the role of databases in WISs, we need to identify the main categories of WIS.

Before entering into the discussion, an observation is appropriate. The Web originated in the scientific world, and it spread first through individual users and not professional ones. Only later did it become a working tool. A term often used to describe use of the Web is *surfing*, which suggests a usage that is superficial and recreational. We will focus on the Web as a device for pursuing processional or business-oriented objectives in the context of databases, where surfing is not a central issue. However, data-intensive applications offer large collections of data to end users, thus supporting forms of surfing.

14.2.1 Publication and consultation on the Web

The original objective of the Web was to make information available, in particular in the form of HTML pages. Many organizations use the Web for making information available to worldwide users. This information is organized in HTML pages that are usually purpose-built, although most of them are based on pre-existing information. The users of these systems *consult* the information *published* on the Web.

As the demand and the quantity of published information increases, it becomes apparent that the manual management of HTML documents is difficult.

- Data may change. These changes need to be propagated to the data content of the Web site, but the process is labour-intensive. Data is interconnected with the hypertext organization and the graphic presentation; this makes Web site evolution more difficult.

- The Web site can store data in a redundant fashion, in order to facilitate legibility and navigation. For example, consider the pages about university professors. On each of these pages there could be not only a link to the main page of the department, but also the name and address of the professor, which is the same as the address of the department. If the department changes its address, the modification would thus affect many pages.

These two problems are eased if data is stored in a database. This allows the pages to be constructed automatically,[1] supports the separation of the various aspects and eliminates the problems of redundancy.

The second main reason for the interaction of Web sites and databases is the fact that the information itself might already be stored in databases. In these cases, the reason for publication on the Web is to enable easier access to a large amount of relevant information, which can be published on the Web at relatively little cost.

14.2.2 Transactions on the Web

Initially, the databases accessible through the Web were updated by other means, such as already existing applications or specific functions for loading and modifying data, managed locally. A natural step at this point was to allow for updates through the Web, possibly through pages structurally

---

1. The fact that the page construction is static or dynamic, that is, on-line or off-line, is not important here. The crucial aspect is that the effort of construction of the pages is supported. We will return to this aspect in Section 14.5.

similar to those used for display, so distributing the work to different individuals. For example, in a university site, the updates concerning the staff of each department could be managed by the administration of the department itself. Access by means of the browser thus substitutes for other user interfaces, bringing the benefit of uniformity.

14.2.3 Electronic commerce and other new applications

Apart from the increased number of users and the uniformity of the interfaces, the applications described above can be thought of as traditional in the context of information systems. On the other hand, the Web has produced many new applications, which are possible due to the spirit of collaboration and participation that animates many of the Internet users.

One of the most important and challenging new applications is *electronic commerce*, that is, the use of the Web for selling goods and services. Many companies sell products on the Web, for example, books, software tools, air tickets, and so on; the information about offered products has to be organized and stored at the company's site, typically by means of a DBMS. This application is largely an extension of existing systems: traditional mail order is often based on information systems and databases, which are used only by company personnel. Now, with Web-based systems, access is offered directly to the purchaser. Clearly, the security problem becomes critical at this point, especially for the payment for sales, which is usually done by communicating credit card numbers on the Web.

Several other new applications of Web technology are less tightly connected with database technology, although they might need the support of a DBMS for the management of large data sets.

One new application is that of *discussion groups*. The discussion group idea has been taken up by commercial organizations; for example, the companies that sell books through the Web usually offer the possibility of writing comments and revisions, which become public property. The management of the information can be carried out by means of simple files, but, if the size increases, it can be useful to have the support of a database.

Further developments of the potential offered by the Web are affecting other types of systems. For example, support is being developed for forms of *co-operative work*. The idea has already been widespread in the technical and scientific community for years, and concerns tools, in particular software, able to harness the power of individual or group activity, also known as *Computer-Supported Cooperative Work* (CSCW). The most advanced forms of co-operative systems require the controlled sharing of documents and the co-ordination of activities and workflow. The software dedicated to this purpose, known as *workflow management systems* (WFMS), enables the organization of work within offices by controlling activities and the flow of the documents that they produce. The Internet provides a very useful infrastructure for the creation of workflow systems and the Web is the natural interface. It should be underlined, however, that a workflow often requires a level of structuring of activities and support of integrated and specific software systems that can be in conflict with the open nature of the Web. We can say that these applications are usually offered to a particular range of users who co-operate according to specific rules and make use of specific tools that are not generally available. Therefore, workflows are often used over intranets. However, sometimes the same infrastructure should be used for both protected and open applications. This need led to the development of *extranets*, networks that are controlled by given organizations, but are also open to some form of external access. On extranets, users are classified and each user is enabled to use different applications. A classical example is the extranet offered by express delivery companies, where information is provided by the company's employees in a protected way, but customers can monitor the delivery of their mail by using the same Web interfaces.

Another original aspect of the Web is the possibility of offering integrated services, handled by different subjects. Co-operation here can be loose or rigid. An example of the former is the 'list of useful links' or 'related sites', which are found on many pages; an example of the second is an interface that allows bibliographical search over many sites. An example of the latter is the activity of *data farming*: given the large amount of data available on the Web, a company or entity can acquire and organize information through the Web, possibly for integration into its data warehouse.

A different direction that is developing in WISs is that of *embedded* systems. These systems do not use traditional terminals or personal computers as interfaces, but use a range of devices, such as mobile phones, wireless palmtop computers, data collection devices or control systems for industrial installations. A common characteristic of these systems is the limitation of the resources (computing power, memory, bandwidth and size of display, if any). Currently, this type of system presents few aspects of specific interest from the point of view of databases. On the other hand, in the near future we expect a rapid growth of 'terminals' connected to the Internet, incorporated into vehicles or domestic appliances for example, and then the demand for database interaction will increase. As an example, consider a system in a vehicle that uses a GPS device to determine the position of the vehicle on any part of the Earth's surface and obtains, from the Web, weather or tourist information for the area. Alternatively, for domestic appliances, think of a system for carrying out maintenance and software updating through the Internet.

14.3 Design of data-intensive Web sites

In this section we will briefly discuss how the techniques for the design of databases, which we described in detail in Chapters 5–7, can be adapted for the design of Web sites. Clearly, the design of Web sites is a complex activity and cannot be dealt with in a few pages; we will therefore give an overview of the main issues.

Let us first clarify the extent of the design activity that we are now going to consider.

One could think of the *entire* Web as a unified source of information. This is not a helpful view, as there is no coherence in the form in which the information is offered, in its quality, substance or usability. At the other extreme, we could consider the Web as a set of 'independent pages', each of which constitutes a specific source of information. This is the point of view of the lists of *bookmarks* managed by browsers and of search engines, which select links to single pages. Both alternatives are obviously inappropriate for setting the scope of Web design. In fact, design has to concentrate on a system that is dedicated to a specific application need and under the control of a single subject, or at least of various co-ordinated subjects who share the same design goals. Since Web sites usually enjoy this property, we set Web sites as the extent of the design activity.

We further concentrate our attention to *data-intensive* Web sites. That is, sites whose primary purpose is to deliver large amounts of information to a variety of users. These needs are best served by sites with very regular structures. For example, the various departments of a university, each with its own professors and courses, often have similar Web pages, homogeneously interconnected. Correspondingly, a database may store information about professors and courses. Given the regularity of Web pages, it becomes convenient to design portions of the Web with techniques similar to those used to design databases. Our attention, therefore, will be mainly centred on sites with at least a certain degree of regularity in the information offered, whose goal can be described as the 'publication of the contents of a database' for consultation purposes.

14.3.1 A logical model for data-intensive hypertexts

Let us consider a company that has a database with the conceptual schema and the logical schema in Figure 14.4. (This is a simplified version of a case shown earlier.) Suppose that the company wishes to organize a Web site that offers the content of the database for consultation. A simplified, but reasonable organization for this site includes:

- a home page, with links to all the branches and two other pages, containing links to all the projects and to all the employees of the company, respectively;

- a page for each branch, with a list of departments, each with a link to the respective manager and a link to another page with a list of employees of the department;

- a page for each project, with a list of links to the employees of the project;

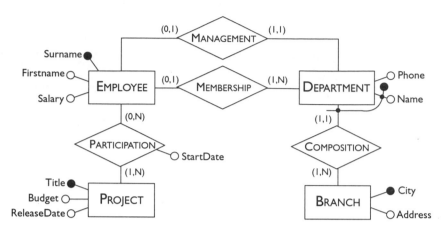

EMPLOYEE(<u>Surname</u>, Firstname, Branch, Department)
DEPARTMENT(<u>Branch</u>, <u>Name</u>, Phone, Manager)
BRANCH(<u>City</u>, Address)
PROJECT(<u>Title</u>, Budget, ReleaseDate)
PARTICIPATION(<u>Employee</u>, <u>Project</u>, StartDate)

Figure 14.4 The E-R schema and the logical schema of a database on the employees of a company.

• a page for each employee, with personal information and links to the branch and to the projects in which he or she is participating.

The pages for projects, employees, departments, and branches, within each of the categories, are certainly similar to each other. For example, in Figure 14.5 we show the pages for two employees: these contain the same information, with different values, and have the same organization. We find here the classical distinction between schema and instance: the regular structure of the page is the schema, while the actual content corresponding to a given employee is an instance that conforms to the schema. Thus, it makes sense to have the notion of a *page schema* to describe the common structure of a set of pages. We can have the page schema EMPLOYEE of which the two pages shown are instances.

Based on the above considerations, we can define a model for Web hypertexts, which describes the page structure and the way in which the pages are correlated. We present a simple model sufficient for the site described above. It uses the sole construct of the page schema, which is analogous to the notion of class in the object-oriented model shown in Chapter 11. Each page can have atomic or complex attributes. Besides the classic ones (integer, character, date, and so on), atomic types also include multimedia types (for describing documents, images and sometimes videos and sound). Complex attributes are built by means of the list constructor (because pages have a physical order). Links connect page schemas as in the object model, but each link instance consists of both a reference and an

Figure 14.5 Web pages for two employees.

associated *anchor*, usually a value whose content identifies the page referred to. Using syntax similar to that of Chapter 11, we can define the page schema EMPLOYEE as follows:

```
page-schema Employee
   (Surname:   string;
    Firstname: string;
    Salary:    integer;
    Dept:      string;
    Branch:    link(City: string; *Branch);
    Projects:  list-of
                     (Project: link(Title: string; *Project);
                      StartDate: date;
                     );
   )
```

In particular, note that each link is made up of an attribute with the role of anchor (for example, City in the Branch link) and of a reference (for example, *Branch in the above example). The anchor is made up by one or more attributes of the referenced page schema. Alternatively, as we will see shortly, the anchor can be a constant.

A peculiar characteristic of the Web is the fact that while in a database each class usually has several instances, there are page schemas that have *one and only one instance*. For example, the home page of each site falls into this category. In the site described above, the pages that contain the list of all the employees and the list of all the projects also have this characteristic. We can say that these pages are *unique*; anchors pointing to unique pages from other pages are constant strings. With the same syntax as above, the other page schemas of the site can be defined as follows:

```
page-schema Company unique
  (Branches:  list-of (Branch: link(City: string; *Branch));
   Employees: link("Employees"; *EmployeeList);
   Projects:  link("Projects"; *ProjectList);
  )
page-schema ProjectList unique
```

```
            (Projects:  list-of(Project: link(Title: string; *Project)))
         page-schema EmployeeList unique
            (Employees: list-of(Employee: link(Surname:string; *Employee)))
         page-schema Branch
            (City:      string;
             Address:   string;
             Depts:     list-of
                         (Name:    string;
                          Phone:   string;
                          Manager: link(Surname: string; *Employee);
                          Employees: link("Employees"; *EmployeesOfDept);
                         )
            )
         page-schema EmployeesOfDept
            (Branch:    link(City: string; *Branch;
             Dept:      string;
             Employees: list-of(Employee: link(Surname:string; *Employee));
            )
         page-schema Project
            (Title: string;
             Budget: integer
             ReleaseDate: date;
             Employees:   list-of(Employee:link(Surname:string; *Employee));
            )
```

A graphic representation of the same schema is shown in Figure 14.6.

14.3.2 Levels of representation in Web hypertexts

The schema described above can be considered as the description of the hypertext at a *logical* level. In fact, it represents the hypertextual structure, but it does not describe all the details of the hypertext itself, such as the actual layout of the pages or some additional links, which are usually included in Web sites. For example, one of the pages about the employees could be that in Figure 14.7, rather than the one in Figure 14.5. Both pages correspond to the same page schema and to the same database content; what changes is the page layout and the graphical presentation.

A further observation we can make on the site illustrated above is that the same data content can be presented through different page schemas. For example, rather than each employee's page having a link to the branch and the list of projects, we could have more information about the branch and a link to a page that lists the employee's projects. The definition of the page schema would become:

```
         page-schema Employee
            (Surname:   string;
             Firstname: string;
             Salary:    integer;
             Dept:      string;
             City:      string;
             Address:   string;
             Projects:  link("CurrentProjects"; *ProjectsOfEmp);
            )
```

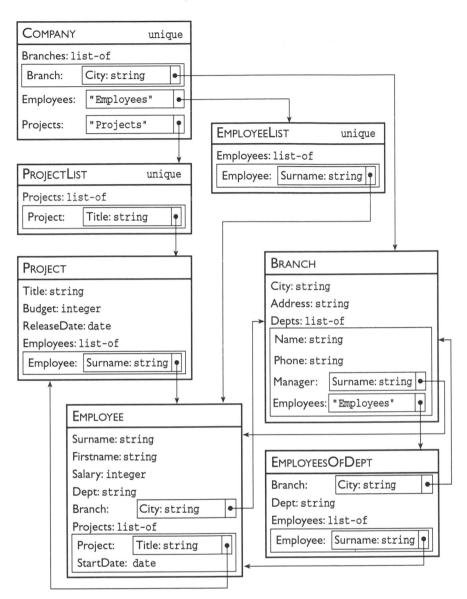

Figure 14.6 Logical schema of a hypertext.

Figure 14.8 shows the pages of our usual employees, according to the new organization.

The above considerations allow us to distinguish among three distinct aspects of a data-intensive Web site.

- The *information content*, which, in a data-intensive site, is made up of data. As in databases, we can distinguish between schemas and instances.

- The *hypertext structure*, which describes how the information content is organized into pages and the links that allow navigation among the pages.

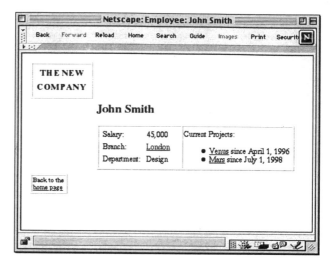

Figure 14.7 Web page with the same information as one of those in Figure 14.5, with a different presentation.

Figure 14.8 Another two employee pages, with different contents.

In a data-intensive site, the hypertext structure can be defined by a hypertext schema, with references to the database schema for the data.

• The *presentation*, which describes the graphic aspects and the deployment of the contents and links within the pages; the definition of the presentation can also refer to the hypertext schema.

This division shows some similarities with the levels in database architectures (external, logical and physical) as discussed in Chapter 1. Keeping with the analogy, we can also extend the notion of independence with a new level, which we can call 'hypertext independence'. In fact, the hypertext structure of a site can be modified without altering the structure of the associated database. Also, the presentation can be modified, without necessarily modifying the hypertext structure or the database structure. Presentation is in a sense the implementation level of hypertexts. In contrast with databases (where physical structures are not visible) presentation characteristics are visible to the users, even if they do not influence the information content.

14.3.3 Design principles for a data-intensive Web site

The distinctions among the various aspects of hypertext, contents, structure and presentation, suggest a design method: it is appropriate first to define the contents, then the hypertext structure, and finally the presentation.

In data-intensive Web sites, the content is made up largely of data, which we can describe on various levels, conceptual, logical and physical.

As regards the contents, the most useful description is undoubtedly the conceptual one, which we can consider as a major input for the design of the hypertext. We can thus think of the design of a data-intensive Web site as made up of two interconnected lines of activity: database design and hypertext design.

To identify the phases of the method, we can make the following observations. First, it is necessary that the analysis of requirements does not concern only the specifically data-oriented aspects, as we assumed in Chapter 6. We must also consider the objectives of the site, the user requirements, and the desired interaction techniques. Thus, hypertext design should use on one hand the products of conceptual database design, and, on the other hand, the requirements specifically focused on Web interaction aspects.

The phase of hypertext design uses the conceptual schema as input and produces a hypertext schema as output. We identify a number of differences between these two models.

- A conceptual model tends to map each class of real world objects to a different entity. In hypertext, the pages are focused upon application objects, which often embody several entities of the conceptual schema.

- In a conceptual model, the relationships are indicated in a non-redundant way and without indications of a 'predefined direction'. In a hypertext, links are oriented (a reference goes from one page to another, and there need not be the inverse link) and multiple links may correspond to the same relationship, yielding redundant navigation opportunities. In addition, links may correspond to paths obtained by traversing two or more intermediate relationships.

- A hypertext has additional page schemas and links that support the navigation (including the home page and some hierarchical structures or forms for accessing page instances).

The logical model of the hypertext also specifies several aspects that are not present in the conceptual data model, including the organization of the concepts into pages and the auxiliary access structures. For this reason, it can be useful to introduce an intermediate level, which we can call the *conceptual level* of the hypertext. This has the aim of keeping track of the aspects just mentioned. We limit ourselves to a simple example, illustrated in Figure 14.9, which illustrates the main features of a conceptual representation for hypertexts. We underline the differences with regard to the conceptual database schema in Figure 14.4.

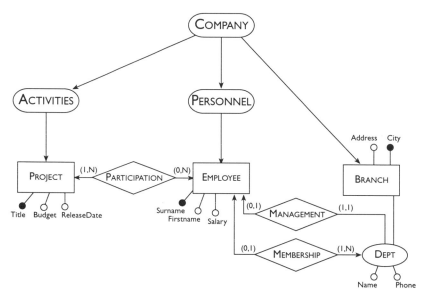

Figure 14.9 Conceptual schema of a hypertext.

- The DEPARTMENT entity has been transformed into an attribute, because the concept has not been considered to be autonomous in the hypertext. It is however, a structured attribute, which is also involved in several relationships.

- The relationships are oriented. Many are bi-directional, but there is one, MANAGEMENT, which is unidirectional: it is assumed that it is important to get from a department to its manager and not vice-versa.

- The concepts COMPANY, ACTIVITIES, PERSONNEL have no counterparts in the E-R schema; they make up the main access structures of the site. In a complex site, there can be many concepts of this type, corresponding to a hierarchical organization for enabling navigation to page instances.

Figure 14.10 illustrates a method for the design of data-intensive Web sites. Let us briefly comment on the various phases.

Requirements analysis, conceptual design and *logical design* of the database component can be carried out as we discussed in Chapter 6 and Chapter 7, with some additional emphasis, in requirements analysis, on the specific needs of the Web framework.

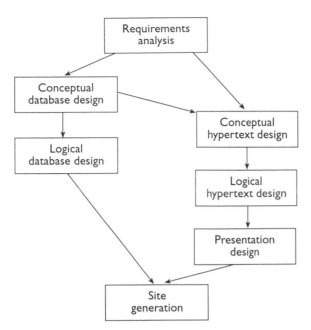

Figure 14.10 A method for the design of data-intensive Web sites.

- *Conceptual hypertext design*, given the requirements and the conceptual data schema, produces the conceptual schema of the hypertext.

- *Logical hypertext design* produces the logical schema of the hypertext given the conceptual one.

- *Presentation design* has the aim of defining the layout and the presentation of each of the page schemas defined in the logical design.

- *Site generation* is concerned with the development of the connection between the database and the Web site according to the technological options that are discussed in the next section.

The proposed approach is modular: if a database exists already, and it is documented by means of a conceptual schema, then the conceptual and logical database design phases can be omitted. If instead only the logical schema is available, then we can proceed with *reverse engineering* to construct the conceptual schema, and then continue with the above method.

In the example we have been using in this section, the schema in Figure 14.9 would be derived in the conceptual hypertext design phase, from the E-R schema in Figure 14.4. Then, in the logical hypertext design phase, the schema in Figure 14.6 would be defined, with the definition of the various page schemas.

In the presentation design phase, we would design the actual appearance of pages, for example, by choosing between that in Figure 14.5 and that in Figure 14.7. Finally, in the site generation phase we would implement the actual construction of pages, by using suitable techniques and tools from among those discussed in the next section. A major point in this final phase is the establishment of the correspondence between the logical database schema (in the example, the relation schemas in the second part of Figure 14.4) and the logical (and presentation) schemas of the hypertext. In the following section we will see some examples that show various alternative solutions.

14.4 Techniques and tools for database access through the Web

In this section, we will present an overview of the techniques that can be used for interfacing a Web site and a database. We will begin by presenting the most common approach, based on the CGI protocol, and will then discuss its limitations and the alternative solutions. We will also have a brief look at the salient aspects of some tools for the development of applications.

14.4.1 Database access through CGI programs

The simplest technique for access to a database from within the Web consists of the CGI protocol, which we described briefly in Section 14.1. The technique is general and the principle on which it is based is simple. The HTTP server receives a request, recognizes that the resource indicated by the URL is a program and launches this program through the CGI protocol. The program accesses the database and returns the results to the server, which then sends them to the browser. We have here two separate environments, the HTTP server and the application program. They interact by means of an interface (the CGI), which is very simple and well defined. Assume now that we are interested in generating, by means of a CGI program, the pages for the employees as shown in Figure 14.8. The HTML source for one of them is shown in Figure 14.11.

```
<html>
<head><title>John Smith</title></head>
<body>
<H3>John Smith</H3>
<table>
<tr><td><em>Department</em> :</td><td> Design</td></tr>
<tr><td><em>City</em> :</td><td> London</td></tr>
<tr><td><em>Address</em> :</td><td> 354 Regent St</td></tr>
<tr><td><em>Salary</em> :</td><td> 45,000 per year</td></tr>
<tr><td><a href="/cgi-bin/Projects?Surname=Smith">Current
        projects</a></td><td></td></tr>
</table>
</body>
</html>
```

Figure 14.11 The HTML source of the first page in Figure 14.8.

In Figure 14.12 we show a simple CGI program written in C, with embedded SQL, that takes a surname as input and generates the page of the employee with that surname. The program could be called up using a URL that includes the surname of the employee as input parameter:

> http://www.nc.com/cgi-bin/Employee?Surname=Smith

```
main(char Surname[])
{
   char Firstname[20], Department[20], City[20];
   char Address[60];
   int Age, Salary;
   $ open connection to NewCompanyDB
   $ select Firstname, Department, City, Address, Salary
       into :Firstname, :Department, :City, :Address, :Salary
     from Employee E, Branch B
     where E.Branch = B.City
       and Surname = :Surname ;
   $ close connection
   if (sqlcode == 0){
     printf("<html>\n<head><title> %s %s",Firstname,Surname,
           "</title></head>\n<body>\n");
     printf("<H3> %s %s",Firstname,Surname,"</H3>\n");
     printf("<table>\n");
     printf("<tr><td><em>Department</em>:</td><td>%s",
           Department,"</td></tr>\n");
     printf("<tr><td><em>City</em>:</td><td>%s",City,
           "</td></tr>\n");
     printf("<tr><td><em>Address</em>:</td><td>%s",Address,
           "</td></tr>\n");
     printf("<tr><td><em>Salary</em>:</td><td>%u",Salary,
           "</td><tr>\n");
     printf("<tr><td><a href=\"/cgi-bin/ProjOfEmp?Surname=%s",
           Surname,"\">Current projects</a></td>
           <td> </td></tr>\n");
     printf("</table>\n</body>\n</html>");
     }
   else {
     printf("<html>\n<head><title>Not found</title></head>
           \n<body>\n");
     printf("No employee has surname %s\n",Surname,"</body>\n
           </html>");
   }
}
```

Figure 14.12 A CGI program that produces pages as in Figure 14.8.

Since **Surname** is the key of the relation, it is guaranteed that the **select** statement returns at most one tuple and so it is not necessary to use cursors. The program opens the connection with the database, executes the query, stores the result in suitable local variables and generates the page. The page is transmitted to the HTTP server, which then sends it to the client. The HTML formatting is specified by means of the constants in the output statements.

14.4.2 Development tools

We briefly mentioned in Chapter 1 the existence of tools to support database development, in particular as regards the production of components of user interfaces, such as forms, menus and reports.

The needs of Web applications have caused the rapid appearance of dedicated development tools that have the same goals. The fundamental idea is that of facilitating the construction of Web pages based on the contents of the databases. HTML pages can be generated by these tools based on a prefixed organization. Many products offer the facility of using *HTML templates*, which are skeletons of HTML pages with a portion of the content defined using an SQL query, possibly with parameters. For example, the first page in Figure 14.8 could be generated using the template in Figure 14.13. In this example template, we use a simplified syntax, which is not used by any current product, but is useful to explain essential concepts.

```
<html>
<! tmplSQL connect database NewCompanyDB>
<! tmplSQL query "select Firstname, Department,
                        City, Address, Salary
               from Employee E, Branch B
               where E.Branch = B.City
               and E.Surname = $Surname
               ">
<head>
<title></title>
</head>
<H3>$1 $Surname</H3>
<table>
<tr><td><em>Department</em> :</td><td> $2</td></tr>
<tr><td><em>City</em> :</td><td>$3</td></tr>
<tr><td><em>Address</em> :</td><td>$4</td></tr>
<tr><td><em>Salary</em> :</td><td> $5 per year</td></tr>
<tr><td><a href="/cgi-bin/tmplSQL?tmpl=ProjOfEmp&Surname=$Surname">
        Current projects</a></td><td> </td></tr>
</table>
</body>
</html>
```

Figure 14.13 An HTML template for the construction of pages such as those in Figure 14.8.

The template produces the same HTML source as the CGI program in Figure 14.2, but without using a program in C (or other programming language). The HTML code is not hidden in the output statements, but directly specified. This is useful when debugging the structure of pages: a browser ignores the HTML elements of the form <!...> and can thus show the template, with the names of the variables ($1, $2 and so on) in place of the respective values. The tools that allow the use of templates operate in a way that is similar to CGI programs: the URLs denote a specific program, which we could call the 'template manager', that receives as input the name of the template and the needed parameters (in the example, the surname), accesses the database and returns an HTML page as the result. The template in Figure 14.3 can be invoked with a URL such as the following:

```
http://www.nc.com/cgi-bin/tmplSQL?tmpl=Employee&Surname=Smith
```

Many other development tools have been proposed, mainly to support access to Web sites using tools similar to those available for traditional database applications. For example, the PL/SQL language, which we will describe in Appendix C, has been recently enriched with features that allow the generation of HTML interfaces.

14.4.3 Shortcomings of the CGI protocol

The use of CGI programs is relatively simple, but has some limitations as follows.

- Since HTTP has no memory, it is not obvious how to manage transactions that require multiple accesses to the database.

- The execution of a CGI program starts with the request and terminates with the return of the results. More precisely, we have an operating system process that is created, carried out and terminated. This means that, at the time of creation, main memory space must be allocated for the process. If this is large, the delay due to memory allocation can be quite high. Furthermore, different requests to the same program generate different processes. This is particularly onerous in the case of systems with many requests and large CGI programs.

- Once initiated, the CGI program in turn requests a new connection with the DBMS (often requiring a user authentication); the session is then closed before the termination of the program. Here also, we have the cost of opening and closing sessions with the DBMS, which can become overloaded, if there are many requests. If the DBMS is also used for other activities, these can be heavily affected.

- It is not easy to create a keyword-based search service over the information on the site, a function regarded as extremely important in many contexts. The standard search tools usually operate only on files that are stored statically on the site and not on dynamically generated files. Using a database, it is necessary to introduce further application modules that carry out the search in the database itself.

Various approaches have been suggested for dealing with these problems. We will look at them briefly in the next subsections.

14.4.4 Simulating long connections for transactions

Various techniques have been proposed to overcome the problem of the stateless nature of HTTP.

The basic idea is to maintain a continuous exchange of information between browser and server with the aim of keeping continuity of a connection, thus enabling transactions spanning over multiple page accesses. To this end, one possibility is to request the user to specify an identifier and to reuse it in every page request, suitably 'hidden' in the HTML code.

Another, simpler solution, requiring a non-standard use of the browsers, is the following. A *cookie* is a small set of data (at most 4Kbytes) that the server can send to the client in a suitable field in the heading of an HTTP reply. The contents of the cookie are stored as part of the configuration of the browser and are sent back to the server that generated it each time the browser is connected with that server. Therefore, the cookie could be used to identify the user and thus to recognize successive actions within the same session. These two approaches partly overcome the limitations of the CGI approach due to the stateless nature of HTTP.

14.4.5 Server-based alternatives to the CGI approach

Materialization   A radical solution to the performance problems due to the interaction of three different entities (the HTTP server, the CGI program and the DBMS) consists of the *materialization* of the HTML pages of a site based on the content of the database. This is sometimes called the *push*[2] approach, to indicate that the data is 'pushed' in advance towards the site (and thus towards the user). In contrast, the CGI solution is called *pull*, as the data is extracted or 'pulled' from the database on request. The same observations made in Section 10.6 about the currency of data in co-operating systems apply to this context as well. If the data changes rather slowly or if it is acceptable to offer on the Web data that is not exactly up to date, then we can periodically generate the entire site from the database. Thus, we eliminate the performance problems caused by the activation and termination of CGI processes and we reduce the load on the database: the requests are managed directly by the HTTP server, which returns files prepared in advance. Another advantage of this solution is the possibility of duplicating the site and moving it to other environments (without constraints for DBMSs, HTTP servers or operating systems). The obvious disadvantage of a materialized solution is the possible obsolescence of information on the site.

Materialization can be obtained with programs similar to those used for a pull approach (for example, that shown in Figure 14.12). The only difference (and additional difficulty) consists of the necessity for generating suitable names for the files that contain the materialized pages. A simple technique

---

2. Note that the term 'push technology' is also used in a different context, to refer to tools that allow the browser to poll a server continuously in order to update the displayed information without user intervention.

involves the use of names made up of the juxtaposition of the names of the page schema and key values of the page itself.[3]

Extension of the HTTP server functionality A solution that is gaining popularity is based on the availability of libraries associated with HTTP servers. This solution is denoted by the term *server API* (*Application Programming Interface*) and indicates the modules of a specific library that allow direct access to the database. In this case, the DBMS client is the HTTP server itself and not another program, as with the CGI architecture. The programs that access the database are called by the HTTP server and are executed within the HTTP process itself.

The main benefit is the reduction of activation operations, with consequent improvement of performance. The functions offered often include the management of transactions and authorizations.

The main disadvantage of this solution is the lack of standardization; the APIs offered by the various servers, although similar to each other, are different, and thus the applications are not easily portable. In addition, the fact that the applications operate as sub-processes of the HTTP server can affect the server, in case of malfunctions of applications.

An extreme version of this approach consists of *dedicated HTTP servers*; these are systems that integrate the functions of DBMS and HTTP server. Obviously, all the services mentioned above, such as the complete management of transactions, management of authorizations and others, such as load balancing, are present. At the same time, there remains the disadvantage of non-portability, accentuated by the fact that the DBMS is also fixed.

Thin CGI To meet the demand for portability and standardization, various suppliers have suggested an intermediate solution. The technique consists of the use of minute CGI programs (known as *thin CGI*), which have the sole aim of receiving the Web server requests and of opening a connection to another module. This module is called the *CGI server*, since it acts as a server for the thin CGI requests. The thin CGI processes are subject to activation and termination, as for each CGI. However, this concerns very small processes, which are unlikely to cause performance problems. Conversely, the CGI server is a permanently active process (a *daemon*) and thus presents no problems of activation and termination. Furthermore, it keeps the connection with the DBMS open, with the double advantage of being able to manage transactions and security.

---

3. We have not discussed the concept of keys with reference to the logical model for hypertexts, but it is similar to that seen in earlier chapters for the relational and the E-R model.

14.4.6 Client-based alternatives to the CGI approach

Radical solutions for avoiding a heavy load of interactions between client and DBMS mediated by the HTTP server and the CGI program consists of the elimination of the mediation itself. The basic idea of this approach is shown in Figure 14.14 compared with the basic CGI solution. For the database client, there are various solutions, which we will illustrate briefly.

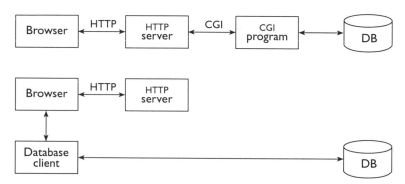

Figure 14.14 Comparison of CGI and client-based solutions.

- **Browser extensions** These are software modules executed by the browser as dynamic libraries. Many browser extensions exist to manage data of a particular type, for example, graphical formats. Among them, there can be modules used to access a remote database. These can be stored on the client machine (creating problems of distribution and software update) or can be incorporated into the HTML code (but the browser has to load them from the network, and this can be expensive).

- **External helpers** As an alternative to extensions, browsers can initiate or hand over control to external tools (*helpers* or *viewers*). This can also be done for an SQL interpreter or a local application that accesses a remote database. In this case, the user interacts only with the helper, and traditional client-server interaction can take place; the browser simply initiates the interaction, without being further involved.

- **Proprietary browsers** Some DBMS vendors have evaluated the possibility of creating browsers specializing in database access. The initiative has not had particular success, because the users are usually interested in having general-purpose browsers. In a small number of cases, this technology could be used to limit the functionality of the client, or to extend it in a controlled way.

In general, client-based solutions are almost exclusively suitable for a known context and predefined user population (typically within an intranet). This is due to the complexity of the distribution and of the updating of tools and to the fact that the compatibility with the various browsers of programs taken from the network is never really complete.

Client-based solutions are usually implemented by means of new languages, whose development is closely related to the Internet and the Web. The first and most popular item here is *Java*, a modern object-oriented language, which was conceived with portability and security in mind. Portability is achieved by means of an intermediate level of representation for its programs (the *byte-code*) for which interpreters are available on many machines. As regards security, the execution environment of a program defines a closed set of resources that the program is allowed to use; explicit authorization is needed for using further resources. Given these features, Java has been widely used to extend browsers: in fact, if a browser includes an interpreter for Java byte-code (called *Java Virtual Machine*, JVM), then it can run any Java application downloaded from a Web server. The security features guarantee that the new potential does not become dangerous. A major use for Java is the development of *applets*, programs that can be embedded in Web pages and then executed by the browser, thus offering extensions to the client side.

Another client-based solution is *Javascript*, a language that allows dynamic extension and modification of the content of HTML pages. It is a scripting language (that is, an interpreted language) with a rich set of browser specific commands that enriches the interface functions, without the need for an execution environment, as required by Java.

Both Java and Javascript are based on interpreters integrated in a browser, and are therefore portable. A proprietary solution has instead been proposed by Microsoft *ActiveX*: this is an architecture that extends the functions of browsers by allowing them to execute applications. This solution takes advantage of the popularity of Windows platforms and can provide good performances, but cannot in general guarantee portability and security.

In the framework of Java solutions, it is important to mention the JDBC (*Java Data Base Connectivity*) protocol. Its goal is to allow Java applications to access relational databases, in a way similar to that used by the ODBC protocol (see Section 10.5), independently from the specific DBMS. The architecture includes a layer (the driver manager) that isolates the application from the server. In practice, there are four options listed below and shown in Figure 14.5.

1. *JDBC on a native driver*: in this solution, a Java module translates the Java calls produced by the JDBC driver manager into a format used by a driver external to the Java environment (typically a pre-existing database driver written in the native language of the machine).

2. *JDBC/ODBC bridge*: this is a special case of the previous architecture (an ODBC driver is used instead of a generic database driver). The JDBC/ODBC bridge translates the Java calls produced by the JDBC driver manager into calls of the ODBC protocol, external to the Java environment. The availability of the ODBC driver for the target DBMS is then needed.

Neither of these solutions is portable, since each requires the presence of natively executable components. These are often considered intermediate solutions that can exploit the availability of pre-existing drivers.

Two other pure-Java and portable solutions are:

3. *Java middleware server*: this architecture entails the use of a Java component responsible for providing the services required by the driver manager, offering a multiplicity of targets. This component is typically implemented by companies specializing in the construction of software gateways.

4. *Java driver*: this solution implements in Java, for a specific DBMS, the services required by the driver manager. These drivers are typically offered by DBMS vendors, for their specific products.

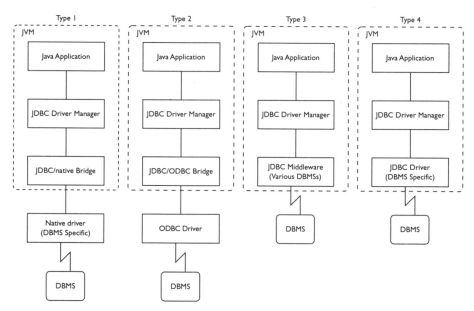

Figure 14.15 JDBC architectures.

Overall, JDBC is an interesting solution with great potential for solving interoperability problems in a portable way. It now presents a few immaturity problems, but its relevance goes beyond the context of Web applications.

14.5 Bibliography

There are many sources of information on the Internet and the Web, in traditional printed form and in electronic format, available though the Web itself. We mention a few general reference sources. A comprehensive discussion of network protocols is provided by Comer [32]; an introductory presentation of information services on the Internet (including the Web but not limited to it) by Liu et al. [55]; a complete presentation of HTML by Graham [43]. Greenspun [47] considers many issues, including a general discussion of WIS, electronic commerce, as well as an introduction to HTML and architectural aspects, such as CGI and Server API. A series of articles on WIS has recently appeared, edited by Isakowitz, Bieber and Vitali [50]. A general discussion on the development of Web sites is carried out by Rosenfeld and Morville [70].

A survey of the research and technological issues related to database approaches to the Web is presented in Florescu, Levy and Mendelzon [42]. They also discuss the solutions based on *semi-structured data models*, which have recently been proposed to take into account the need for flexibility and irregularity of the data managed on the Web.

An overview of the major issues to be faced in the design of data-intensive Web sites is presented in Ceri, Fraternali and Paraboschi [16]. The conceptual and logical models for Web sites, as well as the design methodology we have briefly sketched, are described in more detail by Atzeni, Mecca, and Merialdo [4] & [5].

Discussions of the architectural issues on the interconnection of databases and the Web can be found in the books by Ju [51] and by Cheng and Malaika [24].

Much additional information can be found on the Internet itself, both by means of search engines and by looking at the Web sites of the vendors.

14.6 Exercises

Exercise 14.1 Consider the Web site of your university or company and examine the services it offers, classifying them according to the types discussed in Section 14.2.

Exercise 14.2 Find on the Internet one or more sites that fall in each of the categories discussed in Section 14.2 ('Publication and consultation'; 'Transactions on the Web'; 'Electronic commerce'; 'Co-operative and workflow applications').

Exercise 14.3 Find on the Internet a Web site that could be used as a source for a data farming activity.

Exercise 14.4 Consider the conceptual schema shown in Figure 5.26 and design a Web site that can be used to publish the content of the database. Show both the conceptual and the logical schema of the hypertext.

Exercise 14.5 We want to build a Web site for the training company example discussed in Chapter 6 and Chapter 7. Therefore:

• find the user requirements for the site, by choosing the pieces of information that are interesting for the public (outside the company);

- design the conceptual schema of the hypertext;

- design the logical schema of the hypertext.

Exercise 14.6 Following the same steps as in the previous exercise, design the Web site for the database whose E-R schema is shown in Exercise 5.6.

Exercise 14.7 Using the database for soccer games considered in Exercise 14.4, write a CGI program that generates the list of games played by a given team in a specific period.

Exercise 14.8 Write a CGI program that generates a page for a course (whose code is given as input parameter) offered by the training company, with a list of all the editions.

Part V

Appendices &
Bibliography

Microsoft Access

Access, produced by Microsoft, is the most widespread DBMS for the Microsoft Windows environment. Access can be used in two ways:

- as an independent database manager on a personal computer;

- as an interface to work on data residing on other systems.

As an independent database manager, it suffers from the limits of personal computer architecture: It offers limited support for transactions, with rather simple and incomplete mechanisms for security, data protection and concurrency control. On the other hand, it has a low cost and the applications to which it is targeted do not typically require a sophisticated implementation of these services. The system interface exploits the potential of the graphical environment and offers a user-friendly interface, both for the user and for the database designer.

When it is used as a client of a relational server, Access makes available its own interface features for the interaction with the external system. In this context, Access can be seen as a tool that allows the user to avoid writing SQL code, as it acquires schemas and simple queries using a graphical representation that is easy to understand. These inputs are translated into suitable SQL commands in a transparent manner. The ODBC protocol, described in Chapter 10, is normally used for communication between Access and the database server.

We focus the description of Access on its use as a database manager, placing particular emphasis on the definition of schemas and queries. The version we refer to is Access 97, available as a separate product or as part of the suite of applications in Microsoft Office 97 Professional. For a complete description of the system, we refer the interested reader to the manuals that are provided with the program, and to the on-line guide, accessed using the *Help* menu.

A.1 System characteristics

The system is activated in the traditional way in which Windows applications are started, by selecting the program icon in a window or menu. The icon is shown in Figure A.1.

Msaccess

Figure A.1   The program icon.

At the start, the program asks whether we wish to create a new database or open an existing one. It provides a list of databases that have been used earlier by the program. The creation of a database can begin with an empty database or with a schema selected from a series of predefined models (useful for inexperienced users). Each database corresponds to a file with a standard MDB extension. To open a pre-existing database, we need to select the corresponding file. To create a new database, or open a pre-existing one, the commands *New database* or *Open database* can also be used from the *File* menu. The newly created or opened database is represented by a window, which appears within the main window of the application. Figure A.2 illustrates this situation; we call the window listing the database components the *database window*. The main window contains a set of drop-down menus (*File*, *Edit*, etc.) and the toolbar. The menus and the toolbar vary according to the window appearing on the foreground within Access. Figure A.2 shows the contents of the toolbar when the database window is in the foreground in the application.

The database window contains a list of the families of system components: *tables*, *queries*, *forms*, *reports*, *macros* and *modules*. To move from one family to another, the user clicks on the corresponding button. When a family is selected, all the names of the elements of the family present in the database appear in the window. If there are more elements than the window can contain, a scroll bar makes it possible to navigate along the list. In Figure A.2, we can see the set of elements of the *Table* family present in the database selected. We observe that the database contains two tables, CITY and PERSON.

At this point, for each family, we can select one of the three buttons that appear in the right hand side of the window:

• using the *Open* button, Access shows the contents of a selected element;

• using the *Design* button, Access reopens the design phase on a selected element;

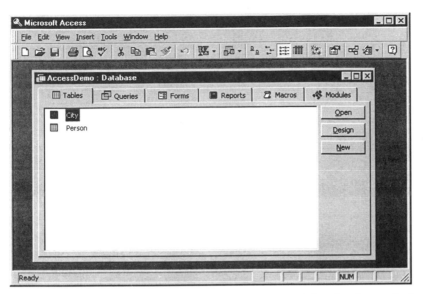

Figure A.2 The window containing the elements of the database window.

- using the *New* button, Access creates a new element of the family.

Thus, the commands *New* and *Design* are for access to the information on the design of the component (to its schema), while *Open* accesses its contents.

We will now describe the definition of tables and queries. Then we will briefly illustrate the functions offered for the management of forms, reports, and macros.

A.2 Definition of tables

To define the schema of a new table, we must select the *Table* family and click on the *New* button. At this point, Access offers a choice of five different table definition mechanisms: *Datasheet view*, *Design view*, *Table wizard*, *Import table* and *Link table*. Using *Datasheet view*, the table schema is defined in a way similar to the definition of a spreadsheet, presenting a grid of cells where the user may define column names. This interface is provided for users experienced in applications like Microsoft Excel or Lotus 123, making the use of a relational system easier for them. The options *Import table* and *Link table* permit the importing of a table from an external source. The first command copies the entire contents in an internal structure at table definition time, whereas the second constructs a connection that allows the table contents to be recovered dynamically from the remote resource. (It actually defines a view on a remote system.) The *Table wizard* option allows the use of a 'wizard', which is a support tool that guides the creation of a table by asking a series of questions and supplying a collection of examples. Access also provides wizards in other contexts, and they are of great help to inexperienced users. For the management of all situations falling outside of the predefined examples, or in the case of expert users, it is more convenient to use directly the services offered by the *Design view* option, on which we concentrate our presentation.

Firstly, the attributes are defined, using the window that appears in Figure A.3. We need to specify the name and the domain for each attribute.

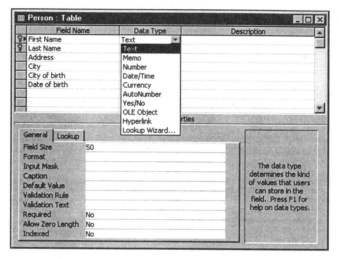

Figure A.3 Window for the definition of the table schema.

In Access, the attributes are called *fields*, the domains *types*. Each attribute is characterized by a set of *field properties*. The set varies according to the domain associated with each attribute. The domains that can be associated with an attribute are similar to the domains of standard SQL, with a few changes. The domains offered by Access are:

- *Text*: allows the representation of strings of characters (corresponds to the SQL domain varchar).

- *Memo*: allows the representation of strings of text as long as 64,000 characters; it is not a domain explicitly allowed by SQL, but it can be intended as a variant of varchar. (Indexes cannot be built on *memo* attributes.)

- *Number*: represents the family of numeric domains, both integer and real. The field properties allow the specification of whether the attribute represents precise or approximate values, and the degree of accuracy of the representation. This domain corresponds to the SQL domains numeric, decimal, integer, smallint, float, double and real.

- *Date/time*: represents temporal instants and corresponds to the SQL domains date, time and timestamp. It can represent only the date, only the time or both (specified in the field properties).

- *Currency*: represents monetary values. It is essentially a special case of the *Number* domain, characterized by an exact numeric representation on eight bytes with two decimal places.

- *AutoNumber*: assigns a unique value to each row of the table. This domain makes it possible to associate a compact key to the table.

- *Yes/No*: corresponds to the SQL domain bit.

- *OLE object*: represents a generic object that can be managed using OLE (Object Linking and Embedding). OLE is a protocol that allows the specification of which application must manage an object in the Windows environment. In this way, word processor documents, spreadsheets, images, or multimedia information can be inserted into the database. The application specified by OLE is given the task of presenting and updating the attribute contents.

- *Hyperlink*: allows the management of references. The reference can be internal (the identifier of a resource internal to the database or accessible on the local machine) or external (such as, for example, the URL of a resource available on the Internet).

- *Lookup wizard*: is used during the insertion phase. It defines a mechanism that on insertion offers the choice of a value among those in a predefined list or extracted using a query on the database.

The field properties appear in the lower half of the schema definition window. They are as follows:

- *Field size*: represents the dimension of the attribute. It is used only for the domains *Text* and *Number*. For the *Text* domain, the dimension is a value that represents the maximum length of the character string. For the *Number* domain, the admissible values are:

  o *Byte*: integer on eight bits (values between 0 and 255);

  o *Integer*: integer on 16 bits (values between −32,768 and 32,767);

  o *Long integer*: integer on 32 bits;

  o *Single*: floating point representation on 32 bits;

  o *Double*: floating point representation on 64 bits;

  o *Replication ID*: identifier of 128 bits, unique for each tuple, even in a distributed system.

- *Format*: describes the representation format of the attribute values. Wherever possible, Access uses the values specified for the Windows environment (*Internationalization* option on the Control Panel). For the representation of dates, numbers, and boolean values, it allows the choice of various predefined formats (seven predefined formats for date, six for number, three for boolean). Other formats can then be defined. We can also specify how to represent values according to whether they are positive, negative, or null.

- *Decimal places*: (definable only for attributes of domain *Single* and *Double*) specifies how many decimal places must be used in the representation.

- *Input mask*: specifies the format that must be used for the input of data. Take, for example, an attribute that holds a telephone number, made up of a three digit prefix and of a seven digit number, separated by a dash. We can specify an entry mask, which distinguishes the two parts and presents the dash, allowing the user to insert only the digits. Access offers a wizard to assist in the creation of input masks.

- *Caption*: represents the name that can be given to the attribute when it appears in a form or in a report. The attribute names are typically short, in order to have a compact schema and to write concise queries. For displaying information to the user, it is instead convenient to use an extended name that better represents the attribute content.

- *Default value*: specifies the default value for the attribute. It corresponds exactly to the `default` option of SQL. Each time a new tuple is inserted, the default value will appear as a value for the attribute. The result of an expression can also be used as a default value, like `=Date()`, which assigns the current date to a field of the *Date/Time* domain.

- *Validation rule*: describes a constraint that the attribute must satisfy. Access automatically verifies that each value inserted belongs to the domain of the attribute. As well as this check, Access allows the specification of a generic constraint for each attribute (similar to the `check` clause in SQL). This constraint is expressed by using the syntax used for the specification of conditions in QBE, which we will see in the next section.

- *Validation text*: specifies the message that must be displayed when an insertion or an update introduces a value that does not satisfy the integrity constraint.

- *Required*: specifies whether the tuples must always present a value on the attribute. This property can be true or false and corresponds to the `not null` constraint in SQL.

- *Allow zero length* (valid only for attributes of the domains *Text* and *Memo*): specifies whether empty strings (that is, strings whose length is zero) can be allowed, or whether an empty string must be considered as a null value. According to the context, it can be useful to manage the empty strings differently from the null value. Bear in mind that the null value is treated in a particular way by SQL; an inequality comparison on strings may be satisfied by an empty string, but not by a null value.

- *Indexed*: specifies whether an index should be constructed on the attribute or not. The possible options are *No*, *Yes (Duplicates OK)* and *Yes (No duplicates)*. The third option defines an index of type *unique* on the attribute. This is also the way in which *unique* constraints are defined. It is not possible to define indexes on the attributes *Memo*, *AutoNumber*, *Yes/No* and OLE. With this technique, it is possible to define indexes only on a single attribute. For the definition of more complex indexes, we must operate at table level.

Once the various attributes are defined, the session terminates with the indication of the attributes that must be considered the primary key of the table. These attributes are specified by selecting them and then choosing the *Primary key* item in the *Edit* menu. The attributes that make up the key are denoted by a key icon in the column preceding the name. Access will automatically define a unique index on the attributes that make up the key.

We can then define further properties at the table level (to which access is gained through the *Property* item in the *View* menu). The table properties are as follows.

- *Description*: a textual description of the contents of the table.

- *Validation rule*: specifies a constraint that must be satisfied by each tuple of the table. Constraints that involve multiple attributes can be defined as table properties. The syntax is identical to the one used to express conditions on queries. The constraint is checked at the end of the insertion of each tuple.

- *Validation Text*: defines the message that appears when the system detects a violation of the constraint.

- *Filter*: specifies a condition that must be satisfied by the tuples that should be shown when displaying the table contents.

- *Order by*: defines which attributes should be used to order the tuples of the table.

To specify indexes on many attributes, we must open the index definition window, by selecting the *Index* button on the toolbar, or selecting the *Index* option in the *View* menu (when the table definition window is in the foreground). The window contains a table (shown in Figure A.4) with columns *Index name*, *Field name*, and *Sort order*. To define an index on more than one attribute, we insert in the first row the index name, the name of the first attribute and the ordering direction. In the next row, we leave empty the name of the index and introduce the name of the second attribute together with the corresponding ordering direction. This is repeated for all the attributes in the index.

Before ending the definition session, we must save the result (by selecting

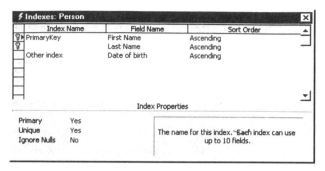

Figure A.4   The index definition window.

the *Save* option in the *File* menu). The system at this point asks for a name to be given to the table. The name can contain spaces.

A.2.1 Specification of join paths

A join path is a relationship between pairs of attributes of two tables and is used to specify that a join between those tables is normally used and is based on equality of those attributes. A join path is graphically represented by a line connecting the two tables (see Section 7.3). For example, in the 'Person and City' database, there is a join path between attribute **City of birth** of PERSON and attribute **Name** of City. Access allows the definition of join paths (called *Relationships* in Access): for each join path, it is possible to specify whether a referential integrity constraint is associated with it. All this happens without the input of any text. The process is exclusively graphical. We briefly describe the procedure.

First, the *Relationships* option in the *Tools* menu is selected. This causes the opening of a window (see Figure A.5) in which we can insert the schemas of the tables created, selecting them from a list. A join path between two tables

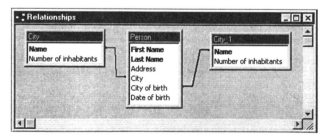

Figure A.5   The join path definition window.

is defined by clicking on an attribute in the graphical representation of the first table, then holding down the mouse button, and moving the pointer to the corresponding attribute in the second table. Once the link between the attributes is built, Access opens a window that presents the attributes involved in the join path. The window allows either the extension of the join condition to other attributes or the modification of the relationship thus defined. This window is shown in Figure A.6. By clicking on the *Join Type* button, we have the possibility of choosing which type of join, *inner, outer left* or *outer right,* must be used when combining the tuples of the two tables (in contrast with SQL, the *full outer join* is not available). Each time we define a query that accesses the two tables, the join condition represented by the join path will be automatically used.

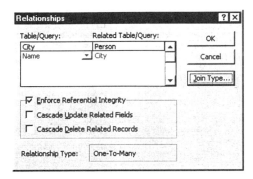

Figure A.6   The join property window.

Once the join path is defined, we can specify whether the path must be associated with a referential integrity constraint. In the same window, Access permits the definition of a policy for reaction to violations. In this way, we can impose that updates and deletions introducing referential integrity violations are followed by corresponding updates and deletions in the joined tables. If the policy is not specified, each modification that introduces a violation is simply refused. Compared with the SQL-2 standard, Access allows a limited set of reactions, corresponding to the two policies of `cascade delete` and `cascade update`. To specify the various referential integrity constraints, we should apply the design criteria described in Chapter 6. Access does not allow more than one path between two tables to appear in the graph. If more than one join path between two tables must be defined, it is necessary to introduce more representations of the same table into the graph (as in Figure A.5).

A.2.2 Populating the table

Once the schema is defined, tuples can be inserted into the tables to populate them. Access provides a simple graphical interface to do this task. By opening a table, clicking on the *Open* button of the main database window, a tabular representation of the table contents is displayed. This consists of a grid with attribute names as column headings, and rows describing the table tuples. At the bottom, there is an empty row for the insertion of new tuples into the table (see Figure A.7).

The insertion is carried out by placing the pointer in the last row and typing a value for each attribute. If the inserted value does not satisfy all the

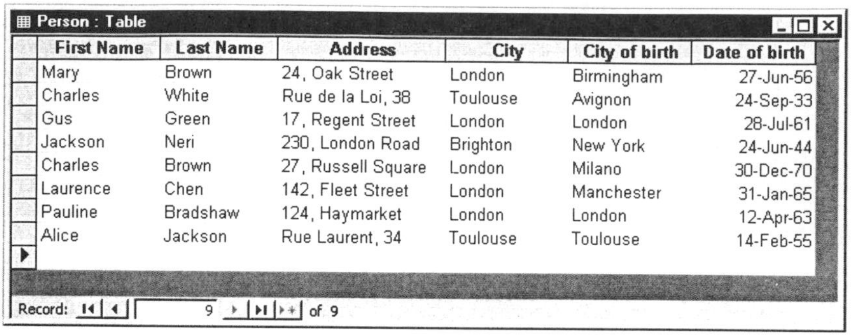

Person : Table

First Name	Last Name	Address	City	City of birth	Date of birth
Mary	Brown	24, Oak Street	London	Birmingham	27-Jun-56
Charles	White	Rue de la Loi, 38	Toulouse	Avignon	24-Sep-33
Gus	Green	17, Regent Street	London	London	28-Jul-61
Jackson	Neri	230, London Road	Brighton	New York	24-Jun-44
Charles	Brown	27, Russell Square	London	Milano	30-Dec-70
Laurence	Chen	142, Fleet Street	London	Manchester	31-Jan-65
Pauline	Bradshaw	124, Haymarket	London	London	12-Apr-63
Alice	Jackson	Rue Laurent, 34	Toulouse	Toulouse	14-Feb-55

Record: 9 of 9

Figure A.7 The window for viewing the instance of the table.

constraints defined on the attribute, the insertion is immediately refused. Moving the pointer out of the row implicitly indicates that the insertion is terminated. At this point the system checks that all the constraints are satisfied; this requires confirmation that the attributes requiring a value have been specified and that the introduced values satisfy the defined validation rules. To modify the value of attributes, it is sufficient to put the mouse pointer on the value to be modified, click on it and type the new value. When the cursor is moved to a different row the constraints are checked and the modification is made permanent.

A.3 Query definition

To define queries, Access makes available two different tools: a graphical tool for the formulation of QBE (Query By Example) queries, and an SQL interpreter. We will first describe the characteristics of the QBE interface, then analyze the SQL interpreter.

A.3.1 Query By Example

The name QBE refers to a family of languages that try to provide a practical implementation of the basic ideas of domain relational calculus (see Section 3.2.1). The major point, as we saw, is that a query is expressed by describing the characteristics which must be possessed by the elements of the result. In the QBE offered by Access, the definition of a query requires the filling of a table schema with all the attributes and conditions that characterize an 'exemplary' row of the result.

To define a new query, the *Query* component must be selected in the main database window. By selecting *New,* and choosing the *Design* view option, the query design window is opened. This window is divided into two halves (see Figure A.8 and Figure A.12). The top half is initially empty and is filled with a description of the schemas of the tables involved by the query, selected from a list. The tables are connected by the predefined join paths. (We can interpret the top half of the window as showing the portion of the *Relationships* diagram relevant for the query.) In the bottom half of the

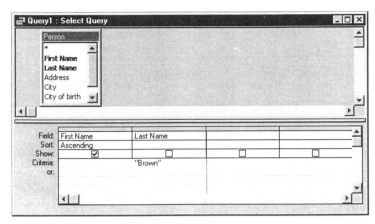

Figure A.8 QBE query that returns the first names of the people called Brown.

window, an initially empty table appears, with a set of columns without names and with predefined rows labelled *Field*, *Sort*, *Show* and *Criteria*.

The cells of the row *Sort* can be empty or can contain one of the options *Ascending* or *Descending*. When the row is not empty, an ordering of the tuples of the result is imposed, according to the values of the attribute associated with the column in which the option appears. If there are many columns with a non-empty value in the *Sort* row, columns are considered from left to right (tuples are first ordered on the first column on the left; for equal values of the first column, the second column is considered, and so on).

The cells of the *Show* row contain a square that may or may not contain a checkmark. If the square contains a checkmark, the attribute that appears in the column must be part of the result of the query. The state of the square changes by clicking on it with the mouse.

The cells of the *Criteria* row contain the conditions that must be satisfied by the tuples in the result of the query. If we are interested only in tuples that have a given constant value for an attribute, we can specify this by simply inserting the constant value into the *Criteria* cell in the column that has that attribute in the first row. The condition can also be more complex and can include richer comparisons, expressions and references to other attributes, as we will illustrate with a sequence of examples.

To put the names of the attributes in the columns, we can use two techniques. Firstly, we can directly type the name of the attribute in the first row of the column, possibly preceded by the name of the table to which it belongs. Otherwise, we can select the attributes that appear in the representation of the schemas on the top half of the window, 'dragging' them to the appropriate columns. Once the query is formulated, to execute it, we select the button on the toolbar that contains the exclamation mark. After the execution, the table resulting from the query appears in place of the query definition window.

Let us look at some examples of query definition. Suppose we have a database with a table PERSON(First Name, Last Name, Address, City, City of birth, Date of birth), and a table CITY(Name, Number of inhabitants). To find the first names, in alphabetical order, of the people called Brown, we can fill the schema as in Figure A.8.

A query applies the conjunction of the distinct conditions when more cells of the same *Criteria* row are filled. If a query needs to select the tuples that satisfy the disjunction of many conditions, different rows should be filled with the distinct criteria. The system automatically uses the label *Or* on the additional rows. Thus, to find the first names, last names and addresses of the people living in Boston called Brown or White, we create a schema as shown in Figure A.9.

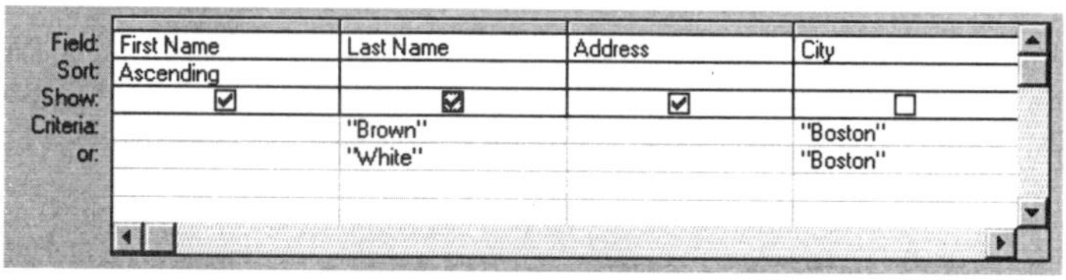

Field:	First Name	Last Name	Address	City	
Sort:	Ascending				
Show:	☑	☑	☑	☐	
Criteria:		"Brown"		"Boston"	
or:		"White"		"Boston"	

Figure A.9   Query that returns the people in Boston called Brown or White.

The list of table attributes presented in the top half also contains an asterisk, which, as in SQL, represents all the attributes. Thus, to extract all the attributes of the tuples of the PERSON table who are resident in their cities of birth, we can formulate the QBE query shown in Figure A.10.

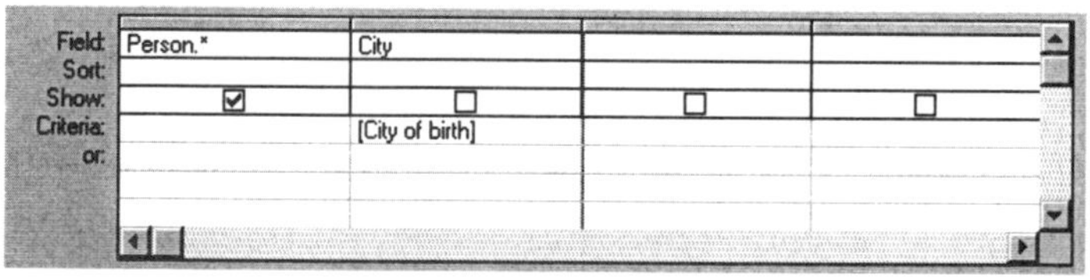

Field:	Person.*	City			
Sort:					
Show:	☑	☐	☐	☐	
Criteria:		[City of birth]			
or:					

Figure A.10 Query that returns the people born in their cities of residence.

In this query, to impose the identity of the two attributes, we put, as selection value on the attribute City, the attribute name City of birth enclosed in square brackets. Square brackets are the syntactic construct that Access uses to distinguish references to schema components from string constants. Access also allows the formulation of conditions using the normal operators of comparison ($<$, $>$, $<=$, $>=$, $<>$) and the operator *Like*, used to compare strings with regular expressions containing the special characters $*$ and $?$ (which correspond respectively to the characters % and _ of standard SQL). To find the first names and last names of the people born before January 31st

1965 and who have a last name beginning with C, we can formulate the query shown in Figure A.11.

Field:	First Name	Last Name	Date of birth	
Sort:				
Show:	☑	☑	☑	☐
Criteria:		Like "C*"	<#31/01/65#	
or:				

Figure A.11   Query that returns the first names and last names of people whose last names begin with C born before January 31st 1965

For each query, it is possible to specify a set of properties, at different levels. At the level of a single column, we can specify a viewing format different from the one chosen in the design of the table schema. Another important property is the elimination of possible duplicates present in the result. To specify that the duplicates must be removed, we must open the window presenting the query properties (using the *Property* option in the *View* menu) and assign the value *Yes* to the property *Unique values*.

To formulate queries that require more than one table, it is a good idea to have all the tables needed by the query appear in the upper window. The tables should be selected from the dialogue box that appears as soon as a new query is created. The tables will appear linked by the join paths that were defined at the end of schema design. In the table in the lower half of the query definition window, we can add a further row, labelled *Table*, by selecting the option *Table names* from the *View* menu. This row presents the name of the table from which the attribute is extracted. The join conditions between the tuples of the tables do not need to be specified when they are predefined. If the query requires join conditions that are different from the predefined ones, it is possible to modify the paths directly in the graphical representation appearing in the top half of the window.

Suppose we wish to formulate a query that finds the people born in cities with fewer than 100,000 inhabitants. If the join condition between the PERSON and CITY tables is predefined by a join path, we can formulate the query in Figure A.12.

Whenever the join path is not predefined, we must make the condition explicit in the table, formulating a query like that in Figure A.13, which uses references to attribute names in the *Criteria* rows.

It can be necessary at times to introduce into the top half tables whose attributes are not part of the query result. An important case of this type is that in which information must be extracted from two tables that do not have a direct join path, but in which the join involves an intermediate table. In this case, even if the query uses only attributes of the two unconnected tables in the result and in the conditions, the intermediate table must be present in the top half, with an approach similar to that used in relational

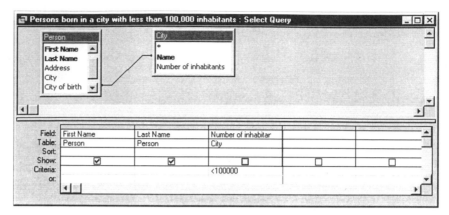

Figure A.12 Query which returns the first names and last names of the people born in cities with fewer than 100,000 inhabitants (using the predefined join path).

Field:	First Name	Last Name	Name	Number of inhabitar	
Table:	Person	Person	City	City	
Sort:					
Show:	☑	☑	☑	☐	
Criteria:			[City of birth]	<100000	
or:					

Figure A.13 Query that returns the first names and last names of the people born in cities with fewer than 100,000 inhabitants (without predefined joins).

algebra and calculus (Chapter 3), and also in SQL (Chapter 4). In fact, without a join path connecting the two tables, the system computes the cartesian product of the two tables, eventually applying the conditions that appear in the schema of the QBE query.

Let us now look at the formulation of QBE queries using aggregate operators. The aggregate operators provided are *Sum*, *Avg*, *Min*, *Max* and *Count*. They correspond to the standard SQL operators with the same names. Access also provides the operators *DevSt* (the standard deviation), *Var* (the variance) *First* and *Last* (the value of the attributes in, respectively, the first and last tuples). To use these operators, we must introduce a new row into the query schema, the *Total* row. This row is introduced by selecting the *Totals* option in the *View* menu. We will look at a simple example of the use of aggregate operators, defining a query that allows us to find the number of tuples present in the PERSON table, as shown in Figure A.14.

Note that the *Count* value appears in the *Total* row. This causes the result of the query to be not the value of the **First Name** attribute of the PERSON table, but the number of tuples. Any of the attributes of the PERSON table can appear in the row *Field*. For the sake of coherence with SQL, Access could have permitted the use of the asterisk in this context (*). However, since in the evaluation of the other aggregate operators the asterisk creates

Field:	First Name				
Table:	Person				
Total:	Count				
Sort:					
Show:	☑	☐	☐	☐	
Criteria:					
or:					

Figure A.14 Query which returns the number of people.

complications, Access does not permit its use when the *Total* row is activated.

In the query in Figure A.15, the **Last Name** attribute is characterized by the value *Group by* in the *Total* row. This specifies that the attribute is used to group the tuples of the PERSON table. The second column represents the application of the *Count* operator to each single grouping.

Field:	Last Name	Last Name			
Table:	Person	Person			
Total:	Group By	Count			
Sort:					
Show:	☑	☑	☐	☐	
Criteria:					
or:					

Figure A.15 Query that returns the number of people having each last name.

Access permits the expression of conditions on the result of the aggregate operators, corresponding to the use of the having clause in SQL. This is obtained with the simple specification of the desired values in the *Criteria* row, in a way similar to the expression of simple conditions on tuples. Thus, to find the last names that are possessed by at least two persons, we could write the QBE query in Figure A.16, which returns the last names possessed by more than one person, indicating for each last name the number of times that it appears in the PERSON table.

Field:	Last Name	Last Name			
Table:	Person	Person			
Total:	Group By	Count			
Sort:					
Show:	☑	☑	☐	☐	
Criteria:		>1			
or:					

Figure A.16 Query which returns the number of people who possess each last name, for the last names possessed by more than one person.

Consider now a query with grouping in which the tuples must be selected beforehand, based on the values of attributes that are not used in the grouping. It then becomes necessary to distinguish the conditions that must be applied before and after the grouping. In SQL this distinction occurs by placing the preliminary conditions in the where clause and the later conditions in the having clause. In QBE, the distinction occurs by placing the value *Where* in the *Total* row for the attributes that are used only before the grouping operation. The presence of the value *Where* is incompatible with an active *Show* cell. The reason is that, as in SQL, the result of the queries that use aggregate operators may contain only the result of the evaluation of the aggregate operators and the attributes on which the grouping is carried out. For example, to find the persons born after January 1st 1975 having the same last name of another person born after the same date, we can use the *Count* operator and formulate the query in Figure A.17.

Field:	Last Name	Date of birth	Last Name		
Table:	Person	Person	Person		
Total:	Group By	Where	Count		
Sort:					
Show:	☑	☐	☐	☐	
Criteria:		>#01/01/75#	>1		
or:					

Figure A.17 Query which returns the homonyms in the set of people born after January 1st 1975.

There are other ways to formulate this query that do not use the *Where* term. One consists of the definition and saving in the database of a preliminary query that extracts only the people born after January 1st 1975; a second query, which starts from the first query result, can then be defined. The first query result is grouped on the last name attribute in order to find the people who share the last name with others. In fact, Access associates a name to each saved query and a query can extract data both from the database tables, and from the queries already defined. Each query that is saved and made persistent can thus be considered as a definition of a view on the database.

A.3.2 The SQL interpreter

As well as the query language QBE, Access provides an SQL interpreter, which can be used as an alternative to QBE. Access allows a rapid switch from the QBE context to that of SQL and vice-versa, by selecting the option on the left-most button of the toolbar or by selecting the options *SQL View* and *Design View* from the *View* menu. The switch from one environment to the other transforms the current query into the corresponding query in the other representation.

The switch from QBE to SQL is always possible. Each time there is a request for the computation of a QBE query, the query is first translated internally into the corresponding form in SQL, and is then executed by the SQL engine. The reverse switch, however, is not always possible, as the SQL language is more powerful than QBE, for example allowing the expression of queries with the union operator. The QBE language is a powerful and friendly language when formulating queries that use only selections, projections and joins. In this case, the possibility of formulating queries without the need of writing a text according to a rigid syntax, is a considerable help. On the other hand, QBE does not provide an adequate mechanism for the representation of complex queries, such as those that require the use of nested queries in SQL. When an SQL query that uses a nested query is translated into QBE, the translation simply returns the text of the entire nested query in the appropriate cell of the *Criteria* row.

As regards the syntax recognized by the interpreter, this is a slight variation of the standard SQL syntax, with support for new functions and a few syntactic and semantic differences. Some of the differences are as follows:

- the top clause can be used to select a certain number of tuples from the result;

- square brackets are used to enclose the identifiers of the tables and attributes (necessary when spaces or special characters appear within the identifiers);

- the join operator must always be qualified by the term inner or outer;

- the evaluation of the count operator is different: if an attribute is given as argument, the operator does not compute the distinct values of the attribute, returning instead the number of not null values for the attribute (as if the all option were explicitly specified); the distinct option is not recognized inside the count argument.

For example, consider the QBE query in Figure A.18, for which the query property is specified that only the first 10 elements have to be returned and for which a join path is predefined. It thus corresponds the following query in the SQL dialect of Access:

Field:	Last Name	Last Name	Number of inhabitant		
Table:	Person	Person	City		
Total:	Group By	Count	Where		
Sort:		Descending			
Show:	☑	☑	☐	☐	
Criteria:		>1	>200000		
or:					

Figure A.18 Query which returns the number of homonyms in a city with more than 200,000 inhabitants.

```
select top 10 Lastname, count (Lastname) as HomonymNumber
from Person inner join City on Person.[City of birth]=City.Name
where [Number of inhabitants] > 200000
group by Lastname
having count (Lastname) > 1
order by count(Lastname) desc
```

A.4 Forms and reports

Forms allow the presentation of the database contents in a pleasing and structured way, often preferable to the flat representation of the rows of the tables.

Forms are normally similar to pre-printed forms, characterized by a set of slots in which data must be inserted, and a set of labels that specify which item of data must be inserted into a particular slot. Forms can be used for the insertion of data, creating an electronic version of the pre-printed form, and can also be used to view and modify the contents of the database.

Form generation tools are a frequent component of the support environment of commercial DBMSs. Access, in place of the simple and old character interface, exploits the potential of the Windows environment and permits the creation of sophisticated graphical forms. The form definition tool allows the definition of the position and meaning of each component of the form, offering a wide choice of character fonts, colours, drawings and graphical symbols.

To create a new form, we must click on the *New* button in the *Form* component on the main database window. The system first asks whether we wish to use the basic design tool or a wizard. Using a wizard, we can create a simple form on the schema of a table in a few moments. Access offers a choice of wizards for the creation of forms. The various wizards differ in the structure of the forms they produce. If the services of a wizard are not used, the tool presents a blank page in which the designer can insert the components of the form. The same interface can be used to explore and modify the structure of a pre-existing form, selecting the form in the main database window and then clicking on the *Design* button.

A form is composed of several elements, which need to be defined one by one. The basic element of a form is the *control*, an object that corresponds to a rectangular area of the screen and can be of three types: *bound*, *unbound* and *calculated*. A *bound* control is a component of the form associated with an attribute of the table. This component is responsible for representing the value of the attribute for the particular tuple considered. The representation of values generally requires the printing of a sequence of characters; for attributes with an OLE domain, the representation is delegated to the application managing the attribute content. An *unbound* control contains a fixed value. This kind of control is typically used to define the form labels. The constant value can be a sequence of characters, or a generic object. For example, if we wish to insert a logo into the form, we can assign the figure that represents the logo to an *unbound* control. Finally, *calculated* controls allow the viewing of the results of expressions, evaluated on an arbitrary combination of constant parameters and attribute values. *Calculated* controls cannot be used to insert or update attribute values.

When a form has been designed, its use permits immediate access to and modification of the database content. The insertion of new tuples occurs by writing the attribute values directly into the corresponding bound controls. Forms also permit querying of the database, offering a friendly search command (*Find* option in the *Edit* menu). To modify the value of an attribute, the tuple is selected and the new value is written directly in the slot presenting the old attribute value. The modification is made permanent by moving to a different tuple (typically by pressing on the *page-up* or *page-down* key, which are used to scroll the elements in the form). Figure A.19 shows a form on the tuples of PERSON, extended with an attribute that contains a picture.

   Forms are generally constructed on a single table. We can define forms that contain other forms within themselves, by specifying links between the values in the forms. In this way, we can, for example, define forms for the management of tables with one to many relationships, in which the included form presents all the elements of the table associated with the element in the including form. Think of a pair of tables that describe orders and items appearing in the orders. A form can illustrate at the most external level the common characteristics of the order, for example, customer, date or payment. An included form can then be used to present all the items included in the order.

   A *report* is defined in a similar way to a form, with almost identical tools and concepts. The main difference lies in the fact that a report has typically the aim of providing a description of the database contents at a summary level. For this reason, reports typically contain *calculated* controls that compute aggregate functions, and do not permit the viewing of particular tuples. Another difference from forms is that, in general, reports are printed, instead of being used interactively.

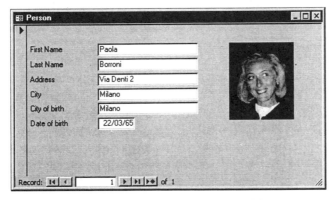

Figure A.19 A form that presents the content of table *Person*.

A.5 The definition of macros

Macros are a way of specifying a set of actions that the system must carry out. In this way, we can automate the execution of a set of tasks. Using macros, we can perform the following actions.

- Let a form interact with other forms or with reports. For example, consider a form that describes the data of clients, and one which describes orders. We can add to the first form a button that activates the second form, presenting the order data for the client presented on the first form. We can also add a button that allows the printing of a report that lists the credit balance of the client, with the total amount of merchandise ordered, delivered and paid for by the client.

- Select and group tuples automatically. In a form, we can insert a button that allows the immediate selection of the tuples that satisfy given conditions.

- Assign values to the attributes. Using a macro, we can assign to a control of a form a value obtained from other controls or other tables of the database.

- Guarantee the correctness of data. Macros are very useful for the manipulation and validation of the data in the form. For example, we can define a macro that reacts to different incorrect values of an attribute with different messages, and guarantee that the inserted data is correct.

- Set properties on forms, reports and attributes. Using macros, we can automate changes of any property of these objects. For example, we can make a form invisible when its contents are needed but not to be seen.

- Automate the transfer of data. If we need to transfer data repeatedly between Access and other applications (both reading and writing), we can automate the task.

- Create a customized environment. We can specify a macro that opens a set of tables, queries, forms and reports each time a database is opened; the toolbar can also be personalized.

- Specify reactions to certain events. For each element of a form, we can specify which macro must be executed after each event of access, selection or modification on the element. This characteristic makes up the basis for the definition of reactive behaviour in Access, which however must not be confused with what is offered by active databases, described in Chapter 12. This behaviour occurs in Access only when a particular form is used for the manipulation of the database; the access or modification event is not detected if the same operation is executed directly in SQL or using another form.

To define a macro, it is necessary to follow the usual steps: first, the *New* option of the *Macro* component in the main database window must be selected. At this point, Access presents the window for macro design. The top half of the window contains a table with two columns: *Action* and *Comment*. The macro is made up of a sequence of actions described in the *Action* column, each on a different row, to which a brief description can be added. In the lower half of the table a set of attributes appears, which, for each single action, specify the parameters of the action. We can specify conditions that must be verified when a command is executed, adding the *Condition* column. We can also use simple control structures.

The available commands can be divided into families. We list the most significant commands in each family.

- Execution: *RunCommand* (invoke a command, like a menu option), *OpenQuery* (execute a query), *RunMacro* (execute a macro), *RunSQL* (execute an SQL command), *RunApp* (execute an external application), *CancelEvent* (disregard an event), *Quit* (close the session), *StopMacro* (terminate the execution of the macro) and *StopAllMacros* (terminate the execution of all macros).

- Access to data: *ApplyFilter* (apply a selection condition to the tuples) *FindNext* (move to next tuple), *FindRecord* (access a tuple), *GotoControl* (position the cursor in a form control), *GoToRecord* (go to a particular tuple).

- Modification of data: *SetValue* (assign a particular value to an attribute), *DeleteObject* (removes an object), *OpenForm*, *OpenQuery*, *OpenReport*, *OpenTable* (commands that open respectively a form, a query a report and a table).

There are other command families, such as those for the transfer of data between Access and other applications, for the modification of the window dimensions and to open dialogue windows with the user.

A simple macro is described in Figure A.20. The macro is associated with modifications on the **Price** attribute of the **ITEM** table. The macro assigns to the attribute **Expensive** the value *Yes*, if the **Price** is greater than 1000, otherwise it assigns the value *No* to the attribute.

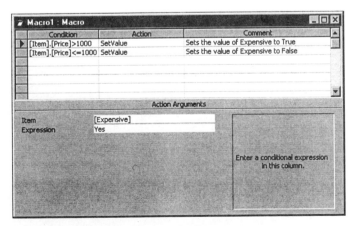

Figure A.20 The macro definition window.

B
DB2
Universal Database

DB2 Universal Database[1] belongs to a 'historic' family of database management systems produced by IBM. The oldest member of this family is SQL/DS, one of the first commercial systems based on the relational model, made available by IBM at the beginning of the eighties. In its turn, SQL/DS has its roots in *System R*, one of the first prototypes of relational DBMSs developed, in the early seventies, in the IBM research laboratories in San José. It was in the development environment of this prototype that SQL was born. This language soon became the standard for all DBMSs based on the relational model.

Together with a complete support for the relational model, DB2 offers some object-oriented features and a rich set of advanced features, including:

- support for the management of non-traditional data types, such as texts, images, sounds and video;

- support for the management of data types and functions defined by the user;

- some extensions of SQL that include powerful On Line Analytical Processing (OLAP) operators and special constructs to specify recursive queries;

- support for parallelisms based on both 'shared memory' configurations, in which a database is managed by a symmetric multiprocessing (SMP) machine, and 'shared nothing' configurations, in which a database is partitioned among different machines connected by a network.

---

1. For the rest of the chapter, we will refer to this product simply as DB2.

The server component of DB2 is available on Windows NT, OS2 and several Unix-based platforms. The client component is also available on Windows and Macintosh environments for personal computers. Client and server can communicate on the basis of diffuse communication protocol standards (TCP/IP, NetBios, etc.). Moreover, DB2 systems can participate in heterogeneous and distributed multi-database environments, using a protocol called *Distributed Relational Database Architecture* (DRDA), adopted by many other database management systems. Finally, DB2 provides support for the main interface standards (such as ODBC, JDBC) and adheres to SQL-2.

In the rest of this appendix, we will describe the general characteristics of the system, paying particular attention to its advanced functionality. We will not discuss the DB2 triggers here, because, although they form an advanced feature of the system, they have already been presented in Chapter 12.

For a more detailed presentation of this system, we refer the reader to the book by Chamberlin [20], one of the inventors of SQL.

B.1 DB2 overview

B.1.1 Versions of the system

The DB2 system is available in four versions, which manage architectures of increasing complexity.

- *Personal edition*: is a version of DB2 for PCs, available on Windows and OS2 environments. It allows the creation and manipulation of single user databases.

- *Workgroup edition*: allows shared access to local databases, by local and remote users and applications. It can be used on symmetric multiprocessor machines having up to four processors.

- *Enterprise edition*: allows shared access to both local and remote databases, by local and remote users and applications. It can be used on symmetric multiprocessor machines having even more than four processors. It can also participate in multi-database system architectures that communicate by means of the DRDA protocol.

- *Enterprise-extended edition*: as well as the functionality of the *Enterprise edition*, this allows the partition of a database among many computers connected by a communication network, each of which can be a parallel machine with even more than four processors.

For each of these versions, the system supplies an application development environment (called Software Developer's Kit) supporting various programming languages (for example, C, C++, Java). There are also several IBM products complementary to DB2, including a tool for the integration of heterogeneous databases (DB2 DataJoiner), a product for the development of data warehouses (Visual Warehouse), an OLAP tool (DB2 OLAP Server), and a set of data mining applications (Intelligent Miner).

B.1.2 Instances and schemas of DB2

We can define many different *instances*[2] of DB2 servers on the same computer. Each instance has a name and its own configuration and can manage many databases, which remain the property of the instance. In this way, we can adapt the system to specific application needs. For example, we can define and configure a DB2 instance for operational applications and another, with different configuration parameters, for decision support applications. There is, however, a predefined instance, created during the installation of DB2, which is simply called DB2. The databases of an instance are organized into *schemas* having a name and composed of collections of tables. The default schema into which the new tables are inserted has the same name as the user account.

DB2 clients possess a list of instances and databases to which they can have access. They are supplied with tools to create new instances, new schemas and new databases. To interact with the server, a client must first access a DB2 instance and then establish a connection with a database of this instance. A client can connect at the same time to many databases of an instance and can then send DB2 commands both at the instance level (for example to create a new database) and at database level (typically an SQL statement). If in a DB2 operation the name of the schema is not specified, then the default schema is referred to.

B.1.3 Interaction with DB2

We can interact with a DB2 database in two ways, as specified below.

- In an interactive manner, in which SQL commands are sent to the system and their results are immediately shown on the screen. Both a simple textual interface and a user-friendly graphical interface are provided.

- Through the execution of programs written in traditional programming languages, in which SQL commands are embedded. Both static and dynamic SQL are available (see Chapter 4). In the former, the structure of SQL statements is known at compilation time, whereas in the latter the SQL statements are generated at run time.

In contrast with other database management systems, DB2 does not offer a 4GL, that is, an ad-hoc application development language. Although this means that we need external compilers to develop applications, it allows the creation of software that is easily portable from one system to another.

---

2. The term 'instance' denotes here an installation of DB2 server and has nothing to do with the notion of 'database instance' introduced in Section 1.3.1.

In the next section, we will describe how a DB2 database is managed, using the above techniques.

B.2 Database management with DB2

B.2.1 Interactive tools

The simplest way to interact with DB2 is by means of a user interface that accepts and immediately executes commands issued by the user. The traditional user interface of DB2 consists of a textual environment, called the *Command Line Processor* (CLP), which is available on all platforms. The CLP is invoked at the operating system level with the db2 command. It accepts both SQL and DB2 administration commands and returns results and messages directly onto the screen. If a command is longer than a line, we must signal the continuation on the following line with the *backslash* (\) character. In the CLP environment, it is not possible to access a database if the database server has not been explicitly activated using the db2start command. An example of interaction with CLP is shown in Figure B.1. The prompt db2 => indicates that the system is ready to receive commands.

```
C:\SQLLIB\BIN>DB2.EXE
(c) Copyright IBM Corporation 1993,1997
Command Line Processor for DB2 SDK 5.0.0

You can issue database manager commands and SQL statements from the command
prompt. For example:
        db2 => connect to sample
        db2 => bind sample.bnd

For general help, type: ?.
For command help, type: ? command, where command can be
the first few keywords of a database manager command. For example:
 ? CATALOG DATABASE for help on the CATALOG DATABASE command
 ? CATALOG           for help on all of the CATALOG commands.

To exit db2 interactive mode, type QUIT at the command prompt. Outside
interactive mode, all commands must be prefixed with 'db2'.
To list the current command option settings, type LIST COMMAND OPTIONS.

For more detailed help, refer to the Online Reference Manual.

db2 => _
```

Figure B.1 The DB2 Command Line Processor.

For Windows and OS2 environments, some advanced tools are also available. They facilitate database management using windows and pop-up menus. These tools can be profitably used in a classic client-server architecture, in which a database resident on a Unix server is accessed and managed by clients made up of PCs. The DB2 interactive graphic tools are described below.

Control Center   This allows the administration of a database using table creation operations, definitions of integrity constraints, authorization controls, backups, restores, and so on. As shown in Figure B.2, the Control Center interface has two main windows. In the one on the left, the DB2 objects available are shown (instances, databases, tables and so on), according to a hierarchical organization. These objects can be declared explicitly by the

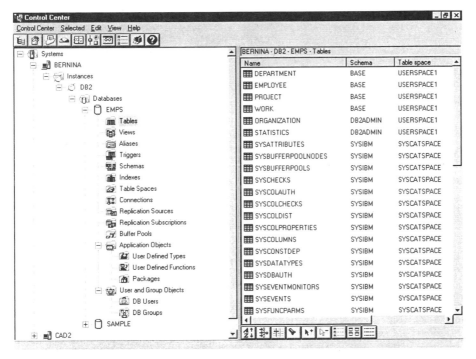

Figure B.2 The DB2 Control Center.

user, or the Control Center can be requested to search on the local network for all the DB2 objects to which access is possible.

In our case, we can observe that two machines containing DB2 objects are available. They are called respectively Bernina and Cad2. The information about the first machine has been expanded, as shown by the minus symbol next to the icon. We can see that this system contains a single DB2 instance (the default instance). This instance contains two databases: one called Emps and another called Sample. For the first of these, all the components are shown, whereas the information about the second is not expanded, as shown by the plus symbol next to the icon.

The window on the right contains information on the object selected in the window on the left. In our case, all the tables of the Emps database are shown. This database contains two schemas: the base schema and the db2admin schema. The tables of the sysibm schema are system tables. By clicking the right mouse button on any object of the screen, we obtain a menu that allows us to perform actions on the selected object. For example, by clicking on the *Tables* icon of a database, we can create a new table. The system guides the user in the execution of many of these actions. Recent releases of DB2 also provide a version of the command center that is accessible from a Web browser.

Command Center This tool allows the user to type and execute SQL commands and to compose *scripts*, that is, sequences of SQL statements to be executed, if necessary, at particular times. The Command Center is made up of three integrated environments: *Script, Results* and *Access Plan*. To move from one to another it is sufficient to click on the corresponding panel. In the first environment, we can type single SQL commands or scripts made up of sequences of SQL commands. This environment also accepts DB2 commands for the administration of a database. For example, commands to create a database, to make a backup copy or to define access privileges. In Figure B.3, an example of an SQL query formulated within the Script environment of the DB2 Command Center is shown.

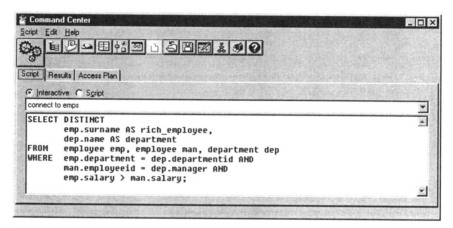

Figure B.3   An SQL query expressed in the DB2 Command Center.

This is a classic query that searches for employees who earn more than their respective managers, in a schema containing the following tables:

EMPLOYEE(<u>EmployeeId</u>, Surname, Department, Salary)
DEPARTMENT(<u>DepartmentId</u>, Name, Location, Manager)

The commands written in the Script environment can be executed by clicking on the *Execute* icon, made up of gears. The result is displayed in the *Result* environment. An example of the contents of this environment following the execution of the query in Figure B.3 is shown in Figure B.4. Moving back and forth between the two environments is then possible to work interactively with a database. The commands or scripts typed in the first environment can be saved in a file or in the Script Center (see below) for successive executions.

The third environment shows the access plans created by the DB2 optimizer for the execution of SQL commands typed in the first environment. The access plans have a tree form: the leaves of the trees correspond to the tables involved in the SQL command and the internal nodes correspond to operations carried out by the system to execute the command. Typical examples are the scanning of a table, a certain type of join between two tables, the ordering of an intermediate result. These trees are created by

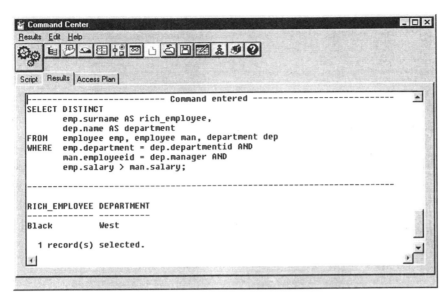

Figure B.4   The result of an SQL query in the DB2 Command Center.

clicking on the appropriate icon on the top of the window. In Figure B.5 a portion of the access plan of the query in Figure B.3 is shown. In the smallest window, the entire graph that represents the access plan is shown and the portion of the graph that is being examined is highlighted. In the selected

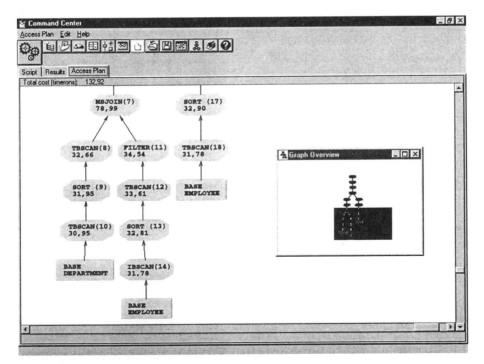

Figure B.5   The access plan generated by DB2 for an SQL query.

portion, a series of preparation operations is reported (scan, sort and filter), which precede the join operation between the DEPARTMENT and EMPLOYEE tables. The values indicated in the node provide an estimate of the cost expected for the operation. By clicking on the single nodes, we can access other data relevant to the corresponding operation, such as more detailed estimates of the cost of execution and of the cardinality of the results. From detailed analysis of the access plans, we can optimize queries, for example by introducing indexes for avoiding an ordering operation.

Script Center The Script Center allows the creation, modification and schedule of sequences of commands that can be SQL, DB2 or operating system statements. A script can run immediately or its execution can be scheduled for particular dates and times. A script can be programmed to be executed repeatedly, for example at '3.00 am each Saturday'. An example of the contents of the Script Center is shown is Figure B.6. Observe that it must be explicitly indicated whether the script contains DB2 statements (including SQL commands) or operating system commands.

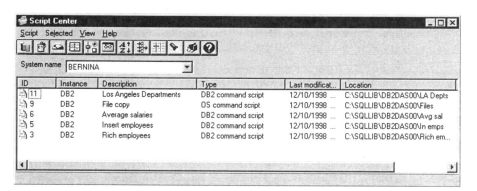

Figure B.6   The DB2 Script Center.

Journal The Journal keeps track of all the events that happen in a database. In particular, we can use the Journal to examine all the query/update operations that have been executed (in the *Jobs* panel), the backup/restore operations performed (*Recovery* panel), the possible signals for attention produced automatically by the system (*Alerts* panel), and all the messages generated by the system on the execution of the various operations (*Message* panel).

Information Center The Information Center supplies a large amount of information on the DB2 system. Using this tool, we can obtain help on various topics. These include subject-oriented descriptions such as 'creation of a table' or 'backup of a database', explanations of the DB2 messages and of the error codes, and a list of example programs that illustrate the various features of DB2.

B.2.2 Application programs

The DB2 system provides many tools for the development of application programs for databases, in which the SQL commands are embedded in host languages, such as C, C++, Java, FORTRAN and COBOL.

As described in Chapter 4, there are two techniques for embedding SQL in a programming language: static SQL and dynamic SQL. The difference is that in the first case, relations and attributes involved in SQL commands are fixed in advance. The only parts of the commands that can remain unknown at compile time are the specific values used for querying and updating. In dynamic SQL, the SQL statements are provided at execution time. Below, we will give a more detailed explanation of the first technique, which is used in most database applications, and we will only look briefly at the tools offered by DB2 for implementing the second.

Static SQL A complete example of a program in static SQL embedded in C for DB2 is shown in Figure B.7. This program accesses a database containing the tables EMPLOYEE and DEPARTMENT mentioned above. It reads the name of an input location and prints names and salaries of the employees of the departments in those locations, ordered by department.

The DB2 prefix indicating an SQL command in a host language is `exec sql`. The program begins with a series of compilation directives that declare the DB2 system library (called `sqlenv.h`) and the `sqlca` structure, used by the system to return status information. In particular, the field `sqlcode` in `sqlca` contains an integer that codes the exit status of the last SQL command executed.

Among the definitions of global variables, note that there are some enclosed in a section delimited by the keywords `declare section`. These variables are called *host* and are the variables that allow the exchange of data between program and database. Note that when a host variable is used in an SQL statement it is preceded by a semicolon: this prefix serves to distinguish variables from attribute names. The `whenever` statement allows us to specify the behaviour of the program after the execution of any unsuccessful SQL command. The statement is not therefore associated to a specific SQL operation, but to the entire program. Three options are possible for this statement: `not found`, `sqlerror`, and `sqlwarning`. With the first option, we can specify what to do when the result of a query is empty ($sqlcode = 100$); with the second, when an error occurs, ($sqlcode < 0$); with the last, when a *warning* occurs, that is, the signalling of an unexpected but not serious event ($sqlcode > 0$). In our program, it has been established that, when an error occurs, the control passes to a routine that loads into a buffer the error message generated, prints it and ends the program. Nothing is specified for empty results and for warnings.

Before interacting with a database, a connection must be established with it by means of the `connect to` statement. Following this, SQL commands can be freely executed. The effects of these commands on the database become

```
                #include <stdlib.h>
                #include <string.h>
                #include <stdio.h>
                #include <sqlenv.h>
                exec sql include sqlca;
                void main() {
                  char CurrDept[10];              /* Program variable declaration */
                  exec sql begin declare section; /* Host variable declaration */
                    char EmpSurname[10];                   /* Employee surname */
                    char DeptName[10];                     /* Department name */
                    char DeptLoc[15];                    /* Department location */
                    long EmpSalary;                        /* Employee salary */
                    char msgbuffer[500];       /* Buffer for DB2 error messages */
                  exec sql end declare section;
                  exec sql declare C1 cursor for          /* Cursor declaration */
                      select distinct emp.surname, emp.salary, dep.name
                      from     employee emp, department dep
                      where    emp.department = dep.department_id and
                               dep.location = :DeptLoc
                      order by dep.name;
                  exec sql whenever sqlerror go to PrintError;
                  exec sql connect to emps;        /* Connection to the database */
                  printf("Enter a location:"); scanf("%s", DeptLoc);
                  exec sql open c1;                          /* Opens the cursor */
                  exec sql fetch c1 into :EmpSurname, :EmpSalary, :DeptName;
                  if (sqlca.sqlcode==100)
                    printf("No department in this location.\n");
                  while (sqlca.sqlcode == 0) {
                    if (strcmp(DeptName,CurrDept)!=0) {
                      printf("\nDepartment: %s\nEmployee\tSalary\n",DeptName);
                      strcpy(CurrDept,DeptName);
                    }                                              /* end if */
                    printf("%s\t%d\n", EmpSurname, EmpSalary);
                    exec sql fetch c1 into :EmpSurname, :EmpSalary, :DeptName;
                  }                                            /* end of while */
                  exec sql close c1;                        /* Closes the cursor */
                  exec sql connect reset;            /* Resets the connection */
                  return;
                PrintError:            /* Retrieves and prints an error message */
                  sqlaintp(msgbuffer, 500, 70, &sqlca);
                  printf("Unexpected DB2 error: %s\n", msgbuffer);
                  return;
                }                                          /* end of main */
```

Figure B.7   An SQL program embedded in C for DB2.

permanent only after the execution of the commit statement. (The example program does not include update operations so it does not use such a statement). To carry out the planned operations, the program makes use of the cursor technique illustrated in Section 4.6. A cursor is first defined over an SQL query that contains the host variable DeptLoc. Then, after having stored in this variable a string read by the input, the cursor is opened and the query is executed. Then, using the fetch statement, the result is first copied, one tuple at a time, into the host variables and then displayed. This operation is controlled by examining the value assumed by the system variable `sqlcode`. In particular, a message is generated when the result is empty (`sqlcode` = 100) and copy and print operations continue as long as there are still tuples to be viewed (`sqlcode` = 0). The cursor is then closed and the connection released.

To create a DB2 application, the program is first precompiled by sending the **prep** *filename* command in the CLP or in the Command Center. The result of the precompilation is then compiled and linked according to the techniques adopted in the environment at disposal for any program written in the chosen host language.

Dynamic SQL   DB2 supplies three different methods for the creation of applications based on dynamic SQL: the *Call Level Interface* (CLI), the *Java Database Connectivity interface* (JDBC) and embedded dynamic SQL. In all three cases special statements are available to perform the following main dynamic SQL operations as described in Chapter 4:

- preparation of an SQL command, with the invocation of the DB2 optimizer that creates the access plan;

- description of the result of an SQL command, specifying the number and type of attributes;

- execution of a prepared SQL command, with the assignment of values to possible host variables used in the command;

- loading of the result, one tuple at a time, into program variables for their later use.

The CLI is based on ODBC (see Chapter 11). This interface provides a library of functions that can be directly invoked by programs to access a database. For example, the function `sqlconnect()` allows connection to a DB2 database, the `sqlprepare()` function prepares an SQL command for its execution, the `sqlexecute()` executes a prepared SQL command and finally the `sqlfetch()` function loads a tuple into host variables of the program. The great advantage of the programs that use the CLI technique is that they have no need to be precompiled. Furthermore, they can be used on other DBMSs that support ODBC.

The JDBC interface (see Chapter 14) is based on the same principle as CLI, but is dedicated to the development of programs written in Java and is thus purely object-oriented. In particular, this interface is supplied with the `executeQuery`(*String*) method. This takes as entry a string containing an SQL command and returns an object of the predefined class RESULTSET, made up of a set of tuples. This class possesses a number of methods that allow the programmer easily to manipulate the tuples contained in the objects of the class. As well as standard Java applications, this interface allows the development of *applets*, that is, programs that can be loaded and executed by a Web browser (see Chapter 14). In this way, DB2 databases can be accessed by any computer connected to the Internet, without needing to install the client component of the DB2 system on it.

Finally, dynamic SQL can be embedded in programming languages in a way similar to static SQL. However, in contrast to the CLI and the JDBC interface, these programs need to be pre-compiled. There are particular statements (preceded by exec sql) that allow the specification of the dynamic SQL operations. In particular, the preparation phase of an SQL command is implemented using the prepare *name* from *variable* statement, where the variable stores an SQL command. This SQL command can contain question marks that indicate the presence of parameters that are to be supplied during the execution phase. In the case of queries, the cursor mechanism can be used, as happens with static SQL.

If the number and type of attributes of the SQL commands are not known in advance, we can use a *describer*. This is a data structure that describes the type, length and name of a variable number of attributes of relations. The DB2 system supplies for this purpose the predefined describer sqlda, which is a record containing a variable number of fields of sqlvar type, one for each attribute to be described. The number of these fields is stored in the sqld field of sqlda. The sqlvar fields are records themselves, containing a number of fields, including sqlname, sqltype and sqlen, which respectively store the name, type and length of an attribute. In the preparation phase, we can indicate the use of this describer with the following syntax: prepare *name* into sqlda from *variable*. After the execution of this statement, the description of the command stored in the variable is loaded into the sqlda. Using this technique, we can easily implement, for example, a personalized user interface, capable of accepting and executing arbitrary SQL commands.

B.3 Advanced features of DB2

As mentioned at the beginning of the chapter, DB2 offers a set of advanced features. Although not standardized, these features give an interesting indication of the system characteristics of current database management systems.

B.3.1 Extension of SQL for queries

DB2 adheres to the entry level of SQL-2, but also provides several extensions. These extensions allow a notable increase in the expressive power of the language, especially as regards the query operations. We will look at some of them by means of examples.

CASE In the select clause of SQL for DB2, we can specify conditional expressions. These expressions allow the generation of values that appear in a column of the result, based on conditions defined on other columns of the result itself. They are specified with the case construct. Assume that we have a table containing information on vehicles, with the schema:

VEHICLE(RegistrationNumber, Type, Manufacturer, Length, NWheels)

Assume now that we wish to calculate a tax on the vehicles registered after 1997, based on a tariff that refers to the type of vehicle. A possible solution is as follows, where the value is calculated on the basis of values that appear in the Type column of the VEHICLE relation.

```
select RegistrationNumber,
  case Type
    when 'car' then 42.50 * Length
    when 'truck' then 25.00 * NWheels
    when 'motorbike' then 37.00
    else null
  end as Tax
from Vehicle
where RegistrationYear > 1997;
```

The case expressions can also be used for update operations. For example, the following SQL command specifies a modification of the salary in the EMPLOYEE relation, based on the values in the Department column.

```
update Employee
set Salary =
  case
    when Department = 'Administration' then Salary * 1.1
    when Department = 'Production' then Salary * 1.15
    when Department = 'Distribution' then Salary * 1.12
    else Salary
  end;
```

It should be observed that in standard SQL the only way to perform the same operation would be to use multiple commands.

Nesting of queries   An interesting facility offered by SQL for DB2 is the ability to nest queries, not only in the where clause, but also in the from clause. This characteristic is based on a principle of *orthogonality* of programming languages, which requires that independent features can be combined without restrictions. In the SQL context, orthogonality suggests that a select statement, returning a table, must be allowed to appear anywhere a table is expected, including the from clause.

As an example, look again at the schema:

EMPLOYEE(EmployeeId, Surname, Department, Salary)

Suppose we wish to find the employees who earn 30% more than the average salary in the department to which they belong. The query can be expressed in DB2 with the following SQL statement.

```
select Surname, Salary
from Employee as Emp, (select Department, avg(Salary)
                       from Employee
                       group by Department)
                       as AvgSalDept(Department, AvgSalary)
where Emp.Department = AvgSalDept.Department and
      Emp.Salary > AvgSalDept.AvgSalary * 1.3
```

This query can also be expressed in a standard way, by moving the nested SQL statement, which determines the average value of salaries, within the where clause. It is however easy to show that this functionality increases the expressive power of the language: we can write SQL queries embedded in the from clause that cannot be expressed in another way.

Suppose for example, that the schema possesses a further table with the schema JOBS(<u>Employee</u>, <u>Project</u>), which stores the projects in which the employees participate. The average number of projects in which the employees of the Production department participate can be retrieved as follows:

```
select avg(NumberOfProjects)
from Employee as Emp, (select Employee, count(Project)
                       from Jobs
                       group by Employee)
                       as NoProjects(Employee, NumberOfProjects)
where Emp.EmployeeID = NoProjects.Employee and
      Emp.Department = 'Production'
```

This query cannot be expressed with a nesting in the where clause, because it requires the use of the result of an aggregation (count) to evaluate another aggregation (avg). However, in the where clause, we can use the result of a nested query only for a comparison of values. (See Chapter 4.)

OLAP operations   DB2 provides some extensions of the group by clause, to specify queries that involve complex aggregations of data. These operations are particularly useful for database analysis oriented to decision making. As we said in Chapter 13, these operations are commonly termed On Line Analytical Processing (OLAP).

Suppose we have a database that registers the sales of a chain of stores, organized according to the following schema:

SALE(<u>Store</u>, <u>Item</u>, Income)

LOCATION(<u>Store</u>, City, State)

PRODUCT(<u>Item</u>, Category)

As we said in Chapter 13, this could be the star schema of a data mart constructed for specific analysis activity. In this data mart, the SALE table stores the facts on which the analysis is focused (centre of the star), while LOCATION and PRODUCT constitute the dimension tables.

A first SQL extension provided by DB2 allows the specification of aggregations on different levels of the same dimension with the rollup construct. For example, the statement that follows allows the calculation of the total income of the chain, grouped by store, city and state (all levels of the 'Location' dimension).

```
select Location.Store, City, State, sum(Income) as TotIncome
from Sale, Location
where Sale.Store = Location.Store
group by rollup(State, City, Location.Store)
```

A possible result of the command is shown in Figure B.8. Observe that this instruction also calculates the global total of the incomes. In the result tables the tuple components for which there is no applicable value (for example, the store in the third tuple) are filled by DB2 with null values. As we said in Chapter 13, these components should instead represent 'all the possible values'. To improve the readability of reports generated with these operations, it is then preferable to fill these spaces with an appropriate term, for example, 'all'. This operation can be easily carried out using the `case` construct.

Store	City	State	TotIncome
White	Los Angeles	CA	34
Black	Los Angeles	CA	32
NULL	Los Angeles	CA	66
Brown	San Francisco	CA	25
NULL	San Francisco	CA	25
NULL	NULL	CA	91
Red	New York	NY	28
NULL	New York	NY	28
NULL	NULL	NY	28
NULL	NULL	NULL	119

Figure B.8 Result of a roll-up operation.

We can also carry out aggregations computed along several dimensions, possibly on different levels. This operation corresponds to the data cube operation described in Section 13.3.3 and is carried out using the `cube` construct. For example, the following instruction calculates the total number of sales by city and by product category.

```
select City, Category, count(Income) as NoOfSales
from  Sale, Location, Product
where Sale.Store = Location.Store and
      Sale.Item = Product.Item
group by cube(City, Category)
```

A possible result of this instruction is shown in Figure B.9. Observe that in this case, too, DB2 does not supply special values for components of the result with no applicable value.

Recursion Suppose we have a table SUPERVISION(Employee, Head), which stores the immediate superior of each employee. Now suppose we wish to know the superiors, the superiors' superiors, and all the other indirect superiors of the employee Jones. It is well known that this query cannot be expressed in either relational algebra or SQL-2 because, intuitively, it would require an unpredictable number of joins of the SUPERVISION table with itself.

City	Category	NoOfSales
Los Angeles	milk	2453
Los Angeles	coffee	988
New York	milk	789
New York	coffee	987
Los Angeles	NULL	3441
New York	NULL	1776
NULL	milk	3242
NULL	coffee	1975
NULL	NULL	5217

Figure B.9   Result of a cube operation.

The query can, however, be expressed in DB2 using the following recursive command.

```
with Superior(Employee, SuperHead) as
     ((select Employee, Head
       from Supervisor)
       union all
      (select Supervisor.Employee, Superior.SuperHead
       from Supervisor, Superior
       where Supervisor.Head = Superior.Employee))
select SuperHead
from Superior
where Employee = 'Jones'
```

In this command, the with clause defines the SUPERIOR table, which is constructed recursively, starting from the SUPERVISOR table. In particular, the construction involves a basic non-recursive query over the SUPERVISOR table (base definition) and a recursive query that expresses a join between the tables SUPERVISOR and SUPERIOR (recursive definition). It is interesting to observe that the schema adopted by DB2 for recursive queries is similar to the definition of intentional predicates adopted in the logical language Datalog, as described in Section 3.3.

B.3.2 Object-oriented features of DB2

DB2 offers three independent features that can be combined for the creation of databases with object-oriented characteristics: complex data types, user data types, and user functions.

Complex data   DB2 provides three types of pre-defined data types that can be used to store complex data in a table (for example, images), which are called generically LOBs (Large Objects).

* *Blob (Binary Large Object)* represents a data item in binary form, up to two gigabytes. Blob data cannot be assigned or compared with data of other types.

- *Clob (Character Large Object)* represents a data item composed of a sequence of one byte characters, up to two gigabytes. The Clob data can be compared with data of string type (`Char` and `Varchar`).

- *Dbclob (Double-Byte Character Large Object)* represents a data item composed of a sequence of two-byte characters, up to two gigabytes. Dbclob data can be used only on databases with a suitable configuration.

A possible table definition that contains LOB data is as follows.

```
create table Employee (
  EmployeeId integer not null unique,
  Name       varchar(20),
  Salary     decimal(7,3),
  HiringDate date,
  Picture    blob(5M) compact,
  Resume     clob(500K)
)
```

In this table, the `Picture` column serves to store images and the `Resume` column, texts. The dimensions specified in brackets indicate a maximum value. The `compact` option specifies that the data item should occupy the least possible space on the disc, possibly trading efficiency.

There are indeed many limitations to the use of LOB data in DB2 SQL commands. In particular, it is not possible to compare directly columns of LOB type with operators such as =, >, < or in. It is however possible to use the `like` operator. For example, the SQL command

```
select EmployeeId, Name
from Employee
where Resume like '%DBA%'
```

retrieves the employees for which the DBA string appears in the `Resume` column.

DB2 manages LOBs in a way that minimizes their movements from one location in the memory to another. In particular, LOBs can be manipulated in applications using suitable variables called *locators*. These represent a LOB without physically storing it. With the appropriate use of locators, we can defer or even avoid the loading of a LOB in main memory. For example, the copy of a LOB happens simply by copying the locator. A locator is defined in the host variable declaration section of a program with the SQL command `type is` *TypeOfLob LocatorName*. The locator can then be used like all the other host variables to manage a LOB of associated type. We can also manipulate locators using special functions. These special functions include `posstr`, which finds the position of the first occurrence of a pattern in a LOB, and `substr`, which returns the substring of a LOB, included in the specified positions.

As well as these basic pre-defined types, DB2 provides, as external packages, a series of *extenders*. These are further data types, more specific than LOBs, for the management of non-traditional data. Extenders are equipped with auxiliary functions for the manipulation of the particular data types. There is, for example, a DB2 extender for text data, whose associated functions allow the indexing of texts and searches based on keywords.

User types   A user type (called *distinct* in DB2) is a type defined from basic data types of DB2. For example, the user types Money, Image and Text can be defined as follows:

```
create distinct type Money as decimal(7,2) with comparisons;
create distinct type Image as blob(100M);
create distinct type Text as clob(500K) compact;
```

The **as** clause specifies the *source data type*, while the **with comparisons** clause specifies that all the comparison operators defined for the source type are also allowed on the user type. Unfortunately, only pre-defined DB2 data types can be used as source types and definitions cannot be nested.

Once defined, the user types can be freely used in the creation of tables. For example, the preceding definition of the EMPLOYEE table can be rewritten as follows:

```
create table Employee (
  EmployeeId integer not null unique,
  Name       varchar(20),
  Salary     money,
  HiringDate date,
  Picture    image,
  Resume     text
)
```

On columns defined on a user type, it is not generally possible to apply the same operations that can be applied to the respective source types. For example, it is not possible to sum two data items of Money type. We can however, obviate this limitation with the definition of suitable user functions, described below.

User functions   The user functions can be declared explicitly using the **create function** statement, which assigns a name to the function and defines its semantics. These functions are associated with a database and can be used only in the context of that database. An important characteristic of DB2 user functions is that they adhere to the principle of overloading, as in object-oriented programming. We can define the same function more than once as long as the input parameters of the various definitions differ in type and/or number. Based on the same principle, we can also redefine pre-defined DB2 functions, for example arithmetical operators. The DB2 user functions can be classified as follows.

• *Internal functions*: these are constructed on the basis of predefined DB2 functions, called *source functions*, in a similar way to user types

- *External functions*: these correspond to external programs written in traditional programming languages (C or Java). They may or may not contain SQL commands. The declaration of an external function contains the specifications of the physical location where the code, which implements the function, is stored. There are two types of external function:

  o *scalar functions*: these can receive many parameters as input but return a single value as output: if the name of the function redefines a basic operator (for example '+') then such functions can be invoked using the infix notation;

  o *table functions*: these return a collection of tuples of values, which are considered as if they were rows of a table; each time that these functions are invoked, they return a new tuple or a special code indicating that no more tuples are available.

Internal functions are mainly used together with user types to allow the application of standard functions to user types. For example, with reference to the user type Salary defined above, we can define some internal functions with the following declarations.

```
create function "*"(Money, Decimal()) returns Money
   source "*"(Decimal(), Decimal())
create Function Total(Money) returns Money
   source Sum(Decimal())
```

In these declarations, we define the name of the function, the types of input parameters (which can also be user types), the type of the result and the *source function*. The source function is a DB2 function that is applied when we invoke the user function that is being defined. In our case, we have redefined the product operator and have defined a new function, based on the aggregate operator sum of SQL. These declarations make SQL commands such as the following legal:

```
select Age, Total(Salary)
from Employee
group by Age;

update Employee
set Salary = Salary * 1.1
where Department = 'Production';
```

Expressions that involve, for example, the sum of a salary with a decimal number are instead not legal because the sum operator is undefined for the Money type.

Suppose now that we wish to define an external scalar function that calculates the salary earned by an employee, based on his length of service, assuming that the length of service is calculated on the basis of the date of hiring. A possible definition of such an external function is as follows:

```
create function StandardSalary(Date) returns Money
   external name '/usr/db2/bin/salary.exe!StdSal'
   deterministic
   no external action
   language c parameter style db2sql
   no sql;
```

This declaration defines the external function StandardSalary, which receives a Date item as input and returns a Money data item. The external clause indicates the path name of the file that contains the code of the function. The name after the exclamation mark indicates the module (C function in our case), within the file that implements the user function. The deterministic clause specifies that many invocations of the function on the same values return the same result. The external action clause specifies whether the function involves actions external to the database, as for example the writing in a file. This information can be useful for the optimizer to decide whether to limit the number of invocations of an external function. The language clause specifies the programming language used to implement the external function and the transfer method of parameters with it. The standard method for C is called db2sql, while the one for Java is db2general. Finally, the last clause indicates whether the function involves access to a database or not.

We will not discuss here the techniques by which an external function is implemented. We will just mention the fact that there are conventions for transforming programming language types into SQL data types and that the implementation of a user function has other parameters, which allows the control of the data flow. As an example of the use of an external function, the following command retrieves surnames and salaries of the employees who earn 20% more than the reference salary, also showing the value of the salary.

```
select Surname, Salary, StandardSalary(HiringDate)
from Employee
where Salary > StandardSalary(HiringDate) * 1.2;
```

Observe that the condition in the where clause is valid because: (a) the user function returns a data item of type Money; (b) the product of this data type by a decimal value has been defined above; and (c) the value returned by the product is of Money type and can therefore be compared with the Salary attribute, as established by the definition of the user type Money (see above).

The table functions constitute a particularly interesting aspect of DB2. They allow the easy transformation of an external information source into a table that can be manipulated in SQL. It is sufficient to write a program that accesses the data source, for example a text file or an MS Excel file, possibly filters the data based on parameters passed as input, and finally returns them one row at a time. The return of the various rows happens as follows. The system allocates an area of memory (called a *scratchpad*), which preserves its content from one execution of the program to another. In this way, a program can access information about the previous execution; for example, the last position accessed in a file.

Suppose we have a function of this type that takes as input the name of a city and returns sequences of values stored on a remote file, corresponding to sales information of stores located in that city. The definition of the corresponding table function could be as follows:

```
create function Sales(Char(20))
   returns table (Store    char(20),
                  Product char(20),
                  Income  Integer)
   external name '/usr/db2/bin/sales'
   deterministic
   no external action
   language c parameter style db2sql no sql
   scratchpad
   final call disallow parallel;
```

Note that, apart from some specific clauses, the definition is similar to the definition of an external scalar function. The main difference is that the result of the function is composed of many parameters, which are interpreted as attributes of a table.

A possible SQL command that uses the table function defined above is as follows:

```
select Store, sum(Income)
from table(Sales('Los Angeles')) as LASales
where Product = 'Toy'
group by Store;
```

This command retrieves the total income taken by the stores in Los Angeles for sales of toys. The table queried is not stored in the database (as indicated by the keyword table), but is generated by the table function Sales, to which is passed, as an entry parameter, the string 'Los Angeles'.

By using user types and user functions together, we can obtain a data management system with object-oriented features. For example, we can define a class 'Polygons' using a LOB user type. We can then define as user functions a series of methods of this class for constructing a new object, modifying it, printing it and calculating its perimeter and area.

C

Oracle PL/SQL

In this appendix, we first describe the general characteristics of *Oracle Server*, illustrating the various tools and the architecture of the system. We then present the object extensions that were recently introduced. We finally focus on the programming language PL/SQL, a procedural extension of SQL, with control structures, definition of variables, subprograms and packages. We refer to version 8.0 of Oracle Server and version 8.0 of the PL/SQL language.

C.1 Tools architecture of Oracle

Oracle is currently one of the main world producers of software, and the range of products offered has as its foundation the database management system Oracle Server, available for most types of computer. An important strength of Oracle is this availability on various platforms, which facilitates the integration among databases at various levels in an organization.

The range of Oracle products consists of the following families.

- *Database servers*. These are available for most platforms, including PCs, local network servers, workstations, mini-computers, mainframes and parallel supercomputers. The servers can then be enhanced by various components, as follows.

  ○ *Video Option*: for the management of multimedia data.

  ○ *Spatial Data Option*: for the management of geographic and spatial data.

  ○ *ConText Option*: for the management of unstructured text-type information. This component adds to the server the functionality of an information retrieval system.

  ○ *On Line Analytical Processing Option* (OLAP): for increasing database efficiency, when the database is used in tasks of data analysis and decision support.

○ *Messaging Option*: to use the database as a tool for the interchange of messages between information system users.

○ *Web Server*: a proprietary HTTP server allowing access to the database with a Web interface (a data access mechanism that will acquire more and more importance, see Chapter 14).

The observation that can immediately be made is that a database server can now manage data of any type, structured or not, extending the range of applications of a DBMS well beyond its traditional domain.

• *Communication Products*. Along with the server, it is indispensable to provide tools that allow dialogue with the outside world, given the wide variety of protocols, systems and network interfaces that exist. To provide efficient communication among many systems, Oracle offers a large selection of products for communication, including the network manager SQL*Net.

• *OLAP tools*. This is an area that is showing increasing importance (see Chapter 13). To satisfy these needs, we have seen that Oracle Server can be extended with an additional OLAP module. As well as these, Oracle provides external support tools and offers database servers (Oracle Express) specially designed for data warehouse management, capable of offering richer functionality and greater services of data analysis. The reference architecture for these systems assumes the existence of a replication mechanism for the central database. The server dedicated to analysis then operates on the copy. The support tools for data analysis are in any case able to operate even on a traditional server.

• *Tool environments*. The Oracle environment comprises many support tools. The tools are organized into three families.

○ *Designer*: provides support tools for the design of information systems, focused on the database role. It consists of a set of tools for the specification of organizational processes and for the description of tasks, interfaces and application components. Then there are tools that use these specifications automatically to generate the SQL code corresponding to the given descriptions. With these tools, the designer can be supported in the definition of the database schema and also in the generation of applications.

○ *Developer*: provides tools for writing applications. For data description and applications, all the tools of this family use the same repository as was constructed by the tools in the earlier environment. This is a good example of an integrated development environment. Among them, we note the *Forms* tool for the definition of applications, based on the definition of forms and targeted to different environments (Windows, Mac, X/Motif or alphanumeric terminals). Other important components are *Reports* (a report generator) and *Procedure Builder*, a support tool for the design of PL/SQL code, which provides an interpreter and a debugger for the language. All these tools offer assistance in the production of advanced applications, such as those for client-server environments and graphical interfaces.

o *Discoverer*: provides tools for the analysis of the database content. Among these, there are tools that provide a graphical interface for navigation on the database, together with tools that allow the execution of more sophisticated data analysis. These tools all offer an interface that does not require knowledge of SQL, and that tries to mask the complexity of the database. A representative tool of this family is *Data Query*.

• *Gateways*. A very important issue in the database world is that of interoperability, or rather the need to make different database managers co-exist and interact (as we have seen in Chapter 10). For this purpose, Oracle provides a set of applications that are capable of making Oracle communicate with various other products.

• *Groupware*. A slowly growing market is that of support tools for co-operation in the work environment, known as *Computer-Supported Cooperative Work* (CSCW). The objective is that of providing tools that exploit the computer network as an organizational resource, in a more structured manner than is actually offered by tools such as electronic mail. Oracle exploits the database server as a basis for co-operation tools.

The presence of so many products makes it very difficult to describe the interaction with the system, as what is important in one context or platform may not be valid in another. For this reason, we will not describe the use of the system, but will concentrate instead on three aspects of Oracle Server: the base domains, the object-relational extensions and the PL/SQL language. The base domains are dealt with because they constitute one of the basic design choices of a DBMS, and this knowledge is necessary for the use of PL/SQL. The object-relational extensions illustrate a concrete application of the ideas presented in Chapter 11. PL/SQL is the main subject of this appendix. It is described because it represents one of the most sophisticated and best known examples of procedural extension of SQL, an important aspect in the exploitation of a DBMS.

C.2 Base domains

Oracle extends the base domains defined in standard SQL.

• `binary_integer`. This is a domain of integers with a binary representation on 32 bits. It allows the sub-domains `natural` (from 0 to $2^{31} - 1$) and `positive` (from 1 to $2^{31} - 1$). The most similar SQL domain is the `integer` domain.

- number. This is the most general domain for the representation of numbers and is characterized by precision and scale. This domain permits the representation of both integer and real values; it has the power to describe the whole family of numeric domains of standard SQL (for example, decimal, double, float and integer). Each declaration of a numeric domain with the SQL syntax is translated by the system in a declaration on the number domain, with appropriate values of precision and scale.

- char. When it is characterized by length, it represents strings of characters, otherwise it defines a domain of a single character. The maximum length of the string is 255. It corresponds exactly to the char domain of SQL.

- varchar2. This allows the representation of strings of characters of variable length. The maximum length is equal to 2000 characters. This corresponds to the domain varchar of SQL. The term varchar can actually be used. The name varchar2 was chosen to prevent future modifications of the varchar domain in standard SQL from having an impact on applications. A designer using the domain varchar2 has the guarantee that the behaviour of the program in future versions of Oracle will remain unchanged; instead, the varchar domain depends on the decisions of the SQL standardization committee. If an application is developed that must be used only in the Oracle environment, there are no strong objections to the use of this domain; otherwise it is preferable to write code that respects the standard as far as possible.

- long. The name would lead us to suppose that this concerns a numeric domain (similar to the type long in C). It is in fact a domain of strings of characters of variable length with a maximum length of $2^{31} - 1$. It is therefore an extension of the varchar2 domain.

- raw. This allows the representation of data in binary form, seen as strings of bytes of variable length. It is managed as if it contained strings of characters, except that the system never tries to interpret it for conversion (as for example happens for characters, when transferring from a system with ASCII codes to a system with EBCDIC codes). The maximum length for an attribute is 255 bytes.

- long raw. This extends the raw domain by allowing a maximum length equal to $2^{31} - 1$ bytes.

- date. This represents instants of time and corresponds to the timestamp domain of standard SQL. As well as the date, hours, minutes and seconds are also represented. There is no domain corresponding to the time domain of standard SQL.

- rowid. Oracle internally allocates a unique identifier to each tuple. The identifier is a binary value using six bytes. The six bytes indicate the file to which the tuples belong, the block number within the file, and the position of the tuple within the block.

• LOB (*LargeOBject*): this is a family of domains that were introduced in version 8 of Oracle Server. These domains can be considered as extensions of the long and long raw domains. The domains of this family are *Binary LOB* (BLOB), *Character LOB* (CLOB), and *National Character LOB* (NCLOB). There are a few differences between long and LOB domains, the main one being that LOBs are managed with *locators*. That is, if a table has a LOB attribute, then its value is a reference to a database area where the actual value of the LOB is kept. Locators are more compact, have fewer restrictions than long attributes, and offer a richer access to the data (possibly identifying a fraction of the LOB content, located anywhere in the data). A variant of the LOB domain is the BFILE (binary file) domain. The BFILE domain represents references to files kept outside the server. Data accessed by a BFILE attribute cannot exploit the transactional support the server offers for internal data.

C.3 The object-relational extension of Oracle

Version 8 of Oracle has introduced several object features into the relational engine. The approach follows the guidelines delineated in Section 11.3: an object-relational system is compatible with previous relational applications and provides object orientation features, minimizing the need for a complex migration of existing data, long retraining of personnel and expensive rewriting of applications.

The basic component of the object extension are the type definition services, which improve significantly the domain definition services of relational systems and are comparable to the type definition mechanisms of modern programming languages. The SQL interpreter offers a create type command, which permits the definition of object types. Each element of an object type is characterized by an implicit identifier (the *object id* or OID). The command:

```
create type EmployeeType as object
(     RegNo      char(5),
      FirstName  varchar(25),
      LastName   varchar(25),
      DateOfBirth date,
      member     function Age() return number )
```

defines an object type EmployeeType, with attributes RegNo, FirstName, LastName and DateOfBirth. EmployeeType also contains a method Age(), available on all the objects of EmployeeType. Types can be used to in the definition of tables, as in the following command:

```
create table Employee of EmployeeType
```

Each row of the EMPLOYEE table is an EmployeeType object, with the attributes and methods described in EmployeeType. The following query extracts information from the objects that return a value for Age between 35 and 45:

```
select E.RegNo, E.FirstName, E.LastName, E.DateOfBirth
from Employee E
where E.Age() between 35 and 45
```

Type definitions can be arbitrarily composed. The following type definition reuses EmployeeType in the definition of an object structure describing departments:

```
create type DeptType as object
(      DeptName varchar(25),
       Director EmployeeType,
       member    function NoOfEmployees() return number )
```

Each object of DeptType contains an object of EmployeeType. A command for the insertion of values into a table DEPT containing objects of DeptType, can be:

```
insert into Dept values ('Administration',
EmployeeType('23456', 'Mary', 'Lafayette', '6/6/1951'))
```

An alternative to the direct import of objects is represented by the use of references to object types, denoted by the keyword ref. A definition of DeptType which does not explicitly contain an object of EmployeeType, but instead makes reference to it, is:

```
create type NewDeptType as object
(      DeptName varchar(25),
       Director ref EmployeeType,
       member    function NoOfEmployees() return number )
```

Each object of NewDeptType refers to an EmployeeType object defined in an external object table. The NewDeptType object keeps an internal representation of the OID of the EmployeeType object.

The create type command can be used for the definition of arrays and typed tables, two constructors absent from the relational model. The definition of arrays uses the construct varray (that is, varying array). This construct permits the definition of a structure that contains an ordered list of elements. Each element is identified by its position in the array, and the array can contain between zero and a maximum number of elements. The maximum number of elements must be specified by the definition command. An example of use of an array is the structure defined in the next two commands. The Polygon varray keeps the geometric coordinates of the vertices of a polygon with at most 10 vertices:

```
create type Vertex as object
(      Xcoord number,
       Ycoord number);
```

```
create type Polygon as varray(10) of Vertex;
```

The definition of a typed table has a similar structure. A typed table is like a varray, except that a table can contain an arbitrary number of elements and that the elements are unordered and there is no direct access mechanism to them. For example, the following command defines a typed table on EmployeeType elements:

```
create type EmployeeTableType as table of EmployeeType
```

Varrays and tables can be used in other table or type definitions, at an arbitrary level of nesting. We offer two definitions that build structures with respectively a nested varray and a nested table. The first creates a table of polygons; the second defines a table representing a department.

```
create table Polygons as
(       Figure Polygon);

create table Dept as
(       DeptName   varchar(25),
        Manager    ref EmployeeType,
        Employees  EmployeeTableType
        member     function NoOfEmployees() return number )
```

Each element of POLYGONS contains a varray of vertices. Each element of DEPT will be associated with a table of EmployeeType rows. To access the content of a nested table, Oracle offers the operator the. Thus, to extract the data contained in the EMPLOYEES nested table, we can write the following statement:

```
select Emp.FirstName, Emp.LastName, Emp.Age()
       from the(select D.Employees
                     from Dept D
                     where D.DeptName = 'Production') Emp
       where Emp.DateOfBirth < 1/1/65
```

An important feature, one that facilitates the integration between the object extensions and the existing relational data, is the definition of *object views*. Object views permit the definition of an object structure on top of existing relational data. This is based on two mechanisms. The first is the with object oid clause, that specifies the attributes that build the identifier of the view elements. In this way, the object identifier is not managed internally by the system, but it is explicitly derivable from the tuple identifiers. The second mechanism is the availability of view updating mechanisms that allow the modification of the object view and automatically propagate the changes to the underlying relational data. For complex view definitions, where the system would not be able to identify an automatic propagation from the object view update to the underlying data (such as when the view computes a join), the system allows the definition of instead of triggers on view updates. These are responsible for implementing the update propagation mechanisms the designer considers adequate. An example of object view definition is:

```
create view EmpView of EmployeeType
with object id (RegNo) as
select RegNo, FirstName, LastName, BirthDate
from Employee
```

This view builds objects of **EmployeeType**, extracting data from a relational table EMPLOYEE. The attribute **RegNo** takes the role of object identifier. In this case, the system is able to propagate automatically updates on the object view EMPVIEW to updates on the relational table EMPLOYEE.

We do not explore further the object-relational extension of Oracle 8. It is important to observe that this extension has a profound impact on all the components of the Oracle architecture (server, tools, gateways, etc). Even if we will not make explicit reference to it, all the functionality of the object-relational extension of Oracle Server is available in the PL/SQL language that we are going to describe.

C.4 PL/SQL language

The name PL/SQL stands for 'Procedural Language/SQL' and describes a procedural extension of SQL. It is thus possible to use the SQL environment to write applications that would otherwise require the use of a host language. This solution offers the advantages of greater portability (from one Oracle server to another) and is indicated for the definition of simple tasks. Another advantage is that often PL/SQL applications are more efficient, particularly when the traditional application would generate many queries similar to each other. PL/SQL can actually reduce both the traffic on the network and the load on the syntactic-semantic analyzer of the server.

The language is a modern programming language that offers characteristics such as control structures, exception management, encapsulation, prototyping and modularization. A generic PL/SQL program is characterized by a set of blocks. Each block has the following structure: first is a declarations part, in which the objects used in the block are defined, then the steps of the program are described, and finally the exceptions are treated. The mandatory part is the specification of the steps of the program. Blocks may be arbitrarily nested. The declarations of a block can be used in all the blocks embedded in it. If a block redefines a term, then in the block itself the term will assume the new definition.

Let us look at a simple example, which can give an idea of the general characteristics of the language:

```
declare
      Sal number;
begin
      select Salary into Sal
            from Employee
            where RegNo = '575488'
            for update of Salary;
      if Sal > 30 then
```

```
            update Employee
            set Salary = Salary * 1.1
            where RegNo = '575488';
      else
            update Employee
            set Salary = Salary * 1.15
            where RegNo = '575488';
      end if;

      commit;
  exception
      when no_data_found then
            insert into Error
            values('The RegNo does not exist', sysdate);
  end;
```

This program updates the salary of the employee with the registration number 575488. The program uses a local variable Sal in which the value of the salary is held. If the salary is higher than 30 thousand, the salary is increased by 10%, otherwise by 15%. If the select returns no tuples, a no_data_found exception is generated and the program returns to the execution inserting a tuple into the ERROR table. This contains a description of the error and the time at which it occurred.

This program is composed of a single block. We distinguish among the declaration part (enclosed between the keywords declare and begin), the execution part (enclosed between begin and exception) and the part that manages exceptions (between exception and end). Observe that the program integrates SQL commands (select, update and insert) with control structures typical of programming languages.

C.4.1 Execution of PL/SQL in a client-server environment

As regards the architecture of the system, Oracle offers two different techniques for the use of PL/SQL in a client-server environment.

The first solution makes the PL/SQL code interpreter reside with the client. This component is responsible for executing step by step the program instructions, sending to the server only the SQL commands to be executed. This solution has the advantage of freeing the server from the task of interpreting the PL/SQL blocks. The client can also send to the server a pre-compiled representation of the SQL command.

The second technique puts the system component responsible for the interpretation of the PL/SQL program directly on the server. In this situation, the client sends the entire program to the server, where it is executed. The advantage of the second solution is that the need to exchange commands between client and server is minimized. The Oracle system allows both solutions, and thus it is up to the designer to choose the best solution; this choice in complex applications depends upon many factors and requires careful consideration.

C.4.2 Declarations of variables and cursors

A PL/SQL program allows the definition of variables. In the declaration, the name of the variable is specified, together with the domain from which the allowable values can be drawn. Variables may be assigned an initial value and the not null option can be used to ensure that the variable cannot assume the null value. The domains that can be assigned are the domains described in Section C.2, with the addition of the domain boolean, which allows the values true, false and null.

Here are some examples of variable declarations:

```
Description varchar(255);
Finished  boolean;
Sal       integer := 10;
RegNo     char(6) not null default '575488';
Increase  constant number := 0.1;
NewSal    number := Sal* (1 + Increase);
```

To assign an initial value to the variables we can use the assignment operator := or use the keyword default. If no value is assigned to the variable, the null value is automatically assumed. An initial value is obligatory whenever the not null clause is used. As the Increase definition shows, we can define constants, that is, identifiers associated to a value that cannot vary. The specification occurs by placing the keyword constant before the domain definition. Note also that in the initial assignments we can refer to variables introduced earlier.

Two interesting options are represented by the keywords %type and %rowtype. Using the option %type, we can specify that the domain of a variable must be identical to the domain of another variable or of any attribute of a database table. With this option, we can write code that is robust with respect to certain schema modifications. To use the option, the attribute identifier is followed by the %type option, as shown in the following example:

```
Sal  Employee.Salary%type;
```

The %rowtype option allows the definition of PL/SQL variables of record type, characterized by a structure similar to that of a tuple of a specific database table. An example of use of this option is shown below:

```
declare
       Emp Employee%rowtype;
       Num Employee.RegNo%type := '575488';
begin
       select * into Emp
              from Employee
              where RegNo = Num;
       … /*continues */
end;
```

PL/SQL allows the definition of cursors. A cursor can also be used as the basis for the use of the %rowtype keyword.

```
declare
      cursor NewCursor is
              select FirstName, LastName
              from Employee;
      Person NewCursor%rowtype;
```

In the example above, `Person` is a variable of a record type, with fields `FirstName` and `LastName`, each having a domain equal to the attributes of table EMPLOYEE with the same name.

Another important feature of PL/SQL is the definition of variables of `table type` and of `record type`. The definition happens in two steps, defining first the structured type and then the variable of the type. The table variables differ from normal tables managed by the database server in several aspects (they are often called *collections* instead of tables). The main difference is that every table type must have one attribute dedicated to the representation of the row identifier. The table variables must also not be subject to deletions, but their content may only be changed by insertions and updates; PL/SQL offers a rich set of predefined commands for the management of table variables. Record types do not have particular restrictions. PL/SQL also allows the definition of nested record types. Let us look at a simple example of the definition and use of these constructs.

```
declare
    type EmpNameTableType is table of Employee.FirstName%type
        index by binary_integer;
    EmpNameTable EmpNameTableType;
    Counter binary_integer := 0;
    type EmpRecordType is record
    (    FirstName Employee.FirstName%type,
         LastName  char(20),
         SalaryEmp integer );
    EmpRecord EmpRecordType;
begin
    for EmpRecord in
    (select FirstName, LastName, Salary
     from Employee) loop
         Counter := Counter + 1;
         EmpNameTable(Counter) := EmpRecord.FirstName;
    end loop;
    /* process the table */
end;
```

This example defines a PL/SQL table `EmpNameTable`, defined from the type `EmpNameTableType`, having an attribute with domain equal to the `FirstName` attribute in EMPLOYEE and a second attribute of domain `binary_integer`, used to access table elements. In the procedural part, the table is filled by copying the names of the employees one at a time. In the example, we define a record type `EmpRecordType` and an `EmpRecord` variable of this type. The variable is used to read the tuples in the EMPLOYEE table.

C.4.3 Control structures

In PL/SQL, there are control structures similar to those of other modern programming languages. Using them, we can specify various forms of conditional, iterative and sequential execution. All these control structures exploit the concept of block of instructions, with a possible declarative and exception part local to the block.

Conditional execution The conditional control structures use the following syntax:

```
if Condition then
    InstructionsBlock
{elsif Condition then
    InstructionsBlock}
[else InstructionsBlock]
end if
```

The interpretation is intuitive: the conditions are evaluated one by one; as soon as one is true, the corresponding block is executed and the remaining branches are not considered; the else branch is executed when no condition is satisfied. Let us look at a PL/SQL program that increases the salary of the employee with the registration number 575488, increasing it by 10% if the salary is above 60 thousand, 15% if between 45 and 60 thousand, 20% otherwise.

```
declare
    EmpRecord Employee%rowtype;
begin
    select * into EmpRecord
        from Employee
        where RegNo = '575488'
        for update of Salary;
    if EmpRecord.Salary > 60 then
        update Employee set Salary = Salary * 1.1
            where RegNo = '575488';
    elsif EmpRecord.Salary > 45 then
        update Employee set Salary = Salary * 1.15
            where RegNo = '575488';
    else update Employee set Salary = Salary * 1.2
            where RegNo = '575488';
    end if;
end;
```

Iteration The basic construct for iteration is the loop. In its most simple form, a sequence of instructions is placed between the keywords loop and end loop. The sequence will be executed until it finds an exit instruction. For a cycle with an initial condition, a while condition is inserted before the keyword loop. The condition is evaluated before each iteration. If the condition is false, execution terminates. The for construct is used to define the number of times that the iteration must be repeated. The for structure specifies a range of values and the instructions enclosed by loop and end loop are executed once for each value. The syntax is as follows:

```
[while Condition |
  for Counter in [reverse] StartValue..EndValue]
loop
     InstructionsBlock
end loop
```

Consider a program that applies the salary updates of the preceding example to all the employees, using a cursor to scan the various elements of EMPLOYEE.

```
declare
    cursor EmpCursor is select Salary
                        from Employee
                        for update of Salary;
    EmpNo integer;
    I     integer;
    Sal   Employee.Salary%type;
begin
    open EmpCursor;
    fetch EmpCursor into Sal;
    while not EmpCursor%notfound
        if Sal > 60 then
            update Employee set Salary = Salary * 1.1
                where current of EmpCursor;
        elsif Sal > 45
            update Employee set Salary = Salary * 1.15
                where current of EmpCursor;
        else update Employee set Salary = Salary * 1.2
                where current of EmpCursor;
        end if;
        fetch EmpCursor into Sal
    end loop;
end;
```

The same program can be written using a loop with an internal exit:

```
loop
    fetch EmpCursor into Sal;
    if EmpCursor%notfound
        exit;
    … /* instructions to increase the Salary */
end loop;
```

In the example, we have seen the use of the operator %notfound on cursors. The operator returns a boolean value *true* if the last operation on the cursor is unsuccessful. In PL/SQL, a cursor is used for each query and update command. The cursor can be explicitly defined in the program; otherwise, PL/SQL uses an implicit one. The operator presented above can be applied both to the explicit and to the implicit cursors. The implicit one is referred to as sql. Thus, sql%notfound is an expression that returns *true* if the last command has recovered no tuples.

Let us look finally at the construct for on cursors. Cursors are used to scan the result of a query. To represent this situation compactly, PL/SQL provides a suitable structure, characterized by the following syntax:

```
for TupleVariable in Cursor loop
    InstructionsBlock
end loop
```

The cursor is opened automatically when the program reaches the cycle and a fetch instruction is implicitly executed on each iteration. The cycle terminates when an exit instruction appears or when all the tuples returned by the cursor have been dealt with. The earlier loop could be written:

```
for EmpRecord in EmpCursor loop
    if EmpRecord.Salary > 60 then
    … /* instructions updating the Salary */
end loop;
```

The cursor can also be defined *in line* (that is, without an explicit definition in the declaration part of a block) as happens in the following code fragment, part of the final example in Section C.4.2.

```
for EmpRecord in
    (select FirstName, LastName, Salary
     from Employee) loop
```

C.4.4 Management of exceptions

The term *exception* denotes anomalous situations that the system detects at execution time. PL/SQL offers an advanced management of exceptions, providing a set of pre-defined errors to which appropriate actions can be assigned. It is also possible to define exceptions adapted to the specific application needs, called *user-defined* exceptions.

When the system detects an exception, execution is suspended and control is transferred to the exception management procedure (called the *exception handler*). The advantage of this approach is that in this way there is no need to introduce repeated checks on the success of the action. It is instead sufficient to write only once the steps that are to be taken in the face of a particular error. This produces cleaner code and permits the construction of a system that reacts consistently to malfunctions.

Some of the predefined exceptions are the following:

- cursor_already_open (when the program executes an open command on an already open cursor);

- dup_val_on_index (if the program tries to insert a duplicate into a table on which a unique index is defined);

- invalid_cursor (if an illegal operation is carried out on a cursor, such as a close on a cursor that is not open);

- invalid_number (if an SQL command produces an inaccurate value, such as the failure of a conversion of a character string to an integer);

- no_data_found (if a query returns an empty result);

- storage_error (if the memory is exhausted, or found to be corrupt);

- `timeout_on_resource` (if it is not possible to access a resource because of a timeout);

- `too_many_rows` (if an instruction `select into` without cursors returns more than one row);

- `value_error` (if a PL/SQL instruction produces an incorrect value in an assignment);

- `zero_divide` (if the program tries to execute a division by zero).

As regards user-defined exceptions, these must be specified in the declaration part of a block, using the predefined type `exception`. The same visibility rules are valid for exceptions as for variables. While pre-defined exceptions are raised automatically at the occurrence of an event in the system, those defined in the program must be activated explicitly in the program by means of the `raise` instruction. This instruction accepts as argument the name of the exception we wish to activate. When the exception management procedure terminates, the program restarts at the end of the block in which the exception was generated (and not on the instruction following the one producing the exception). If we wish the control to be returned to the next instruction, we must make that instruction the last of a block, possibly by introducing a block that contains only that instruction. Let us look at an example, in which a bank procedure withdraws a sum of 100 from the account number 12345. If the amount of the account following the operation falls below the overdraft limit, then the transaction is refused, and a record is written in the OVERDRAFTEXCEEDED table.

```
declare
    OverdraftError exception;
    OldAmount      integer;
    NewAmount      integer;
    Threshold      integer;
begin
    select Amount, Overdraft into OldAmount, Threshold
        from BankAccount
        where AccountNo = '12345'
        for update of Amount;
    NewAmount := OldAmount - 100;
    if NewAmount > Overdraft then
        update BankAccount set Amount = NewAmount
        where AccountNo = '12345';
    else
        raise OverdraftError;
    end if;
exception
    when OverdraftError then
        insert into OverdraftExceeded
            values('12345', 100, sysdate);
    when data_not_found then
        insert into AccessToGhostAccounts
            values('12345', sysdate);
end;
```

C.4.5 Procedures

Procedures, also called *subprograms*, constitute a fundamental tool for the construction of large applications. Procedures permit the construction of PL/SQL programs with important properties like modularity, reusability, maintainability and abstraction.

In the PL/SQL environment, the subprograms have a still more important role, as PL/SQL is used very often as a tool for the definition of *stored procedures*. These are PL/SQL procedures that are stored and may be considered a part of the database schema.

Let us look at how subprograms enrich the language. Considering the example of a bank transaction in the preceding section, it is natural to try to write more general code, producing instructions able to carry out a generic debit on an arbitrary account. The following procedure satisfies the requirement.

```
procedure Debit(ClientAccount char(5), Withdrawal integer) is
    OverdraftError exception;
    OldAmount       integer;
    NewAmount       integer;
    Threshold       integer;
begin
    select Amount, Overdraft into OldAmount, Threshold
        from BankAccount
        where AccountNo = ClientAccount
        for update of Amount;
    NewAmount := OldAmount - Withdrawal;
    if NewAmount > Overdraft then
        update BankAccount set Amount = NewAmount
            where AccountNo = ClientAccount;
    else
        raise OverdraftError;
    end if;
exception
    when OverdraftError then
        insert into OverdraftExceeded
            values(ClientAccount, Withdrawal, sysdate);
    when data_not_found then
        insert into AccessToGhostAccounts
            values(ClientAccount, sysdate);
end Debit;
```

The transfer command above could thus be carried out with a simple call of the procedure:

```
Debit('12345',100);
```

Procedures must be defined in the declaration part of a block. The syntax for the definition is as follows:

```
procedure Name [(Parameter {, Parameter})] is
    LocalDeclarations
begin
    Instructions
[exception
```

      ExceptionHandlers]
   end [*Name*]

The instructions and the exceptions are defined with the syntax previously described. Each parameter follows the syntax:

ParameterName [in | out | in out] *ParameterDomain* [:= *Value* |
                                           default *Value*]

Each parameter is characterized by a name and by a domain. The parameters can be as follows.

- *Input* (type in, the type assumed when no keyword is specified). In this case, a value is assigned to the parameter when the procedure is called, and internally to the procedure, the parameter must be considered as a constant.

- *Output* (type out). When the procedure is called, the parameter must be associated to an *l-value*. An l-value is a term that can appear in the left side of an assignment instruction. The l-value is generally the identifier of a variable to which a value will be assigned at the end of the procedure.

- *Input/output* (type in out). In this case, a variable must still be assigned to the parameter. However, its value can be used within the procedure. A value is assigned to the variable at the end of the execution of the procedure.

From the syntax, we observe that we can associate a default value with a parameter. This is possible only for input parameters, and is forbidden for output or input/output parameters. If the procedure is called without an input parameter, the default value is assigned to the parameter. The presence of this feature complicates the mechanism managing the exchange of values between the procedure and the program calling it. In most programming languages, the correspondence between the parameters that appear in the definition of the procedure (called the *formal* parameters) and the parameters that are used in the call of the procedure (the *actual* parameters) is *positional*. The first formal parameter corresponds to the first actual parameter, and so on until the last actual parameter to which the last formal parameter will correspond. If a domain incompatibility appears, the program is interrupted by a **value_error** exception. If default values for parameters are allowed, some parameters can be missing and the correspondence between formal and actual parameters will require a different mechanism.

A first solution offered in PL/SQL consists in an extension of the positional correspondence between actual and formal parameters, permitting them to differ in number. If the actual parameters are fewer than the formal, the default value is assigned to the last formal parameters. This method requires, however, that the parameters using the default value are always the last.

A further mechanism is name-based, and uses in the call of the subprogram a direct reference to the formal parameters. Thus, with an arbitrary parameter order, the above call could also be written as:

```
Debit(Withdrawal => 100, AccountNo => '12345')
```

One of the advantages of the definition of default values for the parameters is that it becomes possible to extend pre-existing procedures, assigning a default value to every parameter added to the procedure. If the procedure is called using the previous set of parameters, the assignment of default values to the new parameters should keep the previous behaviour, without requiring modification of all the calls to the procedure already present in the program.

A *function* is a particular kind of subprogram, one that returns a value as a result of its call. Functions have a structure identical to the procedures seen above, with only two differences. Firstly, functions are associated with a domain that corresponds to the domain of the result produced and, secondly, in a function we can use the instruction return *Expression*. This instruction terminates the execution of the function, returning as function value the result of the evaluation of *Expression*. The syntax for the declaration of functions is thus:

```
function Name [(Parameter {, Parameter})] return
                                        FunctionDomain is
        LocalDeclarations
begin
        Instructions
[exception
        ExceptionHandlers]
end [Name]
```

A function can also return values using the definition of parameters of type out and in out. However, it is preferable to avoid this, because it corrupts the natural interpretation of a function as a subprogram that returns only a value based on parameters supplied as input data.

An important characteristic of every programming language is the way in which the exchange of parameter values is implemented. We focus on the output parameters, typically managed with two alternative methods. The first is known as *call by copy* and consists in an initial copy of the actual parameter into a variable corresponding to the formal parameter, with an inverse copy at the end of the procedure. The second is known as *call by reference* and considers the formal parameter as an alias for the actual parameter. In PL/SQL the choice of whether to use one mechanism or the other is left to the system, which in each situation will adopt the choice it believes is better. These two mechanisms usually present the same behaviour, but there are two notable exceptions. The first is when it happens that the same parameter is transferred more than once in the same procedure call. The second is when in the procedure an explicit reference is made to a variable that is also assigned to a parameter. Since the system is free to choose the exchange mechanism, programmers must take care to avoid these situations.

PL/SQL provides an overloading mechanism, consisting of the use of the same identifier for many subprograms. A restriction is that the various subprograms differ in the number or domain of parameters. At the time of procedure invocation, the system will choose the particular subprogram that is compatible in its own parameters with the actual parameters of the call.

In PL/SQL, it is also possible to call subprograms recursively. Recursion is useful for solving certain problems, like the computation of a *transitive closure*. These situations cannot be managed in SQL-2, but require the use of a procedural system support. An example of transitive closure is one where a table EMPLOYEE contains the personal details of the employee (RegNo, Salary, Title, and Supervisor). We might need to find, for each employee with title 'Director', the average salaries of the employees supervised by him, directly or indirectly. For this, we can suppose that we have defined in the database a table EMPDIRECTOR with two attributes having the same domain of RegNo. We can fill this table using a recursive function that returns the supervisor for each employee; the procedure analyzes the complete hierarchy moving up one step at a time, until a supervisor is found with title 'Director'.

```
declare
    function RegNoDirector(RegNoEmp Employee.RegNo%type)
        return Employee.RegNo%type is
            RegNoSupervisorEmployee.RegNo%type;
            TitleSupervisorEmployee.Title%type;
    begin
        select Supervisor, Title into RegNoSupervisor, TitleEmp
            from Employee
            where RegNo = RegNoEmp;
        if TitleEmp = 'Director' then
            return RegNoEmp;
        else
            return RegNoDirector(RegNoSupervisor);
        end if;
    end RegNoDirector;

    EmpRecord      Employee%rowtype;
    EmpRegNo       Employee.RegNo%type;
    DirectorRegNo  Employee.RegNo%type;
    cursor EmpCursor is
        select *
        from Employee;
begin
    for EmpRecord in EmpCursor loop
        EmpRegNo := EmpRecord.RegNo;
        DirectorRegNo := RegNoDirector(EmpRegNo);
        insert into EmpDirector values(EmpRegNo,DirectorRegNo);
    end loop;
end;

select D.FirstName, D.LastName, avg(E.Salary)
    from Employee E, EmpDirector ED, Employee D
    where E.RegNo = ED.EmpRegNo and
          D.RegNo = ED.DirectorRegNo
group by D.RegNo, D.FirstName, D.LastName
```

To store the subprograms on the DBMS, making them available to each authorized user, the commands `create procedure` and `create function` are used. These commands transform the PL/SQL subprograms into stored procedures. For example, the `Debit` procedure can be stored by the following command (note the keyword `as` in place of `is`):

```
create procedure Debit(ClientAccount char(5),
                       Withdrawal integer) as
    OverdraftError exception
    … /* the remainder of the procedure */
end Debit;
```

Stored procedures offer many advantages.

- They can improve productivity in the creation of applications, as it becomes possible to construct a library of functions available to all the applications. In this way, we can concentrate several system functions in stored procedures. When the requirements change and it is necessary to modify a procedure, the modifications are automatically propagated to all the applications that use the procedure.

- Another advantage is that a stored procedure can replace the calls to many SQL commands. This simplifies the dialogue between the client and the server, an aspect that is particularly critical when the network has a limited capacity.

- Stored procedures can also permit the saving of space in the memory on the server, as the calls of many users exploit the same area of shared memory.

- We can improve the integrity and the accuracy of applications by requiring, for example, that all the accesses to certain data are carried out using a stored procedure. It is thus possible to have the guarantee that the applications respect the integrity of data.

- Finally, stored procedures are a powerful tool for the definition of access control policies. After the definition of a procedure that implements the desired access policy, this policy can be effectively enforced by granting to the user the right only to call the procedure and revoking the rights to access the data in other ways.

Stored procedures can be called in various contexts: by direct dialogue of a user with the SQL interpreter, by an application using a SQL embedded interface, or by one of the tools in the rich support environment of the DBMS.

We conclude the presentation of procedures in PL/SQL by briefly presenting the possibility offered by PL/SQL of calling *external procedures*. PL/SQL programs can make use of procedures written in a traditional programming language. This is a feature that significantly extends the power of the database server, because there are several functions, typically those characterized by strong algorithmic requirements, that are not efficiently implemented in PL/SQL. For example, functions that manipulate multimedia data must typically implement complex transformations on large amounts of data, requiring a language that allows a translation to machine executable code. The invocation of external procedures thus allows the extension of data management services, importing generic functions into the database server. This extensibility constitutes one of the key technologies necessary for transforming the database server into a *Universal Server,* a system responsible of the storing and managing of any kind of data. The use of external procedures currently incurs in a number of constraints that limit its wide adoption. The first problem is that PL/SQL and the typical programming language have very different environments, and the integration between the two languages requires a complex interface definition. In addition, the mechanisms are currently available only for the C language and for limited platforms. In general, the mechanisms required to use these services are quite complex and usable only by experienced programmers.

C.4.6 Packages

Packages allow the regrouping of type definitions, procedures and cursors into a single component. In a package, we distinguish a specification part (the *head*) and an implementation part (the *body*). The specification part defines all those properties that must be visible from the outside. The body describes the implementation of subprograms and defines all that is needed within the package and need not to be visible from the outside.

The syntax for the definition of a package is:

```
package PackageName is
      InterfaceDeclarations
end [PackageName]

package body PackageName is
      CompleteDeclarations
[begin
      InitializationInstructions]
end [PackageName]
```

Packages offer many advantages.

- They allow the grouping into a single logical unit of all the elements that have to do with a particular aspect or component of the database. In this way, it is easier to understand how the system behaves or to apply modifications.

- They also make it possible to obtain *information hiding.* By separating the interface from the implementation, it becomes possible to modify a procedure without worrying that the applications already written must be modified, as far as the behaviour of the system continues to satisfy the initial assumptions. The development of applications is also facilitated, as it becomes possible to consider only the specification part of a package, ignoring the body and thus considering a set of data that is more restricted and easier to understand.

- Packages can contribute to an improvement in services, as the whole package is loaded into the memory the first time that a reference is made to one of its components, minimizing the transfers from disks to main memory. (In general, when access to a function is required, it is probable that shortly afterwards access will be gained to other functions of the same package.) Objects that are defined in a package remain available for the entire session, shared by all the procedures that are executed during the session.

- Packages also extend the functionality of the system. For example, the body of a package can also contain initialization instructions, which are executed in each session the first time that a package is accessed.

To make a package permanent, the following commands are used:

```
create package PackageName is
        InterfaceDeclarations
end [PackageName]
```

```
create package body PackageName is
        CompleteDeclarations
end [PackageName]
```

To access the components of a package, we use the *dot notation*. Each package component is globally identified by the package name, a dot, and the name of the component internal to the package, be it a subprogram, a cursor, a data type or an exception. The `standard` package is a particularly important predefined package, which contains almost all the basic services that are part of the PL/SQL language. Other system components may provide their packages, which actually extend the functionality of PL/SQL in a particular direction. For example, Oracle Server provides a `dbms_standard` package, loaded each time a PL/SQL statement is executed in the server environment, which offers a rich set of services that let PL/SQL applications interact with the database engine.

Bibliography

[1] Abiteboul, S., Hull, R., Vianu, V., *Foundations of Databases*, Addison-Wesley, Reading, Mass., 1995.

[2] Albano, A., De Antonellis, V., Di Leva, A. (eds.), *Computer-Aided Database Design: The DATAID Project*, North-Holland, Amsterdam, 1985.

[3] Atzeni, P., De Antonellis, V., *Relational Database Theory*, Benjamin-Cummings, Menlo Park, Calif., 1993.

[4] Atzeni, P., Mecca, G., Merialdo, P., 'To Weave the Web', *Proceedings of 23rd International Conference on Very Large Data Bases*, 1997, Athens, Greece, Morgan Kaufmann, San Francisco.

[5] Atzeni, P., Mecca, G., Merialdo, P., 'Design and Maintenance of Data-Intensive Web Sites', *Proceedings of 6th International Conference on Extending Database Technology*, Valencia, Spain, Lecture Notes in Computer Science, vol. 1377, pp. 436–450, Springer-Verlag, Berlin, 1998.

[6] Bancilhon, F., Delobel, C., Kanellakis, P. (eds.), *Building an Object-Oriented Database System: The Story of O2*, Morgan Kaufmann, San Mateo, Calif., 1992.

[7] Batini, C., Ceri, S., Navathe, S. B., *Conceptual Database Design, an Entity-Relationship Approach*, Benjamin-Cummings, Menlo Park, Calif., 1992.

[8] Bernstein, P. A., Hadzilacos, V., Goodman, N., *Concurrency Control and Recovery in Database Systems*, Addison-Wesley, Reading, Mass. 1987.

[9] Bernstein, P. A., 'Middleware: A Model for Distributed System Services', *Communications of the ACM*, vol. 39, no. 2, pp. 89–98, 1996.

[10] Bertino, E., Martino, L., *Object-oriented Databases Systems: Concepts and Architectures*, Addison-Wesley, Reading, Mass., 1993.

[11] Brodie, M. L., Stonebraker, M., *Legacy Systems: Gateways, Interfaces & the Incremental Approach*, Morgan Kaufmann, San Mateo, Calif., 1995.

[12] Cannan, S. J., Otten, G. A. M., *SQL – The Standard Handbook*, McGraw-Hill, New York, 1992.

[13] Cattel, R. G. G., *Object Data Management – Object-Oriented and Extended Relational Database Systems*, revised edition, Addison-Wesley, Reading, Mass., 1994.

[14] Ceri, S. (ed.), *Methodology and Tools for Database Design*, North-Holland, Amsterdam, 1983.

[15] Ceri, S., Fraternali, P., *Designing Database Applications with Objects and Rules: The IDEA Methodology*, Addison-Wesley Longman, Reading, Mass., 1997.

[16] Ceri, S., Fraternali, P., Paraboschi, S., 'Design Principles for Data-Intensive Web Sites', *ACM SIGMOD Record*, vol. 28, no. 1, 1999.

[17] Ceri, S., Gottlob, G., Tanca, L., *Logic Programming and Data Bases*, Springer-Verlag, Berlin, 1989.

[18] Ceri, S., Pelagatti, G., *Distributed Databases: Principles and Systems*, McGraw-Hill, New York, 1984.

[19] Ceri, S., Widom, J., 'Deriving Production Rules for Constraint Maintenance', *Proceedings of the International Conference on Very Large Data Bases*, 1990, Brisbane, Australia, pp. 566–577, Morgan Kaufmann, San Francisco.

[20] Chamberlin, D. D., *A Complete Guide to DB2 Universal Database*, Morgan Kaufmann, San Francisco, Calif., 1998.

[21] Chamberlin, D. D., Astrahan, M. M., Eswaran, P. P., Lorie, R. A., Mehl, J. W., Reisner, P., Wade, B. W., 'SEQUEL 2: A Unified Approach to Data Definition, Manipulation, and Control', *IBM Journal of Research and Development*, vol. 20, no. 6, pp. 97–137, 1976.

[22] Chamberlin, D. D., Boyce, R. F., 'SEQUEL: A Structured English Query Language', *Proceedings of ACM SIGMOD Workshop*, vol. 1, pp. 249–264, 1974.

[23] Chen, P. P., 'The Entity-Relationship Model: Toward a Unified View of Data', *ACM Transactions on Database Systems*, vol. 1, no. 1, pp. 9–36, 1976.

[24] Cheng, J., Malaika, S. (eds.), *Web Gateway Tools: Connecting IBM and Lotus Applications to the Web*, John Wiley and Sons, New York, 1997.

[25] Cochrane, R., Pirahesh, H., Mattos, N., 'Integrating Triggers and Declarative Constraints in SQL Database Systems', *Proceedings of the International Conference on Very Large Data Bases*, Mumbay (Bombay), 1996, pp. 567–578, Morgan Kaufmann, San Francisco.

[26] Codd, E. F., 'A Relational Model for Large Shared Data Banks', *Communications of the ACM*, vol. 13, no. 6, pp. 377–387, 1970.

[27] Codd, E. F., 'Further Normalization of the Data Base Relational Model' in Rustin, R. (ed.), *Database Systems*, pp. 33–64, Prentice Hall, Englewood Cliffs, N.J., 1972.

[28] Codd, E. F., 'Relational Completeness of Database Sublanguages' in Rustin, R. (ed.), *Database Systems*, pp. 65–98, Prentice Hall, Englewood Cliffs, N.J., 1972.

[29] Codd, E. F., 'Extending the Database Relational Model to Capture More Meaning', *ACM Transactions on Database Systems*, vol. 4, no. 4, pp. 397–434, 1979.

[30] Codd, E. F., 'Relational Database: A Practical Foundation for Productivity', *Communications of the ACM*, vol. 25, no. 2, pp. 109–117, 1982.

[31] Codd, E. F., 'Twelve Rules for On-Line Analytical Processing', *Computerworld*, April 1995.

[32] Comer, D. E., *Internetworking with TCP/IP, Volume 1: Principles, Protocols, and Architecture*, 3rd edn, Prentice Hall, Englewood Cliffs, N.J., 1995.

[33] Date, C. J., *An Introduction to Database Systems*, 6th edn, Addison-Wesley, Reading, Mass., 1995.

[34] Date, C. J., Darwen, H., *A Guide to the SQL Standard*, 3rd edn, Addison-Wesley, Reading, Mass., 1993.

[35] Davis, W., *System Analysis and Design*, Addison-Wesley, Reading, Mass., 1983.

[36] Eisenberg, A., Melton, J., 'Standards in Practice', *ACM SIGMOD Record*, vol. 27, no. 3, pp. 53–58, 1998.

[37] Elmagarmid, A. K. (ed.), *Database Transaction Models for Advanced Applications*, Morgan Kaufmann, San Mateo, Calif., 1992.

[38] ElMasri, R. A., Navathe, S. B., *Fundamentals of Database Systems*, 2nd edn, Benjamin-Cummings, Menlo Park, Calif., 1994.

[39] Fairly, R., *Software Engineering Concepts*, McGraw-Hill, New York, 1985.

[40] Fayyad, U. M., Piatetsky-Shapiro, G., Smyth, P., Uthurusamy, R. (eds.), *Advances in Knowledge Discovery and Data Mining*, AAAI Press/MIT Press, Cambridge, Mass. 1996.

[41] Fleming, C. C., von Halle, B., *Handbook of Relational Database Design*, Addison-Wesley, Reading, Mass., 1989.

[42] Florescu, D., Levy, A., Mendelzon, A., 'Database Techniques for the World-Wide Web: A Survey', *ACM SIGMOD Record*, vol. 27, no. 3, pp. 59–74, 1998.

[43] Graham, I. S., *HTML Sourcebook*, 2nd edn, John Wiley & Sons, New York, 1996.

[44] Gray, J., Anderton, M., 'Distributed Computer Systems: Four Case Studies', *IEEE Proceedings*, vol. 75, no. 5, pp. 719–726, 1987.

[45] Gray, J., Chaudhuri, S., Bosworth, A., Layman, A., Reichart, D., Venkatrao, M., Pellow, F., Pirahesh, H., 'Data Cube: A Relational Aggregation Operator Generalizing Group-by, Cross-Tab, and Sub

Totals', *Data Mining and Knowledge Discovery*, vol. 1, no. 1, pp. 29–53, 1997.

[46] Gray, J., Reuter, A., *Transaction Processing Concepts and Techniques*, Morgan Kaufmann, San Mateo, Calif., 1994.

[47] Greenspun, P., *Philip & Alex's Guide to Web Publishing*, Morgan Kaufmann, San Mateo, Calif., 1999.

[48] Hull, R., King, R., 'Semantic Database Modeling: Survey, Applications and Research Issues', *ACM Computing Surveys*, vol. 19, no. 3, pp. 201–260, September 1987.

[49] Inmon, B., *Building the Data Warehouse*, John Wiley & Sons, New York, 1996.

[50] Isakowitz, T., Bieber, M., Vitali, F. (guest eds.), 'Web Information Systems', *Communications of the ACM*, vol. 41, no. 7, pp. 78–117, 1998.

[51] Ju, P., *Databases on the Web: Designing and Programming for Network Access*, IDG Books Worldwide, Foster City, Calif., 1997.

[52] Kim, W. (ed.), *Modern Database Systems: the Object Model, Interoperability, and Beyond*, ACM Press and Addison-Wesley, New York, 1995.

[53] Kimball, R., *The Data Warehouse Toolkit: Practical Techniques for Building Dimensional Data Warehouses*, John Wiley & Sons, New York, 1996.

[54] Lamport, L., 'Time, Clocks and the Ordering of Events in a Distributed System', *Communications of the ACM*, vol. 21, no. 7, pp. 558–565, 1978.

[55] Liu, C., Peek, J., Jones, R., Buus, B., Nye, A., *Managing Internet Information Services*, O'Reilly & Associates, Sebastopol, Calif., 1994.

[56] Loomis, M. E. S., *Object Databases: the Essentials*, Addison-Wesley, Reading, Mass., 1995.

[57] Lum, V. Y., Ghosh, S. P., Schkolnik, M., Taylor, R. W., Jefferson, D., Su, S., Fry, J. P., Teorey, T. J., Yao, B., Rund, D. S., Kahn, B., Navathe, S. B., Smith, D., Aguilar, L., Barr, W. J., Jones, P. E., '1978 New Orleans Data Base Design Workshop Report', *Proceedings of the International Conference on Very Large Data Bases*, Rio de Janeiro, Brazil, 1979, pp. 328–339, IEEE.

[58] Maier, D., *The Theory of Relational Databases*, Computer Science Press, Potomac, Md., 1983.

[59] Mannila, H., Raiha, K. J., *The Design of Relational Databases*, Addison-Wesley, Reading, Mass., 1992.

[60] Melton, J., 'SQL3 Update', *Proceedings of the IEEE International Conference on Data Engineering 1996*, pp. 566–672.

[61] Melton, J., Simon, A. R., *Understanding the New SQL*, Morgan Kaufmann, San Mateo, Calif., 1993.

[62] Obermarck, R., 'Distributed Deadlock Detection Algorithm', *ACM Transactions on Database Systems*, vol. 7, no. 2, 1982.

[63] O'Neil, P., *Database: Principles, Programming, Performance*, Morgan Kaufmann, San Mateo, Calif., 1994.

[64] Oracle Corporation, *Oracle 8 Server: Concepts Manual*, Redwood City, Calif., 1998.

[65] Oracle Corporation, *Oracle 8 Server: SQL Language Reference Manual*, Redwood City, Calif., 1998.

[66] Ozsu, M. T., Valduriez, P., *Principles of Distributed Database Systems*, 2nd edn, Prentice Hall, Englewood Cliffs, N.J., 1999.

[67] Paredaens, J., De Bra, P., Gysses, M., Van Gucht, D., *The Structure of the Relational Database Model*, Springer-Verlag, Berlin, 1989.

[68] Pressman, R. S., *Software Engineering, a Practitioner's Approach*, 3rd edn, McGraw-Hill, New York, 1992.

[69] Ramakrishnan. R., *Database Management Systems*, McGraw-Hill, New York, 1997.

[70] Rosenfeld, L., Morville, P., *Information Architecture for the World-Wide-Web*, O'Reilly and Associates, Sebastopol, Calif., 1998.

[71] Rumbaugh, J., Blaha, M., Premerlani, W., Eddy, F., Lorensen, W., *Object-Oriented Modelling and Design*, Prentice Hall, Englewood Cliffs, N.J., 1991.

[72] Samaras, G., Britton, K., Citton, A., Mohan, C., 'Two-Phase Optimizations in a Commercial Distributed Environment', *Journal of Distributed and Parallel Databases*, vol. 3, no. 4, pp. 325–360, 1995.

[73] Samet, H., *The Design and Analysis of Spatial Data Structures*, Addison-Wesley, Reading, Mass., 1989.

[74] Senn, J. A., *Analysis & Design of Information Systems*, 2nd edn, McGraw-Hill, New York, 1989.

[75] Shasha, D., *Database Tuning: A Principled Approach*, Morgan Kaufmann, San Mateo, Calif., 1994.

[76] Sheth, A. P., Larson, J. A., 'Federated Database Systems for Managing Distributed, Heterogeneous, and Autonomous Databases', *ACM Computing Surveys,* vol. 22, no. 3, pp. 183–236, 1990.

[77] Siegel, J. (ed.), *CORBA: Fundamentals and Programming*, John Wiley & Sons, New York, 1996.

[78] Silberschatz, A., Korth, H. F., Sudarshan, S., *Database System Concepts*, McGraw-Hill, New York, 1996.

[79] Stonebraker, M., *Object-Relational DBMSs – The Next Great Wave*, Morgan Kaufmann, San Mateo, Calif., 1994.

[80]Stonebraker, M. (ed.), *Readings in Database Systems*, 2nd edn, Morgan Kaufmann Publishers, San Mateo, Calif., 1994.

[81]Stonebraker, M., Rowe, L. A., Lindsay, B. G., Gray, J., Carey, M. J., Brodie, M. L., Bernstein, P. A., Beech, D., 'Third-Generation Database System Manifesto', *ACM SIGMOD Record*, vol. 19, no. 3, pp. 31–44, 1990.

[82]Smith, J. M., Smith, D. C. P., 'Database Abstractions: Aggregation and Generalization', *ACM Transactions on Database Systems*, vol. 2, no. 1, pp. 105–133, June 1977.

[83]Subrahmanian, V. S., *Principles of Multimedia Database Systems*, Morgan Kaufmann, San Mateo, Calif., 1998.

[84]Teorey, T. J., *Database Modeling and Design: the E-R Approach*, Morgan Kaufmann, San Mateo, Calif., 1990.

[85]Teorey, T. J., Fry, J. P., *Design of Database Structures*, Prentice Hall, Englewood Cliffs, N.J., 1982.

[86]Teorey, T. J., Yang, D., Fry, J. P., 'A Logical Design Methodology for Relational Databases Using the Extended Entity-Relational Approach', *ACM Computing Surveys*, vol. 18, no. 2, pp. 201–260, 1986.

[87]Tsichritzis, D., Lochovsky, F. H., *Data Models*, Prentice Hall, Englewood Cliffs, N.J., 1982.

[88]Ullman, J. D., *Principles of Database and Knowledge Base Systems*, vol. 1, Computer Science Press, Potomac, Md., 1988.

[89]Ullman, J. D., Widom, J., *A First Course in Database Systems*, Prentice Hall, Upper Saddle River, N.J., 1997.

[90]Vossen, G., *Data Models, Database Languages, and Database Management Systems*, Addison-Wesley, Reading, Mass., 1990.

[91]Widom, J., Ceri, S., *Active Database Systems*, Morgan Kaufmann, San Mateo, Calif., 1996.

[92]Wiederhold, G., *Database Design*, McGraw-Hill, New York, 1983.

[93]Zaniolo, C., 'Database Relations with Null Values', *Journal of Computer and System Science*, vol. 28, no. 1, pp. 142–166, 1984.

[94]Zaniolo, C., Ceri, S., Faloutsos, C., Snodgrass, R. T., Subrahmanian, V. S., Zicari, R., *Introduction to Advanced Database Systems*, Morgan Kaufmann, San Mateo, Calif., 1997.

Index

B

E

P

X

Y

Z